PRINCIPLES AND PRACTICE
OF MANAGEMENT ACCOUNTANCY

PRINCIPLES AND PRACTICE
OF MANAGEMENT
ACCOUNTANCY

J. LEWIS BROWN, M.Sc., A.C.M.A., A.M.B.I.M.
Principal Lecturer in Management Accountancy and Finance,
Kingston Polytechnic

and

LESLIE R. HOWARD, F.C.A.
Principal Lecturer in Financial and Management Accountancy,
City of London Polytechnic

SECOND EDITION

MACDONALD AND EVANS LTD
8 JOHN STREET, LONDON WC1N 2HY
1969

First published January 1966
Reprinted November 1966
Second edition September 1969
Reprinted January 1971
Reprinted July 1973

©

MACDONALD & EVANS LTD
1969

I.S.B.N. 0 7121 1626 5

*Printed in Great Britain by Richard Clay (The Chaucer Press), Ltd.,
Bungay, Suffolk*

AUTHORS' PREFACE TO THE SECOND EDITION

MANAGEMENT accountancy has made significant progress even in the short space of time since this book was first published, and the importance of information for management purposes has become more widely appreciated. In the second edition, therefore, we have incorporated further illustrations of the types of report likely to facilitate the formulation of management policy. The section on working capital statements has been extended, discounted cash flow has been given more extensive treatment and matters covering share valuation and the understanding of the financial aspects of shares and public company finance have been brought up to date.

A special budgetary control project of a practical nature has been introduced to demonstrate the compilation and application of budgets and to emphasise the essential role of the Management Accountant to co-ordinate all the functions of the business. Greater recognition of the usefulness of accounting ratios, properly applied, has warranted fuller treatment of this subject, while the opportunity has been taken to include the latest recommendations of the Institute of Cost and Works Accountants regarding standard costing. The provision of selected questions from the final examination papers of the various accountancy bodies has proved its worth, and these have been adjusted to include the most up-to-date and relevant examples.

This book follows the recommendations of the various accountancy bodies and of the examining bodies responsible for National Further Education syllabuses and examinations, and gives decimal currency equivalents where appropriate. These are set out in the form advised by the Decimal Currency Board, as described in *Decimal Currency: Expression of Amounts in printing, writing and in speech*, H.M.S.O., 1968.

Our acknowledgments are due to those who have written expressing their appreciation and offering suggestions for improvement. We would also express our thanks to the following organisations for permission to use their recommendations and examination questions:

Association of Certified and Corporate Accountants	*C.C.A.*
Association of Cost and Industrial Accountants	*C.I.A.*
Chartered Institute of Secretaries	*C.I.S.*
Corporation of Secretaries	*C.C.S.*
Institute of Bankers	*I.B.*
Institute of Chartered Accountants in England and Wales (designated in the text as "The Institute of Chartered Accountants")	*C.A.*

v

Institute of Chartered Accountants of Scotland	*C.A.(S)*
Institute of Cost and Works Accountants	*C.W.A.*
Joint Diploma Board	*J.Dip. M.A.*
University of London, B.Sc.(Econ.)	*B.Sc. (Econ.)*
Society of Commercial Accountants	*S.C.A.*

J. LEWIS BROWN
LESLIE R. HOWARD

July 1969

INTRODUCTION

MANAGEMENT accounting is not new, though the interest shown in it is of relatively recent origin. Accountants have applied their skill in seeking to maintain or improve business efficiency for centuries past, but they have concerned themselves mainly with obtaining figures of an historical nature—that is, by analysing past results, they have sought to regulate future policies. Until more recently they have been chiefly occupied with matters of a domestic or internal nature, and although they have not been able to ignore affairs outside a company, such as the influence exerted by customers, nevertheless they have not sought to extend the field of their activities. They have concentrated their endeavours on seeking to establish an efficiently run business, leaving those engaged on the various executive activities of the organisation to pronounce on their own particular fields of interest.

Modern business activities and the increasing complexity of present-day manufacture and commerce have necessitated a broadening of the views, knowledge and influence of the accountant, and while greater specialisation has taken place within the profession itself, a new branch of accountancy has evolved, namely, that of management accounting.

"Management accounting" may be defined broadly as that aspect of accounting which is concerned with the efficient management of a business through the presentation to management of such information as will facilitate efficient and opportune planning and control.

The managerial aspect of his work is the management accountant's prime concern. Having satisfied himself as to the efficiency of the organisation of the business—covering such matters as the basic book-keeping and regulation of activities—he may justifiably expect the financial accountant to be concerned with the day-to-day running of affairs. His attention should be directed more particularly towards the extraction of information from records and the compilation and preparation of statements which will enable management to function with the minimum of effort and with the maximum of efficiency.

The expression management *accountancy* has been used advisedly in the title of this book, as it is felt that it covers a broader view than "management accounting," for to carry out his duties effectively the management accountant is now required to extend his knowledge and research into related, but distinct, fields of activity, covering such widely separated areas as taxation, manufacturing processes, electronic data processing, stock exchange activities, economic influences, statistical research and so on.

This does not imply that the management accountant needs to be (for example) a qualified production engineer to be able to concern himself with the efficiency of manufacturing processes, but he must nevertheless have some knowledge of the flow of work through the plant in order to be able to assess what costing, statistical or other records are necessary to ensure effective control. His training and experience must be such as will enable him to comprehend and deal with these allied activities.

The essential characteristics of information required for management are that (a) it must be relevant, and (b) it must be timely. To meet the first requirement, the management accountant will need to have a detailed understanding of the business concerned and the ability to present such information as will enable management to concentrate on essential matters without wasting time on routine activities previously assessed and agreed. It is here that "management by exception" should be operated. At the same time, if capital projects, expansion or proposed mergers are under consideration, it will be the duty of the management accountant to grasp the underlying essentials of the situation and to present them in such a way as will enable management to reach a decision based on possession of all the *relevant* facts.

In the second instance, the management accountant must realise that information, to be useful, should be received in time to enable the executive to act effectively. To be informed after events have reached such a stage as precludes their regulation or adjustment is merely to cause frustration and may lead to wrong decisions aggravating an already difficult situation. It is here that factors of planning and control are manifested as essential to sound management, and in analysing the functions of the accountant regarding his presentation of information to management, his duties may be sub-divided as to:

1. The presentation of forecasts and budgets of a forward-looking nature—so facilitating planning.

2. The supplying of such current information as will ensure efficient control of activities during the fulfilment of the plans formulated.

3. Ensuring that internal control within the business is such that relevant information is automatically prepared and summarised in such a way as provides an easy, rapid analysis and compilation for submission to management.

(1) The application of budgetary control, and more particularly *flexible* budgetary control, presupposes the availability of sufficient information being to hand as will make the necessary budgets possible. The efficient ordering of office routine is essential, as mentioned previously, but—and here the wider aspects of the accountant's experience must be applied—relevant information must also be made available from the shop floor, the warehouse, the sales department, etc. Part of such information should arise in the routine order of work, for example, the preparation of requisitions and their subsequent analysis, or of efficient stock recording. Other information would have to be prepared specially, as, for example, sales budgets and market analysis.

In any case the accountant should know what kind of information is likely to be useful and should ensure that it will be received in time for analysis, interpretation and presentation to management.

But the broader aspects of planning will no doubt require the preparation of statistics and the amassing of information in those wider aspects of the management accountant's field of experience. Where capital projects are to be undertaken, not only will a recommendation as to an adequate return on capital invested be required, but the most suitable method of raising the necessary finance will have to be indicated. Likewise, if any take-over project or investment in a subsidiary company or other concern is contemplated, the management accountant will be expected to be able to express an opinion based upon the ability to interpret accounts, to assess future trading prospects, etc.

(2) The importance of information being received in time for effective action has already been stressed. In this respect, the submission of information covering standards and variances from those standards during the course of actual activities will facilitate management by exception and effective action while control may still be exercised.

(3) The necessity for the efficient recording of essential information has already been dealt with. This assumes efficient internal control and the suitable allocation of duties within the management accountant's department so that information may be rapidly compiled in an orderly manner, especially in the event of some urgent business arising, ensuring that no dislocation occurs.

Being in the nature of an introduction to the field of management accountancy, this brief exposition has sought only to illuminate some of the main aspects of the subject and to emphasise the duties falling to the management accountant; the more detailed aspects are dealt with in the pages of this book.

CONTENTS

PART FOUR: INFORMATION FOR MANAGEMENT
CONTROL

LIST OF ILLUSTRATIONS

PART ONE

CAPITALISATION

CHAPTER I

TYPES OF CAPITAL

No single business has its exact counterpart; each has its own particular facets and these may vary widely in accordance with the type of organisation concerned, whether manufacturing, trading or otherwise. Capital requirements likewise differ: the amount to be raised and the source of finance to be employed are the main factors which must be carefully considered when the nature of the capital to be raised is decided upon. The normal procedure for dealing with these two factors in turn would be first to draw up the capital budget and then to search for the cheapest and most suitable type of capital. However, before proceeding to the aspects of budgeting, capital gearing and the sources from which the required finance may be raised, it is advisable to review briefly the various types of capital available.

SOLE TRADERS AND PARTNERSHIPS

This is the most simple example, for here the capital will be supplied by the owner or partners from their own private resources or such loans as they may be able to raise. It is possible to register limited partnerships whereby certain partners may subscribe to the business while taking no part in the management; such partners are liable only for debts of the partnership up to the amount they have subscribed. Limited partnerships, however, are very rare, and as the method of capitalisation of partnerships is obvious it needs no further elucidation.

LIMITED COMPANIES

In dealing with companies affording to their members liability limited to the amount (if any) unpaid on their shares, we are dealing with the great majority of businesses of consequence to the management accountant. Their method of capitalisation may take any of the undermentioned forms.

1. PERMANENT CAPITAL

Since the permanent capital of the company will be such as will be retained in earning the profits of the business, the proprietors should obviously supply the major part, if not all of it, by way of taking up shares in the company.

(a) *Shares and stock*

There is no specified type of share mentioned in the Companies Act, 1948, nor in the Memorandum of Association of a company, which

3

merely states the authorised capital of the company and its division into shares of a fixed amount. The rights attaching to such shares are usually set out in the Articles of Association and cover the following types of shares.

(i) *Preference shares.* Owing to the incidence of taxation, these are now seldom issued, Debentures—the interest on which is allowable for taxation purposes—being preferred. Provided the Articles so specify, holders are entitled to payment of dividends prior to other classes of shares and also to repayment of capital in the event of winding-up. If they are accorded the right to partake in a second dividend, *e.g.* to an additional 1% dividend for every 2% paid to Ordinary share holders in excess of 10%, they are termed *Participating* Preference shares.

The holders are not usually allowed to vote save in stated instances, *e.g.* when their dividend is six months in arrear, or in the event of a meeting called for the purpose of winding up or altering the rights of such shareholders. The abrogation from voting rights is not invariable, however, and classes of shares ("A" and "B," etc.) may exist, some of which may carry voting rights and others not.

Since, however, the equity, or Ordinary shares, should bear the risks of the company, it seems only right that they should carry the voting rights save where there is the possibility of the Preference shareholders being deprived of some rights which may have prompted them to buy the shares originally.

(ii) *Redeemable Preference shares.* Any company so authorised by its Articles may issue Preference shares which are, or at the option of the company are, liable to be redeemed. The Companies Act, 1948, lays down the circumstances in which such shares only may be redeemed, viz., either out of the proceeds of a new issue of shares made for the purpose or out of profits available for distribution and transferred to a Capital Redemption Reserve Fund; before redemption such shares *must* be fully paid up.

The advantage of being able to pay back, or *redeem*, such shares at a later date is particularly useful where additional capital is required, but it is hoped that earnings will be sufficient to allow of their subsequent redemption, thus enabling a larger distribution to be made on the remaining capital. They are especially useful when additional finance is required during periods when it is expensive to obtain new capital. The shares may be issued at the prevailing high rate and redeemed from the proceeds of a new issue made when rates fall.

It may be noted that the effect of the requirements of the Companies Act is to ensure the maintenance of the capital of the company at its original figure prior to redemption, for either a new issue of shares must be made or distributable profits must be set aside to a Capital Redemption Reserve Fund, (or a combination of both may be applied). In any case, the capital remains effectively at its original figure, so ensuring that outside interests are protected from any reduction in the amount of the capital.

Added inducement may be given to investors to take up Redeemable Preference shares by offering a premium on redemption, which the Companies Act requires shall be provided for out of the profits of the company or the company's share premium account before the shares are redeemed. A right of conversion to Ordinary shares may also be offered, but until recently this has been looked upon as a sign of financial weakness since it is a tacit admittance that the company will be unable to accumulate the necessary funds for ultimate redemption. Lately, however, these terms have been offered by companies of such standing on the stock exchange as to overcome this prejudice and to give the impression that they contemplate being able subsequently to bear the additional burden of larger profit distributions.

(iii) *Ordinary shares.* The Ordinary share holders provide the main risk-bearing capital of the business and normally carry such voting rights as confers ultimate control of the company. Since they bear the risks it is only right that they should be entitled to this and to the greater proportion of the profits available for distribution, after due regard has been paid to the setting aside of amounts to reserves, etc. They are also normally entitled to any surplus arising in the event of winding up.

The "equity share holders," a term which signifies their being entitled to the equity of the business, *i.e.* the profits and assets remaining after the prior claims of all fixed interest bearing stocks have been met, may rightly expect voting powers which give them some say in the running of the business, but by various methods they are sometimes divested of this.

(iv) *Non-voting Ordinary shares.* The issue of non-voting shares is held by some to be justified in certain circumstances, for example, where it is desired to retain control in the hands of the original shareholders. Death duty has caused problems in this respect when it has been necessary to sell certain shares in a company, and various schemes have been devised to overcome this; but if an issue of, say, one for one of non-voting shares is made, no disturbance of the original control need take place. It is also maintained that necessary capital may be obtained without the risk of a take-over bid, as the controlling shares may be retained while no incentive is given to buy up the non-voting shares.

A further justification for the issue of non-voting Ordinary shares is claimed in that the market for the company's shares is widened. This, however, is often belied in practice since it is not unusual for two distinct markets to arise whereby the voting shares are quoted at a premium above those of the later issue. The actual issue may take the form of "B" class shares subsequent to an "A" class share carrying voting rights, and may arise in the case of the one-for-one issue granting restricted voting rights according to a stated nominal value held or, as mentioned, may afford no rights at all.

It would seem that the objections raised outweigh the advantages claimed for such shares, since they appear to be undemocratic, there being holders of equity share capital having to bear their share of the risks, but having little or no chance of exercising any power in the control of the company. Moreover, virtually complete control may be gained by a minority of the shareholders.

(v) *Deferred or founders' shares.* This type of share is sometimes issued to the founders or promoters of a company, either as a signification of their confidence in the company's prospects or as a way of obtaining compensation for the goodwill they are selling to the company. Under the terms of issue dividends may be paid only after a specified time has elapsed or after a stated amount of dividend has been paid to the Ordinary share holders.

Although such shares may form only a small proportion of the total share capital they can prove very remunerative to the holders, as they may be entitled under the Articles to a very high rate of dividend. They may also confer the same voting rights as Ordinary shares or may be stated to be convertible to Ordinary shares after the lapse of a certain period.

(vi) *Stock.* Fully paid shares may be converted into stock or stock units. Although stock may not be issued directly, it has the advantage of allowing transfer fractionally, whereas shares must always be transferred in whole units and consequently according to their numbers. Since stock is not numbered, a considerable saving in clerical work is afforded by its use.

Shares issued at a discount or at a premium

Shares issued at a discount must be of a class already issued and the company issuing them must have been entitled to carry on business for at least one year. Court permission for such an issue must also be obtained. These restrictions, and the fact that to put shares on the market at a discount would be an admission of the fact that the company was in difficulty, make the issue of such shares more of academic interest than practical worth.

Should a company with shares quoted at a figure lower than par wish to put shares on the market it would be more advisable to do so by means of an issue made at a nominal value of the quoted price of the shares on the market and offering at the same time similar voting rights.

Example

> £1 nominal share quoted 15s. entitled to dividend of 6%.
> New issue at 15s. nominal, entitled to dividend of 8%.

The issue of shares at a premium is dealt with in Chapter xvi.

(vii) *Shares of no par value.* Differing opinions have been expressed with regard to the desirability or otherwise of allowing the issue of shares of no par value, but the Gedge Committee in 1954 decided in favour of permitting companies to do this. The Government did not adopt the recommendations, considering that the changes required in the law were not immediately practicable.

This type of share is already issued in Canada and the United States in addition to shares of nominal or par value. The holder of one share where a company has issued, say, 20,000 such shares, is the holder of a fraction representing the right to receive one 20,000th share of the profits and the same fraction of any surplus available after the settlement of prior claims in the event of winding-up.

The total amount paid by those taking up the shares on issue is shown on the Balance Sheet as the paid-up capital. Thereafter the value of the shares on the market is governed by the usual market influences of supply and demand, which are in turn affected by the estimation of future dividends.

The main advantage claimed for such shares is that the anomalies of shares quoted at par value are avoided. These anomalies, held by some to be seriously misleading, are that

1. The uninitiated may consider a par value share to be cheap if quoted below par or dear if quoted above, whereas such values are governed by the more important factors of earning capacity, yield, profits ploughed back, etc.;

2. Dividends may be declared on nominal values which may bear no resemblance to the market value and in no way reflect the true return on the investment. This, it has also been maintained, may have adverse economic effects in engendering dissatisfaction among those receiving rewards as factors of production. Dividends declared on shares of no par value are quoted at a stated amount of cash per share.

(b) *Capital raised from internal sources*

Capital may also be raised internally by the following methods:

(i) *Ploughing back profits.* An efficient company will usually ensure that not all its profits are distributed and adequate funds are ploughed back into the business by creating reserves or sinking funds for such matters as replacement of assets or acquisition of new ones.

Where reserves or sinking funds are set aside for specific purposes and not merely for strengthening the business as a whole, to ensure that such sums are available when required and to avoid their becoming absorbed in various assets of the business, they are usually invested outside the company and realised as and when required.

With regard to programmes of expansion, the procedure of utilising internal capital resources applies more generally to smaller concerns; where large capital projects are contemplated, bigger companies are more easily able to raise capital from outside sources. In the latter case the "watering down" of capital is also less likely than where the proprietors' funds are more limited—the "watering down" of capital signifying here the capitalisation of funds to a larger degree than the earning capacity, and consequently the distributable profits, justify.

(ii) *Bonus issues.* Where reserves have been growing owing to a period of prosperity and conservative policy, "ploughed back" profits may be distributed in the form of bonus issues. Such issues carry two main advantages, viz.

1. The receipt of the bonus share constitutes a non-taxable item in the hands of the recipient and may be sold for cash if so desired;
2. A misleading impression may be overcome, viz., that of the earning of excessive profits and the distribution of abnormally high dividends. The readjustment of capital is an overt acknowledgment of the fact that the company's shareholders have been investing further moneys in the business and not withdrawing the profits which have accrued to them.

Specimen question

During the last six years of trading, a company having an issued share capital of £100,000 and revenue reserves of £20,000 has made profits and distributed dividends as follows:

Year 1	Profit £20,000	Dividends £8,000
2	26,000	8,000
3	32,000	8,000
4	40,000	12,000
5	48,000	12,000
6	60,000	24,000

To encourage the retention of profits in the business for expansion purposes, a bonus issue of one for two was made at the end of the third year and a further scrip issue of one for three was made in the sixth year. Both issues not to rank for dividend in the year of issue.

Ignoring taxation, you are required to show:

(i) The dividends as a percentage of the *original* share capital.
(ii) The dividends as a percentage of the *actual* share capital.
(iii) The total capital employed in the business from 1st January in each year.
(iv) The dividends paid as a percentage of the capital employed at the 1st January in each year.

Answer

	Dividend rate on original capital (%)	Dividend rate on actual capital (%)	Capital employed (£)	Dividend rate on capital employed (%)
Year 1	8	8	120,000	6·6
2	8	8	132,000	6·1
3	8	8	150,000	5·3
4	12	8	174,000	7·0
5	12	8	202,000	6·0
6	24	12	238,000	10·0

NOTES

(i) The dividend rate as calculated on the original capital would appear to have trebled during the period, whereas the dividend on the capital employed shows an increase of only 50% over that of the first year.

(ii) The use of the figure at the 1st January in respect of capital employed in each year is approximate, as this would accrue over the trading period.

(iii) These are the necessary workings:

Share capital	£100,000	Profit brought forward		£20,000
		Profits earned		
		Year 1	£20,000	
		2	26,000	
		3	32,000	
				78,000
				98,000
		Dividends paid		
		Year 1	8,000	
		2	8,000	
		3	8,000	
				24,000
				74,000
Bonus issue, 1 for 2	50,000			50,000
	150,000			24,000
		Profits earned		
		Year 4	40,000	
		5	48,000	
		6	60,000	
				148,000
				172,000
		Dividends paid		
		Year 4	12,000	
		5	12,000	
		6	24,000	
				48,000
				124,000
Bonus issue, 1 for 3	50,000			50,000
	£200,000	Revenue reserve		£74,000

Capital employed	
Year 1	£120,000
Add profit	20,000
	140,000
Less Dividend	8,000
Year 2	£132,000
etc.	—

(iii) *Rights issues.* This procedure is often favoured since:

1. It saves the expense in making an offer to the public.
2. It gives a greater assurance of the sale of the shares.

Both bonus issues and rights issues are dealt with more fully in Chapter xv.

2. LOAN CAPITAL

Where capital is required but not of a permanent nature, it may be obtained by borrowing either on long term loans or for more immediate repayment.

The most important method of raising capital on a long term basis is by means of Debentures. A Debenture is a document given by a company in acknowledgment of a debt, undertaking to repay the stated sum on or before a certain date, and in the meantime to pay interest at a fixed rate, usually in half-yearly intervals.

(a) *"Simple" or "naked" Debentures.* Such Debentures offer no charge on the assets of the company as security for the loan and in the event of winding up the holders of such Debentures rank *pari passu* with ordinary unsecured creditors and can claim no priority of repayment. These naked Debentures, since they offer no charge on the assets of the company, or security, are often termed "Unsecured Notes," and, although in the form of Debentures, need not be registered.

(b) *Mortgage Debentures.* Debentures more usually give a charge over the assets of the company and in such a case are termed "Mortgage Debentures." The charge may be a fixed charge, that is, on certain assets of the company, or a floating charge. Not infrequently a charge may be conferred on some specified assets of the company in the form of a fixed charge, and in addition a floating charge may be given on the whole of the company's undertaking.

In the case of a fixed charge, the effect is to lease the property charged to the Debenture holders, so restricting the company's right to deal in the property in any way until such time as the Debentures are redeemed.

Where a floating charge exists the property may be dealt with as if no such charge existed. If the company makes some default in a condition in the deed, and action is taken by one or more of the Debenture holders to enforce the security, the charge crystallises, or in other words becomes fixed on the assets as they then exist.

It is a requirement of the Companies Act, 1948, that a charge securing any issue of Debentures and various charges shall be void against the liquidators and any creditor unless it is registered with the Registrar of Companies within 21 days after its creation. To protect the interests of the Debenture holders and to safeguard their rights it is not unusual to appoint a Trustee for Debenture holders, the trustee being empowered to sell the property in the event of the company's default in the payment of interest or capital or any other breaches of the covenant.

(c) *Debenture stock.* Debenture stock constitutes, as do Debentures, evidence of a debt, but instead of each lender holding a separate bond he has a certificate entitling him to a specified portion of one loan.

(d) *Bearer Debentures.* Debentures payable to bearer are transferable by delivery and any bona fide transferee for value becomes the legal owner of them.

Debentures are frequently issued at a discount and may be redeemable at a premium. The disadvantage mentioned with regard to the issue of shares at a discount does not apply here, however, since they may be issued without any legal restrictions, and the advantage may be gained of being able to issue them at a lower rate of interest payable on this account.

3. MEDIUM TERM CAPITAL

(a) *Bank loans.* Traditionally, banks have not considered it their policy to make loans for lengthy periods of time. Under official direction they are now willing to assist "small industrial and business units" in the form of loans for the purposes of "enabling them to improve or purchase capital assets." For the larger organisations the Finance Corporation for Industry Ltd and the Industrial and Commercial Finance Corporation Ltd are available; these organisations are mentioned later under "Financial Institutions."

(b) *Hire purchase.* The obvious advantage of being able to use an asset to make it pay for itself is apparent with regard to hire purchase, but such use has to be paid for in interest charges; furthermore, the capital allowances made for income tax purposes are spread over the period of the contract.

While hire purchase is a method of obtaining finance for assets on medium length terms, it is not always favoured. Where possible, businesses prefer to pay outright for an asset to obtain full tax relief, and to be able to look to the earnings received as available for the business and not for payment away, during the life of an asset which is steadily deteriorating. This risk element due to supervening obsolescence, or otherwise, is always present on the purchase of an asset whether on hire purchase terms or by outright purchase. But in the latter case the loss to be borne may be carried out of current earnings without the additional burden of continued hire purchase instalments, and in any case there is always the saving of relatively high interest charges.

It is of interest to note that hire purchase is more particularly used by contracting organisations, such as building companies, whose work necessitates profits and expenses being spread over comparatively long periods of time before ultimate completion.

(c) *Sale and lease-back.* With rising property values this method of finance has been used profitably in a number of instances. Since the sale is of a capital nature only capital allowances already received stand to be lost, leaving substantial non-taxable profits available. At the same time action may be taken when selling property to ensure that the seller can lease the property at an agreed rate for a specified period, as well as to stipulate a renewal option. Such rent as is paid thereafter is then chargeable against profits.

It is this aspect of sale of property at prices greatly in excess of their original cost that strengthens the argument of some accountants for the revaluation of assets and the creation of capital reserves on Balance Sheets in order to ensure that take-over bids are not made according to historic Balance Sheet values.

If a company wishes to expand and to obtain immediate resources, this method of obtaining funds may be used, but it must always be borne in mind that the additional rental charges have to be met over a period of years when profits may fluctuate and its own position, from the point of view of fixed assets, is not so strong.

(d) *Equipment leasing.* This method of obtaining finance is analogous to that of renting a property. A finance company buys the equipment and leases the assets on a contractual basis for a specified period and, since the system is in effect the same as renting, where the contract does not exceed a period of five years this term is commonly applied.

The obvious advantage is that a company with limited resources may obtain capital equipment in the hope that it will more than pay for its hire. The charges are high but not so high in the short period as would be the case if it had to pay a deposit and obtain the equipment on hire purchase terms. The company may also charge the payments against its profits for taxation purposes, but on the other hand it cannot obtain the usual capital allowances it would obtain under the latter system. Over the long period, if it is necessary to renew the contract it will usually prove the more expensive method.

(e) *Selling factors.* The valuable use of funds for working capital purposes may be obtained by the sale of goods to a factor, who then sells the goods to the original seller's customer. This method is used quite widely in the United States, but is not much favoured in Britain. The interjection of a "second" seller's name between contracting parties is not considered conducive to good trading relations.

(f) *Borrowing without recourse.* This quite recent method of financing is growing in favour in Great Britain. Immediate payment can be received on sales where settlement dates may be delayed either for such periods as ninety days or even up to three years in the case of export markets. The method obviates the disadvantage mentioned with regard to factors in that the goods are sold to the company supplying the finance. Up to 85% of the invoiced amount may be obtained at once and the remainder on final settlement by the customer, the latter not being informed that he is buying from any other party than the original seller.

Further advantages derive from this method of finance, for after suitable investigation into the financial standing of the "borrowing" company, insurance is taken out by the financing company to cover any bad debts which might arise, the "borrower" then being freed from any further liability which might arise had, say, the funds been obtained by the more usual method of drawing and discounting a bill which might be subsequently dishonoured.

4. SHORT TERM CAPITAL

(a) *Bank overdrafts.* This is the commonest method of obtaining short term capital and where a business is sound financially or even if it is in difficulty with regard to liquid assets but at the same time can offer evidence of reasonable security and sound management, banks provide one of the easiest and quickest methods of obtaining finance.

Some organisations have used overdraft facilities for comparatively lengthy periods despite the relatively expensive interest charges, since the burden of these may be mitigated by the charge against profits for taxation purposes. However, this policy is not advocated, as more suitable methods of capitalisation are available and the appearance on a published Balance Sheet of a large overdraft may give a misleading impression.

(b) *Acceptance credits.* By the term "acceptance credits" is signified a method of borrowing at a cheaper rate than may be obtained on a bank loan or overdraft.

The well-known discount houses are willing to lend on more favourable terms than the banks provided they are sufficiently satisfied as to security. Where evidence of this can be supplied, facilities are extended to the borrower to draw on the house. The bills drawn may be discounted with the bank, the borrower supplying the necessary funds to the house in due course to enable it to settle the bill.

This method of borrowing presupposes that the transactions will be sufficiently large to justify taking advantage of the better rates to be obtained. Such may be the case with the sale and export of goods, the documents of title being deposited as security.

(c) *Delayed settlement of credit transactions.* This may seem out of place under methods of obtaining short term finance, but it is nevertheless an important method by which capital is obtained for short periods.

Where agreement can be reached with certain associated business organisations to delay settlement for agreed periods, this will have obvious advantages. However if, when liquid resources become short, creditors are kept waiting an unduly long time before settlement, permanent damage may be done to the good name of a business, subsequently leading to loss of trading facilities.

For short term capital the methods of "factorising" or "borrowing without recourse" can also be applied as well as for obtaining medium term finance as outlined above.

FINANCIAL INSTITUTIONS

The brief list of methods of obtaining finance would be incomplete without reference to the two important financial institutions offering assistance to commercial and industrial concerns.

The Finance Corporation for Industry Ltd

Established in 1945 by arrangement between its present shareholders, the Bank of England in collaboration with a number of large insurance companies and investment trusts, the Finance Corporation for Industry exists, in the words of the then Chancellor of the Exchequer, to provide "temporary or longer period finance for industrial businesses of the country with a view to their quick rehabilitation and development in the national interest, thereby assisting in the maintenance and increase of employment."

Operations do not replace but rather supplement the activities of other lenders. Funds are made available only for amounts of £200,000 and over, the intention being to fill the gap which exists between short term facilities on the one hand and the long term loans which are attractive to insurance companies and other institutions on the other. Also, where difficulty may be experienced in raising capital at reasonable rates in times of economic difficulty, the F.C.I. seeks to supply the need for medium term capital without restriction as to any particular industry, so long as it may be considered to further industrial development in the U.K.

The Industrial and Commercial Finance Corporation Ltd

The I.C.F.C., also established with Government approval, is under the control of the Bank of England and the joint stock banks, who are the holders of its equity share capital.

Besides providing share and loan capital, it offers advice and assistance to borrowers while not seeking to take away their independence. Loans are made for the purpose of providing permanent capital but not working capital.

Amounts advanced by the I.C.F.C. range from £5000 to £250,000, or slightly more if further help is required at a later date, interest being at a percentage fixed for the whole period but payable only on the balance outstanding. The repayment period is arranged on a basis unlikely to cause hardship to the company concerned, and may extend to ten or twenty years. The small private company operating on a sound basis is the most favoured for loan purposes.

Further facilities are also available in the form of a hire purchase scheme whereby companies may obtain plant and other fixed assets.

The Estate Duties Investment Trust is managed by the I.C.F.C. and this body assists in making provision for estate duty incident on the estates of shareholders in private companies where holdings are large in relation to total resources, or where continuity of control is desired for family or other reasons.

EXAMINATION QUESTIONS

1. State the different methods of raising temporary funds which might be considered by a trading company requiring additional working capital for a period. [C.A. (1962)

2. A motor accessories manufacturer finds that owing to growing demand it must build a new factory. State the various sources of finance available and the main factors affecting the final choice of such finance. [C.C.A.

3. Mainroad Ltd, an old established private company, has for many years owned and occupied freehold shop property standing in the books at its cost of £50,000 but recently professionally valued for the directors at £150,000. A proposal has been received from a substantial property company that Mainroad Ltd should sell the property to them for £175,000 and that the purchasers should lease it back for a period of 21 years at an exclusive rental of £12,250, the tenant being responsible for all rates, repairs and insurance.

You are required to state the points (excluding taxation) to which you consider that the directors of Mainroad Ltd should have regard in deciding whether to proceed further with this proposal. [C.A. (1962)

4. You are financial adviser to a large privately owned manufacturing company which requires new plant to meet the export drive. The last Balance Sheet was as follows:

Capital	£500,000	Cash at bank	£5,000
Reserves	200,000	Stocks and debtors	900,000
Creditors	800,000	Plant	400,000
		Premises	195,000
	£1,500,000		£1,500,000

It is anticipated that the necessary plant would cost £200,000 and that orders for £400,000 are immediately available on which a 20% return would be obtained. Additional stocks would involve £50,000 and it is expected that three months' credit would be allowed to customers.

(a) Examine the proposition and state whether you consider the return sufficient.

(b) Compare and choose the best method of financing the plant purchase from among the following alternatives:

(i) Hire purchase at an interest rate of 7% (repayable by half-yearly instalments over ten years).

(ii) Bank overdraft at 7%.

(iii) State financing body on 7% redeemable preference shares, voting when in arrear as to dividend, redeemable by annual drawings over ten years.

(c) How would you expect to finance the investment in stocks?

(d) Would any other investment be necessary other than in plant and stock? If so how would you finance it? [C.C.A.

5. The share capital of Excelsior Ltd consists of 2,000,000 Ordinary shares of 10s. each. Profits and dividends have grown steadily over the past decade, the 1961 dividend (14%) being covered nearly three times. Total reserves at the end of 1961 amounted to £1,200,000. The shares are quoted in London, the current price being 29s. 6d. to 31s. 6d.

The company has a short term loan of £600,000 outstanding bearing interest of 6% per annum. The board has decided to raise £1,000,000 to repay the loan, provide additional working capital and buy additional machinery. It is estimated that the additional profits accruing from such expansion will amount to some £50,000 a year.

The following alternative methods of raising finance in the prevailing market conditions have been suggested:

(a) Issue of £1,030,000 6% Convertible Loan Stock 1975–78 at par convertible at the holder's option into Ordinary shares on 1st January 1967 at 32s. per share.

(b) Placing of £1,040,000 5¾% Debentures 1980–83 at 99.

(c) Rights issue of 800,000 Ordinary shares at 25s. 6d. a share.

(d) Placing of 1,020,000 8% Cumulative Preference shares of £1 at par, redeemable at the company's option at 20s. 6d. per share in or after 1975.

Advise the board on such suggestions, stating the major factors which must be considered.   [C.C.A.

6. In recent years many organisations have leased plant and equipment instead of purchasing it. Describe a typical lease arrangement and indicate the factors to be taken into account in deciding whether or not to lease.
                                                                        [C.C.A.

7. Give a brief account of the main institutions providing (a) short term (b) long term finance for British industry.   [C.C.A.

8. A summary of the most recent balance sheet of Quantum Ltd is given in the Appendix below. The company is now (January 1968) appraising a major investment project which would require an initial outlay of £2m. and would be expected to increase earnings by £225,000 per annum for an indefinitely long time.

You are given the following additional information:

(1) The directors have not yet finally decided what dividend to recommend for 1967 (payable 31st March 1968). They estimate that the company has £2m. in cash, surplus to its requirements for the present level of operations; and they had thought to use the whole of this sum to increase the dividend payment to 25%.

(2) The following ordinary dividends have been paid for the last five years:

March 1963   15%
      1964   15%
      1965   15%
      1966   20%
      1967   20%

A bonus issue of one new ordinary share for every five held was made on 1st April 1964. No other bonus issues and no rights issues were made during the period. The market price of the shares on 1st April 1962 was 66 shillings ex. div. and the market price on 31st December 1967 was 80 shillings.

(3) The index of retail prices has increased in recent years at the average rate of 3% p.a. (compound).

(4) The debentures are redeemable at par, £100, on 31st December 1980.

Interest is payable on 31st December in each year. The debentures have a current market price of £75.

You are required to:

(a) Indicate the main sources of capital available to finance the project and explain how you would decide which source, or combination of sources, is best. Discuss the problem of determining a suitable discount rate for use in appraising the project. Illustrate your answer by calculations, using the data given in the question, amplified where necessary, by reasonable (and specified) assumptions. Ignore taxation.

(b) Indicate briefly how your answer to (a) would differ if taxation were to be taken into account.

APPENDIX

QUANTUM LIMITED

Summary Balance Sheet at 31st December 1967

	£m.		£m.
Share Capital		Fixed Assets	18·8
8m. Ordinary Shares of £1	8·0	Current Assets	12·4
Profit and Loss Account	11·6		
4% Debentures (at par)	4·8		
Current Liabilities	6·8		
	31·2		31·2

[J. Dip. M.A.

Chapter II

SOURCES OF CAPITAL

THE ultimate source of capital is, of course, the investor, but there are a number of ways by which a business may endeavour to obtain the finance it requires with the maximum of certainty and the minimum of expense.

When seeking to capitalise a business it is essential to know the amount of finance required, and the type of undertaking and its relevant circumstances. However, it is equally important that the search for funds should be made when the appeal is likely to have the desired effect. It is necessary, therefore, to consider the various methods of raising capital together with the conditions in which a business may find it expedient to apply them.

1. PRIVATE AGREEMENTS

This is the simplest and most common method of raising capital. Where partnerships or sole traders are concerned, private investors may be persuaded to finance such businesses by supplying capital or loans, or by subscribing a share as a limited partner (*see* p. 3). Such business is mostly done on a personal basis and requires no comment here save that where sole traders and partnerships are concerned, proper agreements should always be drawn up with regard to any investments made.

2. ISSUES MADE PRIVATELY

By far the greater number of limited liability companies registered are those of a private nature, which implies that the majority of such bodies obtain their capital by means of issues made privately.

Such issues may be made, on formation, to a sole trader or partnership, there being none of the various requirements that have to be dealt with where a public issue is concerned. Additional shares may be taken up from time to time by existing shareholders or by others introduced to them, but where it is desired to raise considerable amounts of new capital it is necessary to obtain access to the capital market. This may be done by various means, including that of private placings.

3. PRIVATE PLACINGS

Using the services of the company's accountant or stockbroker, negotiations may be entered into with a finance house, not to obtain a loan, but to take up shares or debentures in the company. The broker may also place the shares or debentures with financial institutions, such as investment trust companies or insurance companies, since these organisations are willing to take up such unquoted securities which may not be readily saleable but are sound and promise a favourable earnings yield.

Marketability of shares is an important factor and although a private company may build up its capital resources by means of "ploughing back" profits, such matters as providing against death duties, disposing of holdings or enlarging the number of shareholders prior to an issue to existing shareholders, all necessitate the establishment of a wider market in the shares. To implement this, application may be made to the council of the stock exchange for a quotation of the company's shares by means of an "introduction."

4. INTRODUCTIONS

The company, acting through its broker supported by two dealers, will make formal application for the company's shares to be quoted, whereupon there follows an investigation into the company and its affairs by the various departments of the stock exchange.

The Share and Loan Department of the Exchange must approve the advertisement which is required to be published in at least two London newspapers. This advertisement contains much the same information as required in a Prospectus (*see* below) with a number of additions, *e.g.* whereas a Prospectus is legally required to show the foregoing five years' profits or losses, the stock exchange requirement is for ten years, unless waived at their discretion.

Certificates must be submitted by the company's accountants and/or auditors, who have submitted the report on profits, etc., of the company stating the nature of adjustments made in such profits, for the purposes of the Prospectus and reconciling these with the profits shown on the audited accounts, and also certifying their satisfaction as to the adequacy of depreciation charged in the adjusted profits and that the stocks and work-in-progress have been properly valued throughout the period covered by their certification.

Proofs of certain documents, such as for instance share certificates, must also be submitted for approval, together with the written consent of valuers (whose services may be used in respect of, say, valuation of fixed assets), accountants and any other experts engaged, in respect of their reports appearing in the advertisement. Copies of the company's Memorandum and Articles of Association must be submitted, there being various requirements as to matters to be included in the Articles. Details of directors' qualifications, remuneration and obligations must be shown, together with a short directors' report on the company's trading and financial prospects for the ensuing year.

The advertisement itself must state that it is issued in compliance with the regulations of the council of the stock exchange concerned, and that the directors accept full responsibility both collectively and individually for the accuracy of the information contained therein.

Arrangements must be made to ensure that an adequate number of shares will be made available on the market. Evidence to this effect must be given, and that the support of at least two stock-jobbers has been obtained. The arrangement might take the form of giving jobbers an option to take quite a large number of shares at an agreed price and a further number at a higher figure. If a lively demand for the shares is stimulated by the advertising, the jobbers can then meet it, so obviating a steep rise in price; on the other hand, if demand is disappointing, the shareholders will not obtain the price they had hoped for but the jobber is protected at the agreed figure.

The advertisement of a stock exchange introduction, since it is not "offering to the public for subscription or purchase any shares or debentures . . ." does not appear to constitute a Prospectus as defined by the Companies Act, 1948, and there is no legal obligation therefore to file a copy with the Registrar of Companies, but if the company has converted from a private to a public company, then a Statement in lieu of Prospectus must be filed.

5. STOCK EXCHANGE PLACINGS

If the amount of the issue is not large enough to justify a public issue, considerable expense may be saved by adopting the method of a placing combined with an introduction.

In this case a broker, often in co-operation with an issuing house, will arrange for a number of large investors, such as those mentioned with regard to private placings, to take up the shares or debentures to be issued. Having reached agreement with the institutions concerned, application is made in the same way as for an "introduction." Alternatively, rather than acting as intermediary and using their connections, the broker or issuing house may purchase the securities at an agreed price, at par or above, and then sell them at a disclosed profit to interested investors.

The advertisement published on this occasion, however, is considered to form a Prospectus under the Companies Act, 1948, and must therefore be lodged with the Registrar of Companies.

The stock exchange does not view placings very favourably, partly because no publicity is involved on their issue; also, since the shares have a limited "spread," those who take them up are able to make an immediate profit on any rise in price when the official quotation is given. Furthermore, until the placings are actually made, the stock exchange will not give permission to deal. Such placings, therefore, most often take place where the amount is relatively small, say in the region of £100,000 to £300,000, and where a private company converts to a public company.

6. ISSUES MADE PUBLICLY

Since by such issues the public at large are invited to invest their funds in various undertakings, the legal aspects have received careful consideration and have grown more stringent with the passage of time. Moreover, the stock exchange here again insists upon further safeguards before it will give permission to deal, culminating in the Council's recommendations in 1964 for disclosure of certain additional information by public companies to their shareholders. This information covers, in brief, such matters as the supplying of information about the composition of groups of companies and major interests in associated companies, disclosure of turnover, an analysis of trading results where the operations of a group are diverse, and the issue of quarterly or half-yearly interim reports.

The Council has unhappily been forced to make this move by events which have proved that investors can still lose large sums in circumstances that might never have arisen had such information been disclosed in time.

The numerous stock exchange and other requirements now having become quite complicated, it is advisable for a company intending to make a public issue to seek, through its accountants or other advisers, the aid of an issuing house. The latter institution has already been mentioned and some explanation of its nature and activities is advisable here.

Issuing house services

The issuing house is an institution which acts as an intermediary between investors and companies seeking capital in the form of shares or debentures. The great majority of issues made by stockbroking firms are now marketed by issuing houses which specialise in such work.

The Issuing Houses Association, formed in 1945, numbers almost 60 firms and includes such well-known institutions as the Charterhouse Finance Corporation Ltd, Hambros Bank Ltd and the Industrial Finance & Investment Corporation Ltd. Since the success or otherwise of an issue may largely depend upon their efforts, they conduct the most careful enquiries before agreeing to act on behalf of a company. That they take such care in this direction is understandable, for their name depends upon the success attending their efforts, and since they are looked upon as reputable organisations, investors are prepared to accept their backing as signifying a safe investment.

Before commencing the work involved in marketing the issue, the issuing house will first satisfy itself as to the nature and previous conduct of the company; matters such as efficient management, steady and adequate earnings and other factors, while not necessarily meeting any legal requirement, nevertheless constitute sound business policy, and are taken into consideration.

Having decided to act, full discussions will be entered into with the company's accountants and solicitors as to the nature of the issue and when it is to be made (for timing is a vital factor); the nature of the shares to be offered and their relationship to existing capital; and, in the case of a new company, the capital gearing (*see* Chapter III).

Responsibility will be taken by the issuing house for such matters as advertising, underwriting and compliance with stock exchange and various legal requirements, including that of the issue of the Prospectus.

The Prospectus

This document, as required under the Companies Act, 1948, serves to make available to investors the relevant facts concerning an issue of securities. Certain information *must* be given and a selection of items is given below, but in practice the minimum requirements are often exceeded, since everything that will serve to convince investors and their expert advisers of the soundness of the company and the integrity of its directorate is to the company's advantage.

This selection, much abbreviated, covers some of the items of particular interest to accountants:

1. Before issue of the Prospectus, a copy certified by the chairman and two other directors must be registered with the Registrar of Companies. It must also be signed by any expert (such as an accountant) whose opinion is given thereon.

2. Full details regarding directors, including any qualification shares to be held, any remuneration fixed by the Articles of Association, and details of any director's interest in the promotion of, or in any property to be acquired by, the company.

3. The minimum subscription which in the directors' opinion is necessary to provide for the purchase of any property, payment of preliminary expenses, and working capital.

4. Benefits paid or given to any promoter.

5. Where there are various classes of shares, the voting rights and rights in respect of capital and dividends of the various classes.

6. Auditor's reports to be given:

   (*a*) On profits, losses and rates of dividends for the past five financial years, and assets and liabilities at the last date on which the accounts were made up.

   (*b*) On any business to be acquired out of the proceeds of the issue.

   (*c*) On any company which is to become a subsidiary on the acquisition of shares out of the proceeds of the issue.

For fuller information regarding Prospectus requirements the reader is referred to the relevant sections of the Companies Act, 1948, and in particular to the Fourth Schedule, where the matters affecting the Prospectus are detailed. The recommendations of the Institute of Chartered Accountants in *Accountants' reports for prospectuses: adjustments and other matters* (N16) are also of interest since they are concerned with matters affecting the duties of accountants.

Underwriting

An underwriting agreement is a contract whereby an issuing house or other financial institution or person undertakes to apply for, or to find some third party to apply for, any shares or debentures not taken up by the public. It is essential that all the shares be taken up since the company's plans will have been made in the expectation of obtaining the necessary capital; the underwriting therefore takes the form of an insurance. The issuing house assisting in the marketing of the shares may itself underwrite the whole issue, sub-underwriting in turn if it so wishes, or it may arrange for underwriting with some other institution, charging a so-called overriding commission for the service. The rate or amount of the underwriting commission payable must be disclosed in the prospectus or Statement in lieu of Prospectus.

Again, as with the issuing house, the underwriters will make investigation into the financial standing of the company and its prospective earnings yield. From their intimate knowledge of the market they will be able to judge whether it will be necessary for them to take up a proportion of the shares and they will decide whether or not they are prepared to do so. The fact that the issue is underwritten is a further item in inspiring confidence in investors, but they will also take note of the rate the underwriters have considered necessary for their protection, and take it as an indication of the "quality" of the issue.

The underwriter need not be requested to underwrite the whole issue but only a proportion; he is remunerated according to the amount underwritten. Where the shares appear attractive he may "underwrite firm," that is, while underwriting a proportion he may request that the shares be allotted to him regardless of the amount taken up by the public.

While issues are underwritten to ensure their being fully taken up, nowadays issues are frequently over-subscribed.

Over-subscription

Where issues are over-subscribed, it is not usual to allot shares according to the first letters dealt with, but either to omit small applications or to "scale down" the applications received, so ensuring a spread of shareholding over a larger number of shareholders. Where such scaling-down takes place the applicants are allotted only a proportion of the shares they have applied for, the excess payments submitted are not returned but applied towards the amount due on allotment.

Specimen question

A company invites applications for 100,000 Ordinary shares of £1 each to be issued at a premium of £0·12½ a share, payable as to £0·25 on application, £0·37½ on allotment, including the premium of £0·12½, and £0·50 on first and final call. Any excess above the amount due on allotment is returnable. Applications are received for an aggregate of 180,000 shares.

Shares are allotted to applicants for 60,000 shares in full. Applications in respect of 40,000 shares are scaled down 50% and the remaining applications are scaled down 75%.

Show the Application and Allotment Account and relevant details of the issue up to allotment.

Answer

APPLICATION AND ALLOTMENT ACCOUNT

Cash—excess received on allotment returned	£7,500	Cash received on application	£45,000
Ordinary Share Capital Account	50,000	Cash received on allotment	25,000
Share Premium Account	12,500		
	£70,000		£70,000

DETAILS OF THE ISSUE

Method of issue	Shares applied for	Shares allotted	Cash received	Amount due up to allotment	Amount due (returnable) on allotment
Issued in full	60,000	60,000	£15,000	£37,500	£22,500
Scaled down 50%	40,000	20,000	10,000	12,500	2,500
Scaled down 75%	80,000	20,000	20,000	12,500	(7,500)
	180,000	100,000	£45,000	£62,500	£17,500

7. OFFERS FOR SALE

The alternative method of making a public issue is by an "offer for sale." This method resembles a stock exchange placing save that the issuing house or broker purchases the shares or debentures and then offers them for sale to the public (not to particular clients) at a price which will cover their own expenses plus a disclosed profit margin. This difference is revealed in the advertisement, where details of the company's contracts are mentioned. The advertisement, very similar to that for a placing, will require a slight variation owing to the fact that the company supplies the information, formerly required from them direct, in the form of a chairman's letter addressed to the issuers. The directors' responsibility remains, however, and liability also attaches to the directors of the issuing company. A copy of the "offer for sale" has to be registered with the Registrar of Companies.

This method is considered more favourably than that of placings, since the public are given the opportunity to apply for the securities being offered and, as the company is assured of a definite sum, financial planning is greatly facilitated.

8. ISSUES BY TENDER

Issues by tender are being used increasingly by companies. This method of issue requires the investor to tender for a number of shares at the maximum price he is prepared to pay. A minimum figure for application is announced with specified multiples at which the bids should be made, *e.g.* a minimum of £1·25*s*. for a £1 share with multiples of £0·02½. Every allotment is made at the same price, the only difference between this and the normal share issue being that the price is not fixed in advance by the company.

If the issue is not fully subscribed, the minimum price is applied. If there is an over-subscription, the price fixed is that which is sufficient to cover the whole issue. In order to ensure a reasonable "spread", and the establishment of a market in the shares, allocations are fixed by the company on what is considered by them an equitable basis.

Example

In a recent issue, a company offered 500,000 £0·25 Ordinary shares with a minimum fixed at £1·10, tenders to be made in multiples of £0·02½. The final issue price was fixed at £1·30 after tenders had been received as high as £2·20. Those offering less than £1·30 were repaid. The remainder were allotted shares on the following basis:

(*a*) Applicants at £1·40 and over were allotted in full, subject to a maximum of 5000 shares per application.

(*b*) Applicants at £1·37½ for up to 1000 received full allocation at the striking price of £1·30, those applying for 2000 and over received 1500, *e.g.* an applicant for 100,000 shares received 2500 shares.

(*c*) Applicants at £1·35 and £1·32½ and £1·30 received 100 shares.

This method of dealing with share issues is a further advance in the endeavours being made to stop the unfortunate effects of "stagging" and is most effective when, as frequently happens, issues are heavily over-subscribed.

"Stagging"

This term is used to denote the activities of speculators who apply for shares on new issues when market conditions are such that demand exceeds supply. They have no intention of holding shares but make application with the intention of selling at a profit as the price rises and before the full amount is due and payable on the shares. The demand they create is not a true reflection of the climate of the market and merely serves to raise prices unduly.

As the full price is payable on application when issues are made by tender the "quick profit" tactics of stags are obviously curtailed.

9. ISSUES TO EXISTING SHAREHOLDERS

The "rights" issue to members is an inexpensive and convenient way of raising additional capital. This method and the capitalisation of

internal resources by means of bonus issues are dealt with in Chapter
XVI in connection with the valuation of securities.

EXAMINATION QUESTIONS

1. What are the advantages of the shares in a company being dealt in and
quoted on a stock exchange? [C.A. (1964)
2. You have been approached by the directors of an investment trust
company, who are seeking your advice on obtaining a stock exchange
quotation for their company: details relevant to the company are listed below.

You are required to recommend a method for obtaining a quotation and
outline particulars that may be required by the stock exchange in support of
any application that may be made on the basis of your recommendations.

Ordinary shares of £1 each	—authorised	—£2,500,000
Ordinary shares of £1 each	—issued and fully paid	—£1,200,000

The company carries on the business of an investment trust specialising in
the acquisition of minority holdings in unquoted companies. It is a public
company the shares of which are held by a number of financial institutions.

Details at 31st March 1963.

Investments, at or under cost:

Ordinary shares: quoted in United Kingdom	£1,562,118
unquoted	834,116
	£2,396,234
Capital reserve—investment reserve	£1,144,628
Creditors and accrued expenses	25,189
Debtors and payments in advance	17,612
Taxation recoverable	5,171
Proposed dividend (net)	98,000
Loans to local authorities	150,000
Cash at bank	23,318
Market value of quoted investments at 31st March 1963	2,265,112
Profit and Loss Account	124,518
Commitments outstanding in respect of calls on certain investments	25,000
Contingent liability (being uncalled capital on an investment)	10,000
The directors estimate the value of the unquoted investments to be	£834,116

Profits for the ten years to 31st March 1963 are as follows:

(a) Before charging United Kingdom income tax.

(b) After charging all expenses of management but before writing off
formation expenses.

Year to 31st March	1956—£17,219	Year to 31st March	1960—£114,322
,,	1957— 32,651	,,	1961— 121,171
,,	1958— 62,117	,,	1962— 150,185
,,	1959— 85,441	,,	1963— 178,466

Profits, less losses, on realisations of investments are transferred to capital
reserve. The company distributes approximately 90% of its income by way
of dividend. The dividend for 1963 being 13½% amounting to £160,000 gross.

The directors estimate that the profits to 31st March 1964 will be £200,000 approximately, before taxation, in which case it would be their intention to pay dividends amounting to £180,000 gross. [C.C.A.

3. What sources of additional capital are available to a private limited company?

What factors would the directors of such a company require to take into consideration in making their decision as to the form of such additional capital? [C.A. (S)

4. Stomps Ltd was a private company that had been trading since 1st July 1956. It has recently been converted into a public company and an issue of 750,000 £1 Ordinary shares and 250,000 £1 $7\frac{1}{2}\%$ second Preference shares is to be made; the existing Ordinary shares are to be converted into Founders' shares which give the holders superior voting rights, but otherwise rank *pari passu* with the new Ordinary shares. You are the auditor of Stomps Ltd and you are required to draft the report for the prospectus as laid down by the Fourth Schedule of the Companies Act, 1948.

The summarised Balance Sheets and Profit and Loss Accounts are as follows:

Year ended 30th June:	1957	1958	1959	1960	1961
Ordinary £1 shares	£20,000	£20,000	£20,000	£50,000	£100,000
8% £1 Cumulative Preference shares	—	—	25,000	25,000	25,000
P. & L. account balance	3,000	10,000	10,000	3,000	15,000
Tax reserve	2,000	4,000	1,200	—	27,000
Bank overdraft	—	22,000	28,000	25,000	16,900
Current liabilities	10,700	18,000	14,600	13,000	20,000
Proposed dividends	—	—	1,200	—	12,600
	£35,700	£74,000	£100,000	£116,000	£216,500
Fixed assets, at cost	23,000	43,300	83,400	112,400	154,400
Less: Depreciation	2,300	6,400	13,400	22,400	34,400
	20,700	36,900	70,000	90,000	120,000
Stock	8,000	20,800	23,000	18,000	66,000
Cash and debtors	7,000	16,300	7,000	8,000	30,500
	£35,700	£74,000	£100,000	£116,000	£216,500

		1957	1958	1959	1960	1961
Trading profit		£9,000	£19,000	£15,000	£7,100	£70,700
Less: Depreciation	£2,300	£4,100	£7,000	£9,000	£12,000	
Directors' fees	500	500	500	500	1,000	
Directors' salaries	1,200	2,000	3,000	2,700	3,500	
Bank interest	—	400	1,500	2,300	2,800	
		4,000	7,000	12,000	14,500	19,300
		5,000	12,000	3,000	(7,400)	51,400
Taxation		2,000	5,000	1,200	(400)	25,000
		3,000	7,000	1,800	(7,000)	26,400
Ordinary dividend		—	—	600	—	12,000
Preference dividend		—	—	1,200	—	2,400
				1,800		14,400
						12,000
Balance brought forward		—	3,000	10,000	10,000	3,000
Balance carried forward		£3,000	£10,000	£10,000	£3,000	£15,000

You are informed in addition that:

(a) The money received will be used to purchase additional plant at the factory and open two new branches at Bristol and Sunderland.

(b) The fixed assets have been revalued, and the revaluation figure of £220,000 will be used in future accounts.

(c) Prior to 1959–60, stock, etc., was valued at prime cost only; since then a proportion of the overheads amounting to 10% of prime cost has been included in the stock valuation.

(d) An assumed tax rate of £0·40 in the £ has been used. [C.C.A.

CHAPTER III

PRIORITIES AND GEARING

WHEN it has been decided how much capital is required to finance an undertaking, consideration must be given as to which of the types of capital outlined in Chapter I should be employed and the proportions in which it is to be raised.

ATTRACTING INVESTORS

These matters cannot be considered simply from the point of view of the greatest advantage to the company, however, since investors can only be induced to subscribe for securities which appear sufficiently attractive to them. Different aspects of the return to be received appeal to various types of investors; where they are willing to take a risk on the capital outlay involved they will require a greater income as compensation for the risk factor and Ordinary shares would offer the greatest appeal. If security is considered more important, a lower yield but with more assured return on capital would lead to the favouring of fixed-interest-bearing securities, such as unsecured loan stock giving prior rights on return of capital. If greater security is desired, Debentures having a specific charge would be preferable. Normally, the greater the risk involved the greater the return desired; conversely, the safer the security the lower the income yield. This more usual aspect of expected return has now been modified in the light of present methods of taxation. Investors are willing to accept lower income yields on stocks maintaining an element of risk than on fixed-interest securities, in the hope of mitigating the effects of taxation by the subsequent expansion of the business concerned, and the ploughing back of profits with the related issue of bonus shares. This investment in so called "growth" stocks (*see* p. 356) has led to a willingness on the part of investors to accept lower dividend yields on stocks of a slightly speculative nature.

These broad principles may be varied in order to meet market conditions and to enlarge the area of appeal. To encourage investment by those more inclined to desire safety, participation rights may be given to Preference share holders, likewise redemption rights in respect of Preference shares and Debentures may be enhanced by the promise of a premium on redemption.

Prevailing market rates governing securities issued by similar undertakings will decide what rates must be offered. If the business involves an element of risk and profits are likely to fluctuate, a higher rate will have to be offered on Ordinary shares than on those of a more stable business. Likewise, in the case of a new company, a higher rate will have to be offered than in that of a well established organisation in the same trade. Where the undertaking is of a speculative nature, shareholders may face the prospect of there being times when no dividend can be declared. Therefore a larger distribution is sought when profits *are* available. This rather more extreme example is not the most usual, however, as companies normally endeavour to maintain a regular dividend on their Ordinary shares around a certain figure, after allowing for a surplus to be ploughed back into the business.

This latter is an important point since it serves to increase the capital value of the shares, and capital profits now have an added attraction for investors as mentioned above. Adequate dividends should be maintained, however, since a low yield may lead to a low quotation and the possibility of subsequent take-over bids (*see* Chapter XVI).

CAPITAL GEARING

The term "capital gearing" is used to describe the ratio between the ordinary share capital and the fixed-interest bearing securities of a company. The "gearing" of a company or the relationship between its equity share and preference and/or loan capital, is important. In the first place the equity shareholders may rightly expect to receive the benefits which arise from their having supplied the main capital structure of the business and for having taken the inherent risks—but at the same time they should be prepared also to stand the losses which may arise. The temptation to make others bear such risks and at the same time to obtain cheap capitalisation of the company by issuing fixed-interest-bearing stocks should be avoided.

The capital gearing reveals the suitability, or otherwise of the company's capitalisation. A large ratio of Debentures or—now less usually —Preference shares to Ordinary shares reveals a highly geared company. For example:

Highly geared		*Low-geared*	
Ordinary shares:	£50,000	Ordinary shares:	£200,000
Debentures:	£200,000	Debentures:	£50,000

It will be noted that the gearing is in inverse ratio to the ordinary share capital:

Highly geared—low equity share capital.
Low-geared—high equity share capital.

In the case of a highly geared company, fluctuations in profits are usually followed by disproportionately large increases or decreases in the return to the Ordinary shareholders.

This capital gearing, or "leverage," is important not only to the company, but also to prospective investors. It must be carefully planned since it affects the company's capacity to maintain an even distribution policy in the face of any difficult trading periods which may occur. Furthermore, its immediate effect may be to enable a company to pay higher Ordinary dividends when there is only a narrow margin of profit but its long term effects on the efficiency of the company are far-reaching. Distribution policies and the building up of reserves, as well as an even dividend policy, mentioned above, are all affected by the company's "gear ratio."

When commencing a business venture, the amount of profits available for distribution after the maintenance of reserves must be estimated, and consideration given to the market rates of yields on investments in companies of a similar nature. For example, if the capital assets in the company are to total £150,000 and estimated profits available for distribution are to be £16,000 (ignoring taxation), and Ordinary shares in similar companies yield 12% on the market, then Ordinary shares issued for the total sum will not find a market at par since only 10·6% could be offered. Since it is inadvisable to issue new shares at a rate lower than par (*see* p. 6) the capital must be arranged to overcome this difficulty. It might be done by issuing £50,000 secured Debentures at 8%—market rates being relevant—and the remainder being covered by Ordinary shares. This would allow a distribution as follows:

£50,000	8% Mortgage debentures	£4,000
100,000	Ordinary shares (12% dividend)	12,000
		£16,000

It might be thought that if even more of the fixed-interest-bearing securities were offered at the lower rates, then even more would be available proportionately for the Ordinary share holders, and as profits might increase the Ordinary share holders would have still more to gain. It is at this point that the importance of the ratio of the capital gearing becomes apparent.

Example

The following are two methods which might be used to finance a company with a capital of £250,000 and with distributable profits before payment of debenture interest varying in two years from £27,000 to £18,000 (ignoring taxation).

Capitalisation	Method 1	Method 2
8% Debentures	£80,000	£200,000
Ordinary shares	£170,000	50,000
	£250,000	£250,000

Gearing ratio: 2·12 $\left(\dfrac{£170,000}{£80,000}\right)$ 0·25 $\left(\dfrac{£50,000}{£200,000}\right)$

First year—£27,000		
8% Debentures	£6,400	£16,000
Ordinary shares	20,600 (12%)	11,000 (22%)
	£27,000	£27,000

Second year—£18,000		
8% Debentures	£6,400	£16,000
Ordinary shares	11,600 (7%)	2,000 (4%)
	£18,000	£18,000

This simple illustration serves to reveal how the profits available for Ordinary share holders are subject to a much greater degree of fluctuation in a "highly geared" company (*i.e.* one with a low gear ratio) than in a company with low capital gearing. A reduction in profits by $33\frac{1}{3}\%$ has caused a fall in dividend rates under Method 1 by 42%, whereas under Method 2 the rate has fallen by 82% to 4%.

This fluctuation of dividends available for Ordinary share holders has unfortunate repercussions on share valuation in a period when difficult trading conditions force a reduction in profit distributions. Under such conditions share prices would fall, causing Ordinary shares to be avoided. However, when trading prospects are good, speculation in these shares might take place in the hope of large dividends and sharp increases in capital values.

The incidence of corporation tax has had its influence in recent times on the capital gearing of companies, since it has encouraged them to raise loan capital in larger proportions than would normally be justified as the loan interest paid is allowable for taxation purposes.

The following example shows somewhat more emphatically the effects of capital gearing. If the references to share valuation are not clear, it may be found advisable to study Chapter XVI before seeking to follow the example through to completion.

Specimen question (1)

Given the capitalisation of an old established company at £200,000 by one of the three methods shown, show the effect on Ordinary share prices and dividends where distributable profits, prior to payment of debenture interest, average £20,000 and fall and rise by £4000 respectively. For the purpose of the valuation of the Ordinary shares the rate of dividend yield on similar shares is 8%, the Ordinary share prices shown being calculated on the dividend yield basis, *e.g.* (28%/8%) × £1 = £3·50. (*see* Chapter XVI).

Capitalisation:	Method 1	2	3
5% Mortgage debentures	£80,000	£40,000	—
6% Preference shares	80,000	20,000	—
Ordinary shares	40,000	140,000	200,000
	£200,000	£200,000	£200,000

Answer

Method 1.

Distributable profits	£20,000	£16,000	£24,000
Apportionment of profits:			
5% Mortgage debentures	4,000	4,000	4,000
6% Preference shares	4,800	4,800	4,800
Ordinary shares	11,200 (28%)*	7,200 (18%)	15,200 (38%)
	£20,000	£16,000	£24,000
Ordinary share prices	£3·50	£2·25	£4·75

Method 2.

Apportionment of profits:			
5% Mortgage debentures	£2,000	£2,000	£2,000
6% Preference shares	1,200	1,200	1,200
Ordinary shares	16,800 (12%)	12,800 (9%)	20,800 (15%)
	£20,000	£16,000	£24,000
Ordinary share prices	£1·50	£1·12½	£1·87½

Method 3.

Profit all to Ordinary share holders	£20,000 (10%)	£16,000 (8%)	£24,000 (12%)
Ordinary share prices	£1·25	£1·00	£1·50

NOTES

Method 1

The company under this scheme is highly geared with a gear ratio of 0·25 (£40,000/160,000). This would have the effect of causing wide fluctuations in the profits available for Ordinary share dividends, which in turn would have repercussions on the price of the shares. Dividend equalisation reserves would not be the answer in such a case because Ordinary share holders would press for higher dividends while profits are available since any slight downward trend is immediately felt.

An important point to be emphasised with regard to highly geared companies is that since Ordinary share holders not only bear the risk but also reckon to benefit in times of prosperity, they are expected to contribute the greater part of the capital to be invested in assets of a permanent nature as well as providing sufficient funds to finance intangible assets and a proportion of the working capital. If they do not do so, it is taken as a sign of their lack

* Figures in parentheses show the Ordinary share dividend rate.

of confidence in the company. There are exceptions, *e.g.* in the case of a property owning company, but in general this important rule applies.

Method 2.

This would seem to be the most acceptable scheme. Advantage was taken of lower capitalisation rates with Preference share and loan capital, but the gearing is still quite low at 2·33 (£140,000/£60,000).

The issue of Debentures is often favoured, as the rate of interest is not only relatively low, but is also allowed as an expense against profits for taxation purposes whereas dividends are not. On the other hand, the raising of too great a sum by means of Debentures may cause difficulty in raising further loans, such as bank overdrafts, owing to the reduced security which may be offered.

This method, however, seems balanced adequately between preference and loan capital, and the more even fluctuation of profits available for Ordinary share holders is apparent, while the share prices also show less variation.

Method 3.

This scheme, while acceptable, loses the advantages to be gained from the varied capitalisation shown in method 2, and this is reflected in the lower dividend rates. Nevertheless, a decreased fluctuation in share prices and profits available is again apparent as compared with Scheme 1.

Where there are free reserves it is sometimes considered necessary to include them in ascertaining the capital gearing of a company; on the other hand, this factor can safely be disregarded where the distribution of income is being dealt with. The computation may still be carried out as shown, the omission of the reserves serving to emphasise the fact that the distribution reveals a case of (say) high gearing and that it might be advisable to capitalise the reserves available.

Furthermore, investors will be more concerned with the amount of prior charges on the income receivable by them than with the company's reserves. Prior charges are known as "priority percentages."

PRIORITY PERCENTAGES

Where a company has various classes of capital, it is of paramount importance that profits earned should be sufficient to meet the charges of the fixed-interest-bearing securities as well as allowing for a steady distribution to the Ordinary share holders and adequate transfers to reserve.

This is a matter to which investors will pay careful attention, ensuring that at each stage there are sufficient funds to meet the various charges in their order of preference.

Tables are therefore drawn up in the following form over a number of years to reveal the trends in the amount of dividend cover, and how far distributable profits can vary before interest or dividends may cease to be adequately covered.

Specimen question (2)

A company having a capital structure as shown hereunder is expected to pay an ordinary dividend of 10% and to transfer to reserve any balance remaining. The profits for the past two years prior to the payment of debenture interest have been £51,000 and £42,000 respectively (taxation being ignored)

Capital (inc. loan capital)		Allocation of interest and profit Year 1	Year 2
£100,000	5% Mortgage Debentures	£5,000	£5,000
200,000	6% Preference shares	12,000	12,000
300,000	Ordinary shares	30,000	30,000
	To reserve	4,000	
		51,000	47,000
	From reserve to meet deficiency of dividend earned		(5,000)
		£51,000	£42,000

You are required to compile a list of priority percentages for the two years

Answer

PRIORITY PERCENTAGES

	Debentures	Preference	Ordinary	Reserve
Year 1	$-9\frac{3}{4}$	$9\frac{3}{4}-33\frac{1}{3}$	$33\frac{1}{3}-92$	92–100
2	-12	$12-40\frac{1}{2}$	$40\frac{1}{2}-112$	112–100

(The actual figures are obtained by taking the allocation of profit at each stage and adding this to each prior distribution, e.g.

$$\frac{5,000}{51,000} \times 100 = 9\frac{3}{4}\%, \frac{5,000 + 12,000}{51,000} \times 100 = 33\frac{1}{3}\%, \text{ etc.})$$

The table reveals the insufficiency of earnings in the second year to maintain the proposed dividend and the serious outcome of this for the various classes of capital. Whereas in Year 1 the Debenture interest took $9\frac{3}{4}$% of the earnings and was backed by $90\frac{1}{4}$% of the profits, in Year 2, 12% was taken, leaving a backing of 88%. This is not so serious from the point of view of this first charge, but the backing for the Preference share holders has dropped from $66\frac{2}{3}$% to $59\frac{1}{2}$% and in the case of the Ordinary share holders the 100% of earnings has been exceeded, necessitating a drawing from reserves.

It may be added that Preference share investors can normally expect their dividend to be covered about three times by profits available for dividend purposes.

The following condensed Balance Sheets compiled from actual companies may serve to reveal the varying nature of capital structures and asset ratios. A few points of particular note are appended to each Balance Sheet.

Example (1)

PROPERTY COMPANY

	£000's		£000's
Share capital:		Freehold and leasehold	
6% Cumulative Preference shares	160	property	21,278
Ordinary stock units £0·25 each)	3,200	Fixtures and fittings	39
	——	Trade investments	32
	3,360	Current assets:	
Capital reserves:		Capital redemption policies at cost 19	
Share premium 7,690		Debtors, bank, etc. 1051	
General 455			—— 1,070
	—— 8,145		
Revenue reserve:			
Profit and loss	265		
Amount set aside for future taxation	31		
Secured liabilities:			
6¼% first mortgage debenture stock, 1990/95 4,750			
6½% do. 1986 340			
Mortgages 4,000			
	—— 9,090		
Current liabilities	1,528		
	£22,419		£22,419

NOTES

(i) The capital formation does not follow the usual structure, as it is highly geared, being made up of a large proportion of loan capital. In the case of a property company, this would possibly be due to the security offered on freehold and leasehold properties which form the major part of the company's assets.

(ii) The inclusion of capital redemption policies under "Current assets" would seem to indicate some attempt to set aside funds for ultimate redemption of the loan capital, but as the business is expanding and liquid resources are required the redemption aspect is not being strongly pursued at this stage.

(iii) Note the large proportion of capital made up of the share premium, indicating the success of the company's activities.

Example (2)

CHEMICAL COMPANY

	£m.		£m.
5% Cumulative Preference shares	34	Property, plant and equipment	413
Ordinary shares	246	Interest in subsidiary companies	97
	——	Net current assets:	
	280	Stocks 61	
Reserves:		Other current assets 65	
Capital 142			——
Revenue 90			126
	—— 232	*Less* current liabilities 68	
Unsecured loans	56		—— 58
	£568		£568

NOTES

(i) The large proportion of loan capital in unsecured loans indicates the gilt-edged nature of the company, since a less well-known company would have difficulty in obtaining so much loan capital without offering security.

(ii) Note the capital reserve created on revaluation of the company's properties.

Example (3)

MOTOR COMPANY

	£m.			£m.
5% Cumulative Preference shares	9	Freehold properties		13
Ordinary shares (£0·25 each)	42	Plant and equipment		27
	—			—
	51			40
Reserves:		Stocks and tools	41	
Capital	2	Other current assets	46	
Revenue	20		—	87
	— 22			
Current liabilities	54			
	£127			£127

NOTES

The asset structure of a large engineering concern is normal here but the figure for current liabilities against current assets other than stocks and tools is peculiar to motor manufacturers since immediate finance is often provided to customers, so lessening the sum for debtors as against creditors. Normally, trade debtors may be expected to exceed trade creditors owing to the gross profit addition on sales, assuming the same period of credit is applied.

Example (4)

MINING COMPANY

	£000's				£000's
Ordinary shares:		Fixed assets:			
12,500,000 at £0·20 each	2500	Main shafts, plant and machinery, etc.			3563
Capital reserves	411	Current assets:			
Revenue reserves	666	Investments		2048	
Amount set aside for taxation	856	Sundries		728	
				2776	
		Less current liabilities:			
		Taxation	573		
		Creditors	583		
		Proposed final dividend (Gross)	750		
				— 1906	870
	£4433				£4433

NOTES

(i) The issue of Ordinary capital only is normal in such companies, as investment is represented by a wasting asset, and the attraction of security necessary for low-interest-bearing stocks is not available.

(ii) The dividend for the year proposed by the company amounts to 30% gross. This, together with the large sums provided for taxation, indicates its prosperity but also reveals something of the speculative nature of the undertaking, a further reason for the equity issue.

(iii) The large amount of investments held is a feature of such companies. Depreciation is provided on assets which, owing to exhaustion of the mine, do not call for renewal. The amounts set aside are therefore invested, leading eventually to large holdings of securities. It is not uncommon, on the cessation of mining operations, for such companies to continue as investment trusts or finance companies.

EXAMINATION QUESTIONS

1. State what you understand by the following terms in relation to investment in companies:

(a) Capital gearing ratio.
(b) Dividend cover.
(c) Asset cover.
(d) Cash flow.
(e) Maturity. [C.A.(1963)

2. It has been suggested that British firms rely too much on equity capital and self-financing, paying too little attention to the possibilities of gearing. Comment on this, paying particular attention to the advantages and disadvantages of self-financing (for development and current purposes).
[C.C.A.

3. The XY Manufacturing Company Ltd has been a public company since 1938, its 6% Preference shares and its Ordinary shares being quoted on a provincial stock exchange. The company has recently entered upon a major scheme to expand its production and trading, and it is estimated that this will involve expenditure on fixed assets over the next two years of £500,000, with a further £250,000 for additional working capital. The following are abridged Balance Sheets at 31st December 1966 and 31st December 1967.

You are asked to write a report for the board outlining comprehensive proposals for bringing the company's issued capital more into line with the value of its net assets and for raising the additional capital required to finance the expansion scheme.

	31st Dec. 1967	31st Dec. 1966
Capital, authorised and issued, fully paid:		
300,000 6% Cumulative Preference shares of 13s. 4d. each	£200,000	£200,000
100,000 10% Cumulative 2nd Preference shares of £1 each	100,000	100,000
1,000,000 Ordinary shares of 4s. each	200,000	200,000
	500,000	500,000

Capital reserve:			
Share premiums		100,000	100,000
Revenue reserves:			
Future taxation	£210,000		£200,000
General	650,000		550,000
Profit and Loss Account	180,000		150,000
		1,040,000	900,000
		£1,640,000	£1,500,000

		31 Dec. 1967	31 Dec. 1966
Fixed assets:			
Freehold land, buildings, plant and equipment: at net book value at 31st Dec. 1957, *less* sales, plus additions since at cost		£920,000	£885,000
Less Depreciation		500,000	410,000
		420,000	475,000
Current assets:			
Stocks and work in progress	£985,000		£860,000
Debtors	692,000		570,000
Cash at bank and in hand	3,000		25,000
		1,680,000	1,455,000
Less Current liabilities:			
Creditors	177,250		202,000
Bank overdraft	44,800		—
Dividends, *less* tax:			
On 6% Preference shares	3,450		3,450
On 10% 2nd Preference shares	5,750		5,750
On Ordinary shares (final dividend of 25% making 40% for year)	28,750		28,750
Taxation	200,000		190,000
		460,000	430,000
		1,220,000	1,025,000
		£1,640,000	£1,500,000

[C.W.A.

4. Your clients, Jones & Smith, carry on business in partnership, sharing profits—Jones two-thirds and Smith one-third—after providing interest on capital at 5%. They decide to form their business into a limited company and you are requested to report to them on the capitalisation of the company. Mr Jones also wishes £10,000 of his capital to be registered in the name of his wife, but does not wish his wife to have any say in the running of the company.

You ascertain that the results of the last three years were as follows:

| | Year to 30th September | | |
	1960	1961	1962
Gross profit	£20,900	£23,900	£25,200
Less Overhead expenses	11,000	11,000	12,000
Net trading profit	9,900	12,900	13,200
Add Gain on sale of premises	—	3,900	—
	9,900	16,800	13,200
Interest on capital	1,000	1,200	1,100
Net profit	£8,900	£15,600	£12,100

BALANCE SHEET AT 30TH SEPTEMBER 1962

Fixed assets:		
Premises		£12,000
Plant and machinery		10,000
Motor vehicles		5,000
		27,000
Less Bond over property at 4%		10,000
		17,000
Current assets:		
Stock	£11,000	
Debtors	22,000	
Bank	1,000	
	£34,000	
Less Creditors	30,000	
		4,000
		£21,000
Capital account:		
Jones		16,000
Smith		5,000
		£21,000

You ascertain that the premises are valued at £21,000 and that the services of Jones and Smith are worth £3000 and £1500 per annum respectively. The average return on capital employed in similar businesses is 20%. Draft your report (ignore income tax).   [C.C.A.

5. During the next five years, the nationalised electricity industry in Great Britain is planning to incur capital expenditure to the extent of over £1300 million. It is proposed that over £300 million shall be met out of revenue surpluses which, if necessary, must be obtained by increasing charges to consumers.

Discuss the merits and demerits of using revenue for financing a proportion of capital expenditure in this way.   (C.A. (1963)

6. The share capital of a manufacturing company is as follows:

	Authorised	Issued and fully paid
6% Preference shares (£1 each)	£100,000	£100,000
Ordinary shares (£1 each)	450,000	250,000

The profits of the company have been steadily increasing and for the year to 31st December 1962 amounted to £80,000 before taxation.

For that year, in addition to the dividend on the Preference shares, a dividend was paid on the Ordinary shares of 12½% less tax.

Further expansion of the company's manufacturing activities involves capital expenditure of £250,000, which cannot be financed from existing resources. Consequently it has been suggested that this amount should be provided in one of two ways:

(i) A Debenture Issue of £250,000 at a rate of 6% per annum, associated with an increase to 7% per annum in the rate of dividend on the Preference shares to compensate for the prior ranking of the Debenture issue; or

(ii) A "rights" issue to the existing Ordinary share holders of four Ordinary shares of £1 each for every five Ordinary shares held, at an issue price of £1·25 a share.

You are required:

(a) To prepare statements showing the amount which would have been retained, if any, for Ordinary share holders under each scheme, starting with a profit of £80,000 before charging debenture interest and taxation at current rates; and thereafter make provision for dividends, including a dividend less tax of 12½% on the Ordinary shares.

(b) To calculate the increase in profits required under each scheme to allow the Ordinary dividend of 12½% to be twice covered; and

(c) To comment on which of the suggested methods of financing would be more attractive to the Ordinary share holders, assuming the trend of profits continues.   [C.A. (S)

CHAPTER IV

FINANCIAL PLANNING FOR
INITIAL CAPITALISATION

DETAILED budgets are necessary for the various aspects of a business. These are dealt with in Chapter IX. We are concerned here only with the initial capitalisation of a business. Having considered the types of capital available and the most effective structure to be applied, it remains to co-ordinate them so as to satisfy the capital requirements of a business. These requirements have to be ascertained by careful budgeting, for since capital is not obtained easily it would be expensive and wasteful to estimate broadly merely to avoid shortage. Excessive capitalisation may be just as harmful as a shortage of funds. Funds may be obtained by short-term borrowing, etc., but an over-capitalised business may find it difficult to divest itself of unnecessary funds; at the same time, current profits may be strained in the endeavour to keep up a return on capital comparable with that of competitors.

There is no set period which can be recommended for cash budgets in general. A period of months may be best, or of years, according to requirements.

In the case of a continuing business where budgetary control and standard costing systems are in operation, the forecasting of requirements should present no difficulty. Estimates and their subsequent fulfilment, with the variances which have arisen, will enable quite accurate budgets to be prepared. If methods of control are not maintained, the necessity of budgeting for future needs will reveal the inadequacy of the system and encourage the rectification of such a state of affairs; in either case the records of past transactions will be available.

At the commencement of a business, more has to be left to conjecture. Not only must costs be estimated, but income in the form of sales, etc., is dependent on demand. Businesses of any size, however, are not initiated on the off-chance. Expert opinion can be obtained as to formation expenses and running costs, and market research can give some idea of the likely income.

The expense involved in obtaining and retaining capital finance has already been mentioned. It is, therefore, essential to budget for costs and income over a period. This will ensure that funds are called upon only as needed, not estimated in total, called up and then left idle until required.

In both new and existing businesses, funds may be raised from outside sources in the form of share or loan capital, or by short term borrowing; but in a continuing business, internal resources can be assured by the "ploughing back" of profits. It is here that the creation of sinking funds with concomitant investments becomes apposite, for it is essential that the provision for depreciation should be utilised to replace assets. Inflationary tendencies give rise to the difficulty that such provisions often turn out to be inadequate when the time comes for the replacement of assets against which they have been made. These factors, and the necessity for providing working capital, are dealt with later.

The following specimen questions exemplify the method of preparing cash budgets. The use of a form of cash book showing estimated receipts and payments prior to the inclusion of the funds to be obtained will reveal the most suitable dates on which to call up the finance required.

Specimen question (1)

A and B agree to form a limited company to take over part of an existing business. They are to contribute £25,000 each for Ordinary shares issued at par and C is to supply any additional amount required to finance the business during the first six months without recourse to an overdraft. C is to be given 8% Debentures, to the nearest £1000 above the amount required, secured on the freehold premises.

The company is to purchase freehold premises for £25,000, stock £8000 and plant, fittings and motor vans for an additional £6000. Settlement is to be made in the month of incorporation.

The following estimates are made of transactions for the six months commencing 1st May:

Sales: May, £14,500; June, £16,000; July, £18,000 and £24,000 for each of the following three months. Gross profit on sales to be at the rate of 20%.

Purchases: to be sufficient to secure stock at the end of each month adequate to supply the sales of the following month.

Debtors: to settle their accounts net by the end of the second month after the month of sale.

Creditors: to be paid at the end of the month following the month of purchase.

Expenses:

(a) Preliminary expenses, £800, to be paid in June.
(b) General expenses, £600 per month, payable at the end of each month.
(c) Wages and salaries, £800 payable on the last day of each month for the first four months, and £900 thereafter.
(d) Rates, £400 per annum, payable six-monthly on 31st March and 30th September, to be paid in the month following that in which they are due. Ignore apportionments on purchase of freehold.

Assume shares and debentures are issued on 1st May.
Draw up a cash budget and budgeted final accounts and Balance Sheet to 30th October (ignoring taxation).

Answer

CASH BUDGET

for six months ending 30th October

Receipts	May	June	July	Aug.	Sept.	Oct.	Total
Shares	£50,000						£50,000
8% Debentures	18,000						18,000
Sales			£14,500	£16,000	£18,000	£24,000	72,500
Balance b/f		27,600	9,000	7,700	3,100	400	—
	£68,000	£27,600	£23,500	£23,700	£21,100	£24,400	£140,500

Payments							
Fixed and current assets	£39,000						£39,000
Preliminary expenses		£800					800
Wages and salaries	800	800	£800	£800	£900	£900	5,000
Expenses	600	600	600	600	600	600	3,600
Purchases	—	16,400	14,400	19,200	19,200	19,200	88,400
Rates						200	200
Balance c/f	27,600	9,000	7,700	3,100	400	3,500	3,500
	£68,000	£27,600	£23,500	£23,700	£21,100	£24,400	£140,500

BUDGETED TRADING AND PROFIT AND LOSS ACCOUNT

for the six months ending 30th October

Opening stock	£8,000	Sales		£120,500
Purchases	107,600			
	115,600			
Less Closing stock	19,200			
	96,400			
Gross profit c/d	24,100			
	£120,500			£120,500
Wages and salaries	£5,000	Gross Profit b/d		£24,100
Rates	200			
Expenses	3,600			
Debenture interest	720			
Net profit c/d	14,580			
	£24,100			£24,100
		Net profit b/d		£14,400

NOTIONAL BALANCE SHEET AS AT 30TH OCTOBER

Ordinary share capital		£50,000	Freehold premises	£25,000
Profit and Loss Account		14,580	Plant and fittings	6,000
8% Debentures	£18,000		Stock	£19,200
Add Debenture			Debtors	48,000
interest out-			Bank	3,500
standing	720			70,700
		18,720		
Trade creditors		19,200	Preliminary expenses	800
		£102,500		£102,500

Specimen question (2)

C and D form a limited company to take over a business, settlement to the proprietor being in the form of £40,000 Ordinary shares at par for the following items:

Plant and machinery	£60,000
Premises	30,000
Stock raw material	3,000
Goodwill	5,000

The balance of the purchase price is payable in two equal instalments at 2% interest three months and six months after the formation of the company on 1st April.

Estimates of the company's activities are made as follows:

	April	May	June	July	Aug.	Sept. and forward to Dec.
Production (units)	200	200	300	300	400	500
Sales (units)	100	100	300	450	450	500

Production costs:

Materials	£10 per unit, but from July, £7
Direct labour	£4 per unit, but from July, £3

Purchases are to be made in order to ensure sufficient stock at the month's end for the following month's production. Work in progress is to be ignored.

A new machine is to be installed and paid for in June for the sum of £25,000; it is to be in operation from July. Depreciation on machinery is to be at the rate of 10% on cost.

Selling prices: £20 per unit for the remainder of the current year, but from January 1st in the following year selling prices are to be reduced by £0·50 when it is estimated sales will be increased by 10%.

40% of debtors are expected to pay one month after sale at 2½% cash discount, the remainder to settle net by the end of the second month after sale. Trade creditors are to be paid one month after purchase of materials. Wages are settled by the end of the month and expenses are reckoned on a monthly basis of £1200 for the first four months and £1600 thereafter.

Preliminary expenses are estimated at £5000 payable in May. C and D are to receive directors' salaries of £3000 a year each, payable monthly.

You are asked to draw up a budget and to submit a scheme for outside capitalisation of the company, which would obviate the necessity of any overdraft facilities being required.

Answer

In the first place it is necessary to draw up the cash budget, showing receipts and payments prior to the calling up of capital. This will serve to reveal the periods when the largest requirements of cash arise, nine months being sufficient for this.

A clearer picture of the capital needs having been obtained, it is necessary to see how far the estimated profit is likely to offer a reasonable return on a suitable capital structure. This requires the preparation of a budget on a full year's operations and the capitalisation of the profit at a rate parallel to that offered by other companies of a similar nature.

It now remains to see at what dates the capital should be called up to meet the operational needs.

CASH BUDGET

	April	May	June	July	Aug.	Sept.	Oct.	Nov.	Dec.	Total
Receipts										
Sales	—	£780	£1,980	£3,540	£7,110	£8,910	£9,300	£9,900	£9,900	£51,420
Balance overdrawn before capitalisation *	£2,500	10,220	68,430	70,490	69,480	96,815	94,615	91,815	89,015	—
Capital issues:										
Ordinary shares	15,000		30,000			15,000				60,000
8% Debentures			30,000			10,000				40,000
Balance b/f		12,500	4,780	6,570	4,510	5,520	3,185	5,385	8,185	—
	£15,000	£13,280	£66,760	£10,110	£11,620	£39,430	£12,485	£15,285	£18,085	£151,420
Payments										
Raw materials	—	1,000	3,000	3,000	2,800	3,500	3,500	3,500	3,500	23,800
Wages	800	800	1,200	900	1,200	1,500	1,500	1,500	1,500	10,900
Expenses	1,200	1,200	1,200	1,200	1,600	1,600	1,600	1,600	1,600	12,800
Directors' salaries	500	500	500	500	500	500	500	500	500	4,500
Vendor			29,000			29,000				58,000
Vendor's interest (tax ignored)			290			145				435
Preliminary expenses		5,000								5,000
New machine			25,000							25,000
Total payments	2,500	8,500	60,190	5,600	6,100	36,245	7,100	7,100	7,100	140,435
Balance c/f	12,500	4,780	6,570	4,510	5,520	3,185	5,385	8,185	10,985	10,985
	£15,000	£13,280	£66,760	£10,110	£11,620	£39,430	£12,485	£15,285	£18,085	£151,420

* NOTE

When compiling the cash budget, if estimated receipts and payments are entered this line will reveal the amounts of capital required and the most suitable periods during which to make the calls, *e.g.* May: b/f £2500 + 8500 − 780.

ESTIMATION OF PROFIT TO BE EARNED ON A COMPLETE YEAR'S TRADING

Sales (12 months at 500 units per month increased by 10%) 6600 units at £19·50		£128,700
Less discount allowable (40% at 2½%)		1,287
		£127,413
Expenses:		
Raw material	£46,200	
Wages	19,800	
Expenses	19,200	
Directors' salaries	6,000	
		91,200
		36,213
Depreciation (10% on £85,000)		8,500
		27,713
Corporation tax at 40% less writing down allowances say		7,713
Distributable profit		£20,000

Excess of payment over receipts peak during September		£96,915
Cash required, say		100,000
Total capital required (to vendor £40,000)		140,000
Authorised capital might be		150,000
The capital could be issued as to:		
8% £100 Debentures		£40,000
Payable £75 on application and allotment during June	£30,000	
Payable £25 on first and final call in September	10,000	
	£40,000	
Ordinary shares		100,000
Issued to vendor	40,000	
Remainder payable:		
£0·25 on application and allotment during April	15,000	
£0·50 on first call in June	30,000	
£0·25 on final call in September	15,000	
	£100,000	
		£140,000
With available profits at		£20,000
Allow for transfer to reserve (⅖)		8,000
		£12,000
Debenture interest payable: £40,000 × 8%	3,200	
Less Adjustment to corporation tax charge above to deduct from profits available for distribution	1,280	
		1,920
Leaving available for a dividend of 10% (gross)		£10,080

Alternatively, £60,000 of secured Debentures could be issued, so leaving the possibility of a slightly increased dividend—but to allow for expansion the additional £20,000 of Debentures could be issued later, the security to be offered making their disposal easier.

EXAMINATION QUESTIONS

1. Spring Sales Ltd was incorporated in December 1967 and plans were made to commence a wholesale trading business on 1st January 1968. Fixed assets are to be acquired at a cost of £23,800; payment is to be made on 1st January 1968. Sales for the six months to June 1968 are estimated as follows:

January and February, £10,000 per month	£20,000
March	24,000
April	36,000
May and June, £10,000 per month	20,000
	£100,000

Gross profit will be a uniform rate of 25% of selling price.

Purchasing is to be so arranged that, at the end of each month, the stock of goods will be exactly sufficient to supply all the sales of the following month. It is expected that sales in the month of July 1968 will be £10,000.

It is expected that payment for sales will be received on the last day of the second month after that in which the goods are sold.

Trade creditors are to be paid on the last day of the month after that in which the goods are purchased.

Wages and salaries, amounting to £2200 each month, will be paid on the last day of the month in which they are earned.

General expenses, amounting to £800 each month, will be paid on the last day of the month after that in which they were incurred.

It has been decided that the company will issue, at par, on 1st January 1968, such a number of ordinary £1 shares, to be paid up in full immediately, as will be sufficient to provide for:

(*a*) The cost of the fixed assets.

(*b*) Sufficient working capital for the four months of the half-year to 30th June 1968, in which the requirements are lower than in the two remaining months.

The additional working capital required during the two months in which requirements are higher than in the rest of the period is to be financed by means of a bank overdraft.

You are required:

(*a*) To show your calculation of the number of shares to be issued on 1st January 1968.

(*b*) To prepare a Trading and Profit and Loss Account for the six months to 30th June 1968, and a Balance Sheet at that date.

Ignore bank interest, taxation and depreciation.   [C.C.S.

2. A distributor proposes to start a new business on 1st January 1962. He has £50,000 to invest in it from the outset and a financier has agreed to provide any additional finance needed by way of short monthly loans at £25 a month interest for each £1000 or part of £1000 lent. The following estimates have been made of the volume of sales at sale prices: January £0, February £30,000, March £60,000 and thereafter £120,000 a month. All sales will be made on two months' credit and the gross profit margin is 20% on cost. Goods must

be purchased in the calendar month before that in which they are resold and in addition in January 1962 a buffer stock for display purposes and emergencies is to be bought for £5000 and to be maintained thereafter. Suppliers of goods will give one month's credit. All other expenses are to be paid promptly on cash terms. Wages are £3000 a month for the first three months and £5000 a month thereafter. The equipment to be used in the business from its commencement is to be hired at a rent of £2000 a month: the contract provides for a minimum period of hire of two years. The rent of the business premises is £24,000 a year, payable quarterly in arrear.

For convenience assume that all receipts and payments are made on the last day of the respective month.

Required:

(*a*) A statement showing the amount of the maximum expected need for cash from the financier.

(*b*) The date on which it will be required.

(*c*) Budgeted revenue account and Balance Sheet as at 30th June 1962. Ignore taxation.   [C.C.S.

3. The Goodnight Bedstead Co. Ltd. has recently obtained substantial long-term orders for its products from a West Indian importer and finds itself without sufficient capital to finance the fulfilment of these. The company is unable to raise this capital by borrowing, but the importer has introduced it to a Dr Yess who is willing to invest the necessary money in Ordinary shares on the basis of your opinion as to the amount required and the value to be placed on the shares. The company is private, its shares being held by the three directors.

Profits for the past several years ended 31st March have been at the rate of around £50,000 per annum, after charging directors' remuneration of £10,000, and are expected to continue at this level on the basis of existing business. The dividend for the year ended 31st March 1967 on the 40,000 ordinary shares of £1 each, fully paid, was at the rate of 45%. The balance sheet at that date showed:

Fixed assets:		
Leasehold premises (on long lease)	£10,000	
Plant	40,000	
		50,000
Net current assets (including cash £5,000)		175,000
		225,000

The order in question will involve an annual output of 6000 ornamental brass bedsteads, selling at £40 each, to be despatched evenly at the rate of four shipments per annum. The customer will remit cash by telegraphed order fourteen days after receipt of goods at Kingston, Jamaica; the cargo will be landed at Kingston two and a half weeks after despatch. The price per unit is made up as follows:

Materials	£15
Labour	10
Overheads	5
Shipment expenses	7
Profit	3
	£40

Materials and expenses are paid for at the end of the month following that in which incurred; wages are paid one week in arrear. The factory closes for two weeks per annum. No additional plant is required as this is mainly assembly work.

You are required:

(a) To prepare a statement of working capital required for the new venture.

(b) To compute the number of new ordinary shares of £1 each to be issued to Dr Yess on the basis that the existing dividend policy will continue.

(c) To comment on the effect on the voting position in the event of your suggestion being adopted.

You are *not* required to prepare your report to Dr Yess.   [C.A.(s)]

4. At a management meeting of the Wholesale Trading Company Ltd, held on 20th January 1963, the financing of certain capital commitments is under consideration. These commitments will total £40,000, of which £15,000 will be required by 30th June 1963 and the remainder by the end of the year.

In the absence of any formal system of cash budgeting you are required to prepare from the following information a statement which will indicate the cash positions at the relevant dates, and also a report commenting on the figures disclosed and the assumptions underlying their construction.

(a)   BALANCE SHEET OF THE WHOLESALE TRADING COMPANY
as at 31st December 1962

				Cost	Depreciation	
Capital, authorised, issued and fully paid:			Fixed assets:			
100,000 Ordinary £1 shares		£100,000	Land/Buildings	£100,000	£5,000	£95,000
Reserves		34,490	Equipment	15,500	5,000	10,500
Future taxation		12,000	Trade investments:			
Current liabilities:			(M.V. £8,250)			5,110
Trade creditors	£28,500		Current assets:			
Accrued charges	500		Cash	£5,000		
Dividends	3,060		Debtors	21,540		
Taxation	13,600		Stock	55,000		
		45,660				81,540
		£192,150				£192,150

(b) The Sales Manager estimates that the sales for 1963 will be as follows:

Period 1st January 1963–30th June 1963—£156,000.
Period 1st July 1963–31st December 1963—£178,000.

(c) Over the past few years the ratio of profits (excluding any items which did not reflect cash inflows or outflows such as depreciation) to sales turnover has been 20%.

(d) The Company gives four weeks' credit to its customers and takes six weeks' credit from its suppliers.

(e) Company policy is to turn over stocks four times per annum.

(f) The purchasing manager estimates that purchases will be as follows:

Period 1st January 1963–30th June 1963—£105,000.
Period 1st July 1963–31st December 1963—£115,000.

(g) In addition to the £40,000 of capital expenditure mentioned above it has been decided to install a new packing machine in July 1963, which will cost £5000.

(h) Over the past few years the company has paid a dividend of 15% on the Ordinary shares. This has consisted of an interim dividend of 10% payable in August and a final dividend of 5% payable in January or February.
      [C.C.A.]

CHAPTER V

WORKING CAPITAL

DEFINITION

ALTHOUGH the term "working capital" has been deprecated by the Institute of Chartered Accountants for use in Balance Sheets—the preferred term is "current assets less current liabilities"—nevertheless, for management purposes it is a useful phrase to summarise the factor which is the effective life-blood of any business. In Balance Sheet interpretation, perhaps the most significant measure which can be obtained is the working capital ratio, because the profit-earning cycle of the company is geared to working capital.

A number of definitions have been formulated, but perhaps the most widely acceptable would be something like: "Working capital represents the excess of current assets over current liabilities." In most businesses, this would normally represent:

Current liabilities	Current assets
—	1. Stocks (raw materials, work in progress, finished goods)
2. Creditors	2. Debtors (less provision for bad debts)
3. Bank overdraft Bank loan *Total*	3. Bank balance Cash on hand *Total*

NOTES

(*i*) *Stocks* are needed for continuous production.

(ii) *Debtors* arise as a result of sales while creditors arise as a result of purchases, necessitating the provision of funds while settlement is awaited, and creditors conversely supplying finance until their settlement date.

(iii) *Bank* and *cash* balances are needed to meet the lag in payment which occurs between the expense incurred in purchasing and the payment received for sales. Bank loans or overdrafts may be required where there is insufficient cash otherwise available.

The conversion of all working capital into cash is most important, because only when it is converted is profit realised. If the amount at the end of the cycle was less than at the beginning, a loss would result. Fig. 1 represents the basic flow of working capital.

It must, however, be noted that it is not always as simple as has been suggested; there are two items particularly which put this basic cycle out of phase: (i) stocks and (ii) credit facilities.

(i) *Stocks:* most businesses are obliged to carry stocks of raw materials so as to supply production needs, and carry stocks of finished goods to meet customers' requirements. Thus the longer stocks remain in the business, the more working capital is required to finance them.

(ii) *Credit facilities:* in most manufacturing businesses, cash purchase and cash sales are rare, all transactions being more or less on credit. Thus credit allowed by a supplier will reduce the amount of working capital required for a period, while credit allowed to a customer will increase the amount required.

Working capital is essentially circulating capital; in fact it is often referred to as such. This has been admirably summed up by comparing it with a river which is there from day to day, but the water in it is constantly changing.

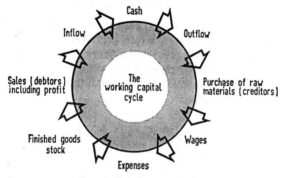

FIG. 1.—*The flow of working capital.*

WORKING CAPITAL REQUIREMENTS

The required amount of working capital in relation to the fixed capital of a business will vary widely between firms in different industries. For example, a company engaged in the shipbuilding industry will need a large amount of fixed or long term capital to finance the shipyard, equipment, etc., for considerable periods, whereas a jobbing builder will require virtually no fixed assets but instead a reasonably large amount of working capital to finance stocks of parts, amounts owing by customers, etc. If a company does not have enough working capital it will soon find its activities restricted. Many firms which seemed to be expanding their activities successfully have come to grief through insufficient working capital being available to finance this expansion. Under normal conditions a steady increase in working capital indicates a successful business, while a steady decrease would be a danger signal demanding immediate action to remedy the situation. It should be noted, however, that working capital requirements may rise owing to external factors such as:

(i) A rising market, which will force up prices of raw materials and possibly other elements of cost,

(ii) Replacement of plant from internal funds, the price of which may be much greater than that of the original equipment.

Current assets cannot invariably be described as part of working capital. For example, in stock valuation there may be "base" stocks, minimum stocks or obsolescent stocks which are really not circulating in the business. Included in the balance at the bank may be cash which is no longer needed and is virtually an investment. But in most instances, and certainly in examination questions, it is usual to interpret current assets as forming part of working capital.

MANAGEMENT CONTROL

In numerous business concerns, control of working capital has not been exercised by management, which probably helps to explain why many companies cease to function every year. In most companies there is a strict control of capital expenditure, yet many still do not realise how important it is to control working capital too. The following items require particular attention:

1. STOCKS

In the majority of businesses, raw materials form the largest element of cost in a product, as a result of which large stocks are often necessary. Frequently, insufficient attention is paid to the levels of stock carried; the adoption of maximum and minimum stock levels, re-order levels and re-order quantities may prove very useful in effecting reductions. Even if it proves impossible to introduce these levels to all items in store, it may well be possible to apply them to the more important or more expensive items. The cost of holding large stocks in terms of capital locked up, storage costs and storage losses must be measured against the economies of buying large quantities—in terms of quantity discounts, reduced purchasing overheads and no risk of hold-ups in production.

2. DEBTORS

Failure of debtors to pay in reasonable time can explain a need for increased working capital. Close checks should be maintained on bad or doubtful debts and an index maintained which shows the performance of debtors in terms of debts in relation to average daily sales. It must be appreciated, however, that it may be dangerous to press debtors too much or the company may lose goodwill.

3. CREDITORS

Creditors' accounts should not be paid before the due date. Where cash discounts are available, they should be accepted; it must be remembered that they usually show a good return. Thus a $2\frac{1}{2}\%$ cash discount for payment within one month represents a rate of 30% p.a., which is a very satisfactory return.

4. CASH

Unnecessarily large balances of cash should not be encouraged, because cash is completely unproductive. Conversely, while bank overdrafts and loans often fulfil a vital need, it should be remembered that they incur overhead costs. Some firms, however, work on bank overdrafts as a matter of policy, considering a bank overdraft a cheap method of finance.

In short, efficient control of stocks and liquid resources in conjunction with credit facilities is an essential part of management control. So-called "safe" policies, ensuring a high ratio of current assets to current liabilities, may only serve to lock up capital which could otherwise be used for more profitable purposes. On the other hand, trying to capitalise cheaply by taking up extended credit facilities may lead to loss of goodwill and business, and, even more drastically, to ultimate disaster—which is often the result of over-trading. There is a grave danger of it in firms which are expanding rapidly. More stocks are needed, more labour is engaged, more equipment purchased and additional overhead costs incurred before the additional sales are realised. This creates a strong pressure on the business's finances and may result in debtors being pressed for early payments by the offer of discounts (which aggravates the position) and bank overdrafts being required. This is discussed more fully in Chapter XXI.

WORKING CAPITAL STATEMENTS FOR MANAGERIAL CONTROL

It is essential for management to receive concise and unambiguous information revealing the uses to which working capital has been put and forecasting, as accurately as possible, future requirements. There are various statements which may be compiled which, though all concerned with working capital, nevertheless present information regarding the different sections and aspects of the business.

It is necessary to be precise in the titles given to such statements, as when these may be called for both in practice and examinations, the information may be supplied which, while being correct, is not the most suitable for the purpose for which it is required. It is proposed, therefore, to deal with these statements under the following headings:

1. Statements of movement of working capital and its sources and application.
2. Funds flow statements.
3. Cash flow statements.
4. Net cash flow.
5. Working capital forecasts.

1. STATEMENTS OF MOVEMENT OF WORKING CAPITAL AND ITS SOURCES AND APPLICATION

We commence by way of introduction to the compilation of such statements with some preliminary examination questions, proceeding thence to a more practical example.

Specimen question (1)

The Balance Sheets of Banstead Products Ltd for two years are as follows:

BALANCE SHEET
as at 31st March

	Year 1	Year 2		Year 1	Year 2
Ordinary share capital	£80,000	£120,000	Freehold land and buildings	£55,400	£113,200
Share premium	8,000	12,000	Plant and machinery	35,600	51,300
General reserve	6,000	9,000			
Profit and Loss Account	19,500	20,800	Furniture and fittings	2,400	1,500
5% Debentures	—	26,000	Stock	22,100	26,000
Corporation tax	9,800	10,900	Debtors	36,500	39,100
Creditors	33,500	36,400	Bank	4,800	4,000
	£156,800	£235,100		£156,800	£235,100

Depreciation written off during year:

Plant and machinery	£12,800
Furniture and fittings	£400

From the foregoing, you are required to show any increase or decrease in working capital and acquisition and disposal thereof.

Answer

MOVEMENT OF WORKING CAPITAL
AND ITS
SOURCES AND APPLICATION
for year ended 31st March 19—

	31st March 19—	31st March 19—
Current assets:		
Stock	£22,100	£26,000
Debtors	36,500	39,100
Bank	4,800	4,000
	63,400	69,100
Less Current liabilities:		
Corporation tax	£9,800	£10,900
Creditors	33,500	36,400
	43,300	47,300
	£20,100	£21,800
Increase in working capital, made up as follows:		£1,700

	Sources	Application
Increase in proprietor's funds:		
Issue of Ordinary shares	£40,000	
Share premium	4,000	
General reserve	3,000	
Profit and loss	1,300	
Depreciation	13,200	
	61,500	
Issue of 5% Debentures	26,000	
Acquisition of fixed assets:		
Freehold property		57,800
Plant and machinery		28,500
Sales of fixed assets:		
Furniture and fittings	500	
	£88,000	£86,300
Increase in working capital	£1,700	

NOTES

(i) Debentures are a deferred liability and should not be included in the working capital computation.

(ii) Depreciation is written back because the profit for the year has materially affected the working capital by an increase in the same amount. Depreciation has necessitated no dispersion of actual funds, yet has been used to reduce the profit figure. From the point of view of working capital this has been merely a double entry book figure, and to show the true increase in working capital, depreciation must be written back. The same position would apply with regard to a loss, except of course that the loss would be reduced.

(iii) The application of the working capital cannot be taken as merely the increase in value of fixed assets, since these have suffered depreciation. To calculate the correct position, abbreviated accounts for fixed assets must be prepared similar to those shown below. The items marked with asterisks are missing when the information given in the question is collated and must be assumed to show purchases, if on the debit side, and sales if on the credit side.

Plant and machinery				Furniture and fittings			
Balance b/d	£35,600	Depreciation	£12,800	Balance b/d	£2,400	Depreciation	£400
*Cash	28,500	Balance c/d	51,300			*Cash	500
						Balance c/d	1,500
	£64,100		£64,100		£2,400		£2,400
Balance b/d	51,300			Balance b/d 1,500			

The same type of question may be set in quite a different way from that above, necessitating working back to show the Balance Sheet.

Specimen question (2)

The following is the summarised Balance Sheet of Jerid & Co. Ltd at 1st January.

BALANCE SHEET

Issued share capital:			Freehold property at cost		£77,000	
80,000 Ordinary shares £1 each		£80,000	Plant and machinery *less* depreciation		47,000	
40,000 5% Redeemable Preference shares £1 each		40,000	Furniture and fittings *less* depreciation		2,000	
		———	Investments (market value £32,000)		25,000	
		120,000	Stock	£20,000		
Share premium		8,000	Debtors	45,000		
Revenue reserve	£35,000			———	65,000	
Profit and Loss Accounts	12,000	47,000				
	———					
Creditors	38,000					
Bank overdraft	3,000					
	———	41,000				
		———			———	
		£216,000			£216,000	

On 31st December the statement shown below was prepared when the stock and debtors amounted to £18,000 and £43,000 respectively, and creditors amounted to £36,000.

SOURCES AND APPLICATION OF WORKING CAPITAL

Revenue receipts:			
Net trading profit for year		£19,000	
Add depreciation:			
Plant and machinery	£10,000		
Furniture and fittings	600		
	———	10,600	
		———	£29,600
Capital receipts:			
Sale of investments	32,000		
Sale of furniture and fittings	300		
	———		32,300
			———
			61,900
Capital payments:			
Redemption of Preference shares	44,000		
Plant and machinery	3,000		
	———	47,000	
Dividend on Ordinary shares		8,000	
		———	55,000
			———
Increase in working capital at end of year			£6,900

You are required to prepare the Balance Sheet at the end of the year, in similar form to that shown above. Ignore taxation.

Answer

BALANCE SHEET AT END OF YEAR

Issued share capital 80,000 Ordinary shares £1 each	£80,000	Freehold property at cost	£77,000
Share premium	4,000	Plant and machinery *less* depreciation	40,000
Capital Redemption Reserve Fund	40,000	Furniture and fittings *less* depreciation	1,100
Profit and Loss Account	25,000	Stock £18,000	
Creditors	36,000	Debtors 43,000	
		Bank 5,900	
			66,900
	£185,000		£185,000

NOTE

The workings involved in this question resemble those in the previous illustration, so no further explanation is given, except to show the calculation of the Profit and Loss Account balance:

PROFIT AND LOSS APPROPRIATION ACCOUNT

Dividend paid	£8,000	Balance b/d	£12,000
Transfer to Capital Redemption Reserve Fund	5,000	Trading profit	19,000
Balance c/d	25,000	Profit on sale of investments	7,000
	£38,000		£38,000
		Balance b/d	25,000

The Profit and Loss Accounts and Balance Sheets shown hereunder will be used for the computation of the statements given in the following sections.

PROFIT AND LOSS ACCOUNTS

	31st December 19—		31st December 19—	
Trading profit		£50,000		£72,000
Investment income		500		—
		50,500		
Profit on sale of investments				3,000
				75,000
Corporation tax		28,000		29,500
		22,500		45,500
Balance b/f from previous year	13,000		19,500	
Taxation over-provided in previous year	—	13,000	3,000	22,500
		35,500		68,000
Proposed dividend	16,000		24,000	
Transfer to general reserve	—	16,000	12,000	36,000
Unappropriated profit c/f		£19,500		£32,000

BALANCE SHEETS

		31st December 19—		31st December 19—
Fixed assets at cost		£62,000		£70,000
Additions during year		8,000		17,000
		70,000		87,000
Depreciation		25,000		36,000
		45,000		51,000
Current assets:				
Investments		£10,000		—
Stock at cost		181,500		£205,000
Trade debtors		131,500		138,700
		323,000		343,700
Current liabilities:				
Bank overdraft	£116,000		55,000	
Trade creditors	71,000		82,200	
Accruals	7,500		8,300	
Taxation	21,300		28,700	
Proposed dividend	16,000		24,000	
		231,800	198,200	
			91,200	145,500
		£136,200		£196,500
Ordinary share capital		75,000		100,000
General reserve		26,000		38,000
Profit and Loss Account		19,500		32,000
Deferred Taxation Account		15,700		16,500
		136,200		186,500
8% Debentures (issued 1st January 19—)		—		10,000
		£136,200		£196,500

For the year ended 31st December 19—, sales amounted to £844,500 and purchases totalled £720,000. Trading profit was arrived at after charging directors' emoluments of £15,000.

We conclude this section with a Statement of Movement of Working Capital compiled from the foregoing final accounts and Balance Sheets.

MOVEMENT OF WORKING CAPITAL AND ITS
SOURCES AND APPLICATION
Year ended 31st December 19—

Current assets:				
Investments		£10,000	—	
Stock in trade		181,500	£205,000	
Trade debtors		131,500	138,700	
		323,000	343,700	
Less current liabilities:				
Bank overdraft	£116,000		£55,000	
Trade creditors	71,000		82,200	
Accrual	7,500		8,300	
Taxation	21,300		28,700	
Proposed dividend	16,000		24,000	
		231,800		198,200
		91,200		145,500

Increase in working capital
made up as follows: £54,300

		Sources	Application
Proprietors' funds:			
Share issue	£25,000		
Trading profit	72,000		
	97,000		
Depreciation	11,000		
	108,000		
Less taxation	£29,500		
Over-provision	3,000		
	26,500		
Transfer of taxation "reserve" *	800		
		25,700	
		£82,300	
Distribution of profit: proposed dividend			£24,000
Acquisition of fixed assets			17,000
Loan capital issued: 8% Debentures		10,000	
Profit on sale of investments*		3,000	
		£95,300	£41,000 £54,300

The taxation referring to the increase in the Deferred Taxation Account is in effect an increase in a reserve; as such, it is merely a transfer of profit from one account to another, not an increase in a

* In compiling the statement these two items are worthy of note as they serve to emphasise that in this type of statement, which explains the movement of working capital, items included in the net current assets themselves should not be repeated within the sources and applications section.

liability affecting the working capital. As the whole of the profit has been shown as a source of working capital, this transfer from one reserve to another is not, therefore, deductible as a liability.

The amount received on the sale of investments might be included in full as a source of working capital if it were not included to the extent of £10,000 in the current assets. As the movement of the £10,000 has already been reflected in the change in current assets, only the additional profit element is included as a source of working capital, being the addition to the current assets, the remaining £10,000 being a transfer from one current asset (investments) to another (bank).

Care should be exercised when using the "trading profit" figure on the Profit and Loss Account as opposed to the final figure on the closing Balance Sheet, for, as explained above, any items affecting the current assets and liabilities must be either deducted or added—*e.g.* taxation charges, or adjustments—but movements on reserves should be ignored.

2. FUNDS FLOW STATEMENT

This is probably the most useful of the working capital statements to be submitted to management. The funds flow statement is, in effect, a financial operational statement—that is, it reveals the methods by which the business has been financed and the uses to which it has applied its funds over the period. Furthermore, it leaves management in no doubt about what sources the company is being financed from when any excess credit is being taken and when any weakness is due to lack of internal capitalisation.

While the necessity of incoming funds to finance expenditure on such items as fixed assets is obvious, the necessity to provide working capital to finance debtors is not so easily understood. Where sales are increased or credit terms to debtors are lengthened, further capital is required, just as in the case of more tangible assets such as plant and machinery. The point needs emphasising because this factor, together with the added expense due to increased activities, has led in some instances to over-trading with unfortunate results. The following statement, compiled from the example on pp. 57–8, should bring any such danger clearly before management, since it reveals the expense involved in the application of funds to provide the necessary increase in current assets.

The "proprietors' funds" section, it will be observed, is similar to that in the previous statement, the adjustments having already been explained. Unlike the Movement of Working Capital statement, however, all the items are shown as to their individual increases and decreases, whereas the working capital was shown previously in summary form. Likewise, the *increase* and *decrease* in assets and liabilities have been revealed as opposed to the *total* expenditure or income arising on the movement of the assets and liabilities.

FUNDS FLOW STATEMENT

Year ended 31st December 19—

Acquisition				*Disposal*		
Proprietors' funds:				Opening bank overdraft		£116,000
Share issue	£25,000			Increase in assets:		
Trading profit	72,000			Fixed assets	£17,000	
				Stock-in-		
	97,000			trade	23,500	
Add depreciation	11,000			Trade debtors	7,200	
						47,700
	108,000					
Less taxation						
£29,500						
Over-						
provided	3,000					
	26,500					
Transfer						
of taxa-						
tion						
"reserve"						
item	800					
	25,700					
		82,300				
Loan Capital issued:						
8% Debentures		10,000				
Increase in liabilities:				Decrease in liabilities:		
Trade creditors	11,200			Settlement of		
Accruals	800			taxation	21,300	
Taxation	28,700					
		40,700				21,300
Disposal of assets:						
Investments	10,000					
Add profit on						
sale	3,000					
		13,000		Profit distributed:		
Closing bank overdraft		55,000		Ordinary dividend		
				paid		16,000
		£201,000				£201,000

NOTES

(i) As the movements on the various assets and liabilities are shown, the reason for the omission, on the acquisition side, of the dividend proposed, may be queried, as this is the only current liability omitted. The omission is due to the inclusion in "acquisition of funds" of the full trading profit, which includes the dividend subsequently deducted on the Profit and Loss Account. It will be noted that the differences on the two Balance Sheets are revealed by this statement; therefore, to commence with a trading profit of £72,000 is to require subsequent adjustment to ensure that both balance sheets remain balanced. The transfer between reserves is also applicable in this sense, as explained on the Statement of the Movement of Working Capital.

(ii) Again, it is emphasised that to increase liabilities has the same result as obtaining funds, as such liabilities finance the acquisition of assets in whatever form. In other words, to increase the liabilities side of the Balance Sheet is to cause a corresponding increase on the assets side.

An example of a Fund Flow Statement prepared from differing information is also given on p. 499 in the section dealing with interpretation of accounts.

3. CASH FLOW STATEMENTS

Cash flow statements are quite distinct from the two foregoing types of statement. Simply explained, they are summarised cash books or actual receipts and payments sectionalised. For their compilation from information given, the actual purchases and sales for the period must be supplied, together with the Balance Sheets and Profit and Loss Account. If the purchases and sales figures are not supplied, it is only possible to prepare either of the two foregoing types of statement. Expenses, on the other hand, can be computed if the purchases and sales figures are given as shown in the workings appended. The following cash flow statement has been compiled from the final accounts and Balance Sheets shown on pp. 57-8.

STATEMENT OF CASH FLOW

Year ended 31st December 19—

Bank overdraft 1st January 19—			£116,000
Amounts of cash received from:			
Share issue		£25,000	
Issue of 8% Debentures		10,000	
Payments by debtors		837,300	
Sale of investments		13,000	
		885,300	
Amounts paid to:			
Trade creditors	£708,800		
Expense creditors	48,400		
Settlement of taxation	18,300		
Directors' emoluments	15,000		
Debenture interest*	800		
Acquisition of fixed assets	17,000		
Dividend paid*	16,000		
		824,300	
Actual net cash flow			61,000
Bank overdraft at 31st December 19—			£55,000

* Shown gross for illustrative purposes.

WORKINGS

Payments to suppliers

Cash payments*	£708,800	Opening balances	£71,000
Closing balances	82,200	Purchases to Trading Account	720,000
	£791,000		£791,000

Payments for expenses

Cash payments*	£48,400	Opening balances	£7,500
Closing Balances	8,300	Expenses to Profit and Loss Account	49,200
	£56,700		£56,700

Payments by debtors

Opening balances	£131,500	Cash received*	£837,300
Sales to Account Trading	844,500	Closing Balances	138,700
	£976,000		£976,000

Calculation of expenses

Opening stock	£181,500
Purchases	720,000
	901,500
Closing stock	205,000
	696,500
Sales	844,500
Gross profit	148,000
Trading profit	72,000
Total charges	76,000
Directors' emoluments £15,000	
Debenture Interest 800	
Depreciation 11,000	
	26,800
Expenses	£49,200*

Payment for taxation

Over-provision transferred	£3,000	Opening balances:	£21,300
			15,700
Cash payment*	18,300	Profit and Loss Account	29,500
Closing balances: £28,700 / 16,500	45,200		
	£66,500		£66,500

It has been questioned whether management is likely to find a cash flow statement of real use and suggested that "the analysis of numerous expenses is not worth the work involved and not of particular interest when compiled." Certainly the presentation of numerous items of expense shown on a cash basis would be superfluous, but an overall picture of the actual use of such reserves is often quite convincing when management is not clear about rather extreme movements shown on working capital. Here, the management accountant must use his discretion in summarising various matters affecting the actual cash flow in order to present an easily understandable and useful guide rather than an elaborate display of figures.

4. NET CASH FLOW

So far only statements for presentation to management have been dealt with. The following reconciliation statement is of greater import-

* These figures are obtained by insertion after all the available information has been entered.

ance to the management accountant than to management. It is essential, however, for the management accountant to understand the nature of this reconciliation, as it may be necessary to explain to a board why certain figures presented may differ from those shown for investment analysis purposes. "Net cash flow" as quoted by the stock exchange information service is not the same as the "actual net cash flow" illustrated in the foregoing section. Using the information given previously, the net cash flow is made up as follows:

Trading profit		£75,000
Add depreciation		11,000
		86,000
Less taxation (over-provision written back)		26,500
		59,500
Less proposed dividend		24,000
Net cash flow		£35,500

This figure can be reconciled with the actual net cash flow as follows:

Net cash flow		£35,500
Add amounts deducted in excess of actual payments:		
Taxation (£26,500−18,300)	£8,200	
Proposed dividend (£24,000−16,000)	8,000	
		16,200
		£51,700
Funds obtained apart from those in profit element:		
Share issue	25,000	
Debenture issue	10,000	
		35,000
		£86,700
Funds accounted for by increase in net current assets (excluding bank, taxation and dividends already dealt with)	8,700	
Acquisition of fixed assets	17,000	
		25,700
Actual net cash flow		£61,000

Although the two figures may be reconciled, the actual net cash flow is of less concern to the prospective investor than that which reveals the self-generating aspect of the company's finances. Although in the foregoing example the net cash flow is shown as £35,500, being only one half of the actual net cash flow, nevertheless the figure is not too far from the position which the investor is concerned with. The taxation and proposed dividend have to be met from the available funds, so leaving a lesser figure for future operations than would be apparent by showing the dividends and tax *paid* during the past year which have influenced the figure given as actual net cash flow.

The investment analyst is interested in the availability of funds to meet (in particular) future capital commitments, since, should sufficient funds not be available internally, recourse may have to be made to raising additional funds by means of a share issue or borrowing by means of Debentures. In any case, as mentioned earlier, it is not possible to compile the actual net cash flow unless figures for purchases and sales are supplied, and although the figure for turnover is published, the figure for purchases is not normally available.

WORKING CAPITAL FORECASTS

Budgetary control is dealt with in detail in Chapters ix and x, but for convenience, some working capital forecasts are included here covering commercial and manufacturing concerns.

1. COMMERCIAL CONCERN

The following example is based on a final examination question. It is useful in bringing out various points but suffers from some over-simplication.

Specimen question (3)

The following is an extract from the draft Balance Sheet of a company dealing in one particular line which is pursuing a course of expansion. It is estimated that in the following year the Company will be able to increase sales by 20% but the board is concerned to find the most suitable method of providing the necessary working capital, as the estimated amount made available by profit is to be used for the completion of capital projects.

DRAFT BALANCE SHEET
31st March 19—

Fixed assets:			
Freehold land and buildings at valuation			£60,000
Other fixed assets			30,000
			90,000
Current assets:			
Stock at cost		£205,000	
Trade debtors		185,000	
Bank		6,000	
		£396,000	
Current liabilities:			
Trade creditors	165,000		
Bank overdraft (unsecured)	108,000		
Taxation	40,000		
Accruals, etc.	15,000		
		£328,000	
			£68,000
			£158,000

The bank does not wish to extend the overdraft above the level already agreed of £110,000, and in order to keep financial requirements to a minimum, the board has agreed not to undertake any further capital projects for the next year.

Net profits have been steadily increasing and, according to draft accounts for the current year, should amount to £78,000 before taxation; it is estimated that they will amount to £95,000 before taxation for the following year.

It will not be possible to extend credit periods beyond those operated, nor to reduce stocks at the present rate of turnover.

Submit your recommendations to the Managing Director in memorandum form as to any additional finance you consider may be required, together with the most suitable method of raising it.

Answer
—— COMPANY LTD

To: *Managing Director*   Date:............
From: *Chief Accountant*

Additional finance for working capital purposes

In reply to your memorandum dated ——, I estimate that working capital requirements for the year ending 31st December 19— will amount to £35,000.*

The most suitable method of raising the necessary sum would appear to be by means of the issue of £35,000 8% redeemable Debentures. The advantages of this proposal are that:

(*a*) The interest payable would be chargeable against profits for taxation purposes.

(*b*) No difficulty should be experienced in raising this sum, as adequate security could be offered on the freehold land and buildings of the company.

(*c*) When sufficient profits have been accumulated, the Debentures may be redeemed.

* This sum has been calculated as follows:

ESTIMATED WORKING CAPITAL POSITION
at 31st March 19—

Current assets:		
Stock in trade	£246,000	
Trade debtors	222,000	
Bank (say)	7,000	
		£475,000
Current liabilities:		
Trade creditors	£198,000	
Bank overdraft	110,000	
Taxation	48,000	
Accruals	18,000	
		374,000
		£101,000
Amount required:		
Forecast working capital		101,000
Present working capital		68,000
		£33,000
	Say	£35,000

(In any case, additional Debenture interest will be payable)

Signed
Chief Accountant ....

NOTES

(i) As sales are to increase by one fifth, those aspects affected by the flow-through of stocks have been increased by that proportion, viz., stock creditors and debtors.

(ii) With fixed and semi-variable overheads as well as those directly variable, accruals would not increase by one fifth, but the approximate figure is adequate.

(iii) *Taxation.* In practice this should be estimated more precisely in consideration of capital allowances, etc.

(iv) Carried to an extreme in this company, the policy of using all available profits to finance capital projects could lead to the unfortunate results consequent upon over-trading (see p. 493).

2. MANUFACTURING COMPANY

Both in practice and in examinations, the question is often asked: "What will be the working capital requirements to finance this level of activity or that new project?" This is a very practical and important problem which may require extensive research and difficult calculations. However, to show the usual requirements in simple form, the following items are tabulated:

(i) The cost of raw materials, wages and overheads.

(ii) The period during which raw materials will remain in stock before issue to production.

(iii) The period during which the product will be processed through the factory.

(iv) The period during which finished goods will remain in the warehouse.

(v) The lag in payment to suppliers of raw materials and services.

(vi) The lag in payment to employees.

(vii) The lag in payment by debtors.

(viii) Frequently an amount is allowed to cover contingencies, e.g. 10% might be added to the total amount.

Most of these points will be included in a computation of working capital requirements. It will be appreciated that most of these figures will not be accurate and are at best estimates. For example, the period during which stocks of finished goods stay in the warehouse can only be an average figure, but by careful observation it should be possible to make a reasonable assessment. This is the reason for allowing an amount to cover contingencies: it is hoped that this figure might cover any inaccuracies in calculation.

Specimen question (4)

On 1st January the board of directors of C. Beeches & Co. Ltd wish to know the amount of working capital that will be required to meet the programme they have planned for the year. From the following information, prepare a working capital requirements forecast and a forecast Profit and Loss Account and Balance Sheet.

Issued share capital £200,000.

5% Debentures (secured on assets) £50,000.

Fixed assets valued at £125,000 on 1st January.

Production during the previous year was 60,000 units; it is planned that this level of activity should be maintained during the present year.

The expected ratios of cost to selling price are: raw materials 60%, direct wages 10%, overheads 20%.

Raw materials are expected to remain in stores for an average of two months before issue to production.

Each unit of production is expected to be in process for one month.

Finished goods will stay in the warehouse awaiting despatch to customers for approximately three months.

Credit allowed by creditors is two months from date of delivery of raw materials.

Credit given to debtors is three months from date of despatch.

Selling price is £5 per unit.

There is a regular production and sales cycle.

Answer

FORECAST REVENUE ACCOUNT

Period...............

Materials consumed	£180,000	Cost of manufacture c/d	£270,000
Direct wages	30,000		
Overheads	60,000		
	£270,000		£270,000
Cost of manufacture b/d	270,000	Sales	300,000
Gross profit c/d	30,000		
	£300,000		£300,000
Debenture interest	2,500	Gross profit b/d	30,000
Net profit	27,500		
	£30,000		£30,000

FORECAST BALANCE SHEET AS AT END OF PERIOD

Issued share capital	£200,000	Fixed assets			£125,000
Profit and loss balance	27,500	Current assets:			
		Stocks—			
	227,500	Raw material	30,000		
5% Debentures	50,000	Work in progress	22,500		
		Finished goods	67,500		
				120,000	
		Debtors		75,000	
					195,000
		Less current liabilities:			
		Creditors	30,000		
		Bank overdraft	12,500		
				42,500	
		Working capital			152,500
	£277,500				£277,500

WORKING CAPITAL REQUIREMENTS FORECAST

Period.................

	Period (months)	Total	Raw materials	Work in progress	Finished goods	Debtors	Creditors
1. *Materials:*							
(a) In stock	2		£30,000				
(b) In work in progress	1			£15,000			
(c) In finished goods	3				£45,000		
(d) Credit to debtors	3					£45,000	
	9						
(e) Credit from creditors	2						£30,000
Total	7	£105,000					
2. *Wages:*							
(a) In work in progress	1			2,500			
(b) In finished goods	3				7,500		
(c) Credit to debtors	3					7,500	
Total	7	17,500					
3. *Overheads:*							
(a) In work in progress	1			5,000			
(b) In finished goods	3				15,000		
(c) Credit to debtors	3					15,000	
Total	7	35,000					
4. *Profit:*							
Credit to debtors	3					7,500	
Total	3	7,500					
Total		£165,000	£30,000	£22,500	£67,500	£75,000	£30,000

It will be observed that this statement includes the elements of cost and profit, and excludes the cash position. Cash is an important element of working capital, so the cash position ascertained from the cash budget or, in this case, from the Balance Sheet, must be introduced to give the final figure or working capital required. Thus:

Requirements as shown in statement	£165,000
Cash as per forecast Balance Sheet	(12,500)
Total working capital required	£152,500

NOTES

(i) *Forecast Revenue Account*

This is easily computed in this illustration, because it is given that the three elements of cost are a certain percentage of sales; sales being 60,000 units at £5 each.

(ii) *Forecast Balance Sheet*

The figures representing current assets and current liabilities are obtained from the working capital requirements forecast, with the exception of cash (or, in this illustration, bank overdraft). This is simply the balancing figure on the Balance Sheet (if the latter is not particularly clear at this point, it is discussed in more detail under "Cash budgets" in Chapter IX).

It is stressed that the Balance Sheet presentation is not meant to portray the form of presentation stipulated by the Companies Act, 1948; it is shown in this form so as to reveal the working capital position to management.

(iii) *Working capital requirements forecast*

(a) *Materials.*—Cost per month is £180,000 ÷ 12. Materials remain in stock two months, in work in progress one month, in finished goods three months, and customers do not settle their accounts for three months; the result is a cycle of nine months from receipt into store until payment by debtors. This figure must, however, be reduced by two months, which is the credit allowed to the company from suppliers. The net result is a seven months' lag in recovering the cost of materials used in production which must be financed by the company. The cost of materials is £15,000 a month, resulting in £105,000 for seven months' delay.

(b) *Labour.*—Cost per month is £30,000 ÷ 12. The cost of labour is un-recovered from customers for seven months at £2500 per month, which is £17,500. It should be noted that this illustration is meant to be relatively simple so as to introduce the subject: the problem of possible lag in payment of wages and length of time the labour force has been engaged in process have been ignored. It is simply assumed for illustrative purposes that there is one month's average delay in work in progress; refinements will be discussed in a later example.

(c) *Overheads.*—Cost per month is £60,000 ÷ 12. This is similar to labour costs in that seven months is the time taken to recover the cost of overheads.

(d) *Sales.*—Profit per month is £30,000 ÷ 12. Profit is earned only on sales, so the working capital requirements are three months at £2500 a month, which is £7500.

Specimen question (5)

You are required to prepare for the board of directors of Vigilant Co. Ltd a statement showing the working capital needed to finance a level of activity of 5200 units of output. You are given the following information:

Element of cost	Amount per unit
Raw materials	£8
Direct labour	2
Overheads	6
Total cost	16
Profit	4
Selling price	£20

Raw materials are in stock on average one month. Materials are in process, on average, half a month.

Finished goods are in stock on average six weeks.

Credit allowed by creditors is one month.

Credit allowed to debtors is two months.

Lag in payment of wages is 1½ weeks.

Cash on hand and at bank is expected to be £7300.

You are informed that production is carried on evenly during the year and wages and overheads accrue similarly.

Answer

WORKING CAPITAL REQUIREMENTS FORECAST

Period..............

	Period (weeks)	Total	Raw materials	Work in progress	Finished goods	Debtors	Creditors
1. Materials:							
(a) In stock	4		£3,200				
(b) In work in progress	2			£1,600			
(c) In finished goods	6				£4,800		
(d) Credit to debtors	8					£6,400	
	20						
(e) Credit from creditors	4						£3,200
Total	16	£12,800					
2. Wages:							
(a) In work in progress	1			200			
(b) In finished goods	6				1,200		
(c) Credit to debtors	8					1,600	
	15						
(d) Credit from employees	1½						300
Total	13½	2,700					
3. Overheads:							
(a) In work in progress	1			600			
(b) In finished goods	6				3,600		
(c) Credit to debtors	8					4,800	
Total	15	9,000					
4. Profits:							
Credit to debtors	8					3,200	
Total	8	3,200					
Total		£27,700	£3,200	£2,400	£9,600	£16,000	£3,500

Requirements as shown in statement   £27,700
Cash as per estimate   7,300

Total working capital required   £35,000

NOTES

(i) *Sales*
Sales are 5200 units at £20 per unit = £104,000 p.a.
Sales are £2000 a week.

(ii) *Materials*
Material cost is (8/20) × £2000 = £800 a week.

(iii) *Wages*
Wages cost is (2/20) × £2000 = £200 a week.

In the above question it is assumed that wages accrue evenly during the time manufacture is in progress. Process time is two weeks and it is assumed that labour is evenly carried on during production, so that on average the total cost of labour is outstanding for only half the time. This is contrary to specimen question 3, where it was not assumed that labour accrued evenly during the period. It is appreciated that there are some sweeping generalisations in these examples, but without going into considerable detail one cannot measure the input of labour during the time manufacture is in process. The effect of two of a number of possibilities has therefore been shown: (i) where labour was introduced at the beginning, and (ii) where it accrued evenly over the period and so was assumed to be completely introduced for half the time. Lag in payment of wages of 1½ weeks is considered as follows: if employees work evenly throughout the week, the employee earns wages from the beginning of the week and they increase daily until the end of the week. Thus on average the employer owes half the week's wages. If this is not paid until the following week-end, as often happens in practice, in effect the employer owes 1½ weeks' wages in arrears.

INTRODUCTION OF SHIFT WORKING

The problem of whether to introduce shift working to a factory is a highly complex one, and it is not within the scope of this book to discuss it at great length. It is however proposed to illustrate some of the effects the introduction of shift working may have on working capital.

The greatest economies of introducing shifts are in the use of fixed capital. No more plant and equipment, or little additional plant and equipment, are needed to work double shifts. Production can be doubled with minimum outlay on fixed capital. The same is not true of *working* capital, for it will probably be necessary to pay higher wages to shift workers, carry increased stocks, etc.

Specimen question (6)

Paulan Products Ltd operate a normal working day of eight hours. There are 25 working days in a month. Production costs per month are as follows:

Raw materials		£20,000
Direct labour		10,000
Overheads:		
Fixed	£7,500	
Semi-variable	3,750	
Variable	3,750	
		15,000
Net profit		5,000
Sales		£50,000

Raw materials are in stock on average	1 month
Materials are in process on average	½ month
Finished goods are in stock on average	1 month
Credit allowed by creditors is	1 month
Credit allowed to debtors is	2 months
Lag in payment of wages	⅛ month
Lag in payment of overheads	1 month
Semi-variable overheads are 50% variable.	

You are asked by management to report on the effects on working capital of introducing shift working. It is proposed to operate two shifts a day, each shift to work for 7½ hours. It is not thought that the hourly rate of productivity will be affected by the introduction of new employees. Employees will receive the same wages per shift as they formerly earned per day. It is assumed that the additional output can be sold.

Answer

WORKING CAPITAL REQUIREMENTS FORECAST
Single shift working Period . . . .

	Period (months)	Total	Raw materials	Work in progress	Finished goods	Debtors	Creditors
1. Materials:							
(a) In stock	1		£20,000				
(b) In work in progress	½			£10,000			
(c) In finished goods	1				£20,000		
(d) Credit to debtors	2					£40,000	
	4½						
(e) Credit from creditors	1						£20,000
Total	3½	£70,000					
2. Wages:							
(a) In work in progress	½			5,000			
(b) In finished goods	1				10,000		
(c) Credit to debtors	2					20,000	
	3½						
(d) Credit from creditors	⅛						1,250
Total	3⅜	33,750					
3. Overheads							
(a) In work in progress	½			7,500			
(b) In finished goods	1				15,000		
(c) Credit to debtors	2					30,000	
	3½						
(d) Credit from creditors	1						15,000
Total	2½	37,500					
4. Profit:							
Credit to debtors	2					10,000	
Total	2	10,000					
Total		£151,250	£20,000	£22,500	£45,000	£100,000	£36,250

WORKING CAPITAL REQUIREMENTS FORECAST
Double shift working Period . . . .

	% change on single shift	Total	Raw materials	Work in progress	Finished goods	Debtors	Creditors
1. Materials:							
(a) In stock	+87·5		£37,500				
(b) In work in progress	—			£10,000			
(c) In finished goods	+87·5				£37,500		
(d) Credit to debtors	+87·5					£75,000	
(e) Credit from creditors	+87·5						£37,500
Total		£122,500					
2. Wages:							
(a) In work in progress	+6·6			5,350			
(b) In finished goods	+100				20,000		
(c) Credit to debtors	+100					40,000	
(d) Credit from creditors	+100						2,500
Total		62,850					
3. Overheads:							
(a) In work in progress	−29·2			5,300			
(b) In finished goods	+32·7				19,900		
(c) Credit to debtors	+32·7					39,800	
(d) Credit from creditors	+32·7						19,900
Total		45,100					
4. Profit:							
Credit to debtors	+72·0					17,200	
Total		17,200					
Total		£247,650	£37,500	£20,650	£77,400	£172,000	£59,900

Notes on double-shift working

It will be observed that in the double-shift working capital requirements forecast, the "Period" column has been changed to read "% change on single shift." This is because the period is the same as that used in the single shift calculations, so we can disregard it in the double-shift calculations. The percentage change figures are to show management the percentage change in costs of the cash element concerned, so that easy reference can be made as required. The notes which follow describe how these percentage changes have been calculated.

1. *Materials*

Productivity under double-shift working has not changed per hour, so production has risen from 8 hours to 15 hours per day, an increase of 87·5%. Thus if production rises by 87·5% it is assumed that a corresponding increase in stocks will be required, of raw materials to meet production demands and of finished goods to meet sales. More sales will mean more debtors. However, the position with work in progress is not the same as the stocks just mentioned.

The amount of material in work in progress will not change. Double-shift working may result in processing output more quickly (which will affect overhead costs favourably) but the amount of materials in work in progress at any one time will remain unchanged; the amount of working capital tied up in materials is the same as with single-shift working.

2. *Wages*

Finished units remain in store for the same length of time as with single shifts; the periods of credit to debtors and from creditors remain the same too, so there is no change in the time factor here. But there are twice as many employees now, so the amount of working capital tied up will be doubled.

The effect of work in progress is not the same as that on the finished goods in stock. The time factor does not change, because work which previously required 12½ days × 8 hours = 100 hours will now take 6¾ days × 15 hours = 100 hours. However, the rate per hour does change. It was proposed by management that the employees would receive the same pay for a 7½-hour shift as for the previous 8-hour day; the result is a premium of 6·6%. The effect on working capital is thus an increase of 6·6%.

3. *Overheads*

To keep this example within reasonable bounds overheads were given as: fixed, £7500; semi-variable (50% variable), £3750; variable, £3750; total £15,000.

If shift working is introduced:

(a) *Fixed overheads* will remain fixed.

(b) *Variable overheads* will increase by the rate of increased production, 87·5%.

(c) *Semi-variable overheads* will increase by 50% of the variable element, i.e. 50% of 87·5 = 43·75%.

This results in the following overheads:

Fixed	£7,500
Semi-variable	5,391
Variable	7,031
	£19,922

For convenience this figure is taken as £19,900, which represents an increase on single shift working of 32·7%.

As with materials and labour, the effect of overheads on work in progress required is now calculated. Work in progress formerly required 12½ days to complete. Now it requires only 6¾ days, representing a saving of 46·7%.

In single-shift working the overheads included in working capital locked up in work in progress were £7500:

Fixed	£3750
Semi-variable	1875
Variable	1875
	£7500

Under double-shift working

(a) *Fixed overheads.*—These will be reduced by 46·7%. It is emphasised again that fixed overheads do not vary with output (at least in the short run) but they usually change with time. Thus the manager's salary may be the same irrespective of the level of activity achieved, but it obviously would increase with a longer period worked. Output is transferred to finished goods more quickly than before, resulting in a reduced amount of working capital being required to finance overheads. Fixed overheads will be reduced by 46·7%, *i.e.* by £1750 to £2000.

(b) *Variable overheads.*—These will continue at the same rate because they vary directly with output.

(c) *Semi-variable overheads.*—These are composed of 50% variable and 50% fixed overheads. The variable element will remain strictly variable, resulting in £937, while the fixed element will be reduced by 46·7%: 46·7% of £938 = £438. Therefore the fixed element will be £938 − £438 = £500. Semi-variable overheads will therefore amount to £1437:

Fixed	£2000
Semi-variable	1437
Variable	1875
	£5312

This figure is regarded as £5300 and represents a decrease of 29·2% on the amount required for single-shift working.

4. Profit

Net profit is one-tenth of turnover, which is equivalent to a ninth of cost. Cost of sales can be calculated from the amount for debtors shown in the working capital requirement forecast. Under double-shift working this is shown to be:

Raw materials	£75,000
Wages	40,000
Overheads	39,800
	£154,800

Profit is therefore $\frac{1}{9} \times$ £154,800 = £17,200. This represents an increase on single-shift working of 72%.

Remarks

It is again stressed that the above example is intentionally over-simplified. The object was to illustrate the principles from which the reader may advance to more complicated problems. In practice the employer would probably have to pay a larger premium for shift working than 6·6% and he would be very lucky to achieve 87·5% more production. But it does not matter here. What is important in this type of problem is that management should be informed of the various effects on working capital which the introduction of shift working will have.

In this instance, shift working resulted in an increase in production of 87·5% and in working capital requirements of 64%, from £151,250 to £247,650. Management thus learns that while fixed capital is scarcely affected, working capital goes up steeply.

EXAMINATION QUESTIONS

1. The following are the summarised Balance Sheets of NVN Ltd as on 31st December 1960 and 31st December 1961:

BALANCE SHEETS

	1960	1961		1960	1961
Issued share capital	£60,000	75,000	Freehold property at cost	£33,000	24,000
Share premium account	—	5,000	Plant and machinery at cost		
Capital reserve (profit on			*Less:* Depreciation	20,800	60,300
sale of freehold premises)	—	17,000	Preliminary expenses	1,200	600
Profit and Loss Account	21,500	21,200	Stock	30,350	32,850
Trade creditors	27,200	32,600	Debtors	20,100	24,750
Proposed dividends	6,000	8,500	Bank	9,250	16,800
	£114,700	£159,300		£114,700	£159,300

The following is a summary of the Profit and Loss Account for 1961:

Proposed dividends	£8,500	Net profit for year	£8,200
Balance c/f	21,200	Balance from 1960	21,500
	£29,700		£29,700

No plant and machinery was sold during 1961. The net profit £8200 is the amount after charging £7500 for depreciation of plant and machinery and after writing off preliminary expenses £600.

You are required to prepare a statement showing:

(a) The net increase in working capital during 1961.

(b) The sources and application of working capital during that year.

Ignore taxation. [C.I.S. (May 1962)]

2. The abridged Profit and Loss Accounts for the years ended 30th June 1963 and 30th June 1964 and the Balance Sheets as on those dates of Beeches Ltd were:

PROFIT AND LOSS ACCOUNTS

	1963	1964
Trading profit	£45,000	£70,000
Profit on sale of investments	—	2,000
	45,000	72,000

Taxation on profits of the year:

Income tax	£21,000		£33,000	
Profits tax	6,700		12,000	
		27,700		45,000
		17,300		27,000
Brought forward from previous year	15,000		17,300	
Income tax over-provided in previous years	—		4,000	
		15,000		21,300
		32,300		48,300
Proposed dividend	15,000		15,000	
Transfer to general reserve	—		10,000	
		15,000		25,000
Balance of undistributed profits		£17,300		£23,300

BALANCE SHEETS

Fixed assets: cost	£50,000		£60,000	
additions during year	10,000		8,000	
		£60,000		£68,000
depreciation		20,000		32,000
		40,000		36,000
Current assets:				
Investments	12,000		—	
Stock, at cost	178,000		200,000	
Debtors	130,000		218,500	
	320,000		418,500	
Current liabilities:				
Bank overdraft	115,000		140,000	
Trade creditors	70,000		90,000	
Expense creditors	8,000		9,200	
Current taxation:				
Income tax	13,000		18,000	
Profits tax	6,700		12,000	
Proposed dividend	15,000		15,000	
	227,700		284,200	
Net current assets		92,300		134,300
		£132,300		£170,300
Ordinary share capital		70,000		80,000
General reserve		25,000		35,000
Profit and Loss Account		17,300		23,300
Future taxation		20,000		32,000
		£132,300		£170,300

For the year ended 30th June 1964, trading purchases totalled £650,000 and sales £800,000; the trading profit was arrived at after charging depreciation £12,000 and directors' remuneration £10,000.

You are required to prepare:

(*a*) A summarised cash flow statement of Beeches Ltd for the year ended 30th June 1964.

(*b*) A statement showing the source of additional working capital that has become available during the year and the manner of its utilisation.

[C.A. (1965)

3. Using the information given in the following Balance Sheets and Profit and Loss Account, draft a Movement of Working Capital and Sources and Applications of Funds Statement for the year ended 31st December 1971.

PROFIT AND LOSS ACCOUNT

Year to 31st December 1971

Sales		£5,750,000
Materials	£1,576,000	
Labour	644,000	
Works overheads	1,837,000	
Depreciation	146,000	
Selling expenses	223,000	
Distribution expenses	334,000	
Administrative expenses	425,000	
		5,185,000
Trading profit		565,000
Dividend from Subsidiary company (gross)		15,000
Profit prior to taxation		580,000
Taxation		232,000
Profit after taxation		348,000
Proposed dividends (gross):		
Preference	20,000	
Ordinary	210,000	
		230,000
Balance c/f		£118,000

Balance sheet at 31st December	1970		1971
Fixed assets:			
Land and buildings		£765,000	£980,000
Plant, machinery and vehicles		662,000	760,000
		1,427,000	1,740,000
Investment in subsidiary company		150,000	175,000
Current assets:			
Stock	£930,000		£1,006,000
Debtors	686,000		763,000
Tax reserve certificates	110,000		180,000
Cash at bank	1,000		15,000
	1,727,000		1,964,000

Current liabilities:

Creditors	678,000	692,000
Bank overdraft	20,000	—
Current taxation	135,000	195,000
Proposed dividends (gross)	129,000	230,000
	962,000	1,117,000

Net current assets	765,000	847,000
	£2,342,000	£2,762,000

Share capital:

5% £1 Preference shares	£400,000	£400,000
£1 Ordinary shares	1,150,000	1,400,000
	1,550,000	1,800,000

Revenue reserves:

General	280,000	400,000
Profit and Loss Account	324,000	342,000
	2,154,000	2,542,000
Deferred liability for taxation	188,000	220,000
	£2,342,000	£2,762,000

Movements on Fixed Assets Accounts

	Land and buildings	Plant, machinery and vehicles
Balance at 31st December 1970	£765,000	£662,000
Additions	371,000	218,000
Disposals (net book value)	(128,000)	(2,000)
	1,008,000	878,000
Depreciation for year	28,000	118,000
	£980,000	£760,000

Movements on Reserve Accounts

	General	Profit and Loss Account
Balance at 31st December 1970	£280,000	£324,000
Profit on sale of fixed assets	20,000	—
Balance of profit for year	—	118,000
Transfer	100,000	(100,000)
Balance at 31st December 1971	£400,000	£342,000

[C.C.A. (adapted)]

4. The following are the summarised Balance Sheets of A. Ltd as on 31st December:

	1962	1963		1962	1963
Share capital:			Fixed assets—at cost	£240,070	£253,730
6% Preference shares—			Depreciation provided	90,020	98,480
redeemable 1959/65 at					
£1·10	£100,000	£80,000		150,050	155,250
Ordinary	75,000	120,000	Subsidiary company—		
Revenue reserves:			Shares at cost	61,000	76,000
Plant replacement	15,000	10,000	Current assets:		
Profit and Loss Account	100,350	102,700	Stocks	98,000	104,000
6½% Debentures	—	40,000	Debtors	88,000	85,000
Current liabilities:			Cash	11,750	32,000
Bank loan	22,000	—			
Creditors and accruals	84,450	75,550			
Proposed ordinary divi-					
dends	12,000	24,000			
	£408,800	£452,250		£408,800	£452,250

You ascertain that during 1963:

(a) £25,000, part of the unappropriated balance on Profit and Loss Account, was capitalised and applied in paying up £0·25 per share on the issued Ordinary shares making them fully paid up.

(b) On 31st December, 20,000 Preference shares were redeemed at the specified premium out of the proceeds of a rights issue of 20,000 new Ordinary shares issued for cash at £1 per share. The premium was written off to Profit and Loss Account.

(c) The movement on plant replacement reserve represents a transfer to Profit and Loss Account.

(d) The Ordinary dividend proposed for the year 1962 was paid and in addition an interim dividend on the Ordinary shares absorbing £4000 was paid. The Preference dividend was paid on 31st December in each year.

(e) In regard to fixed assets (i) £3000 was added to the book value of a property, following a revaluation, and credited to Profit and Loss Account, (ii) expenditure totalling £1700 which, at 31st December 1962, had been carried forward in suspense (included in "debtors") was transferred to fixed assets, (iii) depreciation of fixed assets of £13,260 was charged to Profit and Loss Account and (iv) plant (cost £6000, depreciation provided £4800) was sold for £250 and the loss written off to Profit and Loss Account.

(f) The increase in the investment in the subsidiary company represents the cost of additional shares purchased during the year.

You are required to prepare a statement showing the sources and application of funds during the year.

Ignore taxation.   [C.A. (1964)

5. The managing director of an iron and steel stockist expects its sales of £1 million to increase by 25% over the whole of the next financial year and he seeks your advice on the most appropriate method of financing the increase. He provides the following information:

Estimated Balance Sheet position at 31st December 1968:

Fixed assets:

Freehold property at valuation	£75,000
Other fixed assets	25,000
	100,000

Current assets:

Stocks	£252,000	
Debtors	208,000	
Other	12,000	
		£472,000

Current liabilities:

Bank overdraft (unsecured)	148,000		
Creditors	180,000		
Taxation	46,000		
Other	22,000		
		396,000	
			76,000
			£176,000

Year ending 31st December	Net profit before tax
1964	£38,000
1965	41,000
1966	52,000
1967	68,000
Estimate 1968	96,000
Estimate 1969	120,000

You further ascertain that the bank overdraft limit is £150,000 and has been agreed at that level for the next two years. The company has no plans for capital expenditure in 1969 and it is expected that 50% of the profits after tax will be paid in dividends.

Draft a note to your client, making such assumptions as you consider necessary, setting out clearly:

(a) Your estimate of the additional finance required, taking into account a very approximate estimate (derived from the information above) of the company's cash flow for 1969.

(b) Your practical suggestions for raising the additional finance required.

For business reasons it is not possible to reduce stocks for the existing turnover or lengthen credit taken. [C.C.A.

6. This is the skeleton Balance Sheet of Fairbairn Enterprises Ltd at 30th November 1969:

£ 1968		£	£ 1968		£
100,000	Ordinary shares	150,000	207,000	Plant—at cost	219,000
20,000	Redeemable Preference shares	—	66,000	*Less:* depreciation	53,000
6,000	Capital reserve	—			166,000
10,000	Share premium account	—	141,000		
17,000	Profit and Loss Account,		23,000	Land and buildings	37,000
	unappropriated balance	34,300	22,200	Stocks	49,000
22,000	Deferred Taxation			14,000 Debtors 18,000	
	Account	24,000		800 less provision 1,200	
—	6% Debentures	25,000	13,200		16,800
9,069	Creditors	19,700	2,600	Cash	14,450
16,400	Provision for current		—	Discount on issue of	
	taxation	28,700		debentures	750
1,531	Provision for proposed				
	dividends	2,300			
£202,000		£284,000	£202,000		£284,000

The skeleton Profit and Loss Account for the year ended on that date was:

Trading profit after deducting depreciation		£84,087
Less: loss on sale of fixed assets		1,400
		82,687
Less: taxation		30,700
		51,987
Add: balance b/f		17,000
		68,987
Less: discount on Debentures written off	£500	
Amounts capitalised	25,000	
Dividends	9,187	
		34,687
Balance c/f		£34,300

(*a*) The land and buildings were revalued at 1st December 1968; there were no purchases or sales during the period.

(*b*) Plant costing £27,500 on which the accrued depreciation amounted to £24,300 was sold during the year for £1800.

(*c*) A bonus share issue of one-for-two was made on 31st December 1968, to the Ordinary shareholders.

(*d*) On the same date the redeemable Preference shares were redeemed at a premium of £0·25 per £1 share.

You are required to prepare a movement of working capital and sources and applications of funds statement for the period.   [C.C.A. (adapted)

7. In preparing a financial budget for a six-months period, draft a columnar statement, specifying the headings for the entries without entering any figures, to show the budgeted working capital at the end of each month.

In addition, provide in the lower half of the statement for additions to and deductions from the budgeted figures to reflect monthly the changes in the plan.   [C.W.A.

8. From the following information prepare a statement in columnar form showing the estimated working capital requirements (*a*) in total, and (*b*) as regards each constituent part of working capital:

Budgeted sales	£26,000 per annum
	£
Analysis of £ of sales—	
Raw material	0·30
Direct labour	0·40
Overheads	0·20
	0·90
Profit	0·10
	£1·00

It is estimated that:

(*a*) Pending use, raw materials are carried in stock for three weeks, and finished goods for two weeks.

(*b*) Factory processing will take three weeks.

(*c*) Suppliers will give five weeks' credit and customers will require eight weeks' credit.

It may be assumed that production and overheads accrue evenly throughout the year and that dividends are paid annually.　　　　　　[S.C.A.

9. You are consulted as to the estimated working capital requirements for project XXX.

Data:

Raw material costs £0·75 per unit.
Overheads £15,000 per month.
Labour £0·58½ per unit.
Output and sales 10,000 units per month.
Selling price £5 per unit.
Buffer stocks to be carried:
　Raw materials: 2 weeks' production.
　Finished goods: 3 weeks' supply.
The debtors on average take 2·25 months' credit.
Raw material is received in uniform deliveries daily and suppliers have to be paid at the end of the month goods are received.
Other trade creditors allow an average of 1½ months' credit.

Calculate the working capital required for February in a form for presentation to the board. For this purpose you may assume that a month is a four week period. Append a note(s) as to any comment(s) you may wish to make.　　　　　　[C.C.A.

10. The Liquidator of West Ltd has offered to East Ltd, for £18,000, manufacturing plant which cost £50,000 in 1949 and is estimated to operate efficiently for a further ten years and, for £4500, stocks and work in progress.

If the offer is accepted the tenancy of the factory will be transferred to East Ltd, but not that of the office, as that company's office will suffice. You are given the following information of the last year's trading of West Ltd.:

Sales—average credit two calendar months		£111,678
Purchases—average credit 6½ weeks	£61,381	
Wages—lag in payment, 1½ weeks	20,800	
Factory rent—payable quarterly in advance	2,392	
Other factory expenses—average credit one calendar month	7,212	
Depreciation of plant	2,500	
Decrease of stocks and work in progress	2,219	96,504
Gross profit		15,174
Office rent—payable quarterly in arrear	1,260	
Salaries—lag in payment, half a week	6,656	
General expenses—average credit one calendar month	2,472	
Managing director's salary—paid monthly in arrear	3,000	
Directors' fees—paid quarterly in advance	2,000	15,388
Net loss		£214

You are instructed to assume that:

    (*a*) Sales would be maintained at the former level with no significant seasonal variations.

    (*b*) There would be savings of 4% of the cost of materials used and $2\frac{1}{2}$% of the cost of wages.

    (*c*) The managing director would be appointed manager on the same terms, but directors' fees as well as office rent would be saved.

    (*d*) No profits would be withdrawn until they were surplus to working capital requirements.

    (*e*) It would be necessary to increase immediately the stocks and work in progress offered by the liquidator for £4500 by further stock costing £4000.

The directors of East Ltd are disposed to accept the offer, which remains open until 1st January 1961, but before doing so wish to know the additional amount of money which the business would require for working capital.

You are required to set out your calculations of the additional money required for working capital:

    (*a*) At the maximum during the year 1960, and

    (*b*) At the end of that year.   [S.C.A.

11. Consider the effect of "three-shift working" on production costs in an industry where "one-shift working" has been normal in the past.

                                                          [C.C.A.

12. Your company wishes to acquire adjoining factory premises at a cost of £60,000 to manufacture a new product. The present owner is prepared to take a mortgage on the property for half the purchase price, carrying interest at 5% per annum.

The equipping of the factory with plant, machinery, tools, fittings, etc., is expected to cost £75,000.

The prime cost of the product is estimated at £10 per unit, *i.e.* labour £6 and material £4, the latter being purchased on the usual trade terms for payment in the month following delivery.

Power, stores, tools and other variable expenses are expected to cost £1·50 per unit.

Management, supervision, indirect labour, and all other fixed expenses, including mortgage interest, but excluding depreciation, are budgeted at £9000 per month.

Selling and distribution expenses, apart from advertising, may be taken at £3000 per month.

It is expected that an initial advertising campaign costing £15,000 will be required to establish a market for the product. In addition, normal advertising will cost about £1000 per month.

The selling price is to be £17·50 per unit, and sales are estimated as follows:

First month	1000 units
Second month	2000 ,,
Third and subsequent months	3000 ,,

10% of sales will be for cash, the remainder for settlement in the following month.

Stocks required at the commencement of trading are:

Materials	£20,000
Finished goods	1,000 units

and these will require to be maintained.

The value of work in progress at full production is estimated at £5000.

The patent rights for the new product will cost £15,000, and legal expenses for purchase of property £1000.

A charge of £500 per month will be made against the factory for head office administration expenses.

Compute the amount of capital required to finance this project, and prepare a statement showing the expected earnings for the first and subsequent years.

[C.W.A.

13. A factory consists of:

(a) heavy machine shop,
(b) light machine shop,
(c) electro-plating department,
(d) assembly department,

together with the usual service departments, administrative, selling and distributive organisation.

Owing to pressure of work, which is regarded as likely to last for at least two years, the management is considering:

(a) getting plating done outside or working overtime in the plating shop,
(b) extending the heavy machine shop or working a night shift.

The other production departments have capacity to cope with the additional work.

Assuming a sound costing system to be in existence, explain how you would advise the management, to enable them to make decisions.

[C.W.A.

14. (a) What is the significance of cash budgeting for management purposes and why is the cash budget dependent on both the operating and the capital budgets?

(b) From the following information taken from the budget of the AB Co. Ltd, prepare a statement showing the average amount of working capital required by the company.

Annual sales are estimated at 100,000 units at £1 per unit.

Production quantities coincide with sales and will be carried on evenly throughout the year, and production cost is:

Material	£0·50 per unit
Labour	£0·20 per unit
Expenses	£0·17½ per unit

Customers are given sixty days' credit, and fifty days' credit is taken from suppliers.

Forty days' supply of raw materials and fifteen days' supply of finished goods are kept.

The production cycle is twenty days and all material is issued at the commencement of each production cycle.

A cash balance equivalent to one-third of the average other working capital requirements is kept for contingencies.

[C.C.A.

15. It has been decided to market a new product based on the following forecasts of what will take place in a "normal" year.

Sales	£480,000
Raw material	240,000
Wages	96,000
Factory expenses (see note (f))	42,000
Administration expenses (see note (g))	16,000
Selling expenses (see note (h))	22,000
Profit	64,000

NOTES

(a) Debtors will be allowed three months' credit, two months' credit will be taken from creditors.

(b) Factory and administration expenses accrue evenly throughout the year and are paid at the end of the month following the month in which they are incurred. Wages will be paid weekly in arrears and for this purpose it can be assumed that all months contain four weeks. There will therefore only be 48 pay periods during any one year.

(c) Selling expenses other than the head office allocation (*see* note (*h*)) vary directly in proportion to sales turnover, payment of these is on the same basis as factory and administration expenses.

(d) A raw material stock of £30,000 will be held and will be purchased immediately.

(e) Sales and production will be carried on evenly throughout the year and for this purpose the year can be assumed to contain twelve equal months. To allow finished goods stocks to be accumulated, sales will be restricted to £20,000 per month for the first two months but for the remaining ten months sales will remain at the "normal" monthly level.

(f) Included in the factory expenses are the following items:

   (i) £5000—depreciation being 10% per annum of original cost of equipment;
   (ii) £1000—being a notional rent charge equal to 1/40th of the purchase price of premises to be acquired.

(g) Included in the administration expenses is a sum of £1000 being a re-allocation of existing head office costs. Head office expenses are not paid in cash to the head office but are treated as a loan.

(h) Included in the selling expenses is a sum of £2800 being an allocation of existing head office costs.

(i) Payment for premises and equipment will be made in two equal instalments the first to take place at the commencement of the first month and the second at the commencement of the sixth month.

Using the above you are required to prepare:

   (i) A monthly statement of the cash inflows and outflows for the first twelve months' trading.
   (ii) A statement of the anticipated investment in working capital as at the end of the twelfth month on the assumption that at the commencement of month 10, £150,000 of permanent capital will be paid into the company's bank account.
   (iii) A brief report indicating the various sources of finance—internal and external—which are available to an organisation, indicating the cost of these to the organisation.

Work in progress can be ignored.

Taxation can be ignored for parts (i) and (ii) only.   [C.C.A.

16. The Alpha Company Limited are about to market a new product—Product X. The company has not produced this type of product before and a management meeting has been called to discuss possible selling prices for Product X. As a basis for discussion you, as management accountant, have been asked to prepare a statement indicating the price to be charged in order that the company may earn a return of 25% on the capital invested in this product. It is the practice of the company to divide capital employed into two categories—fixed capital and current capital. Your statement should clearly indicate that part of the mark-up on cost which is due to the desired return on each category. You should also prepare an estimated summary profit/loss account and a capital employed statement and a report commenting on this.

Further Information

1. Product X Unit Cost

		£
	Material	1·20
	Labour	0·80
	Expenses	1·40
		3·40

Non-cash outlays such as depreciation involved in the unit cost figure amount to £0·34.

2. Target figures for current assets are as follows:

(*a*) Sales terms for customers are net 30 days after receipt of goods.

(*b*) Stock—Finished Goods = 3 months
Raw Materials = 1 month
Work-In-Process = 1 month

For work-in-process it can be assumed that raw material is introduced at the beginning of the productive process and that work in progress is 50% complete as far as labour and expenses are concerned.

(*c*) A cash contingency of 20 days requirement is maintained.

(*d*) No allowance for sundry creditors is taken into consideration.

3. Fixed asset invested for the company in total equals £2,000,000, of this £400,000 relates entirely to product X, and £1,200,000 relates directly to other products. The remainder cannot be identified directly with any one product. Over the years the amount invested in fixed assets correlates best with machine hour usage a table of which is given below:

Estimated Machine Hour Usage

	Machine 1	Machine 2	Machine 3	Machine 4	Machine 5	Machine 6
Product T	2000	—	750	—	—	500
Product V	—	—	600	2000	—	500
Product W	—	—	375	—	2000	500
Product X	—	2000	275	—	—	500
	2000	2000	2000	2000	2000	2000

4. Estimated annual unit sales of Product X = 3,000,000. [C.C.A.

PART TWO

INTERNAL CONTROL

CHAPTER VI

INTEGRAL ACCOUNTS

ADVANTAGES

INTEGRAL accounting is a system of recording both financial and costing transactions in one integrated set of books. In other words, to balance the accounts one must include balances of what may be termed the "cost" accounts as well as the "financial" accounts. It is assumed in this text that the reader has a reasonable knowledge of financial and cost accounting; to discuss either is beyond the scope of this book.

There has been considerable controversy over the merits of integrating the accounts of a company. It is not a new idea, as is shown by an article in the *Cost Accountant* in 1950,* where it was stated: "It is common practice in many concerns today to dispense with two sets of books (one for financial accounts and the other for cost accounts) by using the data compiled for costing purposes as the basis for the entries in the general ledger." In actual fact, research has revealed that in Britain as yet there are not many firms which operate a completely integrated system of accounting, but it would appear that use of the system is much more prevalent in the U.S.A. Readers who are particularly interested in this system of accounting should consult the articles noted below,† which give considerable information on such matters as how to install a system, the advantages and disadvantages, the difficulties experienced in installing and operating a system, and mention some important points to be considered.

It is claimed by those who have operated the system in practice that considerable economies are achieved in clerical labour and that confidence in the costing records and information is greater when they form part of an integrated accounting system. In theory there is no doubt that the system is a valuable form of control for management and it seems logical that the two sets of accounts should be integrated. The future may see widespread adoption in the use of integral accounts; in examinations it is already quite a popular subject.

Where separate cost accounting and financial accounting systems are operated, a cost ledger control account has to be maintained as a "link" between the two sets of accounts. At the end of each accounting period,

---

* "The valuation of finished stocks and work in process for periodic accounts," by G. J. Underdown, Nov. 1950.

† "Integrated accounts," by G. P. Souster, April 1962; "Integrated cost accounting systems," by P. C. P. Ford and T. E. Gambling, May 1962; "Accounting integration in a multiple product organisation," by H. P. Southall, Dec. 1961 (all in *The Cost Accountant*); "Integration or reconciliation?" by A. Marshall, Oct. 1951; "Integral accounting," by J. P. Wilson, *The Accountant*, Mar. 1963.

for the sake of confidence in the accounts, it is necessary to reconcile the cost and financial accounts by means of a reconciliation account or statement. The introduction of integral accounting eliminates the need for all this *and* dispenses with a number of accounts which originally appeared in one set and were duplicated in another.

A company wishing to change to integrated accounts from non-integrated cost and financial accounting should not have much difficulty, provided co-operation has been obtained from all staff who are directly concerned with the change, and the switch has been effectively planned to take place at the end of an accounting year. In the financial and cost accounts the original basic transactions were:

Financial accounts	*Cost accounts*
Recording assets and liabilities.	Detailed analysis of costs and sales.
Payments to and from cash.	
Analysis of expenditure and sales.	

In an integrated system the analysis of costs and sales previously made in the financial accounts will be discontinued because it is analysed in far more detail in the cost accounts. Thus the basic transactions are:

Integral accounts
Recording assets and liabilities.
Payments to and from cash.
Detailed analysis of costs and sales.

To illustrate the basic difference in accounting entries, four brief examples are given:

Example 1: sales

Sales for the period were £510,000 compared with budgeted sales of £500,000.

		Dr.	Cr.
(a) *Financial books*	Debtors	£510,000	
	Sales		£510,000
(b) *Cost books*	Cost ledger control	510,000	
	Budgeted sales		500,000
	Sales price variance		10,000
(c) *Integral accounts*	Debtors	510,000	
	Budgeted sales		500,000
	Sales price variance		10,000

Example 2: materials

Purchased goods of £305,000 compared with standard cost of £300,000.

		Dr.	Cr.
(a) *Financial books*	Purchases	£305,000	
	Creditors		£305,000
(b) *Cost books*	Stores ledger control	300,000	
	Material price variance	5,000	
	Cost ledger control		305,000
(c) *Integral accounts*	Stores ledger control	300,000	
	Material price variance	5,000	
	Creditors		305,000

Example 3: wages

Paid production wages of £56,000 compared with standard cost of £55,000.

		Dr.	Cr.
(a) *Financial books*	Wages	£56,000	
	Cash		£56,000
(b) *Cost books*	Wages control	55,000	
	Labour rate variance	1,000	
	Cost ledger control		56,000
(c) *Integral accounts*	Wages control	55,000	
	Labour rate variance	1,000	
	Cash		56,000

Example 4: overheads

Production expenses incurred during the month were £76,000 compared with standard cost of £75,000.

		Dr.	Cr.
(a) *Financial books*	Production expenses	£76,000	
	Expense creditors		£76,000
(b) *Cost books*	Production overhead	75,000	
	Expenditure variance	1,000	
	Cost ledger control		76,000
(c) *Integral accounts*	Production overhead	75,000	
	Expenditure variance	1,000	
	Expense creditors		76,000

It should be observed that in each of these examples the Expense Account in the financial books, and the Cost Ledger Control Account in the cost books, have been eliminated in the integrated accounting system.

VALUATION OF STOCKS

When a system of integral accounting is adopted, difficulty may be experienced in recording stock valuations. It will be recalled that in financial accounting the "golden rule" is that stocks should be valued at "the lowest of cost, net realisable value or replacement price," while in cost accounting, stocks are valued according to whichever system of stores pricing has been operated, *e.g.* actual or standard cost. One of the more difficult questions in the reconciliation of cost and financial accounts is reconciliation where the stock is valued in one set of books at a price different from that in the other. This problem persists in an integrated system: which figures should be shown in the integrated accounts? It can be overcome by operating a Stores Adjustment Account, to which is posted the difference between the valuation required for the final accounts and that shown in the Stores Ledger.

Example

The stock valuations of a company as shown in the financial books and the cost books are as follows:

	Financial books	Cost books
Raw materials	£75,000	£77,000
Work in progress	27,000	29,000
Finished goods	33,000	34,000

The company decides to integrate its accounts, so that the integrated accounts should show:

Raw material stores	Dr.	£77,000	
Work in progress		29,000	
Finished goods		34,000	
Raw materials adjustment	Cr.		£2,000
Work in progress adjustment			2,000
Finished goods adjustment			1,000

In this way the figures which would normally be shown in the cost accounts continue under integration, but to allow for year-end accounting for Balance Sheet purposes the adjustment accounts shown above reveal the changes in valuation.

INTEGRAL ACCOUNTING SYSTEMS

There are two orthodox systems of fully integrating a cost accounting and a financial accounting system:

1. The double entry method.
2. The third entry method.

They are similar in practice, the only difference being that the third entry method utilises a Cost Control Account with memorandum entries. The object of the Cost Control Account is to collect various items of cost into one Control Account which can then be analysed into various classifications of cost, such as direct and indirect wages. The third entries are the record of this analysis in memorandum form, so they perform the same sort of service as a day book in financial accounting. For examination purposes either method may be adopted; where there is considerable detailed analysis of expenditure concerning a number of departments the third entry system might be preferable, but otherwise the double entry system seems to be satisfactory. Both will be illustrated in this chapter.

Examination candidates should realise that the questions set on this subject vary widely. The accounting system in one firm will rarely correspond exactly with that in another—except perhaps with firms which have adopted uniform costing—but even here the systems are rarely identical. Consequently examination questions can cover a very wide range, and a large number of difficult problems have resulted. So it is advisable to note the principles of integral accounting mentioned previously, then to attempt as many questions on the subject as one possibly can. For this reason two relatively orthodox examples are given, followed by two examination questions which are typical of questions set at the final level by professional bodies.

1. THE DOUBLE ENTRY METHOD

Specimen question (1)

The cost and financial accounts of the Vigilant Manufacturing Co. Ltd are integrated. The following transactions and details are to be recorded in the Ledger Accounts, then you are required to prepare a Profit and Loss Account for the year and a Balance Sheet as at the end of the year. Balances as at 1st January are:

	Dr.	Cr.
Debtors	£40,880	
Trade creditors		£25,648
Expense creditors		8,970
Bank	19,924	
Stock of raw materials	36,842	
Work in progress	17,346	
Finished goods	8,648	
Freehold buildings	90,000	
Plant and machinery	135,000	
Issued share capital		200,000
Profit and Loss Account		50,000
Provision for depreciation of freehold buildings		9,000
Provision of depreciation of plant and machinery		54,000
Provision for bad debts		1,022
	£348,640	£348,640

Transactions which took place during the year were:

Materials purchased	£210,453
Materials returned to suppliers	4,687
Materials issued to production	184,830
Indirect materials issued	18,432
Carriage inwards	5,632
Cheques paid to trade creditors	194,665
Cheques received from debtors	586,450
Cheques drawn for salaries and wages	172,925
Cheques drawn for expenses	93,759
Discount allowed	11,496
Discount received	7,423
Salaries and wages:	
Production, direct wages	81,236
Production, indirect wages and salaries	24,328
Administrative salaries	36,562
Sales department salaries	29,738
Distribution department salaries and wages	19,426
Deductions made from salaries and wages	15,468
Expenses:	
Production	32,436
Administration	18,328
Selling	29,462
Distribution	9,387
Production overheads recovered	108,000
Administration overheads recovered	62,000
Selling and distribution overheads recovered	88,000

Depreciation provision:
  5% on freehold buildings
    Production overheads 50%
    Administration overheads 25%
    Selling and distribution overheads 25%
  20% on plant and machinery
  10% on office machinery

Bad debts (provision for bad debts: $2\frac{1}{2}\%$ of debtors)	574
Wages and salaries accrued	2,897
Purchased and paid for computer equipment for accountancy department on 1st January	50,000
Output	369,945
Finished goods sold at cost of production	372,272
Sales	600,000

  Ignore taxation.

Answer

Debtors

Balance b/d	£40,880	Discount allowed	£11,496
Sales	600,000	Bank	586,450
		Bad debts	574
		Balance c/d	42,360
	£640,880		£640,880
Balance b/d	42,360		

Trade creditors

Stores	£4,687	Balance b/d	£25,648
Discount received	7,423	Stores	210,453
Bank	194,665		
Balance c/d	29,326		
	£236,101		£236,101
		Balance b/d	29,326

Expense creditors

Bank	£93,759	Balance b/d	£8,970
Balance c/d	10,456	Production overheads	5,632
		Production overheads	32,436
		Administration overheads	18,328
		Selling and distribution overheads	29,462
		Selling and distribution overheads	9,387
	£104,215		£104,215
		Balance b/d	10,456

Bank

Balance b/d	£19,924	Trade creditors	£194,665
Debtors	586,450	Expense creditors	93,759
		Salaries	172,925
		Office equipment	50,000
		Balance c/d	95,025
	£606,374		£606,374
Balance b/d	95,025		

Freehold buildings

Balance b/d	£90,000

Plant and machinery

Balance b/d	£135,000

Office equipment

Bank	£50,000

Provision for depreciation of freehold buildings

Balance c/d	£13,500	Balance b/d	£9,000
		Production overheads	2,250
		Administration overheads	1,125
		Selling and distribution overheads	1,125
	£13,500		£13,500
		Balance b/d	13,500

Provision for depreciation of plant and machinery

Balance c/d	£81,000	Balance b/d	£54,000
		Production overheads	27,000
	£81,000		£81,000
		Balance b/d	81,000

Provision for depreciation of office equipment

Administrative overheads	£5,000

Provision for bad and doubtful debts

Debtors	£574	Balance b/d	£1,022
Balance c/d	1,059	Profit and loss	611
	£1,633		£1,633
		Balance b/d	1,059

Capital

Balance b/d	£200,000

Profit and loss appropriation

Balance c/d	£120,813	Balance b/d	£50,000
		Profit and loss	70,813
	£120,813		£120,813
		Balance b/d	120,813

Discount allowed

Debtors	£11,496	Profit and loss	£11,496

Discount received

Profit and loss	£7,423	Creditors	£7,423

Wages and salaries payable

Deductions	£15,468	Wages control	£191,290
Bank	172,925		
Balance c/d	2,897		
	£191,290		£191,290
		Balance b/d	2,897

Wages control

Wages and salaries payable	£191,290	Work in progress	£81,236
		Production overhead	24,328
		Administration overhead	36,562
		Selling and distribution overhead	29,738
		Selling and distribution overhead	19,426
	£191,290		£191,290

Raw materials store

Balance b/d	£36,842	Creditors	£4,687
Creditors	210,453	Work in progress	184,830
		Production overhead	18,432
		Balance c/d	39,346
	£247,295		£247,295
Balance b/d	39,346		

Production expenses

Stores	£18,432	Work in progress	£108,000
Expense creditors	5,632	Overhead adjustment	2,078
,, ,,	32,436		
Wages	24,328		
Provision for depreciation	2,250		
,, ,, ,,	27,000		
	£110,078		£110,078

Administration expenses

Expense creditors	£18,328	Cost of sales	£62,000
Wages	36,562		
Provision for depreciation	1,125		
„ „ „	5,000		
Overhead adjustment	985		
	£62,000		£62,000

Selling and distribution expenses

Expense creditors	£29,462	Cost of sales	£88,000
„ „	9,387	Overhead adjustment	1,138
Wages	29,738		
„	19,426		
Provision for depreciation	1,125		
	£89,138		£89,138

Overhead adjustment

Production overhead	£2,078	Administration overhead	£985
Selling and distribution		Profit and loss	2,231
overheads	1,138		
	£3,216		£3,216

Work in progress

Balance b/d	£17,346	Finished goods	£369,945
Stores	184,830	Balance c/d	21,467
Wages	81,236		
Production overhead	108,000		
	£391,412		£391,412
Balance b/d	21,467		

Finished goods

Balance b/d	£8,648	Cost of sales	£372,272
Work in progress	369,945	Balance b/d	6,321
	£378,593		£378,593
Balance b/d	6,321		

Cost of sales

Finished goods	£372,272	Profit and loss	£522,272
Administration overheads	62,000		
Selling and distribution			
overheads	88,000		
	£522,272		£522,272

Sales

Profit and loss	£600,000	Debtors	£600,000

Profit and Loss Account for year

Cost of sales	£522,272	Sales	£600,000
Overhead adjustment	2,231	Discount received	7,423
Discount allowed	11,496		
Provision for bad debts	611		
Balance c/d	70,813		
	£607,423		£607,423

BALANCE SHEET AS AT END OF YEAR

Issued share capital	£200,000		Freehold buildings	£90,000	
			Less depreciation	13,500	
Profit and loss	120,813				£76,500
		£320,813	Plant and machinery	135,000	
			Less depreciation	81,000	
Trade creditors	29,326				54,000
			Office equipment	50,000	
Expense creditors	10,456		*Less* depreciation	5,000	
					45,000
Wages accrued	2,897				175,500
			Stock	39,346	
Wages deductions	15,468		Work in progress	21,467	
		58,147	Finished goods	6,321	
				67,134	
			Debtors	£42,360	
			Less provision for depreciation	1,059	
				41,301	
			Bank	95,025	
					203,460
		£378,960			£378,960

NOTES

(i) Administrative overheads recovered amounted to £62,000. Opinion is divided among accountants on the treatment of administration overheads. Should they be recovered in work in progress, finished goods or in cost of sales? Or, as marginal costing exponents would advise, charged direct to Profit and Loss Account? In this example administration overheads have been recovered, so marginal costing is obviously not in use. The authors think it preferable to recover them in cost of sales, so that stocks of work in progress or finished goods will not bear any charge for these fixed overheads. Valuation of stocks is discussed at greater length in Chapter XIV.

(ii) It will be observed that two accounts have been opened for wages: Wages Control and Wages Payable. It is not strictly necessary to follow this practice, but it is advisable, especially when considerable detail is involved. There may be wages paid, accruals, prepayments, deductions for various items such as P.A.Y.E. tax and National Insurance contributions, and amounts to be recovered as direct charges to production or through overhead recovery rates. By separating wages into two accounts—one essentially "financial" and the other essentially "costing"—transactions can be followed through and interpreted relatively easily.

Specimen question (2)

[This question was set at a final examination of the Institute of Cost and Works Accountants.]

From the following information relating to a year's operations, you are required to compile and close off the cost and financial accounts of a company whose accounts are integrated and prepare a final balance.

Balances at beginning of period:	*Actual*	*Standard*
Customers	£185,000	
Suppliers	84,000	
Cash	39,000	
Materials		£40,000
Fixed assets	200,000	
Depreciation provision	94,000	
Work in progress		60,000
Investments	12,000	
Ordinary share capital	300,000	
Profit and Loss Account (balance)	58,000	

Transactions during year:	*Actual*	*Standard*
Sales	£404,000	£385,000
Cost of sales		249,000
Gross wages (70% direct)	112,000	
Materials issued (85% direct)		106,000
Materials purchased	137,000	131,000
Materials returned	4,000	5,000
Cash paid:		
Wages	102,000	
Expenses	7,000	
Suppliers	125,000	
Interim dividend	23,000	
Cash received:		
From customers	416,000	
Income from investments	4,000	
Overhead allowance		65,000
Variances adverse:		
Direct wages:		

Rate   3% of actual
Efficiency 4% of actual
Methods 3% of actual
Indirect materials: price 4% of standard
Depreciation at 10% per annum is to be charged to costs.

Answer

Total debtors

Balance b/d	£185,000	Cash		£416,000
Sales	404,000	Balance c/d		173,000
	£589,000			£589,000
Balance b/d	173,000			

Creditors

Returns	£4,000	Balance b/d	£84,000
Cash	125,000	Purchases	137,000
Balance c/d	92,000		
	£221,000		£221,000
		Balance b/d	92,000

Cash

Balance b/d	£39,000	Wages	£102,000
Debtors	416,000	Production overheads	7,000
Investments	4,000	Creditors	125,000
		Dividend	23,000
		Balance c/d	202,000
	£459,000		£459,000
Balance b/d	202,000		

Stock of materials

Balance b/d	£40,000	Work in progress	£90,100
Purchases	131,000	Production overheads	15,900
		Returns	5,000
		Balance c/d	60,000
	£171,000		£171,000
Balance b/d	60,000		

Fixed assets

Balance b/d	£200,000

Depreciation provision

Balance c/d	£114,000	Balance b/d	£94,000
		Production overheads	20,000
	£114,000		£114,000
		Balance b/d	114,000

Profit and Loss Account

	Balance b/d	£58,000

Investments

Balance b/d	£12,000

Ordinary share capital

	Balance b/d	£300,000

Interim dividend payable

Cash	£23,000

Income from investments

	Cash	£4,000

Wages payable

Cash	£102,000	Wages control	112,000
Balance c/d	10,000		
	£112,000		£112,000
		Balance b/d	10,000

Wages control

Wages payable	£112,000	Rate variance	£2,352
		Work in progress	76,048
		Production overheads	33,600
	£112,000		£112,000

Production overhead control

Work	£15,900	Work in progress	£65,000
Cash—expenses	7,000	Overhead variance	11,500
Depreciation	20,000		
Wages	33,600		
	£76,500		76,500

Work in progress

Balance b/d	£60,000	Efficiency variance	£3,136
Stores	90,100	Methods variance	2,352
Production overheads	65,000	Cost of sales	249,000
Wages	76,048	Balance c/d	36,660
	£291,148		£291,148
Balance b/d	36,660		

Cost of sales

Work in progress	£294,000

Sales

Debtors	£385,000

Direct material price variance

Purchases	£6,000	Indirect material price	
Returns	1,000	variance	£636
		Balance c/d	6,364
	£7,000		£7,000
Balance b/d	6,364		

Indirect material price variance

Direct material price variance	£636

Labour rate variance

Wages control   £2,352

Labour efficiency variance

Wages control   £3,136

Labour method variance

Wages control   £2,352

Overhead variance

Production overheads   £11,500

Sales variance

Debtors   £19,000

TRIAL BALANCE AS AT END OF PERIOD

	Dr.	Cr.
Debtors	£173,000	
Creditors		£92,000
Cash	202,000	
Stock	60,000	
Fixed assets	200,000	
Depreciation provision		114,000
Investments	12,000	
Ordinary share capital		300,000
Interim dividend payable	23,000	
Income from investments		4,000
Wages payable		10,000
Work in progress	36,660	
Cost of sales	249,000	
Sales		385,000
Direct material price variance	6,364	
Indirect material price variance	636	
Labour rate variance	2,352	
Labour efficiency variance	3,136	
Labour methods variance	2,352	
Overhead variance	11,500	
Sales variance		19,000
Profit and Loss Account		58,000
	£982,000	£982,000

The question asked for the preparation of a trial balance and not a Profit and Loss Account or Balance Sheet; it would be useful practice for the student to prepare them now.

NOTES

(i) *Indirect material price variance*

The question gives this as 4% on standard; it also states that materials purchased were: actual £137,000 and standard £131,000. It has been assumed, therefore, that materials were taken into store at standard, and the variance on indirect materials is 4% × £15,900 = £636. This figure has been transferred from the Direct Material Price Variance Account to the Indirect Material Price Variance Account.

(ii) *Rate variance*

This is 3% × (70% of £112,000).

(iii) *Efficiency variance*

This is 4% × (70% of £112,000).

(iv) *Methods variance*

This is 3% × (70% of £112,000).

2. THE THIRD ENTRY METHOD

Specimen question (3)

The Beeches Co. Ltd operates a system of integrated accounting using the third entry method. At the beginning of the year the balances in the integrated ledger are as follows:

	Dr.	Cr.
Fixed assets	£200,000	
Issued share capital		£300,000
Profit and loss		80,000
Depreciation provision		30,000
Debtors control	50,000	
Trade creditors control		20,000
Expense creditors control		15,000
Bank	25,000	
Stores control	95,000	
Work in progress control	35,000	
Finished goods control	40,000	
	£445,000	£445,000

During the year, transactions were as follows:

Stores purchased		£400,000
Stores returned to suppliers		10,000
Stores issued to production		320,000
Stores issued to production maintenance		30,000
Wages and salaries paid		375,000
Production wages: direct	£150,000	
indirect	35,000	
Production salaries	20,000	
Administration salaries and wages	80,000	
Sales department salaries	60,000	
Distribution department salaries and wages	30,000	
Production wages: direct, accrued		2,500
indirect, accrued		500
Paid to expense creditors		170,000
Production expenses	75,000	
Direct expenses	5,000	
Administration expenses	60,000	
Selling expenses	30,000	
Distribution expenses	20,000	
Administration expenses prepaid	5,000	
Depreciation provision (charge to production) 5%		
Production overheads recovered		172,000
Selling overheads recovered		88,000
Distribution overheads recovered		51,000

Administration overheads are charged to Profit and Loss Account

Output at cost of production	635,000
Goods sold at cost of production	630,000
Sales	1,000,000
Payment by debtors	980,000
Payments to creditors	373,000
Discount received	12,000
Discount allowed	15,000
Transfer to general reserve	50,000

Ignore taxation. Enter these transactions in the integrated ledger, then prepare the Profit and Loss Account and Balance Sheet.

Answer

Fixed assets

Balance b/d	£200,000

Issued share capital

	Balance b/d £300,000

Profit and loss appropriation

General reserve	£50,000	Balance b/d	£80,000
Balance c/d	123,500	Profit and loss	93,500
	£173,500		£173,500
		Balance b/d	123,500

Provision for depreciation

Balance c/d	£40,000	Balance b/d	£30,000
		Cost control	10,000
	£40,000		£40,000
		Balance b/d	40,000

Bank

Balance b/d	£25,000	Cost control	£375,000
Debtors	980,000	Expense creditors	170,000
		Trade creditors	373,000
		Balance c/d	87,000
	£1,005,000		£1,005,000
Balance b/d	87,000		

Discount allowed

Debtors	£15,000	Profit and loss	£15,000

Discount received

Profit and loss	£12,000	Creditors	£12,000

Debtors

Balance b/d	£50,000	Bank	£980,000
Sales	1,000,000	Discount allowed	15,000
		Balance c/d	55,000
	£1,050,000		£1,050,000
Balance b/d	55,000		

General reserve

	Profit and loss appropriation £50,000

Trade creditors

Stores	£10,000	Balance b/d	£20,000
Discount received	12,000	Stores	400,000
Bank	373,000		
Balance c/d	25,000		
	£420,000		£420,000
		Balance b/d	25,000

Expense creditors

Bank	£170,000	Balance b/d	£15,000
Balance c/d	35,000	Cost control	190,000
	£205,000		£205,000
		Balance b/d	35,000

Administration expenses prepaid

Cost control	5,000

Wages accrued

	Cost control £3,000

Stores

Balance b/d	£95,000	Creditors	£10,000
Creditors	400,000	Cost control	320,000
		" "	30,000
		Balance c/d	135,000
	£495,000		£495,000
Balance b/d	135,000		

Work in progress

Balance b/d	£35,000	Finished goods	£635,000
Cost control: direct	477,500	Balance c/d	49,500
indirect	172,000		
	£684,500		£684,500
Balance b/d	49,500		

Finished goods

Balance b/d	£40,000	Cost of sales	£630,000
Work in progress	635,000	Balance c/d	45,000
	£675,000		£675,000
Balance b/d	45,000		

Cost of sales

Finished goods	£630,000	Profit and loss	£769,000
Cost control: selling	88,000		
distribution	51,000		
	£769,000		£769,000

Overhead adjustment

Cost control: selling	£2,000	Cost control: production	£1,500
Profit and loss	500	distribution	1,000
	£2,500		£2,500

PROFIT AND LOSS ACCOUNT FOR PERIOD ENDED.........

Cost of sales	£769,000	Sales	£1,000,000
Administration overheads	135,000	Overhead adjustment	500
Discount allowed	15,000	Discount received	12,000
Net profit	93,500		
	£1,012,500		£1,012,500

COST CONTROL ACCOUNT

Stores: direct		£320,000	Administration expenses	
indirect		30,000	prepaid	£5,000
Bank: wages		375,000	Work in progress:	
Wages accrued		3,000	direct	477,500
Creditors: expenses		190,000	indirect	172,000
Depreciation provision		10,000	Cost of sales:	
Overhead adjustment:			selling	88,000
production	£1,500		distribution	51,000
distribution	1,000		Profit and loss:	
		2,500	administration	135,000
			Overhead adjustment:	
			selling	2,000
		£930,500		£930,500

Third entries

Element of cost	Total	Work in progress	Production	Overhead Administration	Selling	Distribution
Stores	£350,000	£320,000	£30,000	—	—	—
Wages	375,000	150,000	55,000	£80,000	£60,000	£30,000
Expenses	190,000	5,000	75,000	60,000	30,000	20,000
Depreciation	10,000	—	10,000	—	—	—
Wages accrued	3,000	2,500	500	—	—	—
	928,000	477,500	170,500	140,000	90,000	50,000
Administration expenses prepaid	5,000	—	—	5,000	—	—
	923,000	477,500	170,500	135,000	90,000	50,000
Recovered	923,500	477,500	172,000	135,000	88,000	51,000
	£(500)	—	£(1,500)	—	£2,000	£(1,000)

BALANCE SHEET AS AT END OF YEAR

Issued share capital	£300,000		Fixed assets	£200,000	
General reserve	50,000		Less depreciation	40,000	
Profit and loss appropriation	123,500				£160,000
		£473,500	Stores	135,000	
Trade creditors	£25,000		Work in progress	49,500	
Expense creditors	35,000		Finished goods	45,000	
Wages accrued	3,000				
		63,000		229,500	
			Debtors	55,000	
			Prepayments	5,000	
			Bank	87,000	
					376,500
		£536,500			£536,500

NOTE

Administration overheads have been charged direct to the Profit and Loss Account in accordance with the question. This follows marginal costing practice.

Specimen question (4)

[This comes from a specimen paper in management accountancy set by the Incorporated Association of Cost and Industrial Accountants.]

Record the following transactions in the appropriate ledger accounts (which are maintained in integral form) and prepare a trial balance at the end of the period.

(a) *Opening balances*

Stock: raw materials	£24,000
work in progress	26,000
finished goods	18,000
Sundry debtors	35,000
Cash	2,000
Buildings	64,000
Plant and machinery	26,000
Investments	5,000
Share capital	150,000
Profit and loss appropriation	3,000
General reserve	20,000
Sundry creditors	27,000

(b) *Transactions for the period.*

Sales (cost of production plus 20%)	£39,600
Purchase of raw materials	14,200
Payments to creditors	28,000
Received from debtors	34,500
P.A.Y.E. deducted from wages	3,100
National Insurance contributions	1,200

	Production Dept.	Service Dept. 1	Service Dept. 2	Selling and Admin.
Wages and salaries	£16,400	£1,900	£1,440	£2,000
Sundry expenses	2,500	100	160	50
Materials issued	12,700	1,400	800	—

Output for period: 38,600 units at £1 each.

(c) *Further information.*

(i) Depreciation:

On plant and machinery $1\frac{1}{2}\%$
On buildings $\frac{1}{4}\%$

(ii) Apportionment of cost of services:

Dept. 1: 10% of cost of materials, wages and salaries, and expenses.
Dept. 2: 15% of wages and salaries.

Answer

Share capital

Balance b/d	£150,000

Profit and loss appropriation

Balance b/d	£3,000

Buildings

Balance b/d	£64,000

Provision for depreciation on buildings

Cost control	£160

Plant and machinery

Balance b/d	£26,000

Provision for depreciation on plant and machinery

Cost control	£390

Investments

Balance b/d	£5,000

General reserve

Balance b/d	£20,000

Cash

Balance b/d	£2,000	Creditors	£28,000
Debtors	34,500	Balance c/d	8,500
	£36,500		£36,500
Balance b/d	8,500		

Debtors

Balance b/d	£35,000	Cash	£34,500
Sales	39,600	Balance c/d	40,100
	£74,600		£74,600
Balance b/d	40,100		

Creditors

Cash	£28,000	Balance b/d	£27,000
Balance c/d	16,010	Raw materials	14,200
		Cost control	2,810
	£44,010		£44,010
		Balance b/d	16,010

P.A.Y.E.

Wages payable	£3,100

National Insurance

Wages payable	£1,200

Wages payable

P.A.Y.E.	£3,100	Cost control	£21,740
National Insurance	1,200		
Balance c/d	17,440		
	£21,740		£21,740
		Balance b/d	17,440

Raw materials

Balance b/d	£24,000	Cost control	£14,900
Creditors	14,200	Balance c/d	23,300
	£38,200		£38,200
Balance b/d	23,300		

Work in progress

Balance b/d	£26,000	Finished goods	£38,600
Cost control	37,770	Balance c/d	25,170
	£63,770		£63,770
Balance b/d	25,170		

Finished goods

Balance b/d	£18,000	Cost of sales	£33,000
Work in progress	38,600	Balance c/d	23,600
	£56,600		£56,600
Balance b/d	23,600		

Cost of sales

Balance b/d	£33,000

Sales

Debtors	£39,600

Cost control

Wages payable	£21,740	Work in progress	£37,770
Creditors	2,810	Balance c/d	2,230
Stores	14,900		
Provision for depreciation	160		
,, ,, ,,	390		
	£40,000		£40,000
Balance b/d	2,230		

Third entries

Element of cost	Total	Production department	Service departments 1	2	Selling and admin.
Wages and salaries	£21,740	£16,400	£1,900	£1,440	£2,000
Creditors: expenses	2,810	2,500	100	160	50
Stores: materials	14,900	12,700	1,400	800	—
Depreciation	390	390	—	—	—
,,	160	160	—	—	—
	40,000	32,150	3,400	2,400	2,050
Service Dept. 1	—	3,160	(3,160)	—	—
Service Dept. 2	—	2,460	—	2,460	—
	£40,000	£37,770	£240	£(60)	£2,050

TRIAL BALANCE AS AT END OF PERIOD

Share capital		£150,000
Profit and loss appropriation		3,000
Buildings	£64,000	
Provision for depreciation on buildings		160
Plant and machinery	26,000	
Provision for depreciation on plant and machinery		390
Investments	5,000	
General reserve		20,000
Cash	8,500	
Debtors	40,100	
Creditors		16,010
P.A.Y.E.		3,100
National Insurance		1,200
Wages payable		17,440
Raw materials	23,300	
Work in progress	25,170	
Finished goods	23,600	
Cost of sales	33,000	
Sales		39,600
Cost control	2,230	
	£250,900	£250,900

NOTES

(i) *Apportionment of cost of Service Department 1*

10% of cost of materials, wages and salaries and expenses

Materials	£12,700
Wages and salaries	16,400
Expenses	2,500
	£31,600

(ii) *Apportionment of cost of Service Department 2*

15% of wages and salaries

Wages and salaries	£16,400

It has been assumed, owing to lack of information to the contrary, that the service departments have not been apportioned between each other.

EXAMINATION QUESTIONS

1. (a) What do you understand by integral accounts?

(b) Design a code of accounts illustrating the principles of integral accounts in a limited liability company selling a single standardised product which passes through one production department. [C.W.A.

2. You are appointed to a manufacturing business where monthly trading statements are prepared from costing records, while financial accounts are compiled six-monthly, in June and December. The monthly trading statements are prepared in four-weekly and five-weekly periods, and emphasise departmental performances and spending against prepared budgets, whereas the financial accounts follow the traditional pattern of shareholders' accounts.

You are required to advise top management of the advantages to be secured from integration of the two functions, quoting in your report:

(*a*) The main difficulties of this integration.

(*b*) How you propose to overcome such difficulties.   [C.W.A.

3. Design a code for integral accounts illustrating the principles of integral accounts in a limited liability company selling a single specialised product which passes through one production department.   [C.I.A.

4. Some of the balances in a company's integrated accounting system as at 30th November are as follows:

Account code

		£000
10	Creditors	116
11	Materials in stock and in progress—at standard	87
12	Wages in progress—at standard	16
13	Overhead in progress—at standard	32
14	Finished stocks—at standard	110
15	Debtors	236
16	Cash at bank	12
17	Sales budget	1,700
18	Sales variance	24 (credit)
19	Cost of sales—at standard	1,652
20	Materials price variance	12 (credit)
21	Wages variance	2 (credit)
22	Overhead variance	5 (debit)

The following transactions took place in December:

	£000
Sales budget	135
Sales—actual	124
Cash receipts—from debtors	134
Material purchases—actual (on credit)	76
Cash payments to creditors	95
Cash payments—wages	24
Overheads incurred (on credit)	52

Finished output—at standard:

	£	
Materials	64	
Wages	22	
Overhead	44	
	—	130
Cost of sales—at standard		112
The standard cost of material purchased was		78

The closing valuations of work in progress—at standard—were:

Wages	£13,000
Overhead	43,000

(*Work in progress is debited at actual, and credited at standard.*)

You are required to write up the ledger accounts and to bring down the closing balances.   [C.W.A.

5. You are required to record in the accounts in the financial ledger, maintained at head office, the following transactions for the year ended 30th June 19—. All factories, being at a distance from the head office, maintain their own cost accounts, which are integrated with the financial accounts. You

are also required to provide for depreciation at 5% (2½% on additions made during the year) and to transfer the appropriate balances to a Profit and Loss Account.

Credit purchases made by:

Factory A	£146,200
B	97,300
C	103,900
D	72,300
Head office administration	8,970
Head office selling	22,850

Cash paid by head office to or on behalf of:

Factory A	97,800
B	143,200
C	169,500
D	47,900
Head office administration	95,650
Head office selling	49,500

Stocks at 1st July 19— at:

Factory A	23,260
B	15,090
C	36,000
D	9,060

Cash in hand at:

Factory A	600
B	500
C	800
D	500
Cash received from trade debtors	1,376,500
Credit sales	1,196,800
Balance at 1st July 19— on Fixed Assets Account in financial ledger*	1,073,000

* Representing fixed assets at:

Factory A	£280,150
B	228,000
C	400,450
D	84,800
Head office administration	31,850
Head office selling	47,750

Cash paid to trade creditors	509,370

Cost of new plant, equipment, etc., invoiced to:

Factory A	24,500
B	2,600
C	5,900
D	17,200
Head office administration	8,300
Head office selling	8,500

Cost of alterations (capitalised) at:

Factory B	3,800
C	9,200

Stocks at 30th June 19— at:

Factory A	25,900
B	12,600
C	42,500
D	11,300

[C.W.A.

6. Record in ledger accounts in Integral Account form the under noted transactions, give effect to the additional information provided and close off the accounts as at the end of the period.

Trial balance at beginning of period

Cash	£3,000	
Debtors	26,000	
Stock: raw materials	22,000	
work in progress	14,000	
finished goods	6,000	
Plant and machinery	60,000	
Buildings	10,000	
Share capital		£100,000
General reserve		10,000
Profit and loss		2,000
Creditors		29,000
	£141,000	£141,000

Transactions during period

Purchases, credit: materials	£15,000
expenses	500
cash: expenses	500
Materials used: product direct	12,000
Service Dept. A direct	1,000
B direct	500
Production Dept. direct	2,500
"Expense" allotted: to products	200
Service Dept. A	200
B	400
Production Dept.	200
administration and selling	100
Wages and salaries: Service Dept. A	200
B	400
Production Dept.	3,500
administration and selling	900
Deductions from salaries: P.A.Y.E.	700
Funds	100
Sales: production cost plus $16\frac{2}{3}\%$	28,000

Additional information

Rate of apportionment of cost of Service Dept. A	30% of cost of all materials.
Rate of apportionment of cost of Services Dept. B	40% of production dept. wages and salaries.
Rate of absorption of cost of production dept.	£2 per unit of product.
Number of units of product produced and completed at cost of £5 each	4000.
Depreciation	1% of value of plant and machinery and $\frac{1}{2}\%$ of value of buildings to be charged to Production Department.

[C.W.A.

7. The following details apply to a manufactured product:

Standard cost each:

	£
Direct material: A—2 units	0·60
B—6 units	5·40
C—4 units	1·00
	7·00
Direct labour, 0·37½ per hour	1·50
Variable overheads, 25% of direct labour	0·37½
Fixed overheads (based on budgeted production of 1080 units per month)	0·62½
	£9·50

The budgeted selling price is £12·50 each.

The transactions for a month were as follows:

Direct material:

	Purchased		issued to production
Units		Price per unit	Units
A	2080	£0·32½	2010
B	6400	0·87½	6080
C	4260	0·30	4040

	Hours	Rate per hour
Direct wages	3600	£0·37½
	240	0·40
Overheads: variable	£380	
fixed	£650	
Production (units)	1000	

	Units	Each
Sales: home	700	£12·50
export	200	12·25

There was no opening stock of material and no opening or closing stock of work in progress.

An integrated system of accounting is in operation and the raw material stock account is kept at standard.

Journalise the above transactions for the month, reflecting all sales and production variances.   [C.W.A.

8. At the beginning of the current financial year the following list of balances were extracted from the integrated accounts of a manufacturing company:

Debtors	£180,000
Creditors	115,000
Cash	54,000
Fixed assets at cost	350,000
Raw materials at standard	85,000

Finished goods at standard	50,000
Work in progress at standard	90,000
Depreciation, fixed assets	95,000
Investments	20,000
Ordinary share capital	500,000
Profit and loss, credit balance	119,000

The following information is provided of transactions in the first quarter of the current financial year:

	Actual	Standard
Direct wages	£22,000	£21,000
Materials issued to production at standard prices	36,500	35,000
Purchase of raw materials, on credit	41,500	40,000
Factory overhead, including indirect wages and £4000 depreciation	20,100	
Factory overhead absorbed, at 95% normal capacity		19,000
Administration, selling and distribution expenses	13,000	

		Budget
Sales, on credit	97,600	£100,000

The cash transactions are as follows:

Payments:	net wages	£26,500 (after subtracting deductions £3500)
	Creditors	70,000
Receipts	Debtors	100,000

Overhead expenses (except wages) should be regarded as credit transactions. At the end of the quarter the following balances have been calculated on a basis of standard costs:

Work in progress	£95,000
Finished goods	48,000

Wages earned during the quarter have all been paid.

The following adverse variances have been calculated and with the other variances to be ascertained are to be charged against profit:

Overhead expenditure	£100
Sales price	1400
Labour rate	1200

You are required to:

(a) Record the above information in integral form in the books of the company.

(b) Prepare for presentation to management the interim:

    (i) Profit and Loss Account for the quarter.

    (ii) Balance Sheet at end of the quarter.

[C.W.A.

9. An engineering company employing 2,000 people operates an integrated system of cost and financial accounts, using standard costing and budgetary control. From the information given below, you are required to prepare a "profit and loss statement" for periods 1–10, with such supplementary statistics as you think desirable, for presentation to the board:

TRIAL BALANCE, AT END OF PERIOD 10

Sales: product X		£250,000
Y		100,000
Z		150,000
Cost of sales: X	£107,500	
Y	50,000	
Z	67,500	
Administration and selling overhead control	81,300	
Bank interest	465	
Bad debts	40	
Directors' fees	1,000	
Profit on sale of fixed assets		250
Factory variance accounts:		
Overhead efficiency	3,798	
Volume		3,618
Volume in budget	2,000	
Material price	1,895	
Labour rate	1,085	
Labour efficiency	3,165	
Expenditure		2,000
Stock and work in progress	120,250	
Sales ledger control	73,150	
Purchase ledger control		32,500
Fixed assets at cost	350,000	
Depreciation provision		82,500
Share capital		200,000
Profit and Loss Account		50,000
Cash at bank	7,720	
	£870,868	£870,868

Budgeted sales for the ten periods: product X	£275,000
Y	45,000
Z	140,000

The sales price of product Y has been increased by 25% since the budget was established.

Stock and work in progress at the commencement of the year was £147,000 at standard cost, less £10,500 applied variances. Debits to stock and work in progress accounts during the year have been entered in the books at standard cost; and a notional adjustment to actual cost must be made.

Stock and work in progress was assumed in the budget to remain constant.

Budgeted expenditure for the ten periods was:

Direct labour	£50,250
Direct material	98,825
Works overheads (recovered at 120% on direct labour cost)	62,300
Administration and selling overheads	80,800
Financial charges (net)	2,825

For the ten periods

	Budget	Actual
Productive hours worked	100,500	106,530
Standard hours produced	100,500	100,200

[C.W.A.

CHAPTER VII

INTER-FIRM COMPARISONS AND UNIFORM COSTING

THE idea of comparing the results of similar firms is not new, but only in recent years has it been adopted extensively. The development of trade associations, continual amalgamations of firms and the increasing degree of competition in industry have all contributed to the need for the development of systems of inter-firm comparison and uniform costing.

In 1889 the National Association of Stove Manufacturers of the U.S.A. introduced the first scheme of uniform costing; the British Federation of Master Printers introduced a system to the U.K. in 1913. This printers' system is probably the most efficient, widely known and extensively used system of all. An article, "Costing in printing," appeared in *Target*, the bulletin of the British Productivity Council, in December 1956, from which the following extract is taken:

"Forty years ago the British Federation of Master Printers realised the advantages of a uniform costing system which could be adopted throughout the industry. It had to be a system sufficiently simple, accurate and flexible to meet the requirements of the varying types of business which go to make up the printing industry. It had to embrace a number of basic principles.

The fundamentals are much the same now as they were then, only the emphasis has changed. What started out as simply a method of cost finding has been widened to embrace both the control and the reduction of costs.

A great many firms have used the system throughout a period of widely changing conditions and today it is used by most of the Federation's 5000 members. Many printers overseas have either adopted it or modelled their own systems on it.

The use of uniform costing methods does not mean that costs in different businesses will be the same. It does mean, however, that a comparison of the costs of different firms will be logical if they have been computed on similar lines. Uniform costing makes possible the exchange or comparison of cost figures prepared on a similar basis in each business and this provides a means of improving efficiency throughout the industry. By profiting from the experience of the most efficient firms, others are able to reduce costs. It facilitates investigations into specific cost problems of the industry."

INTER-FIRM COMPARISONS

The technique of inter-firm comparison is based on the use of a common definition for items of financial accounts and other records,

120

from which are constructed ratios and comparative data to aid management in making decisions. The ratios of comparable companies are important because they provide a yardstick against which the results of any other company can be measured. An analysis of these ratios should highlight possible inefficiencies that ought to be investigated. A system of inter-firm comparison may be operated in two ways:

1. Firms in a variety of industries submit required information to an independent centre, which analyses the data for each industry and presents reports to subscriber members. An example in the U.K. is the Centre for Inter-firm Comparison, which is described below.

2. Individual firms in an industry submit required information to a trade association established by the industry, which analyses the data and presents reports to each member firm. The Cotton Board, whose scheme is described later, is an example.

THE CENTRE FOR INTER-FIRM COMPARISON

The Centre for Inter-firm Comparison* was set up in 1959 by the British Institute of Management, in association with the British Productivity Council, in order to meet the demands of industry and trade for an expert body to conduct inter-firm comparisons. It was introduced as a result of a survey carried out by the B.I.M. which investigated the extent and usefulness of schemes of inter-firm comparison, both in the U.S.A. and Europe. It is a non-profit-making organisation and charges for its services are based on the actual costs incurred. During the first five years of operation, schemes of inter-firm comparison have been prepared for 40 industries, including those manufacturing chemicals, clothing, food, light and medium–heavy engineering products, and those engaged in electrical, tiling and pipework contracting.

Reports issued by the Centre provide yardsticks by which management can obtain guidance on such problems as:

(i) Is return on capital sufficient?
(ii) Are selling costs too high?
(iii) Is stock turnover adequate?
(iv) Is production efficient?
(v) Is working capital adequate?

The Centre has collected strong evidence of the vast scope for higher profitability which exists in British industry. In all the industries and trades in which it has been operating, the Centre has found striking differences between the profitability of otherwise broadly similar firms.

Some examples (taken from a report on the Centre's first four years) are given in Table I.

* The authors acknowledge with thanks the help given in the preparation of this section by the Centre for Inter-firm Comparison, particularly by Mr L. Taylor Harrington, the Deputy Director of the Centre. Much of the material in this section was prepared by the Centre.

TABLE I. SOME INTER-FIRM COMPARISONS

	AN ENGINEERING INDUSTRY *Averages of the ratios of the three firms which earned the*		A SECTION OF THE FOOTWEAR INDUSTRY *Averages of the ratios of the three firms which earned the*	
	highest operating profit/ operating assets employed	*lowest operating profit/ operating assets employed*	*highest operating profit/ operating assets employed*	*lowest operating profit/ operating assets employed*
1. Operating profit/ operating assets employed (%)	28·4	3·5	38·6	0·2
2. Operating profit/ sales (%)	17·3	2·5	14·4	0·3

Differences of this order have been found in all the comparisons so far prepared or conducted by the Centre, in which over a thousand firms have taken part.

Not only do such differences show *that* there is great scope for improvement; the comparisons which revealed these differences also showed each firm taking part *why* its profitability differed from those of others, *in what respects* it was weak and *which* of its departments or activities should be improved. In this way the Centre's comparisons provided firms with a challenge and incentive to improve, and showed them how improvements could be effected.

After several years of inter-firm comparison, the Centre feels the evidence is clear that differences in profitability between firms are due less to factors like size and location than to others about which their managements really *can* do something; in other words, they seem to be primarily due to differences in managerial efficiency.

The Centre has not found that there is, on the whole, any single cause of low profitability; nor has there been an industry in which the less profitable firms were weak in all major respects. On the contrary, the Centre found a great number of different combinations of strengths and weaknesses in different firms. Some would show high production efficiency, but a lower standard in, for instance, marketing or office administration. Others would excel in purchasing and stock management, but would be weak in utilising labour resources. Yet others would compensate for a slow stock turnover by a relatively fast turnover of debtors. Even the "best" firm usually shows weaknesses in some respects; participation in inter-firm comparison enables it to raise its profitability to still higher levels.

How inter-firm comparison works.

After a comparison group has been formed, each firm is sent a simple questionnaire on which it is asked to return figures of its costs, sales, assets, etc. Participating firms contribute their figures (in confidence) to a common pool and receive in return a report which either shows (anonymously) the data of each individual contributor or presents figures indicating the average and the range of performance of all participants. The report usually contains explanations showing how the results should be interpreted; further help with interpretation is given to individual firms requiring it. Comparisons of this kind not only tell the manager whether the performance of his firm is as good as that of his competitors, but also reveal the reasons for differences and often indicate how performance can be improved.

Confidentiality is ensured by allocating to each firm a code number which appears on questionnaires and other documents, and the results of comparisons are presented in such a way that individual firms' data cannot be identified. Reports are available only to participants in the scheme. In each comparison that it undertakes the Centre makes special arrangements to ensure that figures to be compared are arrived at on an agreed uniform basis.

Example

[The following example has been condensed somewhat.]

Table II gives the ratios of a firm in a light engineering industry for two years:

TABLE II. FIRM C'S FIGURES

Ratio	Unit	Last year	This year
1. Operating profit/Operating assets	%	8·25	10
2. Operating profit/Sales	%	5·5	6·1
3(a). Sales/Operating assets	times	1·5	1·64
3(b). Operating assets/Average daily sales	days*	249	222
4. Production cost of sales/Sales	%	71	70·4
5. Distribution and marketing expenses/Sales	%	17·7	17·7
6. General and administrative expenses/Sales	%	5·8	5·8
7. Current assets/Average daily sales	days*	215	188
8. Fixed assets/Average daily sales	days*	34	34
9. Material stocks/Average daily sales	days*	49	49
10. Work in progress/Average daily sales	days*	53	46
11. Finished stocks/Average daily sales	days*	52	39
12. Debtors/Average daily sales	days*	61	54

* Days required to turn the asset item over once.

From the table it can be seen that the performance of Firm C this year is much better than last year. Profit on assets employed has gone up from 8·25% to 10% owing to an increase in the firm's profit on sales (ratio 2) and the better use it seems to have made of its assets (ratios 3(a) and 3(b)). The higher profit on sales seems to have been achieved through operational improvements, which resulted in a lower ratio of cost of production (ratio 4). The firm's faster turnover of assets (ratio 3(*a*)) is due mainly to a faster turnover of current assets (ratio 7) and this in turn is due to accelerated turnovers of work in progress (ratio 10), finished stocks (ratio 11) and debtors (ratio 12). The management may believe this improvement in performance to be satisfactory, but should be disillusioned when presented with a report in which the ratios of Firm C are compared with those of other light engineering firms of its type. The following table is an extract from the results (it gives the figures of only 5 of the 22 participating firms).

TABLE III. THE INTER-FIRM COMPARISON

Ratio	Firm:				
	A	*B*	*C*	*D*	*E*
1. Operating profit/Operating assets (%)	18	14·3	10	7·9	4
2. Operating profit/Sales (%)	15	13·1	6·1	8·1	2
3 (*a*). Sales/Operating assets (times)	1·2	1·09	1·65	0·98	2
3 (*b*). Operating assets/Average daily sales	304	335	222	372	182
4. Production cost of sales/Sales (%)	73	69·4	70·4	72·5	79
5. Distribution and marketing expenses/Sales (%)	8	13·1	17·7	13·7	15
6. General and administrative expenses/Sales (%)	4	4·4	5·8	5·7	4
7. Current assets/Average daily sales	213	219	188	288	129
8. Fixed assets/Average daily sales	91	116	34	84	53
9. Material stocks/Average daily sales	45	43	49	65	29
10. Work in progress/Average daily sales	51	43	46	62	52
11. Finished stocks/Average daily sales	71	59	39	93	22
12. Debtors/Average daily sales	46	74	54	68	26

This year the firm's profit on assets employed is well below that of two other firms, and this appears to be due to its profit on sales (ratio 2) being relatively low. This in turn is mainly due to the firm's high distribution and marketing expenses (ratio 5). In the actual comparison, further ratios were given helping Firm C to establish to what extent its higher ratio 5 was due to higher costs of distribution and warehousing; higher costs of advertising and sales promotion; or higher costs of other selling activities (*e.g.* cost of sales personnel).

Comparisons between two years may create a feeling of false security. An inter-firm comparison could show that the results achieved by the firm were not good enough. On the other hand a fall in profits will be less worrying to management if an inter-firm comparison shows that many firms in the industry have had a similar experience.

Ratios used by the Centre

In recent years a wide variety of ratios have been devised, many of them an invaluable help to management, others of doubtful use. The Centre has recognised the importance of selecting ratios and using them intelligently, and has developed a series of those which have been found of particular interest in any selected industry. The primary ratio is profit to total assets employed; this measures the overall success of the business. From this ratio has been derived a "pyramid" of subsidiary ratios reflecting the influence of various operational factors. Fig. 2 shows a set of management ratios in a manufacturing industry, while Fig. 3 shows ratios for certain distributive trades.

It will be observed that on both examples on pp. 125–127, ratios reveal that the primary ratio is profit related to capital employed, which is then

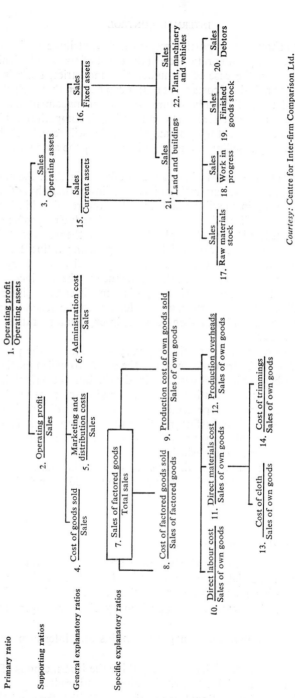

Courtesy: Centre for Inter-firm Comparison Ltd.

FIG. 2.—*Pyramid diagram of ratios of manufacturing industry*

analysed to show the supporting ratios which contribute to the overall result. These supporting ratios reveal the effect of costs and of sales on the business. In the case of manufacturing industries, there is more scope for the analysis of costs and sales: it can be seen that each element of cost is related individually to turnover, and management can detect where there is any excessive cost compared with competitors. If costs are found to be satisfactory, an analysis of sales will reveal whether or not the company is selling enough goods to justify the amount of assets employed.

The value of these ratios will be apparent from Fig. 2. If the management finds that the primary ratio of its firm is lower than that of others, there are two main possible reasons: either the relationship between income and expenditure is less favourable, thus reducing profit; or it is using its assets less intensively; or both. Which of them has contributed to the situation will be revealed by the supporting ratios 2 or 3. If ratio 2 indicates a poor performance, the general explanatory ratios 4–6 will ascertain the cause. Further reference to the specific explanatory ratios 7–14 will reveal any appropriate inefficiencies. Similarly, if ratio 3 indicates a poor performance, reference to the general explanatory ratios 15 and 16 and then to specific explanatory ratios 17–22 will reveal the causes.

The details of such a pyramid may vary according to the particular features of the industry concerned and the extent to which participants wish to probe particular questions in detail, but the principles will remain the same: the identification of the main factors at work, their measurement in ratio or percentage form, and their display in such a way that the cause-and-effect relationship between them is clearly brought out. In this way the reasons for differences between firms can be systematically established.

An important feature of this system of selecting ratios is that it avoids over-proliferation of figures; no ratio should be included in the set unless its relationship to the others and particularly to the overall performance yardstick being used can clearly be shown.

Summary of the Centre's activities

1. It offers a special service to trade associations, acting on their behalf as an impartial, expert organisation for the promotion and conduct of inter-firm comparisons among their members.

2. It undertakes inter-firm comparison by direct arrangement with individual firms.

3. It runs seminars on management ratios and inter-firm comparisons.

4. It carries out research aimed at making the best methods of inter-firm comparison available to British industry and trade.

5. It offers its international connections to British firms wishing to

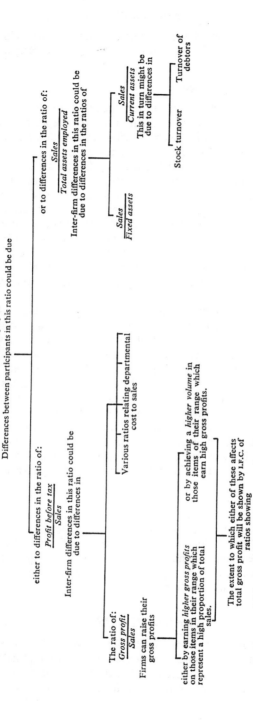

The overall profitability of the operations of the business, and the overall success of its management, are reflected by the ratio of:

$$\frac{Profit\ before\ tax}{Total\ assets\ employed}$$

Differences between participants in this ratio could be due

either to differences in the ratio of:

$$\frac{Profit\ before\ tax}{Sales}$$

Inter-firm differences in this ratio could be due to differences in

The ratio of:

$$\frac{Gross\ profit}{Sales}$$

Firms can raise their gross profits

either by earning *higher gross profits* on those items in their range which represent a high proportion of total sales.

or by achieving a *higher volume* in those items of their range which earn high gross profits.

The extent to which either of these affects total gross profit will be shown by I.F.C. of ratios showing

(a) the composition of sales of participants;
(b) gross profits earned on different items of their range.

Various ratios relating departmental cost to sales

or to differences in the ratio of:

$$\frac{Sales}{Total\ assets\ employed}$$

Inter-firm differences in this ratio could be due to differences in the ratios of

$$\frac{Sales}{Fixed\ assets}$$

$$\frac{Sales}{Current\ assets}$$

This in turn might be due to differences in

Stock turnover

Turnover of debtors

Courtesy: Centre for Inter-firm Comparison Ltd

FIG. 3.—*Pyramid diagram of ratios—certain distributive trades*

compare their efficiency and costs with opposite numbers in such countries as Germany, France, Switzerland, Holland, Belgium and the U.S.A.

TRADE ASSOCIATIONS

As mentioned earlier, some trade associations run inter-firm comparison schemes for the benefit of the industry they represent. The Cotton Board is one of them, its scheme having been introduced with the assistance of the Centre for Inter-firm Comparison.

In 1962 the Cotton Board Productivity Centre announced details of a system of inter-firm comparison available to all firms in the cotton industry. The primary ratio in the scheme is that of profit as a percentage of assets employed (*see* Chapter XXII). Participants in the scheme are arranged in a "league table" in order of their primary ratios; thirty or so further ratios derived from it analyse performances in particular sections of the firms' activities. The C.B.P.C. conducted a pilot scheme of inter-firm comparisons in the spinning section of the industry. Nineteen spinners took part, and the results were very favourably received.

This scheme is now available to the whole industry, providing a uniform and commercially acceptable method of valuing assets employed and calculating profit. The difficulties of comparison which would arise through differing raw material costs have been eliminated by expressing profit and all other costs as a percentage of "value added." The term "value added" represents sales less cost of raw materials and components; it is a sufficiently standard base for firms in one section of the industry to compare their results not only with each other but also with other firms in other sections. But of course the most useful feature of the scheme is that firms engaged in similar activities can make detailed comparisons between one another. This is made possible by the provision of the background information about each firm in terms of activity, size, product group, etc. The information is given in such a way that no firm is identifiable.

Firms participating in a scheme of inter-firm comparison submit information on capital employed, costs, prices, profits and performance to the trade association, which analyses the information and submits reports to members. Members must have confidence in the association, and assurance that the reports will safeguard anonymity yet gives the maximum useful information.

UNIFORM COSTING

Uniform costing is defined by the I.C.W.A. as "The use by several undertakings of the same costing principles and/or practices." Such a system is usually introduced in an attempt to standardise accounting methods and assist in determining prices. An advisory service may be operated to advise members about the recommended approach to accounting techniques.

When is it applicable?

A system of uniform costing may be applied in two different situations: (*a*) in a business which controls numerous firms or factories producing similar products or performing similar operations, (*b*) in firms which are connected with a trade association. Leading associations which have encouraged uniform costing in the U.K. include the British Federation of Master Printers, the British Steel Founders' Association, the Metal Window Association and the National Hosiery Manufacturers' Federation.

Requirements of uniform costing

When uniform costing is to be adopted, it is important that a careful study should be made of conditions in the industry, to ensure that the various operations *are* comparable. This does not mean that firms must be the same size, manufacture the same product or have the same plant and equipment, but they must be sufficiently comparable for rational conclusions to be drawn from reports based on comparisons. It will be necessary to establish a standard procedure for analysing costs, otherwise results could be very misleading. For example, if Firm A recovers overheads as a percentage of direct materials, Firm B as a percentage of prime cost and Firm C on a machine hour rate basis, total costs for a similar product could vary considerably between them.

The following points require special attention:

1. The method of costing. Whether to use process costing, operating costing, etc.
2. The costing techniques to be used: actual, standard or marginal?
3. The unit of cost, *e.g.*, ton, lb or dozen.
4. The adoption of similar classification of accounts and form of statements.
5. The classification of production and service departments.
6. The segregation of direct and indirect materials, direct and indirect wages.
7. The pricing method for stores issues, *e.g.* F.I.F.O., L.I.F.O. and the method of valuing stocks of work in progress, *e.g.* prime cost, marginal cost.
8. The method of remunerating labour, *e.g.* time rate, piece rate.
9. The classification of overheads, *e.g.* production, research.
10. The allocation, apportionment and absorption of overheads.
11. The method and rates of depreciation, *e.g.* straight line at 10% per annum.
12. The inclusion of interest on capital in costs.

Uniform costing manual

A manual is usually provided to firms engaged in a system of uniform costing. This manual may vary in the thoroughness of its treatment, from a simple description to an elaborate book showing in detail every principle and function of the system. However, the usual manual is a reference book outlining the objects, installation and operation of the system. Rules are laid down for the treatment of points like those mentioned above and outlines given of the various forms and reports to be used.

Advantages claimed for uniform costing

1. It establishes the best known way to ascertain costs in any particular industry. However, provision must be made for developments in cost accounting.

2. It stimulates interest in efficiency.

3. It helps to avoid ignorant competition. Uniform costing ensures that participating firms are not ignorant of each other's costs.

4. It underlines the effects of increased productivity, e.g. in terms of reduced costs per unit.

5. It encourages standardisation of materials and components.

6. It reveals profitable and unprofitable products or operations.

7. It encourages research into improved methods of accounting, because research can be undertaken more effectively and economically by the industry as a whole than by any individual firm.

8. It emphasises the advantages usually attributable to any efficient costing system.

Possible disadvantages

1. Difficulty in ensuring comparability. The needs and methods of each business differ from those of others. However, principles in the same industry will usually be the same.

2. A lack of standardised terminology. However, the introduction of a cost accounting manual should overcome this objection.

3. The cost of the service. Some businesses may object to the initial and running costs of the system. However, it is a common experience that the costs incurred are more than compensated for by increased savings from the economies effected.

A number of interesting books and articles have appeared on this subject, and those listed below particularly deserve attention:

Inter-firm comparison for management by H. Ingham and L. Taylor Harrington (B.I.M.).
Efficiency comparison within large organisations (B.I.M.).
"Problems of using return on capital as a measurement of success" by L. Taylor Harrington (Manchester Statistical Society, March 1961).
"Pyramid structure: a pattern for comparative measurements" by H. Ingham and L. Taylor Harrington (*The Manager*, September 1956).

"The value of inter-firm comparisons" by H. Ingham (*The Manager*, February 1961).

"Inter-firm comparisons" by H. Ingham (*The Manager*, June 1961).

"Co-ordination types in i.f.c." by H. Ingham (*The Manager*, September 1963).

"Inter-firm comparisons" by H. W. G. Kendall (*The Cost Accountant*, October 1960).

"The B.F.M.P. management ratios scheme" by H. W. G. Kendall (*The Cost Accountant*, November 1961).

"Successful inter-firm comparisons" by Alan Kershaw (*The Cost Accountant*, June 1960).

"Management ratios and inter-firm comparisons" by J. A. Alderson (*The Chartered Secretary*, March 1963).

EXAMINATION QUESTIONS

1. The chief accountant of a group of companies in the same industry wishes to introduce uniformity of costing methods, and you are charged with investigating this object. Tabulate the fundamental costing principles which need agreement and give an example of each.   [C.W.A.

2. Design a form of cost statement suitable for a number of concerns engaged in the manufacture of the same standard product, adding a note as to the factors which you would consider in order to ensure that the results of the various concerns are strictly comparable.   [C.I.A.

3. You have undertaken an investigation on behalf of a trade association in order to establish the possibility of recommending uniform costing methods for the trade, and you are satisfied that such methods are practicable. You are next called upon to write a uniform costing manual for circulation to members of the association.

Draft a schedule of main and sub-headings for the manual, and indicate briefly the points to be covered under each heading.   [C.W.A.

4. What matters would you expect to find dealt with in a manual issued to members of an association of manufacturers in connection with a system of uniform costing to be adopted by its members?   [C.A. (May, 1960)

5. What are schemes of inter-firm comparison? Explain how they are organised and indicate their value to individual firms and to industry as a whole.   [C.W.A.

6. You are the secretary of a trade association which looks after the general interests of its member firms. Some of these firms feel that it would be useful if a scheme of inter-firm comparison could be introduced within the association. You are required, therefore, to draft a circular pointing out the advantages and limitations of such a scheme and the type of information which could be produced.

After such a scheme has been introduced it is found that in a given year certain of Company A's costs compare with the average costs provided by the association as follows:

COSTS PER UNIT OF PRODUCT (£)

	Average for all firms	Company A
Direct labour	15	10
Direct material	32	30
Overhead	16	26

Give possible explanations of these differences and indicate what investigations it might pay Company A to make.   [C.C.A.

7.

	Profit/ net assets %	Profit/ sales %	Sales/ net assets Times	Fixed Assets/ total assets %	Sales/ net worth Times
Company A	13·3	8·3	1·6	52·0	2·1
Average of other companies in same industry	17·4	11·6	1·5	60·0	2·1

The above information, which has been prepared from the published accounts of companies, has led your managing director to conclude that other companies are obviously much more efficient than Company A. Comment on the figures disclosed above, giving a brief description of the significance of each figure in the table and discuss the dangers which might exist in basing an opinion on figures which have been arrived at from the published accounts of companies. [C.C.A.

8. It has been decided by the employers in the industry in which you work that attempts should be made to introduce a uniform costing system throughout the industry. Prepare a list of items on which agreement would have to be reached about their treatment before such a system could be introduced. [C.C.A.

9. The following figures were taken from the annual accounts of two electricity supply boards working on uniform costing methods:

Meter reading, billing and collection costs:

	Board A (£000's)	Board B (£000's)
Salaries and wages of:		
Meter readers	150	240
Billing and collection staff	300	480
Transport and travelling	30	40
Collecting agency charges	—	20
Bad debts	10	10
General charges	100	200
Miscellaneous	10	10
	600	1000
Units sold (millions)	2880	9600
Number of consumers (thousands)	800	1600
Sales of electricity (£millions)	18	50
Size of area (square miles)	4000	4000

Prepare a comparative cost statement using suitable units of cost. Brief notes should be added, commenting on likely causes for major differences in unit costs so disclosed. [C.W.A.

CHAPTER VIII

STANDARD COSTING

INTRODUCTION

WHAT IS STANDARD COSTING?

BASICALLY, there are two different methods of cost accounting:

(i) The calculation of the cost of a product after it has been completed; this can be referred to as historical costing;

(ii) The detailed estimating of the cost of a product before it is manufactured, so that expenditure can be controlled during production; on completion, the actual result can be compared with the estimate, and variances ascertained and investigated. This method can be referred to as pre-determined or standard costing.

When historical cost figures are analysed carefully they may be useful in remedying past results, but mistakes and inefficiencies are not discovered until after the damage is done. Information of this type is an aid to management, but is not as valuable as it might be because:

(i) The data are not presented to management until some considerable time has elapsed, so management is unable to take the necessary corrective action in good time;

(ii) No suitable yardstick is provided by which management can measure actual performance.

Only through control of costs are profits realised: management is becoming increasingly cost conscious, and the management accountant should be constantly in search of new ways of reducing expenditure and eliminating wastage. Standard costing is one of the most recently developed refinements of cost accounting and has been widely adopted because it is so effective in providing the information needed for control.

Standard costing may be defined basically as a technique of cost accounting which compares the "standard cost" of each product or service with the actual cost, to determine the efficiency of the operation, so that any remedial action may be taken immediately. The "standard cost" is a predetermined cost which determines what each product or service *should* cost under given circumstances.

"Variance" is the difference between a budgeted or standard amount and the actual amount during a given period.

133

Standard costing involves:

(i) The setting of standards,
(ii) Ascertaining actual results,
(iii) Comparing standards and actual costs to determine the variances,
(iv) Investigating the variances and taking appropriate action where necessary.

ADVANTAGES OF STANDARD COSTING

The introduction of a system of standard costing may offer many advantages:

1. Standard costs provide a yardstick against which the actual costs can be measured.

2. The setting of standards involves determining the best materials and methods, which may lead to economies.

3. A target of efficiency is set for employees to reach, and cost consciousness is stimulated.

4. Variances can be calculated which enable the principle of "management by exception" to be operated.

5. Costing procedures are often simplified.

6. Standard costs provide a valuable aid to management in determining prices and formulating policies.

7. The evaluation of stock is facilitated.

8. The operation of cost centres defines responsibilities.

BUDGETARY CONTROL AND STANDARD COSTING

Budgetary control and standard costing are comparable systems of cost accounting in that they are both predetermined or "forward-looking." However, there is one big difference in that budgetary control is concerned with comparison of the estimated and actual results of a department, company or even country, while standard costing is concerned with comparison of estimated and actual results of manufacturing a product or providing a service. Both are valuable aids to management in controlling costs.

It is frequently thought that budgetary control and standard costing cannot function independently because both methods involve estimating costs for a future period. This is not strictly true, but it is a fact that each functions better in conjunction with the other. When standard costs have been determined it is relatively easy to compute budgets for production costs and sales. On the other hand, in determining standard costs it is necessary to ascertain the level of output for the period, and this is much easier when budgeted levels have been set. It would appear that, certainly in the U.S.A. and the U.K., most companies which have a "forward-looking" approach to cost accounting do in fact use both systems.

PRELIMINARIES IN ESTABLISHING A SYSTEM OF STANDARD COSTS

In establishing a system of standard costing there are a number of preliminaries to be considered, including:

1. The establishment of cost centres with clearly defined areas of responsibility.

2. The classification of accounts, with provision for standard and actual costs with variances.

3. The type of standard to be operated.

4. The setting of standard costs for each element of cost.

1. ESTABLISHMENT OF COST CENTRES

A cost centre, according to the I.C.W.A., is "a location, person or item of equipment (or group of these) for which costs may be ascertained and used for the purposes of cost control." A centre which relates to persons is referred to as a personal cost centre, and one which relates to location or to equipment as an impersonal cost centre.

It is important in establishing cost centres that there should be no doubt who is responsible for each cost centre. In many instances, departments or functions will form natural cost centres, but it may happen that there are a number of cost centres in a department, *e.g.* there may be four machine groups in a manufacturing department, each of which may be classed as a cost centre.

2. CLASSIFICATION OF ACCOUNTS

Accounts are classified or grouped to meet a required purpose, *e.g.* by function, revenue item or asset and liability item. Codes and symbols will be used to facilitate speedy collection and analysis of accounts. Thus a code for elements of cost, for example might be as follows:

000–299	Direct materials,
300–399	Direct labour,
400–499	Indirect materials,
600–699	Indirect labour,
700–999	Other expenses.

For a comprehensive discourse on this subject, readers are referred to *The classification and coding of accounts* by J. M. S. Risk, published by the Institute of Cost and Works Accountants.

3. TYPES OF STANDARD

The standard is the level of attainment accepted by management as the basis upon which standard costs are determined. There are four different standards to consider:

(i) *Ideal.* This level of attainment is that which would result if ideal conditions obtained, such as maximum output and sales, best possible prices for materials and most satisfactory rates for labour and overhead costs. This ideal is obviously unrealistic and would not be experienced for any length of time. It does provide a target or incentive for employees, but is usually so unattainable that they become discouraged and adverse variances are experienced.

(ii) *Expected actual.* This is the level which it is actually expected will be achieved in the budget period, based on current conditions. Standards set are on a short term basis and frequent revisions may be necessary.

(iii) *Normal.* This represents an average figure which it is hoped will smooth out fluctuations caused by seasonal and cyclical changes. It should be attainable and provides a challenge to the staff.

(iv) *Basic.* This is the level fixed in relation to a base year. The principle used in setting the basic standard is similar to that used in statistics when calculating an index number. Thus if in 1966, the base year, the standard cost of material B7 is £0·50 per lb. and in 1970 the price is £0·60 per lb., the basic standard must be adjusted by 20%. This standard is set on a long term basis and is seldom revised.

4. SETTING STANDARDS

It is essential that the factory be so organised that departments are clearly designated and that lines of authority are defined. Responsibility for setting standards should be given to a specific person or to a committee, because the success of a system of standard costing depends upon the reliability of the standards. How many people are concerned with setting the standards will depend on the size and nature of the business, but in a large undertaking they will normally include:

(i) *The production controller.* He will give details of production requirements in terms of materials, labour and overheads.

(ii) *The buyer.* He will prepare schedules of prices and give details of market price trends.

(iii) *The personnel manager.* He will provide labour rates of pay and possible forecasts of any changes in rates.

(iv) *The time study engineer.* He will calculate standard times for the many operations involved.

(v) *The cost accountant.* He will provide all necessary cost figures such as overhead recovery rates. However, his main functions will be to co-ordinate the activities of the committee so that the standards set will be as accurate as possible, and to present the standards and standard cost statements in the most satisfactory manner.

THE STANDARD COST CARD

A standard cost card will be prepared for each product or service. The card will normally show the quantity and price of each material to be consumed, the time and rate of labour required, the overhead recovery and the total cost. Once a standard has been prepared, it should be received and approved by the person who will be responsible for the operation concerned, otherwise he is unlikely to co-operate with much enthusiasm in maintaining the standard.

Details of each element of cost must be ascertained. In many cases this will be a complicated matter. Briefly, standard costs will be established as shown below.

1. Direct material

(i) *Quantity.* Material specifications will be produced showing the standard quantity of each type of material required. Normal loss in process must also be estimated before the standard cost can be ascertained.

(ii) *Price.* A standard price will be calculated for each type of material.

2. Direct labour

(i) *Time.* Standard times, based on the best way of performing it, will be computed for each grade of labour for each operation involved.

(ii) *Rate.* The standard rate for the job will be determined.

3. Variable overhead

This is defined by the I.C.W.A. as "a cost which tends to vary directly with volume of output."

It is assumed that the overhead rate per unit is constant, irrespective of the quantity produced, so it is necessary to calculate only a standard cost per unit or per hour.

4. Fixed overhead

By I.C.W.A. definition, "a cost which tends to be unaffected by variations in volume of output."

(i) *Expenditure.* The budgeted expenditure for the period will be ascertained.

(ii) *Volume.* The budgeted output in units or standard hours will be used to calculate the overhead recovery rate.

Example

STANDARD COST CARD

Product: Jaydee

Date of standard:

Element of cost	Code	Quantity hours	Price rate	A	Departments B	C	D	Total	Per unit
1. Direct material	X125	20	£0·50	10					
	Y374	30	1·00			30			
	Z24	50	1·00				50	£90	£1·0
		100							
Normal loss		10							
		90							
2. Direct labour	A3	10	£0·30	3					
	C5	5	0·40			2			
	D1	8	0·50				4	9	0·10
3. Variable production overhead				10		15	20	45	0·50
4. Fixed production overhead		10	£0·60	6					
		5	2·00			10			
		8	2·50				20	36	0·40
								£180	£2·00

THE STANDARD HOUR

In a system of standard costing, the introduction of standard hours can be very valuable. The I.C.W.A. defines a standard hour as "A hypothetical hour which represents the amount of work which should be performed in one hour under standard conditions." Time and motion study engineers can calculate what the output of each process in one hour *should* be. For example, if 20 units of A should be produced in one hour, then an output of 100 units would represent five standard hours.

In most industries, production is expressed in terms of some physical unit such as pounds, tons or gallons, but where different types of product are manufactured it is sometimes impossible or inappropriate to aggregate the production of the factory. If a coke oven produced 1000 tons of coke and 100,000 cu. ft. of gas, it would be difficult to express the total output of the plant in units. However, if in one hour 10 tons of coke and 10,000 cu. ft. of gas should be produced, then the total output in standard hours would be $100 + 10 = 110$ standard hours.

Example

The Cereal Manufacturing Co. produces three brands of cereal: "Corny," "Wheato" and "Branex." Production per hour should be 500, 750 and 1000 packets, respectively. Actual production during May was 15,000, 37,500 and 40,000 packets respectively. Production measured in standard hours would be as follows:

PRODUCTION STATEMENT, MAY

Product	Actual output (packets)	Standard output per hour (packets)	Production (standard hours)
Corny	15,000	500	30
Wheato	37,500	750	50
Branex	40,000	1,000	40
			120

ACCOUNTING METHODS

RECORDING COSTS

A number of accounting methods are available for recording costs in a system of standard costing. Some systems record the actual and standard costs side by side, while others use ratios or percentages to show the relationship between actual and standard performance. However, to avoid confusion in this text only one method is illustrated. It has been found practicable and reasonably easy to follow. It is briefly explained thus:

Dr.	Expense (stores, wages, overheads)	at *actual*
Cr.	Creditors or cash	at *actual*
Dr.	Work in progress	at *standard rate*
Cr.	Expense	at *actual*
Dr./Cr.	Price variance	with difference
Dr.	Finished goods	at *standard cost*
Cr.	Work in progress	at *standard rate*
Dr./Cr.	Volume variances	with difference

MATERIAL PRICE VARIANCE

There are two distinct ways of treating a material price variance in the accounts. It may be calculated when:

(i) the material is taken into stores,
(ii) the material is issued from stores.

Under method (i) the variance on materials purchased is ascertained immediately and the stores are debited at standard cost. This has the effect of eliminating the price variance on all the materials purchased as and when they are received. However, under method (ii) the variance is calculated as and when the materials are issued from stores, so considerable delay may occur before the variance is ascertained, and stores are debited at actual cost.

Example

100 units are purchased at £0·95 each, the standard price being £1. Fifty units are issued to work in progress. In an integral accounting system the entries would be:

Method 1

	Dr	Cr
Stores	£100	
Price variance		£5
Creditors		95
Work in progress	50	
Stores		50

Method 2.

	Dr	Cr
Stores	£95	
Creditors		£95
Work in progress	50	
Price variance		£2·50
Stores		47·50

Either method may be used in practice, and in examinations a knowledge of both may be required, so the reader should be familiar with both. In this text, method (2) will be used throughout.

DEFINITION OF TERMS

There is often confusion in the minds of many students concerning such terms as standard and budget, so to clarify the position the following may be helpful:

1. *Actual production.* The actual quantity produced during the actual hours worked.
2. *Budgeted production.* The budgeted quantity to be produced during the budgeted hours to be worked.
3. *Standard production.* The quantity which should have been produced during the actual hours worked.
4. *Actual cost.* The actual quantity produced at the actual cost per unit.
5. *Budgeted cost.* The budgeted quantity to be produced at the standard cost per unit.
6. *Standard cost.* The actual quantity produced at the standard cost per unit.

VARIANCES

Perhaps the most valuable contribution a standard costing system makes to the principle of "management by exception" is the presentation of variances. Variances highlight those situations where actual results are not as planned, whether better or worse. They represent the difference between standard and actual for each element of work and sometimes for sales. When actual results are better than expected a *favourable* variance arises; where they are not up to standard an *adverse* variance occurs. By reference to the variances, management can concentrate its efforts on the important items.

Variances help to pinpoint responsibilities, in that management can ascertain where the blame lies when results are poor. For example, an adverse Material Usage Variance would indicate that an excess material cost was due not to an increase in price but to inefficient use of materials. In this case responsibility could be placed on the supervisor in charge of the particular operation in which the inefficiency occurred. It may be discovered that the variance was caused by (say) inefficient handling, the purchase of poor quality materials or the employing of trainees. The important point is that the reason for the variance must be found, explained and, where necessary, corrective action taken.

Different variances are used in different industries, and it is not possible to discuss them all here. Attention will be concentrated on those which are frequently met with in practice and in examinations; they will be illustrated in detail.

Variances may be calculated in respect of the following:

1. Direct material.
2. Direct labour.
3. Variable overhead.
4. Fixed overhead:
   (a) Based on units.
   (b) Based on standard hours.
5. Sales:
   (a) Based on turnover.
   (b) Based on profit.

Each of these will be discussed in this text.

Basically there are only two different types of variance:

PRICE

This type of variance relates to prices of materials, rates of labour, expenditure on overheads or selling prices of products. Thus have been developed:

(i) Material Price Variance.
(ii) Labour Rate Variance.
(iii) Variable Overhead Expenditure Variance.
(iv) Fixed Overhead Expenditure Variance.
(v) Sales Price Variance.

VOLUME

This type of variance relates to quantity of units in terms of raw materials consumed, number of hours worked, utilisation of plant and number of articles sold. The following have been developed:

(i) Material Usage Variance.
(ii) Labour Efficiency Variance.
(iii) Fixed Overhead Volume Variance.
(iv) Sales Volume Variance.

For each element of cost there is a total variance, known as the Cost Variance, which is the total of the Price Variance and the Volume Variance. Similarly, for sales there is a total variance known as the

Value Variance, which is the total of the Price Variance and the Volume Variance. We can now build up the basic variances:

1. Material: Cost Variance { Price Variance / Usage Variance

2. Labour: Cost Variance { Rate Variance / Efficiency Variance

3. Variable Overhead: Cost Variance Expenditure Variance

4. Fixed Overhead: Cost Variance { Expenditure Variance / Volume Variance

5. Sales: Value Variance { Price Variance / Volume Variance

It will be observed that Variable Overhead Cost Variance is represented by only one variance, the Expenditure Variance. This is because, as mentioned earlier in this chapter, it is assumed that variable overhead costs vary directly with production so that only a change in expenditure can affect costs. Thus if the variable overhead rate per unit is £0·25, and the actual output 1000 units, the standard cost will be £250. If, however, the actual cost is £260, the difference of £10 will be due to a change in expenditure. In some circumstances it could be argued that a variance may arise through inefficiency, but as these costs are usually so small per unit of output this refinement is generally ignored and any variance in Variable Overhead is attributed to Expenditure Variance.

Basic variances, though useful, do not meet all the needs of the management. It is not enough to know that the volume changed; the important thing is to know the *cause* of the change. From the list above, we can proceed to the sub-variances:

1. Material:
Cost Variance { Price Variance / Usage Variance } { Usage Variance / Mix Variance / Yield Variance

2. Labour:
Cost Variance { Rate Variance / Efficiency Variance } { Efficiency Variance / Idle Time Variance / Mix Variance

3. Variable overheads:
Cost Variance Expenditure Variance

4. Fixed overheads:
Cost Variance { Expenditure Variance / Volume Variance } { Efficiency Variance / Capacity Variance / Calendar Variance

5. Sales:
Value Variance { Price Variance / Volume Variance } { Mix Variance / Quantity Variance

An adverse variance will be designated *adv*. while a favourable variance will be designated *fav*.

These variances will now be discussed and illustrated.

1. MATERIAL VARIANCES

Example (1)

It is estimated that, in the manufacture of a product, for each ton of materials consumed, 100 articles should be produced. The standard price per ton of material is £10. During the first week in January, 100 tons of materials were issued to production, the purchase price of which was £10·50 per ton. The actual output for the period was 10,250 units.

Cost Variance

This represents the difference between the standard cost and the actual cost of output.

$$\text{Standard cost} - \text{Actual cost}$$
$$\text{SC} - \text{AC}$$
$$£1025 - £1050 = £25 \ adv.$$

NOTE

(i) Standard cost = Actual production × Standard rate
10,250 units × £0·10 each

(ii) Standard rate $= \dfrac{\text{Standard cost per ton}}{\text{Standard output per ton}} = \dfrac{£10}{100}$

Price variance

This represents the difference between the actual price and standard price of materials consumed.

$$\text{Actual quantity (Actual price} - \text{Standard price)}$$
$$\text{AQ (AP} - \text{SP)}$$
$$100 \ (£10·50 - £10) = £50 \ adv.$$

This adverse variance shows that unfavourable prices were paid for materials consumed during the period. The buyer would be asked to explain the position.

Usage Variance

This represents the difference between the actual quantity consumed and the standard quantity which should have been consumed, expressed in terms of money.

$$\text{Standard price (Actual quantity} - \text{Standard quantity)}$$
$$\text{SP (AQ} - \text{SQ)}$$
$$£10 \ (100 - 102·5) = £25 \ fav.$$

NOTE

Standard quantity = the standard quantity which should have been required to produce actual output.

$$\dfrac{\text{Actual quantity}}{\text{Standard output}} = \dfrac{10,250}{100}$$

It should be noted that the Price Variance eliminates any difference in price; therefore standard price must be used in the Usage Variance calculations. The supervisor would be asked to explain the variance.

CHECK

Cost Variance = Price Variance + Usage Variance
£25 *adv.* = £50 *adv.* + £25 *fav.*

Accounting entries

A summary of the accounting entries required in an integral accounting system would be as follows:

	Dr	Cr
Stores	£1050	
Creditors		£1050
Work in progress	1000	
Price Variance	50	
Stores		1050
Finished goods	1025	
Usage Variance		25
Work in progress		1000

The above example showed the calculation of the Price Variance and the Usage Variance only, and so was a relatively simple one. The next introduces the rather complicated Mix Variance and Yield Variance. There are two schools of thought regarding the Mix Variance: first, that the change in mix is a fortuitous change; second, that the change in mix is a deliberate change. A fortuitous change would occur, for example, when an employee inadvertently introduced an incorrect mix of input. A deliberate change would occur, if it was decided to change the mix of a product because one of the ingredients was in short supply. Both these situations will now be considered.

Example (2)

The standard mix of a product is:

X	60 units at	£0·15	£9
Y	80 „ „	£0·20	16
Z	100 „ „	£0·25	25
	240		£50

Ten units of the finished product should be obtained from this mix. During June, ten mixes were completed and consumption was:

X	640 units at	£0·17½	£112
Y	950 „ „	£0·18	171
Z	870 „ „	£0·27½	239·25
	2460		£522·25

Actual output was 90 units.

The standard cost for the month can be calculated by multiplying the number of mixes by the standard cost:

X	600 at £0·15	£90	
Y	800 ,, £0·20	160	
Z	1000 ,, £0·25	250	
	2400	£500	

This reveals that the actual quantity used differed from the standard quantity that ought to have been used. It shows too that the total actual input for ten mixes was greater than the total standard input planned. This necessitates calculating the standard proportion of the actual mix to find out which proportions should have been used. It is calculated as follows:

$$\frac{\text{Standard quantity for each material}}{\text{Standard quantity total}} \times \text{Actual quantity total}$$

and will be referred to as the revised standard quantity (RSQ). Thus the figures for the materials used are:

$$\text{RSQ} \quad X \quad \frac{600}{2400} \times 2460 = 615$$

$$\text{RSQ} \quad Y \quad \frac{800}{2400} \times 2460 = 820$$

$$\text{RSQ} \quad Z \quad \frac{1000}{2400} \times 2460 = 1025$$

We can proceed now to calculate the Material Variances.

Cost Variance

$$\text{SC}-\text{AC}$$
$$£450-522·25 = £72·25 \ adv.$$

NOTE

Standard cost = Actual output × Standard rate

$$90 \times \frac{£500}{100}$$

Price Variance

AQ (AP − SP)

X	640 (£0·17½ − £0·15)	£16	adv.	
Y	950 (£0·18 − £0·20)	£19	fav.	= £18·75 adv.
Z	870 (£0·27½ − £0·25)	£21·75	adv.	

Usage Variance

SP (RSQ − SQ)

X	£0·15 (615 − 600)	£2·25	adv.	
Y	£0·20 (820 − 800)	£4·00	adv.	= £12·50 adv.
Z	£0·25 (1025 − 1000)	£6·25	adv.	

Mix Variance

SP (RSQ − AQ)

X	£0·15 (615 − 640)	£3·75	adv.	
Y	£0·20 (820 − 950)	£26·00	adv.	= £9·00 fav.
Z	£0·25 (1025 − 870)	£38·75	fav.	

This represents the difference between the actual proportions of the actual quantity used and the standard proportions of the actual quantity used. In this Example costs have been reduced by using smaller quantities of the higher priced material C, which results in a favourable variance. The supervisor would be asked to explain this situation.

Yield Variance

$$\text{Standard rate (Standard yield} - \text{Actual yield)}$$
$$\text{SR (SY} - \text{AY)}$$
$$\frac{£500}{100} (100 - 90) = £50 \; adv.$$

NOTE

$$\text{Standard rate} = \frac{\text{Standard cost for standard mix}}{\text{Standard output}}$$

This represents the difference between the actual output and the output which should have resulted from the actual input. Here, less output was achieved than expected, resulting in an adverse variance; the supervisor would be asked to explain it.

CHECK

Cost Variance = Price Variance + Usage Variance + Mix Variance
+ Yield Variance

£72·25 *adv.* = £18·75 *adv.* + £12·50 *adv.* + £9·00 *fav.* + £50 *adv.*

Accounting entries

	Dr	Cr
Stores	£522·25	
Creditors		£522·25
Work in progress	503·50	
Price Variance	18·75	
Stores		522·25
Finished goods	450·00	
Usage Variance	12·50	
Yield Variance	50·00	
Mix Variance		9·00
Work in progress		503·50

It should be noted that Yield Variance differs from the other Material Variances—Price, Usage and Mix—in that it is an output variance, while the others are input variances. In other words, Yield Variance represents a gain or loss on output in terms of finished production, while the other variances represent a gain or loss on the cost of materials input.

It should also be noted that the Usage Variance in this illustration was calculated by the formula SP (RSQ − SQ), while in Example 1 the formula SP (AQ − SQ) was used. This change is to allow for the introduction of the Mix Variance, for which the formula is SP (RSQ − AQ). This can be checked:

Usage Variance (as above)   £12·50 *adv.*
Mix Variance (as above)   £9·00 *fav.* = £3·50 *adv.*

Assuming Usage Variance only is calculated, if it is not desired to show a Mix Variance.

Usage Variance   SP (AQ − SQ)
  X   £0·15 (640 − 600)   £6·00 *adv.*⎫
  Y   £0·20 (950 − 800)   £30·00 *adv.*⎬ = £3·50 *adv.*
  Z   £0·25 (870 − 1000) £32·50 *fav.*⎭

Where a deliberate change in mix is made, for example because of a shortage of certain materials, the calculation of Usage Variance and Mix Variance is different from that in Example 2 above. Using the same illustration as in Example 2 but altering it slightly to allow for the deliberate change in mix, we can proceed.

Example (3)

During June it was found that there was a shortage of Material Z, as a result of which the standard mix was changed temporarily from 3:4:5 to 3:5:4, but it was not expected that this change would affect the standard yield. Here the Mix Variance is a form of Revision Variance. A Revision Variance occurs when, after standards have been set, changes in circumstances arise which could not have been envisaged. If the change is temporary, then rather than revise standards a Revision Variance may be calculated.

The revised standard mix can now be calculated, the proportion being 3:5:4. The revised standard quantity will be X, 600 units, Y, 1000 units and Z, 800 units.

Cost Variance

As in Example 2 = £72·25 *adv.*

Price Variance

As in Example 2 = £18·75 *adv.*

Usage Variance

                    SP (RSQ − AQ)
  X   £0·15 (600 − 640)   £6·00 *adv.*⎫
  Y   £0·20 (1000 − 950) £10·00 *fav.*⎬ = £13·50 *adv.*
  Z   £0·25 (800 − 870) £17·50 *adv.*⎭

Mix Variance

                    SP (RSQ − SQ)
  X   £0·15 (600 − 600)   —   ⎫
  Y   £0·20 (1000 − 800) £40 *adv.*⎬ = £10 *fav.*
  Z   £0·25 (800 − 1000) £50 *fav.*⎭

Yield Variance

As in Example 2 = £50 *adv.*

CHECK

Cost Variance = Price Variance + Usage Variance + Mix Variance
                                            + Yield Variance

£72·25 *adv.* = £18·75 *adv.* + £13·50 *adv.* + £10 *fav.* + £50 *adv.*

Accounting entries

	Dr	Cr
Stores	£522·25	
Creditors		£522·25
Work in progress	503·50	
Price Variance	18·75	
Stores		522·25
Finished goods	450·00	
Usage Variance	13·50	
Yield Variance	50·00	
Mix Variance		10·00
Work in progress		503·00

With regard to the Mix Variance discussed in Examples 2 and 3 above, either situation could in practice arise, but in examination questions the change in mix is more likely to be fortuitous.

An alternative way of calculating Material Cost Variances is one based on the revised edition of the I.C.W.A. terminology. According to the 1966 edition, the Direct Materials Mixture Variance and the Direct Materials Yield Variance are sub-variances of the Direct Materials Usage Variance. Illustrated graphically this is:

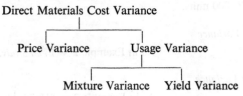

Calculating these variances according to this interpretation, this will result in two minor changes in formula from those discussed in the previous Example 2. Using the same figures, the variances would be calculated as follows:

Direct Materials Cost Variance
As in example 2 = £72·25 *adv.*

Direct Materials Price Variance
As in example 2 = £18·75 *adv.*

Direct Materials Usage Variance
Standard cost of output − standard cost of input
£450 − £503·50   £53·50 *adv.*

NOTE

Standard cost of input is calculated:

	Actual quantity	Standard price	Value
X	640	£0·15	£96
Y	950	0·20	190
Z	870	0·25	217·50
			£503·50

Direct Materials Mixture Variances

$$SP (SQ - AQ)$$

X	£0·15	(600 − 640)	£ 6·00 *adv.*
Y	0·20	(800 × 950)	30·00 *adv.*
Z	0·25	(1000 − 870)	32·50 *fav.* £3·50 *adv.*

Direct Materials Yield Variance

$$SR (SY - AY)$$
$$£5 \quad (100 - 90) \quad £50·00 \; adv.$$

This method is recommended by the authors as being a realistic and useful method of calculating the Direct Materials Cost Variances. A further illustration of this method is given now, based on a question set in the final examination of the Institute of Cost and Works Accountants.

Specimen Question

The standard raw material mix for a ton of finished product is:

Materials	Weight (lbs)	Price per lb.
A	1200	£0·05
B	500	0·50
C	500	0·30
D	100	1·00

Materials used during an accounting period were as follows:

A	2900	£0·05
B	1300	0·47½
C	1350	0·32½
D	260	0·95

During the period 2·5 mixes were processed and actual production was 5500 lbs. Calculate the direct materials cost variances.

Normal cost

Materials	Quantity	Price per lb.	Amount
A	3000	£0·05	£150
B	1250	0·50	625
C	1250	0·30	375
D	250	1·00	250
	5750		1400
Normal loss	150		—
	5600		£1400

Actual cost

A	2900	£0·05	£145
B	1300	0·47½	617·50
C	1350	0·32½	438·75
D	260	0·95	247
	5810		1448·25
Loss	310		—
	5500		£1448·25

Actual quantity used at standard prices

A	2900	£0·05	£145
B	1300	0·50	650
C	1350	0·30	405
D	260	1·00	260
	5810		1460
Loss	310		—
	5500		£1460

Direct Materials Cost Variance

$$SC - AC$$
$$£1375 - £1448·25 \quad £73·25 \ adv.$$

NOTE

Standard cost = Actual quantity produced at standard cost per unit.
5,500 units × £0·25 per unit = £1375

$$\text{Standard cost per unit} = \frac{\text{Normal cost}}{\text{Normal output}} = \frac{£1400}{5600} = £0·25 \text{ per unit.}$$

Direct Materials Price Variance

$$AQ \ (SP - AP)$$

A	2900	(0·05 − 0·05)	—
B	1300	(0·50 − 0·47½)	32·50 *fav.*
C	1350	(0·30 − 0·32½)	33·75 *adv.*
D	260	(1·00 − 0·95)	13·00 *fav.* £11·75 *fav.*

Direct Material Usage Variance

$$SC \text{ of output} - SC \text{ of input}$$
$$£1375 - £1460 \quad £85 \ adv.$$

Direct Materials Mixture Variance

$$SP \ (SQ - AQ)$$

A	0·05	(3000 − 2900)	5 *fav.*
B	0·50	(1250 − 1300)	25 *adv.*
C	0·30	(1250 − 1350)	30 *adv.*
D	1·00	(250 − 260)	10 *adv.* £60 *adv.*

Direct Materials Yield Variance

$$SR\ (SY - AY)$$
$$£0{\cdot}25\ (5600 - 5500)\ £25\ adv.$$

CHECK

(i) D.M. Cost Variance = D.M. Price Variance +
D.M. Usage Variance
£73·25 *adv.* = £11·75 *fav.* + £85 *adv.*

(ii) D.M. Usage Variance = D.M. Mixture Variance +
= D.M. Yield Variance
£85 *adv.*= £60 *adv.* + £25 *adv.*

2. LABOUR VARIANCES

Example (4)

Two hundred employees are engaged in a manufacturing process. A 40-hour week is worked. The standard rate is £0·50 an hour and the standard output is 250 units an hour. During the first week in January, four employees were paid at £0·47½ an hour and two at £0·52½ an hour; the remaining employees were paid at standard rates. Actual output was 10,250 articles.

Cost Variance

$$\frac{SC - AC}{£4100 - £3998} = £102\ fav.$$

NOTES

(i) Standard cost = Actual output at Standard rate
10,250 units × £0·40 per unit

(ii) Standard rate = $\dfrac{\text{Standard cost per hour}}{\text{Standard output per hour}} = \dfrac{200\ \text{at}\ 10s.}{250}$

(iii) Actual cost = 194 employees × 40 hours × £0·50 per hour
4 „ × 40 hours × £0·47½ per hour
2 „ × 40 hours × £0·52½ per hour

Rate Variance

Actual hours (Actual rate − Standard rate)

$$AH\ (AR - SR)$$
$$160\ (£0{\cdot}47\tfrac12 - £0{\cdot}50)\ 4\ fav.$$
$$80\ (0{\cdot}52\tfrac12 - 0{\cdot}50)\ 2\ adv. = £2\ fav.$$

It should be noted that the actual hours relate to the employees who were not paid at the standard rate. Obviously, no variance arises in respect of the 194 employees who were paid at the standard rate.

This favourable variance shows that overall wage rates were lower than standard; the personnel manager would be asked to explain the position.

Efficiency Variance

Standard rate (Actual hours − Standard hours)

$$SR\quad (AH - SH)$$
$$£0{\cdot}50\quad (8000 - 8200) = £100\ fav.$$

This reveals to management that efficiency was such that £100 was saved during the period. Perhaps the foreman could explain how it occurred.

CHECK

$$\text{Cost Variance} = \text{Rate Variance} + \text{Efficiency Variance}$$
$$\text{£102 } fav. = \text{£2 } fav. + \text{£100 } fav.$$

NOTE

SH = Time which should have been taken to produce actual output.

$$\frac{\text{Actual output}}{\text{Standard output per hour}} = \frac{10,250}{250} = 41 \text{ standard hours}$$

200 employees were engaged; therefore $41 \times 200 = 8,200$.

Even though standards are set as carefully as possible, idle time will still occur which could not have been foreseen. This abnormal idle time must be shown separately, not concealed in the Efficiency Variance, otherwise employees may be blamed for inefficiency when the true cause may have been beyond their control—a breakdown in power supply, for example.

Example (5)

Using the illustration in Example 4, but assuming that abnormal idle time occurred of one hour per employee:

Cost Variance

As in Example 4 = £102 *fav.*

Rate Variance

As in Example 4 = £2 *fav.*

Efficiency Variance

$$\begin{array}{ll} \text{SR} & \text{(AH} - \text{SH)} \\ \text{£0·50} & (7800 - 8200) = \text{£200} \, fav. \end{array}$$

Idle Time Variance

Hours idle $\times$ Standard rate
$$200 \times \text{£0·50} = \text{£100 } adv.$$

Idle Time Variance will of course *always* be adverse; it will necessitate investigation to discover the cause of the abnormal idle time.

CHECK

$$\text{Cost Variance} = \text{Rate Variance} + \text{Efficiency Variance} + \text{Idle Time Variance}$$
$$\text{£102 } fav. = \text{£2 } fav. + \text{£200 } fav. + \text{£100 } adv.$$

It will be observed that the actual hours shown have been reduced by 200 hours, to allow for the inclusion of an Idle Time Variance.

Accounting entries

	Dr	Cr
Wages control	£3998	
Wages payable		£3998
Work in progress	4000	
Rate Variance		2
Wages control		3998
Finished goods	4100	
Idle Time Variance	100	
Efficiency Variance		200
Work in progress		4000

Sometimes a change in the grades of labour employed on an operation has to be made, perhaps because of a shortage of one grade during a certain period. When this happens a Labour Mix Variance is calculated to reveal to management how much of the Labour Cost Variance is due to the change in the labour force.

Example (6)

The budgeted labour force for a certain process is:

20 skilled men at £0·50 per hour for 40 hours	£400
40 semi-skilled men at £0·37½ per hour for 40 hours	600
	£1000

During a certain week the actual labour force was:

30 skilled men at £0·50 per hour for 40 hours	£600
30 semi-skilled men at £0·40 per hour for 40 hours	480
	£1080

In this Example it is not proposed to show the Labour Efficiency Variance or Idle Time Variance, because they were shown in Example 5. Thus it is assumed that the actual performance attained was equal to standard performance.

Cost Variance

$$SC - AC$$
$$£1000 - £1080 = £80 \ adv.$$

Rate Variance

$$AH \quad (AR - SR)$$
$$1200 \ (£0·40 - £0·37\tfrac{1}{2}) = £30 \ adv.$$

Mix Variance

Standard cost of Standard mix — Standard cost of Actual mix
$$SC \ of \ SM - SC \ of \ AM$$
$$£1000 - £1050 = £50 \ adv.$$

The shortage of semi-skilled employees has resulted in the utilisation of extra skilled men.

NOTE

Standard cost of actual mix is calculated:

30 skilled men at £0·50 per hour for 40 hours	£600
30 semi-skilled men at £0·37½ per hour for 40 hours	450
	£1050

CHECK

Cost Variance = Rate Variance + Efficiency Variance
+ Idle Time Variance + Mix Variance

£80 *adv.* = £30 *adv.* + Nil + Nil + £50 *adv.*

Accounting entries

	Dr	Cr
Wages control	£1080	
Wages payable		£1080
Work in progress	1050	
Rate Variance	30	
Wages control		1080
Finished goods	1000	
Mix Variance	50	
Work in progress		1050

3. VARIABLE OVERHEAD VARIANCE

This variance is probably the easiest to calculate. Variable overheads tend to move directly with output, so the standard cost per unit will remain the same whatever level of output is reached. It was mentioned earlier that there are only two basic variances, price and volume, so if volume does not affect the cost per unit the only variance to be calculated is a Price Variance known as the Variable Overhead Expenditure Variance. It may be found that, in some examination questions, variable overheads have not moved directly with output; where this occurs Variable Overhead variances are calculated in a similar manner to Fixed Overhead variances (illustrated later in this chapter). Here it is assumed that variable overheads do in fact move directly with output; this follows the pattern adopted by many firms in practice and by a number of writers on the subject.

Example (7)

The standard variable overhead cost per unit is £0·10. During the first week in January actual expenditure on variable overheads was £1075 and actual output 10,250 units.

Expenditure Variance

SC − AC
£1025 − £1075 = £50 *adv.*

An explanation of this adverse variance should be obtained from the buyer. It will be observed that the Expenditure Variance is calculated in the same way as the Cost Variance; because there is only one variance it must be equal to the Cost Variance.

Accounting entries

	Dr	Cr
Variable overheads	£1075	
Expense creditors		£1075
Work in progress	1025	
Variable Overhead Expenditure Variance	50	
Variable overheads		1075
Finished goods	1025	
Work in progress		1025

4. FIXED OVERHEAD VARIANCES

Fixed overhead recovery depends basically on two important items:

(i) The amount of fixed overheads during the period.

(ii) The output of products or standard hours during the period.

As we have seen, when standards are being set two factors must be considered in calculating the overhead recovery rate. The budgeted fixed overhead of the period divided by the budgeted output for the period will show the standard fixed overhead cost per unit. This figure will be used in evaluating the standard cost of production. If this actual figure differs from that budgeted, an over- or under-recovery will result. Differences may arise from either a change in overhead costs (*e.g.* a price increase) or a change in output (*e.g.* loss of production due to a strike).

Fixed overhead costs are highly significant in most firms today: often they are the largest single element of cost. This does not necessarily reflect any inefficiency. It is often a result of the introduction of automation or mechanisation, which increases fixed expenses such as depreciation and maintenance but reduces direct labour costs. However, it is important that management be fully informed of the standard cost of fixed overheads and its attention drawn to any significant variances. Variances may be calculated in two ways:

(*a*) Those based on units of output.

(*b*) Those based on standard hours.

Both methods seem to be widely used, and for examination practice students should be familiar with both. Questions may be set which necessitate calculations based on one method only, so the student has to be versatile. Both methods will be illustrated in this chapter, although the emphasis will be on the first method.

(a) Variances based on units of output

Example (8)

The budgeted output of a product is 500,000 units p.a. For the same period budgeted fixed overheads are £225,000. Each year the factory closes for two weeks' annual holiday. During the first week in January the actual output was 10,250 units, while actual expenditure was £4750. Standard performance is 250 units per hour; a 40-hour week is worked. One hour a week was lost owing to abnormal idle time.

Cost Variance

$$SC - AC$$
$$£4612 \cdot 50 - £4750 = £137 \cdot 50 \ adv.$$

NOTE

$$\text{Standard cost} = \text{Actual output} \times \text{Standard rate}$$
$$10,250 \text{ units} \times £0 \cdot 45$$

$$\text{Standard rate} = \frac{\text{Budgeted fixed overhead}}{\text{Budgeted output}} = \frac{£225,000}{500,000}$$

⟨ Expenditure Variance

$$BC - AC$$
$$£4500 - £4750 = £250 \ adv.$$

This reveals to management that actual expenditure was £250 more than expected; the buyer could investigate.

NOTE

$$\text{Budgeted cost} = \frac{\text{Budgeted fixed overheads}}{\text{Budgeted number of weeks}} = \frac{£225,000}{50}$$

2⟨ Volume Variance

$$\text{Standard rate (Actual quantity} - \text{Budgeted quantity)}$$
$$\text{SR} \qquad \text{(AQ} - \text{BQ)}$$
$$£0 \cdot 45 \quad (10,250 - 10,000) = £112 \cdot 50 \ fav.$$

This favourable variance results from the actual quantity produced being greater than that budgeted, therefore there is an over-recovery of overheads.

NOTE

$$\text{Budgeted quantity} = \frac{\text{Budgeted output p.a.}}{\text{Budgeted number of weeks}} = \frac{500,000}{50}$$

Volume Variance reveals that the volume achieved differs from that budgeted. The cause may be any of a number of factors, the two most important being a change in efficiency or in capacity utilised. Thus the Efficiency Variance and the Capacity Variance are sub-variances of Volume Variance.

7) *Efficiency Variance*

Standard rate (Actual quantity — Standard quantity)

$$SR \quad (AQ - SQ)$$
$$£0.45 \ (10,250 - 9750) = £225 \ fav.$$

This favourable variance shows that there has been considerable efficiency during the month; perhaps the foreman could explain why.

NOTE

Standard quantity = Actual hours × Standard quantity per hour
39 × 250

This variance may be referred to as the Volume Efficiency Variance.

4) *Capacity Variance*

Standard rate (Standard quantity — Budgeted quantity)

$$SR \quad (SQ - BQ)$$
$$£0.45 \quad (9750 - 10,000) = £112.50 \ adv.$$

This shows that the capacity of the factory has not been fully utilised during the week; the production control department should be able to explain why. This variance may be referred to as the Capacity Usage variance.

It sometimes happens that the actual number of days worked differs from the number of days it was expected would be worked, say because an extra day's holiday was given to celebrate the 100th anniversary of the founding of the firm. It is usual to show the effects of such a change because it obviously affects the firm's capacity. Thus the Volume Variance is analysed to show three sub-variances: Efficiency, Capacity and Calendar. The Capacity Variance changes from that shown in Example 8 so as to allow for the introduction of this additional variance.

The Calendar Variance should arise only in exceptional circumstances. Normal holidays should be allowed for in budgeted calculations and forecasts, so unless there is an unexpected increase or decrease in the number of days worked there should be no need for a Calendar Variance. If a company is operating a budget based on twelve monthly periods and the overheads are to be absorbed on the basis that fixed overheads are the same for each period irrespective of the number of working days in each period, then an over- or under-absorption may occur according to whether more of fewer days are worked than was budgeted for an average month. This would result in a Calendar Variance occurring in most months of the year. It should be appreciated, however, that the sum of these monthly Calendar Variances in a complete year would be zero. It is unlikely that many firms will base their cost accounting on such a system as this; more probably, a system of thirteen months of four weeks each would be operated, which is much more satisfactory for comparative purposes and eliminates the need for a Calendar Variance. In those firms which prefer to use twelve calendar months in the year, it is possible to use four quarters of the year divided into months of four, four and five weeks each, which again eliminates the need for a calendar variance.

Example (9)

Using the facts as Example 8, but assuming that only four days were worked instead of the normal five:

Cost Variance
$$\text{As in Example 8} = £137{\cdot}50 \ adv.$$

Expenditure Variance
$$\text{As in Example 8} = £250 \ adv.$$

Volume Variance
$$\text{As in Example 8} = £112{\cdot}50 \ fav.$$

Efficiency Variance
$$\begin{array}{cc} \text{SR} & (\text{AQ} - \text{SQ}) \\ £0{\cdot}45 & (10{,}250 - 7750) = £1125 \ fav. \end{array}$$

NOTE
$$\text{Standard quantity} = \text{Average hours worked} \times \text{Standard quantity per hour}$$
$$31 \times 250$$

Capacity Variance
$$\text{Standard rate (Standard quantity} - \text{Revised budget quantity)}$$
$$\begin{array}{cc} \text{SR} & (\text{SQ} - \text{RBQ}) \\ £0{\cdot}45 & (7750 - 8000) = £112{\cdot}50 \ adv. \end{array}$$

NOTE
$$\text{Revised budgeted quantity} = \text{Budgeted output for period} \times \frac{\text{Actual days}}{\text{Budgeted days}}$$
$$= 10{,}000 \times \tfrac{4}{5}$$

Calendar Variance
$$\begin{array}{cc} \text{SR} & (\text{RBQ} - \text{BQ}) \\ £0{\cdot}45 & (8000 - 10{,}000) = £900 \ adv. \end{array}$$

This adverse variance is the result of the factory being closed unexpectedly for one day, presumably on a management decision to celebrate some special event such as that suggested above.

These Fixed Overhead Variances can be shown by a diagram, which may clarify the position and help the reader to visualise the formulae.

$$\begin{array}{c} \text{Cost Variance} \\ \text{SC--AC} \end{array}$$

$$\begin{array}{cc} \text{Volume Variance} & \text{Expenditure Variance} \\ \text{SC--BC} & \text{BC--AC} \end{array}$$

Volume Variance is then analysed to show the two sub-variances based on quantity of units (multiplied by standard rate).

Volume Variance

AQ—BQ

Efficiency Variance   Capacity Variance
AQ—SQ   SQ—BQ

It should be observed that Volume Variance = Efficiency Variance + Capacity Variance

$$AQ - BQ = (AQ - SQ) + (SQ - BQ)$$

Volume Variance can be analysed further to show three sub-variances based on quantity of units (multiplied by standard rate).

Volume Variance

AQ — BQ

Efficiency Variance   Capacity Variance   Calendar Variance
AQ — SQ   SQ — RBQ   RBQ — BQ

It should be observed that Volume Variance = Efficiency Variance + Capacity Variance + Calendar Variance.

$$AQ - BQ = (AQ - SQ) + (SQ - RBQ) + (RBQ - BQ)$$

For example, in order to find Capacity Variance the formula would be SR (SQ — RBQ).

In the above diagrams the discerning reader may have observed that Volume Variance has been shown as:

(i) Standard cost — Budgeted cost
    SC — BC

(ii) Standard rate (Actual quantity — Budgeted quantity)
     SR (AQ — BQ)

It should be appreciated that these formulae are synonymous:

$$SC = AQ \times SR$$
$$BC = BQ \times SR$$
$$\therefore SC - BC = SR (AQ - BQ)$$

Accounting entries

	Dr	Cr
Fixed overheads	£4750	
Expense creditors		£4750
Work in progress	4500	
Expenditure Variance	250	
Fixed overheads		4750
Finished goods	4612·50	
Calendar Variance	900	
Capacity Variance	112·50	
Efficiency Variance		1125
Work in progress		4500

(b) Variances based on standard hours

Example (10)

Using the same figures as in Example 8, the variances based on standard rates for a standard hour of output can be calculated. It may be remembered that earlier in this chapter the measurement of output in standard hours was discussed. In brief, standard hours represent actual output in terms of standard hours.

Cost Variance

$$SC - AC$$
$$£4612·50 - £4750 = £137·50 \; adv.$$

NOTE

(i) Standard cost $=$ Standard hours $\times$ Standard rate per hour
$$(41 \times 112·50)$$

(ii) Standard hours $= \dfrac{\text{Actual units produced}}{\text{Standard output per hour}} = \dfrac{10,250 \text{ units}}{250}$

(iii) Standard rate $= \dfrac{\text{Budgeted overhead in period}}{\text{Budgeted hours in period}} = \dfrac{£225,000}{50 \times 40}$

Expenditure Variance

$$BC - AC$$
$$£4500 - £4750 = £250 \; adv.$$

Volume Variance

$$SR \, (SH - BH)$$
$$£112·50 \, (41 - 40) = £112·50 \; fav.$$

Efficiency Variance

$$SR \, (SH - AH)$$
$$£112·50 \, (41 - 39) = £225 \; fav.$$

Capacity Variance

$$SR \, (AH - BH)$$
$$£112·50 \, (39 - 40) = £112·50 \; adv.$$

It should be observed that these variances agree with those in Example 8 above. Thus whether one adopts the unit method or the standard hour method, the results should be the same.

If it is desired to show the effect of a change in the number of days worked, it can be calculated by using the standard hour method.

Example (11)

For this illustration the same figures are used as in Example 9

Cost Variance

As in Example 9 = £137·50 *adv.*

Expenditure Variance

As in Example 9 = £250 *adv.*

Volume Variance

As in Example 9 = £112·50 *fav.*

Efficiency Variance

$$\text{SR} \quad (\text{SH} - \text{AH})$$
£112·50 (41 − 31) = £1125 *fav.*

Capacity Variance

$$\text{SR} \quad (\text{AH} - \text{RBH})$$
£112·50 (31 − 32) = £112·50 *adv.*

NOTE

$$\text{RBH} = \text{Budgeted hours for period} \times \frac{\text{Actual days}}{\text{Budgeted days}}$$
$$= 40 \times \tfrac{4}{5}$$

Calendar Variance

$$\text{SR} \quad (\text{RBH} - \text{BH})$$
£112·50 (32 − 40) = £900 *adv.*

These variances are of course the same as those calculated in Example 9 and the accounting entries would be the same. A diagram can be used to show them.

Cost Variance
SC − AC

Volume Variance   Expenditure Variance
SC − BC   BC − AC

Volume Variance is then analysed to show the two sub-variances based on hours (multiplied by standard rate per hour).

Volume Variance
SH − BH

Efficiency Variance   Capacity Variance
SH − AH   AH − BH

It will be observed that Volume Variance = Efficiency Variance + Capacity Variance

$$SH - BH = (SH - AH) + (AH - BH)$$

Volume Variance can be analysed further to show the three sub-variances based on hours (multiplied by standard rate per hour).

Volume Variance
SH — BH

Efficiency Variance	Capacity Variance	Calendar Variance
SH — AH	AH — RBH	RBH — BH

It should be observed that Volume Variance = Efficiency Variance + Capacity Variance + Calendar Variance.

$$SH - BH = (SH - AH) + (AH - RBH) + (RBH - BH)$$

Thus if, for example, we wish to find Capacity Variance, the formula would be SR (AH — RBH).

In the above diagrams, it will again be noted that Volume Variance has been shown as:

(i) Standard cost — Budgeted cost SC — BC.
(ii) Standard rate (Standard hours — Budgeted hours) SR (SH — BH).

$$SC = SH \times SR$$
$$BC = BH \times SR$$
$$\therefore SC - BC = SR (SH - BH)$$

SALES VARIANCES

A number of standard costing systems are designed so as to present the cost variances only, *i.e.* Material, Labour and Overhead. These variances are invaluable, but many accountants think that a system is incomplete if sales variances are not included in the presentation of information to management. They are, however, among the more difficult variance calculations, and can be shown in two different ways. In discussing overhead variances on p. 155, we saw that two alternative calculations were possible, each giving the same result. But with sales variances the different methods produce quite different final results. Both are very useful and both should be understood by management accountants. Examinees in cost and management accounting should be familiar with both methods because some questions are set which demand the use of one of them only. The two methods of calculating sales variances are:

(a) *The turnover method.* This shows the effect of a change in sales on turnover.

(b) *The profit method.* This shows the effect of a change in sales on profits.

Both will be discussed in this chapter but before going on to any involved illustration, it might be helpful if some easy examples are given.

Sales variances are basically caused by two changes which may occur when comparing budgeted sales with actual sales: (i) those due to price and (ii) those due to volume. A change in volume may be caused by (i) changes due to a change in quantity and (ii) changes due to a change in "mix" of sales. These differences are shown in simplified form:

Change in price

Product	Budget		Actual	
A	50 at £5	£250	50 at £6	£300
B	50 at £10	500	50 at £8	400
	100	£750	100	£700

Here the volume of sales is as budgeted, but the selling price has changed.

Change in volume

	Budget		Actual	
A	50 at £5	£250	120 at £5	£600
B	50 at £10	500	80 at £10	800
	100	£750	200	£1400

Here the price is as budgeted, but the volume has changed.

Change in quantity

	Budget		Actual	
A	50 at £5	£250	100 at £5	£500
B	50 at £10	500	100 at £10	1000
	100	£750	200	£1500

Here the price is as budgeted and the "mix," *i.e.* the ratio of A and B to total sales, is the same (A 50%, B 50%) but the physical quantity has increased.

Change in mix

	Budget		Actual	
A	50 at £5	£250	70 at £5	£350
B	50 at £10	500	30 at £10	300
	100	£750	100	£650

Here the price and quantity are as budgeted but the "mix" of products has changed from A 50%, B 50% to A 60%, B 40%.

Total change

A	50 at £5	£250	70 at £4	£280
B	50 at £10	500	40 at £11	440
	100	£750	110	£720

Here neither price, quantity nor mix are as budgeted; this total change is known as a Value Variance.

At this point it should be explained that in addition to the fact that there are two methods of calculating variances, there are also two techniques which can be used:

(i) *The quantity technique.* This uses *quantity* of sales as the basis of calculation.

(ii) *The value technique.* This uses sales *value* as the basis of calculation.

Both techniques are used in practice and either may be required in examination questions. To clarify the position, if we calculate ratios from one of the simple examples above, *e.g.* that for change of mix, we should obtain these ratios:

Budget A : B   Quantity 1 : 1   Value 1 : 2
Actual A : B   Quantity 7 : 3   Value 7 : 6

It will be seen in the examples which follow that ratios are an important calculation in ascertaining variances, so the result will obviously depend on which ratio is used. The value technique will be used here, because it is felt that sales values are more important to management than quantities; moreover, values can represent heterogeneous products more readily than can quantities. This can be shown briefly:

Budgeted sales

20 tons of coke at £10 per ton	£200
10,000 cu. ft. of gas at £1 per 100 cu. ft.	100
10,020	£300

It will be appreciated that a ratio of 2 : 1 seems more reasonable than a ratio of 1 : 500.

(a) Variances based on turnover
Example (12)

The budgeted and actual sales, costs and profits for the month of March of the Jaydee Sales Co. are as follows:

| Product | Sales | | | Cost | | Profit | |
	Quantity	Price	Amount	Price	Amount	Price	Amount
			Budget				
Jay	18,000	£5	£90,000	£4	£72,000	£1	£18,000
Dee	30,000	2	60,000	1·50	45,000	0·50	15,000
	48,000		£150,000		£117,000		£33,000
			Actual				
Jay	21,000	4·75	£99,750	4	£84,000	0·75	£15,750
Dee	25,500	2·50	63,750	1·50	38,250	1	25,500
	46,500		£163,500		£122,250		£41,250

Before calculating the sales variances, it is necessary to ascertain the standard sales and the revised standard sales, so that the "mix" of sales can be established. In other words, it is necessary to find out (i) whether the quantity of sales differs from the estimated and (ii) whether the mix of sales is in a different proportion from that budgeted. Standard sales are simply actual sales at standard prices, while revised standard sales are the budgeted ratio of total standard sales.

Standard

Jay	21,000	£5	£105,000	£4	£84,000	£1	£21,000
Dee	25,500	2	51,000	1·50	38,250	0·50	12,750
	46,500		£156,000		£122,250		£33,750

Revised standard

		Sales		Profit	
Jay	$\frac{3}{5}$ × Standard sales	£93,600	$\frac{1}{5}$	£18,720	
Dee	$\frac{2}{5}$ × „ „	62,400	$\frac{1}{4}$	15,600	
		£156,000		£34,320	

NOTES

(i) Revised standard sales is budgeted ratio of total standard sales:

Jay: $\frac{90,000}{150,000} \times 156,000$ Dee: $\frac{60,000}{150,000} \times 156,000$

(ii) Revised standard profit is budgeted profit % of revised standard sales:
Jay: 20% × £93,600   Dee: 25% × £62,400
(iii) Budgeted profit %:
Jay: £1 profit on £5 sales   Dee: £0·50 profit on £2 sales

Value Variance

	Budgeted sales	—	Actual sales	
	BS	—	AS	
Jay:	£90,000	—	£99,750 =	£9,750 *fav.*
Dee:	60,000	—	63,750 =	3,750 *fav.*
Total	£150,000	—	£163,500 =	£13,500 *fav.*

This variance represents the total variance, made up of Price Variance and Volume Variance. All the Sales Variances are the responsibility of the sales manager.

Price Variance

	Standard sales	—	Actual sales	
	SS	—	AS	
Jay:	£105,000	—	£99,750 =	£5,250 *adv.*
Dee:	51,000	—	63,750 =	12,750 *fav.*
Total	£156,000	—	£163,500 =	£7,500 *fav.*

This reveals to management the effect on turnover of change in prices.

Volume Variance

	Budgeted sales	—	Standard sales	
	BS	—	SS	
Jay:	£90,000	—	£105,000 =	£15,000 *fav.*
Dee:	60,000	—	51,000 =	9,000 *adv.*
Total	£150,000	—	£156,000 =	£6,000 *fav.*

This variance represents the effect of a change in volume on total sales.

Quantity Variance

	Budgeted sales	—	Revised standard sales	
	BS	—	RSS	
Jay:	£90,000	—	£93,600 =	£3,600 *fav.*
Dee:	60,000	—	62,400 =	2,400 *fav.*
Total	£150,000	—	£156,000 =	£6,000 *fav.*

This favourable variance shows that the actual quantity of sales as distinct from the mix of sales was more than expected.

Mix Variance

	Revised standard sales	—	Standard sales	
	RSS	—	SS	
Jay:	£93,600	—	£105,000 =	£11,400 *fav.*
Dee:	62,400	—	51,000 =	11,400 *adv.*
Total	£156,000	—	£156,000 =	£ —

This variance shows that the actual mix of sales was not in the same ratio as that budgeted.

It will be observed that the final variance, while showing the effect of each product on turnover, must inevitably be, in total, *nil*. The reason is obvious—we are utilising total standard sales and total revised standard sales which are, or course, one and the same. On the other hand if the quantity technique had been used this would not necessarily be so, because the revised standard sales would have been in the ratio of budgeted quantities, not of budgeted values.

The above variances can be shown in diagrammatic form:

Value Variance

BS — AS

Volume Variance   Price Variance

BS — SS   SS — AS

It will be observed that Value Variance = Volume Variance + Price Variance.

$$BS - AS = (BS - SS) + (SS - AS).$$

Volume Variance can be analysed further:

Value Variance

BS — AS

Volume Variance   Price Variance

BS — SS   SS — AS

Quantity Variance   Mix Variance

BS — RSS   RSS — SS

It will be observed that Volume Variance = Quantity Variance + Mix Variance.

$$BS - SS = (BS - RSS) + (RSS - SS)$$

(b) Variances based on profits

The revised terminology of cost accounting published in 1966 by the Institute of Cost and Works Accountants favours this method of calculating sales variances. The variances have been restyled *Margin Variances* and are illustrated by using the same figures as those used in the turnover method. Readers should note the change in terminology.

Example (13)

Using the same figures as in the turnover method, the variances based on profit can now be calculated.

Total Sales Margin Variance

Budgeted profit — Actual profit

	BP	—	AP		
Jay:	£18,000	—	£15,750	=	£2,250 *adv.*
Dee:	15,000	—	25,500	=	10,500 *fav.*
Total	£33,000	—	£41,250	=	£8,250 *fav.*

Sales Margin Variance due to Selling Price

Standard profit — Actual profit

	SP	—	AP		
Jay:	£21,000	—	£15,750	=	£5,250 *adv.*
Dee:	12,750	—	25,500	=	12,750 *fav.*
Total	£33,750	—	£41,250	=	£7,500 *fav.*

Note that the variance here is exactly the same as the Price Variance calculated in the turnover method. This must be so, because a price change will affect turnover and profit equally.

Sales Margin Variance due to Volume

Budgeted profit — Standard profit

	BP	—	SP		
Jay:	£18,000	—	£21,000	=	£3,000 *fav.*
Dee:	15,000	—	12,750	=	2,250 *adv.*
Total	£33,000	—	£33,750	=	£750 *fav.*

Comparison of this variance with that calculated on turnover will reveal an obvious relationship. The percentage of profit of Jay is one-fifth and if one calculates one-fifth of the Volume Variance based on turnover one finds that this is the variance based on profit ($\frac{1}{5}$ × £15,000 = £3,000). Similarly with Dee ($\frac{1}{4}$ × £9000 = £2250).

Sales Margin Variance due to Quantity

Budgeted profit — Revised standard profit

	BP	—	RSP		
Jay:	£18,000	—	£18,720	=	£720 *fav.*
Dee:	15,000	—	15,600	=	600 *fav.*
Total	£33,000	—	£34,320	=	£1320 *fav.*

As with Volume Variance, the Quantity Variance can be compared:

Jay: $\frac{1}{5}$ × £3600 = £720
Dee: $\frac{1}{4}$ × £2400 = £600

Sales Margin Variance due to Sales Quantities (Mixture)

Revised standard profit − Standard profit

	RSP	−	SP	
Jay:	£18,720	−	£21,000 =	£2280 *fav.*
Dee:	15,600	−	12,750 =	2850 *adv.*
Total	£34,320	−	£33,750 =	£570 *adv.*

In this instance also we have:

Jay: ⅕ × £11,400 = £2280
Dee: ¼ × £11,400 = £2850

The above variances can be shown in diagrammatic form:

Sales Margin Variance
BP − AP

Volume Variance   Price Variance
BP − SP   SP − AP

Quantity Variance   Mixture Variance
BP − RSP   RSP − SP

A final check should show that the formulae illustrated can be proved quite easily:

Sales Margin Variance = Quantity Variance + Mixture Variance + Price Variance

$$BP − AP = (BP − RSP) + (RSP − SP) + (SP − AP)$$

The rest of this chapter is concerned entirely with a single comprehensive example showing the calculation of variances in standard costing. Most of those discussed in the previous chapter have been computed and the final results presented for management in a typical standard costing statement. So that the reader can try out the techniques discussed earlier, this illustration has been designed to include two products "Jaydee" and "Eejay." It is suggested that the reader who is interested in calculating variances should follow through those for "Jaydee" and then attempt those for "Eejay" independently. Comparison with the text should provide a useful exercise and help to consolidate the reader's knowledge of the techniques of standard costing.

STANDARD COSTING PROJECT

Banstead Products Ltd manufacture two products, Jaydee and Eejay. The company operates a system of standard costing and integral accounting

During the month of May the following information was available:

Direct materials

One hundred tons of material E42 at £155 a ton were issued to the Jaydee process and 50 tons of material D10 at £195 a ton were issued to the Eejay process.

The standard prices of these materials are £150 and £200 a ton respectively. Standard production from each ton of material E42 consumed is 50 units of Jaydee, and from each ton of material D10 is 200 units of Eejay.

Direct labour

The company operates a five-day week of 40 hours. Male and female employees are employed in the factory, standard rates of pay being £0·37½ and £0·25 an hour respectively. The budgeted labour mix has been set as follows:

Jaydee:	8,000 hours at £0·37½ per hour	£3,000
	8,000 „ „ £0·25 per hour	2,000
	16,000	£5,000

Eejay:	20,000 hours at £0·37½ per hour	£7,500
	50,000 „ „ £0·25 per hour	12,500
	70,000	£20,000

During May the company had difficulty in recruiting male workers, and as a result was obliged to employ some females on process operations normally undertaken by male employees. The labour mix was revised as follows:

Jaydee:	6,000 hours at £0·37½ per hour	£2,250
	10,000 „ „ £0·25 per hour	2,500
	16,000	£4,750

Eejay:	16,000 hours at £0·37½ per hour	£6,000
	54,000 „ „ £0·25 per hour	13,500
	70,000	£19,500

At the end of May an analysis of wages revealed the following results:

Jaydee:	6,600 hours at £0·40 per hour	£2,640
	11,000 „ „ £0·22½ per hour	2,475
	17,600	£5,115

Eejay:	15,200 hours at £0·40 per hour	£6,080
	52,000 „ „ £0·22½ per hour	11,700
	67,200	£17,780

There were 21 working days in May, but one of them was a Bank Holiday, leaving 20 working days. Actual results showed that 21 days were in fact worked. Machine breakdowns resulted in the following idle time: Jaydee, 120 hours (male employees); Eejay, 200 hours (female employees).

Variable overheads

The standard variable overhead rates per unit are: Jaydee £0·50, Eejay £0·25. Actual results for the month were: Jaydee £3100, Eejay £2300.

Fixed overheads

The budgeted fixed overhead for the year is: Jaydee £218,750 and Eejay £343,750. Actual overhead incurred in May was: Jaydee £21,500 and Eejay £24,500. There are 50 working weeks in the year.

Budgeted production for the year is: Jaydee 62,500 units and Eejay 125,000 units.

Actual production for the month of May was: Jaydee 6000 units and Eejay 9000 units.

Sales

Sales for May were as follows:

Product	Sales Quantity	Sales Price	Sales Amount	Cost Price	Cost Amount	Profit Price	Profit Amount
			Budget				
Jaydee	5,000	£10	£50,000	£8	£40,000	£2	£10,000
Eejay	10,000	7	70,000	6	60,000	1	10,000
	15,000		£120,000		£100,000		£20,000
			Actual				
Jaydee	4,000	£10	£40,000	£8	£32,000	£2	£8,000
	2,000	11	22,000	8	16,000	3	6,000
	6,000		£62,000		£48,000		£14,000
Eejay	6,000	£7	£42,000	£6	£36,000	£1	£6,000
	3,000	6	18,000	6	18,000	—	—
	9,000		£60,000		£54,000		£6,000

You are required to (*a*) calculate the variances, (*b*) show the accounting entries, and (*c*) present the information to the management.

Answer

(*a*) Calculation of variances

1. Direct materials

Jaydee

(*a*) Cost Variance   SC — AC
£18,000 — £15,500 = £2500 *fav.*

(b) Price Variance   AQ (AP − SP)
                     100 (155 − 150) = £500 *adv.*
(c) Usage Variance   SP (AQ − SQ)
                     150 (100 − 120) = £3000 *fav.*

NOTES

(i) Standard cost   = Actual production × Standard rate
                      6000 units × £3
(ii) Standard rate = Standard cost per ton ÷ Standard output per ton
                      £150 ÷ 50
(iii) Standard quantity = Actual output ÷ Standard output per ton
                      6000 ÷ 50

CHECK

Cost Variance = Price Variance + Usage Variance
£2500 *fav.* = £500 *adv.* + £3000 *fav.*

Accounting entries

	Dr	Cr
Stores	£15,500	
Creditors		£15,500
Work in progress	15,000	
Price Variance	500	
Stores		15,500
Finished goods	18,000	
Usage Variance		3,000
Work in progress		15,000

Eejay

(a) Cost Variance   SC − AC
                     £9000 − £9750 = £750 *adv.*
(b) Price Variance   AQ (AP − SP)
                     50 (195 − 200) = £250 *fav.*
(c) Usage Variance   SP (AQ − SQ)
                     200 (50 − 45) = £1000 *adv.*

CHECK

Cost Variance = Price Variance + Usage Variance
£750 *adv.* = £250 *fav.* + £1000 *adv.*

Accounting entries

	Dr	Cr
Stores	£9,750	
Creditors		£9,750
Work in progress	10,000	
Price Variance		250
Stores		9,750
Finished goods	9,000	
Usage Variance	1,000	
Work in progress		10,000

2. Direct labour

Jaydee

(a) Cost Variance

$$\begin{array}{ll} \text{SC} - \text{AC} \\ \text{£6000} - \text{£5115} & = \text{£885 } fav. \end{array}$$

(b) Rate Variance

$$\begin{array}{ll} \text{AH} \quad (\text{AR} - \text{SR}) \\ 6{,}600 \ (\text{£0·40} - \text{£0·37}\tfrac{1}{2}) & = 165 \ adv. \\ (11{,}000 \ \text{£0·22}\tfrac{1}{2} - \text{£0·25}) & = 275 \ fav. \\ & \overline{\qquad} \quad \text{£110 } fav. \end{array}$$

(c) Mix Variance

$$\begin{array}{ll} \text{SR} \quad (\text{RSH} - \text{SH}) \\ \text{£0·37}\tfrac{1}{2} \quad (7{,}200 - 9{,}600) & = 900 \ fav. \\ \text{£0·25} \quad (12{,}000 - 9{,}600) & = 600 \ adv. \\ & \overline{\qquad} \quad \text{£300 } fav. \end{array}$$

(d) Efficiency Variance

$$\begin{array}{ll} \text{SR} \quad (\text{AH} - \text{RSH}) \\ \text{£0·37}\tfrac{1}{2} \quad (6{,}480 - 7{,}200) & = 270 \ fav. \\ \text{£0·25} \quad (11{,}000 - 12{,}000) & = 250 \ fav. \\ & \overline{\qquad} \quad \text{£520 } fav. \end{array}$$

(e) Idle Time Variance

$$\begin{array}{ll} \text{Hours idle} \times \text{Standard rate} \\ 120 \quad \times \text{£0·37}\tfrac{1}{2} & = \text{£45 } adv. \end{array}$$

NOTES

(i) Standard cost = Actual production × Standard rate
(6000 units × £1)

(ii) Standard hours $= \dfrac{\text{Budgeted mix in hours}}{\text{Budgeted output}} \times$ Actual output

Male $\quad \dfrac{8000}{5000} \times 6000$

Female $\quad \dfrac{8000}{5000} \times 6000$

(iii) Revised standard hours $= \dfrac{\text{Revised mix in hours}}{\text{Budgeted output}} \times$ Actual output

Male $\quad \dfrac{6{,}000}{5{,}000} \times 6{,}000$

Female $\quad \dfrac{10{,}000}{5{,}000} \times 6{,}000$

(iv) Actual hours = Actual hours paid − Hours idle
Male $\qquad$ 6600 − 120

CHECK

Cost Variance = Rate Variance + Mix Variance + Efficiency Variance
+ Idle Time Variance

£885 *fav.* = £110 *fav.* + £300 *fav.* + £520 *fav.* + £45 *adv.*

Accounting entries

	Dr	Cr
Wages control	£5115	
Wages payable		£5115
Work in progress	5225	
Rate Variance		110
Wages control		5115
Finished goods	6000	
Idle Time Variance	45	
Mix Variance		300
Efficiency Variance		520
Work in progress		5225

Eejay

(a) Cost Variance

$$SC \quad - \quad AC$$
$$£18,000 - £17,780 = £220 \; fav.$$

(b) Rate Variance

$$AH \quad (AR \quad - \quad SR)$$
$$15,200 \; (£0·40 \quad - £0·37\tfrac{1}{2}) = 380 \; adv.$$
$$52,000 \; (£0·22\tfrac{1}{2} - £0·25) = 1300 \; fav.$$
$$\overline{\hspace{2cm}} \qquad £920 \; fav.$$

(c) Mix Variance

$$SR \quad (RSH \quad - \quad SH)$$
$$£0·37\tfrac{1}{2} \; (14,400 - 18,000) = 1350 \; fav.$$
$$£0·25 \quad (48,600 - 45,000) = 900 \; adv.$$
$$\overline{\hspace{2cm}} \qquad £450 \; fav.$$

(d) Efficiency Variance

$$SR \quad (AH \quad - \quad RSH)$$
$$£0·37\tfrac{1}{2} \; (15,200 - 14,400) = 300 \; adv.$$
$$£0·25 \quad (51,800 - 48,600) = 800 \; adv.$$
$$\overline{\hspace{2cm}} \qquad £1100 \; adv.$$

(e) Idle Time Variance

$$\text{Hours idle} \times \text{Standard rate}$$
$$200 \quad \times \quad £0·25 \quad = \quad £50 \; adv.$$

CHECK

Cost Variance = Rate Variance + Mix Variance + Efficiency Variance
                                             + Idle Time Variance
£220 *fav.* = £920 *fav.* + £450 *fav.* + £1100 *adv.* + £50 *adv.*

Accounting entries

	Dr	Cr
Wages control	£17,780	
Wages payable		£17,780
Work in progress	18,700	
Rate Variance		920
Wages control		17,780
Finished goods	18,000	
Efficiency Variance	1,100	
Idle Time Variance	50	
Mix Variance		450
Work in progress		18,700

3. Variable overhead

Jaydee

Expenditure Variance
$$\text{SC} \quad - \quad \text{AC}$$
$$£3000 - £3100 = £100 \; adv.$$

NOTE

Standard cost = Actual production × Standard rate
6000 × £0·50

Accounting entries

	Dr	Cr
Variable overheads	£3100	
Expense creditors		£3100
Work in progress	3000	
Expenditure Variance	100	
Variable overheads		3100
Finished goods	3000	
Work in progress		3000

Eejay

Expenditure Variance
$$\text{SC} \quad - \quad \text{AC}$$
$$£2250 - £2300 = £50 \; adv.$$

Accounting entries

	Dr	Cr
Variable overheads	£2300	
Expense creditors		£2300
Work in progress	2250	
Expenditure Variance	50	
Variable overheads		2300
Finished goods	2250	
Work in progress		2250

4. Fixed overhead

Jaydee

The following data will prove helpful in calculating the variances:

Actual production	6000 units
Budgeted production	5000 units
Standard production	5500 units
Revised budgeted production	5250 units

Calculations

Budgeted production:

$$\frac{\text{Budgeted production p.a.}}{\text{Budgeted days in year}} \times \text{Budgeted days in month}$$

$$\frac{62,500}{250} \times 20$$

Standard production:

$$\frac{\text{Actual no. of hours worked}}{\text{Standard no. of hours per product}}$$

$$\frac{17,600}{3\frac{1}{3}}$$

Revised budgeted production:

Days worked × Budgeted output per day
21 × 250

(a) Cost Variance

SC − AC
£21,000 − £21,500 = £500 *adv.*

(b) Expenditure Variance

BC − AC
£17,500 − £21,500 = £4,000 *adv.*

(c) Volume Variance

SR (AQ − BQ)
3·5 (6,000 − 5,000) = £3,500 *fav.*

(d) Efficiency Variance

SR (AQ − SQ)
3·5 (6,000 − 5,500) = £1,750 *fav.*

(e) Capacity Variance

SR (RBQ − SQ)
3·5 (5,250 − 5,500) = £875 *fav.*

(f) Calendar Variance

SR (RBQ − BQ)
3·5 (5,250 − 5,000) = £875 *fav.*

Calculations

Standard cost = Actual production × Standard rate
6000 × £3·50

$$\text{Budgeted cost} = \frac{\text{Budgeted overhead p.a.}}{\text{No. of days in year}} \times \text{No. of days in month}$$

$$\frac{£218,750}{250} \times 20$$

$$\text{Standard rate} = \frac{\text{Budgeted overhead p.a.}}{\text{Budgeted production p.a.}}$$

$$\frac{£218,750}{62,500}$$

CHECK

Cost Variance = Expenditure Variance + Efficiency Variance
+ Capacity Variance + Calendar Variance.

£500 *adv.* = £4000 *adv.* + £1750 *fav.* + £875 *fav.* + £875 *fav.*

Accounting entries

	Dr	Cr
Fixed overheads	£21,500	
Expense creditors		£21,500
Work in progress	17,500	
Expenditure Variance	4,000	
Fixed overheads		21,500
Finished goods	21,000	
Efficiency Variance		1,750
Capacity Variance		875
Calendar Variance		875
Work in progress		17,500

Eejay

The following data will prove to be helpful when calculating the variances:

Actual production	9,000 units
Budgeted production	10,000
Standard production	9,600
Revised budgeted production	10,500

(a) Cost Variance

$$\begin{array}{cc} \text{SC} & - \quad \text{AC} \\ £24,750 & - £24,500 = £250 \text{ fav.} \end{array}$$

(b) Expenditure Variance

$$\begin{array}{cc} \text{BC} & - \quad \text{AC} \\ £27,500 & - £24,500 = £3,000 \text{ fav.} \end{array}$$

(c) Volume Variance

$$\begin{array}{cc} \text{SR} & (\text{AQ} - \text{BQ}) \\ 2 \cdot 75 & (9,000 - 10,000) = £2,750 \text{ adv.} \end{array}$$

(d) Efficiency Variance

$$\begin{array}{cc} \text{SR} & (\text{AQ} - \text{SQ}) \\ 2 \cdot 75 & (9,000 - 9,600) = £1,650 \text{ adv.} \end{array}$$

(e) Capacity Variance

$$\begin{array}{cc} \text{SR} & (\text{RBQ} - \text{SQ}) \\ 2 \cdot 75 & (10,500 - 9,600) = £2,475 \text{ adv.} \end{array}$$

(f) Calendar Variance

$$\begin{array}{cc} \text{SR} & (\text{RBQ} - \text{BQ}) \\ 2 \cdot 75 & (10,500 - 10,000) = £1,375 \text{ fav.} \end{array}$$

CHECK

Cost Variance = Expenditure Variance + Efficiency Variance
+ Capacity Variance + Calendar Variance

£250 fav. = £3000 fav. + £1650 adv. + £2475 adv. + £1375 fav.

Accounting entries

	Dr	Cr
Fixed overheads	£24,500	
Expense creditors		£24,500
Work in progress	27,500	
Expenditure Variance		3,000
Fixed overheads		24,500
Finished goods	24,750	
Efficiency Variance	1,650	
Capacity Variance	2,475	
Calendar Variance		1,375
Work in progress		27,500

5. Sales

Jaydee

To facilitate calculation of the sales variances, standard and revised standard sales are calculated:

Product	Sales Quantity	Sales Price	Sales Amount	Cost Price	Cost Amount	Profit Price	Profit Amount
			Standard				
Jaydee	6,000	£10	£60,000	£8	£48,000	£2	£12,000
Eejay	9,000	7	63,000	6	54,000	1	9,000
	15,000		£123,000		£102,000		£21,000

Revised standard sales

		Sales		Profit
Jaydee	$\frac{5}{12}$ × Standard sales	£51,250	$\frac{1}{5}$	£10,250
Eejay	$\frac{7}{12}$ × Standard sales	71,750	$\frac{1}{7}$	10,250
		£123,000		£20,500

In this illustration, sales variances are to be calculated based on turnover; the reader might care to calculate variances based on profit, thus providing himself with additional exercise.

Calculations

Standard sales = Actual quantity sold at standard prices

$$e.g.\ 6000 \times £10$$

Revised standard sales = Budgeted ratio of standard sales

$$\text{Jaydee: } \frac{50,000}{120,000} \times 123,000$$

$$\text{Eejay: } \frac{70,000}{120,000} \times 123,000$$

Revised standard profit = Budgeted ratio profit of revised standard sales,

$$\text{Jaydee: } \frac{2}{10} \times £51,250$$

$$\text{Eejay: } \frac{1}{7} \times £71,750$$

(a) Value Variance

	BS	—	AS		
Jaydee:	£50,000	—	£62,000	=	£12,000 *fav.*
Eejay:	70,000	—	60,000	=	10,000 *adv.*
	£120,000	—	£122,000		£2000 *fav.*

(b) Price Variance

	SS	—	AS	
Jaydee:	£60,000	—	£62,000	= £2,000 *fav.*
Eejay:	63,000	—	60,000	= 3,000 *adv.*

£123,000 — £122,000   £1,000 *adv.*

(c) Volume Variance

	BS	—	SS	
Jaydee:	£50,000	—	£60,000	= £10,000 *fav.*
Eejay:	70,000	—	63,000	= 7,000 *adv.*

£120,000 — £123,000   £3,000 *fav.*

(d) Quantity Variance

	BS	—	RSS	
Jaydee:	£50,000	—	£51,250	= £1,250 *fav.*
Eejay:	70,000	—	71,750	= 1,750 *fav.*

£120,000 — £123,000   £3,000 *fav.*

(e) Mix Variance

	RSS	—	SS	
Jaydee:	£51,250	—	£60,000	= £8,750 *fav.*
Eejay:	71,750	—	63,000	= 8,750 *adv.*

£123,000 — £123,000   *Nil*

Accounting entries

	Dr	Cr
Debtors	£122,000	
Price Variance	1,000	
Quantity Variance		£3,000
Sales		120,000

The standard cost for a unit and for actual quantity produced during the month can now be shown:

Actual output = 6000 units

May Jaydee	Unit	Total
Direct materials	£3·00	£18,000
Direct labour	1·00	6,000
Variable overhead	0·50	3,000
Fixed overhead	3·50	21,000
Total cost	8·00	48,000
Profit	2·00	12,000
Selling Price	£10·00	£60,000

May *Eejay*	*Actual output = 9000 units*	
Direct materials	£1·00	£9,000
Direct labour	2·00	18,000
Variable overhead	0·25	2,250
Fixed overhead	2·75	24,750
Total cost	6·00	54,000
Profit	1·00	9,000
Selling price	£7·00	£63,000

(*b*) Accounting entries

To enable the reader to follow through the entries in the accounts, those in respect of "Jaydee" have been denoted (J) and those for "Eejay" have been denoted (E).

Trade Creditors Account

Balance c/d	£25,250	Stores (J)	£15,500
		Stores (E)	9,750
	£25,250		£25,250
		Balance b/d	£25,250

Debtors Account

Sales (J)	£62,000	Balance c/d	£122,000
Sales (E)	60,000		
	£122,000		£122,000
Balance b/d	£122,000		

Wages Payable Account

Balance c/d	£22,895	Wages (J)	£5,115
		Wages (E)	17,780
	£22,895		£22,895
		Balance b/d	£22,895

Expense Creditors Account

Balance c/d	£51,400	Variable overhead (J)	£3,100
		Variable overhead (E)	2,300
		Fixed overhead (J)	21,500
		Fixed overhead (E)	24,500
	£51,400		£51,400
		Balance b/d	£51,400

Stores Account

Creditors (J)	£15,500	Work in progress (J)	£15,000
Creditors (E)	9,750	Work in progress (E)	10,000
Price Variance (E)	250	Price Variance (J)	500
	£25,500		£25,500

Wages Account

Wages payable (J)	£5,115	Work in progress (J)	£5,225
Wages payable (E)	17,780	Work in progress (E)	18,700
Rate Variance (J)	110		
Rate Variance (E)	920		
	£23,925		£23,925

Variable Overhead Account

Expense creditors (J)	£3100	Expenditure Variance (J)	£100
Expense creditors (E)	2300	Expenditure Variance (E)	50
		Work in progress (J)	3000
		Work in progress (E)	2250
	£5400		£5400

Fixed Overhead Account

Expense creditors (J)	£21,500	Expenditure Variance (J)	£4,000
Expense creditors (E)	24,500	Work in progress (J)	17,500
Expenditure Variance (E)	3,000	Work in progress (E)	27,500
	£49,000		£49,000

Work in Progress Account

Stores (J)	£15,000	Usage Variance (E)		£1,000
Stores (E)	10,000	Idle Time Variance (J)		45
Wages (J)	5,225	Idle Time Variance (E)		50
Wages (E)	18,700	Labour Efficiency Variance (E)		1,100
Variable overhead (J)	3,000	Fixed Overhead Efficiency Vari-		
Variable overhead (E)	2,250	ance (E)		1,650
Fixed overhead (J)	17,500	Fixed Overhead Capacity Vari-		
Fixed overhead (E)	27,500	ance (E)		2,475
Usage Variance (J)	3,000	Finished goods:		
Mix Variance (J)	300	Materials (J)	£18,000	
Mix Variance (E)	450	Materials (E)	9,000	
Labour Efficiency Variance (J)	520	Wages (J)	6,000	
Fixed Overhead Efficiency Var. (J)	1,750	Wages (E)	18,000	
Fixed Overhead Capacity Var. (J)	875	Variable overhead (J)	3,000	
Fixed Overhead Calendar Var. (J)	875	Variable overhead (E)	2,250	
Fixed Overhead Calendar Var. (E)	1,375	Fixed overhead (J)	21,000	
		Fixed overhead (E)	24,750	
				102,000
	£108,320			£108,320

Finished Goods Account

Work in progress	£102,000	Cost of sales	£102,000

Cost of Sales Account

Finished goods	£102,000	Profit and loss	£102,000

Sales Account

Price Variance (J)	£2,000	Debtors (J and E)	£122,000
Quantity Variance (J)	1,250	Price Variance (E)	3,000
Mix Variance (J)	8,750	Mix Variance (E)	8,750
Quantity Variance (E)	1,750		
Profit and loss	120,000		
	£133,750		£133,750

Material Price Variance Account

Stores (J)	£500	Stores (E)	£250
		Profit and loss	250
	£500		£500

Material Usage Variance Account

Work in progress (E)	£1000	Work in progress (J)	£3000
Profit and loss	2000		
	£3000		£3000

Labour Rate Variance Account

Profit and loss	£1030	Wages (J)	£110
		Wages (E)	920
	£1030		£1030

Labour Mix Variance Account

Profit and loss	£750	Work in progress (J)	£300
		Work in progress (E)	450
	£750		£750

Labour Efficiency Variance Account

Work in progress	£1100	Work in progress (J)	£520
		Profit and loss (E)	580
	£1100		£1100

Idle Time Variance Account

Work in progress (J)	£45	Profit and loss	£95
Work in progress (E)	50		
	£95		£95

Variable Overhead Expenditure Variance Account

Variable overhead (J)	£100	Profit and loss	£150
Variable overhead (E)	50		
	£150		£150

Fixed Overhead Expenditure Variance Account

Fixed overhead (J)	£4000	Fixed overhead (E)	£3000
		Profit and loss	1000
	£4000		£4000

Fixed Overhead Efficiency Variance Account

Work in progress (E)	£1650	Work in progress (J)	£1750
Profit and loss	100		
	£1750		£1750

Fixed Overhead Capacity Variance Account

Work in progress (E)	£2475	Work in progress (J)	£875
		Profit and loss	1600
	£2475		£2475

Fixed Overhead Calendar Variance Account

Profit and loss	£2250	Work in progress (J)	£875
		Work in progress (E)	1375
	£2250		£2250

Sales Price Variance Account

Sales (E)	£3000	Sales (J)	£2000
		Profit and loss	1000
	£3000		£3000

Sales Quantity Variance Account

Profit and loss	£3000	Sales (J)	£1250
		Sales (E)	1750
	£3000		£3000

Sales Mix Variance Account

Sales (E)	£8750	Sales (J)	£8750

(c) Presentation to management

If Banstead Products Ltd had not installed a system of standard costing, only the actual results for the month of May could have been presented to management. A simple form would be as follows:

TRADING AND PROFIT AND LOSS ACCOUNT
for month of May (£'s)

	Jaydee	Eejay	Total	Jaydee	SALES Eejay	Total
Direct materials	£15,500	£9,750	£25,250	£62,000	£60,000	£122,000
Direct labour	5,115	17,780	22,895			
Variable expenses	3,100	2,300	5,400			
Fixed expenses	21,500	24,500	46,000			
Profit	16,785	5,670	22,455			
	£62,000	£60,000	£122,000	£62,000	£60,000	£122,000

This account gives some indication of what profit has been achieved during the month and how much was spent on each product. Profit of Jaydee was £16,785 (27% on turnover) while that of Eejay was £5,670 (9% on turnover), resulting in a total profit of £22,455 (18% on turnover). But the guidance it offers is very limited. Comparative figures for April this year and May last year might be shown, which would give some basis for comparison of results; that is all. What is really needed is a "yardstick" by which actual results can be compared with some pre-determined "target." Standard costing makes this possible. From the results produced by Banstead Products Ltd, the following profit and loss statement could be prepared:

PROFIT AND LOSS STATEMENT
for month of May (£'s)

	Jaydee	Eejay	Total	Jaydee	Eejay	Total
Budgeted sales				£50,000	£70,000	£120,000
Sales variances:						
Price	£2,000 *fav.*	£3,000 *adv.*	£1,000 *adv.*			
Quantity	1,250 *fav.*	1,750 *fav.*	3,000 *fav.*			
Mix	8,750 *fav.*	8,750 *adv.*	—			
				12,000 *fav.*	10,000 *adv.*	2,000 *fav.*
Actual sales				62,000	60,000	122,000
Less:						
Standard cost of sales:						
Materials	18,000	9,000	27,000			
Labour	6,000	18,000	24,000			
Variable overheads	3,000	2,250	5,250			
Fixed overheads	21,000	24,750	45,750			
				48,000	54,000	102,000
Standard net profit				14,000	6,000	20,000
Production variances:						
Materials:						
Price	500 *adv.*	250 *fav.*	250 *adv.*			
Usage	3,000 *fav.*	1,000 *adv.*	2,000 *fav.*			
				2,500 *fav.*	750 *adv.*	1,750 *fav.*
Labour:						
Rate	110 *fav.*	920 *fav.*	1,030 *fav.*			
Mix	300 *fav.*	450 *fav.*	750 *fav.*			
Efficiency	520 *fav.*	1,100 *adv.*	580 *adv.*			
Idle time	45 *adv.*	50 *adv.*	95 *adv.*			
				885 *fav.*	220 *fav.*	1,105 *fav.*
Variable overheads:						
Expenditure	100 *adv.*	50 *adv.*	150 *adv.*			
				100 *adv.*	50 *adv.*	150 *adv.*
Fixed overheads:						
Expenditure	4,000 *adv.*	3,000 *fav.*	1,000 *adv.*			
Efficiency	1,750 *fav.*	1,650 *adv.*	100 *fav.*			
Capacity	875 *fav.*	2,475 *adv.*	1,600 *adv.*			
Calendar	875 *fav.*	1,375 *fav.*	2,250 *fav.*			
				500 *adv.*	250 *fav.*	250 *adv.*
Total				2,785 *fav.*	330 *adv.*	2,455 *fav.*
Actual net profit				£16,785	£5,670	£22,455

This statement gives management a clear picture of the company's results for the month. Figures which are important for control purposes are set out in such a way that any efficiencies or inefficiencies are spotlighted. Expected results are compared with actual results and variances indicated to reveal where difference occurred. Thus management is enabled to operate the "management by exception" technique, reserving its time and effort for those items alone which require attention.

A brief report from the cost accountant should accompany this statement, explaining the main variances. A report on the statement might give such brief details as follow:

1. Sales variances

Consumer demand for Jaydee was greater than could reasonably have been expected, with the result that the proportion of Jaydee sales to total sales rose considerably; thus there was a large Mix Variance in favour of Jaydee. In one sales area it was even possible to increase the price of Jaydee from £10 to £11, showing a favourable variance of £2000.

On the other hand, consumer demand for Eejay was less than expected, which not only resulted in an unfavourable Mix Variance but led to a reduction in price in one area to meet stiff competition there; accordingly there was an adverse Price Variance of £3000, the price falling from £7 to £6 per unit.

2. Material variances

The price of material E142, which is consumed in the Jaydee process, rose by £5 to £155 per ton; but this was partly offset by a fall in price of material D10, used in the Eejay process, from £200 to £195 per ton. However, thanks to efficient handling of material E142, a favourable Usage Variance occurred which was only partly offset by inefficient handling of D10.

3. Labour variances

Owing to a difficulty in engaging male operatives, it was necessary to employ female employees temporarily on some operations normally under-taken by men. This resulted in favourable Mix Variances on both products. Although it was necessary to increase the rates for male operatives to attract them to the company, this was more than offset by a reduction in the rates paid to female employees, made possible by the current excess supply of female labour in the area. Labour efficiency is in line with material handling discussed under (2) above. A small amount of idle time occurred through machine breakdowns, probably due to the overloading of machines. It will be noted by members of the board that a request for new machinery had already been presented for their approval.

4. Variable Overhead Variances

During the month, small rises in the cost of supplies from outside sources occurred. These were, of course, beyond our control.

5. Fixed Overhead Variances

Owing to the success of Jaydee in the markets, some staff and facilities were transferred to this product from Eejay. In addition, rates were increased by the local authority.

One extra day was worked during the month owing to the postponement of the firm's annual outing, which resulted in a favourable Calendar Variance. The increased capacity available was efficiently utilised by the Jaydee process but, as mentioned under (3) above, inefficiency occurred in the Eejay process.

6. Final comment

Investigations into variances and methods are continuing. The final result this month is a good one, showing a profit of £2455 more than expected.

EXAMINATION QUESTIONS

1. Raw Material Price Variance may be reflected at either of two stages in the cost accounting procedure. Illustrate each method separately by posting all the accounts affected where raw material at an actual cost of £1020 is bought and consumed in one month, the standard cost being £1000.

What other main factor may give rise to variance in material costs? Select a single example from practice and show the cost accounting journal entry involved.   [C.W.A.

2. From the data below prepare a tabulation to include analysed variances as well as the details given:

	Departments	
Standard details:	*X*	*Y*
Hours, when working at normal capacity	4000	2000
Overhead hourly rate	£0·50	£2
Allowed hours for actual production	4000	1600
Actual details:		
Hours	4150	1550
Overhead	£2020	£3750

[C.W.A.

3. It sometimes happens that a favourable variance from one standard is directly related to an adverse variance from another, *e.g.* the purchase of processed materials may cause an adverse Material Price Variance but a favourable Labour Efficiency Variance. Give *two* examples, other than the one given above, and explain how you would present and interpret the analysis of variances in such cases.   [C.W.A.

4. In Department X the following data are submitted for the week ended 20th February:

Standard output for 40-hour week	1400 units
Standard fixed overhead	£140
Actual output	1200 units
Actual hours worked	32
Actual fixed overhead	£150

Compute the variances from standard.   [C.C.A.

5. From the following basic data calculate:

(*a*) Efficiency Variance
(*b*) Volume Variance
(*c*) Calendar Variance

Item	Budget	Actual
Number of working days	20	22
Standard man-hours per day	8,000	8,400
Output per man-hour in units	1·0	1·2
Total unit output	160,000	221,760
Standard overhead rate per man-hour	£0·10	

[C.W.A.

6. Doers Ltd operates a standard costing system. In connection with the weekly cost report for Process 9 you have been informed:

(*a*) That the standard costs per hour of the process, based on a normal week of 40 hours' work, are:

Wages	£0·90
Variable expenses	0·25
Fixed expenses	1·25
	———
	£2·40
	═══
Standard output in units per hour	20

(*b*) That the following information has been recorded in respect of the process for the week ended 23rd November:

Hours worked	36
Non-productive hours (waiting work)	4
Total hours paid for	40
Output	850 units
Actual wages paid	£37
Actual variable expenses	£12
Actual fixed expenses	£50

You are required to compute the variances relating to Process 9 for the week.   [C.A. (November 1962)

7. Delaware Ltd has computed the following information for the calendar year, 19—:

Budgeted production	10,000 units
Budgeted fixed overhead	£5,000
Budgeted total machine hours	25,000 hours
Budgeted variable overhead	£6,000

It is also found that each unit requires 1 lb of raw material at a standard cost of £0·25 per lb. Labour rates are £0·33½ per hour and a unit of output requires 1½ standard hours.

Labour rates have been stable, but raw material prices have proved to be 5% above standard.

In the present budget period (March) the following information is obtained:

Fixed expenses	£550
Normal machine hours	2000 hours
Machine hours paid for (these differ from the standard time because of a strike)	1600 hours
Idle time (machine)	60 hours
Actual production	450 units
Raw materials	£125
Variable overhead	£280
Direct wages	£210

You are required to set out the variances under their separate heads for the period March 19— showing precisely how each is calculated, together with variances summary and analysis.   [C.A.

8. A manufacturing company operates a system of standard costing and budgetary control. The following costing information relates to Department 4 for period 6 ended 27 August:

Work in progress

Standard value at 30th July	£6,000
Transferred to finished stock in period at standard value	£14,400

Raw material

Issued to production during period at standard value	£8,200

Production

Budgeted production in direct labour standard hours	6,360 hours
Actual production in direct labour standard hours	7,000 hours

Labour

Wages rate per standard hour	£0·30
Actual direct labour hours	7,200 hours
Actual wages paid	£2,340

Departmental overheads

	Budgeted	Actual
Variable	£2,500	£2,700
Fixed	1,700	1,800
	£4,200	£4,500

Overheads rate per standard hour   £0·66

Using the above information you are required:

(a) To prepare a cost and variance schedule bringing out:

    (i) Activity and efficiency ratios.
    (ii) Labour efficiency and rates of pay variances.
    (iii) Overhead volume and expense variances.

(b) To explain briefly what is meant by each of the ratios and variances brought out; and

(c) To prepare the work in progress control account.   [C.A.(S)

9. In standard costing, certain "ratios" are used to illustrate the effective use of the resources of the company. Define these ratios and illustrate your answer by using the following figures, which are in respect of a four-week period. In this period there was a special one-day holiday due to a national event.

Standard working: eight hours per day, five days per week
Maximum capacity: 50 employees
Actually working: 40 employees

Actual hours expected to be worked per four weeks	6400 hours
Standard hours expected to be earned per four weeks	8000 hours
Actual hours worked in the four-week period	6000 hours
Standard hours earned in the four-week period	7000 hours
	[C.W.A.

10. The Alfa Manufacturing Company has, at your instigation, introduced a system of standard costing. The operating statement covering the first three months has just been prepared and is detailed below. Prepare a report for the management of the organisation in non-technical language outlining the meaning and significance of the figures disclosed.

Operating statement for three months ended . . .

		Budget	Variation from budget (increase/ decrease)	(increase/ decrease)
Sales		£100,000		£4,500
Standard cost of sales		75,000		7,500
Standard gross profit		25,000		3,000
Selling expenses	£6,500		£500	
Administration expenses	4,500		150	
Research expenses	5,000		650	
		16,000		300
Standard net profit		£9,000		£2,700

Factory variances   *Favourable Adverse*

	Favourable	Adverse
Material price	£50	
Material usage	200	
Labour rate		£550
Labour mix		210
Labour efficiency	65	
Variable overhead expenditure		10
Fixed overhead expenditure		375
Fixed overhead calendar	125	
Fixed overhead efficiency		140
	£440	£1,285

845

Total variation from budget profit   £3,545

[C.C.A.

11. The weekly budget for performance and overhead costs in a manufacturing department is based upon the following figures:

Number of operators	20
Working week	40 hours
Budgeted lost time	$12\frac{1}{2}\%$ of total hours worked
Budgeted efficiency	one standard hour per actual hour worked

Budgeted overheads:

Fixed	£350
Variable with operator hours	£525
Variable with output	£175

Detail, on a suitable statement, the overhead variances which have arisen in a week when the actual performance and costs were as follows:

Net operator working hours	620
Standard hours produced	650

Overheads:

Fixed	£350
Variable with operator hours	£510
Variable with output	£190

[C.W.A.

12. Nightlight Ltd are manufacturers of electric torches. The company operates a standard costing system. Standard figures for Model I torches, based on production of 8000 torches per month, are as follows:

Standard cost per torch:

Components	£0·10
Labour	0·07½
Variable expenses	0·02½
Fixed expenses	0·05
	£0·25

Standard selling price per torch   £0·33½

Stocks of Model I components and finished torches on 31st October 1964 and on 30th November 1964 were established by physical stock-taking, as follows:

	31st October 1964	30th November 1964
Sets of components	12,000	8,100
Finished torches	3,000	3,600

There was no work in progress on either date.

The following information relates to Model I for the month of November 1964:

(a) Number of sets of components purchased		5000
(b) Cost of sets of components purchased		£550
(c) Finished torches produced		8400
(d) Actual hours worked		2000
(e) Idle time in hours		100
(f) Direct wages paid (for 2100 hours)		£670
(g) Variable expenses		£220
(h) Fixed expenses		£380

(i) All finished torches produced were either sold at standard selling prices or are included in stocks of finished torches on 30th November.

You are required to produce a profit statement for Model I torches for November 1964, reconciling standard profit on actual sales with actual profit and providing a full analysis of variances. Working papers should be included with your answer, showing how all figures used in the profit statement are arrived at.   [C.A., (1965)

13. The standard mix of a compound of four materials is as follows:

Material	A	B	C	D
% by weight	30%	40%	20%	10%
Price per lb	£0·06½	£0·07½	£0·17½	£0·15

This compound should be used at the rate of 4lb of compound per cu ft of production. During a period in which 1000 cu ft of finished product were made, actual usage was:

Material	A	B	C	D
Lb used	1180	1580	830	440
Price per lb	£0·06	£0·08½	£0·16½	£0·15

Present these figures to the management of an undertaking where standard costing is used.   [C.W.A.

14. A plastic floor covering is produced in rolls 72 in wide and 60 ft long. The materials used are mixed in batches and fed into a continuous processing machine.

The standard mixture used in a batch, which should produce 600 square yards of floor covering, is as follows:

1000 lb material A at £0·10 per lb
600 lb material B at £0·15 per lb
100 gallons material C at £0·80 per gallon

During a period in which 1830 standard sized rolls are produced, 120 batches of materials were made up, and the actual usage of materials was found to be as follows:

114,000 lb material A at £0·11 per lb
75,000 lb material B at £0·16 per lb
12,500 gallons material C at £0·85 per gallon.

Present figures to management to explain the variances arising during the period. [C.W.A.

15. A company manufacturing a special type of facing tile, 12 in × 8 in × ½ in, uses a system of standard costing. The standard mix of the compound used for making the tiles is:

1200 lb material A at £0·07 per lb
500 lb material B at £0·15 per lb
800 lb material C at £0·17½ per lb

This compound should produce 12,000 sq ft of tiles of ½ inch thickness.
During a period in which 100,000 tiles of the standard size were produced, the material usage was:

7000 lb material A at £0·07½ per lb
3000 lb material B at £0·16 per lb
5000 lb material C at £0·18¼ per lb

Present the cost figures for the period showing:

(a) Material Price Variance.
(b) Material Mixture Variance.
(c) Yield Variance. [C.W.A.

16. The standard mixture per batch for the manufacture of a certain product is:

Material A	30 lb at £0·15 per lb
B	30 lb at £0·08½ per lb
C	50 lb at £0·05 per lb
D	5 gal at £0·60 per gallon

This mixture should produce 100 units of the product.
During a period in which 70 batches were made the following materials were used:

2200 lb material A at £0·15½ per lb
2100 lb material B at £0·07½ per lb
3400 lb material C at £0·06 per lb
360 gal material D at £0·62½ per gallon

Actual production totalled 7100 units of the product.
Compute the variances which you would present to management when operating a system of standard costing. [C.W.A.

17. The sales and product cost budget for an engineering company for November, 19—, is as follows:

Product	Units	Sales value	Product cost
A	1,000	£10,000	£9,000
B	500	8,000	6,000
C	1,000	12,000	10,800
D	500	18,000	14,200
		£48,000	£40,000

When the analysis of sales for November has been completed, the following statement of actual sales is compiled:

Product	Units	Sales value
A	920	£9,200
B	700	11,000
C	1,200	14,600
D	200	7,800
		£42,600

Calculate the variation in profit from that budgeted, and show how much is due to the factors of sales price, volume and mix.   [C.W.A.

18. The AB Co. Ltd budgets to sell, in the month of January, 2500 lb of Product A at £3 per lb; 1200 lb of Product B at £2 per lb; and 2000 lb of Product C at £2·50 per lb. During the month, actual sales were 2000 lb of Product A for £5500; 1800 lb of Product B for £4050; and 2200 lb of Product C for £4950. Budgeted costs of A (£2 per unit), B (£1·50 per unit) and C (£2 per unit) were in line with actual.

You are required to calculate the effect of sales variances (Price, Quantity and Mix) on budgeted profit, and to prepare a statement showing how each product has contributed to the increase or decrease in budgeted profit.
[C.C.A.

19. The sales budget of Blueblack Ltd for the month of October was as follows:

Product	Quantity	Standard selling price each	Standard sales	Standard profit on budgeted sales
A	1000	£1	£1000	£100
B	400	£1·50	600	100
			£1600	£200

The actual sales in October were:

Product	Quantity	Actual selling price	Actual sales
A	1050	£1·10	£1155
B	500	£1·70	850
			£2005

You are required to show the budgeted and actual sales for the month of October together with the relative variances, as you would expect them to appear in the costing profit and loss statement of Blueblack Ltd for the month of October.   [C.A.

20. In accounting for materials, what do you understand by:

(a) Usage Variance,
(b) Mix Variance,
(c) Yield Variance?

Give examples of each of these variances.

As the management accountant of a manufacturing concern, what steps would you advise to remedy adverse variances of this kind?   [C.A. (S)

21. It has been stated that one of the objects of a scheme of standard costing and budgetary control is to provide a means of measuring the efficiency of the operations of a company and that this is not available from historical costing procedures.

Discuss this statement, using as a background a factory manufacturing a wide range of products in a relatively small number of processes.

Bring out clearly what you believe to be the differences between standard costing and budgetary control on the one hand and historical costing on the other. [C.A. (S)

22. A firm which manufacturers a single product (a drink, sold in cases of 144 bottles) installed a standard costing system at the beginning of January 1968. Standard cost and revenue data are shown in Appendix I. After the end of January the new management accountant produced the report given in Appendix II. He claimed that the system, by allowing each manager's performance to be evaluated against a target, should greatly increase efficiency.

However, at a management committee meeting his report was not received very warmly and the following comments were made:

(1) The Sales Manager, "The sales volume variance, which you say is my responsibility, reflects the recent unexpected ice and snow. In fact, I think we have done a good job; last month our sales dropped by less than those of our competitors. Anyway, I think part of the blame for this variance lies with the factory. I could have sold at least 500 more cases if I could have got them from production. I don't think your report means much."

(2) The Purchasing Manager, "That price variance reflects increases in taxation of 5%, but I persuaded our supplier not to pass on the whole increase. Besides, it is only a 2% variance and I do not believe that I should be judged against such a tight standard. And another thing, how can we use this kind of data for pricing our products. Your figures are based on historical material prices and they do not reflect the 14% increase in the market price of material following devaluation."

(3) The Chairman, "If fixed overheads are indeed fixed, I do not see what that capacity variance tells us."

You are required to:

(a) Answer shortly the above comments and explain briefly any reservations you may have about the accountant's report.

(b) Suggest any amendments you would make to the report so that it will be as helpful as possible to management in planning and control.

APPENDIX I

STANDARD COST AND REVENUE DATA

	per case
Materials 10 lb. at £0·1	£1·0
Labour 4 hours at £0·37½	1·5
Overheads* Standard recovery rate	2·0
Standard Profit	0·5
Standard Selling Price	5·0

* Fixed overheads per month are made up of: administration £2000; factory overheads £13,000 and advertising £5000. Normal volume is assumed to be 10,000 cases a month, which is also the maximum that could be produced in January as only a small staff is employed at this time of year.

APPENDIX II

BUDGET PERFORMANCE REPORT

January 1968

(*unfavourable variances in brackets*)

Budgeted sales at standard price			
10,000 cases at £5 per case			£50,000
Less Sales volume variance			
1000 cases at £5 per case			(5,000)
Actual sales at standard price			45,000
Less standard cost of sales			40,500
Standard profit on actual sales			4,500
Less Manufacturing variances			
Materials price variance		£(180)	
Labour efficiency variance		(759)	
Fixed overheads:			
Expense variance	£(1,000)		
Under recovery (capacity) variance	(2,000)	(3,000)	(3,939)
Actual profit			£561

Commentary

9000 cases were produced and sold. No stocks of finished products were held at the start or the end of the month.

The sales volume variance is due to the sales department selling 1000 cases less than budgeted. Responsibility: Sales Manager.

The material price variance results from a 2% increase in material prices. Responsibility: Purchasing Manager.

The labour efficiency variance, which results from using 4·225 instead of 4·000 labour hours per case, is due to inadequate supervision. Responsibility: Production Manager.

The overhead expense variance results from advertising costs being £1000 over budget. All other fixed costs were as budgeted.

The overhead capacity variance (1000 cases at the standard recovery rate) reflects lower than budgeted production. Responsibility: Production Manager.   [J. Dip. M.A.

CHAPTER IX

BUDGETARY CONTROL

DEFINITION

BUDGETARY control appears to have been operating for a considerable time—about two centuries in fact—in Government departments in the U.K., where it is necessary to attempt to equate revenue with expenditure. On a smaller scale, the idea of budgeting is familiar to most people who have to balance their earnings with their expenditure. However, it is only during the last fifty years that this vital concept of cost control has been tried and developed in industry. Since its introduction to industry and commerce, however, adoption has been spreading rapidly, particularly during the last 25 years, and it is true to say that most large companies in the U.S.A., U.K. and Europe now operate the system. In fact many of the smaller-sized companies are using budgets in some form or another as a tool of management. Some small concerns have partial budgetary control whereby only one aspect of the business is considered, *e.g.* the sales budget. However, the greatest benefit accrues when budgets are set and co-ordinated for all activities of the business.

A *budget* is a predetermined statement of management policy during a given period which provides a standard for comparison with the results actually achieved.

Budgetary control is a system of controlling costs which includes the preparation of budgets, co-ordinating the departments and establishing responsibilities, comparing actual performance with that budgeted and acting upon results to achieve maximum profitability.

Budgeting is essentially concerned with planning, and can be broadly illustrated by comparison with the routine a ship's captain follows on each voyage. Before the voyage he will plan his route, taking into account such factors as shipping hazards, tides and possible adverse weather forecasts. During the voyage he will check on his plans and record any unusual conditions. If necessary he may even have to deviate from his plan if prevailing circumstances require it. On completion of the voyage he will compare the conditions he encountered with those he expected and use the experience gained in planning similar voyages in the future. This simple analogy is perhaps not as detailed as it should be, but it does serve to illustrate the basic practice used in budgetary control.

Certain fundamental principles can be outlined and these are:

195

1. Establish a plan or target of performance which co-ordinates all the activities of the business.
2. Record the actual performance.
3. Compare the actual performance with that planned.
4. Calculate the differences, or variances, and analyse the reasons for them.
5. Act immediately, if necessary, to remedy the situation.

Budgets are essentially forward looking: they provide yardsticks for purposes of comparison. They are concerned with people, in that they delegate responsibilities to one person, whether he is head of a Government department, a company or a small budget centre. A budget is a means to an end, not an end in itself. It covers the area of responsibility of one specified person, so that his performance can be measured at the end of a budget period. It follows, therefore, that the budget should be prepared in conjunction with those who are to be responsible for achieving the budgeted performance. In this way a head of department knows his goal, which tends to induce precision and confidence. This technique, with its stress on personal responsibility, differs from standard costing, for the latter is concerned with standards for products or services.

THE OBJECTIVES OF BUDGETARY CONTROL

Briefly, the main objectives of budgetary control are:

1. To combine the ideas of all levels of management in the preparation of the budget.
2. To co-ordinate all the activities of the business.
3. To centralise control.
4. To decentralise responsibility onto each manager involved.
5. To act as a guide for management decisions when unforeseeable conditions affect the budget.
6. To plan and control income and expenditure so that maximum profitability is achieved.
7. To direct capital expenditure in the most profitable direction.
8. To ensure that sufficient working capital is available for the efficient operation of the business.
9. To provide a yardstick against which actual results can be compared.
10. To show management where action is needed to remedy a situation.

ORGANISATION FOR BUDGETARY CONTROL

It is essential that there should be an efficient organisation if budgetary control is to be operated effectively. Budgetary control is not only an accounting exercise, but a tool of management at all levels. In organising a system, it is essential to obtain the full co-operation of each member of the management team. A number of preliminaries will be necessary if staff are to have confidence in the system; these include:

1. *The creation of budget centres.* Centres or departments should be established, for each of which budgets will be set with the help of the head of department concerned.

2. *The introduction of adequate accounting records.* It is imperative that the accounting system should be able to record and analyse the information required. A chart of accounts should be maintained which corresponds with the budget centres.

3. *The general instruction in technique* of all concerned in operating the system. Each person must know what a budget is, what it hopes to accomplish and how he fits into the plan. He must feel that he is capable of carrying out the budgeted programme.

4. *The preparation of an organisation chart.* This defines the functional responsibilities of each member of management, and ensures that he knows his position in the company and his relationship to other members. The organisation chart will obviously depend upon the nature and size of the company but a simplified specimen is given in Fig. 4

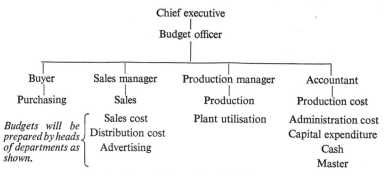

Fig. 4.—*Organisation chart for budgetary control.*

to show the general principles involved. Other budgets such as the raw materials or labour budget may be prepared by heads of departments; for example by the accountant in conjunction with the production manager. It should be appreciated that in the preparation of each of these budgets the accountant will play a big part, especially those involving costs, such as the sales cost budget.

5. *The establishment of a budget committee.* In small companies a budget officer or the accountant may co-ordinate all the work connected with budgets, but in large companies a budget committee is often established to formulate a general programme for preparing budgets and

exercising overall control. The chief executive of the company may establish guiding principles but usually he delegates the responsibility for operating the system to the budget officer as secretary of the committee. This committee is composed of the chief executive, budget officer and heads of the main departments such as those shown in Fig. 4. Each member will prepare his own initial budget or budgets, which will then be considered by the committee, and all budgets will be co-ordinated. Usually many changes are necessary before the budgets can be finally integrated and then approved.

The main functions of the committee are:

(a) To provide historical information to help managers in forecasting.

(b) To issue instructions regarding budget requirements, deadline dates for the receipt of budgets, etc.

(c) To define the general policies of management in relation to the budget.

(d) To advise in the preparation of budgets.

(e) To review budgets.

(f) To suggest revisions and amendments to budgets.

(g) To approve budgets.

(h) To ensure that budgets are submitted in due time.

(i) To prepare budget summaries where necessary.

(j) To prepare the master budget after functional budgets have been approved.

(k) To analyse comparison of budgeted and actual results, and to recommend corrective action where necessary.

(l) To co-ordinate the budget programme.

6. *The preparation of a budget manual.* This is defined (by the I.C.W.A.) as "a document which sets out, the responsibilities of the persons engaged in, the routine of, and the forms and records required for, budgetary control." It is usually in loose-leaf form, so that alterations can easily be made as and when required; appropriate sections can be issued to executives requiring them. An index will be provided so that information can be located quickly. Such a manual will usually prove invaluable, as it will include such information as:

(a) Description of the system and its objectives.

(b) Procedure to be adopted in operating the system.

(c) Definition of responsibilities and duties.

(d) The reports and statements required for each budget period.

(e) The accounts code in use.

(f) Deadline dates by which data are to be submitted.

7. *Budget periods.* There is no "right" period for any budget: budget periods vary between short term and long term. If a business

experiences seasonal fluctuations, the budget period will probably extend over one seasonal cycle. If this cycle covers (say) two or three years the long term budget would cover that period, while short term budgets would be prepared perhaps monthly for control purposes.

Short term budgeting is usually costly to prepare and operate, while long term budgeting may be considerably affected by unforeseen conditions. Budget periods frequently used in industry vary between one month and one year, the latter probably being the most commonly used as it fits in with the normally accepted accounting period. However, forecasts of much longer periods than a year may be used in the case of capital expenditure budgets, for example, which must be planned well in advance. This is particularly so in the electricity industry, where the need for new power stations must be forecast possibly ten years ahead.

A common practice in industry is to have a series of budget periods. Thus the sales budget may cover the next five years, while production and cost budgets may cover only one year. These yearly budgets will be broken down into quarterly or even monthly periods.

Where long term budgets are operated, it is usual to supplement them by short term ones. Thus it is necessary for industries with heavy capital expenditure, such as the aircraft industry, to plan ahead for five to ten years so as to outline the general policy to be pursued, but short term budgets of one year or less may be produced to enable management to control the day-to-day running of the business. The short term budget will be much more detailed than the long term one.

8. *The key factor.* This is the factor the extent of whose influence must first be assessed in order to ensure that functional budgets are reasonably capable of fulfilment. The key factor—known variously as the "limiting" or "governing" or "principal budget" factor—is of vital importance. It may not be the same for each budget period, as circumstances may change. It determines priorities in functional budgets, and among the many key factors which may affect budgeting are the following:

(*a*) Materials
    (i) Availability of supply.
    (ii) Restrictions imposed by licences, quotas, etc.

(*b*) Labour
    (i) General shortage.
    (ii) Shortage in certain key processes.

(*c*) Plant
    (i) Insufficient capacity due to lack of capital
    (ii) . . . or lack of space
    (iii) . . . or lack of markets.
    (iv) Bottlenecks in certain key processes.

(*d*) Sales
    (i) Low market demand.
    (ii) Shortages of experienced salesmen.
    (iii) Insufficient advertising due to lack of money.

(*e*) Management
    (i) Lack of capital, restricting policy.
    (ii) Lack of "know-how."
    (iii) Inefficient executives.
    (iv) Insufficient research into product design and methods.

The factor which is most often the key factor in industry is probably sales demand. Very often the success or otherwise of budgetary control rests on the forecast of sales during the budget period. If the sales figure proves to be inaccurate most of the budgets will be affected.

The sales forecast and production forecast must be correlated. Usually the sales manager will prepare his forecast, and the production manager will consider whether he can produce a sufficient quantity to meet the expected sales demand. If the sales manager can sell more than the production manager can produce, then production will be the key factor; conversely, if the sales manager feels he is unable to market the possible output of the factory, sales demand is a key factor. When the sales manager and the production manager agree on a figure, the accountant must ensure that the company's financial resources can support the expenditure involved.

The key factor is not necessarily a permanent factor; indeed it is often only temporary. In the long run, opportunities should be provided for management to overcome the limitations imposed by key factors. It may be possible to issue new shares in the company or to accumulate internal funds to finance new developments or improved plant and machinery; alternative sources of supply of raw materials or substitutes for raw materials required in production may be found; labour may be attracted to the area or new operatives trained by the company; experts may be appointed to the management team; new product designs or effective advertising may stimulate sales.

In the short run, it may be possible partially to overcome key factor limitations by working overtime or shifts, sub-contracting work, hiring new machinery, introducing new methods, buying new equipment on hire purchase, providing incentive schemes or giving preference to jobs which yield the greatest contribution per hour.

    9. *Level of activity.* It will be necessary to establish the normal level of activity, that is, the level the company can reasonably be expected to achieve. This level is important in forecasting, for example, material and labour requirements, and particularly production overhead budgets which are to be recovered on machine-hour rates.

FUNCTIONAL BUDGETS

A functional budget is one which relates to a function of the business, *e.g.* the sales budget. Functional budgets are prepared for each function and are subsidiary to the master budget for the business. There are many types of functional budget, depending on the size and nature of the business, but those which are frequently used include:

1. Sales.
2. Selling and distribution cost.
3. Production.
4. Production cost.
5. Materials.
6. Purchasing.
7. Labour.
8. Production overhead.
9. Plant utilisation.
10. Capital expenditure.
11. Administrative cost.
12. Cash.

Budgetary control relates expenditure to the person responsible for each function, thus affording an effective method of control. It is an important principle of the system that an executive is held responsible *only* for expenditure within his control.

SALES BUDGET

In most companies the sales budget is not only the most important but also the most difficult to prepare. It forecasts what the company can reasonably expect to sell to its customers during the budget period. The company earns profits only when it sells its products, not when it produces them. It is no good producing goods that are not likely to be sold and for which there is a limited demand. In some industries it is necessary to establish that the product will sell even before it is produced —a large luxury liner would not be built without a prospective customer agreeing to buy it on completion. On the other hand, a company producing bars of chocolate would go ahead with manufacture in the hope that the sales manager's forecasts were reasonably accurate.

It is only during "boom" times, when a company has a full order book, that the sales budget is of less than prime importance. In normal times of keen competition the sales forecast must be realistic and whether or not the sales manager actually prepares the budget it is still his responsibility. The sales forecast is usually based on a quantitative statement which is analysed under various classifications, such as:

1. Products or groups of similar products.
2. Territories, areas or countries.

3. Salesmen or agents.
4. Types of customer.
5. Period: quarters, months, etc.

When preparing the budget, the sales manager will work closely with the budget officer, the accountant and his own staff. A number of aids will be used in estimating sales, among which are:

1. *Reports by salesmen.* Each salesman will be requested to prepare a detailed estimate of sales he expects to be able to make in his area during the budget period. Salesmen are "on the spot" and can appraise the prevailing local conditions. For example, they can note the effect of advertising both by the company and by competitors, the movement of population, the local employment situation, the trend in sales requirements and the activities of competitors.

2. *Analysis of sales.* Statistical analysis of sales will show trends to date and any cyclical or seasonal fluctuations. From the analysis it should be possible to suggest future trends. An estimate should be made of the total market demand for the type of product made by the company, and of the proportion of this demand which the company can expect to achieve. In analysing sales, considerable help can often be obtained from Government publications, statistical reports produced by trade associations and economic intelligence units.

3. *Market analysis.* Many large companies either employ their own analysts or the services of a firm of market analysts to report on the state of the market, fashion trends, the sort of product design required by customers, the activities of competitors and the prices the consumers are likely to pay.

4. *Company conditions.* Any change in company policy or methods should be considered. For example, a new design for a product, the introduction of a new product, new or additional advertising campaigns should all have some effect on a sales budget. Other possible changes might include the setting up of an after-sales service or new channels of distribution.

5. *Business conditions.* A change in political or economic conditions should be noted and foreseeable changes considered. For example, increased Government spending on public developments and schools will lead to increased demand for a wide range of products. The trend of prices on the market should be followed and regard taken of Governmental influences on prices, such as purchase tax.

6. *Special conditions.* The sales manager should watch any new external developments with a view to introducing company products. Thus the compulsory introduction of a "smokeless zone" in a sales area would lead to increased demand for electric heaters, anthracite, etc. When an industry manufactures products for another industry it will be necessary to analyse the trend of sales in that industry: a tyre manufacturer would estimate the sales of cars on which his tyres were

used. Restrictions on imports imposed by a foreign country could seriously affect the company's exports. A flood might affect one business adversely and others favourably.

When the sales forecast is eventually completed it is evaluated and becomes the sales budget, which is presented to the budget committee for approval. The sales and production budgets will then be co-ordinated and form the basis for the preparation of the master budget.

Example

The GPJ Engineering Co. Ltd operate three sales divisions, which sell three branded products G, P and J. The budget committee of the company require a sales budget for the next year. To meet this objective the following information has been made available:

Budgeted sales for the current year are as follows:

Product	Division 1	Division 2	Division 3
G	8,000 at £5	12,000 at £5	12,000 at £5
P	6,000 at £10	16,000 at £10	8,000 at £10
J	4,000 at £20	24,000 at £20	10,000 at £20

Actual sales for the current year, based on actual sales to date and estimated sales for the remainder of the year, are:

Product	Division 1	Division 2	Division 3
G	10,000 at £5	16,000 at £5	14,000 at £5
P	4,000 at £10	20,000 at £10	10,000 at £10
J	2,000 at £20	20,000 at £20	8,000 at £20

Discussions with the divisional sales managers have resulted in the following suggestions and estimates:

It is found that Product G is selling at a higher rate than expected. Investigations have revealed that it is popular and possibly under-priced. It is considered that even if the price were increased to £5·50 it would still find a ready market. On the other hand it is observed that Product J is not selling at the expected rate. Investigations have revealed that customers feel it to be over-priced, and that the market could absorb more if the price were reduced by £1. The management has agreed in principle that these price changes should be effected.

The divisional sales managers have prepared estimates based on these price changes and on reports from salesmen, as follows:

PERCENTAGE INCREASE/DECREASE ON PREVIOUS BUDGET

Product	Division 1	Division 2	Division 3
G	+30	+40	+20
P	-10	+30	-10
J	+10	+20	+10

In view of these estimates an intensive advertising campaign is decided on to boost sales of Product P, particular attention being paid to Divisions 1 and 3. It is thought that this may lead to an increase in sales of P as follows: Division 1, +10%; Division 2, +5%; Division 3, +20%.

It is the practice in the GPJ company to prepare sales budgets which show, in addition to the budget, the budgeted sales and the actual sales for the current period.

SALES BUDGET

Period . . . .

Division	Product	Budget for future period Quan.	Pr.	Val.	Budget for current period Quan.	Pr.	Val.	Actual sales for current period Quan.	Pr.	Val.
1	G	10,400	5·5	£57,200	8,000	5	£40,000	10,000	5	£50,000
	P	5,940	10	59,400	6,000	10	60,000	4,000	10	40,000
	J	4,400	19	83,600	4,000	20	80,000	2,000	20	40,000
	Total	20,740		200,200	18,000		180,000	16,000		130,000
2	G	16,800	5·5	92,400	12,000	5	60,000	16,000	5	80,000
	P	21,840	10	218,400	16,000	10	160,000	20,000	10	200,000
	J	28,800	19	547,200	24,000	20	480,000	20,000	20	400,000
	Total	67,440		858,000	52,000		700,000	56,000		680,000
3	G	14,400	5·5	79,200	12,000	5	60,000	14,000	5	70,000
	P	8,640	10	86,400	8,000	10	80,000	10,000	10	100,000
	J	11,000	19	209,000	10,000	20	200,000	8,000	20	160,000
	Total	34,040		374,600	30,000		340,000	32,000		330,000
Total	G	41,600	5·5	228,800	32,000	5	160,000	40,000	5	200,000
	P	36,420	10	364,200	30,000	10	300,000	34,000	10	340,000
	J	44,200	19	839,800	38,000	20	760,000	30,000	20	600,000
	Total	122,220		£1,432,800	100,000		£1,220,000	104,000		£1,140,000

SELLING AND DISTRIBUTION COST BUDGET

This budget is the forecast of all costs incurred in selling and distributing the company's products during the budget period. It is closely concerned with the sales budget in that it is mainly based on the volume of sales projected for the period. However, it must be noted that expenditure may be contemplated during the budget period which will have no effect on sales until a future budget period. For example, an advertising campaign may be launched this year which will have no immediate effect but should influence sales in the future.

The sales manager will be responsible for the budget, but will co-operate with the budget officer, the sales office manager, distribution manager and either the advertising manager or the company's advertising agents. Advertising is becoming an increasingly important and costly item in selling-cost budgets, so much so that some companies now prepare an advertising budget. To give some idea of its importance, one U.K. company alone has in the past spent nearly £100 million a year on advertising and publicity, and it is foreseeable that this figure will increase in the future.

Example

The budget committee of the GPJ Engineering Co. Ltd requires a selling and distribution cost budget for the next year. It is to be based on:

1. The sales budget (*see* previous Example).
2. The selling and distribution cost budget for the current period.
3. The actual selling and distribution costs for the current period, where appropriate and where possible.

The selling and distribution budget for the present period is:

SELLING AND DISTRIBUTION COST BUDGET (a) THIS YEAR

Element of cost	Division 1	2	3	Total
Direct selling expenses	£	£	£	£
Salesmen's salaries	2,500	8,000	4,950	15,450
commission	9,000	35,000	17,000	61,000
expenses	1,200	3,500	2,100	6,800
Entertaining	600	2,800	1,600	5,000
Car expenses	1,800	4,500	2,800	9,100
depreciation	1,500	4,800	2,850	9,150
Total	16,600	58,600	31,300	106,500
Sales office expenses				
Salaries	1,600	2,800	2,000	6,400
Rent and rates	200	400	300	900
Light and heat	100	150	120	370
Postage, stationery and telephone	450	950	750	2,150
Depreciation	50	120	80	250
General expenses	120	280	150	550
Total	2,520	4,700	3,400	10,620
Advertising				
Press	2,500	6,000	4,000	12,500
Television	6,000	14,000	9,000	29,000
Radio	1,200	1,800	1,500	4,500
Coupon offers	4,500	9,600	7,400	21,500
Shop window displays	800	2,000	1,000	3,800
Total	15,000	33,400	22,900	71,300
Distribution expenses				
Warehouse wages	1,200	3,500	2,200	6,900
Divers' wages	1,250	3,000	2,000	6,250
Rent and rates	500	1,000	800	2,300
Vehicle expenses	2,500	6,000	4,500	13,000
depreciation	1,500	3,600	2,400	7,500
General expenses	200	500	300	1,000
Total	7,150	17,600	12,200	36,950
Total all items	£41,270	£114,300	£69,800	£225,370

The divisional sales managers, in conjunction with the cost accountant, personnel manager, warehouse manager and advertising executive, have decided on the following items which affect the budget:

1. Salesmen's salaries to be increased by 10%.
2. An extra salesman at £500 per annum is required in Divisions 2 and 3.

3. Salesmen's commission to continue at 5% of sales.

4. An extra commission of 5% will be paid to salesmen for additional budgeted sales of Product P during the advertising campaign.

5. Salesmen's expenses and entertainment expenses to be increased by 5%. Entertainment to be additionally increased in Divisions 2 and 3 by £160 for each division.

6. Car expenses to be increased by 5%.

7. Owing to the extra salesman in each of Divisions 2 and 3, car depreciation in those divisions to be increased by £200 each.

8. Salaries of office staff to be increased by 5%.

9. An extra clerk is to be employed in Division 1 and in Division 3, each to be paid £600 p.a.

10. Postage, printing and stationery to be increased by 10%.

11. Television advertising to be increased by 20%.

12. Coupon offers in Divisions 1 and 3 to be increased by £2,400 and £1,600 respectively.

13. Shop window displays in Divisions 1 and 3 to be increased by £500 each.

14. Warehousemen's wages to be increased by 5%; drivers' wages by 10%.

15. Lorry expenses to be reduced by 10%.

The budget which will be prepared in view of these considerations is as follows:

SELLING AND DISTRIBUTION COST BUDGET   (b) NEXT YEAR

Period................

| | Budget | | | | Budget for previous period | | | |
| | Division | | | | Division | | | |
Element of cost	1	2	3	Total	1	2	3	Total
Direct selling expense								
Salesmens' salaries	£2,750	£9,300	£5,945	£17,995	£2,500	£8,000	£4,950	£15,450
commission	10,280	43,420	19,450	73,150	9,000	35,000	17,000	61,000
expenses	1,260	3,675	2,205	7,140	1,200	3,500	2,100	6,800
Entertaining	630	3,100	1,840	5,570	600	2,800	1,600	5,000
Car expenses	1,890	4,725	2,940	9,555	1,800	4,500	2,800	9,100
depreciation	1,500	5,000	3,050	9,550	1,500	4,800	2,850	9,150
Total	18,310	69,220	35,430	122,960	16,600	58,600	31,300	106,500
Sales office expenses								
Salaries	2,280	2,940	2,700	7,920	1,600	2,800	2,000	6,400
Rent and rates	200	400	300	900	200	400	300	900
Heat and light	100	150	120	370	100	150	120	370
Postage, printing and stationery	495	1,045	825	2,365	450	950	750	2,150
Depreciation	50	120	80	250	50	120	80	250
General expenses	120	280	150	550	120	280	150	550
Total	3,245	4,935	4,175	12,355	2,520	4,700	3,400	10,620
Advertising								
Press	2,500	6,000	4,000	12,500	2,500	6,000	4,000	12,500
Television	7,200	16,800	10,800	34,800	6,000	14,000	9,000	29,000
Radio	1,200	1,800	1,500	4,500	1,200	1,800	1,500	4,500
Coupon offers	6,900	9,600	9,000	25,500	4,500	9,600	7,400	21,500
Shop window display	1,300	2,000	1,500	4,800	800	2,000	1,000	3,800
Total	19,100	36,200	26,800	82,100	15,000	33,400	22,900	71,300
Distribution expenses								
Warehouse wages	1,260	3,675	2,310	7,245	1,200	3,500	2,200	6,900
Drivers' wages	1,375	3,300	2,200	6,875	1,250	3,000	2,000	6,250
Rent and rates	500	1,000	800	2,300	500	1,000	800	2,300
Vehicle expenses	2,250	5,400	4,050	11,700	2,500	6,000	4,500	13,000
depreciation	1,500	3,600	2,400	7,500	1,500	3,600	2,400	7,500
General expenses	200	500	300	1,000	200	500	300	1,000
Total	7,085	17,475	12,060	36,620	7,150	17,600	12,200	36,950
Total all items	£47,740	£127,830	£78,465	£254,035	£41,270	£114,300	£69,800	£225,370

PRODUCTION BUDGET

The compilation of the initial sales budget prompts the question: can the goods be produced? The production manager in his preliminary forecast will have ascertained what production facilities are available and what output he could normally expect. This forecast and the initial sales budget will be compared and the result will show whether the sales department is keeping the production departments at optimum capacity. If production facilities are not available to meet sales requirements, various alternatives can be considered:

1. Purchase of additional plant and equipment.
2. Introduction of overtime working.
3. Introduction of shift working.
4. Sub-contracting production of components or products.
5. Hiring machinery.

However, it may happen that the sales forecast will not fully utilise production capacity, in which case revision of the sales budget may be necessary. Possible courses of action are:

1. To promote an advertising and selling campaign in an effort to increase sales.
2. To offer customers better terms or reduced prices so as to increase sales.
3. To reduce output of a slow-selling product and increase output of a better selling line, if this will take up the surplus capacity.
4. To sell or scrap the excess capacity.

These problems occuring between functions are considered and decisions recommended by the budget committee.

The production budget frequently involves many complicated problems. The production manager will devise production schedules determining the products to be manufactured during the budget period. Schedules will be required for each budget centre and machine, showing the standard hours available. An important factor to be considered is the setting-up cost of an operation. For example, it might be possible to produce to meet all the sales demand for one of the company's products in a continuous production run of a month, rather than produce intermittently throughout the year; thus the budget committee must choose between a reduction in storage costs or in operating costs. In the same way seasonal fluctuations of sales could be smoothed out in the production forecast so as to ensure regular production.

Stocks of finished goods must also be considered. If there are considerable stocks on hand, production requirements will be less than sales requirements. On the other hand if it is desired to build up stocks for a future selling campaign, production requirements will be greater than immediate sales requirements.

The production budget will be presented to the budget committee for approval, and will be analysed to show:

1. Manufacturing departments or budget centres.
2. Products or groups of products.
3. The budget period broken down into months.

Example

A production budget is required for the GPJ Engineering Co. Ltd. It is to be based on sales requirements as shown in the sales budget. Information has been prepared showing the estimated stocks at the beginning of the budget period, and estimates prepared of stock requirements at the end of the period:

STOCKS FOR BUDGET PERIOD

Product	Estimated 1st Jan.	Required 31st Dec.
G	8,000 units	10,400 units
P	6,000	5,580
J	10,000	13,800

The production budget will then be drawn up as follows:

PRODUCTION BUDGET

Period............

	Product		
	G	P	J
	units	units	units
Required stock on 31st December	10,400	5,580	13,800
Sales during period	41,600	36,420	44,200
	52,000	42,000	58,000
Estimated stock on 1st January	8,000	6,000	10,000
Production requirements	44,000	36,000	48,000

In this example it has been assumed that there is no normal loss in process, but it must be appreciated that this is not always so. In many process industries there is an inherent loss in production due to factors such as evaporation, handling, etc., so it is usual to allow for a normal loss in process. The figure will be based on past experience and estimates, and such a normal loss will be established for each product at each process. Thus if, in our present Example, it is found that in manufacturing Product J a normal loss of 4% is to be expected, production requirements will differ from sales requirements. The production requirements are 48,000 units, therefore it will be necessary to process 50,000 units of Product J in order to produce 48,000 finished units. In preparing production forecasts it is, therefore, very important to consider this normal loss factor in any industries affected by such losses. It should be borne in mind that the normal loss factor will influence other functional budgets, especially the raw materials and production cost budgets.

PRODUCTION COST BUDGET

This budget shows the estimated cost of carrying out the production plans set out in the production budget. It will show each element of cost incurred—material, labour and overhead (the latter is usually sub-divided into fixed, variable and semi-variable costs). Costs will be analysed by departments and/or products.

Example (*pro forma*)

PRODUCTION COST BUDGET

Period............

Element of cost	Departments 1	2	3	4	Total
Raw materials [*main groups listed here*]	£	£	£	£	£
Total	———	———	———	———	———
Direct labour [*main groups listed here*]					
Total	———	———	———	———	———
Factory overheads [*main items listed here*]					
Total	———	———	———	———	———
Total all items	£				

RAW MATERIALS BUDGET

This budget shows the estimated quantities and costs of all the raw materials and components needed for the output demanded by the production budget. The completed budget will provide details of raw materials which will be required for the production cost budget and data for the purchasing department.

Example

A materials budget is required by the GPJ Co. which is to be based on the production budget. There are four departments in the factory, through which each of the products are processed before being transferred to the finished goods store. The materials used in each department are as follows:

Department 1: materials A and B
2: materials C and D
3: material E
4: material F

and the consumption of materials in the manufacture of the products is:

Product G: 1 unit of B, 2 units of E and F
P: 2 units of A, 1 unit each of C, D and F
J: 1 unit of A, 2 units of C and 1 unit of F.

Standard prices per unit are: A, £0·25; B, £0·05; C, £0·15; D, £0·10; E, £0·20; and F, £0·30.

RAW MATERIALS BUDGET

Period...............

Product	Department	Raw materials (units)					
		A	B	C	D	E	F
G	1	—	44,000	—	—	—	—
	2	—	—	—	—	—	—
	3	—	—	—	—	88,000	—
	4	—	—	—	—	—	88,000
P	1	72,000	—	—	—	—	—
	2	—	—	36,000	36,000	—	—
	3	—	—	—	—	—	—
	4	—	—	—	—	—	36,000
J	1	48,000	—	—	—	—	—
	2	—	—	96,000	—	—	—
	3	—	—	—	—	—	—
	4	—	—	—	—	—	48,000
Consumption		120,000	44,000	132,000	36,000	88,000	172,000
Standard price per unit		£0·25	£0·05	£0·15	£0·10	£0·20	£0·30
Total		£30,000	£2,200	£19,800	£3,600	£17,600	£51,600

PURCHASES BUDGET

This budget provides details of the purchases which must be made during the period to meet the needs of the business. It includes costs of all direct and indirect materials which have been detailed in the raw materials budget and expense budgets such as the research and development cost budget. A number of factors must be considered in preparing this budget, including the following:

1. *Opening and closing stocks.* If it is planned to run down opening stocks or build up closing stocks, this will affect material requirements.

2. *Internal manufacture.* Adjustments will have to be made in material requirements, where some materials or components are manufactured internally.

3. *Purchase orders placed before the budget period.* Adjustments in material requirements will be necessary to allow for orders already placed with outside suppliers.

4. *Maximum and minimum stock quantities.* Where maximum and minimum stock levels are set, adjustments to budgeted material requirements may be necessary to replenish or reduce stocks.

Example

The purchases budget for the GPJ Co. will be based on the raw materials budget. Estimates have been prepared to show the estimated stock of raw materials at the beginning of the budget period, and forecast requirements made of closing stocks. These estimates show the following:

RAW MATERIALS FOR BUDGET

Period...............

	A	B	Materials (units) C	D	E	F
Estimated stock on 1st January	16,000	6,000	24,000	2,000	14,000	28,000
Required stock on 31st December,	20,000	8,000	28,000	4,000	16,000	32,000
Standard price per unit	£0·25	£0·05	£0·15	£0·10	£0·20	£0·30

PURCHASES BUDGET

Period...............

	A	B	Materials (units) C	D	E	F
Required stock on 31st December	20,000	8,000	28,000	4,000	16,000	32,000
Consumption during period	120,000	44,000	132,000	36,000	88,000	172,000
Total	140,000	52,000	160,000	40,000	104,000	204,000
Estimated stock on 1st January	16,000	6,000	24,000	2,000	14,000	28,000
Purchases	124,000	46,000	136,000	38,000	90,000	176,000
Price per unit	£0·25	£0·05	£0·15	£0·10	£0·20	£0·30
Cost	£31,000	£2,300	£20,400	£3,800	£18,000	£52,800

LABOUR BUDGET

This represents the forecast of direct and indirect labour requirements to meet the demands of the company during the budget period. The labour budget must be linked with the production budget as well as the production cost budget. Product specifications will normally detail the operations involved, types of labour required and number of hours allowed to complete the finished product. From these details the total standard hours of direct labour can be found for each grade of labour engaged on each product or in each department. The total number of standard hours can then be estimated to meet the production budget. Finally the standard rates of each grade of labour can be introduced to ascertain the total direct labour cost for the budget period. Indirect labour is within limits normally a fixed amount, so should be relatively easy to calculate in total for the budget period. In calculating the standard rates of labour, the possibility of new wage agreements should be considered.

The final labour budget is useful in many ways, some of which are:

1. It defines the direct and indirect labour force required.

2. It enables the personnel department to plan ahead in recruitment and training of labour. Training new employees is sometimes a long and expensive operation, so adequate warning of labour requirements is essential. On the other hand, if any of the employees are to be made redundant it is necessary for the personnel department

to make them aware of the situation in good time, so that talks between employer and trade union can be held and the employees given every chance and encouragement to find alternative work.

3. It provides the labour cost involved in producing and selling products, which will be required in the preparation of the manufacturing cost budget and the cash budget.

Example (*pro forma*)

LABOUR BUDGET

Period............

Classification	Number of employees	Hours	Employee/ hours	Standard rate per hour	Amounts £
Direct labour					
[*grades of labour listed here*]					
Total					
Indirect labour					
[*grades of labour listed here*]					
Total					
Total all items					£

PRODUCTION OVERHEAD BUDGET

This budget represents the forecast of all the production, fixed, variable and semi-variable overheads to be incurred during the budget period. It will be necessary to apportion the fixed overheads and the fixed portion of semi-variable overheads to departments, and to calculate the variable overheads and the variable portion of semi-variable overheads for departments in view of the production budgeted.

Budgeted overhead costs of any service department will be totalled for control purposes, the apportionment to production departments according to the service it is estimated each such department has received from each service department.

Example

A production overhead budget is required by the Jervid Engineering Co. Ltd. The production overhead apportionment has been prepared to show overheads for each of the production and service departments. Service departments are recovered as follows:

Service department	Production departments		
	A	B	C
1	30%	20%	50%
2	25%	30%	45%

PRODUCTION OVERHEAD APPORTIONMENT

Period...................

Overhead	Basis of apportionment	Total	Production department A	B	C	Service department 1	2
Salaries } Indirect wages }	Standard or actual }	£14,700	£4,000	£3,000	£5,000	£1,500	£1,200
		31,600	9,000	7,000	10,000	3,000	2,600
Consumable stores	No. of employees	1,650	400	350	500	300	100
Depreciation	Straight/line	22,200	6,000	5,000	10,000	700	500
Insurance	Insured amounts	2,480	750	650	900	100	80
Rent/rates	Floor space	3,790	1,200	1,000	1,500	50	40
Power	Metered	2,170	600	700	800	40	30
Heat/light	Floor space	395	100	110	140	20	25
Maintenance	Estimated	2,525	800	700	1,000	15	10
National Insurance	Number of men	3,150	900	800	1,000	250	200
Scrap	Standard	775	225	205	345	—	—
General	Estimated/standard	1,105	375	235	455	25	15
Total		£86,540	£24,350	£19,750	£31,640	£6,000	£4,800
Service Dept. 1			1,800	1,200	3,000		
Service Dept. 2			1,200	1,440	2,160		
Total		£86,540	£27,350	£22,390	£36,800	—	—

PRODUCTION OVERHEAD BUDGET

Period...................

Overhead	Total £	£	A £	£	Department B £	£	C £	£
Variable								
Consumable stores	1,250		400		350		500	
Scrap	775		225		205		345	
		2,025		625		555		845
Semi-variable								
Indirect wages	26,000		9,000		7,000		10,000	
Power	2,100		600		700		800	
Heat/light	350		100		110		140	
Maintenance	2,500		800		700		1,000	
National Insurance	2,700		900		800		1,000	
		33,650		11,400		9,310		12,940
Fixed								
Salaries	12,000		4,000		3,000		5,000	
Depreciation	21,000		6,000		5,000		10,000	
Insurance	2,300		750		650		900	
Rent/rates	3,700		1,200		1,000		1,500	
General	1,065		375		235		455	
Service Dept. 1	6,000		1,800		1,200		3,000	
Service Dept. 2	4,800		1,200		1,440		2,160	
		50,865		15,325		12,525		23,015
Total		£86,540		£27,350		£22,390		£36,800

PLANT UTILISATION BUDGET

This budget covers the plant and machinery requirements to meet the budgeted production during the period. Schedules will be produced showing the available load in each department, probably expressed in standard hours or units. Comparison of the schedules with production requirements will reveal over or underloading of plant and machinery. This results in a number of advantages, including:

1. Where overloading is expected, action can be taken in time to arrange for working shifts or overtime, purchase of new plant or sub-contracting some operations.

2. Where underloading is estimated, the sales manager may be required to try to boost sales of certain products by price reductions, discounts, increased advertising or change of package. If this fails, or is thought to be unprofitable, it may be necessary to dispose of some machinery.

Example (*pro forma*)

PLANT UTILISATION BUDGET

Period............

Department	Machine	Number of hours available in period	Normal lost time	Standard capacity in hours	Output per standard hour	Standard quantity (units)
A	1	2000	200	1800	5	9000
	2					
	3					
B	4					
	5					
	6					
	etc.					
Total						

CAPITAL EXPENDITURE BUDGET

The capital expenditure budget represents estimated expenditure on all fixed assets during the budget period. It should be noted, however, that the budget period in the case of capital expenditure may differ from that of other budgets. Capital expenditure is frequently planned a number of years in advance, perhaps five or ten, in which case for control purposes it will have to be broken down into convenient periods like years or months. This budget is subject to strict management control, because it may involve large amounts of expenditure which need top-management approval. The cost accountant or budget officer will have to co-operate closely with the plant engineer in its preparation. Long term and short term developments must be forecast and many factors considered, such as capital costs, the period of expenditure and the expected earnings.

The preparation of the budget is based on such information as:

1. Overloading, as detailed in the plant utilisation budget.
2. Future development plans of the company to increase output by extending plant or buying new and better equipment.
3. Requests from the manufacturing or service department for new machinery.
4. Requests from the transport manager for new vehicles.
5. Requests from the accountant for new office machinery.

The capital expenditure budget provides the following advantages:

1. It outlines the capital development programme and estimated capital expenditure during the budget period.
2. It enables the company to establish a system of priorities in expenditure. If sufficient capital is not available to meet the programme, the board can decide in advance which developments should have priority.
3. It provides a tool for controlling capital expenditure.
4. It provides some of the fixed-asset figures which will be required for the forecast Balance Sheet.

A number of companies have run into serious financial trouble by proceeding with capital expenditure projects that were beyond the financial resources available to them. This could have been avoided by the use of an effective capital expenditure budget.

Example

A capital expenditure budget is required by the directors of Chriseme Ltd, based on the following information:

Production departments:

1. There is a balance brought forward of £100,000 for the building of an additional can-making department; the authorisation for this was for £200,000. This will be completed during the period.
2. It is proposed to purchase two automatic can-making machines, at an estimated cost of £120,000, all of which will be expended during this budget period.
3. Purchase of a new lathe at an estimated cost of £30,000.

Administration department:

1. There is a balance brought forward of £15,000 for building a new machine-room; the authorised amount for this project was £20,000.
2. Purchase of a new computer at a cost of £50,000.

Sales department:

1. Purchase of ten new cars at a cost of £8,000, of which £6,000 will be expended during the budget period.
2. Building of showroom at a cost of £25,000, of which £5,000 will be expended in this period.

Distribution department:

1. Purchase of one fork-lift truck at a cost of £2,000.
2. Purchase of two new vans costing £1,500 each.

The resulting budget is shown below. Note that in this case it refers to the budget period adopted—one year.

CAPITAL EXPENDITURE BUDGET

Period................

Total cost appropriated but outstanding (£)	Budgeted expenditure to date (£)	Project	Balance b/d (£)	Budgeted appropriation for period (£)	Total (£)	Budgeted expenditure during period (£)	Balance c/d (£)
		Production department					
200,000	100,000	Build additional can-making department	100,000	—	100,000	100,000	—
—	—	Buy two automatic can-making machines	—	120,000	120,000	120,000	—
—	—	Buy new lathe	—	30,000	30,000	30,000	—
		Administration department					
—	—	Buy new computer	—	50,000	50,000	50,000	—
20,000	5,000	Build new machine room	15,000	—	15,000	15,000	—
		Sales department					
—	—	Buy ten new cars	—	8,000	8,000	6,000	2,000
—	—	Build showroom	—	25,000	25,000	5,000	20,000
		Distribution department					
—	—	Buy fork-lift truck	—	2,000	2,000	2,000	—
—	—	Buy two vans	—	3,000	3,000	3,000	—
£220,000	£105,000		£115,000	£238,000	£353,000	£331,000	£22,000

ADMINISTRATION COST BUDGET

This budget represents the costs of all administration expenses such as managing director's salary, office lighting and cleaning. Most of the expenses will be fixed within defined limits, so should not be too difficult to prepare. Each department or budget centre will be responsible for the preparation of its own budget, which will then be incorporated in the administration cost budget.

Example (*pro forma*)

ADMINISTRATION COST BUDGET

Cost Centre: *57*   Period............

Department: *Cost accounting*   Budget agreed: *J. D. B.*

Code No.	Description	Total	Jan.	Feb.	Mar.	Apr.	May	June
	Indirect materials	£	£	£	£	£	£	£
	General supplies							
	Stationery							
	Printing							
	Photographic supplies							
	Indirect wages and salaries							
	Executives' salaries							
	Clerical salaries							
	National Insurance							
	Meal allowances							
	Overtime							
	Overtime premium							
	Depreciation							
	Office equipment							
	Cars							
	Repairs							
	Buildings							
	Office equipment							
	Cars							
	Miscellaneous							
	Rent and rates							
	Insurance							
	Personnel service expenses							
	Conference expenses							
	Training expenses							
	Subscriptions to periodicals							
	Postage							
	Telephone							
	General							
	Total	£						

CASH BUDGET

The cash budget is one of the most important and one of the last to be prepared. It represents the cash requirements of the business during the budget period; in other words, it makes certain that the business has sufficient cash available to meet its needs as and when they arise. It is often not appreciated by some executives that making a profit may depend upon the availability of cash resources. The budgeted Profit and Loss Account may show a very favourable profit forecast, but if the estimates of sales and costs have not been integrated with cash requirements the company may be unable to achieve the level forecast.

The cash budget should extend over the same period as the master budget, but it is essential for control purposes that it be analysed to show monthly flow of cash. In fact it is frequently necessary in some businesses to have even shorter periods than this, and weekly or even daily budgets are not unknown. The cash budget offers many advantages, among them the following:

1. It ensures that sufficient cash is available when required.
2. It shows whether capital expenditure projects can be financed internally.
3. It reveals the availability of cash so that advantage may be taken of cash discounts, etc.
4. It reveals the need for additional cash requirements in good time so that action can be taken to secure loans, bank overdrafts, etc.
5. It reveals the availability of excess cash so that short term investments can be made; in some cases, even, long term investments may be considered. With regard to short term investments, it is important that these should be readily realisable when required. As for long term investments, it would be necessary to consider very carefully the expected return on them. It should be borne in mind that too much cash on hand may reduce the rate of return on capital employed.

The cash forecast will reflect changes in liquid resources and reveal the cash position, at selected times—times which are convenient to the requirements of the company. Thus in a long term forecast the position may be computed at the end of every five years; a company engaged in an industry that experiences seasonal fluctuations may find it important to show the cash position at each of the stock peak times. A build-up of stock to meet peak sales will mean locking up working capital, which must be allowed for at the time it is to be incurred: it is no good hoping that the "peaks" will level out with the "troughs," and show only the position at the end of the year. The company must be solvent continuously throughout the year and not just at the end of the budget period.

Where an expected shortage of cash is revealed by the cash forecast, the company should try to arrange for short term or long term borrowing. In the case of short term requirements it may be possible to secure a bank overdraft or loan, to take longer credit from creditors or to purchase plant and equipment on hire purchase. In the case of long term requirements, an issue of Debentures or new shares could be considered, bearing in mind that additional income would be required to meet the interest on Debentures or the dividends on capital. Where the company is unable or unwilling to raise money to finance capital projects, it may be necessary to curtail expenditure on these projects. This may lead to the authorisation of only those projects which yield a certain return on investment, or have a short pay-back period. The subject of return on investment and pay-back period is discussed in more detail in Chapter XXII.

There are three recognised ways of preparing a cash budget:

1. The receipts and payments method.
2. The adjusted profit and loss method.
3. The Balance Sheet method.

The first method is usually used as a short term forecast and is much more detailed than either 2 or 3. Methods 2 and 3 are usually used as long term forecasts, but where monthly budgeted Profit and Loss Accounts and Balance Sheets are prepared, monthly cash forecasts can be produced.

1. Receipts and payments method.

All cash payments and receipts which are expected during the budget period must be considered. Care must be taken to ensure that adjustments and accruals are not shown in the cash budget. Details of cash transactions can be ascertained from the various budgets which have been discussed earlier in this chapter. For example, the main details could be obtained as follows:

(*a*) Sales from the sales budget, but it must be remembered that monthly sales and cash receipts must be adjusted in cash forecasting because of the lag in payment by debtors.

(*b*) Material costs from the purchase budget, but here again there will be a lag in payment to creditors.

(*c*) Labour costs from the labour budget. Again, there may be some lag in payment of wages to employees.

(*d*) Overhead costs from the expense budgets, such as the production overhead budget and selling and distribution cost budgets. Lag in payment to expense creditors must be considered.

(e) Capital expenditure from the capital expenditure budget. It will depend on the method of showing capital expenditure as distinct from capital appropriation but, where appropriate, attention should be paid to lag in payment of creditors.

Example

The Jaydee Co. Ltd has completed most of the functional budgets and it is now time to prepare the cash budget. An analysis of the various budgets concerned reveals the requirements:

REQUIREMENTS FOR CASH BUDGET (£)

Month	Sales	Materials	Wages	Overheads				
				Production	Administration	Selling	Distribution	Research and development
Oct.	80,000	40,000	10,000	8,400	3,400	5,000	3,000	1,000
Nov.	60,000	30,000	9,000	8,000	3,300	4,500	2,500	1,000
Dec.	40,000	20,000	8,000	7,500	3,500	4,000	2,000	1,000
Jan.	50,000	40,000	9,000	8,000	3,700	4,400	2,400	1,200
Feb.	60,000	50,000	10,000	8,500	3,900	4,800	2,600	1,200
Mar.	80,000	60,000	11,000	9,000	3,600	5,200	2,900	1,200
Apr.	70,000	50,000	9,000	8,000	3,500	5,000	2,600	1,500
May	60,000	30,000	8,000	7,500	3,700	4,800	2,500	1,500
June	50,000	40,000	9,000	8,000	3,900	4,500	2,400	1,500

Period of credit allowed by creditors	2 months
„ „ „ „ to debtors	3 months
Lag in payment of overheads	1 month
„ „ „ „ wages	$\frac{1}{8}$ month.

The cash balance on 1st January is expected to be £100,000.

The capital developments budgeted for are as follows:

(a) Plant and machinery to be installed in April at a cost of £50,000 will be payed for monthly by instalments of £10,000 a month as from 1st May. Extensions to the Research and Development Department at a cost of £10,000 will be completed on 1st January, payment to be made on 1st February.

(b) A sales commission of 10% on sales is to be paid within the month following actual sales.

(c) Cash sales of £5000 per month are expected; no commission is payable on them.

(d) The company has a hire purchase agreement under which £5000 a month is being paid for plant purchased before this budget period. Payment will continue throughout this budget period.

(e) Preference share dividends of 8% on capital of £2 million are to be paid on 1st April.

(f) Tax of £100,000 is due on 1st April.

(g) Dividends from investments amounting to £70,000 are expected on 1st May.

(h) £0·25 calls on Ordinary share capital of £200,000 are due on 1st January, 1st March and 1st June.

The overall cash budget is then drawn up as follows:

CASH BUDGET (a) RECEIPTS AND PAYMENTS METHOD

Period.................

	January	February	March	April	May	June
	£	£	£	£	£	£
Receipts						
Balance b/d	100,000	169,125	164,550	176,675	2,525	1,800
Debtors	80,000	60,000	40,000	50,000	60,000	80,000
Cash sales	5,000	5,000	5,000	5,000	5,000	5,000
Dividends	—	—	—	—	70,000	—
Capital	50,000	—	50,000	—	—	50,000
Total	235,000	234,125	259,550	231,675	137,525	136,800
Payments						
Materials	30,000	20,000	40,000	50,000	60,000	50,000
Labour	8,875	9,875	10,875	9,250	8,125	8,875
Production overheads	7,500	8,000	8,500	9,000	8,000	7,500
Administration overheads	3,500	3,700	3,900	3,600	3,500	3,700
Selling overheads	4,000	4,400	4,800	5,200	5,000	4,800
Distribution overheads	2,000	2,400	2,600	2,900	2,600	2,500
Research overheads	1,000	1,200	1,200	1,200	1,500	1,500
Commission	4,000	5,000	6,000	8,000	7,000	6,000
Income tax	—	—	—	100,000	—	—
Dividends	—	—	—	160,000	—	—
Capital	5,000	15,000	5,000	5,000	15,000	15,000
Total	65,875	69,575	82,875	354,150	110,725	99,875
Cash available	169,125	164,550	176,675	(122,475)	26,800	36,925
Loan or overdraft	—	—	—	125,000	100,000	65,000
Balance c/d	£169,125	£164,550	£176,675	£2,525	£1,800	£1,925

It can be seen from the cash budget that the company has insufficient internal resources to finance operations during April, May and June. Owing to forward planning of cash requirements, it has been possible to approach the bank manager with a view to raising an overdraft of £125,000, which has been agreed. This amount has been reduced by internal flow of cash to £100,000 in May and to £65,000 in June, while still leaving a small surplus in hand to meet contingencies. It may well be considered that the amount of surplus cash in April, May and June is too small, in which case it may be necessary to take appropriate action, such as enlarging the bank overdraft or cutting down expenditure.

2. Adjusted profit and loss method.

This method is often termed the cash flow statement because it converts the Profit and Loss Account into a cash forecast.

It is rather more difficult to understand than the relatively easy to follow receipts and payments method. It is less detailed than the previous method, but is particularly useful for long term forecasting, say over a period of five years. When management is considering long term plans, it is more interested in the overall picture than in details of income and expenditure, so this method of forecasting cash requirements can play a valuable part in budgetary control. The following information will be used in preparing the budget:

(a) Expected cash balance at beginning of period.
(b) Net profit forecast for period (before write-offs and depreciation).
(c) Changes in working capital.
(d) Capital expenditure and sales of plant and machinery.

(e) Capital receipts.

(f) Dividends.

The reader may have observed that, in the receipts and payments method, consideration was given to all those items which necessitated cash transactions. Cash receipts from various sources were added to the balances of cash on hand at the beginning of the period, and from the resulting total were deducted the total cash payments to various sources so as to ascertain the cash available. The adjusted profit and loss method differs from the receipts and payments method mainly in that it considers particularly the non-cash transactions. The theory is based on the elementary assumption that profit = cash. Thus if there were no credit transactions, capital transactions, accruals, provisions, stock fluctuations or appropriations of profit, the balance of profit on the Profit and Loss Account should be equal to the balance of cash in the cash book. It is appreciated that such a situation would never exist in practice, so the elementary assumption needs adjustment. In preparing the cash forecast one proceeds with the budgeted profit for the period, then adjusts this figure by the items mentioned above.

CASH FORECAST FOR THE FIVE YEARS 19— TO 19—

	1	2	Year 3	4	5	Total
Balance b/d	£	£	£	£	£	
Additions to cash						
Budgeted net profit for year						
Depreciation						
Write-offs						
Provisions						
Sales of plant						
Accrued expenses						
Reduction in stocks						
Reduction in debtors						
Increase in liabilities						
Issue of capital						
Issue of debentures						
Total additions						
Total cash available						
Deductions from cash						
Dividends						
Prepayments						
Capital payments						
Increase in stocks						
Increase in debtors						
Decrease in liabilities						
Total deductions						
Loan or bank overdraft						
Balance c/d	£					

Preparation of such a forecast will be relatively easy if a budgeted Profit and Loss Account and a budgeted Balance Sheet are available for each budget period. Most of the items shown can be ascertained by comparing balances shown in the Balance Sheet of one year with those of the succeeding years. An example now follows showing most of the items to which reference has been made, culminating in the forecast cash position at the end of the budget period.

Example

A cash forecast is required by the management of the Jerid Manufacturing Co. Ltd. You are required to prepare this forecast based on the budgeted Profit and Loss Account for the budget period and the budgeted Balance Sheets for the current period and the budget period.

FORECAST BALANCE SHEET
as at 31st December

Current period.................

Issue share capital		£3,500,000	Freehold buildings	£1,750,000	
Capital reserve		350,000	Depreciation	175,000	
Profit and loss appropriation		560,000			£1,575,000
		4,410,000	Plant and machinery	2,800,000	
5% debentures		350,000	Depreciation	560,000	
Creditors	£210,000				2,240,000
Dividend proposed	140,000		Motor vehicles	560,000	
Accrued expenses	28,000		Depreciation	140,000	
		378,000			420,000
					4,235,000
			Stocks		
			Raw materials	£175,000	
			Work in progress	105,000	
			Finished goods	70,000	
				350,000	
			Debtors	315,000	
			Bank	238,000	
					903,000
		£5,138,000			£5,138,000

FORECAST PROFIT AND LOSS ACCOUNT
for year ending 31st December

Budget period.................

Administrative expenses			Gross profit b/d	£1,050,000
Office salaries	£170,170		Interest received	8,680
Expenses	53,480		Discount received	50,820
Rent and rates	17,570			
		£241,220		
Selling expenses				
Salaries	86,940			
Expenses	39,760			
Car expenses	50,680			
Advertising	140,000			
Carriage	32,200			
		349,580		
Financial expenses				
Debenture interest	17,500			
Audit fees	14,000			
Discount allowed	35,000			
		66,500		
Net profit c/d		452,200		
		£1,109,500		£1,109,500
Dividends paid		£280,000	Balance b/d	£560,000
Balance c/d		732,200	Net profit b/d	452,200
		£1,012,200		£1,012,200

FORECAST BALANCE SHEET

as at 31st December

Budget period.................

Issued share capital		£3,850,000	Freehold buildings	£1,750,000
Capital reserve		350,000	Depreciation	210,000
Profit and loss appropriation		732,200		——— £1,540,000
		4,932,200	Plant and machinery	3,500,000
5% debentures		525,000	Depreciation	840,000
Creditors	£245,000			——— 2,660,000
Accrued expenses	31,500		Motor vehicles	700,000
		276,500	Depreciation	280,000
				——— 420,000
				4,620,000

Stocks		
Raw materials £154,000		
Work in progress 126,000		
Finished goods 98,000		
	378,000	
Debtors	280,000	
Bank	455,700	
	——— 1,113,700	

£5,733,700 £5,733,700

Following the method shown on p. 221, one can prepare the cash budget:

CASH BUDGET (b) ADJUSTED PROFIT AND LOSS METHOD

Period.........

Cash balance			£238,000
Additions to cash			
Income		£452,200	
Depreciation:			
Freehold buildings	£35,000		
Plant and machinery	280,000		
Motor vehicles	140,000		
		455,000	
Accrued expenses	3,500		
Stock reductions: raw materials	21,000		
Reduction in debtors	35,000		
Increase in creditors	35,000		
Issue of capital	350,000		
Debentures	175,000		
		619,500	
			1,526,700
Cash available			1,764,700
Deductions from cash			
Dividends proposed	140,000		
Dividends paid	280,000		
		420,000	

Purchases of plant and machinery	700,000		
Purchases of motor vehicles	140,000		
		840,000	
Stock increases:			
Work in progress	21,000		
Finished goods	28,000		
		49,000	
			1,309,000
			£455,700

NOTE

Perhaps the only difficult point here concerns the dividends proposed and paid. It should be observed that the opening Balance Sheet shows "Dividends proposed" of £140,000 which apparently have been paid during the year because there are no arrears at the end of the period, while the Profit and Loss Appropriation Account shows that £280,000 has been appropriated during the budget period and has in fact been paid. Thus the total amount to be paid during the budget period is £420,000.

3. Balance Sheet method.

This method of preparing a cash forecast is rather similar in theory to that of the adjusted profit and loss method. A budgeted Balance Sheet is prepared for the next period showing all items such as fixed assets, capital, etc., but excluding cash. The two sides of the Balance Sheet are then balanced, and the balancing figure is considered to represent cash. If the asset side is larger than the liabilities side, this would reveal a bank overdraft; if the liabilities side is the larger this would reveal a balance at the bank.

Example

If one uses the information stated in the previous example the Balance Sheet would be built up to show liabilities of £5,733,700, fixed assets of £4,620,000, stocks of £378,000 and debts of £280,000. The balancing figure of £455,700 would be inserted as "balance at bank."

THE MASTER BUDGET

The master budget is the one which projects the activities of the business during the budget period. It commonly takes the form of a budgeted Profit and Loss Account and Balance Sheet. It is prepared by the budget officer, and incorporates the details shown in the subsidiary budgets. When it is complete the budget committee will consider all the details and, if approved, it will be submitted to the board of directors. It would be very unusual if the master budget were approved on first presentation; amendments are invariably necessary. However, once it is finally approved it becomes the target for the company during the budget period.

MASTER BUDGET (*a*) BUDGETED PROFIT AND LOSS ACCOUNT
for year ending......

	Budget period Amount	%	Previous period Amount	%
Net sales	£1,000,000	100·0	£950,000	100·0
Production cost	575,000	57·5	535,000	56·3
	425,000	42·5	415,000	43·7
Less operating expenses:				
Administration	90,000	9·0	85,000	8·9
Selling	65,000	6·5	60,000	6·3
Distribution	55,000	5·5	50,000	5·3
Advertising	75,000	7·5	100,000	10·5
Research and development	25,000	2·5	20,000	2·1
Financial	15,000	1·5	15,000	1·6
Total	325,000	32·5	330,000	34·7
Operating profit	100,000	10·0	85,000	9·0
Plus other income	10,000	1·0	10,000	1·0
Net profit before tax	110,000	11·0	95,000	10·0
Less provision for tax	40,000	4·0	35,000	3·7
Net profit	£70,000	7·0	£60,000	6·3

MASTER BUDGET (*b*) BUDGETED BALANCE SHEET AS AT.........

	Budget period £	£	£	Previous period £	£	£
Fixed assets						
Buildings	300,000			300,000		
Less depreciation	30,000			22,500		
		270,000			277,500	
Plant and machinery	100,000			100,000		
Less depreciation	40,000			30,000		
		60,000			70,000	
Motor vehicles	50,000			50,000		
Less depreciation	40,000			30,000		
		10,000			20,000	
			340,000			367,500
Current assets						
Stocks: Raw materials	60,000			50,000		
Work in progress	25,000			20,000		
Finished goods	35,000			30,000		
		120,000			100,000	
Debtors	120,000			100,000		
Less Bad debt provision	5,000			5,000		
		115,000			95,000	
Bank and cash		30,000			27,500	
		265,000			222,500	
Less Current liabilities						
Creditors	35,000			50,000		
Accruals	10,000			5,000		
Tax	40,000			35,000		
		85,000			90,000	
			180,000			132,500
Total fixed assets and working capital			£520,000			£500,000
Financed by capital and reserves						
Issued share capital		400,000			400,000	
General reserve		40,000			40,000	
Profit and loss		80,000			60,000	
			£520,000			£500,000

THE BUDGET REPORT

The work of the budget officer is not concluded when the budgets have been prepared and approved. A continuous flow of reports is required each month to show comparison of actual performance with that budgeted. Reports will be issued to heads of budget centres showing favourable or adverse variations from the budget. Heads of budget centres may be required to report to the managing director on the day following the issue of the report, to explain any variances. Efficiency or inefficiency will be revealed so that where necessary remedial action may be taken before it is too late. These reports may also provide valuable guides in future planning. An example is shown below.

BUDGET REPORT

Cost centre: *42*   Month: *March*

Department: *Accounting*

Performance: Month 102%   Cumulative 101%

Code		Month: Budget £	Actual £	Variance £	Cumulative: 3 months Budget £	Actual £	Variance £
	Indirect materials						
01	Printing	60	50	(10)	180	160	(20)
02	Stationery	80	85	5	240	225	(15)
03	Photographic supplies	40	30	(10)	120	130	10
04	Cleaning material	10	12	2	30	25	(5)
05	General supplies	20	15	(5)	50	60	10
	Indirect wages and salaries						
10	Executive salaries	800	800	—	2300	2300	—
11	Clerical salaries	1500	1450	(50)	4000	3900	(100)
12	Other wages	50	46	(4)	140	135	(5)
13	National Insurance	60	57	(3)	150	144	(6)
14	Overtime	50	60	10	100	120	20
15	Overtime premium	20	24	4	40	48	8
	Depreciation and repairs						
20	Plant and machinery depreciation	50	50	—	150	150	—
21	Vehicles depreciation	—	—	—	—	—	—
22	Plant and machinery repairs	10	20	10	30	40	10
23	Vehicle repairs	—	—	—	—	—	—
	Miscellaneous						
30	Executive expenses	70	60	(10)	300	280	(20)
31	Staff expenses	20	25	5	40	50	10
32	Training expenses	90	70	(20)	160	120	(40)
33	Conference expenses	40	45	5	60	55	(5)
34	Personnel dept. expenses	60	90	30	100	135	35
35	Postage	10	9	(1)	30	28	(2)
36	Telephone	70	54	(16)	210	215	5
37	General	10	6	(4)	30	35	5
	Total	£3120	£3058	£(62)	£8460	£8355	£(105)

Prepared by: *P.J.*   Date issued *6th April*
Checked by: *J.D.*

It is essential in budgetary control that management should receive budget reports as soon after the end of each period as possible. Relative speed of presentation is more important than relative accuracy. Delay in reports reaching management makes the task of investigating variations more difficult. As a result adverse costs go undetected for some time, with consequent delays in remedial action.

An investigation into the activity of Cost Centre 42 would be called for as part of the routine operation of a budgetary control system. In

this case it can be observed from the report that variations from budget
are not significant. The performance for the month is 102% while for
the three months to date it is 101%, which is quite satisfactory. Investigation may reveal that the saving on Code 11 is due to an unfilled
vacancy. This will have led to an increased cost in the personnel department, which is advertising to remedy the situation. Training expenses
also show an under-spending because the training of specialist accounting staff will have been delayed until the vacancy is filled.

MANAGEMENT BY EXCEPTION

Budgetary control, as we have remarked, is essentially a tool of
management. It enables management to consider only the items that
do not go according to plan; to concentrate on exceptions. Variations
from budget reveal a complete picture of the activity of the business
in as convenient a form as possible. Time is not wasted sorting through
masses of figures: variations point to the root of any inefficiencies.
The use of ratios is another valuable technique in illustrating pertinent
facts concerning the progress of the business; these are discussed further
in Chapter XIX.

The preparation of all the budgets discussed in this chapter involves
a considerable amount of work, but it is suggested that it would be
justified if nothing more were achieved than this contribution to
management planning. Such planning ensures that a company knows
where it is going and how it plans to get there. But, this is not the only
benefit to be gained from operating a system of budgetary control:
its invaluable contribution for control purposes is the provision of a
yardstick against which performance can be compared.

BUDGETARY CONTROL PROJECT

The Jeraul Co Ltd is a medium-sized company situated in the South
of England which produces three products, Aye, Bee and Cee. In the
factory there are five departments; Departments 1, 2 and 3 are manufacturing units and Departments X and Y are service units. There are
three sales divisions in the company.

The Company operates a budgetary control system and preliminary
details for next year's budget have been completed. It has been established that the key factor is sales demand. Budgets are to be prepared
for the accounting year ending 30th June Year 3, for presentation to the
Budget Committee. You are required to prepare the following functional budgets:

1. Sales.
2. Selling and distribution cost.
3. Production.
4. Raw materials.
5. Purchases.
6. Wages.
7. Production overhead.
8. Production cost.
9. Administration overhead.
10. Capital expenditure.

On completion of these functional budgets you should then prepare the Budgeted Profit and Loss Statement and Budgeted Balance Sheet, also the Cash Budget. Comment briefly on the main points to which the attention of management should be drawn.

PRELIMINARY DATA

Division	Product	Budgeted Sales Year 1/2			Actual Sales Year 1/2		
		Quantity	Price	Value	Quantity	Price	Value
			£	£		£	£
1	Aye	2,000	12	24,000	2,500	12	30,000
	Bee	1,500	20	30,000	1,000	20	20,000
	Cee	1,000	50	50,000	500	50	25,000
2	Aye	3,000	12	36,000	4,000	12	48,000
	Bee	4,000	20	80,000	5,000	20	100,000
	Cee	6,000	50	300,000	5,000	50	250,000
3	Aye	3,000	12	36,000	3,500	12	42,000
	Bee	2,000	20	40,000	2,500	20	50,000
	Cee	2,500	50	125,000	2,000	50	100,000

The Sales Manager in consultation with his divisional managers and salesmen, has forecast the following changes in relation to last year's budget:

Division 1	Aye + 30%	Bee − 5%	Cee − 5%
2	Aye + 40%	Bee + 30%	Cee − 10%
3	Aye + 20%	Bee + 30%	Cee − 10%

In view of the poor forecasts for Product Cee, the sales manager is proposing an intensive sales campaign. It is hoped that this will result in the following sales increase:

Division 1   20%;   Division 2   10%;   Division 3   30%.

BUDGETED SELLING AND DISTRIBUTION COSTS YEAR 1/YEAR 2

Element of cost	Division			
Direct selling expenses	1	2	3	Total
	£	£	£	£
Salesmens' salaries	2,500	8,000	4,750	15,250
commission	4,950	19,300	9,425	33,675
expenses	400	900	600	1,900
Car expenses	2,000	6,400	3,800	12,200
Entertaining	1,200	3,500	2,100	6,800
Car depreciation	1,500	4,800	2,850	9,150
Total	12,550	42,900	23,525	78,975
Advertising				
Press	10,000	12,783	14,000	36,783
TV	6,000	14,000	9,000	29,000
Shop window display	800	2,000	1,000	3,800
Total	16,800	28,783	24,000	69,583
Sales Office				
Salaries	1,600	2,800	2,000	6,400
Rent and rates	200	400	300	900
Light and heat	100	150	120	370
Depreciation	50	120	80	250
Postage, stationery and telephone	450	950	740	2,150
General expenses	120	280	150	550
Total	2,520	4,700	3,400	10,620
Distribution expenses				
Warehouse wages	1,200	3,500	2,200	6,900
Drivers' wages	1,250	3,000	2,000	6,250
Rent and rates	500	1,000	800	2,300
Lorry expenses	2,500	6,000	4,500	13,000
Lorry depreciation	1,500	3,600	2,400	7,500
General expenses	200	500	300	1,000
Total	7,150	17,600	12,200	36,950
TOTAL	£39,020	93,983	63,125	196,128

The following changes in selling and distribution costs are to be considered in preparing next year's budget:

1. Salesmens' salaries increased by 10%.
2. Salesmens' commission is based on 5% of turnover.
3. In Divisions 2 and 3 an extra salesman is required at £1000 p.a. each from 1st April Year 3.
4. An extra commission of 10% will be paid to salesmen for additional sales of Product Cee during the sales campaign.

5. Salesmen's expenses and entertainment expenses to be increased by 10%. A further increase is to be allowed for in Division 2 and 3 of £160 each, for entertainment.

6. Car expenses to be increased by 5%.

7. Car depreciation to be increased in Division 2 and 3 by £150 each.

8. Wages increased by 5%.

9. Lorry expenses reduced by 10%.

10. Office salaries increased by 5%.

11. One extra clerk is to be employed in Division 1 and 3 at £12 per week each, from 1st January, Year 3.

12. Printing, stationery and telephone charges up by 10%.

13. Shop window displays in Division 2 and 3 to be increased by £500 each.

14. TV advertising to be increased by 20%.

In the manufacture of Products Aye, Bee and Cee, four types of raw material are used. Standard product cost details are as follows:

Material	Price per unit	Department
M1	£0·25	1
M2	£2·00	1
M3	£0·50	2
M4	£1·00	3

Standard usage of material is:

Material (in units)	Aye	Bee	Cee
M1	1	—	2
M2	—	2	1
M3	2	1	1
M4	1	2	2
Normal loss on completion	10%	5%	20%

Budgeted stocks			
1st July, Year 2	1,600	1,225	1,405
30th June, Year 3	2,000	1,500	1,800

	M 1	M 2	M 3	M 4
1st July, Year 2	5,000	4,000	6,000	8,000
30th June, Year 3	7,000	6,000	9,000	10,000

The number of employees in the manufacturing departments of the company are as follows:

	Dept. 1	Dept. 2	Dept. 3
Male	21	25	29
Female	24	24	44

The company operates a 40-hour week, and there are two weeks holiday per annum.

Standard cost of labour is:

Product	Employee	Dept. 1		Dept. 2		Dept. 3	
Aye	Female	1 hour	0·25	1 hour	0·25	—	
	Male	½ hour	0·25	½ hour	0·25	½ hour	0·25
			0·50		0·50		0·25
Bee	Female	1 hour	0·25	1 hour	0·25	1 hour	0·25
	Male	1 hour	0·50	½ hour	0·25	—	
			0·75		0·50		0·25
Cee	Female	2 hours	0·50	2 hours	0·50	6 hours	1·50
	Male	2 hours	1·00	3 hours	1·50	4 hours	2·00
			1·50		2·00		3·50

The budget fixed overheads for departments for the Year 2/3 are agreed as follows:

Dept. 1   £7,200   Dept. 2   £32,000   Dept. 3   £60,800
Dept. X   £20,000   Dept. Y   £10,000

Service department costs are apportioned as follows:

	1	2	3	X	Y
X	30%	10%	40%	—	20%
Y	20%	20%	50%	10%	—

Production overheads are absorbed as a percentage of direct wages.

Administration overheads are recovered by products on the basis of total cost of production.

Selling and distribution overheads are recovered on the basis of cost of production and administration overheads (*i.e.* total cost incurred to date).

The budgeted and actual administration overheads for Year 2/3 are as follows:

	Budget	Actual	*Forecast for Year 2/3. Estimated change on budget for Year 1/2*
Indirect materials			
General supplies	1,500	1,520	
Stationery	2,500	2,410	5% increase
Printing	2,000	1,980	
Photographic supplies	1,000	1,030	
Indirect wages and salaries			
Executive salaries	30,000	30,500	+10%
Clerical salaries	54,000	55,200	+10% + £1,800
National insurance	2,500	2,500	+100
Meal allowance	500	550	−£50
Overtime	1,000	1,020	−£100
Overtime premium	1,500	1,580	−£300

Depreciation

Office equipment	3,000	3,000	+£2,000
Cars	5,000	5,000	+£500

Repairs

Buildings	6,000	6,100	
Office equipment	1,000	920	+5%
Cars	2,000	2,050	

Miscellaneous

Rent and rates	14,940	14,940	+£1,000
Insurance	5,000	5,000	+£200
Personnel service expenses	2,000	2,040	+£50
Conference expenses	1,000	960	no change
Training expenses	500	500	+£100
Journals and periodicals	100	100	no change
Postage	3,400	3,450	+£100
Telephone	2,000	2,060	+£100
General	1,000	1,020	no change

Capital Expenditure

Dept. 1

There is a balance brought forward of £20,000 in respect of a new process line, which was initiated during Year 1/2, at a cost of £50,000. This work should be completed and paid for in Year 2/3.

Dept. 2

A new machine is required at a cost of £5000 to be installed and paid for in Year 2/3.

Dept. 3

A new section is to be built at a cost of £25,000; £15,000 to be incurred this year and the remainder in Year 3/4.

Sales Department

Purchase of two new cars at a cost of £1000 each during Year 2/3.

Administration Department

New equipment amounting to £20,000 will be paid for during Year 2/3.

Assets and liabilities as estimated at the 30th June, Year 2 include the following:

Capital	350,000 Ordinary Shares of £1 each.
Capital reserves	£42,000
Revenue reserves	30,000
Profit for the year	5,950
Creditors	6,000
Buildings	105,000
Plant and machinery	150,000
Office equipment	30,000
Motor vehicles	120,000

Finished goods stock is valued at marginal cost, the figures for each product
being Aye £5, Bee £10, Cee £20

Debtors	16,000
Bank	4,000
Depreciation—Buildings	5,000
Depreciation—Plant and machinery	30,000

Assets and liabilities as estimated at the 30th June, Year 3
include the following:

Capital	360,000 ordinary Shares of £1 each.
Creditors	£8,275

Finished goods stock is valued at marginal cost, Aye £5, Bee £10, Cee £20.

Debtors	£20,000
Depreciation—Buildings	£5,000
Plant and machinery	40,000

In Year 2/3, provide for a dividend on Ordinary Shares of 5%. Taxation
to be ignored.

SALES BUDGET (1)

Details		Budget year 2/3			Budget year 1/2			Actual year 1/2		
Division	Product	Quantity	Price	Value	Quantity	Price	Value	Quantity	Price	Value
1	Aye	2,600	£12	£31,200	2,000	£12	£24,000	2,500	£12	£30,000
	Bee	1,425	20	28,500	1,500	20	30,000	1,000	20	20,000
	Cee	1,140	50	57,000	1,000	50	50,000	500	50	25,000
	Total	5,165		116,700	4,500		104,000	4,000		75,000
2	Aye	4,200	12	50,400	3,000	12	36,000	4,000	12	48,000
	Bee	5,200	20	104,000	4,000	20	80,000	5,000	20	100,000
	Cee	5,940	50	297,000	6,000	50	300,000	5,000	50	250,000
	Total	15,340		451,400	13,000		416,000	14,000		398,000
3	Aye	3,600	12	43,200	3,000	12	36,000	3,500	12	42,000
	Bee	2,600	20	52,000	2,000	20	40,000	2,500	20	50,000
	Cee	2,925	50	146,250	2,500	50	125,000	2,000	50	100,000
	Total	9,125		241,450	7,500		201,000	8,000		192,000
TOTAL	Aye	10,400	12	124,800	8,000	12	96,000	10,000	12	120,000
	Bee	9,225	20	184,500	7,500	20	150,000	8,500	20	170,000
	Cee	10,005	50	500,250	9,500	50	475,000	7,500	50	375,000
	Total	29,630		£809,550	25,000		£721,000	26,000		£665,000

PRODUCTION BUDGET (2)

Details	Product		
	Aye (units)	Bee (units)	Cee (units)
Closing Stock	2,000	1,500	1,800
Sales	10,400	9,225	10,005
	12,400	10,725	11,805
Opening stock	1,600	1,225	1,405
Net requirements	10,800	9,500	10,400
Normal loss	1,200	500	2,600
Gross requirements	12,000	10,000	13,000

NOTES

(i) Normal loss of product Aye; 10% of gross requirements; $\frac{1}{10}$ of gross $= \frac{1}{9}$ of net; $\frac{1}{9} \times 10,800 = 1,200$.

(ii) Normal loss of product Bee: 5% of gross requirements; $\frac{1}{20}$ of gross $= \frac{1}{19}$ of net; $\frac{1}{19} \times 9,500 = 500$.

(iii) Normal loss of product Cee: 20% of gross requirements; $\frac{1}{5}$ of gross $= \frac{1}{4}$ of net; $\frac{1}{4} \times 10,400 = 2,600$.

RAW MATERIAL BUDGET (3)

Product	Department	Raw material				
		M1 (units)	M2 (units)	M3 (units)	M4 (units)	Total (£)
Aye	1	12,000				
	2			24,000		
	3				12,000	
Bee	1		20,000			
	2			10,000		
	3				20,000	
Cee	1	26,000	13,000			
	2			13,000		
	3				26,000	
	Units	38,000	33,000	47,000	58,000	
	Standard price (£)	0·25	2·00	0·50	1·00	
	Value (£)	9,500	66,000	23,500	58,000	157,000

NOTE

The raw materials required are ascertained as follows, using product Aye as an illustration:

Material	Units	Production required	Raw materials required
M1	1	12,000	12,000
M2	—		—
M3	2		24,000
M4	1		12,000

PURCHASES BUDGET (4)

Details	Material				
	M1 (units)	M2 (units)	M3 (units)	M4 (units)	Total (£)
Closing stock	7,000	6,000	9,000	10,000	
Consumption	38,000	33,000	47,000	58,000	
	45,000	39,000	56,000	68,000	
Opening stock	5,000	4,000	6,000	8,000	
Purchases	40,000	35,000	50,000	60,000	
Standard price (£)	0·25	2·00	0·50	1·00	
Value (£)	10,000	70,000	25,000	60,000	165,000

NOTE

It is important to observe the sequence of details in this budget. Many students are inclined to prepare this budget in the form of a traditional trading account, *i.e.* showing the opening stock, to which is added the purchases, then subtracting the closing stock to obtain the consumption for the period. It should be appreciated that in the purchases budget we require the amount to be purchased during the future budget period. It is therefore important to ascertain the stocks required, to which is added the materials to be consumed; from the resulting figure is subtracted the stocks already on hand.

DIRECT WAGES BUDGET (5)

Product	Employee	Department 1			Department 2			Department 3			Total Amount (£)
		Hours	Rate (£)	Amount (£)	Hours	Rate (£)	Amount (£)	Hours	Rate (£)	Amount (£)	
Aye	Female	12,000	0·25	3,000	12,000	0·25	3,000	—	—	—	6,000
	Male	6,000	0·50	3,000	6,000	0·50	3,000	6,000	0·50	3,000	9,000
	Total			6,000			6,000			3,000	15,000
Bee	Female	10,000	0·25	2,500	10,000	0·25	2,500	10,000	0·25	2,500	7,500
	Male	10,000	0·50	5,000	5,000	0·50	2,500	—	—	—	7,500
	Total			7,500			5,000			2,500	15,000
Cee	Female	26,000	0·25	6,500	26,000	0·25	6,500	78,000	0·25	19,500	32,500
	Male	26,000	0·50	13,000	39,000	0·50	19,500	52,000	0·50	26,000	58,500
	Total			19,500			26,000			45,500	91,000
Total	Female	48,000	0·25	12,000	48,000	0·25	12,000	88,000	0·25	22,000	46,000
	Male	42,000	0·50	21,000	50,000	0·50	25,000	58,000	0·50	29,000	75,000
	Total			33,000			37,000			51,000	121,000

NOTE

Wages are calculated as follows, taking product Cee for illustration:

Department 1: Female 2 hours × 13,000 units produced at £0·25.
Male 2 hours × 13,000 units produced at £0·50.

PRODUCTION OVERHEAD DISTRIBUTION SUMMARY

Details	Production Departments			Service Departments	
	1	2	3	X	Y
Balance b/d	£7,200	£32,000	£60,800	£20,000	£10,000
X	6,000	2,000	8,000	(20,000)	4,000
Y	2,800	2,800	7,000	1,400	(14,000)
X	420	140	560	(1,400)	280
Y	56	56	140	28	(280)
X	8	3	11	(28)	6
Y	16	1	(11)	—	(6)
Total	£16,500	£37,000	£76,500	—	—

NOTE

These figures have been "rounded off" for ease of calculation. The distribution of service department costs to production departments is based on estimated service given, so must inevitably be inaccurate; it is therefore unrealistic to consider these figures as warranting accurate calculations.

Production overhead recovery rate

Production overheads are normally absorbed on one of the following bases:

   (a) As a percentage of direct materials.
   (b) As a percentage of direct wages.
   (c) As a percentage of prime cost.
   (d) As a machine hour rate.
   (e) As a labour hour rate.
   (f) As a cost per unit produced.

In this project, production overheads are being absorbed as a percentage of direct wages. This method is not as suitable as methods (d) or (e) above, but it is nevertheless widely used in industry, and is more easily operated than either of the two superior alternatives. In this project, it is used for convenience so as to limit calculations.

The production overhead distribution summary shown above has been calculated by using a method of distributing service department costs known as the *repeated distribution* method. It will be observed that department X is apportioned to the other departments according to the percentages of service rendered to those departments (as estimated in the basic data given for this project). Department Y is then apportioned in a similar way. This operation is repeated until the balance remaining is eliminated. An alternative method is one using simultaneous equations; this method is shown below:

Let x = the cost of service department X and y = the cost of service department Y. Then:

$$x = £20,000 + 0.1y$$
$$y = £10,000 + 0.2x$$
$$10x = £200,000 + y$$
$$5y = £50,000 + x$$
$$10x - y = £200,000$$
$$-x + 5y = £50,000$$
$$10x - y = £200,000$$
$$-10x + 50y = £500,000$$

$$49y = £700,000$$
$$y = £14,285$$
$$x = £21,428$$

Service department		Production departments			
		1	2	3	Total
X	£21,428	£6,428	£2,143	£8,571	
Y	£14,285	2,857	2,857	7,142	
Balance b/d		7,200	32,000	60,800	
		£16,500	£37,000	£76,500	£130,000

NOTE

The above totals have been rounded off for ease of calculation. The production overhead absorption rate is calculated as follows:

$$\text{Production department 1:} \frac{\text{Production overhead}}{\text{Direct wages}} \times 100$$

$$= \frac{16,500}{33,000} \times 100 = 50\%$$

$$\text{Production department 2:} \frac{37,000}{37,000} \times 100 = 100\%$$

$$\text{Production department 3:} \frac{76,500}{51,000} \times 100 = 150\%$$

PRODUCTION OVERHEAD BUDGET (6)

Product	Employee	Departments						Total
		1		2		3		
		Overhead (£)	Absorbed on Wages (£)	Overhead (£)	Absorbed on Wages (£)	Overhead (£)	Absorbed on Wages (£)	(£)
Aye	Female	1,500	3,000	3,000	3,000	—	—	4,500
	Male	1,500	3,000	3,000	3,000	4,500	3,000	9,000
	Total	3,000	6,000	6,000	6,000	4,500	3,000	13,500
Bee	Female	1,250	2,500	2,500	2,500	3,750	2,500	7,500
	Male	2,500	5,000	2,500	2,500	—	—	5,000
	Total	3,750	7,500	5,000	5,000	3,750	2,500	12,500
Cee	Female	3,250	6,500	6,500	6,500	29,250	19,500	39,000
	Male	6,500	13,000	19,500	19,500	39,000	26,000	65,000
	Total	9,750	19,500	26,000	26,000	68,250	45,500	104,000
Total	Female	6,000	12,000	12,000	12,000	33,000	22,000	51,000
	Male	10,500	21,000	25,000	25,000	43,500	29,000	79,000
	Total	16,500	33,000	37,000	37,000	76,500	51,000	130,000

NOTE

Production overheads have been absorbed on the basis of a percentage of direct wages.

Thus in Department 3:

Female wages, £19,500. Absorption rate, 150%. £29,250.
Male wages, £26,000. Absorption rate, 150%. £39,000.

PRODUCTION COST BUDGET (7)

Element of cost		Aye		Bee		Cee		Total	
Direct materials:	DM1	£3,000		—		£6,500		£9,500	
	DM2	—		£40,000		26,000		66,000	
	DM3	12,000		5,000		6,500		23,500	
	DM4	12,000	£27,000	20,000	£65,000	26,000	£65,000	58,000	£157,000
Direct wages:	Dept. 1	6,000		7,500		19,500		33,000	
	2	6,000		5,000		26,000		37,000	
	3	3,000	15,000	2,500	15,000	45,500	91,000	51,000	121,000
Production	Dept 1	3,000		3,750		9,750		16,500	
Overhead:	2	6,000		5,000		26,000		37,000	
	3	4,500	13,500	3,750	12,500	68,250	104,000	76,500	130,000
Total			£55,500		£92,500		£260,000		£408,000

NOTE

Direct materials have been calculated as follows:

D.M. 1: 12,000 units at £0·25
D.M. 2:   Nil
D.M. 3: 24,000 units at £0·50
D.M. 4: 12,000 units at £1·00

ADMINISTRATION COST BUDGET (8)

Element of cost	Budget year 2/3		Budget Year 1/2		Actual Year 1/2	
Indirect materials						
General Supplies	£1,575		£1,500		£1,520	
Stationery	2,625		2,500		2,410	
Printing	2,100		2,000		1,980	
Photographic supplies	1,050	£7,350	1,000	£7,000	1,030	£6,940
Indirect wages and salaries						
Executive salaries	33,000		30,000		30,500	
Clerical salaries	61,200		54,000		55,200	
National insurance	2,600		2,500		2,500	
Meal allowances	450		500		550	
Overtime	900		1,000		1,020	
Overtime premium	1,200	99,350	1,500	89,500	1,580	91,350
Depreciation						
Office equipment	5,000		3,000		3,000	
Cars	5,500	10,500	5,000	8,000	5,000	8,000
Repairs						
Buildings	6,300		6,000		6,100	
Office equipment	1,050		1,000		920	
Cars	2,100	9,450	2,000	9,000	2,050	9,070
Miscellaneous						
Rent and rates	15,940		14,940		14,940	
Insurance	5,200		5,000		5,000	
Personnel service	2,050		2,000		2,040	
Conference expenses	1,000		1,000		960	
Training expenses	600		500		500	
Periodicals	100		100		100	
Postage	3,500		3,400		3,450	
Telephone expenses	2,100		2,000		2,060	
General	1,000	31,490	1,000	29,940	2,020	30,070
TOTAL		£158,140		£143,440		£145,430

SELLING AND DISTRIBUTION COST BUDGET (9)

Element of cost	Budget Year 2/3				Budget Year 1/2			
	Divisions				Divisions			
	1	2	3	Total	1	2	3	Total
Selling Expenses								
Salesmen's salaries	£2,750	£9,050	£5,475	£17,275	£2,500	£8,000	£4,750	£15,250
commission	6,785	25,270	15,447	47,502	4,950	19,300	9,425	33,675
expenses	440	990	660	2,090	400	900	600	1,900
Car expenses	2,100	6,720	3,990	12,810	2,000	6,400	3,800	12,200
Entertainment	1,320	4,010	2,470	7,800	1,200	3,500	2,100	6,800
Car depreciation	1,500	4,950	3,000	9,450	1,500	4,800	2,850	9,150
Total	14,895	50,990	31,042	96,927	12,550	42,900	23,525	78,975
Advertising								
Press	10,000	12,783	14,000	36,783	10,000	12,783	14,000	36,783
Television	7,200	16,800	10,800	34,800	6,000	14,000	9,000	29,000
Shop window display	800	2,500	1,500	4,800	800	2,000	1,000	3,800
Total	18,000	32,083	26,300	76,383	16,800	28,783	24,000	69,583
Sales office								
Salaries	1,992	2,940	2,412	7,344	1,600	2,800	2,000	6,400
Rent and rates	200	400	300	900	200	400	300	900
Light and heat	100	150	120	370	100	150	120	370
Depreciation	50	120	80	250	50	120	80	250
Postage, telephone	495	1,045	825	2,365	450	950	750	2,150
General expenses	120	280	150	550	120	280	150	550
Total	2,957	4,935	3,887	11,779	2,520	4,700	3,400	10,620
Distribution expenses								
Warehouse wages	1,260	3,675	2,310	7,245	1,200	3,500	2,200	6,900
Drivers' wages	1,312	3,150	2,100	6,562	1,250	3,000	2,000	6,250
Warehouse rates	500	1,000	800	2,300	500	1,000	800	2,300
Lorry expenses	2,250	5,400	4,050	11,700	2,500	6,000	4,500	13,000
Lorry depreciation	1,500	3,600	2,400	7,500	1,500	3,600	2,400	7,500
General expenses	200	500	300	1,000	200	500	300	1,000
Total	7,022	17,325	11,960	36,307	7,150	17,600	12,200	36,950
TOTAL	42,874	105,333	73,189	221,396	39,020	93,983	63,125	196,128

NOTE

Salesmen's commission

Division 1	Division 2	Division 3
$\frac{5}{100} \times$ £116,700 5,835	$\frac{5}{100} \times$ £451,400 22,570	$\frac{5}{100} \times$ 241,450 12,072
$\frac{10}{100} \times$ 9,500 950	$\frac{10}{100} \times$ £27,000 2,700	$\frac{10}{100} \times$ 33,750 3,375
£6,785	£25,270	£15,447

CAPITAL EXPENDITURE BUDGET (10)

Total cost appropriated but uncompleted (£)	Budgeted expenditure to date (£)	Project	balance b/d (£)	Budgeted amount appropriated this period (£)	Total (£)	Budgeted expenditure during this period (£)	balance c/d (£)
50,000	30,000	Department 1: new process line	20,000	—	20,000	20,000	—
		Department 2: new machine	—	5,000	5,000	5,000	—
		Department 3: new section	—	25,000	25,000	15,000	10,000
		Sales department: two new cars	—	2,000	2,000	2,000	—
		Admin. department: new equipment	—	20,000	20,000	20,000	—
50,000	30,000	Total	20,000	52,000	72,000	62,000	10,000

BUDGETED PROFIT AND LOSS STATEMENT (11)

Year ending 30th June (year 2/3)

Details	Aye		Bee		Cee		Total	
Sales		£124,800		£184,500		£500,250		£809,550
less Production cost	£53,500		£89,750		£252,100		£395,350	
Administration overhead	21,400		35,900		100,840		158,140	
	74,900		125,650		352,940		553,490	
Selling and distribution overhead	29,960	104,860	50,260	175,910	141,176	494,116	221,396	774,886
Net profit		19,940		8.590		6,134		34,664
Balance b/f	P/S ratios 16%		5%		1%		4%	5,950
								40,614
5% dividend								18,000
Balance c/f								£22,614

NOTES

(i) Production cost

Product

	Aye		Bee		Cee	
	units	£	units	£	units	£
Cost of production	12,000	55,500	10,000	92,500	13,000	260,000
Opening stock	1,600	8,000	1,225	12,250	1,405	28,100
	13,600	63,500	11,225	104,750	14,405	288,100
Closing stock	2,000	10,000	1,500	15,000	1,800	36,000
	11,600	53,500	9,725	89,750	12,605	252,100
Normal loss	1,200	—	500	—	2,600	—
Cost of sales	10,400	£53,500	9,225	£89,750	10,005	£252,100

Stocks have been priced at marginal cost.

(ii) Administration Overhead

Administration overheads are recovered on the basis of production cost.

Thus: $\dfrac{\text{Administration overhead}}{\text{Production cost}} \times 100 \quad \dfrac{£158,140}{395,350} \times 100 \quad\quad 40\%$

e.g. Produce Aye will absorb 40% × £53,500   £21,400

(iii) Selling and Distribution Overhead

Selling and Distribution overheads are recovered on the basis of total cost incurred to date.

Thus: $\dfrac{\text{Selling and Distribution overhead}}{\text{Production cost} + \text{Admin. overhead}} \times 100 \quad \dfrac{£221,396}{553,490} \times 100 \quad 40\%$

e.g. Product Cee will absorb 40% × £352,940   £141,176

BUDGETED BALANCE SHEET END YEAR 1/2 (12)

Issued share capital:			*Fixed Assets*		
350,000 ordinary			Buildings	£105,000	
shares of £1 each		£350,000	*Less* depreciation	5,000	
Capital reserve		42,000			£100,000
Revenue reserve	£30,000		Plant and machinery	150,000	
Profit and Loss Balance	5,950		*Less* depreciation	30,000	
		35,950			120,000
Current Liabilities			Office equipment	30,000	
Creditors		6,000	*Less* depreciation	3,000	
					27,000
			Motor vehicles	120,000	
			Less depreciation	21,650	
					98,350
					345,350
			Current Assets		
			Stock:		
			Finished goods	48,350	
			Raw materials	20,250	
				68,600	
			Debtors	16,000	
			Bank	4,000	
					88,600
		£433,950			£433,950

NOTES

(i) *Depreciation of Motor vehicles*
Administration budget: cars £5,000
Selling and distribution budget:
Cars 9,150
Lorries 7,500
£21,650

(ii) *Depreciation of office equipment*
Administration budget £3,000

(iii) *Stock: finished goods*
Aye: 1,600 units at £5 = £8,000
Bee: 1,225 units at £10 = 12,250
Cee: 1,405 units at £20 = 28,100
£48,350

(iv) *Stock: raw materials*
DM1 5,000 units at £0·25 = £1,250
DM2 4,000 units at £2·00 = 8,000
DM3 6,000 units at £0·50 = 3,000
DM4 8,000 units at £1·00 = 8,000
£20,250

BUDGETED BALANCE SHEET END YEAR 2/3 (13)

Issued share capital:			*Fixed Assets*			
360,000 ordinary			Buildings	£115,000		
shares of £1 each	£360,000		*Less* depreciation	5,000		
Capital reserve	42,000				£110,000	
Revenue reserve	30,000					
Profit and Loss			Plant and			
Balance	22,614		machinery	145,000		
		52,614	*Less* depreciation	40,000		
		454,614			105,000	
Current Liabilities			Office equipment	47,000		
Dividends proposed	18,000		*Less* depreciation	5,000		
Creditors	8,275				42,000	
		26,275	Motor vehicles	100,350		
			Less depreciation	22,450		
					77,900	
						334,9
			Current Assets			
			Stock:			
			Finished goods	61,000		
			Raw materials	28,250		
					89,250	
			Debtors		20,000	
			Bank		36,739	
						145,9
	£480,889					£480,8

NOTES

(i) *Depreciation of motor vehicles*

Administration Budget: cars	£5,500	
Selling and Distribution Budget:		
Cars	9,450	
Lorries	7,500	
		£22,450

(ii) *Depreciation of office equipment*

Administration Budget	£5,000

(iii) *Purchase of Assets*
The increase in assets is taken from the Capital Expenditure Budget.

(iv) *Stock: finished goods*

Aye:	2,000 × £5	£10,000
Bee:	1,500 × 10	15,000
Cee:	1,800 × 20	36,000
		£61,000

(v) *Stock: raw materials*

DM1	7,000 × £0·25	£1,750	
DM2	6,000 × 2·00	12,000	
DM3	9,000 × 0·50	4,500	
DM4	10,000 × 1·00	10,000	
			£28,250

CASH BUDGET YEAR 2/3 (14)

Balance b/f		£4,000	
Sources of cash			
Net profit		34,664	
Issued share capital		10,000	
Creditors		2,275	
Depreciation—Buildings	£5,000		
Plant and machinery	40,000		
Office equipment	5,000		
Motor vehicles	22,450	72,450	
			123,389
Application of cash			
Stocks—Finished goods	12,650		
Raw materials	8,000		
		20,650	
Debtors		4,000	
Buildings		15,000	
Plant and machinery		25,000	
Office equipment		20,000	
Motor vehicles		2,000	
			86,650
			£36,739

Main points to be considered

(i) The budgeted profit and loss statement (11)* shows a poor result, a profit of only £34,664. Product Aye appears to be reasonably satisfactory with a return on turnover of 16%, but Product Bee with 5% and Product Cee with 1% return are most unsatisfactory. The overall result of 4% return on turnover is clearly unacceptable. Investigations must be made into the costs and selling prices of each product, particularly Bee and Cee. The direct wages cost of product Cee (7) is particularly high which results in a heavy absorption of production overheads due to the system of recovering overheads as a percentage of direct wages. This heavy burden of overheads leads to a high cost of production which incurs a large proportion of administration overheads (11) and a further large share of selling and distribution overheads. Market research should be undertaken to ascertain whether or not the selling price could be increased.

(ii) It would be advisable to prepare a profit and loss statement based on the concept of marginal costing. It may well be that product Cee is carrying too much fixed overheads and perhaps an investigation may show that products Aye and Bee should carry a larger proportion of these overheads. However, a re-distribution of overheads will not improve the overall picture. A marginal costing presentation would show which products contribute most to the pool of fixed overheads and profit, and it may mean that one product must be abandoned, if the company is to progress. However, any decision which involves the non-production of any product must be taken

* Numbers in brackets refer to the relevant budgets.

after considering the implications of the fixed overheads being carried by the remaining products, unless of course, idle facilities can be utilised for expansion of sales of the remaining products, or the assets can be sold without incurring heavy losses. This is a marginal costing problem but is noted here for reference purposes; this technique is discussed in more detail in Chapter XI.

(iii) The cash position appears to be very satisfactory (14)*. If any improvements such as those suggested in (i) above are effected, more cash should be generated which may lead to the company having an amount of cash which is surplus to requirements.

(iv) The current ratio is very high at 5·5:1 (13). It would seem that creditors are being paid much too quickly; purchases are about £14,000 per month on average, so with creditors of £8,275 this represents only 2 weeks lag in payment.

Stocks would appear to be rather large, unless there is a specific reason for a stock build-up, such as for example may occur in an industry affected by seasonal demand. A cost of production of £157,000 (7) and an average stock of raw materials of about £24,000, shows a stock turnover of approximately 6 times per year, or every 2 months. As a very general guide, a stock turnover every 2–3 months would seem to be acceptable, but many conditions including the type of industry concerned must be considered in determining a reasonable turnover rate. It is suggested that it may be prudent to consider the introduction of a stock control system which uses maximum, minimum and re-order levels.

(v) The acid test ratio is rather high at just over 2:1 (13), but this is due to a relatively high bank balance. Ratios are discussed more fully in Chapter XIX.

(vi) The return on investment is very low at $7\frac{1}{2}\%$ before taxation (11 and 13) i.e. £34,666/454,614—the year end profit figure being included in capital employed. This item is discussed in detail on the subject of Profitability in Chapter XXII.

It seems very probable that the budget committee will be unable to accept the budgets which have been prepared. As mentioned above, the main areas to be considered appear to be in the costs of production and the selling prices; these would be investigated by the cost accountant and the sales manager. In many companies, it is necessary to draft the budget a number of times before an acceptable budget is achieved. In this project, the sales budget was the principal budget factor, which is experienced in many companies. A re-draft of the sales budget usually affects most of the other functional budgets and the master budget. The budget committee must co-ordinate the activities of the various functions of the business, so that the most realistic master budget is presented to the Board of Directors. Of course, the Board may reject the proposed budget, which results in a further re-drafting of the budgets.

* Numbers in brackets refer to the relevant budgets.

[*Examination questions will be found at the end of Chapter X.*]

CHAPTER X

FLEXIBLE BUDGETARY CONTROL

DEFINITION

THE I.C.W.A. defines a *flexible* budget as "a budget which is designed to change in accordance with the level of activity attained." This is in contrast to *fixed* budgetary control, which was discussed in Chapter IX, a fixed budget being defined as "a budget which is designed to remain unchanged irrespective of the level of activity actually attained."

In fixed budgetary control, the budgets prepared are based on one level of output, a level which has been carefully planned to equate sales and production at the most profitable rate. If the level of output actually achieved differs considerably from that budgeted, large variances will arise. In some companies it is extremely difficult to forecast sales with even a reasonable chance of success.

This situation may occur in the case of companies:

(*a*) Which are greatly affected by weather conditions, *e.g.* the soft drink industry,

(*b*) Which frequently introduce new products, *e.g.* the food canning industry,

(*c*) In which production is carried out only when orders are received from customers, *e.g.* shipbuilding,

(*d*) Which are affected by changes in fashion, *e.g.* the millinery trade,

(*e*) Where a large part of the output is intended for export, *e.g.* the production of air conditioning equipment.

Basically the idea of a flexible budget is that there shall be some standard of expenditure for varying levels of output. Flexible budgetary control has been developed with the objective of changing the budget figures progressively to correspond with the actual output achieved. Thus a budget might be prepared for each level of activity from, say, 70% up to 100% capacity. Some companies operate flexible budgets in conjunction with a fixed budget. A company with a steady production run but seasonal, uncertain sales might conveniently operate a flexible budget for sales and a fixed budget for production. There can be cases of a company having monthly flexible budgets, but a fixed annual budget to allow for variations in the monthly budget periods.

In a system of flexible budgetary control, a series of fixed budgets is set for each manufacturing budget centre so that, within limits, whatever the level of output reached it can be compared with an appropriate budget. The preparation of flexible budgets necessitates the analysis of all overheads into fixed, variable and semi-variable costs. This analysis, of course, is not peculiar to flexible budgeting but it is more important that it should be carried out in flexible than in fixed budgeting because varying levels of output need to be considered and they will have a different effect on each class of overhead.

TERMS USED

Before going any further let us be quite clear about the meaning of the terms we are using. The I.C.W.A. defines them as follows:

Fixed cost: a cost which tends to be unaffected by variations in volume of output.
Semi-variable cost: a cost which is partly fixed and partly variable.
Variable cost: a cost which tends to vary directly with volume of output.

Example (1)

(a) BUDGET WITH OVERHEADS ANALYSED

Department: *X*   Period: *January*

| | Level of activity | | | |
Type of cost	70% (700 *units*)	80% (800 *units*)	90% (900 *units*)	100% (1000 *units*)
Prime cost	£14,000	£16,000	£18,000	£20,000
Variable overhead	2,100	2,400	2,700	3,000
Semi-variable overhead	3,400	3,600	3,800	4,000
Fixed overhead	5,000	5,000	5,000	5,000
Total	£24,500	£27,000	£29,500	£32,000

It can be observed from this budget that variable overheads increase proportionately as the level of output rises, showing that costs are £3 a unit. Semi-variable overheads rise in steps of £200 for each increase in output of 100 units, showing that the variable portion must be £2 a unit and the fixed portion £2000. Fixed overheads remain constant at £5000 throughout. This example is deliberately over-simplified, but it demonstrates the basic principle of flexible budgetary control.

To complete our simple example, the budget can be compared with some "actual" results. Assume that at the end of January actual output was 800 units and actual costs were:

Prime cost	£15,750
Variable overhead	2,450
Semi-variable overhead	3,500
Fixed overhead	5,000

The budget report would be presented as follows:

(b) BUDGET REPORT

Department: *X*

Period: *January*
Production: 800 units

Type of cost	Budget	Actual	Variation Favourable	Adverse
Prime cost	£16,000	£15,750	£250	—
Variable overhead	2,400	2,450	—	£50
Semi-variable overhead	3,600	3,500	100	—
Fixed overhead	5,000	5,000	—	—
Total	£27,000	£26,700	£350	£50

Example (2)

This illustrates in more detail how much overheads are affected by level of activity. The Paulid Co. Ltd operates a system of flexible budgetary control. A flexible budget is required to show levels of activity of 80%, 90% and 100%. The following information is available:

1. *Sales*, based on normal level of activity of 80%, are 800,000 units at £10 each. If output is increased to 90%, it is thought that the selling price should be reduced by $2\frac{1}{2}$%, and if output reached 100% it would be necessary to reduce the original selling price by 5% in order to reach a wider market.

2. *Prime costs* are:

Direct material	£3·50
Direct labour	£1·25
Direct expenses	£0·25
	£5·00

If output reaches a 90% level of activity as above, the purchase price of raw material will be reduced by 5%.

3. *Variable overheads*: salesmen's commission is 5% on sales value.
4. *Semi-variable overheads* at normal level of activity are:

Supervision	£80,000
Power	70,000
Heat and light	40,000
Maintenance	50,000
Indirect labour	100,000
Salesmen's expenses	60,000
Transport	200,000

Semi-variable overheads are expected to increase by 5% if output reaches a level of activity of 90%, and by a further 10% if it reaches the 100% level.

5. *Fixed overheads* are:

Rent and rates	£100,000
Depreciation	400,000
Administration	750,000
Sales department	200,000
Advertising	500,000
General	50,000

Period............   Normal level of activity: 80%

Level of activity

	80%	90%	100%
Prime cost	£	£	£
Direct materials	2,800,000	2,992,500	3,325,000
Direct labour	1,000,000	1,125,000	1,250,000
Direct expenses	200,000	225,000	250,000
	4,000,000	4,342,500	4,825,000
Variable overhead			
Salesmen's commission	400,000	438,750	475,000
Semi-variable overhead			
Supervision	80,000	84,000	92,400
Power	70,000	73,500	80,850
Heat and light	40,000	42,000	46,200
Maintenance	50,000	52,500	57,750
Indirect labour	100,000	105,000	115,500
Salesmen's expenses	60,000	63,000	69,300
Transport	200,000	210,000	231,000
	600,000	630,000	693,000
Fixed overhead			
Rent and rates	100,000	100,000	100,000
Depreciation	400,000	400,000	400,000
Administration	750,000	750,000	750,000
Sales department	200,000	200,000	200,000
Advertising	500,000	500,000	500,000
General	50,000	50,000	50,000
	2,000,000	2,000,000	2,000,000
Total cost	7,000,000	7,411,250	7,993,000
Sales	8,000,000	8,775,000	9,500,000
Profit	£1,000,000	£1,364,250	£1,507,000

ANALYSING SEMI-VARIABLE OVERHEADS

In the two examples above, semi-variable overheads have been shown separately from fixed and variable overheads, mainly for the purpose of illustration. However, in practice it is often found desirable to show only fixed and variable overheads in the budget. This means dividing semi-variables into the fixed and variable portions so that each can be added to its respective class. It is not easy to split semi-variable overheads—some of the ways of doing it are discussed in Chapter XI. However, in budgetary control another method which can be used is the *degree of variability* technique or, as it is often called, the *analytical method*.

This technique is based on the careful analysis of each item to determine how far the cost varies with volume. It may be ascertained that some expenses have a 50% degree of variability, while others have only a 30% degree. This method is not accurate but it is relatively easy to use. There is probably no accurate method of apportioning the fixed and variable factors of semi-variable overheads. One can only approximate.

Example (1)

Analysis of distribution overheads may reveal a 60% degree of variability. At 100% level of activity, budgeted overheads are £1200. What would they be at 75% level of activity?

At 100% level of activity, distribution overheads are £720 variable (60%) and £480 fixed. Therefore at 75% level of activity variable overheads would be 75/100 × £720 = £540, while fixed overheads would remain at £480. Therefore the budgeted distribution overhead at 75% level of output would be £1020. Example 2 is a more detailed illustration of this method.

Example (2)

The Jeraul Engineering Co. Ltd manufactures only one product, which passes through six departments. A study has been made by the Cost Accountant in conjunction with various specialists, including the Time Study Engineer, of the variability of overheads. Each item has been carefully analysed, and among the results are the following:

ANALYSIS OF OVERHEADS

Department No. 1
Budget period: *May*   Normal level of activity: 10,000 machine hours

Overhead	Fixed amount	Variable rate per machine hour
Factory supplies	£300	£0·05
Supervision	2400	
Indirect labour	600	0·10
Maintenance	450	0·07½
Power	900	0·25
Heat and light	150	0·05
Water	300	0·02½
Telephone	600	0·02½
Insurance	750	
Rates	450	
Depreciation	1950	
General	150	0·02½
Total	£9,000	£0·60

This shows the expected fixed and variable overheads at the normal level of activity. The budget at this level would therefore be:

Variable overheads for 10,000 machine hours at	£0·60	£6,000
Fixed		9,000
Total		£15,000
Machine-hour rate		£1·50

Flexible budgets are to be prepared for the company to show budget allowances for levels of activity of 8000, 12,000 and 14,000 machine hours. Study of the expected behaviour of overheads at these levels has produced the following results for a level of activity of 14,000 machine hours:

Indirect labour will increase by £200.
Overtime will be involved, necessitating a premium of £800.
Increased supervision will be needed, at a cost of £350.
Machinery will require increased maintenance of £150.
Machinery will depreciate more rapidly than estimated at the normal level of activity to the extent of £350.

The resulting budget for a 10,000 machine-hour level of activity will then be shown as follows:

FLEXIBLE BUDGET

Department No. 1

Budget period May: Normal level of activity: 10,000 machine hours

Level of activity in machine hours

Overhead	8,000	10,000	12,000	14,000
Factory supplies	£700	£800	£900	£1,000
Supervision	2,400	2,400	2,400	2,750
Indirect labour	1,400	1,600	1,800	2,200
Overtime premium				800
Maintenance	1,050	1,200	1,350	1,650
Power	2,900	3,400	3,900	4,400
Heat and light	550	650	750	850
Water	500	550	600	650
Telephone	800	850	900	950
Insurance	750	750	750	750
Rates	450	450	450	450
Depreciation	1,950	1,950	1,950	2,300
General	350	400	450	500
Total	£13,800	£15,000	£16,200	£19,250
Machine-hour rate	£1·725	£1·5	£1·35	£1·373
	£1·72½	£1·50	£1·35	£1·37½

It can be observed from the budget that the machine-hour rate at normal level of activity is £1·50 but if output falls below that, the machine-hour rate rises. On the other hand if output is increased to 12,000 units, which may be the optimum capacity, the machine-hour rate falls to £1·35. This would obviously be an ideal level which the firm could set as its goal, but the output at such a level may be above what the market would absorb. Some market research could be done to discover the potential sales for the product. If this level of activity is exceeded and output rises to 14,000 units the rate per machine hour rises to £1·37½ owing to the introduction of overtime working and its corresponding effect on supervision costs, etc.

Actual results for the period would be compared with the appropriate level of activity and variances investigated. Assuming that 8000 machine hours were worked during the period, a report might be presented to the management as follows:

BUDGET REPORT

Department No. 1   Normal level of activity: 10,000 machine hours
Budget period................   Actual level of activity: 8,000 machine hours

Overhead	Budgeted allowance at 8,000 machine hours level of activity	Actual expenses at 8,000 machine hours level of activity	Variation Favourable	Adverse
Factory supplies	£700	£750		£50
Supervision	2,400	2,510		110
Indirect labour	1,400	1,360	£40	
Maintenance	1,050	1,020	30	
Power	2,900	2,840	60	
Heat and light	550	610		60
Water	500	470	30	
Telephone	800	820		20
Insurance	750	750		
Rates	450	450		
Depreciation	1,950	1,950		
General	350	320	30	
Total	£13,800	£13,850	£190	£240

It will be observed that so far in this example the actual level of activity achieved has corresponded with one of the flexible budget levels of activity. In practice, of course, this would be quite a coincidence. The reader may naturally ask, "This seems all right if enough flexible budgets are produced so that one or other of the levels budgeted for corresponds with actual output. But what happens if it does not correspond with any flexible budget level?" A technique has been developed to meet the situation. Like the degree of variability method, it does not claim to be 100% accurate but it is certainly a very useful guide to management in measuring the results of a budget centre. The technique is based on what is termed the flexible budget allowance.

THE FLEXIBLE BUDGET ALLOWANCE

This can be defined as "the expense which should be allowed for the level of activity achieved." This allowance, which is regarded here as the flexible budget, involves rather complex calculations, so it is proposed to show how it operates by means of two illustrations. One calculates the allowance from a formula based on standard hours (which are discussed in detail in Chapter VIII). The other introduces ratios, which provide management with useful guides to the performance of the operation concerned, in addition to the presentation of variances.

The introduction of the allowance gives even more "flexibility" to flexible budgetary control. Thus if a company has, for example, a flexible budget for levels of activity of 8000, 10,000 and 12,000 hours and an actual activity of 11,000 hours, the allowance for 11,000 hours would be determined somewhere between 10,000 and 12,000 hours. The vital question is, where? The Examples which follow should answer the question. It is suggested that the reader might care to follow through both Examples and then, if sufficiently interested, rework each example using the alternative method.

Example (1)

Jeraeme & Co. Ltd operate a system of flexible budgetary control which incorporates standard costing. For a budget period, the flexible budgets for Department No. 3 are as follows:

BUDGET

Department No. 3
Budget period...............   Normal level of activity: 5000 machine hours

Level of activity

Machine hours	4,000	5,000	6,000
Units	8,000	10,000	12,000
Variable overheads	£200	£250	£300
Fixed overheads	1,500	1,500	1,500
Total	£1,700	£1,750	£1,800

Actual results for the period are:

Machine hours	4,800
Output in units	11,000
Variable overheads	£260
Fixed overheads	£1,600

It will be noted that in this example machine hours have been used to show the level of activity; direct labour hours could be used as an alternative if desired and are so used in the next example.

Fixed overheads

The actual machine hours worked were 4800, which corresponds approximately to the 5000 machine hours level of activity budgeted, which is the normal level of activity. It is now necessary to calculate the standard hours of output and the allowance, or flexible budget.

To ascertain the flexible budget one can use the formula:

(Budgeted hours + [Standard hours − Actual hours]) × Standard rate

This formula can be analysed as follows:

Budgeted hours × Standard rate per hour = Budgeted amount
(Standard hours − Actual hours) × Standard rate = Efficiency Variance

Thus the formula applies the efficiency variance (*see* 5 below) to the budgeted amount so as to ascertain the amount to be allowed as the flexible budget for this period.

Flexible budget
= (Budgeted hours + [Standard hours − Actual hours]) × Standard rate
= (5000 + [5500 − 4800]) × £0·30.
= £1710

NOTE

Standard hours = Actual output × $\dfrac{\text{Budgeted hours}}{\text{Budgeted output}}$

$= 11,000 \times \dfrac{5,000}{10,000}$

= 5,500

Standard rate $= \dfrac{\text{Budgeted overhead}}{\text{Budgeted machine hours}}$

$= \dfrac{£1,500}{5,000}$

= £0·30

Variances can be calculated which are rather similar to those discussed in Chapter VIII.

1. *Cost Variance:*

Standard cost − Actual cost
£1650 − £1600 = £50 *fav.*

This shows that the total variance for the period was a favourable one. An analysis of this variance will reveal the causes of over or under expenditure.

NOTE

Standard cost = Standard hours × Standard rate
5500 × £0·30

2. *Expenditure Variance:*

Budgeted cost − Actual cost
£1500 − £1600 = £100 *adv.*

This shows that the actual expenditure for the period exceeded that budgeted.

3. *Volume Variance:*

Standard cost − Budgeted cost
£1650 − £1500 = £150 *fav.*

This shows that the volume of output achieved was greater than that budgeted, more than offsetting the adverse variance on expenditure.

4. *Capacity Variance:*

Standard cost − Flexible budget cost
£1650 − £1710 = £60 *adv.*

This shows that the capacity of the firm was not utilised as fully as it should have been.

5. *Efficiency Variance:*

Flexible budget cost − Budgeted cost
£1710 − £1500 = £210 *fav.*

Although the capacity of the firm was not fully utilised, during the time it *was* utilised a considerable degree of efficiency was reached. This favourable efficiency variance more than compensated for the adverse capacity variance; the result was a favourable volume variance overall.

6. *Controllable Variance*

$$\text{Flexible budget cost} - \text{Actual cost}$$
$$£1,710 \quad - \quad £1,600 \quad = £110 \, fav.$$

This variance is a particularly useful one in that it pinpoints responsibility for over or under expenditure on the person who is in a position to control expenditure. The controllable variance comprises the efficiency variance and the expenditure variance, both of which are the direct concern of the head of department concerned. In this example an unfavourable expenditure was more than offset by a very favourable performance. The costs represented in this calculation can be controlled, as distinct from capacity variance, which may be affected by external factors such as low sales demand or internal factors such as low output caused by inefficiency in a preceding production department.

The following checks on the variances are available:

Check I
$$\text{Cost Variance} = \text{Expenditure Variance} + \text{Volume Variance}$$
$$£50 \, fav. \quad = \quad £100 \, adv. \quad + \quad £150 \, fav.$$

Check II
$$\text{Volume Variance} = \text{Capacity Variance} + \text{Efficiency Variance}$$
$$£150 \, fav. \quad = \quad £60 \, adv. \quad + \quad £210 \, fav.$$

Check III
$$\text{Flexible budget} = \text{Budgeted cost} + \text{Efficiency Variance}$$
$$£1710 \quad = \quad £1500 \quad + \quad £210 \, fav.$$

Check IV
$$\text{Controllable Variance} = \text{Expenditure Variance} + \text{Efficiency Variance}$$
$$£110 \, fav. \quad = \quad £100 \, adv. \quad + \quad £210 \, fav.$$

To help the reader understand the connection between the variances and remember the formula used in calculating the variance, the following diagrams may be helpful (A, actual; B, budget; S, standard; FB, flexible budget).

Cost Variance

S–A

Volume Variance   Expenditure Variance
S–B   B–A

It should be observed that $S-A = (S-B) + (B-A)$

Volume Variance

S–B

Capacity Variance   Efficiency Variance
S–FB   FB–B

Again, it should be observed that $S-B = (S-FB) + (FB-B)$

Controllable Variance

FB−A

Efficiency Variance   Expenditure Variance
FB−B   B−A

Again, FB−A = (FB−B) + (B−A)

Complete diagrammatic form

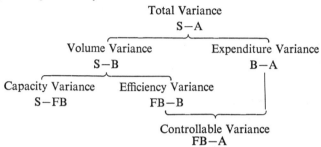

Total Variance
S−A

Volume Variance   Expenditure Variance
S−B   B−A

Capacity Variance   Efficiency Variance
S−FB   FB−B

Controllable Variance
FB−A

Variable overheads

It is assumed that variable overheads move directly with output, so any changes in output can be disregarded in calculating variable overhead variances. In other words, as output rises variable overhead cost rises and *vice versa*. It is, therefore, only necessary to consider the variance due to a change in price, which is termed the Expenditure Variance. However, if it is considered that variable overheads do not move directly with output, calculations of the variances will be made in a similar way to those for fixed overheads.

Expenditure Variance:

$$\text{Standard cost} - \text{Actual cost}$$
$$£275 \quad - \quad £260 \quad = £15 \ fav.$$

NOTES

1. Standard cost = Standard hours × Standard rate = 5500 × £0·05

2. Standard rate = $\dfrac{\text{Budgeted variable overhead}}{\text{Budgeted hours}}$ = $\dfrac{£250}{5000}$

ACCOUNTING ENTRIES

	Dr	Cr
Fixed overhead	£1600	
Variable overhead	260	
Expense creditors		£1860
Work in progress	1775	
Fixed Overhead Expenditure Variance	100	
Fixed overhead		1600
Variable overhead		260
Variable Overhead Expenditure Variance		15
Finished goods	1925	
Capacity Variance	60	
Efficiency Variance		210
Work in progress		1775

Example (2)

The flexible budgets for Department 5 of Jeraeme & Co. Ltd are as follows:

Department No. 5

Budget period......... Normal level of activity: 8000 direct labour hours

Level of activity

Direct labour hours	8,000	10,000	12,000
Units	4,000	5,000	6,000
Variable overhead	£800	£1,000	£1,200
Fixed overhead	2,000	2,000	2,000
Total	£2,800	£3,000	£3,200

Actual results for the period were:

Direct labour hours	7500
Output in units	4200
Variable overheads	£720
Fixed overheads	£2050

The fixed overhead recovery rate will have been based on a budgeted amount of £2000 at a level of activity of 8000 hours, because recovery would be calculated on normal level of activity. It is now necessary to calculate three ratios, because this method of ascertaining the allowance or flexible budget is based on ratios. These ratios are:

1. Efficiency ratio:

$$\frac{\text{Standard hours}}{\text{Actual hours}} \times 100$$

$$= \frac{8400}{7500} \times 100$$

$$= 112\%$$

NOTE

$$\text{Standard hours} = \text{Actual output} \times \frac{\text{Budgeted direct labour hours}}{\text{Budgeted output}}$$

$$= 4200 \text{ units} \times \frac{8000}{4000}$$

This ratio is defined (by the I.C.W.A.) as "the standard hours equivalent to the work produced, expressed as a percentage of the actual hours spent in producing that work." It will be noticed that even though it is called the efficiency *ratio*, it is usually in percentage form.

2. Actual usage of budgeted capacity ratio:

$$\frac{\text{Actual hours}}{\text{Budgeted hours}} \times 100$$

$$= \frac{7500}{8000} \times 100$$

$$= 93 \cdot 75\%$$

This may be defined as "the relationship between the actual number of working hours and the budgeted number."

3. *Activity ratio:*

$$\frac{\text{Standard hours}}{\text{Budgeted hours}} \times 100$$

$$= \frac{8400}{8000} \times 100$$

$$= 105\%$$

This is defined as "the number of standard hours equivalent to the work produced, expressed as a percentage of the budgeted standard hours."

It should be noted that the calculation of these variances can be checked as follows:

$$\frac{\text{Activity ratio}}{\text{Actual usage of budgeted capacity ratio}} = \text{Efficiency ratio}$$

$$\frac{105\%}{93 \cdot 75\%} = 112\%$$

NOTE

$$\text{Standard hours} = \text{Actual output} \times \frac{\text{Budgeted hours}}{\text{Budgeted output}}$$

$$= 4200 \times \frac{8000}{4000}$$

In this method the formula used to calculate the allowance or flexible budget is:

$$\text{BFO} - \text{BFO (AUR} - \text{AR)}$$

where BFO is the budgeted fixed overhead, AUR the actual usage of budgeted capacity ratio and AR the activity ratio.

The flexible budget is £2000 − £2000 (93·75% − 105%)
$$2000 - \quad 2000\,(-11\cdot25\%)$$
$$2000 + \quad 225$$
$$£2225.$$

Fixed overheads

The fixed overhead variances can be calculated in the same way as those in Example 1 were calculated. However, if the reader cares for a change in technique—it is good practice to make a habit of interpreting results in different ways so that one really grasps the principles involved—the variances can be calculated by the standard hours technique.

1. *Cost Variance:*

$$\begin{array}{ccc} \text{Standard cost} & - & \text{Actual cost} \\ £2100 & - & £2050 \end{array} = £50 \; fav.$$

NOTE

$$\text{Standard cost} = \text{Standard hours} \times \text{Standard rate}$$
$$8400 \times £0\cdot25$$

$$\text{Standard rate} = \frac{\text{Budgeted overhead}}{\text{Budgeted hours}}$$

$$\frac{£2000}{8000 \text{ hours}}$$

2. Expenditure Variance:

$$\text{Budgeted cost} - \text{Actual cost}$$
$$\text{£2000} \quad - \quad \text{£2050} \quad = \text{£50 } adv.$$

3. Volume Variance:

Standard rate (Budgeted hours − Standard hours)
£0·25 (8000 − 8400) = £100 fav.

4. Capacity Variance:

Standard rate (Budgeted hours − Actual hours)
£0·25 (8000 − 7500) = £125 adv.

5. Efficiency Variance:

Standard rate (Standard hours − Actual hours)
£0·25 (8400 − 7500) = £225 fav.

6. Controllable Variance:

Flexible budget cost − Actual cost
£2225 − £2050 = £175 fav.

Check I

Cost Variance = Expenditure Variance + Volume Variance
£50 fav. = £50 adv. + £100 fav.

Check II

Volume Variance = Capacity Variance + Efficiency Variance
£100 fav. = £125 adv. + £225 fav.

Check III

Flexible budget = Budgeted cost + Efficiency Variance
£2225 = £2000 + £225 fav.

Check IV

Controllable Variance = Expenditure Variance + Efficiency Variance
£175 fav. = £50 adv. + £225 fav.

Variable overheads

Expenditure Variance = Standard cost − Actual cost
£840 − £720 = £120 fav.

NOTE

Standard cost = Standard hours × Standard rate
8400 × £0·10

ACCOUNTING ENTRIES

	Dr	Cr
Fixed overheads	£2050	
Variable overheads	720	
Expense creditors		£2770
Work in progress	2840	
Fixed Overhead Expenditure Variance	50	
Variable Overhead Expenditure Variance		120
Fixed overhead		2050
Variable overhead		720
Finished goods	2940	
Capacity Variance	125	
Efficiency Variance		225
Work in progress		2840

Flexible budgetary control is assuming great importance in management accounting, not only in practice but equally so in examining questions. The reader who is preparing for examinations should practice these techniques so as to become fully conversant with them.

EXAMINATION QUESTIONS

1. In connection with budgetary control, enumerate and describe briefly the usual subsidiary budgets which make up the master budget. [S.C.A.

2. Explain the principles which may be followed in fixing budgets and expenses of departments under the control of a departmental manager. Will the principles differ as between a manufacturing and non-manufacturing department? [C.C.A.

3. (a) Sales forecasting is an essential element in budgetary control. Set out in short notes the points you would make to a sales manager to enlist his effective co-operation in a budgetary scheme.

(b) Prepare a ruling of a sales forecast form, providing for certain details to be entered by the cost accountant, and others to be entered by the sales manager, for use in connection with budgeting. [C.W.A.

4. You are asking the works engineer to produce a maintenance costs budget for the first time. Prepare the outline, with expense headings, of such a budget, and indicate the sources of all the relevant data required for its construction. [C.W.A.

5. Set out, point by point, the purpose of and procedure for preparing an annual capital expenditure budget in a medium-sized manufacturing company. [C.W.A.

6. What purposes are served by the preparation of a capital expenditure budget? Outline the procedure necessary to its preparation. [C.W.A.

7. "Budgeting is profit planning." Elaborate this statement. What accounting devices would you use where output varies? [C.W.A.

8. Write a critical survey of a budgetary control system with particular reference to (a) the various types of budget and (b) changing production and sales levels. [C.C.A.

9. Explain what is meant by the principal budget factor, and indicate its significance in the fields of

(a) Setting long-term budgets,
(b) Assessing product profitability, and
(c) Fixing selling prices. [C.W.A.

10. (a) "Budgets and standards may be set on different bases of achievement." Explain this statement. Which basis do you recommend and why? Is your opinion affected by the use of flexible budgetary control?

(b) A business can be affected by external conditions resulting in marked changes in the level of output or sales; raw material prices or selling prices may sometimes move substantially away from the budgeted prices. If substantial variances are constantly occurring, what action, if any, would you take regarding the budgets themselves? State your reasons. [C.W.A.

11. A company making a single product has a factory in the South, and distributes its production through three depots situated in the South, Midlands and North.

It is estimated that during the coming year 100,000 units will be manufactured and sold at a price of £20 per unit, the sales being spread as follows:

South	70,000 units
Midlands	20,000 ,,
North	10,000 ,,

Standard costs of production are:

Direct materials		£4·80 per unit
Direct wages		£3
Factory variable overheads		140% on direct wages
Factory fixed overheads		£400,000 per annum

The costs of selling and distribution incurred by the depots are estimated as follows:

Fixed costs	South	£80,000 per annum
	Midlands	£50,000
	North	£30,000
Variable costs	South	5% of sales value
	Midlands	8%
	North	10%

From the budget for the business prepared from these figures, management is considering the desirability of closing the depots and selling organisations in the Midlands and/or North. If this is done it is expected that all sales in these areas will be lost, but that sales in the South will remain unaffected.

Prepare a budget for the business from the figures provided, indicating why management is thinking of closing the depots in the Midlands and/or North.

Present additional information to help management make a decision in regard to this problem, and make recommendations from your figures.

[C.W.A.

12. A company manufactures a single product, which is sold at a standard selling price of £5 per unit. The standard costs of this product are as follows:

Direct materials	5 lb at £0·40 per lb
Direct wages	3 hours at £0·25 per hour
Variable factory overheads	£0·33⅓ per direct labour hour
Fixed factory overheads	£300,000 per annum
Variable administration, selling and distribution overheads	£0·10 per unit sold
Fixed administration, selling and distribution overheads	£200,000 per annum

The capital employed in the business amounts to £1,000,000 and it is forecast that during the coming year 440,000 units of the product will be made and sold.

From these figures management requests that you prepare a forecast of the results for the coming year.

Show clearly the order in which you make your calculations, and from them prepare the figures requested by management. State whether you would recommend acceptance of your forecast as the budget for the coming year; if not what suggestions would you make? [C.W.A.

13. (a) Explain the nature of a system of budgetary control, and list the advantages to management of such a system.

(b) A company prepares the following main budgets:

(i) Sales budget.
(ii) Manufacturing budget.
(iii) Purchasing budget.
(iv) Selling and administrative overheads budget.
(v) Budgeted Balance Sheet.

You are required to describe briefly the relationship between these budgets and the content of each. [C.A., 1965

14. XYZ Engineering Ltd proposes to increase its output by reorganising the factory layout, installing some additional plant and increasing the labour force. The plan is intended to be put into operation during the four months to 31st December 1966, and has the following financial implications:

(a) The forecast balance sheet as on 31st August 1966 is as follows:

Issued share capital		£700,000	Plant and machinery at cost		£600,000
Reserves		100,000	Less: Depreciation		264,000
					336,000
Profit and Loss Account		140,000	Raw material stocks		115,000
		940,000	Work in progress and finished stocks		125,000
Trade creditors		85,000	Debtors		300,000
Accrued charges:			Cash		163,000
Rent	£8,000				
Other	6,000				
		14,000			
		£1,039,000			£1,039,000

NOTE

Trade creditors represent the purchases of raw materials during August 1966. Debtors represent sales in July and August 1966 at the rate of £150,000 per month.

(b) The additional plant, costing £200,000, will be delivered and paid for in September.

(c) Raw materials to be consumed per month:

	September	October to December
	£70,000	£100,000

(d) Stocks of raw materials are to be increased to £130,000 at the end of September and maintained at that level.

(e) Monthly figures of other costs of production:

	September	October to December per month
Direct wages	£16,000	£24,000
Indirect wages	5,000	7,000
Other factory expenses	3,000	5,000

One quarter of each of the above costs would be outstanding at the end of the respective month and would be paid in the following month.

Rent of the factory at £4000 per month is paid quarterly in arrears on 30th September and 31st December, etc.

Depreciation on plant and machinery is to be provided throughout at the rate of £7000 per month.

(f) Administration and selling expenses monthly:

	September	October to December per month
Salaries	£20,000	£22,000
Other office expenses	2,000	3,000

Advertising and publicity will continue at £10,000 monthly, but will be increased to £30,000 in October and November.

Each of the above expenses is to be considered as paid in the month in which they arise.

(g) Forecast sales are:

September and October	£150,000 per month
November	£160,000
December	£250,000

(h) To meet the higher level of sales planned, work in progress and finished stocks are to be increased to £160,000 at the end of October and to £195,000 at the end of November. A fall to £175,000 is expected at 31st December.

(i) It is expected that existing credit terms will continue to be observed.

(j) The parent company has agreed to advance on a loan account monthly such sums as may be necessary to limit to £100,000 the bank overdraft of XYZ Engineering Ltd. (Interest on overdraft and loan is to be ignored.)

As chief accountant, you are required to prepare the following for discussion with your managing director:

(i) A forecast Trading and Profit and Loss Account for each of the four months September to December 1966, and a supporting forecast Balance Sheet as on 31st December 1966.

(ii) A cash forecast, month by month, for the four months to 31st December 1966, showing when any advance on the parent company Loan Account will be required.

Ignore taxation and investment grants. [C.A., (1966)

15. From the undernoted information you are required:

(a) To prepare a cash forecast statement for each quarter of a company's year to 30th June 1968.

(b) To indicate briefly the recommendations you would make to the board to alleviate any points of difficulty revealed by the statement.

(1) The cash on hand and in the bank at 1st July 1967 totalled £14,500.

(2) Estimates of sales and purchases:

Quarter ended	Cash sales	Credit sales	Credit purchases
30th June 1967	£2,000	£150,000	£120,000
30th September 1967	2,500	180,000	150,000
31st December 1967	1,500	120,000	150,000
31st March 1968	3,500	225,000	120,000
30th June 1968	2,000	210,000	120,000

The company generally pays creditors in the month following the receipt of goods, receiving an average cash discount of $2\frac{1}{2}\%$. The company's debtors take one month's credit and take an average cash discount of 5%.

(3) Wages and salaries and all other revenue charges have been estimated at £30,000 per quarter, including depreciation of £7500 per quarter.

(4) Corporation tax liability of £10,500 is due to be paid in the quarter to 30th September 1967.

(5) In the quarter to 31st December 1967, it is intended to replace four of the company's motor vehicles at a cost of £3900. The vehicles sold are expected to realise £1500.

(6) The directors propose to pay a dividend of £10,000 gross in November 1967 in respect of the year to 30th June 1967. Dividends in previous years have normally been paid in January. [C.A.(S)

16. Mr Planet will commence business, manufacturing Elektraps, on 1st January 1969. His plans for the first six months are as follows:

(1) He will manufacture 1000 units per month.

(2) He will purchase machinery costing £300,000 on 1st January 1969; an initial payment of £210,000 is to be made on 1st January and the balance will be paid in twelve monthly instalments, the first on 31 January. This machinery has the capacity to produce up to 3000 units per month. Depreciation is to be provided at the rate of £30,000 p.a.

(3) Each man employed in the factory can produce ten units per month, and will require a wage of £80 per month. The minimum number of men required for the planned output will be employed.

(4) Each unit requires 1 lb of material at £4 per lb. An initial stock of material of 250 lbs will be purchased and paid for on 1st January. Subsequently material will be replaced immediately it is used and paid for in the following month.

(5) Factory rent will amount to £6000 p.a. and it will be payable by the firm, quarterly in advance, on 1st January, etc.

(6) Other overhead expenditure will require payments of £3000 per month.

(7) Sales will be 600 units per month for the first three months and 1000 units per month for the second three months, at the price of £25 per unit. Customers will pay in the second month after receiving the goods.

(8) Mr Planet has been offered a bank overdraft of £30,000.

(9) Stocks are to be valued at direct cost (labour plus materials).

Required: (1) Budget showing the minimum amount of cash that Mr Planet must pay into his business bank account in order just to keep within the agreed bank overdraft during the first six months of operation (assume that Mr Planet will draw no cash for his personal use): and (2) budgeted balance sheet at 30 June 1969, assuming that this sum is paid in as capital.

[B.Sc.(Econ.)

17. The controllers' committee of Modern Scottish Enterprises Ltd has made the following forecasts:

	As at 31st December 1965	As at 31st March 1966	As at 30th June 1966
Fixed assets	£1,137,000	£1,170,000	£1,300,000
Depreciation reserve	480,000	499,000	525,000
Investments	22,000	22,000	26,000
Stocks	1,250,000	1,300,000	1,340,000
Debtors	480,000	470,000	495,000
Creditors	525,000	530,000	528,000

It is expected that the bank overdraft at 31st December 1965 will be £275,000 and that a long-term loan for £500,000 will be obtained in March 1966.

The sales budget for the first quarter of 1966 is £1,650,000 and for the second quarter £1,850,000. The budgeted cash profit is 12% on sales.

Taxation for 1965–66 amounts to £290,000 and a dividend of £76,500 (net) in the ordinary shares is expected to be paid in May.

Prepare a statement in tabular form to show the cash position at the end of March and at the end of June 1966.   [C.A.(S)

18. The Brown Shoe Company Ltd has prepared the following forecasts:

| | | Raw | | | Overheads | | | Capital expendi- |
	Sales	material	Wages	Production	Admin.	Selling	Research	ture
1960 Oct.	£135,000	£53,000	£12,500	£8,100	£3,450	£9,000	£1,600	£1,000
Nov.	120,000	42,000	11,506	7,600	3,400	8,000	1,600	2,000
Dec.	108,000	45,000	9,080	6,000	3,800	7,500	1,600	61,000
1961 Jan.	90,000	48,000	9,790	6,500	3,600	6,400	1,800	4,000
Feb.	82,000	46,000	9,400	6,100	3,500	6,200	1,800	6,000
March	96,000	48,000	10,212	6,700	3,350	6,500	1,800	3,000
April	94,000	49,000	9,300	6,100	3,400	6,400	1,800	—
May	108,000	47,000	10,304	6,900	3,250	7,300	1,900	8,000
June	105,000	40,000	10,032	6,600	3,500	7,400	1,750	63,000

From the above, and taking into account the following, you are required to prepare a cash budget for the first six months of 1961:

(a) Assume that the cash balance on 1st January 1961 will be £87,500.

(b) Debtors are normally allowed two months' credit but only 90% pay within this period. The remainder pay in three months with the exception of bad debts, which are equal to 1% of sales.

(c) Creditors for goods and services allow one month's credit.

(d) 40% of creditors for raw materials allow 2½% cash discount for payment in the same month and advantage is taken of this.

(e) The budget figure for wages is for those earned in the month. Workers are on a five-day week and wages are paid one week in arrears on Fridays (1st January 1961 is a Sunday). Ignore bank holidays and assume 20 working days in December 1960.

(f) Interest on £30,000 5% Debentures is due in February and August.

(g) It is anticipated that an Ordinary share dividend of £31,000 net will be paid in April.

(h) Income from investments amounting to £80 per half year is due in March and September.

(i) Capital expenditure is payable in the month indicated in the table.   [C.I.A.

19. The following is a summary of the Balance Sheet of Perseus Ltd as on 31st December 1961:

Issued share capital	£50,000	Fixed assets	£14,000
Profit and Loss Account	12,000	Stock, at cost	36,000
Bank overdraft	18,000	Trade debtors	50,000
Trade creditors	20,000		
	£100,000		£100,000

The trade creditors represent the December 1961 purchases: the trade debtors represent the November and December 1961 sales, which were £25,000 in each month.

The sales for the six months ended 31st December 1961 were £157,500 and the gross profit was at a uniform rate of 20% of selling price.

On 1st January 1962 the company's suppliers increased the prices of all goods by 25% and Perseus Ltd increased its selling prices by 20%.

The following plans and estimates were made for the six months ended 30th June 1962:

(*a*) Sales would be, in quantities, 10% greater than in the preceding six months. Sales for the month of March would be £42,900 and the remainder of the sales would be evenly spread over the other five months.

(*b*) The stock at the end of each month would be the same, in quantity, as on 31st December 1961 except that, on 31st March, it would be 10% above that level. All stock on 31st December 1961 would be sold during the period.

(*c*) The period of credit allowed would be the same as in 1961, *i.e.* one month by suppliers, and two months to customers. Payments would be made and received, in accordance with these terms, punctually, except that one supplier would be paid £3000 in advance in February 1962 for goods to be purchased in March.

(*d*) Wages and expenses would be £2025 per month, all paid within the month to which they relate.

(*e*) Planned receipts and payments for each month would be effected at an even rate throughout the month.

(*f*) No fixed assets would be acquired, scrapped, or sold during the period.

You are required to prepare:

(i) Statements in the form of a notional Balance Sheet as on 30th June 1962 and notional Trading and Profit and Loss Accounts for the six months ending on that date, as they would appear if the estimates were realised, and

(ii) A statement showing the date and amount of the maximum bank overdraft during the six months ending 30th June 1962 if the estimates were realised.

Ignore taxation, bank interest and depreciation of fixed assets.

[C.A. (1962)

20. The production manager provides the following information regarding his plant requirements during the next three years:

	Year 1 (£)	Year 2 (£)	Year 3 (£)
Lathes for Machine Shop A	16,000		
Replacement of heavy press		20,000	
Conveyors to convert Department C to semi-automatic operation		12,000	
Plant required in new Department X		8,000	184,000

The accounts department proposes to install a mechanised accounting system in Year 1, machinery and equipment for which are estimated to cost £8400.

The distribution manager estimates that he will require three new vans in Year 1, costing £3100. He estimates that in the following year eight vans having a saleable value of £800 will be replaced by eight new vans costing a total of £6400.

A new building to cost £210,000 will be commenced in Year 2 to house Department X. This sum will be paid as to £80,000 in Year 2 and the balance of £130,000 in Year 3.

All the above-mentioned expenditure is approved in principle. Final approval of a further project involving the purchase of land in Year 3 and costing approximately £50,000 is to be deferred until the end of Year 1.

Prepare a long-term capital expenditure budget covering the three years.

[C.I.A.

21. Two companies, Alpha and Beta, are members of a group. Alpha manufactures a raw material for use solely by Beta. Beta processes this

material into a product for sale in a specialised market. Cost and other data for each company for 1968 are given in the Appendix to this question.

As part of a plan to establish responsibility centres, the group management give the management of Alpha and Beta a high degree of freedom in their budgeting and operations. They are told that for the purposes of management accounting in each company the raw material produced by Alpha is to be transferred to Beta at a price of £10 per ton (this having been calculated to give Alpha an acceptable rate of return on the group investment in it).

The management of Beta are told to buy their raw material from Alpha at this transfer price and to plan their output and sales on this basis. Alpha's management are told to produce as much as Beta demands. Both managements are instructed to act, within these rules, so as to maximise their accounting profits.

You are required, on the basis of the data provided, to show, appending appropriate calculations:

(a) Beta's profit and loss budget for 1968 if its management observes the group directive.

(b) Alpha's profit and loss budget for 1968 on the assumption that Beta plans as shown in (a) and informs Alpha how much raw material it proposes to buy in that year.

(c) State, supporting your answer with reasons and appropriate figures, whether the consolidated group budget based on the budgets of (a) and (b) represents the best plan for the group. If not, provide a group profit and loss budget based on the optimal plan.

(d) What conclusions do you draw from the results of (c)?

Work to the nearest 10,000 units of product in budgeting output and sales.

APPENDIX TO QUESTION 21
Data for 1968

ALPHA

Total fixed costs	£500,000
Variable costs per unit of output	£4
Full capacity output (units)	100,000

BETA

Total fixed costs	£130,000
Variable costs per unit of output excluding raw material bought from Alpha	£3
Full capacity output (units)	100,000

Estimated demand conditions for final product

Sales units	Price £
100,000	13
90,000	14
80,000	14½
70,000	15
60,000	15¼
50,000	15½

One unit of raw material from Alpha is required for each unit of output of final product.

It can be assumed that, in both companies, fixed costs are constant and that variable costs have a linear relation to output, within any relevant range of output.

There is no other market available for Alpha's product. Policies followed in 1968 will have no effect on future demand or costs. Stocks are not to be increased or reduced. [J.Dip. M.A.

22. The machine shop of a factory using flexible budgetary control has a budget for April of:

Budgeted machine hours	10,000
Budgeted overheads:	
Variable with machine time	£6,000
Variable with output	4,000
Fixed	5,000

The actual performance and cost details for the month are:

Machine hours worked	9,500
Standard hours produced	10,200
Variable overheads varying:	
With machine time	£6,400
With output	4,300
Fixed overheads	5,200

Present the above details on a statement for works management, analysing the variances which have arisen. [C.W.A.

23. (a) How are (i) volume variance, and (ii) budget variance, as measures of the degree of efficiency, affected when budgeted and actual levels of activity do not coincide?

(b) Illustrate your answer to (a) by calculating the total overhead cost variance and the individual overhead variances for budget, efficiency, and volume in respect of a production department to which the figures given below apply, assuming the budget is (i) fixed, (ii) flexible.

Potential hours	5000	5500	6000
Budgeted costs	£21,000	£22,000	£23,000

The product takes 5 hours to produce, and normal capacity is 5500 standard hours. The actual results for the periods were:

Overheads	£23,000
Output	1000 units of product
Hours	5200 [I.C.W.A.

24. Demand for the output of a certain company is very elastic, and modern plant recently installed is capable of greatly increased production. Output at present is 80,000 units per year, and half a million units annually are estimated to be within the capacity of the new plant.

The present selling price per unit is £15.

The need for flexible budgeting is recognised and six alternative levels of output in addition to the present level are contemplated. Six equal increments in annual output level, up to a maximum of 500,000 units, would involve corresponding reductions of £1 each in unit price to £9 per unit at the maximum output.

The present variable costs amount to £400,000. Fixed costs which at present amount to £200,000 are not expected to increase for any of the six alternative output levels contemplated. Semi-fixed costs are expected to vary from the present annual figure of £230,000 to £320,000, the upward steps being to £260,000 at 220,000 units, £280,000 at 360,000 units, and £320,000 at

500,000 units. The costs classified as variable at the six projected levels of output are calculated to be as follows:

£750,000; £1,100,000; £1,500,000; £1,750,000; £2,050,000; £2,500,000

(a) Tabulate the above data and show total costs, incremental costs, total and incremental sales income at the various output levels.
(b) Which volume should be set for budgeted output?
(c) What is the selling price at that volume? [C.W.A.

25. The annual flexible budget of a company is as follows:

Production capacity	40%	60%	80%	100%
Costs:				
Direct labour	£16,000	£24,000	£32,000	£40,000
Direct material	12,000	18,000	24,000	30,000
Production overhead	11,400	12,600	13,800	15,000
Administration over-head	5,800	6,200	6,600	7,000
Selling and distribution overhead	6,200	6,800	7,400	8,000
	£51,400	£67,600	£83,800	£100,000

Owing to trading difficulties the company is operating at 50% capacity. Selling prices have had to be lowered to what the directors maintain is an uneconomic level and they are considering whether or not their single factory should be closed down until the trade recession has passed.

A market research consultant has advised that in about twelve months' time there is every indication that sales will increase to about 75% of normal capacity and that the revenue to be produced in the second year will amount to £90,000. The present revenue from sales at 50% capacity would amount to only £49,500 for a complete year.

If the directors decide to close down the factory for a year it is estimated that:

(a) The present fixed costs would be reduced to £11,000 per annum.
(b) Closing down costs (redundancy payments, etc.) would amount to £7500.
(c) Necessary maintenance of plant would cost £1000 per annum.
(d) On re-opening the factory, the cost of overhauling plant, training and engagement of new personnel would amount to £4000.

Prepare a statement for the directors, presenting the information in such a way as to indicate whether or not it is desirable to close the factory.
[C.W.A.

CHAPTER XI

MARGINAL COSTING

DEFINITIONS

MARGINAL costing is probably the most controversial subject in the whole sphere of management accounting. Many articles have been written on the subject and it would appear that most writers feel strongly about it, whether they are for or against. It is not proposed here to explore the various points of view that have been expressed; the reader who is interested should refer to a number of articles recommended for those who wish to pursue the matter further.*

Controversy has arisen not only over the usefulness of marginal costing, but even about what the phrase means. "Marginal costing" is used in Britain and Europe, while "direct costing" or sometimes "variable costing" is preferred in the U.S.A., but the techniques used follow the same pattern. The Institute of Cost and Works Accountants publication *A report on marginal costing* gives the following definitions:

Marginal cost. The amount at any given volume of output by which aggregate costs are changed if the volume of output is increased or decreased by one unit.

Marginal costing. The ascertainment, by differentiating between fixed costs and variable costs, of marginal costs and of the effect on profit of changes in volume or type of output.

Fixed cost and variable cost were defined in the previous chapter.

To the economist, marginal cost is an incremental cost; he considers the addition to total cost which results from the production of one more unit of output. The accountant's version has been defined by the Institute of Chartered Accountants in *Developments in cost accounting* as "every expense (whether of production, selling or distribution) incurred

* "Marginal costing—caution!" John Sizer, *The Cost Accountant*, March 1963; "Marginal costing and break-even analysis," G. H. Lawson, *The Cost Accountant*, September 1960; "A case for marginal costing," D. R. C. Halford, *The Manager*, June 1961; "Marginal costing," *Accountancy*, August 1958; "Pricing and costing," *Accountancy*, June 1957; "Why direct costing is rapidly gaining acceptance," Wilmer Wright, *Journal of Accountancy*, July 1962; "Direct costing—handle with care," Thomas S. Dudick, *Journal of Accountancy*, October 1962; "The concept and practice of marginal costing," E. J. Broster, *The Accountant*, February 1964; "The characteristics of cost," R. N. Anthony, *Management Accounting*, September 1965; "The validity of marginal costing," A. H. Taylor, *The Accountant*, 18 September 1965; "The terminology of marginal costing," J. Sizer, *Management Accounting*, August 1966; "Direct costing is a useful management tool," R. S. Fraser, *The Accountant*, 6 August 1966.

by the taking of a particular decision." Marginal cost will be regarded here as the prime cost plus all overheads which vary with volume.

Marginal costing is not a system of costing such as process or job costing, but a technique which presents management with information enabling it to measure the profitability of an undertaking by considering the behaviour of costs. Companies which use marginal costing to aid management decisions frequently operate an orthodox costing system. In other words, overheads may be recovered in the recognised way so that total costs can be ascertained; but fixed and variable overheads will be analysed so that management can be supplied with marginal cost statements when necessary.

HOW IT WORKS

In orthodox costing systems, fixed overheads are recovered in product costs by some agreed recovery method. This usually involves classification of overheads; apportionment to production, administration, selling and distribution departments; apportionment to cost centres and services; recovery in product costs. This recovery can never be accurate and may even sometimes be misleading. In addition, overheads absorbed by production may be carried forward to a future period in work in progress, which is considered by many accountants to be bad accounting practice. It is felt that fixed overheads (such as rates and insurance) are predominantly concerned with time rather than volume of output and so should be recovered during the current period, not carried forward to burden the next. Largely for these reasons, marginal costing was introduced in the 1930's and has been gradually developed since. Statistics show that a number of large U.S. companies now use this technique.

Marginal costing necessitates the analysis of costs into fixed and variable. Semi-fixed costs—those of which part is fixed and part tends to vary with output, such as maintenance—must be analysed and apportioned as appropriate to fixed or variable costs. How to do it will be considered later (*see* p. 279). This procedure will show the effect of costs on the level of output obtained or planned.

Example (1)

Paulid Ltd produce one standard type of article. Their results during the last five months of the year were as follows:

Output:	August	50 units
	September	100 „
	October	150 „
	November	200 „
	December	250 „

Prime cost: £5 per unit

Variable overheads: £1 per unit

Fixed overheads: £36,000 per annum

COST STATEMENT

Level of activity (units)	August 50		September 100		October 150		November 200		December 250	
	Total	Per unit	Total	Per unit	Total	Per unit	Total	Per unit	Total	Per unit
Marginal cost	£300	£6	£600	£6	£900	£6	£1200	£6	£1500	£6
Fixed cost	3000	60	3000	30	3000	20	3000	15	3000	12
Total cost	£3300	£66	£3600	£36	£3900	£26	£4200	£21	£4500	£18

It can be seen from the Cost Statement that total costs have risen steadily each month but the cost per unit has decreased rapidly, owing to the decreasing incidence of fixed overheads. This situation can be illustrated graphically (see Fig. 5).

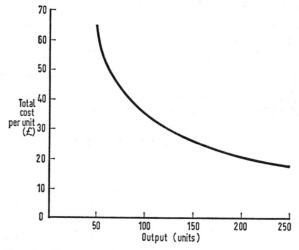

FIG. 5.—Cost curve showing the effect of fixed overheads.

CONTRIBUTION

If a system of marginal costing is operated in an organisation with more than one product, it will not be possible to ascertain the net profit per product because fixed overheads are charged in total to the Profit and Loss Account rather than recovered in product costing. Instead, the contribution of each product to the firm's total overheads and profit is ascertained. The *contribution* is the difference between sales value and the marginal cost of sales; it is sometimes termed the "gross margin." Thus in effect each product is required to contribute to a "fund" which is the total of all fixed overheads, any balance being net profit or loss. This can be shown in an example.

Example

ABSORPTION COSTING STATEMENT

Period..................

Product

	A	B	C	Total
Direct materials	£5,000	£8,000	£9,000	£22,000
Direct labour	1,000	4,000	9,000	14,000
Direct expenses	500	2,000	1,500	4,000
Prime cost	6,500	14,000	19,500	40,000
Production overheads	6,000	18,000	26,000	50,000
Production cost	12,500	32,000	45,500	90,000
Administrative overheads	2,500	4,000	10,500	17,000
Selling and distribution overheads	7,000	14,000	37,000	58,000
Cost of sales	22,000	50,000	93,000	165,000
Net profit	8,000	20,000	27,000	55,000
Sales	£30,000	£70,000	£120,000	£220,000

If we assume these figures had been analysed to show fixed and variable costs, a marginal cost statement may result as follows:

MARGINAL COSTING STATEMENT

Period.....................

Product

	A		B		C		Total
Sales	£30,000		£70,000		£120,000		£220,000
Direct materials	£5,000		£8,000		£9,000		£22,000
Direct labour	1,000		4,000		9,000		14,000
Direct expenses	500		2,000		1,500		4,000
Prime cost	6,500		14,000		19,500		40,000
Variable production over-heads	1,000		6,000		6,000		13,000
Production marginal cost	7,500		20,000		25,500		53,000
Variable sales and distribution overheads	2,000		6,000		15,000		23,000
Total marginal cost		9,500		26,000		40,500		76,000
Contribution		20,500		44,000		79,500		144,000

Fixed overheads:

Production	37,000
Administration	17,000
Selling and distribution	35,000
	89,000
Net profit	£55,000

On first acquaintance with these two statements it might appear that the absorption costing statement gives more information than the marginal costing statement. This may be so, but is the information as useful? If management wishes to consider the effects of increasing the volume of production, it cannot calculate the effect on profit from the absorption costing statement. But it can with the marginal method. If, for example, it was suggested that output of A should be doubled, the contribution of A would be increased to £41,000, giving a net profit of £75,500. This example has been over-simplified in that the possibility of a change in prices or of increased facilities has been ignored. However, it does illustrate the technique as an introduction to marginal costing.

The contribution made by a product is a very important consideration in marginal costing. If the contribution of Product A is less than that of Product B, it may be desirable to stop manufacture of A in favour of B, assuming that the market will absorb the increased output of B. In general, if the selling price of a product is greater than the marginal cost, and a reasonable contribution is made towards fixed overheads and profit, it may be desirable to continue manufacture.

Example

Beeches Products Ltd manufacture four products. The budgeted Profit and Loss Statement for a year is as follows:

PROFIT AND LOSS STATEMENT

Budget period.................

Products

	1	2	3	4	Total
Prime cost	£30,000	£20,000	£50,000	£40,000	£140,000
Production overheads	20,000	12,000	30,000	25,000	87,000
Administration overheads	6,000	4,000	10,000	8,000	28,000
Selling and distribution overheads	10,000	6,000	15,000	12,000	43,000
Total cost	66,000	42,000	105,000	85,000	298,000
Profit	14,000	(2,000)	25,000	15,000	52,000
Sales	£80,000	£40,000	£130,000	£100,000	£350,000

From this statement one could assume that the profit for the year would be greater if Product 2 was not expected to make a loss of £2000. It could be argued that manufacture of this product should be stopped unless the selling price could be increased or economies in production achieved. It could be suggested that, if possible, more of the other products should be produced in preference to Product 2. However, if it is not possible to increase the price and sell more of the other products, is it then advisable to stop manufacture of Product 2? A marginal cost presentation might show the following:

PROFIT AND LOSS STATEMENT

Budget period..................

	Product				
	1	2	3	4	Total
Prime cost	£30,000	£20,000	£50,000	£40,000	£140,000
Variable production over-heads	6,000	5,000	9,000	7,000	27,000
Production marginal cost	36,000	25,000	59,000	47,000	167,000
Variable selling and distri-bution overheads	3,000	1,000	4,000	5,000	13,000
Marginal cost	39,000	26,000	63,000	52,000	180,000
Sales	80,000	40,000	130,000	100,000	350,000
Contribution	41,000	14,000	67,000	48,000	170,000

Fixed overheads:		
Production	60,000	
Administration	28,000	
Selling and distribution	30,000	
		118,000
Profit		£52,000

If sales of Product 2 were to be stopped, the position would then be (assuming the facilities were not transferred) as follows:

PROFIT AND LOSS STATEMENT

Budget period..................

	Product			
	1	3	4	Total
Prime cost	£30,000	£50,000	£40,000	£120,000
Variable production overheads	6,000	9,000	7,000	22,000
Production marginal cost	36,000	59,000	47,000	142,000
Variable selling and distribution overheads	3,000	4,000	5,000	12,000
Marginal cost	39,000	63,000	52,000	154,000
Sales	80,000	130,000	100,000	310,000
Contribution	41,000	67,000	48,000	156,000

Fixed overheads:		
Production	60,000	
Administration	28,000	
Selling and distribution	30,000	
		118,000
		£38,000

This statement reveals a different situation altogether. Management is shown quite clearly what would be the result if production and sales of Product 2 were stopped. It will be observed that the fall in profit of £14,000 (£52,000 − £38,000) is equal to the contribution yielded by Product 2.

MARGINAL COSTING AND PRICING

Determining the prices of products manufactured by a company is often considered to be a difficult problem, particularly in non-repetitive production such as the shipbuilding industry. The difficulty is to equate the demand and the supply. Marginal costing is sometimes used to determine prices, a simple and familiar example being the railway ticket. If you want to go by train from A to B you may find that the price is £6 return. But if you travel between the same towns when an excursion train is running, perhaps because there is a football match on at B and A's supporters are travelling by special train, you may find that the price is £3 return. How is this possible? The normal fare is calculated to cover all the railway's costs, including fixed overheads, which are a considerable item; whereas the excursion fare will probably cover only the marginal cost (which is relatively small) and some contribution towards profit, since the fixed overheads should be absorbed by the normal fares.

In times of depression or low demand for a product, marginal costing is often used as a basis for determining prices. For example, during the world slump in shipping a number of shipbuilding yards chose to accept orders at below total cost, on the theory that if they could cover marginal costs any contribution towards fixed expenses would at least reduce losses and keep together their facilities and employees in the hope of better times to come.

The marginal costing technique can help management in fixing prices in such special circumstances as:

(*a*) A trade depression in the industry.

(*b*) Spare capacity in the factory.

(*c*) A seasonal fluctuation in demand.

(*d*) When it is desired to obtain a special contract.

(*e*) Where alternative levels of activity are being considered.

A number of questions have appeared in recent examinations concerning the effects of a policy decision to change selling price. The following is typical:

Specimen question

Paulan Ltd manufacture a uniform product, the selling price of which is £10. At present the company is operating at 60% level of activity, at which level sales are £60,000. The following information regarding costs is available:

Variable costs are £2 per unit.

Semi-variable costs may be considered as being fixed at £6000 with a variable cost of £0·50 per unit.

Fixed costs are £20,000 at the present level of activity but it is estimated that achievement of an 80%–90% level would increase costs by £4000.

A proposal has been made to the directors that the price of the product should be reduced by 10% so as to reach a wider sales market. The board are considering it and require a statement showing:

(*a*) The operating profit if the factory is operating at levels of activity of 60%, 70%, 80% and 90%, assuming that selling price (i) remains as at present, (ii) is reduced to £9:

(*b*) The percentage increases on present output which will be required to maintain the present profit if the company reduces the selling price.

Answer

	Level of activity			
	60%	70%	80%	90%
Output (units)	6,000	7,000	8,000	9,000
(i) Sales at £10	£60,000	£70,000	£80,000	£90,000
(ii) Sales at £9	54,000	63,000	72,000	81,000
Variable costs	15,000	17,500	20,000	22,500
(i) Contribution	45,000	52,500	60,000	67,500
(ii) Contribution	39,000	45,500	52,000	58,500
Fixed costs	26,000	26,000	30,000	30,000
(i) Profit	19,000	26,500	30,000	37,500
(ii) Profit	13,000	19,500	22,000	28,500

Increase in production required: to maintain the present profit margin, one must ascertain the contribution change. At 60% level the contribution is:

(i) Contribution	£45,000
(ii) Contribution	39,000
	£6,000

Thus if the price is reduced from £10 to £9 per unit, contribution falls by £6000. To offset this fall, production must be increased by £6000/£39,000= 15⅓%. This can be checked approximately, as follows.

A 15⅓% increase in production would result in a level of activity of 69·2%. At this level sales would be 6920 units. This can be checked as follows:

Sales 6920 units × £9 (approx)	£62,300
Variable costs 6920 units × £2·50	17,300
Contribution	45,000
Fixed overheads	26,000
	£19,000

NOTE

The sales figure has been rounded off because of the approximation used in the calculation of the increase in production: the 15⅓% is actually 15·3846%.

If, after inspection of the above statements the board of directors wish to know the level of activity which would be required to enable the existing profit to be maintained after effecting a price reduction of 20%, the following calculations would be necessary:

	Level of activity			
Output (units)	60% 6,000	70% 7,000	80% 8,000	90% 9,000
Sales at £8	£48,600	£56,000	£64,000	£72,000
Variable costs	15,000	17,500	20,000	22,500
Contribution	33,000	38,500	44,000	49,500
Fixed costs	26,000	26,000	30,000	30,000
Profit	£7,000	£12,500	£14,000	£19,500

At 60% level of activity the contribution at £10 selling price and at £8 selling price is:

(a) Contribution	£45,000
(b) Contribution	33,000
Reduction of contribution	£12,000

To meet this reduction in contribution caused by a 20% decrease in price, the level of activity must be increased by £12,000/£33,000 = 36·36%. Such an increase in production would result in a level of activity of 81·82%. This level of activity would be sufficient to meet the required profit of £19,000, if there had not been an increase at 80% level of activity in the fixed overheads incurred. At this level there is an increase of £4000, probably due to increased supervision costs. It is necessary therefore to obtain an increase in contribution to cover this amount of additional overhead.

The contribution per unit can be calculated by subtracting the marginal cost from the sales price of a product. Thus in this case £8·0 − £2·5 results in a contribution per unit of £5·5. To obtain the contribution required to meet the £4000 increase in fixed overheads, the following calculation is required:

$$\frac{\text{Fixed overhead to be absorbed}}{\text{Contribution per unit}} = \frac{\text{£4000}}{\text{£5·5}} = 728 \text{ units}$$

The level of activity required to maintain the existing profit of £19,000, after a price reduction of 20%, is therefore:

81·82%, which represents an output of	8,182 units
Plus production to absorb overheads of £4000	728 units
	8,910

This result can be checked as follows:

Sales, 8910 units at £8	£71,280
Marginal cost, 8910 units at £2·50 (approx.)	22,280
	49,000
Fixed overheads	30,000
Profit	£19,000

A similar illustration is shown on page 307, in which a different technique is used to obtain the required level of activity. This technique uses the P/V ratio, which is discussed in the following chapter.

NET PROFIT

The net profit as ascertained by marginal costing will not be the same as with absorption costing. There are two main reasons:

1. *Over- or under-recovered overheads.* In absorption costing the overheads will never be recovered exactly because of the difficulty in forecasting costs and volume of output. This may lead to over- or under-recovery of overheads. If these balances are not written off to the Costing Profit and Loss Account, the actual amount incurred will not be shown in it. In marginal costing fixed overheads are charged direct to the Costing Profit and Loss Account.

2. *Difference in stock valuation.* In a marginal cost system, stocks of work in progress and of finished goods will be valued at marginal cost; in absorption costing, stocks may be valued at total production cost. Stock discrepancies will affect profits accordingly.

LEVEL-OF-ACTIVITY PLANNING

Marginal costing can be applied to a variety of problems in industry, for example determining the contribution at a certain level of activity. In examination questions, particularly, problems are often posed which need an application of this technique to obtain a satisfactory solution.

Specimen question

Production costs for a factory in the Jervid group of companies are as follows:

	Level of activity		
	60%	70%	80%
Output (units)	1,200	1,400	1,600
Costs (£)			
Direct materials	£24,000	£28,000	£32,000
Direct labour	7,200	8,400	9,600
Production overhead	12,800	13,600	14,400
Production cost	£44,000	£50,000	£56,000

The factory is considering an increase of production to 90% level of activity. It is not expected that there will be any increase in fixed overheads at this level. The factory management requires the following information:

(a) The total prime cost of producing at this proposed level.

(b) The average marginal cost per unit of producing the additional output.

(c) The total marginal cost at this level of activity.

(d) The total production cost at this level of activity.

Answer

MARGINAL COST STATEMENT

Level of activity: 90%

	Total	Per unit
Output (units)	1800	
Costs (£)	Total	Per unit
Direct labour	£10,800	
Direct materials	36,000	
Prime cost	46,800	
Variable production overheads	7,200	
Marginal production cost	54,000	£30·00
Fixed production overheads	8,000	
Total production cost	£62,000	£34·45

NOTE

Production overheads increase by £800 at each level of activity. Therefore variable overheads must be £800/200 units = £4 per unit. At 60% level of activity production overheads are £12,800, of which variable costs are £4800 (1200 × £4), resulting in fixed overheads of £8000.

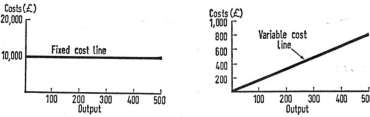

FIG. 6.—*Graph showing fixed costs.*   FIG. 7.—*Graph showing variable costs.*

DIVISION OF SEMI-VARIABLE OVERHEADS INTO FIXED AND VARIABLE OVERHEADS

It was mentioned earlier in this chapter that a system of marginal costing necessitates the division of cost into fixed and variable. This does not necessarily mean that a non-marginal costing system will not divide costs in this way: such a system may well do so in, for example, a combination of standard costing and flexible budgetary control. But in marginal costing the division is absolutely essential. Any semi-variable overheads must be divided into fixed and variable elements. These costs may be shown graphically so as to make the position quite clear.

Fixed costs: a company's budgeted levels of output range up to 500 units per annum. Fixed costs for the year amount to £10,000 (*see* Fig. 6).

Variable costs: the variable costs of the same company are £2 per unit (*see* Fig. 7).

Semi-variable costs: the company's semi-variable costs have been analysed to show a fixed overhead element of £1500 and a variable overhead element of £5 per unit (*see* Fig. 8).

The division of semi-variable costs into fixed and variable elements is a difficult process. A number of methods are available, including the following:

1. THE RANGE METHOD

This as the name suggests, is based on an analysis of past records of overhead behaviour, from which expenditure at a high and a low level of activity is ascertained. From the information it is possible to

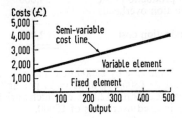

FIG. 8.—*Graph showing division of semi-variable costs into fixed and variable costs.*

calculate the fixed and variable elements of the particular expense which has been analysed. It must be emphasised that this method is not considered to be scientific or accurate.

Example

The following figures are available for the first six months of the year:

Date	Machine hours	Maintenance costs
January	2,000	£300
February	2,200	320
March	1,700	270
April	2,400	340
May	1,800	280
June	1,900	290
Total	12,000	£1,800

These figures are now re-arranged to show the hours in ascending order:

	Machine hours	Increase in machine hours	Maintenance cost	Increase in cost	Increase per machine hour
March	1,700	—	£270	—	£0·10
May	1,800	100	280	£10	£0·10
June	1,900	100	290	10	£0·10
Jan.	2,000	100	300	10	£0·10
Feb.	2,200	200	320	20	£0·10
April	2,400	200	340	20	£0·10
Total	12,000		£1,800		

This statement shows that the variable element is £0·10 per machine hour. It is now possible to calculate the fixed element:

	Machine hours	Variable cost per machine hour	Variable cost	Total cost	Fixed cost
March	1700	£0·10	170	270	100
May	1800	£0·10	180	280	100

and so on.

The high–low method abbreviates this monthly analysis by taking only the high and low points:

Level of activity	Machine hours	Decrease in machine hours	Maintenance cost	Decrease in maintenance cost	Decrease per machine hour
High	2400		£340		
Low	1700	700	270	£70	£0·10
Difference	700		£70		

Variable costs are £0·10 per machine hour, so fixed costs can be ascertained as £100.

THE SCATTERGRAPH METHOD

The "scattergraph" or regression line is being used more widely in practice than ever before, and questions have appeared in examinations recently which required a sound knowledge of this method. A graph is prepared showing costs on the vertical axis and the unit of measurement (such as level of activity) on the horizontal axis. Thus it is necessary to prepare a table to show the cost of the overhead for the period and the corresponding level of activity. In this case (see Fig. 9) the same figures are used as those in the previous example. It is emphasised that this and the following examples have been deliberately over-simplified. The authors have found that many students do not understand these methods, particularly where involved calculations are required. Thus, in this example, it may be fairly obvious what the result is going to be before the end is achieved, but that may be a good thing. If the student can master the basic principles of these admittedly rather advanced techniques, he can attempt the more involved problems with reasonable confidence.

It will be observed that in the scattergraph (Fig. 9) the points plotted for each month conveniently follow a straight line; this is intentional. In practice, of course, it will rarely happen, but this is not a major problem because once the points are plotted a line of "best fit" can be drawn. It is important to draw the line so as to include as many points as possible, or at least to be representative (see Fig. 10).

3. THE ANALYTICAL METHOD

This method is discussed in Chapter x.

4. THE METHOD OF LEAST SQUARES

The method is probably the most difficult of those discussed here,
but is possibly the most accurate. It requires some knowledge of mathe-
matics because formulae are used, but it is not within the scope of this
book to explain the derivation of mathematical formulae.

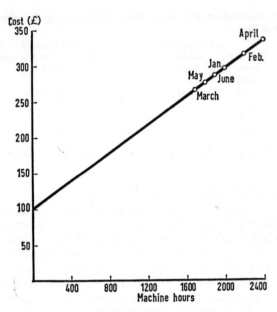

FIG. 9.—*Scattergraph showing maintenance costs*
(simplified).

Example

The figures are again those in the Example under (1) "Range method"
above, but developed further so as to meet the requirements of the formula.

	Machine hours (a)	Difference from average (b)	Cost of mainten- ance (c)	Difference from average (d)	Column (b)²	Columns (b) × (d)
Jan.	2,000	—	£300	—	—	—
Feb.	2,200	+200	320	+20	40,000	+4,000
Mar.	1,700	−300	270	−30	90,000	+9,000
Apr.	2,400	+400	340	+40	160,000	+16,000
May	1,800	−200	280	−20	40,000	+4,000
June	1,900	−100	290	−10	10,000	+1,000
Total	12,000	—	£1,800	—	340,000	34,000

NOTES

(i) Average machine hours $= \dfrac{\text{Total machine hours}}{\text{Number of months}}$

$$= \frac{12,000}{6} = 2,000$$

(ii) Average cost of maintenance $= \dfrac{\text{Total maintenance cost}}{\text{Number of months}}$

$$= \frac{1,800}{6} = £300$$

The variable element of maintenance cost is therefore:

$$\frac{34,000}{340,000} = £\frac{1}{10} = £0·10$$

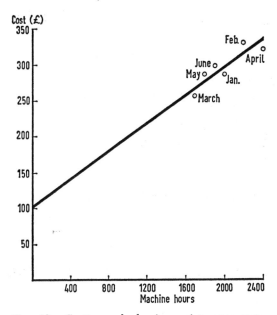

FIG. 10.—*Scattergraph showing maintenance costs, with representative curve.*

In this method the calculations have been easy to follow, but again by using the same approach one can calculate the correlation of costs with level of activity even when large amounts are involved. The reader is recommended to develop his knowledge of this technique by attempting a few past examination questions or by compiling his own figures and applying the technique demonstrated.

MARGINAL COST EQUATION

In marginal costing much emphasis is placed upon the contribution which a product or project will make towards the fixed overheads and profits of the undertaking. The contribution can, therefore, be considered as representing sales less direct costs or fixed costs and profit. Thus the marginal cost equation, which is of fundamental importance, is:

$$\text{Sales} - \text{Variable costs} = \text{Fixed costs} + \text{Profit}$$
$$S - V = F + P$$

This basic formula can be applied in simple cases to find one factor when the other three are known. From it has been developed a formula for ascertaining the sales at break-even point (break-even point is the level of activity at which the costs of the business are equal to the sales; in other words, there is neither profit nor loss):

$$\text{Sales at break-even point} = \frac{\text{Fixed costs} \times \text{Sales}}{\text{Sales} - \text{Variable costs}}$$

or

$$BEP = \frac{F \times S}{S - V}$$

Specimen question

The fixed costs of a company are £25,000 per annum.
Prime costs are £5 per unit.
Variable overheads are £1 per unit.
Selling price is £10 per unit.
Present sales are 10,000 units a year.
What is the break-even point?

Answer

$$\text{Sales at break-even point} = \frac{F \times S}{S - V}$$
$$= \frac{25,000 \times 100,000}{100,000 - 60,000}$$
$$= £62,500$$

Thus when sales are £62,500 per annum the company will make neither a profit nor a loss. This can be checked:

		£62,500
Sales:		
Prime costs: 6250 × £5	£31,250	
Variable overhead: 6250 × £1	6,250	
Fixed overheads	25,000	
		62,500
Profit		—

The importance of the break-even point cannot be over-stressed; a company should know what its turnover must be before a profit will be realised. This is of particular importance in times of depression when sales are falling and management must know at which level profits will change into losses. Management must be aware of what is termed the *margin of safety*, the amount by which current or forecast sales may fall before reaching the break-even point. This is calculated as follows:

$$\text{Margin of safety} = \frac{\text{Profit} \times \text{Sales}}{\text{Sales} - \text{Variable cost}}$$

$$\text{Margin of safety} = \frac{P \times S}{S - V}$$

Example

Current sales are 100,000 units p.a.
Selling price is £6 per unit.
Prime costs are £3 per unit.
Variable overheads are £1 per unit.
Fixed costs are £150,000 p.a.

$$\text{Break-even point} = \frac{F \times S}{S - V}$$

$$\frac{£150,000 \times 600,000}{£600,000 - 400,000}$$

$$= £450,000$$

$$\text{Margin of safety} = \frac{P \times S}{S - V}$$

$$\frac{£50,000 \times 600,000}{£600,000 - 400,000}$$

$$= £150,000$$

CHECK

Sales at break-even point		£450,000
Prime cost, 75,000 × £3	£225,000	
Variable overheads 75,000 × £1	75,000	
Fixed overheads	150,000	
		450,000
Profit		£—
Current sales		£600,000
Sales at break-even point		450,000
Margin of safety		£150,000

ACCOUNTING ENTRIES

The marginal costing technique is usually applied only in reports and statements to management, absorption cost accounting being used otherwise. In companies using this technique throughout, the accounting entries will differ slightly from those where absorption costing is used. Differences will occur in the overhead accounts because of the division into fixed and variable overheads rather than the orthodox production, administration, selling and distribution overheads. It will therefore be necessary to pass these entries through the cost journal:

Dr. Variable overhead control
Fixed overhead control

    Cr.   Production overhead control
           Administrative overhead control
           Selling and distribution overhead control.

In this way the overheads will be analysed according to their fixed and variable elements and charged to the appropriate accounts. Variable overheads will be charged to products in the usual way, fixed overheads direct to the marginal Profit and Loss Account.

THE PROS AND CONS OF MARGINAL COSTING

Many advantages have been claimed for marginal costing but, as with most tools of management, a lot depends on the use made of the technique. However, if management realises its limitations it can offer several advantages.

Possible advantages

1. It eliminates the need to allocate, apportion and absorb overheads.
2. There is no complication of over- or under-absorbed overheads.
3. Stocks of work in progress and finished goods are valued at marginal cost, which is a uniform and realistic figure.
4. Management usually finds it easier to understand marginal cost statements than those produced under absorption costing. This is particularly so in the case of foremen, who are given statements which are influenced by their actions and not obscured by the allocation of fixed costs such as establishment charges.
5. Marginal costs are the same irrespective of the volume of output (within limits).
6. The contribution per product can be revealed, which is a valuable yardstick for management decision.
7. Management is presented with useful figures of marginal cost in quoting sales prices and in tendering for contracts during times of severe competition. This may be particularly useful information when it is important to quote low prices.
8. To aid profit planning, data can be presented to management showing cost–volume–profit relationships. Useful aids such as break-even charts and profit–volume graphs can be used to facilitate planning.
9. Marginal costing provides a measure of income which is more accurate than absorption costing can give.
10. It delineates responsibility clearly, thus providing for management control.
11. It gives greater scope for manoeuvre as between choice of products. So long as total contribution is maintained, some products can be used as "loss leaders" (goods sold at a lower price than is normally acceptable in the hope that sales of other products in the company's range will be encouraged).

Possible disadvantages

1. Danger of too many sales being made at marginal cost or marginal cost plus some contribution, possibly resulting in losses or low profits.
2. Where some products incur high capital outlay, the contribution yielded may be insufficient to warrant such an outlay. Marginal costing would not reveal this situation unless the contributions were perhaps related to capital employed.
3. Danger of misinterpretation of some of the results revealed. It must be remembered that such items as the break-even point are rarely exact—they are essentially guides. Overheads are rarely capable of analysis into precise fixed or variable categories, so this must be remembered in interpreting break-even point calculations.
4. Difficulty of analysing overheads into fixed and variable elements.
5. Difficulty of applying the technique in industries where large stocks of work in progress are locked up, particularly in contracting firms. If overheads were not included in the closing value of work in progress for each year of the contract, there would be losses; while at the end of the contract, when revenue was received, there would be a large profit. This fluctuation in profits is partly evened out by valuing work in progress at total cost plus some element of profit.

APPLICATION OF MARGINAL COSTING

A variety of questions have appeared recently in examinations which are typical of the type of problem which arises in industry and which demands the use of marginal costing for a solution. One recurrent question is to inform management which is the most profitable mix of sales from a number of selected alternatives.

PROFITABLE MIX OF SALES

Specimen question

The directors of Jeravid Ltd are considering the sales budget for the next budget period. You are required to present to the board a statement showing the marginal cost of each product and to recommend which of the following sales mixes should be adopted:

    (*a*) 450 units of A and 300 units of B.
    (*b*) 900 units of A only.
    (*c*) 600 units of B only.
    (*d*) 600 units of A and 200 units of B.

You ascertain the following information:

	Product A	Product B
Fixed overheads: £10,000 p.a.		
Direct labour at £0·50 per hour	20 hrs.	30 hrs.
Variable overheads: 100% of labour		
Direct material	£20	£25
Selling price	£60	£100

MARGINAL COST STATEMENT

	Product A	Product B
Direct materials	£20	£25
Direct labour	10	15
Variable overheads	10	15
Marginal cost	40	55
Contribution	20	45
Selling price	£60	£100

Answer

Sales alternatives:

(i) 450 units of A and 300 units of B

	A	B	Total
Contribution	£9,000	£13,500	£22,500
Fixed overheads			10,000
			£12,500

(ii) 900 units of A

	A	B	Total
Contribution	18,000		£18,000
Fixed overheads			10,000
			£8,000

(iii) 600 units of B

	A	B	Total
Contribution		27,000	£27,000
Fixed overheads			10,000
			£17,000

(iv) 600 units of A and 200 units of B

	A	B	Total
Contribution	12,000	9,000	£21,000
Fixed overheads			10,000
			£11,000

Thus alternative (iii) is the one recommended.

EFFECT OF CHANGE IN SALES PRICE

Another problem which is raised frequently is the effect of a change in sales price. This problem may arise when management is considering an expansion of output, which may involve a reduction in selling price in order to attract a wider market to the product. It does not necessarily follow that expansion *must* result in price reductions, but very often sales managers consider that such a reduction would enable a larger volume of sales to be reached. It is important, therefore, to consider what are the effects of such a proposal.

Specimen question

The management of the Graemy Co. Ltd is considering the results of trading during the past year. The revenue account has been summarised as shown below:

Sales		£1,500,000
Direct materials	£450,000	
Direct wages	300,000	
Variable overheads	120,000	
Fixed overheads	430,000	
		1,300,000
Profit		£200,000

The budgeted capacity of the company is £2,000,000, but the key factor is sales demand. The sales manager is proposing that in order to utilise the existing capacity, the selling price of the only product manufactured by the company should be reduced by 5%.

Management has requested the cost accountant to prepare a forecast statement which should show the effect of the proposed reduction in selling price, and to include any changes in costs expected during the coming year. The cost accountant has ascertained the following information:

Sales forecast: £1,900,000.
Direct material prices are expected to increase by 2%.
Direct wage rates are expected to increase by 5% per unit.
Variable overhead costs are expected to increase by 5% per unit.
Fixed overheads will increase by £20,000.

Answer

STATEMENT SHOWING THE EFFECT OF CHANGE IN SELLING PRICE

Sales		£1,900,000
Direct materials	£612,000	
Direct wages	420,000	
Variable overheads	168,000	
Marginal cost		1,200,000
Contribution		700,000
Fixed overheads		450,000
Profit		£250,000

This statement shows clearly to management that even though costs have increased owing to price increases and wage rates, etc., the profit forecast for the coming year is still in excess of that achieved last year. The increased volume of sales at the reduced sales price will result in increased contribution more than sufficient to cover the increased fixed overheads.

NOTES

(i) Sales volume has increased by 33⅓%. £1,900,000 represents sales at the reduced selling price. 5% reduction, or one twentieth of the old selling price represents one nineteenth on the new selling price. Therefore sales volume would have been £1,900,000 + $\frac{1}{19}$ at the old selling price. This figure of

£2,000,000 compared with last year's sales volume of £1,500,000 represents an increase in volume of 33⅓%. It is essential to compare sales volumes based on the same selling price in order to calculate the change in volume.

(ii) Direct material costs will rise by 33⅓%, owing to the increase in production volume required. To this figure must be added the 2% price change. Thus:

Last year's cost	£450,000
+33⅓% volume change	150,000
	600,000
+2% price change	12,000
	£612,000

(iii) Direct wages are treated similarly to direct materials. Thus:

Last year's cost	£300,000
+33⅓% volume change	100,000
	400,000
+5% rate change	20,000
	£420,000

(iv) Variable overheads are treated similarly to direct wages.

A problem which is rather similar to the previous one arises when management wishes to know which factors have contributed to a change in profits when comparing two revenue statements. The factors which are normally combined are (a) a change in sales volume, (b) a change in sales price and (c) a change in costs. A change in any or all of the factors can have a considerable affect on profits for the period.

Specimen question

The summarised revenue statements of Jeraul Ltd for two successive years are as follows:

	Year 1	Year 2
Sales	£500,000	£840,000
Marginal cost of sales	300,000	400,000
Contribution	200,000	440,000
Fixed overheads	150,000	210,000
Net profit	£50,000	£230,000

Towards the end of year 1, management planned a reorganisation of production methods and this was put into effect as from the beginning of the second year. In addition to this reorganisation, selling prices were increased by 20%. The cost accountant is required to prepare a brief statement which analyses the increase in contribution according to the following factors:

(a) The increase in sales volume.
(b) The increase in sales price.
(c) The reduction in cost due to the reorganisation.

Answer

Contribution, year 1	£440,000
year 2	200,000
Increase	£240,000

Increase in contribution

(*a*) Increase in sales volume	£80,000
(*b*) Increase in sales price	140,000
(*c*) Reduction in cost	20,000
	£240,000

NOTES

(i) *Increase in sales volume*

The sale price was increased 20%, or one fifth. Therefore sales of year 2 at the year 1 price would be:

$$\tfrac{5}{6} \times £840{,}000 = £700{,}000$$

Sales in year 2 at year 1 price	£700,000
Sales in year 1 at year 1 price	500,000
Change in volume	£200,000

Percentage change in volume 40%

Contribution change

Sales increase	£200,000
Marginal cost	120,000
	£80,000

(ii) *Increase in sales price*

Sales in year 2 at year 1 price	£700,000
Sales in year 2 at year 2 price	840,000
Change due to price	£140,000

(iii) *Reduction in cost*

Change in sales volume, 40%

Marginal cost in year 1	£300,000
Marginal cost in year 2 should be £300,000 $+ \frac{40}{100} \times £300{,}000$	420,000
Marginal costs in year 2 were	400,000
Reduction in cost	£20,000

[*Examination questions will be found at the end of Chapter* XII]

BREAK-EVEN ANALYSIS AND PROFIT GRAPHS

MANY industries today are encountering the problems raised by expansion through increased sales and the introduction of new products. Some, on the other hand, are facing problems of contraction due to the introduction of substitute materials or products, or reduced demand for their product. Whichever is the case, it is vitally important that management should be in a clear position to plan for these changing levels of activity. Information must be available showing the forecasted sales, fixed and variable costs for the period so that a general picture can emerge of the company's expected position. Profit planning has been simplified by the introduction of several new techniques. One of the most important is the preparation and analysis of profit graphs.

In Chapter XI, the segregation of costs into fixed and variable elements was discussed. It will be recalled that variable costs are those which tend to vary with output, in other words costs associated with each unit of input, while fixed costs are unaffected by a minor change in input. Fixed costs are, in fact, sometimes analysed to show "committed" costs and "policy" costs. *Committed* costs are those which have been incurred in the setting up of the company and are necessary to carry on the business, such as formation expenses, management salaries, rent and rates. These costs will continue even if there is no output or sales. *Policy* costs are those incurred as a matter of management policy to influence volume of output, such as additional departmental and supervision salaries necessitated by an increase in production facilities. However, for the purpose of profit-graph presentation, these costs can conveniently be considered as fixed.

THE BREAK-EVEN CHART

A very useful device for presenting management with information showing the effects of costs and revenue at varying levels of output is the break-even chart. It is an elementary form of profit graph and has the advantage of being easily prepared and (perhaps more important) easily understood. This chart shows quite clearly the break-even point of the business, hence the name. It has certain limitations, which will be discussed later, but is nevertheless an important aid to profit planning.

In such a chart, costs and revenue are usually shown on the vertical axis and sales or production on the horizontal axis. It will be observed that sales or production can be shown, expressed in terms of units, value or percentage level of activity; sales is perhaps the more widely used because profit is realised only when goods produced are actually sold.

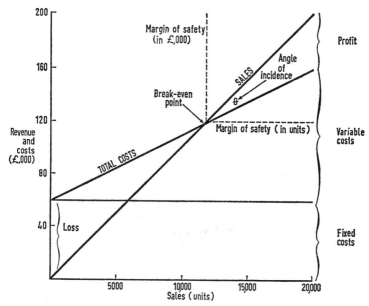

FIG. 11.—*Typical break-even chart.*

CONSTRUCTION OF BREAK-EVEN CHART

1. Select a scale for sales on the horizontal axis.
2. Select a scale for costs and revenue on the vertical axis.
3. Draw the fixed cost line parallel to the horizontal axis.
4. Draw the variable cost line, starting from the point on the vertical axis which represents fixed costs.
5. Draw the sales line, starting from the point of origin (zero) and finishing at point of maximum sales.

Example

You are required to present to the board of directors of Vidjer Ltd a break-even chart based on the following information:

Volume of sales (units)

Sales at £10:	5,000	10,000	15,000	20,000
Fixed costs:	£60,000	£60,000	£60,000	£60,000
Variable costs:	£5 per unit			

The break-even chart will be drawn up as in Fig. 11.

Break-even point

From Fig. 11 it can be observed that the break-even point occurs when sales are 12,000 units valued at £120,000. This can be checked by using the formula discussed in the previous chapter:

$$\frac{F \times S}{S - V} = \frac{£60,000 \times 200,000}{£200,000 - 100,000} = £120,000.$$

ANGLE OF INCIDENCE

This is the angle at which the sales line cuts the total cost line. The management's aim will be to have as large an angle as possible, because this indicates a high rate of profit once the fixed overheads are absorbed. A narrow angle would show that even when fixed overheads are absorbed, profit accrues at a relatively low rate of return, indicating that variable costs form a large part of cost of sales.

This angle of incidence is important in boom times when sales are expanding. Once the break-even point is reached, additional sales show a good profit return.

MARGIN OF SAFETY

This represents the amount by which volume of sales exceeds the break-even point. It is important that there should be a reasonable margin of safety, otherwise a reduced level of activity may prove disastrous. A low margin usually indicates high fixed overheads so that profits are not made until there is a high level of activity to absorb the fixed costs.

The margin of safety is important in times of depression when sales are receding. The greater the margin of safety, the further sales can fall before the break-even point is reached. Of course, once this point is passed, a loss will result.

From Fig. 11 it can be observed that the margin of safety is at £80,000. The break-even point is at 12,000 units of sales and the maximum level of activity at 20,000 units of sales; therefore the difference is 8000 units at £10 each. This can be calculated by using the following formula:

$$\frac{\text{Profit} \times \text{Sales}}{\text{Sales} - \text{variable costs}} = \frac{P \times S}{S - V}$$

$$\frac{£40,000 \times 200,000}{£200,000 - 100,000} = £80,000$$

The margin of safety may be expressed in percentage form rather than as an amount of sales volume; thus:

$$\frac{£80,000}{£200,000} \times 100, \; i.e. \; 40\%.$$

EFFECT OF CHANGE IN PROFIT FACTORS

The break-even chart can be used to show the effect of a change in any of the profit factors, which are:

1. Change in selling price.
2. Change in fixed costs.
3. Change in variable costs.
4. Change in volume of sales.

These changes will now be illustrated, using the same figures as in the above Example, but assuming the changes mentioned in each example.

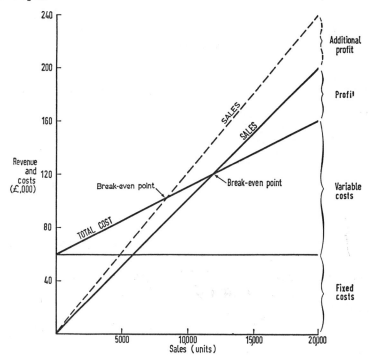

FIG. 12.—*Break-even chart showing effect of 20% increase in selling price.*

1. *Effect of 20% increase in selling price* (Fig. 12)

It can be observed that there is an additional profit of £40,000, decreasing gradually until zero level of activity is reached, and that the break-even point is now at approximately £102,000. This can be checked:

$$\frac{F \times S}{S - V} = \frac{£60,000 \times 240,000}{£240,000 - 100,000} = £102,857.$$

Note that an increase in selling price results in additional profit equal to the increase in sales, because no additional fixed costs are incurred. This is in contrast to an increase in sales volume, which is shown on p. 298.

The margin of safety has increased from £80,000 to approximately £138,000. This can be calculated by the formula:

$$\frac{P \times S}{S - V} = £80,000 \times \frac{240,000}{140,000} = £137,143$$

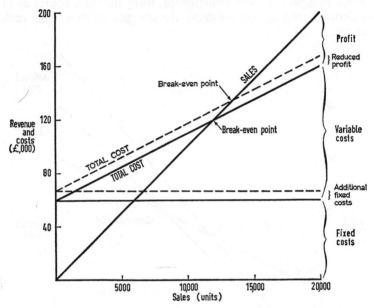

FIG. 13.—*Break-even chart showing effect of 10% increase in fixed costs.*

2. *Effect of 10% increase in fixed costs* (Fig. 13)

Profit has been reduced by £6000 at each level of activity until the break-even point is reached, then additional loss is incurred. The break-even point is now at £132,000; by formula:

$$\frac{F \times S}{S - V} = \frac{£66,000 \times 200,000}{£200,000 - 100,000} = £132,000$$

The margin of safety has decreased from £80,000 to £68,000; by formula:

$$\frac{P \times S}{S - V} = £34,000 \times \frac{200,000}{100,000} = £68,000$$

3. *Effect of 20% decrease in variable costs* (Fig. 14)

Profit has been increased by £20,000 at maximum sales, decreasing sharply until the break-even point is reached, when a reduced loss is incurred. The break-even point is now at £100,000.

$$\frac{F \times S}{S - V} = \frac{£60,000 \times 200,000}{£200,000 - 80,000} = £100,000$$

The margin of safety has increased from £80,000 to £100,000; by formula:

$$\frac{P \times S}{S - V} = 60,000 \times \frac{200,000}{120,000} = £100,000$$

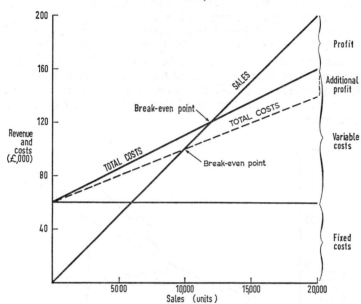

FIG. 14.—*Break-even chart showing effect of 20% decrease in variable costs.*

4. Effect of 10% increase in volume of sales (Fig. 15)

Profit has been increased by £10,000. From the chart it can be observed that originally sales were £200,000 and total costs £160,000, yielding a profit of £40,000. Now sales are £220,000 and total costs £170,000, yielding a profit of £50,000. Break-even point remains as before at £120,000, while the margin of safety increases to £100,000.

ALTERNATIVE FORM OF BREAK-EVEN CHART

An alternative form of break-even chart shows the contribution more clearly than the orthodox type. A number of accountants favour it because they consider it reveals more clearly the effects of fixed overheads on volume of sales. The graph is constructed in a similar way to Fig. 11, except that variable costs are shown first, *then* fixed costs and sales.

Example

Assuming the same figures as were used in the previous Example (p. 293) the break-even chart can be prepared (*see* Fig. 16).

It will be observed that the chart reveals the same results as before, except that the contribution is clearly shown.

COMPLICATIONS IN CONSTRUCTING A BREAK-EVEN CHART

The break-even chart in Fig. 17 shows that costs and revenue cannot always be represented by straight lines. In this instance it is necessary, at 15,000 units of sales, to introduce additional fixed costs for any increase in output; the reason would probably be increased depreciation of new plant, additional maintenance, supervision, etc. At this level variable costs start to decline slightly, the result perhaps of quantity discounts on purchase of raw materials. To exceed the level of sales it may be necessary to reduce prices, so the sales line curves less steeply as lower prices show their effect on revenue. These charges may result in more than one break-even point being reached; in fact in this case there are three.

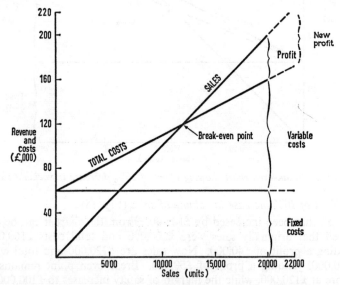

FIG. 15.—*Break-even chart showing effect of 10% increase in sales volume.*

LIMITATIONS OF BREAK-EVEN CHARTS

Break-even charts have been shown to provide a useful guide to management in making decisions on cost–volume problems. However, it must be stressed that there are limitations to their usefulness. Their function is to provide guidance, imperfect though it may be. It must not be imagined that the results shown are completely accurate under all conditions because there are a number of factors which could influence them appreciably. The following considerations should be borne in mind when preparing a break-even chart:

1. A change in one factor may influence another factor; for example, an increase in selling price may lead to a reduction in sales volume.

2. If the company sells more than one product it must be realised that break-even charts for the company as a whole will show costs and revenue which are not representative of any one product. It may be necessary to draw up a break-even chart for each product or group of products.

3. The break-even chart does not take into account capital employed, which may be a very important factor.

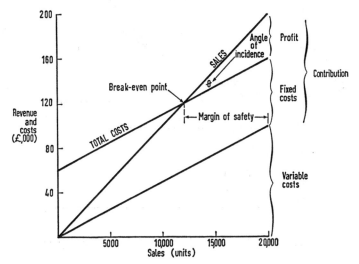

FIG. 16.—*Alternative form of break-even chart, showing contribution.*

CASH BREAK-EVEN CHART

This chart has been developed from the break-even chart to show cash requirements. It is essential that costs for the period are divided into those requiring cash payment during the period and those not requiring cash payments. It may be used when presenting cash budgets, which are discussed on p. 217.

Fixed and variable costs

It will be necessary to analyse variable costs into such items as direct materials, direct wages and variable overheads. Any lag in payment of these items, such as credit allowed by suppliers, must be taken into consideration because this break-even chart shows actual payments, not expenses incurred.

Fixed costs must be analysed to show any deferred, accrued or prepaid expenditure.

Sales

Any credit allowed to debtors must be taken into consideration in arriving at cash to be received from debtors.

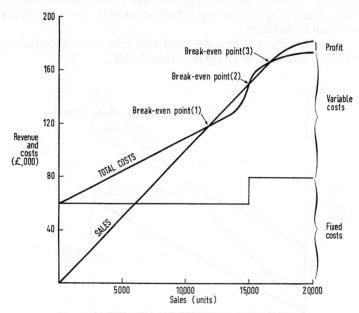

FIG. 17.—*Break-even chart with three break-even points.*

Example

The following information is available in respect of Chriseme Ltd, for the budget period:

Sales, 20,000 units at £10 per unit.
Variable costs, £4 per unit.
Fixed costs £50,000, including depreciation, £10,000.
Preference dividends to be paid, £20,000.
Taxation to be paid, £25,000.

For convenience it is assumed that there are no lags in payment. The cash break-even chart will then be drawn as in Fig. 18.

PROFIT–VOLUME RATIO

The profit–volume ratio is a very useful figure which indicates the relation of contribution to turnover. The formula used to calculate it is:

$$\frac{\text{Contribution}}{\text{Sales}} \text{ or } \frac{\text{Sales} - \text{Variable costs}}{\text{Sales}}$$

It is common practice to express this measurement in percentage form, so the usual version is

$$\frac{S - V}{S} \times 100$$

The profit–volume ratio may be used to measure the relative contribution of products, or of a company, or to measure the relative contribution of a product or a company for various periods.

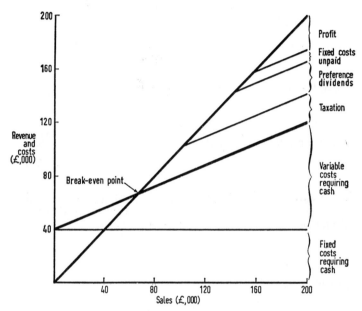

FIG. 18.—*Cash break-even chart showing cash receipts and payments during period.*

It should be noted that "P/V ratio" is rather a misnomer, but nevertheless it is widely used. Perhaps a more accurate definition would be the C/S percentage, or contribution/sales percentage. It does, in fact, relate contribution to sales turnover, and is shown invariably as a percentage. However, the term P/V ratio has been adopted and continues to be used. The fact that the name is anomalous matters little; what is important is its effective use as a tool of management—as will be illustrated in this chapter.

Example

Paulan & Co. Ltd manufacture one uniform product, A. The following figures are available for Year 1 and Year 2:

	Year 1	Year 2
Sales	£100,000	£120,000
Fixed costs	30,000	40,000
Variable costs	50,000	65,000

These figures can now be re-arranged in marginal costing form:

	Year 1	Year 2
Sales	£100,000	£120,000
Variable costs	50,000	65,000
Contribution	50,000	55,000
Fixed costs	30,000	40,000
Profit	£20,000	£15,000

$$Profit\text{–}volume\ ratio: \frac{S-V}{S} \times 100 = \frac{£50,000}{£100,000} \times 100 \qquad \frac{£55,000}{£120,000} \times 100$$

$$50\% \qquad\qquad 46\%$$

$$Break\text{-}even\ point: \frac{Fixed\ costs}{P/V\ ratio} = \frac{£30,000}{50\%} \qquad \frac{40,000}{46\%}$$

$$£60,000 \qquad\qquad £87,000$$

When the profit–volume ratio has been calculated, it may then be used in calculating the break-even point and the margin of safety. It will be recalled that the formula used to calculate the break-even point was:

$$\frac{F \times S}{S - V}$$

The formula for calculating the profit–volume ratio is

$$\frac{S-V}{S} \text{ From this is developed } \frac{F}{P/V\ ratio}.$$

$$Margin\ of\ safety\ \frac{Profit}{P/V\ ratio} \text{ or } \frac{P}{P/V}$$

$$= \frac{£20,000}{50\%} \qquad\qquad \frac{£15,000}{46\%}$$

$$£40,000 \qquad\qquad £33,000$$

Again it will be recalled that the formula used to calculate the margin of safety was:

$$\frac{P \times S}{S - V}$$

The formula for calculating the profit–volume ratio is $\dfrac{Contribution}{Sales}$

from which is developed $\dfrac{Profit}{P/V\ ratio}$

PROFIT–VOLUME RATIO AND MARGIN OF SAFETY

The profit–volume ratio reveals the effect on profit of changes in volume, while the margin of safety reveals the amount by which the volume of sales may decrease before the break-even point is reached. These two measurements may be utilised to find the percentage of net profit. The formula used is:

Profit % = Profit–volume % × Margin of safety %, *i.e.* P = P/V × MS.

Thus if the profit–volume ratio of a company is 50% and the margin of safety is 20%, net profit will be:

$$\frac{50}{100} \times \frac{20}{100} = 10\%$$

APPLICATIONS OF THE PROFIT–VOLUME RATIO

Management may request information from the accountant concerning a variety of problems which require calculations involving profit–volume ratios, such as, for example:

1. What is the company's break-even point?
2. What would the profit be if sales volume is £x?
3. What volume of sales would be required to achieve a profit of £y?
4. What volume of sales would be required to maintain the present level of profit if selling prices were reduced by 10%?

The use of profit–volume ratios and graphs can provide answers to such problems, although it is again stressed that these answers are *guides* only and may not be accurate. However, they do at least provide a measuring tool which can form the basis of decision-making.

Specimen question (1)

Marart Ltd are considering a reduction in the price of their product by 10%, because it is felt that such a step may lead to a greater volume of sales. It is thought that there is no prospect of a change in total fixed costs or variable costs per unit. The directors wish to maintain profit at the present level, so the loss which will be incurred by reducing the selling price must be offset by a gain due to increased volume of sales. You are given the following information:

Sales (10,000 units)	£200,000
Variable costs £15 per unit	
Fixed costs	£40,000

State the volume of sales required to maintain the existing profit.

Answer

The present level of profits is:

£200,000 − (£150,000 + £40,000) = £10,000

and the profit–volume ratio:

$$\frac{S - V}{S} \quad \frac{£50,000}{£200,000} \times 100 \qquad 25\%$$

If the selling price were reduced with no corresponding increase in sales volume, the profit–volume ratio would be:

$$\frac{S - V}{S} \quad \frac{£30,000}{£180,000} \times 100 = 16\tfrac{2}{3}\%$$

It is not expected that fixed costs will change; the directors wish profit to remain at its present level, so the volume of sales required is:

$$\frac{F + P}{P/V \text{ ratio}} \quad \frac{£40,000 + £10,000}{16\tfrac{2}{3}\%}$$

$$£300,000$$

CHECK

Sales of £300,000 at £18 each will necessitate a production of 16,667 units. Revenue and cost figures at this level of activity will be:

Sales	£300,000
Variable costs (16,667 at £15)	250,000
Contribution	50,000
Fixed costs	40,000
Profit	£10,000

Management can see from these results that to reduce selling prices by only 10% would require an increase in sales volume of 50%. It is now a management decision whether or not to reduce the price in view of the huge increase in sales volume which is required. The accountant presents the information in as clear a manner as possible: the final decision rests with management.

Specimen question (2)

The directors of Chriseme Ltd wish to know the volume of sales required to achieve a profit of £20,000. Selling prices are not expected to change, nor should variable costs per unit or total fixed costs change. The following information is given:

One product only is produced.
Fixed overheads for the period are £40,000.
The profit–volume ratio is 60%.

Answer

$$\text{Sales volume required} = \frac{F + P}{P/V \text{ ratio}} \quad \frac{£40,000 + £20,000}{60\%}$$

$$£100,000$$

CHECK

Sales	£100,000
Marginal cost (40%)	40,000
Contribution (60%)	60,000
Fixed costs	40,000
Profit	£20,000

Specimen question (3)

The budgeted results for Graul Ltd include the following:

		£	P/V ratio
Sales:	G	50,000	50%
	R	60,000	40%
	A	100,000	20%
	U	30,000	30%
	L	40,000	25%
	Total	£280,000	31·43%

Fixed overheads for the period, £100,000.

The directors are concerned at the results forecast for the company. They have requested you to (a) produce a statement showing the amount of loss expected, and (b) recommend a change in the mix of sales which will eliminate the expected loss.

Answer

(a)

Product	Sales	Contribution	Additional volume of sales required
G	£50,000	£25,000	£24,000
R	60,000	24,000	30,000
A	100,000	20,000	60,000
U	30,000	9,000	40,000
L	40,000	10,000	48,000
	£280,000	88,000	£38,180
Fixed overheads		100,000	
Loss		£12,000	

NOTE

Contribution = Sales × Profit–volume ratio, e.g.:

G	£50,000 × 50%	£25,000

(*b*) Additional volume of sales required to break even (the additional sales required of any one product, or of current total sales, to meet break-even point). Formula (where F = under-recovery of overheads):

$$\frac{F}{P/V \text{ ratio}}, \text{ } e.g.:$$

G	£12,000	
	——	
	50%	£24,000
		——
Total	£12,000	
	——	
	31·43%	£38,180
		——

Thus if the company can increase sales of one product by the amount shown for that product, such as sales of G by £24,000, the company will break even for the period.

Specimen question (4)

Davaul Ltd manufactures one product, selling price £5. The company is operating at 60% level of activity, at which level sales are £120,000. Variable costs are £3 per unit. Semi-variable costs may be considered as fixed at £9000 when output is nil and the variable element is £25 for each additional 1% level of activity. Fixed costs are £15,000 at the present level of activity, but if a level of activity of 80% or above is reached, these costs are expected to increase by £5000.

The directors of the company are considering a proposal that the selling price should be reduced by 5%. A statement is required showing the operating profit at levels of activity of 60%, 70%, 80% and 90%, assuming that:

(*a*) The selling price remains at £5.
(*b*) The selling price is reduced by 5%.

Show also the level of activity which will be required to maintain the present profit if the company decided to reduce the selling price of the product by 5%.

Answer

	Level of activity			
	60%	70%	80%	90%
Units	24,000	28,000	32,000	36,000
Sales at £5 (1)	£120,000	£140,000	£160,000	£180,000
Sales at £4·75 (2)	114,000	133,000	152,000	171,000
Variable costs	73,500	85,750	98,000	110,250
Contribution (1)	46,500	54,250	62,000	69,750
(2)	40,500	47,250	54,000	60,750
Fixed overheads	24,000	24,000	29,000	29,000
Profit (1)	22,500	30,250	33,000	40,750
(2)	16,500	23,250	25,000	31,750

The sales volume required at selling price of £4·75 to maintain existing profit of £22,500 is:

$$\frac{F + P}{P/V \text{ ratio}} \text{ } \frac{£24,000 + £22,500}{35·52\%} = £130,910$$

$$\text{Level of activity} = \frac{£130,910}{£4·75} = 27·560 \text{ units}$$

NOTE

$$P/V \text{ Ratio } \frac{£40,500}{£114,000} \times 100 = 35 \cdot 52\%$$

CHECK

Sales of 27,560 units at £4·75	£130,910
Marginal cost of 27,560 units at £3·06½	84,410
Contribution	46,500
Fixed overheads	24,000
Profit	£22,500

If management wishes to know the level of activity required to maintain the existing profit, following a reduction of 10%, this is calculated as follows:

$$\frac{F + P}{P/V \text{ ratio}} \quad \frac{£29,000 + 22,500}{31 \cdot 94\%} \quad £161,240$$

$$\text{Level of activity: } \frac{£161,240}{4 \cdot 5} \quad 35,830 \text{ units}$$

NOTE

$$P/V \text{ ratio is } \frac{£34,500}{108,000} \times 100 = 31 \cdot 94\%$$

CHECK

Sales of 35,830 units at £4·50	£161,240
Marginal cost of 35,830 units at £3·06½	109,740
Contribution	51,500
Fixed overheads	29,000
Profit	£22,500

This illustration is similar to that on p. 275, but it will be observed that the P/V ratio technique has been used here. Readers who are interested in this technique may care to answer the question on p. 275, using the P/V ratio technique.

Readers may have observed that the formula used in this illustration and in preceding illustrations has been an adaptation of the break-even point formula. The break-even point formula, which is based on the P/V ratio, is:

$$\frac{\text{Fixed cost}}{\text{P/V ratio}} \text{ or } \frac{F}{P/V}$$

If one requires a specified profit, then by adding P to the formula, one ascertains:

$$\text{Profit required} = \frac{F + P}{P/V}$$

THE PROFIT–VOLUME GRAPH

This graph is a development of the break-even chart and portrays the relationship of profit to volume. It requires the same basic data as the break-even chart and suffers from the same limitations. But if these limitations are borne in mind it provides a valuable aid to management in making decisions concerning volumes of output.

CONSTRUCTION OF PROFIT–VOLUME GRAPH

1. Select a scale for sales on the horizontal axis.

2. Select a scale for profit and fixed costs on the vertical axis.

3. Divide the graph into two areas, one representing profit and the other representing loss. These areas are formed by the sales line, which bisects the graph horizontally.

4. On the vertical axis, the area below the sales line represents fixed costs and that above it represents profit.

5. Points are plotted for the required fixed costs and for profit, and a line drawn to connect the two points.

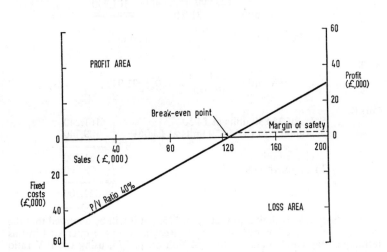

FIG. 19.—*Profit–volume graph.*

Example

The Mart Co. Ltd reports the following results for one year:

Sales	£200,000
Variable costs	120,000
Fixed costs	50,000
Net profit	30,000

The profit–volume graph will then be drawn as in Fig. 19.

From the graph the following can be observed:

(*a*) Profit–volume ratio is 40%

$$\frac{S - V}{S} \quad \frac{£80,000}{£200,000} \times 100$$

(*b*) Break-even point is £125,000

$$\frac{F}{P/V} \quad \frac{£50,000}{40\%}$$

(*c*) Margin of safety is £75,000

$$\frac{P}{P/V} \quad \frac{£30,000}{40\%}$$

When producing a profit–volume graph it may be observed that the profit–volume ratio line is drawn from the fixed costs point through the break-even point to the maximum profit point. Thus if any two of these three points are known the line may be drawn.

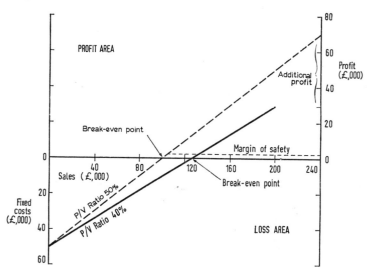

FIG. 20.—*Profit–volume graph showing effect of 20% increase in selling price.*

EFFECT OF CHANGE IN PROFIT FACTORS

Earlier in this chapter, the effect of a change in profit factors was discussed with regard to the presentation of such changes in a break-even chart. The effect of these changes can be shown similarly in a profit–volume graph.

1. *Effect of a 20% increase in selling price*

(The same figures as in the previous Example are again used.) From the graph (Fig. 20):

(*a*) Profit–volume ratio is 50%

$$\frac{S - V}{S} \quad \frac{£120,000}{£240,000} \times 100$$

(b) Break-even point is £100,000

$$\frac{F}{P/V} \qquad \frac{£50,000}{50\%}$$

(c) Margin of safety is £140,000

$$\frac{P}{P/V} \qquad \frac{£70,000}{50\%}$$

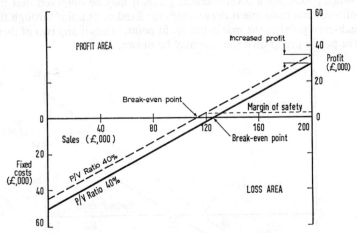

FIG. 21.—*Profit–volume graph showing effect of 10% decrease on fixed costs.*

2. *Effect of 10% decrease in fixed costs*
   From the graph (Fig. 21):
   (a) Profit–volume ratio is 40%

$$\frac{S - V}{S} \qquad \frac{80,000}{200,000} \times 100$$

   (b) Break-even point is £112,500

$$\frac{F}{P/V} \qquad \frac{45,000}{40\%}$$

   (c) Margin of safety is £87,500

$$\frac{P}{P/V} \qquad \frac{35,000}{40\%}$$

3. *Effect of 10% increase in variable costs*
   From the graph (Fig. 22):
   (a) Profit–volume ratio is 34%

$$\frac{S - V}{S} \qquad \frac{68,000}{200,000} \times 100$$

(b) Break-even point is £147,000

$$\frac{F}{P/V} \quad \frac{50,000}{34\%}$$

(c) Margin of safety is £53,000

$$\frac{P}{P/V} \quad \frac{18,000}{34\%}$$

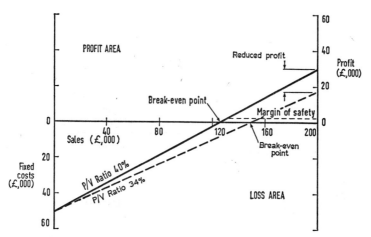

FIG. 22.—*Profit–volume graph showing effect of 10% increase in variable costs.*

4. *Effect of 5% decrease in sales volume*
   From the graph (Fig. 23):
   (a) Profit–volume ratio is 40%

$$\frac{S-V}{S} \quad \frac{76,000}{190,000} \times 100$$

   (b) Break-even point is £125,000

$$\frac{F}{P/V} \quad \frac{50,000}{40\%}$$

   (c) Margin of safety is £65,000

$$\frac{P}{P/V} \quad \frac{26,000}{40\%}$$

ANALYSIS BY PRODUCTS

A profit–volume graph may be used to show the profit–volume ratios for the individual products manufactured by the company. This graph shows the cumulative effect of each product on the profit of the business. It is important that management should be presented with figures showing not only the overall picture of profit–volume ratio but also the ratio for each product, so that action can be taken to deal with any product showing a low ratio. Where many products are manufactured and it is impracticable to show ratios for every one, it may be possible to show them for groups of similar products.

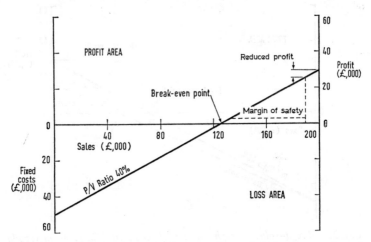

Fig. 23.—*Profit–volume graph showing effect of 5% decrease in sales volume.*

Example

Mechris Ltd produce three products A, B and C. The following are the results for one year:

Product	Sales	Marginal cost
A	£50,000	£20,000
B	30,000	18,000
C	20,000	25,000
Total	£100,000	£63,000

	Fixed overheads	£22,000

These results can be analysed:

Contribution:	A	£30,000
	B	12,000
	C	(5000)

Profit–volume ratio: Company $\dfrac{S - V}{S}$ $\dfrac{£37,000}{£100,000} \times 100$ 37%

A $\dfrac{£30,000}{£50,000} \times 100$ 60%

B $\dfrac{£12,000}{£30,000} \times 100$ 40%

C $\dfrac{(£5000)}{£20,000} \times 100$ (25%)

Break-even point: $\dfrac{F}{P/V}$ $\dfrac{£22,000}{37\%}$ £60,000

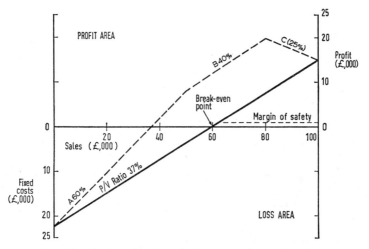

FIG. 24.—*Profit–volume graph showing analysis of products.*

Construction of profit–volume graph showing product analysis (Fig. 24)

1. Draw a graph in the same way as that suggested previously for a profit–volume graph (*see* Fig. 19) for the company, determining the break-even point.

2. Assemble the data so that the products are in order of descending profit–volume ratios; in other words, the product showing the greatest profit–volume ratio is first. In Fig. 24 the products happen to be in current sequence.

3. Plot the first product (in this case a 60% profit–volume ratio). A's contribution is £30,000; sales volume £50,000. From the fixed-cost point (£22,000) draw a line to the point where sales of £50,000 (on the horizontal axis) and contribution of £30,000 (on the vertical axis, starting from £22,000) coincide.

4. Plot the second product (B, 40% profit–volume ratio). B's contribution is £12,000; sales volume £30,000.

Plot the point where sales of £80,000 (A £50,000 and B £30,000) on the horizontal axis and contribution of £42,000 (A £30,000 and B £12,000) on the vertical axis coincide. Draw a line connecting the profit–volume ratio for A to that of B.

5. Plot the third product (C, (25%) profit–volume ratio). C's contribution

is (£5000); sales volume £20,000. Plot the point where sales £100,000 and contribution £37,000 coincide. Draw a line connecting the profit–volume ratio for B to that for C.

IMPROVING THE PROFIT–VOLUME RATIO

It can be noted from the profit–volume graphs that the larger the profit–volume ratio the steeper is the profit–volume ratio line. The aim of a company should be to maintain the profit–volume ratio and where possible to increase it. From Fig, 24 it would appear that Product C is not contributing to profit or overheads, nor is it even recovering its marginal cost. This is affecting the results of the business adversely and should be investigated. Possible ways of increasing the ratio should be considered, such as:

1. Increasing the selling price.
2. Changing the mix of sales. Products which yield an unsatisfactory ratio may be replaced by new products, or sales of other existing products may be increased if facilities allow it.
3. Reducing variable costs.

EXAMINATION QUESTIONS

1. State what you consider to be the advantages and disadvantages of the marginal cost method of costing as compared with other methods.
[C.A. (1960)
2. (a) What benefits are to be gained from marginal costing? Are there pitfalls in the application of marginal costs? Discuss these matters critically.
(b) Give a brief account of a practical application of marginal costing *which you consider sound from a policy viewpoint.* [C.C.A.
3. "Marginal costs reveal the lowest price at which a product can be sold during a trade depression, but they also reveal to management the most profitable lines during a period of intense trade activity."
Explain, with examples, the second part of this statement. [C.W.A.
4. Discuss the practical disadvantages which may be experienced in basing the export prices of goods on a system of marginal costing. [S.C.A.
5. Your directors have decided to commence the manufacture of a product similar to those already manufactured, which will be sold in an entirely new market where the selling price must be kept to a minimum, possibly below total cost. How would you determine the selling price in such an instance?
[C.W.A.
6. Explain what is meant by break-even analysis. Discuss (a) the assumptions that underlie the technique and (b) its uses. [C.W.A.
7. A well-known writer commenting on the break-even chart said, "It [the break-even chart] must be applied with an intelligent discrimination, with an adequate grasp of the assumptions underlying the technique and of the limitations surrounding its practical application." Expand on this statement, giving illustrations of the points which the writer had in mind. [C.C.A.
8. Owing to increases in steel costs being greater than increases in labour costs in metal working companies, material costs over the past two years have risen by 20%, whereas other costs have risen by 10%. Assuming that selling prices have advanced by 10% and that material costs represent $33\frac{1}{3}\%$ of total costs, indicate the effect on the break-even point of a typical break-even chart.
[S.C.A.

9. (a) X Ltd and Y Ltd each anticipate sales turnover amounting to £2,500,000, 10% of which is expected to be profit if each achieves 100% of normal capacity. The variable costs are £1,350,000 for X Ltd and £2,000,000 for Y Ltd.

Present the necessary details graphically on a single break-even chart, and determine therefrom the capacity at each of the break-even points.

(b) What observation can you make regarding the effect of increased or decreased business for each company in the future? [C.W.A.

10. Given the following information, you are required to:

(a) Calculate and present the marginal product cost and contribution per unit;

(b) State which of the alternative sales mixes you would recommend to management, and why.

Per unit

Selling price	X	£25
	Y	£20
Direct materials	X	£8
	Y	£6
Direct wages	X	24 hrs. at £0·25 per hour
	Y	16 hrs. at £0·25 per hour
Fixed overhead		£750
Variable overhead		150% of direct wages

Alternative sales mix:

(i) 250 units of X and 250 units of Y.
(ii) Nil units of X and 400 units of Y.
(iii) 400 units of X and 100 units of Y. [C.W.A.

11. The budget of a large manufacturing company shows that for the following twelve months fixed overheads are estimated at £10,000. The production budget indicates that during this period 200,000 units will be produced, for which variable overheads will be £30,000. Each unit of production requires two machine hours and these figures have been used to calculate a predetermined overhead (absorption) rate per machine hour which is applied to each unit of output. To indicate the possible effects of any under- or over-absorption of cost you are required to prepare a graph on which is plotted the total budget overhead cost line for output levels in machine hours from 0 to 600,000. On the same graph and for the same range of output levels, plot the line of absorbed cost based on the predetermined rate calculated from above. From the graph read off the over- or under-absorption of overheads for the following levels of output:

180,000 machine hours	400,000 machine hours
300,000	450,000
370,000	600,000 [C.C.A.

12. The budget of Nalgonut Ltd includes the following data for the forthcoming financial year:

Fixed expenses—£30,000.

Contributions per unit:

Product A—£5; Product B—£2·50; Product C—£3.

Sales forecast:

Product A—2000 units at £10 each;
B—10,000 units at £6·50 each;
C—5000 units at £7 each.

You are required to:

(a) Calculate the profit–volume ratio for each product.

(b) Plot the above data on a graph.

(c) On the same chart show also the break-even point for the company as a percentage of the budgeted activity. [C.I.A.

13. (a) A factory is divided into three departments, A, B and C, in each of which the capacity available during the six months commencing 1st January 1962 is 1000 hours. The fixed and variable overhead expenses budgeted for each department for this period are as follows:

Department	Fixed	Variable
A	£500	£0·35 an hour
B	£600	£0·25
C	£1750	£0·30

On 31st December 1961 two orders were received for each of which a selling price of £5000 can be charged and on each of which prime costs are expected to be £1700. The use which the two orders would make of factory capacity differs, and is expected to be as follows:

Department	Order X	Order Y
A	500 hours	1000 hours
B	200	300
C	1000	500

You are required to state which of the two orders should be accepted and to show the calculations on which your opinion is based.

(b) The overhead expenses of a factory for the year 1963, all of which are fixed, are estimated to amount to £15,200. The prime cost of the normal output of the year 1963 is expected to be £76,000.

A special order has been received for goods, the prime cost of which would be £4000; the selling price would be £4500. There is sufficient capacity in the factory to carry out this order in 1963 without any increase in factory overhead expenses.

A statement of estimated costs and profits for 1963 has been prepared, in which factory overhead expenses have been allocated to output as a percentage of prime cost. The statement concludes with a suggestion that the special order should not be accepted since the figures show that it would result in a loss.

Do you agree? Show the calculations on which your opinion is based. Ignore administration and selling expenses. [C.I.S.

14. A company manufactures a single product which sells at £2·50 per unit. The marginal cost of this product is £1·75 per unit, and at present the fixed expenses of the organisation are £50,000 per annum, with a maximum capacity of 100,000 units per annum.

Capacity can be increased in stages by making changes which will increase the annual fixed expenses of the business, as follows:

(a) At 100,000 units per annum, the addition of £10,000 per annum fixed charges will increase capacity to 150,000 units per annum;

(b) At 150,000 units per annum, the addition of a further £20,000 per annum fixed charges will increase capacity to 200,000 units per annum.

(c) At 200,000 units per annum, the addition of yet a further £30,000 per annum fixed charges will increase capacity to 250,000 units per annum.

Sales beyond 200,000 units per annum can be achieved only if the selling price of the product is reduced to £2·40 per unit. It is estimated that maximum demand is 250,000 units per annum.

The marginal cost per unit will not be affected at any point in the expansion programme.

Present this information graphically, and make recommendations to management in respect of each addition to capacity.   [C.W.A.

15. A company making and marketing a single product contemplates expansion of output. With the existing type of factory equipment the variable cost of £200 per unit of output is practically constant from 1000 to 8000 units, but more equipment than at present will be required if output in excess of 3000 units annually is produced. This extension of equipment would increase total annual fixed costs from £900,000 to £1,200,000.

You are asked to provide the management with a graph from which profit, or loss, for any level of sales, can be determined. The following figures should be used to plot the sales curve:

Units of output	Selling price per unit
1500	£1000
2000	950
2500	900
3000	850
4000	760
5000	700
6000	600
7000	500
8000	400

Read from the graph the output figure at which the sales curve overtakes total costs, and the output figure at which profit is at its maximum. [C.W.A.

16. As a newly appointed management accountant in a manufacturing company, you have undertaken a survey of the data readily available to you. These include the following figures:

Month	Sales	Loss/profit on sales	
January	£325,000	Profit	£10,000
February	360,000		15,000
March	380,000		25,000
April	400,000		25,000
May	420,000		40,000
June	470,000		50,000
July	450,000		50,000
August	440,000		40,000
September	315,000		10,000
October	280,000	Loss	5,000
November	250,000		10,000
December	230,000		20,000

Using graphical methods, determine the break-even point. What other information may be derived from your graph?   [C.W.A.

17. The trading results of Blank Ltd for the years 1963 and 1964 were as follows:

	1963	1964
Wages	£30,000	£33,750
Materials consumed	50,000	66,500
Variable overheads	5,500	7,500
Fixed overheads	9,000	11,800
Profit	4,000	8,250
	£98,500	£127,800

Material prices and wage rates increased in 1964 by 10% and 12% respectively and the sale prices were increased by 10%.
What factors have contributed to the increase in profit?
Prepare a statement showing how much each factor has contributed to the variation of profit.   [C.I.A.

18. A company has been selling a certain product at £10 per unit. Sales have been static at a level of 1500 units per year.
Careful research has produced the following forecasts:

(1) *Sales*

At £8 per unit there would be a demand for up to 6500 units per annum. Sales of 9000 units per annum would be possible if the price were reduced to £6.

(2) *Fixed costs*

The present level of fixed costs is £5000 per annum. To produce more than 3000 units additional equipment giving rise to £2000 of fixed costs would be required. To exceed 7000 units new premises would be necessary and total fixed costs would be £15,000 per annum

(3) *Variable costs*

Variable costs are £5 per unit through the whole range envisaged, but semi-variable elements would require an increase of £1000 per annum to control production over 2000 units per annum and a further £4000 if production exceeded 6000 units.

You are required:

(a) To present the foregoing information in the form of a graph.
(b) To indicate the optimum level of activity at which the company should endeavour to stabilise.
(c) To indicate the margin of safety relative to present profit level.
                                                                 [C.A. (S)

19. "When deciding between alternative courses of action it is necessary to recognise that certain fixed costs will be unaffected.... In brief, the course of action which yields the greatest contribution will be the most profitable."
In considering the above statement the undernoted product costs should be used for illustration purposes:

	Product A	Product B
Material	£2	£4
Labour	2	1
Works expenses: Variable	1	1
Fixed	1	1
Other fixed expenses	3	1
Total cost	9	8
Selling price	10	10
Net profit	1	2

You are required:

1. (a) To define "contribution."
   (b) To state, with reasons:

   (i) on which product you consider that the effort of the marketing force should be concentrated; and
   (ii) what your answer would be if the "limiting factor" were labour.

2. To discuss the statement quoted above. [C.A. (S)]

20. In a company where the fixed costs remain constant the results for two periods are as follows:

	Sales	Costs	Profits
Period 3	£200,000	£155,000	£45,000
Period 4	220,000	166,000	54,000

Using the above information, you are required:

(a) To determine the profit–volume ratio.
(b) By using the P/V ratio formula, to determine the break-even point.
(c) To prove your results by means of a graph. [C.A. (S)]

21. The imports for 19— of a firm of wine and brandy shippers were as follows:

Description	Quantity (gallons)	Cost per gallon
Wine up to 25° proof spirit	30,000	£2
Wine, from 26° to 42° proof spirit	20,000	3
Brandy, in cask	40,000	10

The sales value of these imports is £825,000. Distribution and bottling costs average £0·33½ per gallon. Management, clerical and selling costs tend to remain fixed in the short-term at £100,000 per annum. Rates, depreciation and cellarage costs amount to £50,000. Additional sales of 20% all round are proposed and these are likely to add £50,000 per annum in respect of advertising, selling, and cellarage costs.

Prepare a break-even chart to reflect operations in the existing and proposed scales. Read from the chart:

(a) Break-even point before and after sales expansion.
(b) Margin of safety before and after sales expansion. [C.W.A.]

22. A manufacturing company with spare capacity proposes to increase its range of products in order to utilise its resources more fully. The fixed costs, which amount to £57,500, are unlikely to be affected by the contemplated increase in output. Budgeted sales, now running at £245,000 per month, are to be increased so that the budgeted total will be £367,500 per month.
Expected figures for variable overhead per month are as follows:

	Production	Selling and distribution	Administration
Present scale of manufacture	£25,000	£23,750	£17,500
Proposed future scale of manufacture	37,500	60,000	25,000

The direct material cost per month is expected to rise from a total of £27,500 to £42,500, and direct wages per month from a total of £42,500 to £75,000.

Using a marginal costing technique, tabulate these data in the form in which you would present it to management to give assistance in reaching a decision upon the proposal. Add your recommendation to management.
[C.W.A.

23. Summarised figures from a manufacturer's budgets are as follows:

	Quantity	Unit price	Total
Sales	17,500 units	£180	£3,150,000
Marginal costs:			
Material		50	875,000
Wages		45	787,500
Variable overheads		36	630,000
		£131	£2,292,500

Assuming that the period costs, which are £500,000, remain unaffected, calculate:

(a) Unit margin.
(b) Profit–volume percentage.
(c) Total contribution.
(d) Effect on profit of making and selling a further 2500 units.
(e) Additional sales required to produce the same profit with unit sales price reduced to £162 each.

24. (a) Marginal income has been defined as selling value less variable cost. From the following tabulation plot a curve on a price–volume chart representing the overall marginal income for the three products; and another representing each product's marginal income in order of descending magnitude.

Product	Sales value	Marginal income	Cumulative marginal income
A	£1,000,000	£300,000	£300,000
B	500,000	100,000	400,000
C	2,000,000	200,000	600,000

(b) What conclusions do you draw from the chart? [C.W.A.

25. The following figures relate to a company manufacturing a varied range of products:

	Total sales	Total costs
Year ended 31st December 19—	£3,900,000	£3,480,000
19—	4,300,000	3,760,000

Assuming stability in prices, with variable costs carefully controlled to reflect pre-determined relationships, and an unvarying figure for fixed costs, calculate:

(a) The profit–volume ratio, to reflect the rates of growth for profit and for sales.
(b) Any other cost figures to be deduced from the data.

How may the profit–volume ratio be improved, apart from increasing selling prices or reducing costs?
[C.W.A.

26. Joe Banger contemplates starting a workshop for production of metal stampings of uniform pattern and has supplied the following technical and financial information:

(a) Sales will be made on a long term contract requiring delivery of a regular number of stampings per week.

(b) The rent of the workshop, inclusive of general and water rates, heating, lighting and all services, will be £4 per week.

(c) He will install as many stamping presses as are required to produce the number of stampings sold. Each press will involve depreciation and maintenance at the rate of £8 per week and electrical power costing £0·05 per productive hour worked.

(d) For each press installed he will employ an operative whose wages (including national insurance and holiday pay) will cost £12 for a guaranteed 42-hour week. No overtime will be worked.

(e) The maximum productive hours for a press will be 40 hours per week and each press will produce stampings of the sale value of £1·75 per productive hour. Two hours weekly will be required for maintenance of each press and, if necessary, output will be restricted to the number of stampings to be delivered in each week.

(f) In addition to operatives he will employ one labourer whose wages, together with other fixed overhead expenses, will cost £16 per week.

(g) Each press will require to be fed with strip metal costing £0·62½ per operating hour and sale of scrap will realise 4% of the cost of strip metal processed.

(h) Use and maintenance of tools will be allowed for at the rate of £0·10 per press per productive hour.

You are required to:

(i) Submit a break-even chart based on weekly operations covering sales up to £250 per week.

(ii) State the level of sales at which a profit of £16 per week could be expected. [C.A. (June 1964)

27. (a) Explain what is meant by a break-even chart and state its uses.

(b) Illustrate by a graph, based on the following information:

Product	Budgeted sales	Budgeted variable cost
A	£10,000	£4,000
B	5,000	4,000
C	15,000	12,000
	£30,000	£20,000

Fixed charges for same period, £6000.

(c) Show on the same graph the effect of eliminating Product B while increasing Product A by 100% and increasing the fixed charges by £1000.
[C.A. (S)

28. The following figures relate to a manufacturing company:

Annual sales	£700,000
Direct material	£100,000
Direct wages	150,000
Semi-variable overheads	120,000
Fixed overheads	80,000
Fixed administrative and selling cost	40,000
Variable selling and distribution cost	100,000

Apart from the cost described as fixed overheads there is included in the semi-variable overhead figure a fixed element amounting to £50,000.

On a single graph, display the cost–volume relationship for each category of cost, and also for the total costs.

Plot the sales line on the graph. What is the break-even point? [C.W.A.

29. A company which allocates all service department costs to production to arrive at overhead rates produces a single product in large quantities. Fixed factory cost is £80,000 annually, and normal production volume is 160,000 units. You are asked, as management accountant, to review the following figures applicable to three years of trading:

	First year	Second year	Third year
Sales (quantity)	160,000	128,000	160,000
Production (quantity)	176,000	192,000	128,000
Sales (value)	£480,000	£384,000	£480,000
Cost of sales at standard	384,000	307,200	384,000
Production cost variance (loss)	1,760	1,920	1,280
Volume variance (gain)	8,000	16,000	
Volume variance (loss)			16,000
Administrative and selling overheads	48,000	48,000	48,000
Profit before tax	54,240	42,880	30,720
Closing stock	38,400	192,000	115,200

(a) From the data above, calculate the profit percentage of sales yearly. Account for the profit difference between the first and third years.

(b) Apply a marginal costing technique to the figures given to ascertain for each year: (i) contribution; (ii) net profit; and (iii) closing stock valuation. [C.W.A.

30. A manufacturing company produces and sells three products X, Y and Z. From the accounts of the past year, the following information is available:

Product	Selling price per unit (£)	Profit-volume ratio (%)	Percentage of total sales by units
X	50	10	50
Y	37·50	20	40
Z	25	40	10
Total fixed costs	£32,500.		

Management is concerned that the overall profit picture might be improved by selling a greater proportion of more profitable lines. After a full investigation it is found that the following sales mix should be possible in future.

Product		Percentage by units
	X	30
	Y	50
	Z	20

Present the following information to management:

(a) A break-even chart for the existing sales mix, showing the combined units of sale in 1000 unit intervals up to a maximum of 7000 units.

(b) A profit–volume graph for both the existing and proposed sales mix over the same range as in (a) above. [C.W.A.

CHAPTER XIII

INTERNAL AUDITING
(I) AN AID TO MANAGEMENT

ON first consideration it may seem strange to bring the subject of internal auditing within the purview of management accounting, but the definition of internal auditing adopted by the Institute of Chartered Accountants may serve to give some indication as to the reason for its inclusion.

DEFINITION

In their publication *Notes on the relation of the internal audit to the statutory audit*, internal auditing is defined as "a review of operations and records, sometimes continuous, undertaken within a business by specially assigned staff."

It is the use of the word "audit" that may be misleading, as it encourages the idea that internal and external (or "statutory") audits are identical in purpose and only differ in personnel. This is not so.

Originally the work carried out by the two kinds of auditor was much the same. However, the statutory audit is made on behalf of the shareholders, and its report is addressed to them; the internal audit report is to the management. The external auditor is not bound to comment on whether the business is being run efficiently, while this consideration is becoming more and more important to the internal auditor. These essential differences, and the more immediate controlling authority of the management as compared with the shareholders, result in the function of the internal auditor being both dynamic and constructive.

Unfortunately, some businesses still cling to the older conception. This results in a restriction of the internal auditor's role to mere duplication of the work of the statutory auditor. Most progressive businesses increasingly place greater emphasis on the reviewing of operations.

There is no doubt that, as industry tends to amalgamate into larger units and management becomes more scientific, there will be yet further developments in this field. The internal audit will increasingly concentrate on its function as an instrument of management while still allowing the annual accounts to be verified before they are accepted by the statutory auditors. Thus, the internal audit:

(*a*) verifies all the multifarious accounting statements produced for management,

(*b*) examines the accounting methods and principles adopted to prepare them, and (*c*) investigates the administrative system upon which they are based.

SCOPE

The coverage of an internal audit depends upon several factors. A good general rule is that this department should have as much freedom as possible. No fixed rules can be laid down as to the exact demarcation of duties to be carried out. The latter can extend to many matters which are not directly of an accounting nature, especially in the larger business where no department for the study and installation of new organisation or methods exists. In such circumstances the internal auditor will have a greatly increased share in recommending new systems, conducting investigations, etc.

The internal auditor's terms of reference should be clearly defined. Lack of a clear statement of his duties, etc., is deleterious to his confidence, morale and prestige, and can result in friction between him and other members of the staff. Management should issue clear directions to all staff at the inception of an internal audit department and keep all staff informed when there are changes in its scope and duties.

It may be thought desirable to exclude certain confidential matters, such as salary agreements, from the scope of the audit. This is a regrettable inhibition, since it indicates a lack of confidence, but where the management insists upon it the auditor should obtain a written statement of the items to be omitted from his programme.

ADVANTAGES

The advantages of an internal audit are that:

1. It avoids the high cost of a continuous audit by external professional auditors and indeed when an internal audit department is properly run it greatly decreases the external auditors' work, audit time and fees.

2. The internal auditors become intimately acquainted with the business, as they are continuously employed in the same concern and have access to much confidential information and to all levels of management. Thus the internal auditor becomes a repository of a great deal of correlated knowledge available to few other members of the staff.

3. It maintains a group of highly skilled people available to cope with non-recurring and exceptional jobs which few other employees could deal with efficiently.

4. It provides a check on the accuracy of the large and ever-increasing number of financial statements issued for management. It ensures enforcement of the organisation's standard practice and is conducive to the efficiency and integrity of the various accounts departments; its work is continuous, as opposed to the great majority of external audits, which are not always continuous; it is more selective in the

information and methods examined; it is rarely as detailed in investigation.

5. It ensures a constant examination of internal check controls and the detailed application of normal auditing methods. This is especially valuable in larger organisations, where the management becomes increasingly remote from the executive as expansion takes place.

6. It provides an excellent training ground for future executives. Trainee personnel obtain intimate knowledge of the business: they can study problems of all kinds at different levels, and critically compare techniques, systems and organisation.

HUMAN RELATIONSHIPS

Before proceeding to the general principles governing the conduct of the internal audit, it is necessary to mention the very important bearing which human relationships have on its efficient execution.

Individual personalities are as important in business as in everyday social intercourse. The internal auditor must never forget that although in the last resort employees of his company have perforce to co-operate with and assist him, his work will be much easier if they find his personality agreeable and his attitude reasonable. This is not to say that he should abandon a healthy scepticism towards the statements of others, but he should not parade such scepticism before the members of the staff. The most innocent question, if phrased in what is construed as a menacing manner, can lead to considerable upset, ill feeling and resultant lack of goodwill.

The internal auditor nearly always starts at a disadvantage—few people take kindly to their work being checked by someone they know has immediate access to high authority and whose primary function is to be critical. While it is usually recognised that the statutory auditor has no alternative but to probe various matters, the internal auditor may be regarded as over-meticulous if he examines too closely, since he may be expected to rely simply on the statements of those who regard themselves as his fellow-workers. The internal auditor should proceed with great patience and tact; such an attitude promotes goodwill and speeds results, particularly from the viewpoint of efficient management. The willing co-operation of staff may lead to their pointing out anomolies of procedure not apparent to anyone not engaged in the actual work.

INTERNAL CONTROL AND INTERNAL CHECK

In his "review of operations and records" the internal auditor will be immediately concerned with the system of internal control and the internal check which forms a constituent part of it.

Internal control is defined by the Institute of Chartered Accountants (in *Statements on auditing*) as "the whole system of controls, financial and otherwise, established by the management in the conduct of a business, including internal check, internal audit and other forms of control."

At the same time, internal check is defined as being "the checks on the day-to-day transactions which operate continuously as part of the routine system, whereby the work of one person is proved independently or is complementary to the work of another, the object being the prevention or early detection of errors and fraud."

The internal control mentioned is the basis upon which the whole internal audit is formed. It comprises the whole body of regulations made by the management for the running of the business, and can be analysed under three main heads: (*a*) organisation, (*b*) accounting and (*c*) administration.

ORGANISATION CONTROL

This is the primary of all management controls. It is concerned with the inter-relation of the whole complex of activities of the different companies, divisions and departments which constitute a business. It not only regulates the standard methods of conducting the transactions which take place between different parts of the concern, but also the precise function and purpose of every section and its authority in relation to the others. There should be no ambiguity about the mechanics of co-ordinating departments for any necessary objective.

In the larger concern the top management, *i.e.* the board of directors, has to beware of the creation of "private empires" and the warping of company policy by powerful and authoritative members of the staff. Therefore every department, section and employee should have comprehensive terms of reference, and all new tasks that arise should be officially allocated to the person or department best able to execute them.

Hence this form of control indicates to the internal auditor the authority which should support projects and the demarcation of responsibility between all sections and employees of the concern.

ACCOUNTING CONTROL

This control utilises the accounting system of the company; its efficiency depends upon the system in operation.

Simple accounts

This is the normal method of opening various accounts for assets, liabilities, expenses and receipts, and for the correct allocation of all transactions relating to them. The auditor's duty is to assure himself that the allocations are properly effected. This control is not of great assistance to management.

Standard cost accounts

These consist in the comparison of actual production results with previously calculated standards. There are nearly always variances from the standards for different divisions of expenditure, owing to miscalculations in the standard or the effect of circumstances different from those anticipated. The standard result and the aggregate of all the different variances will equal the actual result. This is real control accounting and the internal auditor can obtain much assistance from it. Consideration will show that if the auditor, having satisfied himself as to the validity of the standards, sees that in any particular period some of the actual expenses agree with them, then all such cases can be assumed to be substantially correct.

Budgetary control

Under this system the various sections of the business pre-calculate their estimated budgets for a fixed period. Provided production and sales are planned in advance too, the preparation of estimates of expenditure and receipts is fairly straightforward. On the basis of previous experience and present conditions, it is nearly always possible to estimate accurately the expenses and receipts that will accrue in the production and sale of a given estimated quantity of goods.

ADMINISTRATIVE METHODS CONTROL

This consists of all the arrangements made by the company to check the accuracy of the clerical work:

Reconciliation of cost and financial accounts

It is evident that if the company keeps separate cost accounts, their comparison and reconciliation with the financial accounts will be of great assistance to the internal auditor.*

Control accounts

This is the commonest method of control accounting. Practically any series of transactions can be controlled in total in this way. The most usual controls in financial accounts are for:

> (a) Sales Ledger, *i.e.* total debtors for sales,
> (b) Purchases Ledger, *i.e.* total creditors for purchases,
> (c) Nominal Expenses Ledger, *i.e.* for total expenses.

In cost accounts there are other forms of total account, among others those for (d) Material, (e) Labour, (f) Stock, (g) Work in progress.

Documentation

Numbered and counterfoil documents, pre-lists and proof sheets are among other forms of control arising from the accounting methods used.

* See *Wheldon's Cost accounting and costing methods* (Macdonald & Evans, 1970).

Internal check

So far as the internal auditor is concerned, this is the most important form of internal control that exists. It consists of such an arrangement of the work that the duties performed by every individual are checked at some time or another by another employee. Thus, before any fraud can be committed or error pass undetected, at least two people have to be in collusion or make, or overlook, the same error.

Importance of physical as well as financial controls. The auditor must be constantly on guard against the attitude that frauds are always centred around the loss of cash. For example, in a diamond merchant's business the control of the stock is infinitely more difficult and vulnerable than that for the cash at the bank. Similarly, in a business such as a catering establishment which has a large number of deliveries of fairly easily marketable supplies, one must ensure by adequate controls that everything invoiced as "delivered" is in fact physically taken into stock.

It will be apparent from the above that the internal auditor's most important task before going on to consider where internal check should be most stringent is for him to visualise *what the business consists of.* What items of value are bought or produced? Where are they stored? Are they portable? Such questions are prompted by common sense. It is often surprising how an auditor, having become enmeshed in the niceties of (say) the system of checking the petty cash float of £1200, can omit to see whether the yard outside containing stocks of scrap iron worth £100,000 is subject to proper physical controls.

Major requirements of internal check to be considered by the auditor when reviewing the system:

(a) The sequence of staff who examine documents, the reasons why they examine them and the extent of their responsibility for them.

(b) Who should authorise transactions; how the transactions will appear in the records of the company and whose control they will be under.

(c) He must satisfy himself that all the organisation, accounting and administrative controls are being properly applied. Many of the conditions laid down in theory represent the ideal. Often for reasons like shortage of staff or the adoption of streamlined accounting systems (*e.g.* the "slip" method) practice falls short of the ideal standards.

In all considerations—as regards both what he should pay special attention to, and which acts or deviations from the system on the part of the staff are likely to affect the efficient running of the business—the auditor must be essentially practical.

Thus, in many organisations, a deviation from the theoretically perfect forms of check takes the form of a "calculated risk." This is especially so where the business is split into many branches. For example, in a multiple chain store a near-perfect form of stock and counter control could be simply evolved. The disadvantage would be that

CHEQUES AND CASH RECEIPTS

Date.....................

No.	Question	Yes or No	Comments	Initials
1.	Is mail opened by persons other than the cashier or debtors' ledger clerks under the supervision of a responsible official?			
2.	Are cheques, postal orders and money orders crossed immediately mail is opened?			
3.	Can unopened letters, other than private mail, go direct to any employees?			
4.	Is a list of monies received prepared when the mail is opened?			
5.	Is this list checked by someone other than the cashier?			
6.	Is a reconciliation prepared daily between the total cheques and cash received and total credited to debtors?			
7.	Are receipts used by the cashier for all cash received in the form of notes and coin?			
8.	Are such receipts numbered?			
9.	Is a record kept of serial numbers of cash receipt books issued?			
10.	Are unused books kept securely and recorded on issue?			
11.	Can receipts be issued by the cashier for special purposes?			
12.	Is there a control to prevent fictitious discounts being allowed to customers?			
13.	Are all cash and cheques received banked daily?			
14.	Are the paying-in slips prepared by the cashier? If not, by whom?			
15.	Are duplicate paying-in slips stamped by the bank retained and checked?			
16.	Are bank debit advices notified to anyone other than the cashier?			
17.	Are bank reconciliations prepared regularly?			
18.	Has the cashier any connection with debtors' control or writing off bad debts?			
19.	Has the cashier any connection with the keeping of the nominal ledger or any other ledger?			
20.	Is the cashier in any way concerned with the preparation of the purchases day book?			
21.	Does the cashier make journal entries or originate any entries otherwise than through his own book?			
22.	Are rent, dividends, interest received, etc., controlled so that if not received on due dates it would be observed?			
23.	Does the cashier count and balance his cash daily?			
24.	Are the staff permitted to cash personal cheques?			
25.	If so, are the cheques made payable to "Cash"?			

FIG. 25.—*Internal control questionnaire.*

the cost of the extra staff required to stop pilferage and errors altogether would be prohibitive.

Internal check questionnaires. These questionnaires are vital for illustrating the detailed workings of the administrative control system and must be kept accurate and up to date. A priority task of commencing the internal audit is to compile such questionnaires, and they should be revised from time to time in conjunction with the appropriate administrative and executive personnel.

An example of such a questionnaire in respect of cheques and cash receipts is given in Fig. 25. It is necessary to draw up similar questionnaires for all the various aspects of the business which come under the purview of the internal audit.

General. We are not concerned here with the more detailed aspects of the whole system of internal audit but rather with the broad principles. It should be emphasised, however, that in dealing with the more particular aspects it is important to preserve a detached attitude so that commonsense principles can be applied.

This will be easier if the basic rules on which the whole system rests are borne in mind—that in a double entry system there are always two aspects to a transaction, and one person should never cover both. For transactions and events which occur before the double entry stage, a minimum of two people should check the same work. Thus in the case of "cash received" the cash and cheques are first pre-listed and recorded before the cashier receives them for entering into the cash records. There are of course numerous collateral checks, but the foregoing, based on the premise that collusion—though possible—is unlikely, constitutes the main deterrent to deviations from the company's laid down procedure.

INTERNAL AUDIT AND THE PREVENTION OF FRAUD

In short, prevention is better than cure. The upkeep of sound systems of organisation and internal check is far better than any subsequent dramatic discovery of fraud. If fraud *is* discovered the most important point is not that it has been discovered but *how it was possible.* The auditor should make sure that it did not occur through an unknown weakness in the system of internal check (*i.e.* it was *not* the result of a calculated risk that failed), because if such is the case, it reflects upon the ability of the auditor. In an otherwise well organised business the reason for fraud occurring is almost invariably a loophole in the internal check system.

The main factors in the prevention of fraud are:

1. A system of internal check.
2. Internal audit.
3. The use of machines (a person cannot easily alter a machine entry).
4. Examination of comparative figures. This is extremely useful

for detecting frauds (or genuine errors) which have been completely wrong in principle but correct in detail. It can happen that over-emphasis on the detailed checking work results in a more fundamentally incorrect state of affairs being overlooked—the omission, for example, of a whole set of transactions. Such errors can sometimes be glaringly obvious from a study of comparative figures. These should be examined in the same way as estimated and actual results in standard costs, *i.e.* by careful investigation and full explanation of all variances; in this case, however, it is usually the variances between actual figures which have resulted for different periods.

5. Personnel management. The two most important points are the enforcement of holidays for all staff and the careful control of clerical overtime. Obviously nothing is more conducive to defalcations than that someone should have the run of an empty office and access to the records in it.

MANAGEMENT AND THE INTERNAL AUDITOR

The valuable assistance the internal auditor can render to management must by now be apparent, assuming always that management is far-sighted enough to make full use of his services and that he in turn is able to apply himself to his work in such a manner as to preclude "routine checking."

The increasing size of businesses today creates an ever-widening gap between management and the actual field of operations, and it is here that the internal auditor can provide the essential connecting link throughout the whole organisation. For as the chain of responsibility lengthens, so does the possiblity grow of delays, misinterpretations and misjudgments which hinder the running of what would otherwise be an efficient and prosperous business.

This broader and, if anything, more important aspect of the internal auditor's work is facilitated by:

1. Observation and investigation of the actual working of the system during the course of his detailed audit.

2. Comparing the schedules of operations which come under his scrutiny when finally prepared, *i.e.* not only checking the accuracy of statements but also making a critical and comparative appraisal of the budgeted figures and results obtained, and comparing matters which influence various procedures but do not form part of a budgeted estimate.

3. The probing from time to time of the system of internal check, to see not only whether it is still working effectively but whether it is still the best system available.

4. Examination of the organisation's contracts, including those

of a continuing nature. Often contracts for the supply of materials, etc., are allowed to continue simply because they are adequate for the original purpose. But as time passes, conditions and prices may change to an extent where the terms could be improved upon.

5. By the instigation of special enquiries at the request of management.

Such work will range over the organisation's whole field of operations and may extend beyond the more obvious factors to such matters as:

1. The checking of the accuracy of financial statements. The internal auditor can take the more objective view when verifying the accuracy of the statements laid before management: costing standards and established budgets can be scrutinised with a detachment that is sometimes difficult for the busy cost accountant or production expert to achieve. He may be able to draw the management's attention to matters which require decision at the highest level, and thus so speed operations as to make it possible to accept a contract in time to cut production costs.

2. The checking of primary functions, *e.g.* the examination procedures involved in the purchasing and ordering of goods. This has been touched upon in (4) above. Contracts may be allowed to continue for convenience's sake but the internal auditor should see whether new tenders ought to be invited and by comparison ensure that competitive prices and delivery are obtained.

3. The examination of stores procedures to see that there are no delays due to bad storage, no waste of space and no locking up of capital in slow-moving stocks.

4. Ensuring that the standards laid down in the organisation's manual of responsibilities and procedures are maintained. Where necessary, he may advise on alterations to meet changing conditions.

5. Making recommendations for promotion when informed of any vacancies to be filled. These may take the form of reports to management and could ensure promotion on a reasoned and fair basis.

6. Storage of information. Management can call for an independent and urgent report on any matter and, with their intimate yet wide knowledge of the organisation, the internal audit department may be able to supply valuable information at any time.

7. The promotion of harmonious relations between management and staff. As one who has access to top management at all times, the internal auditor may do much to remove the feeling of remoteness in the members of the staff. He should be tactful and may smooth out difficulties or resentments as they arise; likewise, any genuine causes of friction can be brought to the attention of management, facilitating action to preserve a harmonious atmosphere and good relations.

REPORTS TO MANAGEMENT

These have been mentioned at various stages throughout this chapter. A specimen is given in Chapter XXIII, in the form of a report on an investigation by the internal audit department undertaken at the request of management.

OPERATIONAL TIME

This is of vital importance to the whole field of the internal auditor's work, but it is an aspect which management may sometimes be in danger of overlooking.

To allow the internal auditor to preserve the necessary objectivity his working time must allow opportunity to investigate and give careful thought to matters not immediately concerned with routine tasks. On the other hand, urgent reports may be called for at any time. The whole department should be allowed a freedom of movement and adequate time to conduct work on a calculated basis. If work goes on under continual pressure the essential object of the internal auditor's work is lost sight of.

EXAMINATION QUESTIONS

1. Discuss management auditing. What is its function? Set out the terms of reference for a management audit.   [C.C.A.

2. Into what divisions may internal control be subdivided? Comment on the suggestion that internal auditing is useful for checking purposes but has little to do with management and control.

3. The directors of a newly-formed private company which amalgamates the businesses of a number of separate manufacturing concerns, propose to institute an Internal Audit Department. You are asked to advise the directors, in your capacity as the Chief Accountant of the company, as to the general constitution of the proposed Internal Audit Department and the procedure to be adopted to ensure the efficiency of such a department. Submit your report to the board of directors, assuming any data you may require for the purpose of your report.   [S.C.A.

4. State the functions of an internal auditor and indicate his relationship to management.   [C.C.A.

5. In addition to the audit required by statute, many large companies have an internal audit carried out by staff appointed for this purpose.

Discuss, briefly, the fundamental differences between the two forms of audit and the extent to which the statutory and internal auditors can cooperate to their mutual benefit.   [C.C.A.

6. It has been stated that internal audit staff may render a valuable service in conducting special enquiries at the request of management. Give examples of such enquiries and their usefulness to management.

7. "The overall objective of internal auditing is to assist all members of management in the effective discharge of their responsibilities." Comment on this statement outlining the general functions which an internal auditing department should have in order to satisfy this objective. Your answer

should indicate clearly an appreciation of, and the interconnection between the security function and the appraisal function of internal audit.   [C.C.A.

8. You are the internal auditor of a firm in which one cashier is responsible for both incoming cash and cash payments. State the most common ways in which misappropriation of cash might occur. Indicate what systems you would recommend and what checks you would carry out to minimise the risk of loss.   [C.W.A.

CHAPTER XIV

INTERNAL AUDITING
(II) VALUATION OF STOCKS AND WORK IN PROGRESS

THE valuation of stocks and work in progress will be dealt with in some detail here, since it can materially affect the profit or loss position of a company. Moreover the internal auditor can render a valuable service to management by ensuring that efficient stock records are maintained and that stocks are properly valued in accordance with the type of business. He can also ensure that stocks are kept at a minimum level consistent with safety, so obviating the unnecessary tying up of expensive capital.

No definite rules can be laid down as to the method of valuation which should be employed in any particular concern, as the nature of the business and the type of stock carried may vary considerably. Each must be considered on its own merits.

Certain methods are, however, applied generally. They are outlined in the I.C.A. publication *Accounting principles*, which is quoted here by courtesy of the Institute of Chartered Accountants. The accepted basis for the valuation of stocks and work in progress is, briefly, either (*a*) cost, (*b*) net realisable value or (*c*) replacement price, whichever is the lowest. It is computing just what cost and net realisable value *are* that often causes difficulty. The I.C.A. recommendations (quoted verbatim, pp. 275–8) are as follows:

COST

Cost can be said to comprise three elements:

(i) The actual purchase price of goods bought for resale or for use in manufactured finished goods.

(ii) Direct expenditure, such as carriage inwards on goods purchased and direct labour in the manufacture of finished articles.

(iii) An element of overhead expenditure justifiably considered to increase the stock value.

It is the inclusion of overhead expenditure, under the third head, that warrants careful attention. Such overhead expenditure may include expenses incurred in production, administration, selling or finance—although the last two are normally excluded in the valuation of stock. Since production and administration expenses may be included, the I.C.A.'s definitions of cost (given below) are relevant.

The internal auditor will be concerned to see that only overheads which may be justifiably included are added to the value of the stock or work in progress. In this respect it is important to exclude all

overheads that occur purely on a time basis as opposed to those which
vary with the volume of output.

(a) *"Unit"* cost

The total cost of stock is computed by aggregating the individual
costs of each article, batch, parcel or other unit. The method is not
always capable of application, either because the individual units lose
their identity (notably where stocks are bulked or pass through a number of processes) or because it would involve undue expense or complexity to keep individual records of cost, particularly where these
necessitate allocations of expense.

(b) *"First in, first out"*

Cost is computed on the assumption that goods sold or consumed are
those which have been longest on hand and that those remaining in
stock represent the latest purchases or production.

(c) *"Average"* cost

Cost is computed by averaging the amount at which stock is brought
forward at the beginning of a period with the cost of stock acquired
during the period; consumption in the period is then deducted at the
average cost thus ascertained. The periodical rests for calculating the
average are as frequent as the circumstances and nature of the business
require and permit. In times of rising price levels this method tends
to give a lower amount than the cost of unsold stock ascertained on a
"first in, first out" basis and in times of falling prices a higher amount.

(d) *"Standard"* cost

A predetermined or budgeted cost per unit is used. The method is
particularly convenient where goods pass through a number of processes
or are manufactured on mass production lines; but it will not result in a
fair approximation to actual cost unless there is a regular review of
the standards with appropriate adjustment and revision where necessary.

(e) *"Adjusted selling price"*

This method is used widely in retail businesses. The cost of stock is
estimated by calculating it in the first instance at selling prices and then
deducting an amount equal to the normal margin of gross profit on such
stocks. It should be appreciated that where the selling prices have been
reduced the calculation will bring out cost only if appropriate allowance
for price reductions is included in fixing the margin to be deducted;
if no such allowance is made it may bring out amounts which approximate to replacement price as defined (below). The calculations under
this method may be made for individual items or groups of items or by
departments.

REDUCTION TO NET REALISABLE VALUE

When the cost of the stock has been determined it is then necessary to establish whether any portion of the outlay on stock is irrecoverable; to that extent a provision for the loss needs to be made. This calculation may be made either (i) by considering each article separately or (ii) by grouping articles in categories having regard to their similarity or interchangeability or (iii) by considering the aggregate cost of the total stock in relation to its aggregate net realisable value. The third method involves setting foreseeable losses against expected but unrealised profits and would not normally be used in businesses which carry stocks which are large in relation to turnover.

The irrecoverable portion of the cost of the stock is the excess of its cost, as computed by the method of cost ascertainment which is deemed appropriate for the business, over the net realisable value of the stock. *Net realisable value* means the amount which it is estimated, as on the Balance Sheet date, will be realised from disposal of the stock in the ordinary course of business, either in its existing condition or as incorporated in the product normally sold, after allowing for all expenditure to be incurred on or before disposal.

"Net realisable value" is estimated by taking account of all available information, including changes in selling prices since the Balance Sheet date, so far as the information is of assistance in determining, as on the Balance Sheet date, the net realisable value of the stock in the ordinary course of business. This involves consideration of the prospects of disposal, having regard to the quantity and condition of the stock in relation to the expected demand (particular attention being given to obsolete or excessive stock) and to the expected effect, if any, on selling prices of any change which has taken place in buying prices of materials or goods.

REDUCTION TO REPLACEMENT PRICE

In many businesses it is important to have regard to the price at which stock can be replaced if such price is less than cost. These considerations may be influenced by such matters as the following:

(a) *Uncertainty as to net realisable value*

Where the volume of stock carried is large in relation to turnover or there is a long period between the purchase of raw material and its conversion into and disposal as finished goods, selling prices current at the Balance Sheet date for the volume of orders then available may afford an unreliable guide to the prospective net realisable value of the stock as a whole. Replacement price may be considered to be the best available guide for this purpose.

(b) *Selling prices based on current replacement prices*

In some businesses where selling prices are based on or reflect current replacement prices it may be considered that the trading results of a subsequent period will be prejudiced if they are burdened with any amount for stock which exceeds its replacement price; where this view is taken it is regarded as important in reporting the results of the activities of a period, as compared with those of its successor or predecessor, that the period in which a reduction in buying prices occurs should bear the diminution in profit rather than the period of disposal whose realisations will be adversely affected by the events of the previous period.

(c) *Recognition of uneconomic buying or production*

Skill in buying or efficiency in production are most important matters in many businesses; the inclusion of stock in the accounts on a replacement price basis (where lower than net realisable value and cost) may be considered to reflect inefficiency in these respects on the ground that it involves the writing down of stock by an amount which represents approximately the result of misjudged buying or inefficient production.

Where the replacement price basis is adopted the stock is stated at the lowest of (*a*) cost, (*b*) net realisable value, (*c*) replacement price, with the effect that the Profit and Loss Account is charged with any reductions necessitated by an excess of (*a*) over (*b*) or (*c*) as the case may be.

Replacement price for this purpose means an estimate of the amount for which, in the ordinary course of business, the stock could have been acquired or produced either at the Balance Sheet date or during the latest period up to and including that date. In a manufacturing business this estimate would be based on the replacement price of the raw material content plus other costs of the undertaking which are relevant to the condition of the stock on the Balance Sheet date.

The importance of the Institute of Chartered Accountants' Recommendation N.22 has warranted its quotation at length, since every internal auditor should be fully conversant with its details, and reference to it is strongly advocated.

The following illustrations include some of the principles mentioned above.

Specimen question (1)

Stock purchased at £2 per unit.
Market price at Balance Sheet date: permanent fall in value to £1·75.
Cost of disposal of stock if sold: £0·05 per unit.
State the price for inclusion in the Balance Sheet.

Answer

Applying the recommendation as to lowest of cost, net realisable value, or replacement price:

Cost	£2·00
Replacement price (*i.e.* market price for sale purposes also)	£1·75
Net realisable value:	
Market price	£1·75
Less Disposal costs	£0·05
Price for inclusion in Balance Sheet	£1·70 per unit

Specimen question (2)

Purchase of raw material £2 per unit.
Processing costs:

Wages	£0·25	
Materials	£0·20	
		£0·45

Selling price at Balance Sheet date £3 per unit.
Cost of putting finished product on market: £0·15
At Balance Sheet date raw material obtainable at £1·75 per unit.
State the price for inclusion in the Balance Sheet.

Answer

The price for inclusion in the Balance Sheet is calculated as follows:

Selling price of finished units	£3·00
Cost of disposal	0·15
Net sale proceeds	£2·85
Processing costs	0·45
Net realisable value of the raw material*	£2·40

* This is in effect the raw material at cost plus the profit of £0·40 per unit to be made after it has been processed.

Price for inclusion in Balance Sheet is that of cost, £2, this being lower than the net realisable value, £2·40.

NOTE

It is not necessary to reduce the units to their replacement price of £1·75 since no loss will be incurred—rather, in effect, will less profit be made than might otherwise have been the case. Some accountants might wish to show the stock at the replacement price of £1·75, but this would be rather conservative policy.

Specimen question (3)

Given the details as in (2) above but with selling prices at £2·50, state the Balance Sheet price.

Answer

Price for inclusion in Balance Sheet:

Net realisable value, *i.e.* as above, less £0·50	
(£3·00 − £2·50)	£1·90
Replacement price, *i.e.* as mentioned above	£1·75

M

The lower of these two prices would be included, viz., replacement price. £1·75.

ELIMINATION OF INTER-PROCESS PROFIT

This aspect of stock valuation is of particular interest to the internal auditor. Not only may periodic profits be vitally affected by their inclusion or otherwise, but production cost comparisons may be vitiated and competitive prices misquoted if they are not carefully compiled and checked. The following example is, therefore, dealt with in detail.

Specimen question

A newly formed company operates two production departments in which a primary and a finishing process are carried out. The output of Department P is transferred to Department F, with the addition of a profit on transfer of 10% and from Department F to warehouse with a further addition of 20%.

Relevant details extracted from the books at the end of the financial year are as follows:

Materials purchased for store	£102,500	
Manufacturing wages:		
Department P	60,000	
F	84,500	
Factory expenses:		
Department P	19,000	
F	25,500	
Sales, 80,000 units		£280,000
Materials issued from store during year:		
Department P	50,000	
F	47,500	
Depreciation on plant and machinery to be charged as to:		
Department P	9,000	
F	12,000	

Output of units completed in Department P and transferred, 100,000.

Work in progress in the same department consisted of half-completed units, 2000.

Output of units completed in Department F and transferred to warehouse 84,000.

Work in progress consisted of 10,000 units taken as half completed and 6000 units from Department P unworked.

The price of raw materials had fallen by 15% at the end of the financial period and was not expected to rise. Sale prices were not expected to be affected until a lapse of some three months after the closing date.

You are required to value the stocks on hand in accordance with the recommendations of the Institute of Chartered Accountants. All workings to be shown.

Answer

This type of problem may be dealt with in two ways. The first method given below is correct and ensures a knowledge of the underlying principles involved; for this reason it is often required for examination purposes. In practice, the second method would be applied, as any efficient manufacturing company using various processes in the course of production will apply process costing methods. One important difference between the two methods of accounting is the complete segregation of the profit addition in the second case.

Method 1.

	Department P		Department F
Materials	£50,000		£47,500
Wages	60,000		84,500
	110,000		
Transfer from Department P			150,297
			282,297
Factory expenses	19,000		25,500
Depreciation	9,000		12,000
	138,000		319,797

Less work in progress

$\left(\dfrac{£138,000}{101,000} \times 1,000\right)$ 1,366

(Unworked $\dfrac{£150,297}{100,000} \times 6,000$)   9,018

(Partly finished

$\dfrac{£150,297}{100,000} \times 10,000$ 15,029

$\dfrac{£169,500}{89,000} \times \dfrac{10,000}{2}$)   9,524

   24,553

   33,571

	136,634		286,226
Add inter-departmental profit	13,663		57,245
Produced 100,000 units	£150,297	Produced 84,000 units	£343,471

Stock of finished goods $\dfrac{4,000}{84,000} \times £343,471 = £16,356$.

STOCK VALUATION

	Total cost	Provision	Cost value
Raw material	£5,000	£750	£4,250
Work in progress:			
Department P	1,366	—	1,366
Department F:			
Unworked (6/100 × £13,663)	9,018	820	8,198
Partly finished (10/100 × £13,663)	24,553	1,366	23,187
Finished goods $\left(\dfrac{4,000}{84,000} \times £57,245 +\right.$			
$\left.\dfrac{4,000}{100,000} \times £13,663\right)$	16,356	3,273	13,083
	£56,293	£6,209	£50,084

NOTE

As selling prices are not likely to be affected until some three months after the Balance Sheet date, no adjustment has been made for the fall in price of raw materials included in the stocks of finished goods and work in progress, as the rate of turnover would indicate their sale by the lapse of the time stated.

Method 2.

(a) STATEMENT OF EQUIVALENT PRODUCTION

Department P

Input		Output	Equivalent complete units
100,000	Complete transferred	100,000	100,000
2,000	Closing w.i.p. 50% complete	2,000	1,000
102,000		102,000	101,000

Department F

Input		Output	Materials from P	Material direct	Lab. and o.h.
100,000	Complete	84,000	84,000	84,000	84,000
	Closing w.i.p.	10,000	10,000	5,000	5,000
	Unworked	6,000	6,000	—	—
100,000		100,000	100,000	89,000	89,000

(b) STATEMENT OF COSTS

Department P

		Equivalent units	Cost per unit
Materials	£50,000		
Wages	60,000		
Expenses	19,000		
Depreciation	9,000		
	£138,000	101,000	£1·366337

Department F

Materials from P	£136,634	100,000	£1·366337
Materials	47,500	89,000	0·5337
Wages	84,500		
Expenses	25,500	89,000	1·37
Depreciation	12,000		
	£306,134		

(c) STATEMENT OF EVALUATION

Department P

	Units	Cost per unit	Amount
Complete units	100,000	£1·366337	£136,634
Closing work in progress	1,000	1·366337	1,366
			£138,000

Department F

Complete units:			
Transferred from P	84,000	£1·366337	£114,772
Material direct	84,000	0·5337	44,831
Labour overheads	84,000	1·371	115,164
		(say)	£274,749
Closing work in progress			
Materials from P	10,000	1·366337	13,663
Material direct	5,000	0·5337	2,669
Labour overheads	5,000	1·371	6,855
			23,187
Unworked:			
Materials from P	6,000	1·366337	8,198
			306,134

(d) PROCESS ACCOUNT *
Department P

	Total	Cost	Profit		Total	Cost	Profit
Materials	£50,000	£50,000	£—	Closing stock	£1,366	£1,366	£ —
Wages	60,000	60,000	—	Transfer	150,297	136,634	13,663
Expenses	19,000	19,000	—				
Depreciation	9,000	9,000	—				
	138,000	138,000	—				
Profit added	13,663	—	13,663				
	£151,663	£138,000	£13,663		£151,663	£138,000	£13,663

Department F

	Total	Cost	Profit		Total	Cost	Profit
Materials from P	£150,297	£136,634	£13,663	Closing stock:			
direct	47,500	47,500	—	6,000 un-worked	£9,018	£8,198	£820
Wages	84,500	84,500	—	10,000 w.i.p.	24,553	23,187	1,366
Expenses	25,500	25,500	—	84,000 transfer	343,471	274,749	68,722
Depreciation	12,000	12,000	—				
	319,797	306,134	13,663				
Profit added	57,245	—	57,245				
	£377,042	£306,134	£70,908	100,000	£377,042	£306,134	£70,908

(e) SALES ACCOUNT

	Units	Total	Cost	Profit		Units	Total	Cost	Profit
Transfer from F	84,000	£343,471	£274,749	£68,722	Sales	80,000	£280,000	£261,666	£18,334
					Closing stock	4,000	16,356	13,083	3,273
					Loss		47,115	—	47,115
		£343,471	£274,749	£68,722			£343,471	£274,749	£68,722

(f) STOCK VALUATION

Raw material	£5,000	£750	£4,250
Dept. P work in progress	1,366	—	1,366
F work in progress (unworked)	9,018	820	8,198
(partly finished)	24,553	1,366	23,187
Finished goods	16,356	3,273	13,083
	£56,293	£6,209	£50,084

* Inter process profits and work in progress is discussed fully in *Wheldon's Cost accounting and costing methods* (Macdonald & Evans, 1970).

EXAMINATION QUESTIONS

1. Write an essay of not more than three pages upon the principles underlying the valuation (as distinct from verification) of stock in trade and work in progress of a manufacturing company for the purpose of the annual accounts.   [C.A. (1959)]

2. Assuming that the principles adopted by the management of a manufacturing company to ascertain stock in trade are satisfactory, you are required to state the audit procedure you would apply, including appropriate tests by way of an overall assessment, to verify the amount at which stock in trade is stated in a Balance Sheet.

You are not required to deal with the ascertainment of physical quantities. Work in progress may be ignored.   [C.A. (1964)]

3. As recently appointed Chief Accountant to a company, you discover that stocks of certain components, amounting to a substantial sum, are valued at works cost plus departmental profit additions. Upon enquiry, you are informed that this is a reasonable practice since if such components were purchased outside the business, profit would be included in the purchase price. Set out your views in a report for discussion at the next board meeting.

4. Although stock levels may remain practically the same year by year, circumstances affecting stocks may vary, e.g.:

Present costs	Future possibilities
(a) Prices low	Prices likely to rise
(b) Prices high	Prices likely to fall

Draw up a tabulation, providing for the circumstances mentioned, to show four methods of pricing issues, with the effect each method has on current production costs and on year-end valuation of stock.   [C.W.A.]

5. Hammer carries on business as a manufacturer from a factory, which he manages, and a warehouse, which is managed by Tongs: separate operating accounts are kept for each. All manufactured goods are invoiced to the latter at provisional prices which are subsequently adjusted to factory cost plus 10% and stocks of manufactured goods in both the factory and the warehouse are valued, for departmental purposes, on this basis. In ascertaining the net profit of the business as a whole the excess over factory cost is adjusted through the general Profit and Loss Account.

All sales are effected by the warehouse.

Tongs is entitled to (a) a salary of £500 per annum and (b) a commission of 25% of the balance shown by the operating account of the warehouse, after charging his commission and his salary.

The following particulars relate to the year 1961, but exclude the salary of and any commission due to Tongs:

Factory

Stock of manufactured goods:		
on 1st January (at departmental value)	160 units	£7,040
on 31st December	270	
Stocks of raw materials:		
on 1st January		19,560
on 31st December		10,840
Purchases of raw materials		98,400
Wages and manufacturing expenses		57,580

Deliveries to warehouse (including all manufactured goods in stock on 1st January)	2,635	
Faulty goods returned by warehouse and scrapped	80	

Warehouse

Stock of manufactured goods on 1st January (at departmental value)	100	4,400
Sales	2,556	217,260
Shortages disclosed by inventory	4	
Returns to factory (all part of opening stock)	80	
Selling expenses		35,260

NOTE

No goods of 1960 manufacture remained in stock on 31st December, 1961 at either the factory or the warehouse.

General

Administration expenses not specifically allocatable to the factory or to the warehouse	18,250

It was agreed that the actual loss arising from the faulty goods scrapped should be borne as to 75% by the factory and as to 25% by the warehouse, and the allowance to the warehouse was adjusted accordingly. No portion of the loss was to be treated as part of the cost of manufacture in 1961.

You are required to prepare for the year 1961:

    (a) the Operating Accounts for the factory and for the warehouse, and
    (b) the Profit and Loss Account.   [C.A. (1962)]

6. S. commenced business on 1st January 1958. He manufactures one standard product only. His factory consists of two departments, A and B, in which a primary and a finishing process respectively are carried on. The output of Department A is transferred to Department B at the factory cost of Department A, and the finished articles are transferred from Department B to the warehouse at a price equal to the factory cost of Department B plus 10%. The factory cost of Department B includes the cost of the output transferred from Department A.

The following trial balance was extracted from S.'s books as at 31st December 1958:

Trial balance

Capital		£45,000
Freehold property, at cost	£14,000	
Plant and machinery, at cost	10,000	
Materials purchased for store	62,500	
Manufacturing wages: Department A	40,000	
Department B	64,500	
Factory expenses: Department A	9,400	
Department B	15,600	
Sales		240,000
Administration and selling expenses	50,000	
Debtors and creditors	27,300	16,800
Drawings	2,450	
Balance at bank	6,050	
	£301,800	£301,800

You are given the following information relating to the year 1958:

(a) Materials issued from store and used in production, at cost:

Department A	£30,000
Department B	£27,500

(b) Number of output units completed in Department A   100,000

Number of completed Department A units transferred to Department B   90,000

The stock in Department A at 31st December 1958 consisted entirely of completed units ready for transfer to Department B; there was no work in progress.

(c) All Department A units transferred to Department B were there converted into finished articles, and the whole output of Department B (90,000 articles) was transferred to the warehouse.

(d) Number of articles sold   80,000

(e) Provision is to be made for depreciation of plant and machinery at 10% of cost. Three-fifths is to be charged to Department A and two-fifths to Department B.

NOTE

The trading account is to be charged with the output of Department B at the price at which it is transferred to the warehouse. Stocks of Department A units and finished articles are to be shown in the Balance Sheet at factory cost.

You are required to prepare a separate manufacturing account for each factory department for the year 1958, a Trading and Profit and Loss Account for the year 1958, and a Balance Sheet at 31st December 1958.

[C.I.S. (1959)]

7. XY Ltd are manufacturers of rubber tubes. During the three years ended 31st December 1961, output has been constant and 5000 tons of rubber have been used in production each year to produce 5000 tons of tubing. The entire output has been sold as soon as it has been produced and no stocks of finished goods have been held. It has been the company's practice, however, to hold substantial stocks of raw rubber, and movements in the company's rubber stocks have been as follows:

	Year ended 31st December		
	1959	1960	1961
Opening stocks (tons)	—	5,000	4,000
Purchases (tons)	10,000	4,000	6,000
	10,000	9,000	10,000
Used in production (tons)	5,000	5,000	5,000
Closing stocks (tons)	5,000	4,000	5,000

You may assume that the price of rubber has changed on 1st January each year and that rubber purchases have cost £200 per ton throughout 1959, £300 per ton throughout 1960 and £275 per ton throughout 1961.

In addition to the cost of rubber, the company incurs other manufacturing costs, overheads and depreciation amounting to £1 million a year. The selling price of rubber tubing has been varied on 1st January each year so as to allow for changes in the market value of rubber and has been arrived at as follows:

	Method of arriving at selling price per ton of rubber tubing sold during		
	1959	1960	1961
Value of rubber used in production at current market prices	£200	£300	£275
Other manufacturing expenses, overheads and depreciation	200	200	200
Margin of profit	50	50	50
Selling price of rubber tubing	£450	£550	£525

You are required to:

(a) Describe any two recognised bases of valuing the company's rubber stocks and show what the profits of the company would be on each basis during the years 1959, 1960 and 1961, using the facts set out above.

(b) Show to what extent the profits of the company on each basis have been affected by profits or losses arising through the holding of rubber stocks and discuss to what extent any useful purpose is served in disclosing the basis of stock valuation in the company's published accounts without disclosing the amount of such stock profits or losses.   [C.A. (S)

PART THREE

FINANCIAL CONTROL

CHAPTER XV

INVESTMENT OF FUNDS

AN efficiently managed business will not normally have sums of any consequence surplus to its ordinary requirements—efficient budgeting should ensure adequate funds with a sufficient margin to meet contingencies—but in certain circumstances it is expedient to invest funds outside the business for such purposes as the redemption of debentures or the renewal of assets. In such a case it is important to ensure that the investments plus interest accruing will realise the amount needed by the time it is needed. Interest tables are one way of doing it, but continuous inflation can upset the calculations by capital losses on the investments themselves. This difficulty can be overcome by taking out an insurance policy to mature at the required date; but even this may be unsatisfactory if the purpose is renewal of assets, for they in turn may be affected by a fall in the value of money. Despite complications like these, it is still good sense to invest funds outside the business so that there will be no risk of their being absorbed into the general assets and not available when needed.

Investments can be made in other companies associated with the business "vertically" or "horizontally" for such purposes as gaining control or ensuring supplies of essential products. Investments of this nature are dealt with in Chapter xix.

The governing principles which apply generally in the setting aside of funds outside a business are:

(a) *The security offered.* Whereas individual investors may be inclined to take a risk to ensure a higher return, it will not usually be advisable in the case of a trading or manufacturing company.

(b) *The highest return available,* subject to the requirement of security mentioned.

(c) *Ease of realisation.* While the envisaged date of realisation may be in the distant future, it does sometimes happen that the finance may be needed earlier—for example, where a sinking fund is created for the redemption of debentures, in accordance with a term in the deed, debentures may be purchased on the market if they fall below par at any time.

SUITABLE INVESTMENTS

Some of the types of security in which funds may be invested are given below. The list does not claim to be in any way exhaustive, but in view of the foregoing principles a wide range need not be considered.

1. GILT-EDGED

The term is used to describe fixed interest bearing securities which involve virtually no risk factor so far as interest is concerned, although from the capital aspect they are still vulnerable. They include:

(a) *British Government stocks*, which are by far the largest group and may be divided into:

(i) *Short-dated* securities: having only up to five years to run to maturity, they afford a convenient outlet for such organisations as banks and discount houses with short term funds at their disposal. "Shorts," as they are termed, are used for day-to-day borrowing transactions and are frequently dealt in "firm," *i.e.* accrued interest is excluded, and added to the selling price instead. Examples are Treasury $6\frac{1}{2}\%$ 1971 and Exchequer $6\frac{3}{4}\%$ 1971.

(ii) *Medium-dated* securities with 5–15 years to run, *e.g.* Conversion $5\frac{1}{4}\%$ 1974 and British Transport guaranteed stock 4% 1972–7.

(iii) *Long-dated* securities with more than 15 years to run, *e.g.* Treasury 5% 1986–96, British Gas guaranteed stock 3% 1990–5.

(iv) *"Irredeemables."* Such stocks, also termed "undated," are redeemable at the option of the Government but, as their name implies, the chance of it happening is regarded as negligible. Examples are Consolidated stock 4% and War Loan $3\frac{1}{2}\%$.

"Guaranteed" stocks are stocks on which the liability of some other government or body is guaranteed by the British Government under Act of Parliament.

The passage of time will obviously influence the classification of the stocks. As redemption dates draw nearer the more stable the market price becomes, for redemption is at par. Owing to this stability of price, "shorts" normally carry a fairly low yield, as there is more chance of fluctuation with stocks having longer to run. Fluctuations are often caused by such things as temporary economic disturbances or anticipation of changes in interest rates or rates of taxation (*see* Chapter XVII).

The various stocks carry different rates of interest and varying provisions as to redemption, the majority having a specified date for this with the Government retaining the right to redeem at any time within two, five or ten years before that date. Some issues do not specify a date for repayment, but the right to repay after a certain date is retained, *e.g.* $3\frac{1}{2}\%$ War Loan, which is repayable on or after 1st December 1952.

Investment in Government stocks will be decided mainly by the policy it is desired to pursue. If ease of realisability without loss of capital is the prime factor, then investment in "shorts" is advisable. If a higher income is required, a moderately long term investment is preferable and if, in this case, purchases are made below par a capital gain ensues on maturity. If a certain income is required for (say) an annuity, long-dated stocks such as 2½% Consols would be suitable since redemption seems unlikely in view of their low market quotation as against par value.

(b) *British corporations* (including various local councils, *e.g.* G.L.C. stocks) and public boards (*e.g.* the Port of London Authority). This type of stock also offers security of capital with, sometimes, slightly higher rates than Government stocks.

(c) *Commonwealth government and provincials.* Dominion stocks are of higher standing than the others owing to the more stable economic and political conditions of the countries concerned, hence they offer greater security.

The great advantages of gilt-edged stocks are ease of marketability and the undoubted security which accounts for their low yield. They are nearly all free of stamp duty.

Dealings in gilt-edged are for "cash," *i.e.* settlement is to be made on the day following dealing, but in practice a few days are usually allowed except where dealings are in very large amounts. It is also customary to send certificates for such stocks to brokers when giving sale orders to facilitate the preparation of transfer deeds at once.

2. EQUITIES

The rapid fall in the value of money during the years following the Second World War meant substantial losses for those with investments in fixed interest bearing stock. Consequently there has since been a strong tendency to transfer funds from Government stocks to equities. Equities (Ordinary shares), unlike fixed interest bearing stocks, are inclined to maintain or increase their value in times of inflation since companies are able to increase their profits and dividend distribution; hence their shares may increase, or at least maintain, their capital value.

The position has become more stable in recent years, but the effect has been an inclination on the part of investors to buy this type of stock more generally than formerly. "Blue chip" securities such as the equities of I.C.I., Unilever and similar large groups are used extensively for investment purposes by business concerns. The subject of equities and their valuation is dealt with further in Chapter xvi.

3. TAX RESERVE CERTIFICATES

The Institute of Chartered Accountants' recommendation that the charge for taxation shown in the Profit and Loss Account should be in respect of the year's profit, is now generally complied with. Thus in many instances payment of the actual tax may not be made for twelve months, or even longer where negotiations are protracted, after the amount has been set aside. So that settlement can be made without difficulty and at the same time interest earned on the funds set aside, tax reserve certificates can be purchased for £25 (or multiples thereof) and surrendered in respect of income tax, profits tax or land tax, but not Schedule E.

The certificates, which are obtainable through a bank, carry interest as specified in the prospectus applying to the current series issued by the Treasury. The rate, which varies from time to time, is allowed tax free for up to two years, calculated on the basis of each complete month the certificate is held. The interest is not paid over but is added to the value of the certificate when surrendered.

4. TREASURY BILLS

Sums may be set aside by tendering for Treasury bills and holding them until maturity, usually 91 days after date of issue. Tenders are invited every Friday for sums of varying amounts, with a minimum of £5000. They may only be made through the agency of a bank.

If a tender is accepted for, say, £98·75%, the difference represents a discount, or on maturity the interest accrued on the loan.

5. BANK DEPOSITS

Funds can be deposited for short periods with the joint stock banks, merchant banks or discount houses: short periods only, because, as has been remarked, companies should not normally carry excess funds for any length of time. If the investment is long term, better rates can be obtained by the purchase of securities.

YIELD FACTORS

Before proceeding to the valuation of securities in Chapter XVI it is necessary to explain the influence of certain factors that affect both the incentive to invest and the earnings received on investments.

The return on an investment is termed its *yield*. If £100 is invested for one year at 4%, then the interest received of £4 constitutes the *nominal* yield. The nominal yield, however, may differ from the actual yield, which is termed the *flat* or *current* yield. Stocks are bought more often than not for a price other than their par value. For example, a £100 stock with a nominal yield of 4% might be bought for £50. The current yield would then be 8%, since £4 interest would be received per annum on the £100 face value of the stock, or $(100/50) \times 4 = £8$. There may be various reasons why a stock of £100 nominal value sells at £50. They are discussed later, but one of the most likely is a rise in interest rates.

For a fuller explanation of how governmental activity may influence interest rates the reader should consult the economic textbooks, but if rates of interest are stable at (say) 4% and the rate is made to rise to 5%, it means that anyone with £100 to invest will not buy a stock offering only 4%. To obtain a sale, therefore, of a stock yielding 4%, the price must be dropped from £100 to $(4/5 \times 100) = £80$, thus giving a current yield of £4 for £80, or 5%. It will be noted that the current yield ignores taxation.

The capital profit that may accrue on Government stocks was mentioned above. It arises through the purchase of stocks below their face value and redemption on maturity at the nominal value. The difference represents a capital profit which is free of income tax, save in the case of an investment business.

This profit—or it may be a loss—applies not only to Government stocks but to all securities of a redeemable nature. The redemption price payable is taken into consideration in fixing the current price.

Example

Current market rate of interest, 4%.

(a) £100 3% "irredeemable" stock:

$$\text{Market price} = \tfrac{3}{4} \times 100 = \text{£75.}$$

(b) £100 3% redeemable stock, redeemable in five years at par:

(i) Value of 3% irredeemable stock as above	£75
(ii) Add the present value of £25 payable in five years' time at 4%	£20·55
Market price	£95·55

or

(i) Present value of £3 per annum for five years	£13·36
(ii) Present value of £100 at 4%	£82·19
Market price ($95\tfrac{9}{16}$)	£95·55

Compound interest tables are used to make the actual calculations.

It will be seen that over the five years, not only is interest of £3 per annum received, but also the additional sum of £4·45 or, in effect, £4·45/5 annually as a capital profit. These two sums together give a *gross redemption yield*. Where, more practically, income tax is deducted, a *net* redemption yield is obtained.

None of the costs involved in purchase have been included so far, nor has the accrued interest from date of last payment to date of purchase. Where they are included the price or the cost so calculated is termed the "clean price" or "clean cost" respectively. Likewise, if an exact yield is required, the expenses incurred must be taken into consideration, *e.g.*

$$\frac{\text{Rate of interest or dividend receivable}}{\text{Clean cost (cost including expenses)}} \times 100 = \text{Flat yield}$$

Slight complications arise where redeemable stocks are concerned, since the annual income is subject to taxation. Any capital appreciation or loss is not, nor does it occur up to the time of redemption, *i.e.*

year to year: the full appreciation so far as the stockholder is concerned takes place on the date of redemption itself.

We give below an illustration of the type of details shown in the financial columns of the daily papers. As they do not all give the same information, we have included an overall selection.

BRITISH FUNDS

| 19— | | | | | Gross yields % | |
| | | | | | Interest | Redemption |
High	Low	Security	Closing price	+ or −	£	£
101·44	99·12½	Conv. 5½% 1974	100·44 ·70	+·20	£5·20	£5·15

The "High/low" column gives the highest and lowest price quoted during the current year. The "Closing price" column shows, first, the price at which jobbers were willing to buy and, second, the price at which they were willing to sell at the close of the previous days' business. The "+ or −" column shows the increase or decrease on the price since the previous day's closing price. The "Gross interest" and "Gross redemption" yields have been explained above.

GROWTH STOCKS

Where equities are concerned, the dividend yield may not be a true reflection of a stock's value. If, for example, one company distributes a large part of its profits in dividends its shares will show a greater yield than one which ploughs back most of its profits. In the latter case, prudent management may be building up a profitable company, whereas the distribution of dividends at a higher rate *may* be draining a business of necessary resources.

Those who invest in a progressive company may be willing to accept a lower dividend yield in the hope of (a) larger returns later when the business has expanded and (b) the prospect of bonus issues to capitalise reserves. A bonus issue, being regarded for the purposes of taxation as a capital profit and so not subject to tax, may constitute a more profitable distribution than the regular payment of higher dividends.

Since an investor is concerned with the development of a company that ploughs back its profits, the investment is regarded as a "growth" stock. Where dividends are withheld, the stocks may be quoted at a price lower than would otherwise be the case owing to the smaller dividend yield, and this may give rise to the danger of a take-over bid (*see* Chapter XVII).

EARNINGS AND DIVIDEND COVER

It was implied above that a company which distributed all its profits would be regarded as imprudently managed, since neglect of such things as working capital and replacement of assets would lead rapidly to disaster. Investors are concerned, therefore, with a company's ability to continue its dividend payments *and* have adequate resources to plough back. A way of testing for "cover" is by the formula:

$$\text{Cover} = \frac{\text{Earnings available (Profit after tax)}}{\text{Dividend or interest payable}}$$

It can be applied to various classes of shares in order of priority. Priority percentages have already been dealt with in Chapter III.

A further illustration is now given covering the industrial type of security, differing slightly from the government stock shown above. Only the last three columns need any explanation: (i) the most recent dividend was 15% (ii) which was covered 1·3 times, (iii) yielding 3·75% on an investment of £4 or 15% × £1/£4 = 3·75%.

INDUSTRIALS

19— High	Low	Security	Closing price	+ or −	Dividend % or amount	Times covered	P/E	Gross yield %
£3·95	£3·6	XYZ Co. (£0·25)	£3·99 £4·0	+ £0·01	15	1·3	20	3·75

The formula can be used further, for if the Ordinary dividend is covered 1·3 times and the dividend represents 15% on the issued capital, then the yield on investment is 5%, or 20% × £1/£4 or 1·3 × 3·75%.

Assuming for convenience that the Ordinary share capital consists of 400,000 £1 shares (*i.e.* £400,000); the profit ploughed back can be calculated by taking the dividend of 15% or £60,000 from the cover of 1·3 times that amount (*i.e.* £80,000). £20,000 has been ploughed back.

In calculating the dividend cover, it is necessary to deduct priority percentages. The formula is:

$$\text{Dividend cover} = \frac{\text{Earnings available less Prior charges}}{\text{Dividend payable}}$$

Had the capital of the XYZ Company consisted also of £40,000 6% Preference shares, the Ordinary dividend cover would remain the same, since the original calculations would have taken this into consideration, but the total profits would have been greater to the extent of the Preference dividend and the computation would then have been:

$$\frac{£82,400 - 2,400}{£60,000} = 1·3$$

EARNINGS YIELD

The earnings yield has already been touched upon above. It is a useful guide to investors, and is calculated by the formula:

$$\frac{\text{Profit available for Ordinary share holders*}}{1} \times \frac{\text{Nominal share value}}{\text{Purchase price}} = \frac{\text{Earnings}}{\text{yield}}$$

* Expressed as a percentage of the Ordinary share capital.

The earnings yield comprises the profits available to ordinary shareholders if those profits were distributed up to the hilt, or more precisely, the earnings yield represents the amount available to Ordinary shareholders after the settlement of prior charges, expressed as a percentage of the Ordinary share capital taking into consideration the purchase price. Since dividend policies may vary for a number of reasons, *e.g.* in the case of growth stocks mentioned earlier, it is important to know the actual earnings yield of a company for purposes of comparison.

Using the formula above, the earnings yield is:

$$20\% \times £1/£4 = 5\%$$

PRICE–EARNINGS RATIO

The price–earnings ratio (P/E ratio) is the ratio between the market price of a share and the distributable equity earnings per share. Inflationary tendencies have caused investors to be concerned more with the growth aspect of stocks, covering such matters as capital gains, expansion, bonus issues, etc., than with immediate returns in the form of dividends—as evidenced by the fact that on fixed-interest stocks it is possible to obtain 8% whereas, despite the risks involved, 5% is received on equities. This preference has led to the use of the P/E ratio rather than the E/P (earnings yield) ratio, which was formerly used as a measurement of share value. In effect the P/E ratio shows how long it would take for the investor to recover his outlay if the equity earnings were to remain constant.

There are those who still favour the use of the earnings yield as a comparative measurement of share values, and certainly it has the advantage of facilitating the calculation of the dividend cover where the dividend yield is known. In any case, the P/E ratio is merely the reciprocal of the E/P ratio, *e.g.*: earnings yield, 5%; P/E ratio, 100/5 = 20.

Example

Share capital: 100,000 shares of £1 nominal value.
Market price of shares, £2 each.
Distributable profits, *i.e.* profit after taxation and settlement of prior charges, such as Preference dividend: £15,000.
Dividend declared at 10% (gross).

$$\text{P/E ratio} = \frac{\text{Market price of shares}}{\text{Earnings per share}} = \frac{£2 \cdot 00}{£0 \cdot 15} = 13 \cdot 3$$

$$\text{Earnings yield} = \frac{£15,000}{100,000} \times \frac{£1}{£2} = 7\tfrac{1}{2}\%$$

$$\text{Dividend yield} = 10\% \times \frac{£1}{£2} = 5\%$$

The dividend cover is easily calculable in conjunction with the earnings yield *i.e.* $7\tfrac{1}{2}\%/5\% = 1\tfrac{1}{2}$ times.

The following example summarises the various points made above.

Specimen question

A company is capitalised as follows:

> £600,000   7% Preference shares, £1 each.
> 1,600,000   Ordinary shares, £1 each.
> ──────────
> £2,200,000
> ══════════

The following information is relevant as to its financial year just ended:

Profit, after taxation at 40%, £542,000.
Ordinary dividend paid, 20%.
Depreciation, £120,000.
Market price of Ordinary shares, £4.
Capital commitments, £240,000.

You are required to state the following, showing the necessary workings:

(a) The dividend yield on the Ordinary shares.
(b) The cover for the Preference and Ordinary dividends.
(c) The earnings yield.
(d) The price–earnings (P/E) ratio.
(e) The priority percentages.
(f) The net cash flow (*see* Chapter v for explanation).
(g) The reason for the comparison of net cash flow with capital commitments.

Answer

(a) Dividend yield on ordinary shares:

$$20\% \times \frac{£1}{£4} = 5\%$$

(b) Cover for Preference and Ordinary dividends:

(i) *Preference dividend:* £542,000/£42,000 = 12·9 times.
(ii) *Ordinary dividend:* £500,000/£320,000 = 1·56 times.

(c) Earnings yield:

$$\frac{\text{Profit after tax less prior charges}}{\text{Ordinary share capital}} \times 100 \times \frac{\text{Nominal share value}}{\text{Market price}}$$
$$= \text{Earnings yield}$$

$$\frac{£542,000 - £42,000}{£1,600,000} \times 100 \times \frac{£1}{£4} = 7·8$$

or dividend yield × Dividend cover = 5% × 1·56 = 7·8.

(d) P/E ratio = 100/7·8 = 12·8

or

$$\frac{\text{Ordinary share capital}}{\text{Profit after tax less prior charges}} \times \frac{\text{Share's market price}}{\text{Share's nominal value}}$$

i.e.

$$\frac{£1,600,000}{£542,000 - £42,000} \times \frac{£4}{£1} = 12·8$$

(e) Priority percentages:

Preference dividend	Ordinary dividend	Retained net profit	
£42,000	£320,000	£180,000	= £542,000
0–7¾%	7¾%–66⅔%	66⅔%–100%	= 100%

(f) Net cash flow:

Trading profit		£903,333
Taxation 40%		361,333
		542,000
Add depreciation		120,000
		662,000
Less Dividends:		
Preference	£42,000	
Ordinary	320,000	
		362,000
Net cash flow		£300,000

(g) The comparison of net cash flow with capital commitments is important —particularly from the viewpoint of investors—because if sufficient funds are not available internally, recourse may have to be had to raising finance externally by means of a share or loan issue or otherwise. Such action would no doubt have an influence on the market price of existing shares.

EXAMINATION QUESTIONS

1. A produce merchant is concerned about a large balance of £100,000 which he has to keep on current account at his bank in case he has the opportunity of spot purchases of goods, which normally occurs about once a month, but he never knows when. Advise him. [C.C.A.

2. Here are two excerpts from the list of stock exchange closing prices from a daily newspaper published on 18th February (the names and prices of the securities are fictitious):

(a)

BRITISH FUNDS

"*Shorts*" (*lives up to five years*)

19— High	Low	Security	Closing price	21st August Closing price	Interest £	Gross yield % Redemption £
103⅞	98	Macs. 5% 1967	100⅜ ½	99⅞	4·97½	4·82¼

(b)

INDUSTRIALS (MISCELLANEOUS)

19— High	Low	Security	Closing price	21st August Closing price	Dividend % or amount	Times covered	Gross yield %
£0·12½	£0·07	Pop Bttlrs (£0·10)	£0·10 £0·12½	£0·10½	10	1·4	8·0

In a brief essay, explain (i) what the various headings mean, (ii) why this information is thought to be of interest to holders and prospective holders of these securities, and (iii) how the last two items in each line are calculated.
[C.C.A.

3. Discuss the merits and demerits of the following forms of investment:

(a) Short dated British Government stocks,
(b) Loans on mortgage of freehold houses,
(c) High class industrial equity stocks,
(d) High class industrial Preference stocks,

from the point of view of:

(i) The directors of a trading company with surplus funds to invest, and

(ii) The trustees of a staff pension fund enjoying unrestricted powers of investment. [C.A. (1960)

4. Explain how management accounting methods can assist in ensuring the best utilisation of the cash resources of a business. [C.A.

5. (a) Indicate:

(i) The principal factors governing the normal expected price–earnings ratios of particular groups of industries or commercial undertakings.
(ii) Your view as to the reasons for differentials in the average price–earnings ratios, as derived from a recent financial publication, in respect of the following industrial groups:

Tobacco	13·9
Breweries	16·4
Electronics	24·0
Heavy electrical	20·2
Textiles	17·5

(iii) The reasons for the movement away from the use of dividend yield in favour of the price–earnings ratio, in comparing the investment potential of quoted companies.

(b) Summarised figures from a company's accounts to 31st March 1968 show the following:

Profit and Loss Account:

Pre-tax profit	£400,000
Taxation	120,000
Tax equalisation	50,000
Preference dividend	30,000
Ordinary dividend	99,000

Balance Sheet:

Fixed assets	£1,900,000
Current assets	1,550,000
Current liabilities	1,250,000
Long-term liabilities and provisions	200,000
Issued 6% preference stock in £1 units	500,000
Issued ordinary stock in £0·25 units	600,000
Reserves	900,000

Note. Middle market quotations for issued stocks are:

Preference   £0·80
Ordinary   £0·91½

From the above information you are required to state:

(i) Preference dividend yield.
(ii) Ordinary dividend yield.
(iii) Price–earnings ratio.
(iv) Market capitalisation of Ordinary stock.
(v) Net assets value per unit of Ordinary stock.
(vi) Net current ratio.   [C.A. (S)

6. From an examination of the undernoted summarised accounts of a company whose redeemable Preference shares and Ordinary shares have market values of £0·95 and £3 per share respectively you are required to state:

(a) The dividend yields for the redeemable Preference and Ordinary shares.
(b) The price–earnings ratio on the Ordinary shares.
(c) The dividend and asset covers on the Preference shares.
(d) The priority percentages of earnings.
(e) The net cash flow, giving details of the factors contributing thereto.
(f) The percentage (to the nearest 1%) of fixed to net current assets at 31st March 1965 and 1966. (You may assume that no new share capital was introduced during 1965–66 and you may include future taxation with current liabilities.)

GROUP PROFIT AND LOSS ACCOUNT

for year to 31st March 1966

Trading profit		£279,225
Less: depreciation	£40,150	
Less: gains on sale of fixed assets	1,450	
	38,700	
Directors' emoluments	20,000	
		58,700
Profit subject to tax		220,525
Corporation tax		88,500
		132,025
Preference dividend	30,000	
Ordinary dividend	70,000	
	100,000	
Preference share redemption reserve	20,000	
		120,000
Carried to group Balance Sheet		12,025

GROUP BALANCE SHEET

as at 31st March 1966

Issued share capital:

7½% redeemable preference shares of £1 each (*Note 1*)	£400,000
Ordinary shares of £1 each	350,000
	750,000
Capital reserve (*Note 2*)	207,500
Revenue reserves	369,000
	1,326,500

Current assets	2,610,500
Less: current liabilities	1,742,500
	868,000
Less: corporation tax payable 1st January 1967	88,500
	779,500
Fixed assets (*Note 3*)	547,000
	1,326,500

Note 1. The preference shares fall to be redeemed on 31st March 1979 at £1·10 per share.

Note 2. Capital reserve:

Preference share redemption reserve		£180,000
General:		
At 31st March 1965	£7,000	
Add: development grant received during year	20,500	
		27,500
		207,500

Note 3. Fixed asset movements in year (summarised):

	Cost	Depreciation	Net
At 31st March 1965	£842,500	£374,850	£467,650
Gross additions	123,500	—	123,500
Realisations	−20,250	−16,250	−4,000
Depreciation	—	40,150	−40,150
	945,750	398,750	547,000

[C.A. (S)

7. The particulars in the undernoted table have been taken from a financial journal and show certain statistics brought out by analysing a company's accounts:

Explanations

Company	XY Ltd	
Year end	30th June 1962	
Earnings on capital		Profits before tax and before deducting Debenture interest as a percentage of share and loan capital and reserves less goodwill
employed	13·2%	
Net earnings	£1,688,000	
Price–earnings ratio	19	Number of times the latest earnings after tax are covered by the current market value of the issued share capital
Net dividend	£795,000	
Depreciation	£2,573,000	
Net cash flow	£3,466,000	
Capital commitments	£2,515,000	
Price–net cash flow		Number of times the net cash flow is covered by the current market value of the issued share capital.
ratio	9	
Net quick resources	£222,000	

Using the information given above, where appropriate, you are required to answer the following questions:

(a) *Earnings on capital employed*

In arriving at capital employed for the purpose of calculating earnings thereon:

(i) Is it correct in all circumstances to deduct goodwill?
(ii) Should future income tax be treated as capital employed?
(iii) How should fixed assets appearing in the Balance Sheet at figures based on out-of-date historical cost be dealt with?

Give reasons for your answers and comment in the light thereof on the shortcomings of statistics based on capital employed.

(b) *Price–earnings ratio*

(i) In your view, is it advisable to use "the latest earnings after tax" in the denominator in determining the ratio? What alternative denominator would you recommend?
(ii) What is the relationship between price–earnings ratio and earnings yield and which do you consider the more helpful statistic?
(iii) What is the purpose of giving another related ratio, *i.e.* price–net cash flow?

(c) *Miscellaneous points*

(i) How much of the profit did the company plough back in the year?
(ii) What is the significance of the juxtaposition in the table of "Net cash flow" and "Capital commitments"?
(iii) What is meant by the term "Net quick resources" and what is its significance?   [C.A.(S)

8. The following information has been obtained from the accounts of a public company, AB Ltd:

(a) *From the Profit and Loss Account for the year ended 31st March 1962:*

Profit before taxation but after providing all other expenses, including directors' remuneration and depreciation		£600,000
Taxation based on profit for the year:		
Income tax	£232,500	
Profits tax	90,000	
		322,500
Profit after taxation		£277,500
Appropriations:		
Paid:		
Dividend for year on 6% Preference shares (net)		3,675
Proposed:		
Dividend for year at 33⅓% on Ordinary shares (net)		122,500
Profit for year unappropriated		£151,325

(b) *From the Balance Sheet as at 31st March 1962:*

Share capital:		
Ordinary shares of £1 each, fully paid	£600,000	
6% Preference shares of £1 each, fully paid	100,000	
		£700,000
Reserves including Profit and Loss Account		900,000
Future income tax		232,500
		£1,832,500

The quoted price of the Ordinary shares on the stock exchange is currently £5 a share.

From the above information you are required to calculate:

(a) The maximum gross dividends that can be paid out of the profits of the year, and explain the relationship between such gross dividends and the profit of the company before taxation.
(b) The Preference dividend cover.
(c) The earnings yield on the Ordinary shares.
(d) The dividend yield on the Ordinary shares. [C.A. (S)

CHAPTER XVI

VALUATION OF SECURITIES

THIS subject covers a much wider field of study than management accountancy alone.

INFLUENCES ON SHARE PRICES

Political action, economic trends, psychological factors, all have a bearing upon prices quoted on the stock exchange, which is considered to be the nearest approach to a "perfect market." These various factors influence dealings to such an extent that the stock exchange is commonly regarded as a barometer of public reactions.

1. GENERAL

Factors which have an overall effect on share prices generally include those listed below. The list may with little imagination be extended.

(*a*) Government policies regulating interest rates, for example, or direct and indirect taxes. An impending budget may affect prices if it is feared a heavier tax may be imposed on certain commodities—or, on the other hand, there are hopes it may be reduced or removed. Budget uncertainty has on occasion so affected prices as to lead to demands for pre-budget announcements.

(*b*) Rising employment and fears of trade recession may depress the prices of industrial shares while raising those of gilt-edged. Conversely, encouraging export figures may raise prices in expectation of additional activity.

(*c*) Rumours (which may be quite unfounded) often have an influence, and fears of hostilities breaking out in various areas may depress some prices and raise others, such as those of armament manufacturers.

2. PARTICULAR

Factors likely to influence the price of shares in individual companies, on the other hand, include:

(*a*) The present position and future prospects of the industry of which the company is part.

(*b*) The amount and the trend of dividends paid, and expected future dividends, taking into consideration the dividend cover and the yield compared with similar shares.

Announcements by companies themselves may affect prices, for instance if a company increases or "passes" (*i.e.* does not pay) its interim dividend.

(c) The capital gearing of the company concerned (see Chapter III).

(d) The amount and trend of the company's profits and the "earnings yield," i.e. the profits available for distribution to Ordinary share holders after meeting all prior charges, expressed as a percentage of the market value of the share capital (see Chapter xv).

(e) Opinion as to the efficiency and status of the directorate and any contemplated changes due, for example, to retirement.

(f) The net assets according to the company's Balance Sheet (this is dealt with below).

(g) Whether there is a reasonably active market in the shares and the amount of the "turn" (the difference between the higher and lower prices as quoted).

(h) The possibility of "rights" issues or the issue of bonus shares (see below).

3. BONUS AND RIGHTS ISSUES

(a) Bonus issues

In valuing securities the effect of bonus issues, not only on the ordinary capital on which they are paid out, but on any other Debentures or classes of shares in the company, cannot be ignored.

The following are illustrative extracts from the Balance Sheet of a company before and after a "one for one" bonus issue:

(i)

Balance Sheet			
Issued share capital	£50,000	Net assets	£100,000
Reserves (capital and/or revenue)	50,000		

(ii)

Balance Sheet			
Issued share capital	£100,000	Net assets	£100,000

It is apparent that on a "net assets" basis the shares are worth £2 each in the first instance and £1 each in the second.

Although shareholders may be gratified to receive a "tax free" bonus issue, they have not made any gain from the point of view of capital. In fact, as the issue does not increase the profit-earning capacity of the company, it is necessary to ensure that profits are sufficient to justify any additional dividends payable. It may be advisable, therefore, to spread such a capitalisation over a period of years, for not only may the market price of the shares rise to its original figure after a short time, but it will also be easier to maintain the annual dividend at its former figure.

Any Debenture holders in the company may benefit from a bonus issue, since profits, if capitalised from revenue funds, are no longer distributable, so enhancing the Debenture holders' security.

Preference share holders are likely to benefit in the same way as

Debenture holders where, as is usually the case, they have priority of repayment in the event of winding-up. But winding-up may take place only in extreme circumstances, and the Preference share holders stand to lose some security of dividends where revenue reserves are capitalised since such funds are no longer available for payment of dividends in difficult periods. Moreover if the Preference shares carry participation rights after a specified dividend has been paid to Ordinary share holders, these may be adversely affected by the fact that a greater sum has to be paid on the Ordinary dividends at the specified rate, with consequently lower dividends. Ordinary share holders may not object, though, since they may still receive more on their now larger shareholding than previously. *Should the Preference share holders not have priority of repayment of capital, any increase by capitalisation of reserves is likely to be to their detriment, since the Ordinary share holders have increased participation rights.*

The bonus shares may rise slightly in price above the original shares because bonus shares are issued in the form of allotment letters which are negotiable without the buyer having to pay the Government stamp duty of 1%. The bonus shares then carry a premium which may rise to a little below the sum which would have been payable as stamp duty.

(b) *Rights issues*

Companies often favour the raising of funds by means of a rights issue to existing shareholders since:

(i) the expense involved in making an offer to the public is avoided;
(ii) there is more certainty of the shares being sold, since the issue is on favourable terms to those who have already seen fit to invest in the company.

The procedure involved is for a provisional Allotment Letter to be sent to each shareholder entitling the recipient to take up a specified number of shares in proportion to his existing holding, *e.g.* "one for three." The price being less than the market price, the "rights" may be sold if desired.

Owing to the possibility of fractions of shares arising (*e.g.* one for three on a capital of 80,000 shares, which might be rounded off to 30,000 by the issue of 3334 rights shares), or a shareholder not taking up shares he is entitled to, a form of application for excess shares may be allotted to a trustee for sale on behalf of those who fail to apply, or for the company's benefit, to be used for writing off issue expenses or otherwise.

Valuation of "rights." The actual value of the rights may be calculated as follows:

Assuming shares of £1 nominal value are quoted at £2 and a "rights" issue of the same class is made of one for two at £1·50, then the position is:

Value of two £1 shares at £2 each	£4·00
One share on rights issue at £1·50	£1·50
Value of three shares now £1·83½ each	£5·50

The old shares should now stand at the revised value of £1·83½ each, this being £0·33½ greater than the rights issue of £1·5, 0·33½ being the value to the shareholder of his "rights" on one new share, or on his original holding of two shares, £0·16½ each.

But care has to be exercised by the company making the issue, for share prices are not regulated according to purely mathematical formulae. The prospects of the company are an important factor since, as mentioned with regard to bonus issues, the profits have to be spread over a larger amount of capital. If there is likely to be any danger of the price of the shares falling below the price set by the company, the shares may not be taken up. Thus it is advisable to fix the "rights" issue price well below the market price of the existing shares.

4. TAKE-OVER BIDS

To many, the term "take-over bid" signifies a modern way of making money on a large scale by doubtful methods. Some people may have siezed opportunities to further their own interests rather than the community's, but it would be an exaggeration to assume that all bids are to be condemned.

The take-over bid is not a new phenomenon since it is a natural step forward in an organisation's growth, offering advantages in economies of scale and more efficient control of production and selling.

The term is usually understood to mean the offer of cash, shares or both, by one company which seeks to gain control of another by purchasing a majority of the voting shares. The majority need only be 51%, but if subvention payments allowable for income tax purposes are to be obtained a 75% control of the equity is necessary, and a 90% holding for advantage to be taken of Section 209 of the Companies Act, 1948.

As mentioned, take-over bids are not new. It has been established practice when a company has grown and the advantages of combination are obvious for boards of directors to agree between them that the shareholders be recommended to accept a cash payment or exchange their shares for those of another company. Sometimes, however, this co-operation does not take place and negotiations have to be carried on in a very different atmosphere.

The methods employed are varied. The party seeking to acquire the shares may buy as many as possible on the market through a nominee, and then make an offer for the rest direct to the shareholders. Or the offer may be made direct in the first place, naming a date for final acceptance. The directors of the company "threatened" may then circulate their shareholders recommending non-acceptance (it could be that they recommend acceptance, but if the offer were so favourable their co-operation would obviously have been sought in the first place). Further approaches may be made, if necessary increasing the offer. If the shares are widely spread resistance to such pressure is more difficult than where a few investors hold large blocs of shares.

Such offers are not always successful. When they are, and a majority holding has been obtained, the quoted price of the remaining shares may drop considerably. Even the rumour of an impending bid may drive up prices. A rumour may be started by heavy buying thought to be by a nominee. Regrettably, shares offered in exchange often carry no voting rights, a point which may not seem very important to the offerees at the time of acceptance. Institutional investors such as insurance companies do their best to discourage the practice.

One of the main causes of such bids had already been mentioned—growth of a business. There are other factors. Inflation is not always reflected in company Balance Sheets and fixed assets shown at book value may give a misleading picture of the company's true worth. Dividend limitation may lead to a lower quotation on the market than actual profits justify: it may be for the long-run good of the company but tempt bids for the shares at the low price quoted.

Economic development and complexity of production have all inclined towards a combining of productive resources; businessmen have tended to seek established firms amalgamation with which would lead to economies in production and greater control of primary supplies and selling outlets.

On the other hand, control has sometimes been acquired of a variety of companies and the expected profits failed to materialise because the new management had insufficient knowledge to develop all the group's activities properly.

From the shareholders' point of view, there are a number of factors to consider. In most cases the value of their shares will increase; if they have patiently retained them despite growth policies, they may receive the full value of advantage in the form of a capital profit. Directors are given an incentive to maintain fair dividends and efficient working as well as to keep up to date with accounting conventions. They are encouraged to take Ordinary share holders into their confidence more freely, and all this favours the Ordinary share holder, though Preference share holders on their part may find their position weakened owing to their lack of voting power.

Various methods have been employed to resist take-over bids, such as the execution of directors' service agreements, which make it difficult to displace them, the conversion of non-voting to voting shares (so making the bid more expensive), excluding shareholders by the Articles from voting rights unless they are on the register, say, two years, and in certain circumstances the issue of non-voting shares (*see* Chapter I). None of them has met with much success. The best way of avoiding the wrong sort of take-over bid is an enlightened attitude to preparation of accounts, with revaluation of assets where justified (*see* Chapter xx), adequate dividend distributions and the supply of full information to shareholders about the company's activities.

RELEVANCE OF STOCK EXCHANGE PRICES

Although the stock exchange quotations do represent the market price obtainable for any share, a statement issued by the Council of the London Stock Exchange may perhaps be quoted to avoid any possible misunderstanding:

> "We desire to state authoritatively, that stock exchange quotations are not related directly to the value of a company's assets, nor to the amount of its profits, and consequently these quotations, no matter what dates are chosen for reference, cannot form a fair and equitable or rational basis for compensation. The stock exchange may be likened to a scientific recording instrument which registers, not its own actions and opinions, but the actions and opinions of private and institutional investors all over the country and, indeed, the world. The actions and opinions are the result of hope, fear, guesswork intelligent or otherwise, good or bad investment policy and other considerations. The quotations that result definitely do not represent a valuation of a company by reference to its assets and earning potential."

Thus in valuing a business—ownership of which is represented by ownership of its share capital—the stock exchange quotation alone is insufficient, but for a normal sale of shares on the market the quoted price would obviously be taken.

METHODS OF VALUATION

Various methods are applied in the actual valuation of securities since not all are quoted on the stock exchange and, even where they are, the figure may not be satisfactory for various purposes. None of the methods claims to give an exact figure—that is impossible owing to the inherent nature of the valuation concerned and the numerous factors to be considered—but they do serve as a reasonable basis for negotiation. Those most commonly applied are:

1. The stock exchange quotation.
2. Net assets or Balance Sheet basis.
3. Yield bases (both dividend and earnings yield).
4. Revenue or earning capacity basis.

Illustrations of the way in which such bases are applied are given below, but it is emphasised that the methods employed will depend on the particular securities being valued and the purpose of the valuation. Moreover, the methods tend to overlap, yield bases as well as net assets, etc., being considered.

Before considering the aspects enumerated above as to the value set upon securities, we summarise briefly some of the numerous factors and their method of measurement which influence the final price.

    (*a*) The dividend yield.

    (*b*) The earnings yield, or

    (*c*) The price–earning (P/E) ratio.

    (*d*) The prospects of the company.

    (*e*) The value of the company's net assets.

    (*f*) The company's capital commitments and any expansion programme contemplated.

    (*g*) The industrial or commercial prospects of the company's field of operation.

    (*h*) The position and prospects of subsidiary or other companies in which the company has made investments.

    (*i*) Budget, or estimated budget changes.

    (*j*) The composition of the company's board of management.

    (*k*) The prospect of foreign action likely to affect the company's trading prospects.

    (*l*) The general prosperity or otherwise of the country.

2 STOCK EXCHANGE QUOTATIONS

For a normal sale on the market, the ruling price will obviously be the one to use. But if a take-over bid is made or amalgamation proposed, some further incentive will have to be given to shareholders to part with their shares. The price then fixed will depend upon such matters as (*a*) the value of the business as a going concern, *i.e.* computed on a net assets basis, plus any addition for goodwill; (*b*) future prospects as to earnings and other yields; (*c*) the bargaining powers of the parties concerned. The price offered will therefore have to be higher than the quoted price.

The actual prices of the quoted shares prevailing on the market will depend upon the factors discussed above and those which were dealt with in Chapters III and XV with regard to yield factors, priority percentages and earnings yield. All are carefully considered and analysed, such organisations as the Exchange Telegraph Company and Comtelburo offering their services to meet this need.

2. NET ASSETS OR BALANCE SHEET BASIS

With unquoted securities there is no immediate pointer available as there is for quoted shares, but in valuing any business as a going concern the guiding principles are the same: earning power and the subsequent prospect of reasonable dividends. The company's net assets will be considered too, but the fact that the assets may be valuable is a fact to be viewed in a relative sense. An expensively equipped factory built in the middle of open country for a specific purpose would fetch little of its true value if sold as such since, being far from staff and transport facilities, it would be of doubtful use to any other commercial concern.

Nevertheless, it is not possible to disregard the "net assets" valuation of a business. It could be that the net assets are not employed in the best manner possible, owing to inability on the part of management to make full use of them or to exploit available markets, in which case the earnings and dividend yield bases would not give a true value were the business to be purchased. Earnings and dividend yields *and* the net assets employed must be considered.

From the practical point of view, in valuing the shares, such data as are required by the stock exchange for an introduction should be compiled (*see* p. 19). The similarity is obvious, but there is one complication: the holding of shares in a subsidiary. Here, the same method of valuation would have to be used as for the main company. In examination questions it is merely necessary to value the subsidiary company in the same way as a holding company, including the shareholding proportion as an asset in the holding company's net assets statement.

(*a*) *Fixing the issue price*

By way of illustration before proceeding to more practical examples, consider the commencement of a company issuing shares at par for initial capitalisation.

BALANCE SHEET

Ordinary share capital:			
10,000 £1 shares	£10,000	Bank	£10,000

After trading for one year and profits having been made, the Balance Sheet might appear as follows:

BALANCE SHEET

Ordinary share capital:			
10,000 £1 shares	£10,000	Net assets	£12,000
Profit and Loss Account	2,000		

The company's shares are now worth a net asset basis £1·20 each or £12,000/10,000.

Should the company now desire to raise more capital by means of 10,000 £1 Ordinary shares, it would not, as in the first instance, charge £1 each, as the position would then be:

BALANCE SHEET

Ordinary share capital:			
20,000 £1 shares	£20,000	Net assets	£22,000
Profit and Loss Account	2,000		

In this case the share value would be £1·10 each, or £22,000/20,000. In other words, by the issue of 10,000 additional shares the original shareholders would have lost £0·10 per share, this being due to the fact that the new shareholders would be entitled to participate in profits made prior to their admission or assets representing those profits. To eliminate this anomaly, the incoming shareholders should be charged £1·20 each for the shares they take up, the excess above par being credited to a Share Premium Account. This would then leave the position as follows:

BALANCE SHEET

Ordinary share capital	£20,000		
Share premium	2,000	Net assets	£24,000
Profit and Loss Account	2,000		

—the price of the shares on a net asset basis now being £1·20 each, or £24,000/20,000, so leading to an equitable position from the point of view of both the original and the new shareholders.

(b) Revaluation of assets

In the 1950s a spate of take-overs took place, owing to the fact that numerous companies had not revalued their assets when these had increased with inflation. As the assets were shown on the Balance Sheets at cost, the companies' reserves, and consequently their share values, were understated when viewed from a net assets basis.

Using the company illustrated above, suppose the assets prior to the new share issue should have been valued at say £16,000. If such a revaluation were not put through the books, the value would be as stated above prior to the new issue at £1·20, or £12,000/10,000. If, however, the assets were revalued to reveal their true worth, the Balance Sheet would appear as follows:

BALANCE SHEET

Ordinary share capital:			
10,000 £1 shares	£10,000		
Reserve on revaluation		Net assets (as revalued)	£16,000
of assets	4,000		
Profit and Loss Account	2,000		

This would have led to a valuation of £1·60, or £16,000/10,000. The new share issue should therefore be made at the price of £1·60, not £1·20 as shown above. The new Balance Sheet would therefore appear as:

BALANCE SHEET

Ordinary share capital:			
20,000 £1 shares	£20,000		
Share premium	6,000	Net Assets (as revalued)	£32,000
Reserve on revaluation	4,000		
Profit and Loss Account	2,000		
	£32,000		£32,000

The share value would then be as before the new issue at £1·60 or £32,000/20,000.

The foregoing should illustrate the fact that where any valuations of shares are made on the net assets basis, the asset values used should be those as given on revaluation where these differ from those shown on the Balance Sheet.

(c) Computing goodwill

The computation of a value for goodwill to be included in the net assets of a company may also cause some difficulty. The method which takes super-profits into consideration is generally regarded as acceptable, but opinions sometimes differ as to how it should be calculated.

The following question demonstrates the most common methods employed.

Specimen question

The net tangible assets of a company are valued at £80,000. Earnings for the past five years have been £13,000, £16,000, £19,000, £25,000 and £27,000. Companies of a similar nature give a fair return of 17½%. What values might be placed on goodwill? Ignore taxation.

Answer

Goodwill might be computed on the following bases:

(a)		
	Average earnings	£20,000
	Fair return, 17½% × 80,000	14,000
	Super-profits	£6,000
	Goodwill: 5 years' purchase of super-profits	£30,000

(b) Applying a weighted average to the profits:

£13,000 × 1	£13,000	
16,000 × 2	32,000	
19,000 × 3	57,000	
25,000 × 4	100,000	
27,000 × 5	135,000	
15)£337,000		£22,500

£22,500 capitalised at 17½%: 100/17½ × 22,500		£128,570
Net assets employed		80,000
Goodwill (balance)		£48,570

or

(Weighted) Average profits	£22,500
Expected yield, 17½% × £80,000	14,000
	£8,500
Super-profits capitalised, 100/17½ × £8,500—say	£48,570

Of the two methods the second is to be preferred, since it takes into consideration the expected return on the net assets, whereas the first uses an arbitrary assessment of a number of years' purchase of the super-profits.

The weighted average is also to be preferred where profits show a distinct trend, either up or down, to give weight to the more recent profits. If the first method is employed, the specified years' purchase of super-profits may be adjusted to, say, only three years' purchase if profits are falling.

An example is now given of the use of the net assets basis of share valuation.

Specimen question

BALANCE SHEET, *31st March 19—*

Authorised and issued share capital:			Fixed assets:		
30,000 6% Preference shares		£30,000	Freehold premises at cost		£48,000
80,000 Ordinary shares		80,000	Plant and machinery *less* depreciation		74,500
		110,000	Investments at cost (market value £21,000)		18,000
Revenue reserves:					
General reserve	£14,000				140,500
Profit and Loss Account	25,000		Current assets		36,500
		39,000	Capital expenditure not written off		1,000
		149,000			
5% Debenture stock		10,000			
Current liabilities		19,000			
		£178,000			£178,000

Above is the summarised Balance Sheet of a company, the profits of which for the past five years to date have been: £31,500, £30,400, £28,700, £29,900 and £33,400.

The net profits shown are prior to dividend appropriations which, on the Ordinary shares, have been made at an average rate of $17\frac{1}{2}\%$, but include income on investments at a rate of 5% on cost.

The revenue return on similar companies is $17\frac{1}{2}\%$ while the dividend yield is 10% on Ordinary shares and 5% on Preference shares of similar classes respectively.

At the Balance Sheet date the freehold premises were considered to be worth £62,000.

You are required to state what valuation should be put upon both classes of shares as valued on the basis of the underlying assets of the company viewed as a going concern. Ignore taxation.

Answer

(a) *Valuation of shares on a net assets basis:*

   (i) 6% Preference shares

      As the preference capital is covered more than four times by net tangible assets and no complications arise as to participation rights, the shares are worth their par value, £1 per share.

(ii) Ordinary shares

Freehold property (as revalued)		£62,000
Plant and machinery		74,500
Total fixed assets		136,500
Current assets		36,500
		173,000
Less Current liabilities		19,000
		154,000
Add Investments (market value)	£21,000	
Goodwill (*see* below)	20,000	
		41,000
Total net asset value		£195,000

Total net asset value (see above)		£195,000
Apportioned as to:		
6% Preference shares	£30,000	
5% Debentures	10,000	
		40,000
Net assets attributable to Ordinary share holders		£155,000

Net asset value for Ordinary shares £155,000/£80,000 = £1·94.

Ordinary share valuation: £1·94 per share

(iii) Computation of goodwill

Average profits of past five years (a simple average is taken, as profits are fairly even) + Debenture interest		£31,280
Less Investment income		900
		30,380
Revenue return on net tangible assets employed (17½% on £154,000)		26,950
Super-profits		£3,430

Super-profits capitalised at 17½%
$£3430 \times 100/17\frac{1}{2} = £19,600$
Goodwill (say) £20,000

(b) *Alternative method of valuing Ordinary shares:*

(i)

Freehold property (as revalued)		£62,000
Plant and machinery		74,500
		136,500
Current assets		36,500
		173,000
Less 6% Preference shares	£30,000	
5% Debentures	10,000	
Current liabilities	19,000	
		59,000
		114,000

Add Investments (market value)	21,000	
Goodwill (*see* below)	46,000	
		67,000

Net assets representing equity capital	£181,000

Net asset value for Ordinary shares £181,000/80,000 = £2·26.
Ordinary share valuation: £2·26 per share

(ii) Computation of goodwill

Average profits of past five years (say)		£30,780
Less Preference dividend	£1,800	
Investment income	900	
		2,700
		28,080
Less Revenue return on net assets employed, $17\frac{1}{2}\%$ ×		
£114,000 (*see* above)		19,950
Super-profits		£8,130

Super-profits capitalised at $17\frac{1}{2}\%$
£8,130 × $100/17\frac{1}{2}$ = (say) £46,000

The discrepancy in value set upon the Ordinary shares shown above derives from the different valuation placed upon goodwill.

To exemplify the principles involved, a simplified example is given of the valuation of the equity share capital of a company.

Example

Equity share capital	£100,000
5% Debentures	£20,000
Net assets employed	£180,000
Average profits earned	£20,000

Revenue return on similar companies 10% (before charging Debenture interest). Ignore taxation.

(i) Valuation of Ordinary shares

	Method 1		*Method 2*
Net assets employed	£180,000		£180,000
Less Debentures			20,000
			160,000
Goodwill (*see* below)	20,000		30,000
Total net assets value	£200,000	Total equity share of net assets	£190,000

Apportionment of business value:	
5% Debentures	£20,000
Ordinary share holders	180,000
	£200,000

Value of Ordinary shares:

£180,000/100,000 = £1·80 per share   £190,000/100,000 = £1·90 per share

(ii) Computation of goodwill

	Method 1		Method 2	
Profit	£20,000		£20,000	
Less Debenture				
interest	—		1,000	
Profit for				
capitalisation	£20,000		£19,000	
	20,000 × 100/10 =	£200,000	19,000 × 100/10 =	£190,000
Less Net assets		180,000		160,000
Goodwill as above		£20,000		£30,000

In Method 2 it will be observed that cheaper capitalisation by means of Debentures leaves larger profits available for the Ordinary share holders, and this is taken to justify a larger figure for goodwill.

The actual difference in working consists, in the first instance, of taking the return on the whole business and calculating goodwill according to this figure before deducting Debenture interest. Thereafter, the net asset value (including goodwill) of the whole business is apportioned between those supplying the capital, including loan capital. In the second case, the income after deducting Debenture interest and Preference dividends (if any) is calculated as a return on the equity share of the assets only. The goodwill thus computed is added to the equity assets value, the resulting figure being attributable to the Equity share holders only.

Whichever method is employed, goodwill is a matter for agreement and therefore neither can be advocated as correct. It would appear, however, that the first might be preferred in valuing the business for a proposed merger or acquisition as a whole; whereas, if certain shares only are being valued for acquisition, the second method might be applied.

A further example, involving valuation of shares on the net assets basis is given on p. 381, but as the yield valuation is also mentioned there the method of valuation according to yields will now be dealt with.

3. YIELD BASES

The dividend yield basis provides a useful guide but is not sufficient for valuation in itself because the dividend rate may be lower on account of, say, ploughing back of profits, than would otherwise be the case. Growth stocks are an example. In the case of private, director-controlled companies, surtax considerations might influence the dividend rate. Likewise, the benefits to be obtained from non-distribution relief may cause a reduction. It is here that the earnings yield mentioned in Chapter xv is important; it is not a method of valuation but serves as a useful guide to that end.

When calculating the earnings yield, prior charges against the sum available for distribution to Ordinary share holders must be deducted. To obtain the value on the dividend yield basis, it is only necessary to divide the average dividend percentage paid by that of similar percentages in other companies. Simply stated, the average dividend distributions as compared with those of similar companies are calculated proportionately, *e.g.* £0·50 share, company with 10% average dividends, similar companies distribute 5%. [£0·50 × 10/5 = £1.]

Example

Using the figures in the example on p. 376 you are required to value both classes of shares on the dividend yield basis.

Valuation of shares on a yield basis:
  (i) 6% Preference shares
$$\frac{6}{5} \times £1 = £1\cdot20 \text{ per share}$$

  (ii) Ordinary shares
$$\frac{17\frac{1}{2}}{10} \times £1 = £1\cdot75 \text{ per share}$$

Where details of dividends paid are not made available, it will be necessary to calculate the profits which may be prudently distributed before comparing them with the yields available in other companies.

Example

Had dividends not been specified in the Example on p. 376 and a valuation based on yield been requested, then a reasonable amount available for distribution would have to be calculated first. As it is normally first necessary to plough back a certain sum (for expansion and other purposes) an amount of, say, two-fifths of the profits would have to be allowed for the purpose, *e.g.*:

Average profits as shown above (including investment income here, as it is available for distribution)	£30,780
Less Transfer to reserve, say two-fifths	12,780
	18,000
Less Preference dividend	1,800
say	£16,000

$$\frac{£16,000}{£80,000} \times 100 = 20\%$$

Fixing the value of the Ordinary shares on the yield basis at
$$\frac{20}{10} \times £1 = £2 \text{ per share.}$$

The following example necessitates the calculation of both the earnings yield and the dividend yield valuation.

Specimen question

BALANCE SHEET OF X LTD (SUMMARISED

6% Preference shares,		Fixed assets	£3,150,000
800,000 £1 each	£800,000	Current assets	1,600,000
Ordinary shares,			
3,200,000 £1 each	3,200,000		
	4,000,000		
Revenue reserves	450,000		
Current liabilities	300,000		
	£4,750,000		£4,750,000

The profit figure shown in the accounts of the company whose Balance Sheet is shown above, for the year ended on the same date, prior to any appropriation, was £660,000.

Average Ordinary dividends have been at the rate of 12%. The dividend yield on similar shares is 6%. Preference shares of a comparable nature yield 5½%.

You are required to value the shares according to the information given and to state what the earnings yield on the Ordinary shares would be if sold at the price computed. Ignore taxation.

Answer

(a) Value of Ordinary shares on dividend yield basis:

$$\frac{12\%}{6\%} \times £1{\cdot}00 = £2{\cdot}00 \text{ per share}$$

(b) Value of Preference shares on dividend yield basis:

$$\frac{6\%}{5\frac{1}{2}\%} \times £1{\cdot}00 = £1{\cdot}09 \text{ per share}$$

(c) Calculation of earnings yield:

Profit prior to appropriations	£660,000
Less Preference dividend	48,000
	£612,000

£612,000 on £3,200,000 Ordinary share capital = 19·1%
19·1% × £1·00/£2·00 = 9·5% earnings yield.

The following example involves a simple share valuation necessitating the use of both the underlying assets and dividend yield methods of computation.

Specimen question

H Ltd and its subsidiary, S Ltd, are dependent upon an outside supplier, O Ltd, for certain essential components. In conjunction with a scheme of co-ordinated production, H Ltd and O Ltd enter into an agreement involving each company in the acquisition of a quarter share in the other's authorised share capital by means of an exchange of shares. The terms of the agreement are as follows:

(i) While H Ltd's shares are quoted at £1·40 the value to be taken for the purposes of the exchange is the greater of the two values, (a) as quoted, and (b) on the basis of a Balance Sheet valuation.

(ii) As O Ltd's shares are unquoted for the purposes of the agreement, the higher of the two values is to be taken, viz. (a) on a yield basis, and (b) on a Balance Sheet basis. Future profits are estimated at £10,500 but one-third of such profits is to be retained for development purposes. Shares of similar companies yield 8% on the market.

(iii) Goodwill is to be ignored but the freehold properties of O Ltd are estimated to be worth £45,000.

(iv) In order not to deplete liquid resources any balance due on settlement by one company to the other is to be left as a loan.

(v) The summarised Balance Sheets of the companies at the relevant date of 30th June were as follows:

	H Ltd	S Ltd	O Ltd
Authorised share capital, Ordinary shares	£120,000	£50,000	£100,000
Issued share capital, Ordinary shares fully paid	80,000	50,000	75,000
Share premium	8,000	—	—
Profit and Loss Account	23,000	21,000	20,000
5% Debentures	30,000	—	—
Current liabilities	28,000	18,000	21,000
Proposed dividend	10,000	5,000	—
	£179,000	£94,000	£116,000
Fixed assets:			
Freehold properties	66,000	29,000	33,000
Plant and machinery, etc.	45,000	41,000	44,000
Investments:			
40,000 shares in S Ltd	47,000	—	—
Current assets	21,000	24,000	39,000
	£179,000	£94,000	£116,000

You are required to compute the value of the shares according to the terms of the agreement and to present the final settlement, showing all workings. Ignore taxation.

Answer

(i) Valuation of shares in H Ltd and O Ltd at the 30th June:

		H Ltd	S Ltd	O Ltd
Freehold properties		£66,000	£29,000	£45,000
Plant and machinery, etc.		45,000	41,000	44,000
Shares in S Ltd as valued (⅘ × £71,000)		56,800	—	—
Current assets		21,000	24,000	39,000
Dividend receivable from S Ltd.		4,000	—	—
		192,800	94,000	128,000
Less				
5% Debentures	£30,000			
Current liabilities	28,000		£18,000	£21,000
Proposed dividend	10,000		5,000	—
		68,000	23,000	21,000
Net assets		£124,800	£71,000	£107,000
Value per share on underlying assets basis (approx.)		£1·56	—	£1·42½

(ii) Valuation of O Ltd's shares on a yield basis:

Estimated future profits	£10,500
Less Profit to be ploughed back	3,500
	£7,000

Yield on shares £7,000/75,000 = 9·3%
Yield on similar shares 8%
Value on yield basis 9·3/8 × £1·00 = £1·16

(iii) Share value to be taken for agreement purposes:

H Ltd—Greater of £1·56 and £1·40
O Ltd—Greater of £1·42½ and £1·16

(iv) Statement of final settlement between H Ltd and O Ltd:

Shares issued by:

H Ltd to O Ltd	30,000 at £1·56	£46,800
O Ltd to H Ltd	25,000 at £1·42½	35,625
Loan by H Ltd to O Ltd		£11,175

NOTES

(i) It will be observed that four-fifths of the proposed dividend in S Ltd has been brought into the assets of H Ltd.

(ii) The holding of shares in S Ltd has been brought into H Ltd's assets at their valuation according to the worth of the underlying assets.

4. REVENUE OR EARNING CAPACITY BASIS

Although the revenue or earning capacity of a business may be considered in the valuation of the equity share capital, it is not sufficient in itself for the establishment of a reasonable price. It may be used in conjunction with valuation of the net assets as exemplified on p. 372 but is too vague to provide a firm basis for a price. However, it is used to compute a price for equity shares in examinations and is, therefore, included in this list.

Specimen question

A business earns an average return of 17½% prior to an appropriation, on its net assets, whereas the average rate of return in similar concerns is 12½%. The net assets are £120,000, while the equity share capital amounts to 100,000 Ordinary shares of £1 each. What value may be placed upon the Ordinary shares?

Answer

Computation of Ordinary share valuation:

$$17\tfrac{1}{2}/12\tfrac{1}{2} \times £120,000 = £168,000$$
$$£168,000/100,000 = £1·68$$

EXAMINATION QUESTIONS

1. (a) Irish Shops Ltd is a public company with £0·50 Ordinary units quoted on the stock exchange at £5. The dividends for the past several years have been 48% per annum.

A resolution has been passed:

(i) Issuing bonus shares to the shareholders in the ratio of one new Ordinary unit for every Ordinary unit already held.

(ii) Giving the shareholders a right to take up three further Ordinary £0·50 units at par for every five held after the bonus has been issued. The directors have indicated that they expect to be in a position to pay a dividend of 24% on the capital as increased by the bonus and rights issues.

You are required to compute the value of the "rights." [C.C.A. (*extract*)

2. The following is the Balance Sheet of the Ballyfermot Manufacturing Co. Ltd at 31st March:

Ordinary stock (£1 units)	£100,000	Premises	£50,000
Trade creditors	30,000	Plant	180,000
General reserve	250,000	Stock	70,000
Profit and Loss Account	150,000	Debtors	60,000
		Cash at bank	170,000
	£530,000		£530,000

The profits for the last three years have been averaging £90,000 per annum and the dividends have for many years been 10% per annum. The £1 units are quoted on the Dublin Stock Exchange at £2·50 and the stock is widely held by some 500 shareholders.

Competitors who are clients of yours—Bagsnatch Ltd—consult you regarding the possibility of a take-over offer and ask you to report fully under the following headings:

(a) As to whether it is considered that the Ballyfermot company might be taken over by Bagsnatch Ltd.

(b) As to what prices should be offered for the shares of Ballyfermot either in,

(1) cash,

(2) cash and shares in Bagsnatch Ltd, or

(3) shares in Bagsnatch Ltd (whose capital is £300,000 in units of £0·25 each, quoted at £1·50).

(c) To outline the general procedure of the take over:

(i) To whom the offer should be made by Bagsnatch Ltd in the first instance, *i.e.* to the directors or the shareholders?

(ii) Whether, if the offer was first made to the directors, it would be advisable to proceed if the directors were not prepared to recommend it.

(iii) As to the requisite information which should be made available to the Ballyfermot shareholders.

(iv) As to how secrecy might be maintained.

(v) As to whether the offer should be for the whole capital or merely for a controlling interest.

(vi) As to whether it might be an advantage to attempt to buy, say, 10% of the stock on the stock exchange before making the approach.

(d) To indicate what procedure should be adopted with the stock exchange authorities. Draft your report.   [C.C.A.

3. Tarrant Ltd have been approached by another company to dispose of their undertaking. The Balance Sheet of Tarrant Ltd at 31st March 1963 was as follows:

Share capital and reserves:

Ordinary shares of £1 each		£30,000	
Capital reserves		4,000	
General reserves:			
General	£12,000		
Profit and Loss Account	12,029		
		24,029	
			£58,029
Reserve for future taxation			8,200
			66,229
Current liabilities:			
Creditors		9,375	
Profits tax		1,150	
Proposed dividend (net)		3,450	
			13,975
			£80,204
Fixed assets:			
Freehold property at cost		12,000	
Plant and machinery at cost	8,000		
Less Depreciation	3,000		
		5,000	
			£17,000
Current assets:			
Stocks		31,072	
Debtors		20,332	
Bank balance		11,700	
Cash		100	
			63,204
			£80,204

The turnover, net profits and dividends for each of the five years ending 31st March 1963 were:

	Turnover	Profit before taxation	Dividend (net)
1959	£128,322	£12,785	10%
1960	175,412	16,469	12½
1961	220,053	13,824	10
1962	254,435	18,329	15
1963	248,349	19,773	20

The Profit and Loss Accounts have been prepared on a uniform basis and no adjustments are necessary for non-recurring or extraordinary income and expenditure.

The directors of Tarrant Ltd ask for your advice as to a fair price for the company's business.

Draft your report, showing your workings.

You may make any assumptions you consider necessary.   [C.C.A.

4. The following is the Balance Sheet at 31st December 19— of a bill-posting company of which you are chief accountant.

Fixed assets:			
Purchase of businesses			£135,000
Land and buildings			30,000
Plant, furnishings and fittings			1,000
Motor vehicles			4,000
			170,000
Investments (market value £150,000)			80,000
Current assets:			
Stores in hand		£3,500	
Sundry debtors		51,000	
Cash in bank and on hand		30,500	
		85,000	
Less Current liabilities:			
Sundry creditors	£10,000		
Provision for current taxation	14,000		
Proposed dividend	13,000		
		37,000	
			48,000
			298,000
Provision for future taxation			28,000
			£270,000
Capital reserves:			
Investment reserve		10,000	
Revenue reserves and unappropriated profits:			
General reserve		100,000	
Profit and Loss Account		60,000	
			160,000
Share capital:			
Authorised—			
100,000 6% Cumulative redeemable participating Preference shares of £1 each		100,000	
200,000 Ordinary shares of £1 each		200,000	
		300,000	
Issued and fully paid:			
25,000 6% Cumulative redeemable participating Preference shares of £1 each		25,000	
75,000 Ordinary shares of £1 each		75,000	
			100,000
			£270,000

The chairman asks for your opinion on the following questions which have been discussed at a directors' meeting:

(*a*) Is it appropriate to make an issue of bonus shares to the Ordinary share holders? If so, on what basis should it be made?

(b) Would such an issue of itself help to discourage a possible take-over bid?

(c) Should the Preference shares be repaid, or converted into Ordinary shares?

(d) Should the Ordinary shares be sub-divided into shares of a smaller denomination?

You are aware of the following facts:

(a) The billposting hoardings, which form the basis of the company's earnings and which have been maintained in excellent condition, have no value in the Balance Sheet, having been fully written off. Their replacement value at the present time is estimated at £150,000. On the other hand, in the event of a winding-up, their value would be scrap and considerable expense might be occurred in dismantling them.

(b) "Land and buildings" includes properties which were acquired many years ago at modest values. Their present value is estimated at £50,000.

(c) "Purchases of businesses" represents the amounts paid for goodwill from time to time on the acquisition of other businesses.

(d) The investments are being built up to provide funds for further acquisitions as opportunity affords.

(e) The 6% Cumulative redeemable participating Preference shares are entitled to an additional non-cumulative 4% dividend after the Ordinary shares have received a 10% dividend.

(f) The trading results and appropriations for the year to 31st December, which are very similar to those of recent years, are as follows:

Trading profit			£49,500
Interest on investments gross			5,500
			55,000
Provision for taxation		£28,000	
Provision for dividends:			
On 6% Cumulative participating Preference			
shares net	£900		
Additional 4% on ditto	600		
On Ordinary shares at 25%	11,250		
		12,750	
Carried to reserve		10,000	
			50,750
Balance added to carry forward			£4,250

(g) The shares are quoted on a local stock exchange. The present quotation for the Preference shares is £0·80. Transactions in the Ordinary shares are infrequent; the last, dated 30th September, was at £2·00 per share, which is the highest-ever price.

Prepare your answers to the chairman's queries in the form of notes with explanations supported by a *pro forma* Balance Sheet incorporating any recommendations you make. [C.W.A.

5. The maintainable future profits before taxation of the Whitehall Cabinet Co. Ltd, a private company, have been estimated at £75,000 after charging total remuneration for its three directors, Heath, Brown and Thorpe, of £10,000 and depreciation including amounts written off freehold shop

properties of £2500 and from other assets £8000 (the latter closely approximating to the writing-down allowances available for corporation tax purposes). The Balance Sheet as at 31st March 1967 shows:

Fixed assets (at cost less depreciation):

Shop property		£142,500
Vehicles, fittings, etc.		39,500
		182,000

Net current assets:

Stocks		£15,500	
Debtors		31,500	
Cash in bank		102,000	
		149,000	
Creditors	£17,000		
Proposed dividend (including schedule F tax thereon)	27,600		
		44,600	
			104,400
			286,400
Less: Directors' loan accounts		10,000	
Corporation tax payable 1st January 1968		31,000	
			41,000
			£245,400

Representing:

Issued ordinary share capital in shares of £1 each, fully paid	69,000
Reserves	176,400
	£245,400

You have been asked by the directors, who are also the holders of the whole issued capital, for your opinion as to the value of their holdings in the company on which estate duty would be charged were they to die in the near future.

The following additional information has been made available to you:

(a) The shop property was valued on 31st March 1967 at £250,000. Its value at 6th April 1965 was £225,000 and its cost in April 1964 was £150,000.

(b) The cash in bank includes £40,000 on deposit receipt. No credit has been included in the estimated maintainable profits for interest thereon, nor was there such a credit in the profits for the year ended 31st March 1967. Accrued interest at that date would have been £3500.

(c) Directors' loan accounts represent balances of £3500, £3500 and £3000 due to Heath, Brown and Thorpe respectively.

(d) The shareholdings are as follows: Heath, 53,000 shares; Brown, 8500 shares; Thorpe, 7500 shares.

Using the above information, you are required to prepare statements setting out your computation of the valuations as at March 1967 of the above holdings for estate duty purposes, giving your reasons for the methods adopted. [C.A. (S)

6. The summarised Balance Sheet of Alpha Ltd at 30th June is as follows:

Share capital:			Sundry assets		£510,000
100,000 7% Preference shares of £1 each, fully paid		£100,000	Discount on Debentures		5,000
			Preliminary expenses		10,000
300,000 Ordinary shares of £1 each, fully paid		300,000	Profit and Loss Account	£75,000	
Reserve for obsolescence		10,000	Less General reserve	10,000	
Debenture redemption fund		30,000			65,000
7% Debentures		50,000			
Sundry creditors		100,000			
		£590,000			£590,000

The preference shares are non-cumulative and no dividend arrears are payable on liquidation. Preference dividends have been passed for two years, and one year's interest on Debentures is due. The book value of assets has been brought in line with their current value.

Over the past five years profits of £180,000 and losses of £80,000 have accrued. Investors expect to earn about $8\frac{1}{3}\%$ on their capital in this industry.

Calculate the approximate value of the shares, using more than one method. Ignore taxation. [C.C.A.

7. The undernoted information has been obtained from the published accounts of a public company and from stock exchange information relating thereto:

BALANCE SHEET ANALYSIS

	As at 31st December	
	1962	1963
Current assets:	(£000's)	(£000's)
Cash at bank and on hand	15	20
Debtors less Provisions	1580	1730
Stock and work in progress	1350	1160
	2945	2910
Less Current liabilities and provisions:		
Creditors	928	871
Bank overdraft	804	647
Current taxation	62	136
Proposed dividend (net)	107	107
	1901	1761
Net current assets	1044	1149
Add Fixed assets less depreciation	1797	1819
	2841	2968
Less Deferred liabilities:		
Future tax	80	146
Minority interest	4	5
Net tangible assets	£2757	£2817

Representing:

6½% Cumulative Preference stock in £1 units	160	160
Ordinary stock in £0·50 units	1751	1751
Capital reserve	334	334
Revenue reserves:		
General	287	287
Carry forward	225	285
	£2757	£2817

PROFIT ANALYSIS

	Year ended *31st December 1963*
Trading profit	£515,860
Other income	1,190
	517,050
Less:	
Depreciation	120,730
Directors' remuneration	20,000
Profits tax	56,000
Income tax	145,600
Minority interest	930
Earned for dividends	173,790
Preference dividend, paid (net)	6,370
Earned for Ordinary dividend	167,420
Ordinary dividend, 10% (net)	107,249
Increase in carry forward	£60,171

STOCK EXCHANGE INFORMATION

The current mid-prices of the stocks are as follows:

6½% Preference stock in £1 units	£1·00
Ordinary stock in £0·50 units	£0·75

You are required:

    (*a*) To state the following, showing clearly your calculations:

        (i) The dividend yield on the Preference shares.

        (ii) The number of times the Preference dividend is covered by earnings.

        (iii) The number of times the Preference shares are covered by net tangible assets.

        (iv) The dividend yield on the Ordinary stock.

        (v) The earnings yield on the Ordinary stock.

        (vi) The price–earnings ratio on the Ordinary stock.

        (vii) The number of times the Ordinary stock is covered by net equity assets.

        (viii) The net cash flow.

    (*b*) To prepare a statement showing the sources from which funds have been obtained during the year, and how these have been utilised.

                                         [C.A. (S)

8. "The take-over bid movement has taught us how important it is to tell shareholders what their company's assets are worth in the market."

You are asked to state some of the methods that have been advocated to indicate to shareholders the market value of their company's assets and to write fully on the advantages or disadvantages to shareholders and others of declaring such values. [C.A. (S)

9. Summarised accounts for Beaver Enterprises Ltd, for 1967 are shown below:

PROFIT AND LOSS ACCOUNT

for the year ended 31st December 1967

	(£000's)
Operating profit	97
Less debenture interest	10
	87
Less corporation tax	32
Net profit after taxation	55
Balance brought forward from last year	178
	233
Less dividend	45
	£188

BALANCE SHEET

31st December 1967

	(£000's)		(£000's)
Ordinary shares of £1	180	Fixed assets—cost	538
Capital reserve	72	*Less* depreciation	114
Profit and Loss Account	188		
5% Debenture stock 1977	200		424
Creditors, etc.	96	Stocks	191
		Debtors	89
		Cash	32
	£736		£736

You are required to:

(a) Calculate the following from the given data:

(i) Balance Sheet value of a £1 Ordinary share of Beaver Enterprises.

(ii) Market value of a £1 Ordinary share on the basis that the current dividend yield on similar shares is 8%.

(iii) Ratio of net profit after taxation to Ordinary shareholders' interest.

(iv) Market value of £100 debenture stock, *ex div.*, if the appropriate gross redemption yield is 7% and this stock is redeemable at par in exactly ten years. (Interest is paid on 31st December each year.)

(b) Discuss shortly the usefulness and limitations of the ratio in (a) (iii) above as a measure of the efficiency of management. [B. Sc. (Econ.)

10. Early in 1968, J.B. is negotiating for the purchase of a controlling block of ordinary shares in L.S.T. Ltd. The summarised Balance Sheet of the company as on 31st December 1967 was as follows:

Authorised and issued share capital:		Goodwill, at cost, less amounts written off		£14,000
42,000 7% cumulative preference shares of £1 each	£42,000	Freehold land and buildings at cost		70,000
84,000 ordinary shares of £1 each	84,000	Plant and machinery: at cost	105,070	
		Less depreciation	47,180	
	126,000			57,890
Profit and loss account	34,010			
Reserve for contingencies	40,000	Investments at cost (market value £23,100)		12,320
Provision for deferred repairs to buildings	10,500	Stocks		43,008
Current liabilities	62,854	Debtors		60,998
		Balance at bank		15,148
	£273,364			£273,364

(1) The profits shown by the annual accounts, after writing off goodwill, but before other appropriations, for the three years ended 31st December 1967 have been:

1965	£36,260
1966	43,302
1967	38,458

These figures include the investment income which was £1200 in each of the three years.

(2) £700 has been written off goodwill in each of the three years 1965, 1966 and 1967.

(3) The land included in the balance sheet cost £14,000 and the buildings were erected in 1957 for £56,000. The land has recently been valued at £28,000 and the buildings at £118,000.

(4) The current valuation of the plant and machinery is agreed at £72,800 and depreciation thereon will in future be increased by £2800 per annum.

(5) Stock thought to be worthless at 31st December, 1967, was sold in January, 1968 for £4200. Apart from this, the values of the current assets shown in the balance sheet have been accepted by both parties.

(6) Since December, 1967, a contract has been entered into for the modernization of the heating plant in the building at a cost of £14,000. Work has not yet started.

(7) In December, 1967, L.S.T. Ltd paid the following dividends:

(*a*) the preference dividend for the year 1967, and

(*b*) an ordinary dividend, for the year 1967, of 25 per cent. of the ordinary share capital. These dividends have been debited to the profit and loss account.

(8) The preference shareholders have no right to share in surpluses.

Required:

A calculation of the value you would place, in the light of the above information, on each of the ordinary shares (*a*) on the basis of the company's net assets (excluding goodwill), and (b) on the basis of the capitalised value of maintainable net revenue, defined for this purpose as the average profit (including investment income) of the years 1965, 1966 and 1967, suitably adjusted in the light of the above information. The capitalisation rate to be used for ordinary shares is 10 per cent.

Ignore taxation.   [C.I.S. (1968)

CHAPTER XVII

MERGERS AND RECONSTRUCTIONS

MERGERS

WITH constant changes in production methods, owing to automation and the modernisation of procedures, the commercial and accounting sides of a business can no longer afford to remain static for any length of time. More complex production techniques demand additional capital and where the advantages of large scale production may be applied there is every incentive for firms to combine to take advantage of mass output and avoid duplication of work. In short, business mergers and the capital and other adjustments they cause are likely to prove important to the management accountant.

The treatment of this subject in a single chapter precludes any detailed treatment, but the following may serve to illustrate the main principles involved.

ADVANTAGES AND DISADVANTAGES

Business mergers will be encouraged by the prospect of gaining such advantages, apart from those mentioned above, as:

1. Elimination of competition.

2. Greater bargaining power in purchasing raw materials and selling products.

3. Elimination of some overheads by closing down unprofitable sections and centralising control.

4. More intensive use of capital assets, which may be of an expensive nature.

5. More efficient use of staff and resources by eliminating duplication of work.

6. Strengthening of financial resources and consequently better standing with the capital market.

Any of the following disadvantages *may* arise:

1. Monopolistic powers if competition has been eliminated.

2. Loss of the personal element and over-centralisation, with duplication of work and personal "empire building" by executives.

3. Loss of trade name. This is frequently overcome in practice

by continuing to use an old trade name despite the liquidation of the business concerned. The holding-company type of merger also overcomes this difficulty.

4. Over-capitalisation or "watering" of capital where excess prices are paid to buy out businesses, especially in boom periods.

TYPES OF MERGER

While mergers may take the loose form of pooling agreements and interlocking directorates, we are here concerned with those which affect companies more closely. They may be in any of the following forms:

1. *Absorption*, involving the acquisition by an existing company of another or other companies which are liquidated. It differs only from

2. *Amalgamation* in that here a new company is formed to take over the old ones.

3. *External reconstruction*, the winding-up of an existing company and the formation of a new one to take over.

4. *Holding company:* a new company may be formed to acquire majority holdings of equity shares in the other companies concerned, or one of the existing companies may be designated to acquire the shares in the others.

The method adopted will depend upon the particular situation. As between amalgamation and absorption, absorption has the advantage of saving the expense of incorporating a new company and the transfer costs. In the case of a holding company, control may be gained without purchasing the whole share capital of the companies concerned —anything over 50% would be sufficient. Moreover there is no need to obtain the Preference share capital, whereas for amalgamation the Preference share capital or Debentures would have to be acquired and the benefits of cheap capitalisation might be lost. The preservation of separate indentities in a holding company may be an advantage.

RECONSTRUCTIONS

PRINCIPLES INVOLVED

The following question illustrates by practical example some of the main principles involved in reconstruction.

Specimen question

The summarised Balance Sheet of X Ltd at 31st March was as follows:

BALANCE SHEET

Issued share capital:			Goodwill	£25,000
100,000 Ordinary shares			Freeholds	46,000
(£1 each)		£100,000	Plant and machinery	81,000
30,000 8% cumulative			Stock	28,000
Preference shares (£1			Debtors	33,000
each)		30,000	Bank	1,600
			Discount on Debentures	400
		130,000	Profit and Loss Account	20,000
5% Debentures	40,000			
Interest accrued	1,000			
		41,000		
Trade creditors		64,000		
		£235,000		£235,000

NOTE. The preference share dividends are £4800 in arrears.

As the company expects better trading conditions in the near future, the following scheme was agreed upon and put into effect from 1st April:

(i) A new company, X (19—) Ltd, was formed, with an Ordinary share capital of £125,000 divided into shares of £1 each and Preference share capital as shown hereunder, to take over the assets of X Ltd, which was put into liquidation.

(ii) (a) The holders of the 5% Debentures accepted 400 £100 5% Debentures in lieu of their holding, and two fully paid Ordinary shares of £1 each for each £1 of interest in arrears.

(b) The Preference share holders received £30,000 6% Preference shares and two £1 Ordinary shares all fully paid, for each £3 of arrears of interest.

(c) The creditors accepted £3 in cash for every £4 due to them and three Ordinary £1 shares for every further £2 due.

(d) The Ordinary share holders received two new Ordinary shares for every five in the old company.

(iii) The plant and machinery were valued at £63,000, the remaining assets being taken over at their book values. The expenses involved, including those of formation, were settled by the new company in the sum of £1500.

(iv) The remaining Ordinary share capital unissued to the members of the old company was issued at par and duly paid up.

You are required to close the books of the old company and to draft the Balance Sheet of the new company after all the foregoing matters have been carried out. Ignore taxation.

Comments and answer

Although it may not always be fair to analyse such examination questions too carefully from the point of view of the agreement involved, since the main object is to test the candidate's ability in the financial accounting entries, nevertheless it may form an introduction to the principles to be applied when drawing up such schemes of external reconstruction.

It is convenient in the first place to use the summary which it is always advisable to prepare when answering such questions, for having compiled it, the information is not only neatly tabulated, but may also be used (a) to make the necessary financial entries, (b) to compile the purchase consideration and (c) to prepare the new company's Balance Sheet. It is as follows:

	Old company	Ordinary shares	New company 6% Preference shares	5% Debentures	Cash	Total purchase consideration
5% Debentures	£40,000	£2,000		£40,000		£42,000
8% Preference share holders	30,000		£30,000			
8% Preference share holders re dividends	4,800	3,200				33,200
Creditors	64,000	24,000			£48,000	72,000
Ordinary share holders	100,000	40,000				40,000
		£69,200	£30,000	£40,000	£48,000	£187,200
New issue		55,800			55,800	
		£125,000			7,800	
Formation, etc., expenses					1,500	
					£6,300	

Before dealing with each section of the agreement separately, it is observed that the company "expects better trading conditions." If it were rapidly failing, the Debenture holders and others would obviously see no point in accepting Ordinary shares or in suffering any loss or inconvenience when they still have the opportunity of enforcing liquidation.

Where the expected future profits are given in questions requiring the preparation of a reconstruction scheme, care should be taken in drawing up the terms to make certain that the profits are adequate to absorb any increase in interest rates, etc., promised, as well as allowing for reasonable reserves to be built up.

We now turn to the more particular aspects of the scheme.

(a) *5% Debenture holders.* It is assumed that the Debentures are secured on the freehold property of the company, and when their security is sound the Debenture holders are obviously in a strong position. So they cannot be expected to suffer any loss but must, rather, be given something to encourage them not to enforce their security. In this scheme, their interest being in arrears, they are given double the amount in Ordinary shares, which helps to conserve liquid resources in the new company and at the same time affords the Debenture holders the prospect of ultimate profit. In any case, they might sell the Ordinary shares. However, although the question states that the remainder of the Ordinary shares were issued at par—such a sale might be to parties with some connection through directors or otherwise—it might be difficult to sell the shares of the newly reconstructed company at par.

(b) *Preference share holders.* As with Debenture holders when the assets are sufficient for their repayment on winding-up—it is assumed they have priority of repayment—it is unlikely they will accept any loss, but in this case, as their rate at 8% seems rather high (in so far as they have been paid), they have agreed to accept a lower rate. This saves a drain on the new company's profits; they are compensated for the reduction and loss of their dividends by the issue of Ordinary shares. Frequently, however, on reconstruction or amalgamation the converse may apply, in that the benefits of cheap capitalisation may be lost because *higher* rates have to be given to Debenture and Preference share holders.

(c) *Trade creditors.* Since the creditors would normally be unsecured, the offer of an immediate cash payment on account would be attractive. The addition of Ordinary shares above the full amount due would also help to secure their agreement, for they would no doubt be aware that after settlement of the secured creditors (*i.e.* the Debenture holders) the break-up value of the assets would usually be considerably lower than book value. Under the scheme outlined they would be adequately covered and so some additional offer had to be made to secure their agreement.

(d) *Ordinary share holders.* It is only fair that the Equity share holders should bear the losses concerned in the reconstruction. They have had to make little sacrifice in this case, but as Ordinary share holders have voting rights it is obvious that any losses they *are* called upon to bear must appear reasonable in the circumstances. Although we are not here concerned with the legal aspects, the requirements of the Companies Act, 1948, must be borne in mind: under it the rights of minorities are protected, so that the influence of one or two large shareholders could not force an unacceptable scheme through.

PROSPECTIVE EARNINGS

Prospective earnings are an important factor in any merger agreement. Share-price fluctuations are most difficult to estimate, but future earnings are to some extent predictable; earnings therefore may be the over-riding factor in ultimate agreement.

Example

	X Ltd	Y Ltd
Earnings after tax	£240,000	£600,000
Ordinary share capital	£600,000	£1,200,000
Earnings per share	£0·40	£0·50
P/E ratio	10	8
Market price per share	£4·0	£4·0

As the basis of share valuation a first offer might be that of one for one by Y Ltd, the larger company leading to the position of

		Earnings per share Before merger	After merger
X Ltd shareholders	600,000	£0·40⎫	
Y Ltd shareholders	1,200,000	£0·50⎭	£0·47 approx.

£0·47 being the total earnings of £840,000 divided by the total number of shares 1,800,000.

As such mergers usually anticipate increased earnings, then the market value of the shares might retain the P/E ratio of 10 with a share value of approx. £4·7; if on the other hand, future earnings are not viewed so favourably the P/E ratio of 8 might hold with a price fixed at £3·76, *i.e.* 8 × £0·47. Such market movements are, however, not predictable with much degree of certainty.

In both cases Y Ltd shareholders would stand to suffer dilution of earnings, so this might give them bargaining power to offer slightly less value in shares, *e.g.* 4 for 5. This would not affect the market price and its related P/E ratio of the shares, as the same number would still exist, held wholly by Y Ltd, the final position being:

	Shareholding in Y Ltd	Earnings per share Before merger	After merger
X Ltd shareholders	480,000	£0·4⎫	
Y Ltd shareholders	1,200,000	£0·5⎭	£0·5

To summarise the principles involved in reconstruction, both external and internal:

1. The scheme should be as straightforward as possible and likely to secure the agreement of all concerned without controversy.

2. The earning power of the company is the prime factor, so the latest figures, backed by carefully estimated budgets, should be made available.

3. As far as possible, no alteration should be made in status or contractual rights.

4. Ordinary shareholders are assumed to accept risks, and should therefore be prepared to accept any losses arising. Effectually, the reduction of the *nominal* value of Ordinary shares is immaterial and dividends can be declared on any sum, *e.g.* 10% on £1 shares or 100% on £0·10 shares, without any adverse effect to shareholders. Whereas any loss written off against fixed-interest-bearing stocks will reduce their income thereafter for ever.

5. Debenture holders, if required to make any sacrifice, will expect adequate compensation by way of shares, shares plus cash, or otherwise.

6. The right time for reconstruction must be chosen, as sound prospects must be envisaged to obviate further complications later on.

7. Provision must be made by way of shares or otherwise to ensure adequate working capital.

8. It is necessary to eliminate any losses already suffered as well as writing off any capital expenditure still shown on the Balance Sheet.

ASSETS AND GOODWILL

In the above example the settlement with the Ordinary share holders took the form of additional equities. It is now considered advisable to issue Debentures instead of Preference shares in respect of the tangible assets taken over and Ordinary shares for the goodwill acquired, as the debenture interest is allowable for taxation purposes.

Example

Consider the method by which settlement could be made between two companies on amalgamation, the details being as follows:

	X Ltd	Y Ltd
Net assets	£80,000	£36,000
Average profits	8,000	4,500
Fair commercial return on similar companies 10%		
Actual rates on net assets employed	10%	12½%

Goodwill may be calculated by capitalising the profits at the fair commercial return rate or the super-profits; either case will reveal the goodwill as follows:

X Ltd	Y Ltd
$\dfrac{100}{10} \times £8,000 = £80,000$	$\dfrac{100}{10} \times £4,500 = £45,000$
Net assets 80,000	36,000
Goodwill —	£9,000

If Ordinary shares were offered for the full business values and profits remained as previously, the position would be:

	New company Shares	Profits
X Ltd	80,000	£8,000
Y Ltd	45,000	4,500
	125,000	£12,500

This scheme would overlook the important factor of the net tangible assets taken over, yet in the event of liquidation it would be the tangible assets that would be realised and not the then useless goodwill. Debentures might be issued to overcome this difficulty but the position would still not be entirely satisfactory:

	New company Debentures	Ordinary shares
X Ltd	80,000	—
Y Ltd	36,000	9,000
	116,000	9,000

The objections here are that (a) the Debentures would have to carry a rate of 10%, which is not practical, and (b) if profits increased, only the shareholders of Y Ltd would be entitled to them, although the Debentures might be given additional rights.

Alternatively, the original companies might be capitalised on a lower percentage basis, e.g.:

	X Ltd	Y Ltd
Average net profits	£8,000	£4,500
5% on net assets employed	4,000	1,800
Super profits	£4,000	£2,700

This would mean issuing Ordinary shares on the capitalisation of the super profits, the Debentures at the lower rate being the same as before:

	New company 5% Debentures	Ordinary shares
X Ltd	£80,000	$\frac{100}{5} \times £4,000 = £80,000$
Y Ltd	36,000	$\frac{100}{5} \times £2,700 = 54,000$
	£116,000	£134,000

At this stage it may be noted that the overall settlement in shares has amounted to £160,000 and £90,000 respectively, i.e. twice the figure for the total net assets, including goodwill of £80,000 and £45,000 respectively; whereas the settlement in Debentures just covers the amount of the original tangible net assets of £80,000 and £36,000 of each company.

As the goodwill figure would appear excessive at £134,000 the amount might be reduced by issuing two £0·25 Ordinary shares for every £1 due (it will be remembered that the nominal value of an Ordinary share is not very important).

The company at this stage would be highly geared but, since only the original shareholders would be concerned, it would not be to their detriment and could be dealt with subsequently by capitalising profits.

The principles of amalgamation as exemplified above may now be applied in the following circumstances:

Specimen Question

Three companies, the summarised Balance Sheets of which are shown below, are to be amalgamated by the formation of a new company, XYZ Ltd.

You are required to draft briefly a scheme which would be equitable and would not require the obtaining of capital from outside sources.

Ignore taxation and amalgamation expenses.

	X Ltd	Y Ltd	Z Ltd
Goodwill	—	£12,000	—
Freehold property	£22,000	24,000	£8,000
Plant, etc.	19,000	8,000	10,000
Stock	12,000	9,000	3,000
Debtors	33,000	22,000	18,000
Bank	5,000	3,000	7,000
	91,000	78,000	46,000
Less Current liabilities	31,000	16,000	14,000
	£60,000	£62,000	£32,000

Financed by:

Issued share capital

	X Ltd		Y Ltd		Z Ltd	
	40,000 £1 Ordinary shares	£40,000	50,000 £1 Ordinary shares	£50,000	20,000 £1 Ordinary shares	£20,000
					10,000 5% Preference shares	10,000
Revenue reserves	20,000		12,000			2,000
		£60,000		£62,000		£32,000

Profits for the last three years have been:

X Ltd	Y Ltd	Z Ltd
£5000	£6400	£5200
6050	7150	4000
6300	8100	3600

A fair commercial return on the net assets employed in similar companies is 10%.

Answer

[In questions like this the various stages as illustrated above should be shown, to avoid repetition; here, however, only points requiring some further elucidation are given.]

The average profits may be calculated on the weighted average method, as the profits in Z (assumed to be before dividend appropriations) are falling. This gives

	X Ltd	Y Ltd	Z Ltd
Average profits	£6000	£7500	£4000

It is necessary now to capitalise the profits to arrive at the amount due, if any, in respect of goodwill. For the reason given above, the fair return rate may be reduced to 7%, but in this question there is the further complication with respect to Preference share capital already held in Z Ltd. As these Preference shares must be taken over it necessitates the adjustment of the average profits available for distribution to the remaining shareholders on amalgamation:

	Z Ltd
	£4,000
Average net profit	
Less Payable to original 5% Preference shareholders	500
	3,500
Less Amount required for payment on 7% Debentures to be issued for net tangible assets (7% × £22,000)	1,540
Super profit	£1,960

Super profit capitalised at 7% (100/7 × £1,960) = £28,000.

The position arising before the reduction of the goodwill value will now be:

	X Ltd		Y Ltd	Z Ltd	Total
7% Debentures	60,000		50,000	22,000	132,000
5% Debentures				10,000	10,000
Ordinary shares (units) 100/7 × £1,800 (say)	25,500	100/7 × £4,000	57,500	28,000	111,000
	85,500		107,500	60,000	253,000

The summarised Balance Sheet of the new company would be as follows:

XYZ LTD

Authorised share capital (*say*)	20,000	Goodwill	£11,100
		Freehold property	54,000
Issued share capital 110,000		Plant, etc.	37,000
£0·1 Ordinary shares	£11,100	Stock	24,000
7% Debentures	132,000	Debtors	73,000
5% Debentures (secured)	10,000	Bank	15,000
	153,100		
Current liabilities	61,000		
	£214,100		£214,100

NOTES

(i) To preserve the priority of the original 5% Preference share holders in Z Ltd it would be necessary to accord this right to them by a fixed charge.

(ii) That the scheme is equitable is borne out by the fact that should liquidation ensue any amount above £142,000 (*i.e.* the original value of the tangible net assets) would be distributable on the former companies' capacity to earn super profits. Anything below that sum would be borne according to the original contribution of net assets.

A somewhat more practical example is now given, involving the preparation of a report.

Specimen Question

A ENGINEERING CO. LTD

Authorised and issued share capital:		Fixed assets:	
8% Preference shares		Freehold property	£180,000
80,000 (£1 each)	£80,000	Plant and machinery *less*	
Ordinary shares 220,000		depreciation	185,000
(£1 each)	220,000		365,000
	300,000	Investments (market value	
Capital reserve	50,000	£18,000)	20,000
Revenue reserve	40,000	Current assets:	
6% Debentures	40,000	Stock	50,000	
Current liabilities and		Debtors	43,000	
provisions	61,000	Bank	13,000	
			106,000
	£491,000		£491,000

B ENGINEERING CO. LTD

Authorised and issued share capital:		Goodwill	£10,000
Ordinary shares 100,000		Freehold property	88,000
(£1 each)	£100,000	Plant and machinery *less*	
Revenue reserve	10,000	depreciation	80,000
6% Debentures	60,000	Current assets:	
Current liabilities and		Stock	7,000	
provisions	48,000	Debtors	30,000	
		Bank	3,000	
			40,000
	£218,000		£218,000

Above are the summarised Balance Sheets of two companies at 31st March. The B Engineering Co. Ltd is experiencing difficulty with regard to working capital, and negotiations are entered into for a business merger with the A Engineering Co. Ltd.

Profits for the last three years to date of the two companies have been:

A Engineering Co. Ltd	B Engineering Co. Ltd
£43,400	£20,500
52,000	16,000
58,600	14,000

In business of a similar nature, $12\frac{1}{2}\%$ is regarded as a fair commercial return for a company such as the A Engineering Co., and 10% for a company such as the B Engineering Co.

The freehold property of the B Engineering Co. is considered to be worth £100,000. The investments shown on the first Balance Sheet bring in an income of 6% on their original cost.

A dividend of 10% is due to be paid to the A Engineering Co. This has not been provided for in the accounts, but the Preference dividend has been paid.

As an independent accountant you are requested by the directors to give a preliminary report suggesting the methods and terms by which the proposed merger may be carried out, giving reasons for your conclusions.

Answer   [Address]
                                                                              [Date]

The Directors,
A Engineering Co. Ltd and B Engineering Co. Ltd
[Address]

Gentlemen,

   Proposed merger of A Engineering Co. Ltd and B Engineering Co. Ltd

In accordance with your request, dated .... I have pleasure in submitting my report herewith.

1. *Information supplied*

I would point out that the following proposals are submitted in accordance with the information supplied, but before a final conclusion is reached further and more detailed information would be required.

2. *Valuation of companies*

   (*a*) Net assets valuation:

	A Engineering Co. Ltd	B Engineering Co. Ltd
Freehold properties	£180,000	£100,000 (as revalued)
Plant and machinery	185,000	80,000
Stock	50,000	7,000
Debtors	43,000	30,000
Bank	13,000	3,000
	471,000	220,000
Less Current liabilities and provisions £61,000		£48,000
Proposed dividend (gross) 22,000		—
	83,000	48,000
Net tangible assets employed	388,000	172,000
Add Goodwill per computation (*see* below)	52,500	21,500
Investments (market value)	18,000	—
	£458,500	£193,500

(b) Computation of goodwill:

	A Engineering Co. Ltd		B Engineering Co. Ltd	
Profits:				
£43,400 × 1	£43,400	£20,500 × 1		£20,500
52,000 × 2	104,000	16,000 × 2		32,000
58,600 × 3	175,800	14,000 × 3		42,000
6	)323,200	6		)94,500
	53,867			15,750
Less Investment income (gross)	1,200			
	52,667			
Add Debenture interest (gross)	2,400			3,600
	£55,067			£19,350
Profits capitalised:				
at 12½%		at 10%		
£55,067 × 100/12½	£440,536	£19,350 × 100/10		£193,500
Less Value of net tangible assets employed	388,000			172,000
Goodwill, say	£52,500	Goodwill		£21,500

(c) Apportionment of business values:

	A Engineering Co. Ltd	B Engineering Co. Ltd
8% Preference shares	£80,000	
6% Debentures	40,000	£60,000
Ordinary shares (balancing figure)	338,500	133,500
Total valuation of businesses	£458,500	£193,500
Revised value of equity per share:	£338,500/£220,000 £1·54	£133,500/£100,000 £1·33½
Share ratio (approx.)	15	13

3. *Methods of merger available*

There are three methods by which the merger may take place:

(a) *Absorption by one company of the other.* In this case it would be preferable for the A Engineering Co. Ltd to absorb the B Engineering Co. Ltd, assuming the liabilities and issuing approximately 13 new Ordinary shares for every 15 held in B Engineering Co. Ltd according to their valuations as shown above. It would be advisable to increase the authorised capital of the A Engineering Co. Ltd by £100,000 to take advantage of the relief from stamp duty available under s. 55, Finance Act, 1927 (since this sum does not exceed the authorised share capital of the B Engineering Co.

Ltd) although only 86,850 shares, approximately, at a premium of £0·54 would be issued to the shareholders of that company.

(b) *Amalgamation*, involving the formation of a new company to take over both the old companies. It would be necessary here to register a new company with an authorised share capital equal to that of both companies, and since this would not exceed the combined capitals of the two old companies it too would qualify for relief from stamp duty. The new company would have to assume the liabilities of both companies, issuing 8% Debentures to the holders of the Preference capital in the A Engineering Co. Ltd and 6% Debentures of comparable amount to the Debenture holders of both companies.

The Ordinary share holders of each company would be issued with 320,000 £1 Ordinary shares at a premium of £0·47½ as to:

A Engineering Co. Ltd, 229,500 $\left(\dfrac{£338,500}{£472,000} \times 320,000\right)$

B Engineering Co. Ltd, 90,500 $\left(\dfrac{£133,500}{£472,000} \times 320,000\right)$

An important point with both the foregoing methods is that the security available to the Debenture holders and Preference share holders would be increased. This means that, should the security of the Debenture holders be enforced at any time, the interests of both companies could be sold instead of each company's separately. It is considered, however, that as liquidation is not envisaged this should not be a deciding factor.

(c) *Formation of a holding company.* If a holding company were formed it would have to acquire, in addition to the Ordinary share capitals of both companies, £50,000 of the Preference share capital of the A Engineering Co. Ltd; this would be necessary to comply with the requirement that at least 90% of the authorised share capital must be acquired to obtain exemption from stamp duty. If the Preference shares were not acquired, then stamp duty would be payable in respect of the Ordinary share capital of the A Engineering Co. Ltd.

The B Engineering Co. Ltd would be preserved as a separate entity if the name is considered to be of value for goodwill purposes.

4. *Taxation*

The taxation position under schemes (b) and (c) would scarcely be affected, since under (b) no cessation and commencement of a new business could be claimed as there is no substantial change in the ownership of the shares; and under (c) no adjustment would be made as to ultimate tax liability, save for the debenture interest chargeable under (b).

Under (a), however, the cessation rules would apply and some saving in tax should result as the profits of the B Engineering Co. have been falling.

5. *Recommendation*

A merger under scheme (a), absorption of the B Engineering Co. Ltd by the A Engineering Co. Ltd, is recommended since (i) the formation of a new company would be unnecessary, so avoiding the expense involved although it would be necessary to wind up the B Engineering Co. Ltd; (ii) no stamp duty under s. 55, Finance Act, 1927, would be payable; and (iii) a saving would be effected in taxation.

I shall be pleased to be of further assistance to you in this matter should it be desired.

Yours faithfully,

INTERNAL RECONSTRUCTION

Internal reconstruction most commonly takes place where a company, after passing through a difficult trading period, now looks forward to more settled conditions. It is in any case unwise to make changes in the capital structure until the company's prospects are clarified since once such a scheme has been put through it cannot soon be repeated.

Why it may be necessary

Reconstruction is not always undertaken solely for the reason mentioned. The aim may be to simplify the capital structure, eliminate unusual share denominations that might have arisen from some earlier reconstruction (*e.g.* £0·66½ Preference shares) or to prepare for a new issue if there are several classes with different rights. In the more drastic situation where capitalisation and earning power have got out of line, action is necessary to correct it.

It may be that the company's profits are sufficient to meet the prior charges, but if they offer no hope of future dividends on the equity shares there will obviously be pressure for some alteration in the capital structure. Furthermore, unless Preference share dividends are cumulative, the Ordinary share holders may exercise their power to "pass" the Preference dividends.

When there is only one class of Ordinary share holder, matters are much simpler. For example, take a company whose available profits on a capital of £400,000 are only expected to be £25,000 in future as against £50,000 formerly, the yield on shares in similar companies being 10%. By reduction in the nominal value to, say, £0·50 a share, they would be quoted at the figure of £0·62½ since the yield would stand at 12½%. An Ordinary share quotation above par would make the issue of Preference shares, if additional capital were required at a lower capitalisation rate, much easier than if the Ordinaries were below par.

As the Equity share holders have the main voting power (although Preference shares in arrears of dividend may be accorded voting rights), it is unlikely that the fixed interest shareholders would be able to defeat a scheme which, while proposing to alter their rights, is not unfair in the circumstances. In any case, if liquidation is the only alternative, they may consider the losses entailed in selling the company to be greater than the prospects offered by reconstruction. But it would be in their own interest to ensure that any scheme proposed did offer some compensation for any losses they would bear. This is a generally recognised principle, and any scheme should be considered in that light.

Compensating Preference share holders

As any reconstruction scheme will no doubt mean losses for the Preference share holders in view of the lower rate of profit, compensation must be of a nature to ensure that if circumstances improve and larger profits are earned they will be able to participate.

The fact that the nominal value of Ordinary shares may be changed and losses written off makes no difference to the possible return on them, as has already been explained (*see* p. 399); but if Preference share holders are asked to accept any writing down of their shares they stand to suffer a permanent loss. Any scheme, therefore, to be at all fair must allow them to participate somewhat at the higher profit levels.

Specimen Question

A company with capital made up of £1,500,000 6% non-cumulative Preference shares and £300,000 Ordinary shares finds that its immediate earning prospects will leave only £70,000 for distribution. It is proposed, therefore, that the Ordinary shares be written down by £0·80 each but that only £0·33½ be written off the Preference shares.

Show what the effect of this scheme would be with profits at the level of £60,000 and rising by steps of £10,000 per year for the next three years, as compared with the present position. Ignore taxation.

Answer

	PREFERENCE SHARE HOLDERS		ORDINARY SHARE HOLDERS	
Profits	*Present position*	*New scheme*	*Present position*	*New scheme*
£60,000	£60,000	£60,000	—	—
70,000	70,000	60,000	—	£10,000
80,000	80,000	60,000	—	20,000
90,000	90,000	60,000	—	30,000

This simple case shows that from the figure of £60,000 onwards the Preference share holders lose and the Ordinary share holders gain at their expense.

A seemingly obvious answer at this stage is to offer participation rights after their reduced dividend has been met, but the idea has to be examined carefully. To compensate for the loss already borne, a large profit margin may have to be earned, which would not seem feasible in the circumstances. For example, if participation rights of 33⅓% (the proportion of their loss of dividend) were offered on all profits exceeding their lower dividend, profits would have to rise to the sum of £150,000 before they even reached their former level, whereas the Ordinary share holders would in the meantime have received £60,000, *i.e.* £150,000 − (£60,000 + [⅓ × 90,000]):

Profit	*Preference* + ⅓		*Ordinary shares*		
£70,000	£60,000	£3,333	£6,667	=	£70,000
£150,000	£60,000	£30,000	£60,000	=	£150,000

The fairer method would be to give the Preference share holders Ordinary shares.

If, according to the above scheme, the Preference share holders were offered four Ordinary shares of £0·20 each for every £0·80 Preference share, profits would have to rise to £135,000 before they could receive their original amount due. It would be better if five £0·20 Ordinary shares were offered for each original amount due of £1, leaving profits to rise to £126,000 before the Preference share holders received their original amount. At the same time, they would be entitled to five-sevenths of the equity.

Terms accepted by those with Preference capital may to some extent depend on their bargaining power. If their shares are non-cumulative they are in a weaker position since, as mentioned, their dividends may be passed and profits used to build up the company until the earning power can pay both Preference and Ordinary dividends. On the other hand those with cumulative rights can afford to wait if dividends are passed, for as soon as the company is sufficiently profitable they can expect arrears and current dividends.

Numerous variations on the scheme above are possible, with settlement partly in Ordinary shares and partly in new rate Debentures. In each case it is necessary to calculate the position at various profit levels as, in practice, such schemes are usually proposed when a company is thought to have entered upon a more prosperous period even though profits are still uncertain. If this is so, a larger share of future profits may be offered for the loss of present rights. Preference share holders may thus wish to wait as long as possible whereas those in favour of the scheme try to reach a settlement while their bargaining powers are strongest.

The effect on the stock exchange price of the shares may be a guide as to whether the scheme is likely to benefit the company, although it would not of course reflect the justice of the scheme towards any particular class of shareholders. Furthermore, a rise in the price might discourage one class from objecting in case it fell again.

Specimen Question

BALANCE SHEET (SUMMARISED)

at 31st March 19—

Authorised and issued share capital:		Freehold property	£25,000
		Plant and machinery *less*	
6% non-cumulative Preference shares (£1		depreciation	15,000
each)	£120,000	Development of scientific projects	190,000
Ordinary shares (£1		Trade debtors	22,000
each)	140,000	Bank	3,000
		Profit and Loss Account	40,000
	260,000		
Creditors	35,000		
	£295,000		£295,000

The foregoing is the Balance Sheet of a company which has been engaged on developing its own scientific projects and has made a series of losses. It is now considered that by undertaking work for outside concerns it will be able to make an annual profit of £9000 provided it can plough back 25% for re-equipment and modernisation. It is hoped that the estimated sum of future profits will increase considerably in the foreseeable future.

"Development of scientific projects" asset is estimated to be worth £77,000.

In accordance with the information given, you are required to submit a scheme of internal reconstruction assessing the present position and stating your proposals. Ignore taxation.

Answer

1. *Present position*

The amounts to be written off are:

Profit and Loss Account	£40,000
Scientific projects	113,000
	£153,000

The whole of the Ordinary share capital subscribed has been lost, in addition to £13,000 of the Preference capital.

The estimated future profits after ploughing back, £6750, would be insufficient to meet the Preference dividend of £7200.

2. *Proposals*

It is proposed, therefore, that:

(a) The losses should be written off mainly against the Ordinary share capital by reducing the shares to a denomination of £0·05 each.

(b) The remaining £20,000 loss to be borne by the Preference share holders by reducing their shares to £0·83.

(c) To compensate the Preference share holders, they should be offered 60,000 £0·05 Ordinary shares.

(d) The effect of the adjustment on the distribution of future profits may be illustrated as follows:

		Preference share holders		Ordinary share holders	
		Before	*After*	*Before*	*After*
Profit	£9,000	£7,200		£1,800	
Reserve	2,250				
	6,750		6,225 (6,000 + 225)		£525
Profit	12,000	7,200			
Reserves	3,000				
	£9,000		**£6,900**		**£2,100**

NOTES

(i) It will be observed that if profits increased to $33\frac{1}{3}\%$ above their estimated level, *i.e.* £9000 + £3000, the Preference share holders would almost be receiving their original share in distributable profit and at the same time benefiting to the extent of their proportion of profits ploughed back. With the promise of increased profits in the not too distant future, it could be argued that the settlement is over-generous to the Preference share holders, but it should be remembered that it *is* still only a promise.

(ii) This internal reconstruction problem is simplified by the relatively small sums involved. If the whole business were on a large scale it might be more difficult to settle: the increase in profits, from £6750 to £9000, is quite reasonable for a company of this size but might be less so if the figures were proportionately larger, say £67,500 to £90,000.

(iii) Such schemes cannot be submitted on a definite basis. Expert opinions may differ and such things as bargaining powers and the rights of various groups all have to be considered in practice.

INCOME TAX AND STAMP DUTY

It is important to take account of the effects of income tax and stamp duty on any proposed scheme of amalgamation or reconstruction.

INCOME TAX

The position likely to arise on amalgamation or reconstruction would need careful consideration. Such requirements as those operating to prevent companies from obtaining the benefit of the discontinued and new business rules where there is no substantial change in the ownership of the shares would have to be taken into consideration (*Finance Act*, 1954, *s.* 17).

STAMP DUTY

This may be reduced by a sum equal to the duty on the share capital of a vending company in connection with a scheme for reconstruction or amalgamation where the acquiring company takes over not less than 90% of the issued share capital of another company, the consideration for the purchase (excluding the taking over of liabilities) being discharged in the form of shares.

There is also a concession with regard to conveyance or transfer duty on any documents in connection with the transfer of the undertaking, or of shares, or the assignment of liabilities taken over (*Finance Acts*, 1927, *s.* 55; 1928, *s.* 31; 1930, *s.* 41).

EXAMINATION QUESTIONS

1. What reasons can you suggest for the growing number of amalgamations in recent years? Distinguish between take-overs and conventional mergers.
[C.A.A.

2. In drafting a scheme for the reconstruction of a limited company burdered with an accumulation of losses, to what points would you pay particular attention? [C.C.A.

3. The following is the latest Balance Sheet of P Ltd:

7% £1 Preference shares	£100,000	Goodwill	50,000
Ordinary £1 shares	250,000	Premises	40,000
		Plant	100,000
	350,000	Stock	30,000
Bank overdraft (secured		Debtors	70,000
by floating mortgage)	135,000	Profit and Loss Account	260,000
Trade creditors	65,000		
	£550,000		£550,000

Trading results have recently improved and the current profits are £25,000 per annum. You are asked to:

(*a*) Draft a scheme of capital reduction—assuming the Preference dividend to be ten years in arrears,

(b) Show the Balance Sheet as it would look if your scheme were carried out,

    (c) Indicate the procedure involved.   [C.C.A.

4. During recent years there have been innumerable integrations between companies large and small. Discuss the reasons for this and the benefits which it is hoped will be gained from integration.   [C.C.A.

5. River Ltd and Lake Ltd having agreed on a closer trading association, it was decided that each company should acquire (as on 31st December 19—) a minority interest in the other by an exchange of new shares to be issued for the purpose.

The shares of River Ltd (which had one subsidiary, Stream Ltd) were quoted on a stock exchange. The shares of Lake Ltd were unquoted.

As an initial step towards reaching final agreement on the values of the shares for the purpose of exchange, values of the underlying assets in each of the companies were agreed and it was decided to make two calculations:

    (a) To calculate the value of the existing shares in River Ltd and Lake Ltd on the basis of the agreed values of the underlying net assets, and

    (b) To calculate an estimated market value of Lake Ltd shares on the assumption that such value would be arrived at on the basis that:

        (i) the maintainable annual profit would be £17,500, of which £14,000 would be distributed as dividend, and

        (ii) an investor would require a dividend yield of $7\frac{1}{4}\%$ if the dividend were covered $1\frac{1}{2}$ times by earnings and the issued capital covered as to 75% by net tangible assets (to be taken at the agreed values). To adjust for variation of the actual cover from that stipulated, it was agreed that the basic required dividend yield of $7\frac{1}{4}\%$ should be increased or reduced according to the following scale: at the rate of 1% for 100% earnings cover of dividend and at the rate of $\frac{1}{2}\%$ for 75% of asset cover of issued capital.

The Balance Sheets of the companies as on 31st December 19— and the agreed values of the assets may be summarised as follows:

	River Ltd Balance Sheet	River Ltd Agreed values	Stream Ltd Balance Sheet	Stream Ltd Agreed values	Lake Ltd Balance Sheet	Lake Ltd Agreed values
Capital and liabilities:						
Authorised capital	£150,000	—	£50,000	—	£100,000	—
Issued capital in shares of £1 each fully paid	80,000	—	40,000	—	60,000	—
Revenue reserves	57,000	—	21,000	—	27,000	—
Current liabilities	61,000	—	12,000	—	30,000	—
Proposed dividend	10,000	—	8,000	—	—	—
	£208,000		£81,000		£117,000	
Assets:						
Freeholds	38,000	£57,000	—	—	20,000	£30,000
Other fixed assets	45,000	37,000	14,000	£21,000	26,000	18,000
Goodwill	13,000	22,000	15,000	6,000	12,000	47,000
Current assets	77,000	79,000	52,000	49,000	59,000	72,000
30,000 shares in Stream Ltd at cost	35,000		—		—	
	£208,000		£81,000		£117,000	

No credit has been taken in the accounts of River Ltd for the proposed dividend receivable from Stream Ltd.

You are required to prepare:

    (a) A statement showing the value per share of the existing shares of each company on the basis of the agreed values of the underlying net assets.

(b) A computation of the estimated market value of the existing shares of Lake Ltd.

For the purposes of your answer you are to ignore any possible effect of the proposed exchange on the values of the existing shares. Ignore taxation.

[C.A. (1964)

6. Following a period of years during which losses were incurred, the business of Upandown Ltd has been reorganised, with the help of additional directors, and profits are now being made at a fairly steady rate of approximately £15,000 per annum.

The liquid position, however, is still the cause of much anxiety and a critical stage has been reached through the imperative need, if production is to continue, to replace within the next six months worn out plant at a cost of £10,000 and the need to pay off within the same period the loan of £10,000 due to the estate of a deceased director, renewal having been refused.

The latest Balance Sheet of the company (as on 30th September 19—) is summarised below:

Share capital:			Freehold land and buildings,		
Authorised, issued and fully paid:			at cost		£27,000
30,000 6% cumulative Preference shares of £1 each		£30,000	Plant and machinery, at cost	£120,000	
50,000 Ordinary shares of £1 each		50,000	*Less* depreciation	85,000	
					35,000
		80,000	Motor vehicles at cost	10,000	
Profit and Loss Account debit balance		40,000	*Less* depreciation	6,000	
					4,000
		40,000			66,000
Trade creditors	£30,000		Trade debtors	22,000	
Unsecured loan	10,000		Stock	20,000	
Bank overdraft, secured by mortgage on freehold property and floating charge on other assets	28,000				42,000
		68,000			
		£108,000			£108,000

The following information concerning the situation has been ascertained:

(a) The company's bankers are not prepared to increase the amount of the overdraft limit of £30,000.

(b) The Preference shares (dividends on which are in arrears since five years ago), are held by trustees under a trust, the terms of which permit them to retain the shares but preclude them from making any further investment in the company.

(c) The Ordinary shares are held by the directors, who are not themselves able to provide further finance.

(d) The freehold land and buildings and the plant and machinery were professionally valued as on 30th September 19— at £34,000 and £40,000 respectively.

All efforts to obtain loan capital having been unsuccessful, the directors are anxious to accept an offer from an investment company to subscribe £20,000 for Ordinary shares carrying 50% of the equity in the business, subject to a satisfactory reorganisation scheme being previously carried through which would allow for the possibility of some dividends on the Ordinary shares being paid within the next year or two.

You are required:

(a) To state four important points which would need to be dealt with in a suitable reorganisation scheme, and (*b*) To outline what you consider would be an equitable basis for the reorganisation of the capital of Upandown Ltd, stating the consequential alterations (if any) to the other items in the Balance Sheet. [C.A. (1958)]

7. The summarised Balance Sheets of Alpha Ltd and Beta Ltd as on 31st March 1966 were as follows:

	Alpha Ltd	Beta Ltd
Fixed assets	£12,000	£10,000
Investments:		
£2000 3% stock at cost (market value £1000)	1,800	—
Quoted security at cost (market value £4000)	—	2,400
Debtors	2,000	1,500
Stock at cost	6,000	7,000
Balance at bank	4,000	2,000
	25,800	22,900
Current liabilities	6,700	6,150
	£19,100	£16,750

	Alpha Ltd	Beta Ltd
Represented by:		
Share capital (authorised, issued and fully paid shares of £1 each)		
Ordinary	9,200	12,300
Redeemable preference	1,000	—
Reserves	8,900	4,450
	£19,100	£16,750

A new company, Gamma Ltd, was formed to acquire, on 31st March 1966, from the members of Alpha Ltd and Beta Ltd, their shareholdings in those companies, the consideration being the allotment of shares in Gamma Ltd.
You ascertain the following:

(*a*) The trading profits, including investment income, for each of the last three years to 31st March, were:

	1964	1965	1966
Alpha Ltd	£2560	£3100	£3800
Beta Ltd	2150	1850	3150

(*b*) The investments of each company had been held for more than three years, and the investment income received by Beta Ltd was £150 in each of the above years.

It is agreed that:

(*a*) The fixed assets of Alpha Ltd and Beta Ltd are to be valued at £14,000 and £9000 respectively.
(*b*) The stocks of each company are to be written down by 5% of their book values.
(*c*) The preference shares of Alpha Ltd are to be redeemed at par.
(*d*) An earnings yield of 15% on net trading assets should be obtained from businesses of the type carried on by the companies.
(*e*) To arrive at a net trading assets figure for share valuation purposes, the average profits of the last three years, weighted in the proportion 1 : 2 : 3 to give more bias to the results of later years, are to be considered the earnings of the companies.

(*f*) The authorised and issued capital of Gamma Ltd is to be the aggregate capital of Alpha Ltd and Beta Ltd in order to obtain maximum relief from capital duty.

You are required to compute:

(i) The basis of allotment of shares in Gamma Ltd to the existing shareholders in Alpha Ltd and Beta Ltd, and the share premium on issue.

(ii) The value attributable to goodwill in the revised figure for net trading assets in each company.

Ignore taxation.   [C.A. (1966)

8. The summarised Balance Sheet of HTR Ltd, a private company, on 31st March 1965, was as follows:

Balance Sheet

Issued share capital:		Goodwill, at cost		£15,000
75,000 Ordinary shares of £1 each	£75,000	Fixed assets, at cost, *Less* depreciation:		
18,000 6% Cumulative Preference shares of £1 each	18,000	Leasehold property	£14,175	
	———	Plant and machinery	88,155	
	93,000			102,330
Less Profit and Loss Account, debit balance	7,050	Preliminary expenses		270
	———	Current assets:		
	85,950	Stock in trade	10,650	
5% Debentures	15,000	Debtors	17,250	
Current liabilities:				27,900
Trade creditors £41,025				
Bank overdraft 3,525	44,550			
	———			———
	£145,500			£145,500

Note. The dividend on the Preference shares is £2160 in arrears.

The following scheme of reconstruction was accepted by all parties and was completed on 1st April 1965.

(*a*) A new private company, HTR (1965) Ltd, took over all the assets of HTR Ltd and assumed responsibility for all the current liabilities. The purchase consideration was satisfied by the issue, at par, of shares and debentures in the new company, in accordance with the following arrangements:

(i) The holders of the 5% Debentures of the old company were satisfied by the issue of such an amount of 6% Debentures of the new company as is sufficient to discharge the 5% Debentures at a premium of 2%. The 6% Debentures are to be redeemed on 31st March 1970.

(ii) The holders of the Preference shares in the old company received one fully-paid 6½% Cumulative Preference share of £1 in the new company for every two Preference shares in the old company and one fully-paid Ordinary share of £1 in the new company for every four Preference shares in the old company. The arrears of Preference dividend were cancelled.

(iii) The Ordinary share holders of the old company received one fully-paid Ordinary share of £1 in the new company for every two Ordinary shares in the old company.

(*b*) The Ordinary share holders of the old company subscribed to the issue, at par, by the new company, of 22,500 Ordinary shares, of £1 each. This issue was fully paid up on 1st April 1965, and the preliminary expenses of the new company, £630, were paid on the same date.

(*c*) The leasehold property was valued at £12,000. The current assets were taken over at the amounts shown in the Balance Sheet of the old company. The balance of the purchase consideration is to be taken as the value of the plant and machinery.

It is estimated that the net profit of the new company, before charging debenture interest, will be £3750 per annum.

You are required:

(*a*) To set out the summarised Balance Sheet of HTR (1965) Ltd on 1st April 1965, as it would appear after the completion of the above transactions, and

(*b*) To give, with reasons, your opinion of the scheme of reconstruction.

Ignore taxation.   [C.I.S. (1965)

CHAPTER XVIII

CONSOLIDATED ACCOUNTS

HOLDING COMPANIES AND SUBSIDIARIES

MANY factors encourage the creation of larger units in modern industry and trade, such as economies of scale, the easier raising of finance, and others mentioned below. The holding company is a convenient way of obtaining these desirable benefits and in consequence the number of such companies has grown rapidly in recent years.

The efficient financial and managerial control of the group is extremely important, for size alone may constitute its main weakness. For this reason the management accountant must be fully conversant with the characteristics of groups of companies.

Before proceeding with the accounting aspects which require special application in consolidating the information made available by the parent company and its subsidiaries, some of the advantages and disadvantages of this type of organisation should be indicated.

Advantages

1. Vertical combination will ensure regular and cheaper supplies of raw material and other supplies.

2. Production can be unified and cheapened by the elimination of unnecessary processes.

3. Greater use can be made of expensive machinery. The electronic computer is an obvious example.

4. Goodwill may be retained by the continued use of the trade names of companies taken over.

5. A larger organisation which confines its activities to one line of business will be subject to fluctuations or—worse—long term decline in demand for its product or service. Some groups are therefore inclined to bring in other types of business on a lateral basis through acquisitions by the parent company. But *see* (4) under "Disadvantages."

6. Control may be centralised, so speeding decisions. But this centralised control may also have the contrary effect: *see* (1) under "Disadvantages".

7. Rival companies may be acquired to eliminate expensive competition. For the same reason advertising costs may be cut.

8. Finance is raised more easily by a larger group than by smaller undertakings.

9. The firm's bargaining powers are increased. Negotiations are more easily conducted between a few large companies and trade unions

417

than small ones. But here again there is a converse—that an impersonal attitude to employees may tend to added discontent.

Disadvantages

1. Size alone may create difficulties in management and organisation. Care must be taken to maintain an efficient organisation and pay due regard to the human aspect of industry and commerce. Discontent, production stoppages and other labour difficulties may arise through labour relations being governed more by rules and regulations than by a responsible attitude on the part of the ultimate management, who may seem far removed from such matters.

2. It is not always easy to find executives capable of managing large organisations and some groups have suffered from changes made during periods of re-orientation.

3. If the amalgamations eliminate most competition, monopoly powers may encourage the inclination to charge prices which cover inefficient production that healthy competition might eliminate. It may be noted that it is not always easy to create competition to a group, owing to the large amount of initial capital required.

4. Although diversification will help to cushion the group against fluctuations in the fortunes of any one of its companies, the converse has in practice often been found to apply: just as there will always be at least one or two doing well, so there may always be one or the other in difficulties to prevent the group achieving full profitability.

In what follows, a knowledge of the requirements of the Companies Acts, 1948 and 1967, is assumed.

CONSOLIDATED BALANCE SHEETS

No great difficulty should be experienced in the preparation of consolidated accounts and Balance Sheets, provided the basic principles are mastered before proceeding to more complicated examples.

It may be mentioned before going on to practical examples that consolidation of the Balance Sheets means, in effect, merely bringing together the assets and liabilities of the separate companies, subject to the cancellation of inter-company indebtedness (dealt with hereafter), and showing the interests of minority shareholders.

Specimen question (1)

The following is a simple example of a holding company with one subsidiary. Assuming the shares of S Co. have just been acquired by the holding company, H Co., you are required to prepare a Consolidated Balance Sheet.

HOLDING COMPANY'S BALANCE SHEET

Share capital:			
100,000 shares	£100,000	Net assets	£99,000
Profit and Loss Account	37,000	Shares in S Co. (30,000)	38,000
	£137,000		£137,000

SUBSIDIARY COMPANY'S BALANCE SHEET

Share capital:

40,000 shares	£40,000	Net assets	£48,000
Profit and Loss Account	8,000		
	£48,000		£48,000

As H Co. owns only 30,000 shares in S Co., there must be a minority holding of 10,000 shares.

The working schedule usually requires the use of the following three accounts (unless, of course, the subsidiary is wholly owned, when the omission of (b) is obvious):

(a) Cost of control,
(b) Minority shareholders' interests,
(c) Profit and Loss Account (S Co.).

Double entry should be carefully maintained throughout all the workings.

Answer

The remark immediately preceding this specimen question should be borne in mind. It may seem obvious, but if the point is fully understood the first set of entries will be clear. The items in the subsidiary that represent net assets (*i.e.* the shares and reserves) and the cost of the shares in H Co. must be eliminated, since it is the *actual* net assets that are being combined.

So without any alteration, save to divide the S Co. shares, the items to be eliminated are shown in the relevant accounts.

Cost of control

Cost of shares (from H Co.		Shares purchased	£30,000
Balance Sheet)	£38,000		

Minority shareholders' interests

Shares	£10,000

Profit and Loss Account (S Co.)

Balance (per Balance Sheet)	£8,000

As the subsidiary has just been taken over, all the profit must have been earned prior to the take-over date and so is pre-acquisition profit. As such profit is not considered by the holding company to be of a revenue nature, it must either be transferred to a capital reserve or deducted from any sum paid in respect of goodwill. The next step, therefore, will be to debit S Co.'s Profit and Loss Account to transfer out such profit to the credit of the cost of control.

As H Co. owns only three-quarters of S Co., it is only entitled to three-quarters of the profit; the remaining quarter is transferred to the minority shareholders. When this has been done the accounts appear as follows:

Cost of control

Cost of shares	£38,000	Shares purchased	£30,000
		Pre-acquisition profit transferred (¾)	6,000

Minority shareholders' interests

Shares	£10,000
Pre-acquisition profit transferred (¼)	2,000

Profit and Loss Account (S Co.)

Transfer to cost of control	£6,000	Balance	£8,000
Transfer to minority share-			
holders	2,000		

No further adjustments being necessary, the accounts may be completed and the Consolidated Balance Sheet compiled.

As the Cost of Control Account reveals that £38,000 was expended in obtaining shares and profit represented by net assets valued at £36,000, then a sum of £2000 has been paid in respect of goodwill. Had the value received exceeded the actual cost, a capital reserve would have arisen. (*Note:* in order to comply with the Institute of Chartered Accountants' recommendation in *Terms used in published accounts of limited companies*, the term "goodwill" should be used, not "cost of control" as in the heading of the account. This heading is retained since at the commencement of the computation it may not be apparent whether goodwill or a capital reserve will arise.)

The accounts are now completed:

Cost of control

Cost of shares	£38,000	Shares	£30,000
		Pre-acquisition profit	6,000
		Balance c/d	2,000
	£38,000		£38,000
Balance (goodwill) b/d	£2,000		

Minority shareholders' interests

		Shares	£10,000
		Profit	2,000
			£12,000

The Profit and Loss Account of S Co., having no balance remaining, is omitted from the Consolidated Balance Sheet.

CONSOLIDATED BALANCE SHEET

Share capital:		Goodwill		£2,000
100,000 shares	£100,000	Net assets:		
Profit and Loss Account	37,000	H Co.	£99,000	
Minority shareholders'		S Co.	48,000	
interest in the group	12,000			147,000
	£149,000			£149,000

Specimen question (2)

Using the figures in the previous specimen question, if the shares in S Co. had been acquired by H Co. at an earlier date than that of consolidation and the Profit and Loss Account of S Co. had shown a credit balance of, say, £6000, then this £6000 would be pre-acquisition profit and the remaining £2000, having been earned since acquisition, post-acquisition profit. The latter, being revenue profit as far as the holding company is concerned, would be transferred to H Co.'s Profit and Loss Account.

The foregoing accounts would then have appeared as follows:

Cost of control

Cost of shares	£38,000	Shares		£30,000
		Pre-acquisition profit		4,500
		Balance c/d		3,500
	£38,000			£38,000
Balance (goodwill) b/d	£3,500			

Minority shareholders' interests

Shares		£10,000
Pre-acquisition profit		1,500
Post acquisition profit		500
		£12,000

Profit and loss Account (S Co.)

Pre-acquisition profit transferred:			Balance	£8,000
Cost of control ($\frac{3}{4}$)	£4,500			
Minority shareholders ($\frac{1}{4}$)	1,500			
		£6,000		
Post-acquisition profit transferred:				
H Co. Profit and Loss Account	1,500			
Minority shareholders	500			
		£2,000		
	£8,000			£8,000

CONSOLIDATED BALANCE SHEET

Share capital:				
100,000 shares		£100,000	Goodwill	£3,500
Profit and Loss Account	£37,000		Net assets	147,000
Add from S Co.	1,500			
		38,500		
Minority shareholders' interest in the group		12,000		
		£150,500		£150,500

NOTES

(i) The transfer of the £1500 post-acquisition profit to H Co.'s Profit and Loss Account may be noted next to the balance shown on that account as an item to be added to the Profit and Loss Account on consolidation. It is not necessary to prepare a separate Profit and Loss Account for H Co. unless there are sufficient adjustments to justify it.

(ii) It may be observed that the total amount due to the minority shareholders has not varied, at £12,000, and that one-quarter share of all the profits could have been transferred to them at once; but it is preferable to divide the pre- and post-acquisition profits as shown since it facilitates working in more difficult examples.

Specimen question (3)

Had there been a debit balance on the Profit and Loss Account of the subsidiary at the date of acquisition, it would have been necessary to transfer out the pre-acquisition loss first. It will be noted that this increases the subsequent amount of profit to be transferred, thus revealing the true position; for if the Profit and Loss Account reveals a credit balance on the date of consolidation of (say) £8000 and that there was a debit balance of (say) £2000 on the date of acquisition, then £10,000 profit must have been earned since the date of take-over—£2000 to eliminate the pre-acquisition loss and a further £8000 subsequently. The Profit and Loss Account of S Co. would then have appeared as follows:

Profit and loss Account (S Co.)

Post-acquisition profit transferred:		Balance		£8,000
H Co. Profit and Loss Account (¾)	£7,500	Pre-acquisition loss transferred:		
Minority shareholders (¼)	2,500	Cost of control (¾)	£1,500	
		Minority shareholders (¼)	500	
				£2,000
	£10,000			£10,000

At this stage, the reader is referred to Question 1 at the end of this chapter (p. 445), which involves the use of the principles exemplified above.

VARIOUS ADJUSTMENTS

Having dealt with the basic principles of consolidating Balance Sheets, a number of miscellaneous adjustments will now be dealt with, using the following question to exemplify them.

Specimen question

The following are the summarised Balance Sheets of a holding company and its two subsidiaries at the 31st December 19—.

H Co. Ltd acquired its shares in S Ltd one year previously, when there was a balance on S Ltd's Profit and Loss Account of £12,900, out of which it was proposed to pay a dividend of 10%. This dividend was subsequently paid in March of the year just ended.

S Ltd acquired its shares in SS Ltd two years previously, when the balance on the Profit and Loss Account of SS Ltd showed a debit balance of £4800.

Included in the trade debtors of H Co. Ltd. is a debt due from SS Ltd. of £1800.

Of the £5200 bills payable shown on S Ltd's Balance Sheet, £3000 are payable to H Co. Ltd, the latter company having discounted £2000 of them with its bankers.

During the year just ended H Co. Ltd had sold to S Ltd goods to the value of £24,000 at a cost to H Co. Ltd of £20,000. Of these goods £5400 were still in the stock figure of S Ltd at the closing date.

H COMPANY LTL

Balance Sheet, 31st December 19—

Share capital: 150,000			Fixed assets	£89,700
£1 Ordinary shares		£150,000	Shares in S Ltd (40,000)	44,000
Profit and Loss Account		38,000	6% Debentures in	
Current liabilities:			SS Ltd (£20,000)	19,500
Creditors	£30,300		Current assets:	
Proposed dividend	10,000		Stock-in-trade	£26,000	
		40,300	Debtors	40,200	
			Bills receivable	2,500	
			Cash and bank	6,400	
				75,100
		£228,300		£228,300

S LTD

Balance Sheet, 31st December 19—

Share capital: 50,000			Fixed assets	£32,100
£1 Ordinary shares		£50,000	Shares in SS Ltd (30,000)	28,000
Profit and Loss Account		19,400	Current assets:	
Current liabilities:			Stock-in-trade	£12,600	
Creditors	£19,300		Debtors	24,000	
Bills payable	5,200		Cash and bank	2,200	
Proposed dividend	5,000			38,800
		29,500		
		£98,900		£98,900

SS LTD

Balance Sheet, 31st December 19—

Share capital: 45,000			Fixed assets	£55,700
£1 Ordinary shares		£45,000	Current assets:	
Profit and Loss Account			Stock-in-trade	£15,000	
(profit for year, £3,000)		2,400	Debtors	28,200	
6% Debentures		30,000	Cash and bank	1,800	
Current liabilities:				45,000
Creditors	£22,400			
Deb. interest payable	900			
		23,300		
		£100,700		£100,700

You are required to prepare the Consolidated Balance Sheet of H Co. Ltd and its subsidiaries at 31st December 19—. Ignore taxation.

Answer

In a problem of this nature the facts to note carefully are:

(*a*) The dates of acquisition of shares in both cases, so as to distinguish between pre- and post-acquisition profits.

(*b*) The proportionate amounts of share holdings and any various classes of shares held in subsidiary companies. In this example the proportions are (i) H Co. Ltd in S Ltd, four-fifths and (ii) S Ltd in SS Ltd, two-thirds. There are no Preference or other classes of shares to be dealt with.

It is proposed to deal with the miscellaneous adjustments required and explain them before going on to prepare the three accounts for each company within the group.

1. Inter-company indebtedness

Since the Consolidated Balance Sheet is to show the holding company and its subsidiaries as a group, *i.e.* as one business, then debts due to and from various members of the group must be eliminated. Obviously a single concern cannot owe itself anything.

The necessary adjustment is quite straightforward since the amount shown as a credit on one Balance Sheet will be cancelled against the corresponding debit on the other Balance Sheet. As all workings in questions must be shown, a journal entry may be given:

Trade creditors, SS Ltd   *Dr.* £1800

    To trade debtors, H Co. Ltd   £1800
    (being elimination of inter-company indebtedness)

2. Bills payable and receivable within the group

Bills which are payable and receivable within the group represent inter-company indebtedness and will cancel one another out, as mentioned in (1) above. But when a bill receivable has been discounted, the bill payable is no longer a debt to be settled by the acceptor within the group; it is due and payable to the bank which discounted the bill. Cancellation of such indebtedness does not therefore arise and, since the cash received by the company which had the bill discounted will have been set against the bill receivable, it will no longer be shown on that company's Balance Sheet. So only the bills receivable still shown on the Balance Sheet will be dealt with as contras against the bills payable.

There is no need to show a contingent liability on bills discounted as a note on the Consolidated Balance Sheet, since the actual liability is shown by the inclusion of the respective bills payable.

The journal entry required here will therefore be:

Bills payable, S Ltd   *Dr.* £1000

    To bills receivable, H Co. Ltd   £1000
    (being cancellation of bills due and receivable within the group)

3. Unrealised profit on stock

If goods are sold by one company to another within the group at a profit and any such goods are held by the purchasing company at the Balance Sheet date, the profit charged on the original sale by the seller company is unrealised in so far as the shareholding proportion is concerned. For example, in this question, four-fifths of H Co. Ltd's sale of goods to S Ltd has in effect been made to itself, and since £5400 of the goods are still in stock the profit on them has not been realised.

The fact that the total sales to S Ltd amounted to £24,000 is not relevant to the consolidation save in revealing that the goods are sold at cost plus 20% profit. (It will be remembered that an addition of one-fifth will require a reduction of one-sixth to bring it to the original price.)

The profit element contained in the stock is therefore £900, but as H Co. Ltd's holding is only four-fifths the remaining one-fifth may be taken as having been sold to "outsiders" and to that extent can be considered as realised. The provision to be created against unrealised profit is, then, £900 *less* £180 = £720, the adjustment being:

H Co. Ltd Profit and Loss Account   *Dr.* £720

    To stock, S Ltd   £720
    (being provision against unrealised profit on stock)

It may be added that in the opinion of some accountants it is more expedient to eliminate the *whole* of such unrealised profit, *i.e.* in this case the provision would be £900.

S LTD

Cost of control

Cost of shares	£44,000	Shares	£40,000
Balance c/d	8,560	Pre-acquisition profit transferred	6,320
		Pre-acquisition profit from SS Ltd	2,240
		Dividend transferred from H Co.'s Profit and Loss Account	4,000
	£52,560		£52,560
		Balance (Capital Reserve) b/d	£8,560

Minority shareholders' interest

Shares	£10,000
Pre-acquisition profit transferred	1,580
Post-acquisition profit transferred	3,300
Profit from SS Ltd	960
	£15,840

Profit and Loss Account

Transfer pre-acquisition profit to:		Balance b/d	£19,400
Cost of control	£6,320	Proposed dividend transferred back	5,000
Minority shareholders (£12,900—5,000)	1,580	Profit from SS Ltd	4,800
Transfer post-acquisition profit:			
H Co. Ltd	13,200		
Minority shareholders	3,300		
	24,400		
Transfer profit from SS Ltd:			
Minority shareholders (⅕) £960			
H Co. Profit and Loss Account (⅘—2,000) 1,600			
Cost of control 2,240			
	4,800		
	£29,200		£29,200

SS LTD

Cost of control

Cost of shares	£28,000	Shares	£30,000
Pre-acquisition loss transferred	3,200	Balance c/d	1,200
	£31,200		£31,200
Balance (Goodwill) b/d	£1,200		

Minority shareholders' interest

Pre-acquisition loss transferred	£1,600	Shares	£15,000
Balance c/d	15,800	Post-acquisition profit transferred	2,400
	£17,400		£17,400
		Balance b/d	£15,800

Profit and Loss Account

Post-acquisition profit transferred:		Balance b/d	£2,400
S Ltd	£4,800	Pre-acquisition loss transferred:	
Minority shareholders	2,400	Cost of control	3,200
		Minority shareholders	1,600
	£7,200		£7,200

4. Debentures held within the group

It will be noted that there is a holding of £20,000 Debentures by H Co. Ltd in SS Ltd which cost £19,500. Since these Debentures represent inter-company indebtedness they must be cancelled; but the holding of £20,000 cannot be cancelled against the £30,000 issued unless the £19,500 be first increased to nominal value of £20,000. This may be done by adding the amount at which the purchase was made below nominal value of £500, the corresponding entry being a credit of £500 to a reserve, in this case preferably a Capital Reserve.

H Co. Ltd 6% Debentures	£500	
Capital reserve, H Co. Ltd		£500
(being adjustment to bring 6% Debentures to nominal value prior to cancellation of inter-company indebtedness)		

5. Debenture interest outstanding

On the Balance Sheet of SS Ltd is shown an amount (six months') of Debenture interest payable. Since two-thirds is due to H Co. Ltd, the rule about eliminating inter-company indebtedness applies. As the H Co. Ltd Balance Sheet reveals no figure for an amount of Debenture interest receivable it can be assumed that the sum due has not been dealt with.

The following journal entries reveal that the sum due was brought into H Co. Ltd and the internal indebtedness subsequently cancelled:

H Co. Ltd Debenture interest receivable	*Dr.* £600	
To H Co. Ltd Profit and Loss Account		£600
SS Co. Ltd Debenture interest payable	*Dr.* £600	
To H Co. Ltd Debenture Interest Receivable Account		£600
(being amount of Debenture interest for half year due brought into accounts of H Co. Ltd and cancellation of inter-company indebtedness)		

6. Dividend paid by S Ltd during year

Since this dividend was paid in March out of the profits of the previous year, it constitutes a dividend paid out of pre-acquisition profits so far as H Co. Ltd is concerned, *i.e.* H Co. bought the share cumulative dividend. As there is no indication to the contrary, it is assumed that the £44,000 shown on the Balance Sheet of the holding company is the original cost price of the shares and that the four-fifths proportion of the dividend subsequently received has been credited to the Profit and Loss Account. Since the dividend received is of a capital nature, it will be necessary to transfer it out of the Profit and Loss Account of H Co. Ltd to the Cost of Control Account of S Ltd. This will be shown on the working accounts, so no journal entry need be made.

NOTE

Such dividends paid out of pre-acquisition profits are often purposely credited incorrectly to the Revenue Account in examination questions. It is important not to overlook this necessary adjustment.

7. Proposed Ordinary dividend in S Ltd

Proposed Ordinary dividends in subsidiary companies should always be ignored since the whole of the available profits are allocated to the holding company and minority shareholders in their respective share holding ratios. Matters concerning income tax and dividends paid or proposed will be dealt with later.

The three accounts mentioned previously should now be prepared, beginning with the subsidiary. Since their working has already been explained, they are shown completed (pp. 425–6), with the addition of the H Co. Ltd Profit and Loss Account:

H CO. LTD
Profit and Loss Account

Transfer of dividend received out of pre-acquisition profit to cost of control, S Ltd	£4,000	Balance	£38,000
		Debenture interest	600
		Profit from S Ltd	
		(£13,200 + £1,600)	14,800
Provision for unrealised profit and stock	720		
Balance c/d	48,680		
	£53,400		£53,400
		Balance b/d	£48,680

NOTE

As SS Ltd became a member of the Group when H Co. Ltd acquired shares in S Ltd twelve months previously, only the profit for the year just ended, £3000, is in the nature of post-acquisition profit. Of this post-acquisition profit £2000, or two-thirds, has been transferred to S Ltd. Only four-fifths is transferable to H Co. Ltd as revenue. The remainder of the £4800 transferred over, after deducting the minority shareholders' proportion, is transferred to cost of control.

H COMPANY LTD AND SUBSIDIARIES
Consolidated Balance Sheet, 31st December 19—

Share capital: 150,000			Fixed assets		£177,500
£1 Ordinary shares		£150,000	Current assets:		
Capital reserve:			Stock-in-trade	£52,880	
On acquisition of			Debtors	90,600	
S Ltd	£8,560		Bills receivable	1,500	
Less Goodwill SS			Cash and bank	10,400	
Ltd	1,200				155,380
	7,360				
On Debs. purchased	500				
		7,860			
Profit and Loss Account		48,680			
Loan capital:					
6% Debentures		10,000			
Interest of minority shareholders:					
S Ltd	15,840				
SS Ltd	15,800				
		31,640			
Current liabilities:					
Creditors	70,200				
Bills payable	4,200				
Deb. interest payable	300				
Proposed dividend	10,000				
		84,700			
		£332,880			£332,880

CONSOLIDATED PROFIT AND LOSS ACCOUNTS

The combination of constituent companies' Profit and Loss Accounts will be dealt with separately before proceeding to the consolidation of Balance Sheets and Revenue Accounts. In the working of examination questions, owing to the amount of time required for the preparation of both group Revenue Accounts and Balance Sheets combined, consolidation of Revenue Accounts is often dealt with in isolation.

The following simplified example illustrates the basic principles involved.

Specimen question (1)

H CO.

(with three-quarter holding in S Co.)

Profit and Loss Account

Corporation tax	£7,400	Balance b/f	£24,000
Balance c/f	30,600	Net profit b/d	14,000
	£38,000		£38,000

S CO.

Profit and Loss Account

Corporation tax	£1,600	Balance b/f	£6,000
Balance c/f	7,400	Net profit b/d	3,000
	£9,000		£9,000

Prepare a Consolidated Profit and Loss Account, assuming all profits have been earned since acquisition.

Answer

In this instance the consolidation is simple but the method of combining the figures should be noted carefully in anticipation of working more difficult examples.

	H Co.	S Co.	Total
Balances brought forward	£24,000	£6,000	£30,000
Less Minority interest (¼)	—	1,500	1,500
	24,000	4,500	£28,500
Corporation tax	7,400	1,600	9,000
Share of current profit due to minority shareholders:			
Trading profit		3,000	
Less corporation tax		1,600	
		£1,400	
¼ thereof		£350	

NOTE

The minority shareholders' proportion of current profits must always be computed separately because of adjustments made to the net profit figure.

CONSOLIDATED PROFIT AND LOSS ACCOUNT

Current year's profit divisible as to:

Minority shareholders	£350	Trading profit	£17,000
Group c/d	16,650		
	£17,000		£17,000
Corporation tax	9,000	Balance b/d	16,650
Balance c/f	36,150	Balance b/f	28,500
	£45,150		£45,150

Specimen question (2)

If in the previous example there had been a balance of £2000 on S Co.'s Profit and Loss Account when H Co. acquired its majority holding, this would be pre-acquisition profit and could not therefore have been left on the Consolidated Profit and Loss Account as distributable profit. It would be dealt with as follows:

	H Co.		S Co.	Total
Balances b/f	£24,000		£6,000	£30,000
Less Minority shareholders' proportion (¼)			1,500	1,500
	24,000		4,500	28,500
Less Pre-acquisition profits		£2,000		
Less Minority shareholders' proportion (¼)*		500		
			1,500	1,500
	£24,000		£3,000	£27,000

The Consolidated Account would then be shown as follows:

CONSOLIDATED PROFIT AND LOSS ACCOUNT

Current year's profit divisible as to:		Trading profit	£17,000
Minority shareholders (as before)	£350		
Group c/d	16,650		
	£17,000		£17,000
Corporation tax	9,000	Balance b/d	16,650
Balance c/f	34,650	Balance b/f	27,000
	£43,650		£43,650

* As the minority shareholders have been credited with one-quarter share of all the profits brought forward, their share of pre-acquisition profits is included in the sum of £1500. So when the pre-acquisition profit is transferred to cost of control, the amount credited to minority shareholders must be excluded.

Where Profit and Loss Accounts only are being dealt with, to ensure that the "balance carried forward" is not just a balancing figure inserted it may be checked by taking the original net balances carried forward as on the left-hand side of the Balance Sheet and checking the total of such balances after making the transfers outlined above, *e.g.* as in the last example.

Original "balances carried forward" (*see* Specimen
    Question (1)):

H Co.	£30,600	
S Co.	7,400	
		£38,000
Balance c/f on Consolidated Profit and Loss Account	34,650	
Add Transfer to cost of control	1,500	
Add Transfer to minority shareholders of balance b/f	1,500	
Add Minority shareholders' share of current profit	350	
		£38,000

The following example will serve to illustrate the basic rules for eliminating inter-company dividends.

Example

H CO.

Profit and Loss Account

Transfer to reserve	£6,000	Balance b/f	£35,000
Proposed dividend	8,000	Trading profit	16,000
Balance c/d	38,500	Dividends received	1,500
	£52,500		£52,500

S CO.

(H Co. three-quarter holding)

Profit and Loss Account

Transfer to reserve	£2,000	Balance b/f (£2,000 pre-	
Interim dividend paid	2,000	acquisition profit)	£8,000
Final dividend proposed	4,000	Trading profit	14,000
Balance c/f	14,000		
	£22,000		£22,000

NOTES

(i) As H Co. has a three-quarter holding in S Co., £1500 of the £2000 dividend paid will have been received by H Co. Inter-company dividends must be eliminated, since the Consolidated Profit and Loss Account reveals the profit earned by the group and how it is dealt with; the fact that such profits have been transferred, in effect, from one bank account to another is irrelevant.

Having eliminated the £1500, the £500 remaining on S Co.'s Profit and Loss Account is the sum paid to the minority shareholders. This is not shown on the consolidated account but deducted from the amount shown due to minority shareholders on the Balance Sheet.

(ii) It may be observed that Note (i) has dealt only with the dividend paid. Proposed Ordinary dividends in subsidiary companies are always completely ignored since the whole of the profits earned by the subsidiary are divided between the H Co. and the minority shareholders.

Preference dividends should be written back as in the case of Ordinary dividends. In computing the amount due to minority shareholders, the full amount of Preference dividends paid or payable must be deducted from the trading profits in order to arrive at the share of profit due to minority (Ordinary) share holders.

The Preference dividends due or paid to outside shareholders may be included with the amount due to minority holders of Ordinary shares on the Consolidated Profit and Loss Account; those *paid* should be deducted from the sum shown to the credit of minority interests on the Balance Sheet.

The consolidation proceeds as follows:

	H Co.		S Co.	Total
Balances brought forward	£35,000		£8,000	£43,000
Less Amount due to minority shareholders (¼)			2,000	2,000
	35,000		6,000	41,000
Less Pre-acquisition profit		£2,000		
Less Minority shareholders' proportion		500		
			1,500	1,500
	£35,000		£4,500	£39,500
Transfer to reserve	6,000		2,000	8,000
Less Minority shareholders' proportion			500	500
	£6,000		£1,500	£7,500

NOTE

All profits due to minority shareholders must be credited to their account. Therefore such transfers to reserve of subsidiary profits must be diminished by profits already given to minority shareholders.

Minority shareholders' proportion of current profits—as there are no further charges against trading profit	£14,000
¼ thereof	£3,500

CONSOLIDATED PROFIT AND LOSS ACCOUNT

Profit distributable to:		Trading profit	£30,000
Minority shareholders	£3,500		
Group c/d	26,500		
	£30,000		£30,000

Transfer to reserve	£7,500	Balance b/d	£26,500
Proposed dividend	8,000	Balance b/f	39,500
Balance c/f	50,500		
	£66,000		£66,000

The following is a more comprehensive example again demonstrating, *inter alia*, the method of dealing with inter-company dividends on consolidation.

Specimen question

Below are the summarised revenue accounts of H Co. Ltd and its two subsidiaries for the year ended 31st December 19—.

	H Co. Ltd	S1 Ltd	S2 Ltd
Debits:			
Directors' emoluments	£13,000	£4,000	£3,200
Depreciation	14,000	2,900	2,700
Auditors' remuneration	1,200	525	420
Interim dividend paid (gross)	—	4,000	—
Proposed dividends (gross)	12,000	3,500	—
Corporation tax	10,800	4,200	1,200
Transfers to reserve	5,000	—	4,000
Balance c/f	9,800	2,175	980
	£65,800	£21,300	£12,500
Credits:			
Balance b/f	£21,000	£8,500	£4,900
Trading profit	41,800	12,800	7,600
Investment income	3,000	—	—
	£65,800	£21,300	£12,500

H Co. Ltd acquired its three-quarter holding in S1 Ltd when the balance on the Profit and Loss Account was £1200 in credit; its four-fifths holding in S2 Ltd was acquired when the adverse balance on Profit and Loss Account was £2000.

H Co. Ltd sold goods during the year valued at £15,000 to S1 Ltd at 25% above cost, of which £3500 at purchase price to S1 Ltd remained unsold at the year end.

Prepare the Consolidated Profit and Loss Account for the group at 31st December 19—.

Before showing the necessary workings, it may be observed that it is not necessary to show the directors' emoluments paid by subsidiaries for services to those subsidiaries, but it is usual to combine them in the Consolidated Revenue Account.

The obvious aggregations of expenses have been omitted from the following workings.

Answer

	H Co. Ltd	S1 Ltd	S2 Ltd	Total
Balances c/f	£21,000	£8,500	£4,900	£34,400
Add Post-acquisition profit			2,000	2,000
	21,000	8,500	6,900	36,400
Less Minority shareholders' proportion thereof		2,125	1,380	3,505
	21,000	6,375	5,520	32,895
Less Pre-acquisition profits		£1,200		
Less Minority shareholders proportion		300		
		900		900
	£21,000	£5,475	£5,520	£31,995
Trading profit	41,800	12,800	7,600	62,200
Less Unrealised profit on stock (£3,500 × ⅕)	£700			
Less Minority shareholders' proportion	175			
	525			525
	£41,275	£12,800	£7,600	£61,675
Interim dividend		4,000		
Less Dividend received from S1 Ltd	3,000 →	(3,000)		
Deduct from minority interest on Balance Sheet		1,000		
Transfers to reserve	5,000		4,000	9,000
Less Minority shareholders' proportion			800	800
	£5,000		£3,200	£8,200
Minority shareholders' proportion of trading profit		12,800	7,600	
Less Directors' emoluments		4,000	£3,200	
Depreciation		2,900	2,700	
Auditors' remuneration		525	420	
Corporation tax		4,200	1,200	
		11,625	7,520	
		£1,175	£80	
		¼ thereof 294	⅕ thereof 16	£310

H CO. LTD AND SUBSIDIARIES

Consolidated Profit and Loss Account for the year ended 31st December 19—

Director's emoluments	£20,200	Trading profit	£61,675
Depreciation	19,600		
Auditors' remuneration	2,145		
Balance distributable:			
To minority shareholders	£310		
To group c/d	19,420		
	19,730		
	£61,675		£61,675

Corporation tax on current profit	£15,000	Balance b/d	£19,420
Proposed dividend (Gross)	12,000	Balance b/f	£31,995
Transfer to reserve	8,200		
Balance c/f	16,215		
	£51,415		£51,415

CONSOLIDATED BALANCE SHEETS AND REVENUE ACCOUNTS

Finally, in this consideration of group accounts, we come to the amalgamation of Balance Sheets and Revenue Accounts. One further matter of importance will be dealt with before proceeding to the final workings.

In the following specimen question, under (c), machinery is mentioned as being acquired at £15,000, whereas in the books of the subsidiary the asset concerned is dealt with according to its original book value. This implies that on acquisition a further sum of £5000 was in the nature of a capital reserve divisible between the holding company and the minority shareholders.

As consolidation is being applied two years after acquisition, the assets will have depreciated on the full sum, but only the depreciation on the lesser figure will have been put through the books of the subsidiary. The amount, therefore, to be credited to capital reserve will be the excess on revaluation, less depreciation to the beginning of the year under review, the additional figure for depreciation for the year being charged against current profits.

It may be observed that this procedure is not strictly correct. It would be more accurate to charge the depreciation on the full amount incurred since acquisition against post-acquisition profits and to credit the full sum on revaluation to capital reserve. This is not advocated, mainly because adjustments might be required after acquisition on subsequent dividend declarations by the subsidiary; also, the amount involved should not be great. If the sum were large enough to justify more exact treatment, a better method would be to revalue the asset on take-over, for to continue to show an asset considerably below its true value would contravene the Companies Acts, and reveal unenlightened accounting policies. Opinions differ, however, and instead of the treatment in the specimen question, some accountants might add £5000 to "Plant and machinery," include a further £1000 on the depreciation and so increase the amount of the capital reserve.

Specimen question

Below are shown the Balance Sheets and Revenue Accounts of a holding company and its subsidiary for the year ended 31st December 19—, from

which the Balance Sheet and Profit and Loss Account for the group are to
be prepared.

H COMPANY LTD

Balance Sheet, 31st March 19—

Authorised and issued share capital:			Fixed assets:		
150,000 Ordinary			Freehold property		£80,000
shares		£150,000	Plant and ma-		
Reserves:			chinery	£64,000	
General reserve	£9,000		*Less* Deprecia-		
Profit and Loss			tion	13,300	
Account	16,400			———	50,700
		25,400			130,700
Deferred Taxation			Investments:		
account		9,000	At cost, sundries	22,000	
Current liabilities:			Shares in S Co. Ltd:		
Trade creditors	7,400		20,000 Ordinary	23,000	
Corporation Tax	7,400		5,000 Preference	5,000	
Bills payable	3,000			———	50,000
Proposed divi-			Current assets:		
dend (net)	9,000		Stock-in-trade	10,000	
	———	26,800	Trade debtors		
			(£1,000 due		
			from S Co. Ltd)	10,400	
			Bills receivable		
			(all from S Co.		
			Ltd)	2,000	
			Bank	8,100	
				———	30,500
		£211,200			£211,200

Profit and Loss Account for year ended 31st March 19—

Directors' emoluments	£6,000	Trading profit	£38,200
Depreciation	8,200	Investment income	
Net profit c/d	28,000	(Unquoted)	4,000
	£42,200		£42,200

Transfer to reserve	£4,000	Net profit b/d	£28,000
Corporation tax	10,600	Balance b/f	12,000
Proposed dividend 10%			
(gross)	9,000		
Balance c/f	16,400		
	£40,000		£40,000

S COMPANY LTD

Balance Sheet, 31st March 19—

Authorised and issued share capital:			Fixed assets:			
25,000 Ordinary shares (£1 each)		£25,000	Freehold property			£27,700
15,000 5% Preference shares (£1 each)		15,000	Plant and machinery	30,000		
		———	*Less* Depreciation	12,000		
		40,000			———	18,000
Reserves:						
General reserve	£6,000					45,700
Profit and Loss Account	4,950					
	———	10,950	Current assets:			
Deferred taxation account		5,500	Stock-in-trade	11,000		
Current liabilities:			Trade debtors	13,425		
Trade creditors	8,400		Bank	7,100		
Bills payable (all due to H Co.)	3,000				———	31,525
Corporation tax	4,500					
Proposed dividends (net):						
Ordinary	£4,500					
Preference	375					
	———					
	4,875					
	———	20,775				
		£77,225				£77,225

Profit and Loss Account for year ended 31st March 19—

Directors' emoluments		£2,000	Trading profit	£16,000
Depreciation		4,300		
Net profit c/d		9,700		
		———		———
		£16,000		£16,000

Transfer to reserve		£4,000	Net profit b/d	£9,700
Corporation tax		5,500	Balance b/f	10,000
Proposed Ordinary dividend				
30% (gross)		4,500		
Preference dividend				
gross:				
Interim paid	£375			
Proposed final	375			
	———			
		750		
Balance c/f		4,950		
		———		———
		£19,700		£19,700

The following matters were to be taken into consideration on consolidation:

(*a*) When H Co. Ltd acquired its Ordinary shares in S Co. Ltd two years previously, there was a credit balance on Profits and Loss Account of £3000.

(*b*) Of the figure for stock-in-trade shown in S Co. Ltd's Balance Sheet, £9000 had been purchased from H Co. Ltd, the gross profit on sales by that company being at the rate of 20%.

(*c*) When H Co. Ltd acquired its holding in S Co. Ltd, certain machinery shown at a book value of £10,000 was revalued at £15,000. No alteration was made in the books of S Co. Ltd. The depreciation rate of the machinery concerned is 20% per annum.

You are required to prepare the Consolidated Balance Sheet and Profit and Loss Account for the group.

Answer

	H Co. Ltd.	S Co. Ltd.	Total
Balances b/f	£12,000	£10,000	
Less Minority shareholders' proportion (⅕)		2,000	
		8,000	
Less Pre-requisition profits		£3,000	
Less Minority shareholders' proportion		600	
		2,400	
	12,000	5,600	£17,600
Trading profit	38,200	16,000	
Less Unrealised profit on stock	£1,800		
Less Minority shareholders' proportion	360		
	1,440		
	£36,760	£16,000	£52,760
Investment income and Preference dividend (gross)	4,000	375	
Less Interim dividend from S Co. Ltd (gross)	125	(125)	
	3,875	250	3,875
Deduct from minority shareholders' interest in Balance sheet		250	—
Depreciation	8,200	4,300	
Add Additional charge on machinery revalued		1,000	
	8,200	5,300	13,500
Transfers to reserve	4,000	4,000	
Less Minority shareholders' proportion		800	
	4,000	3,200	7,200

Minority shareholders' share of current profit:

Trading profit		16,000	
Less Depreciation (4,300 + 1,000)	5,300		
Directors' emoluments	2,000		
Corporation tax	5,500		
Preference dividends	750		
	13,550		
	£2,450		
⅕ thereof	490		
Preference shareholders' dividends (gross)	500		
	£990		

Cost of control of S Co. Ltd

Cost of shares	£23,000	Ordinary shares	£20,000
Capital reserve c/d	2,600	Pre-acquisition profit	2,400
		Excess on revaluation of machinery (4/5 × (5,000 − 1,000))	3,200
	£25,600		£25,600
		Balance b/d	£2,600

Minority shareholders

Preference dividend paid	£250	Ordinary shares	£5,000
Balance c/d	18,540	Preference shares	10,000
		Pre-acquisition profit	2,000
		Share of excess on revaluation of machinery	800
		Share of current profit	490
		Preference share dividends (gross)	500
	£18,790		£18,790
		Balance b/d	£18,300

H COMPANY LTD AND SUBSIDIARY

Consolidated Balance Sheet, 31st March 19—

Authorised and issued share capital:			Fixed assets:		
150,000 Ordinary			Freehold property		£107,700
shares (£1 each)		£150,000	Plant and machinery	£94,000	
Capital reserve		2,600	*Add* Revaluation	4,000	
Revenue reserves:					
General reserves	£14,200			98,000	
P. & L. Account	19,445		*Less* Depreciation	26,300	
		33,645			71,700
Deferred taxation			Investments at cost		22,000
account		14,500	Current assets:		
Minority shareholders' interest			Stock-in-trade	19,560	
in the Group		18,540	Trade debtors	22,825	
Current liabilities:			Bank	15,200	
Trade creditors	14,800				57,585
Bills payable	4,000				
Corporation tax	11,900				
Proposed dividend (gross)	9,000				
		39,700			
		£258,985			£258,985

Consolidated Profit and Loss Account for year ended 31st March 19—

Directors' emoluments	£8,000	Trading profit	£52,760
Depreciation	13,500	Investment income	
Minority shareholders' share of current profit	990	(Unquoted)	3,875
Balance c/d	34,145		
	£56,635		£56,635

Transfer to reserve		£7,200	Balance b/d	£34,145
Corporation tax		16,100	Balance b/f	17,600
Proposed dividend	10%			
(gross)		9,000		
Balance c/d		19,445		
		£51,745		£51,745

NOTE

As the detailed workings of the items on the Profit and Loss Account are shown, no separate revenue account in respect of the subsidiary has been made. The account should still be prepared where Balance Sheets only are to be consolidated.

HOLDING COMPANY'S PROFIT AND LOSS ACCOUNT FRAMED AS A CONSOLIDATED PROFIT AND LOSS ACCOUNT

Under section 149 of the Companies Act, 1948, a holding company which published a consolidated Profit and Loss Account need not also publish its own Profit and Loss Account, provided that the consolidated Profit and Loss Account: (a) complies with the requirements of the Act relating to consolidated Profit and Loss Accounts; and (b) shows how much of the consolidated profit or loss for the financial year is dealt with in the accounts of the company. More simply stated, provided the Profit or Loss Account shows how much of the consolidated profit or loss *for the financial year* is dealt with in the holding company's account, the company need not also publish an additional account in respect of its own affairs.

In presenting the holding company's Profit and Loss Account under section 149, it is advisable to consider initially on a summarised basis the adjustments which have to be made:

1. All the profits of the group are brought together, less total taxation.

2. Inter-company dividends are not shown as such.

3. The proportion of net profits attributable to minority shareholders is deducted.

4. The net profits of the subsidiaries are taken out, less the dividends paid and less the minority interests' profits already deducted.

5. This automatically leaves in the trading profits of the subsidiaries received by the holding company as dividends, so returning to the end figure shown on the original holding company's Profit and Loss Account.

6. In order to reveal the full amount of profits retained in the subsidiaries which refer to the group, the current net profit as retained

in the subsidiaries, plus the balances brought forward on the subsidiaries, are added.

The following is a simplified example to illustrate the first five points shown above.

Example

	Holding company ($\frac{3}{4}$ holding in S Co.) £10	Subsidiary £8
Trading Profit	£10	£8
Investment income (from subsidiary)	3	—
	13	
Taxation	2	2
	11	6
Proposed dividends	8	4
	3	2

Holding company's Profit and Loss Account framed as a consolidated Profit and Loss Account

Trading profit	£18
Taxation	4
	14
Minority shareholders' proportion of current profit ($\frac{1}{4} \times 6$)	1·5
	12·5

Profit retained in subsidiary $6 - 4 = 2$ (*i.e.* less dividend)	2·0	
Less minority shareholders' proportion (above)	5	
	—	1·5
		11·0
Proposed dividend		8
Per holding company's Profit and Loss Account		£3

Regarding the deduction from the retained profit in the subsidiary of the minority shareholders proportion, a quarter is deducted, as this proportion has been deducted from the *total* net profit above. Only three-quarters of the retained profit should therefore be deducted at this stage.

(a) Holding company and subsidiary with equity holdings

Continuing with a practical example of a holding company with two subsidiaries, a further matter is dealt with: retention in the subsidiaries of distributable profit brought forward from previous periods.

The workings in respect of the balances brought forward are similar to those explained for consolidated Profit and Loss Accounts, being the deduction of minority shareholders' interests and the elimination of preacquisition profit less that already credited to the minority equity. The workings for this are shown beneath the completed account.

	H Co. Ltd	S1 Ltd	S2 Ltd
Trading profits (after charging directors' emoluments, etc.)	£60,000	£30,000	£12,500
Investment income (unquoted)	1,800	500	
Dividends receivable from subsidiaries:			
From S1 Ltd	7,000	—	—
From S2 Ltd	3,000		
	10,000		
Profit prior to taxation	71,800	30,500	12,500
Corporation tax	23,200	11,500	4,100
	48,600	19,000	8,400
Profit b/f from previous year	18,000	3,200	4,500
	66,600	22,200	12,900
Transfer to general reserve	10,000	5,000	—
Proposed dividend (gross)	20,000	8,000	5,000
	30,000	13,000	5,000
	£36,600	£9,200	£7,900

H Co. Ltd holds 75% of the equity capital of S1 Ltd and 80% of S2 Ltd. When H Co. Ltd acquired its shares in S1 Ltd, the profit and loss credit balance amounted to £1400. H Co. Ltd acquired its shares in S2 Ltd when that company was first formed.

H CO. LTD

Consolidated Profit and Loss Account for year ended 19—

Trading profit	£102,500
Investment income	2,300
Profit prior to taxation	104,800
Corporation tax	38,800
	66,000

Proportion of current profit attributable to minority shareholders:

	S1 Ltd		S2 Ltd	
Profit after tax	£19,000		£8,400	
One quarter:	4,750	One fifth:	1,680	6,430
				59,570

Profit retained in subsidiaries:

	S1 Ltd	S2 Ltd	
Profit after tax	19,000	8,400	
Less dividends	8,000	5,000	
	11,000	3,400	
Less	2,750 (¼)	680 (⅕)	
	8,250	2,720	10,970
			48,600
Balance b/f from previous year			18,000
			66,600

Transfer to general reserve	£10,000	
Proposed dividend (gross)	20,000	
		30,000
		36,600

Add total profit retained by subsidiaries and attributable to the group:

Current profit	10,970	
Profit brought forward	4,950	
		15,920
		£52,520

WORKINGS

Balances brought forward

		S1 Ltd	S2 Ltd	
		£3,200	£4,500	
Less minority shareholders' proportion		800 (¼)	900 (⅕)	
		2,400	3,600	
Pre-acquisition profit	£1,400			
Less minority shareholders' proportion (allocated in above)	350			
		1,050		
		£1,350	£3,600	£4,950

(b) *Holding company with Preference share holdings*

The holding of Preference shares by the holding company, or others within the group, would necessitate adjustment to the proportions due to shareholders and retained profits.

Example

If in the preceding example the holding company had owned 20,000 7% preference shares in S1 Ltd out of a total issued of 40,000, the Revenue Account and the necessary calculations would have been as follows:

Trading profit	£102,500
Investment income	2,300
Profit prior to taxation	104,800
Corporation tax	38,800
	66,000

Proportion of current profit attributable
to minority shareholders:

	S1 Ltd	S2 Ltd	
After tax	£19,000		
Less Preference dividend	2,800	As shown	
		previously	
	16,200		
¼ thereof	4,050		
Add preference dividend to outside shareholders (½)	1,400		
	5,450	1,680	7,130
			58,870

Profit retained in subsidiaries:

	S1 Ltd	S2 Ltd	
Net profit	£19,000		
Less dividends	10,800	As shown	
		previously	
	8,200		
Less ¼	2,050		
	6,150	2,720	8,870
			50,000
Balance b/f from previous year			18,000
			68,000
Transfer to general reserve		10,000	
Proposed dividend (gross)		20,000	
			30,000
			38,000*

Add total profit retained by subsidiaries and attributable to the group:

Current profit	8,870	
Profit b/f	4,950	
		13,820
		£51,820

In actual practice the working papers of a group may seem, at first glance, different from the theory as presented above, more especially where a group is made up of a large number of companies. But on further examination it will become apparent that the underlying principles have still to be applied, their utilisation merely being adjusted to suit particular needs. The analysis entailed in combining a large number of items may necessitate numerous working papers, but if a summary is prepared of the various sections involved and these are reviewed in the first instance, a grasp of the situation can be obtained more rapidly.

* Agreeing with the holding company's balance of £36,600, plus £1400, due to the receipt of the preference dividend of £1400.

EXAMINATION QUESTIONS

Balance Sheets

1. At a given date the Balance Sheet of a holding company (H) is as follows:

H

Capital	£100	General assets	£84
Profit	10	Shares in subsidiary (S)	56
Liabilities	30		
	£140		£140

At the same date the Consolidated Balance Sheet of H and its subsidiary S is as follows:

H and S

Capital	£100	Goodwill on consolidation	£4
Profit	26	General assets	185
Minority interest	17		
Liabilities	46		
	£189		£189

H has an 80% interest in the capital of S (which consists entirely of Ordinary shares).

When H acquired S, the latter's profit balance was £5.

Construct the Balance Sheet of S at the given date. Show your calculations clearly. [B.Sc. (Econ.)]

2. On 1st January 1966 Weapons Investments Ltd, a new company, raised its first capital of £225,000 from the issue of 225,000 £1 shares at par, and on that date acquired the following shareholdings:

Axe Ltd: 30,000 shares of £1 each, fully paid, for £35,000.
Bow Ltd: 100,000 shares of £1 each, fully paid, for £72,000.
Club Ltd: 80,000 shares of £1 each, fully paid, for £92,000.

Apart from these transactions and those detailed below, Weapons Investments Ltd neither paid nor received other monies during 1966.

The following are the summarised draft Balance Sheets of the subsidiary companies as on 31st December, 1966:

	Axe Ltd	Bow Ltd	Club Ltd
Goodwill	£4,000	—	£15,000
Freehold property	18,000	£41,000	50,000
Plant	16,000	30,000	12,000
Stock	11,000	32,000	21,000
Debtors	4,000	8,000	17,000
Cash at bank	1,000	2,000	11,500
Profit and Loss Account	—	18,000	—
	£54,000	£131,000	£126,500

Share capital	40,000	120,000	100,000
Reserves (as on 1st January 1966)	3,000	—	7,500
Profit and Loss Account	6,000	—	15,000
Creditors	5,000	11,000	4,000
	£54,000	£131,000	£126,500

The following information is relevant:

(a) The freehold property of Club Ltd is to be revalued at £65,000 as on 1st January 1966.

(b) Additional depreciation for the year 1966 of £3000 on the plant of Bow Ltd is to be provided.

(c) The stock of Axe Ltd as on 31st December 1966 has been undervalued by £2000 and is to be adjusted.

(d) As on 31st December 1966 Weapons Investments Ltd owed Axe Ltd £3000 and is owed £6000 by Bow Ltd; Club Ltd is owed £1000 by Axe Ltd and £2000 by Bow Ltd.

(e) The balances on Profit and Loss Account as on 31st December 1965, were: Axe Ltd, £2000 (credit); Bow Ltd, £12,000 (debit); Club Ltd, £4000 (credit). The credit balances of Axe Ltd and Club Ltd were wholly distributed as dividends in March 1966.

(f) During 1966, Axe Ltd and Club Ltd declared and paid interim dividends of 8% and 10% respectively. No final dividends are to be provided.

You are required to prepare the consolidated Balance Sheet of Weapons Investments Ltd and its subsidiary companies as on 31st December 1966. Ignore taxation. [C.A. 1967

3. Bough Ltd made an offer to acquire all the shares in Twig Ltd at a price of £2·50 per share, to be satisfied by the allotment of five shares in Bough Ltd for every four shares in Twig Ltd.

By the date of expiration of the offer, which was 1st January 1966, shareholders owning 75% of the shares in Twig Ltd had accepted, and the acquisition was effective from that date.

The accounting date of Twig Ltd was 31st March in each year, but, to conform with Bough Ltd, accounts were prepared to 30th June 1966, covering the fifteen months to that date.

The draft summarised accounts of the companies as on 30th June 1966, which do not include any entries regarding the acquisition of shares in Twig Ltd, were as follows:

BALANCE SHEETS

as on 30th June 1966

	Bough Ltd	*Twig Ltd*
Share capital—Ordinary shares of £1 each		
Authorised	£300,000	£75,000

Issued and fully paid	150,000	60,000
Revenue reserves		
Profit and Loss Account	£62,000	20,000
General Reserve	55,000	—
	117,000	
Current liabilities	27,000	7,000
Corporation tax	33,000	6,000
	£327,000	£93,000

Freehold property, at cost		200,000		38,000
Plant and machinery, at cost	50,000		£12,000	
Less depreciation	18,000		3,000	
		32,000		9,000
		232,000		47,000
Quoted investments, at cost		7,000		—
Stock, at cost		32,000		21,000
Debtors		41,000		17,000
Balance at bank		15,000		8,000
		£327,000		£93,000

PROFIT AND LOSS ACCOUNTS

	Bough Ltd Year	Twig Ltd Fifteen months
Period ended 30th June 1966		
Balance b/f	£14,000	£12,000
Profit for period	80,000	18,000
	£94,000	£30,000
Taxation for period	32,000	6,000
Interim dividend paid 30th November 1965	—	4,000
Balance c/f	62,000	20,000
	£94,000	£30,000

The directors of Bough Ltd had recommended the payment of a final dividend of 20% to all shareholders on the register on 30th June 1966. The directors of Twig Ltd had proposed a final dividend of 12½%, payable on 30th September 1966.

You are required to prepare the consolidated Balance Sheet of Bough Ltd as on 30th June, 1966.

Ignore income tax.   [C.A. (1966)

4. The summarised Balance Sheets of Trunk Ltd and Bough Ltd as on 31st December 1964 were as follows:

	Trunk Ltd	Bough Ltd
Authorised and issued share capital—Ordinary shares of £1 each	£120,000	£60,000
Share Premium Account	18,000	—
Capital reserve on 1st January 1964	8,000	6,000
General reserve on 1st January 1964	15,000	10,000
Profit and Loss Account on 1st January 1964	40,000	8,000
Profit for 1964	16,000	5,000
Creditors	35,000	11,000
Current Account—Bough Ltd	2,700	—
	£254,700	£100,000
Goodwill, at cost	25,000	7,500
Plant, at cost, *less* depreciation	72,000	45,000
Fixtures, at cost, *less* depreciation	13,000	5,700
Stock, at cost	18,000	12,000
Debtors	62,700	21,100
Trade investment, at cost	—	2,500
Balance at bank	10,000	3,000
Current Account—Trunk Ltd	—	3,200
Shares in Bough Ltd—48,000 shares, at cost	54,000	—
	£254,700	£100,000

The following information is relevant:

(a) On 1st January 1964 Trunk Ltd had allotted 36,000 shares at a premium of £0·50 each in exchange for 48,000 shares in Bough Ltd.

(b) In arriving at the consideration for the shares in Bough Ltd, plant was revalued at £54,000 and fixtures at £5000, and the trade investment was deemed to be valueless. No adjustment was made in the books in respect of these valuations, and there were no purchases or sales of these assets during 1964, but the directors wish to give effect to the revaluations in the consolidated accounts.

(c) The depreciated figures for plant and fixtures at 31st December 1964 are after providing depreciation for 1964 on the book values at 1st January 1964 at the rates of 10% and 5% per annum respectively.

(d) The stock of Bough Ltd. included £4000 goods from Trunk Ltd, invoiced at cost plus 25%.

(e) A cheque for £500 from Trunk Ltd to Bough Ltd sent before 31st December 1964 was not received by the latter company until January 1965.

You are required to prepare the summarised consolidated Balance Sheet of Trunk Ltd, and its subsidiary Bough Ltd as on 31st December 1964.

[C.A. (1965)]

5. The summarised Balance Sheets of Shellfish Ltd and its subsidiary companies, Lobster Ltd and Limpet Ltd at 31st December 1960 were as follows:

Shellfish Ltd

Issued share capital:		Fixed assets	£28,000
100,000 shares of £1 each	£100,000	40,000 shares in Lobster Ltd	
Profit and Loss Account (in-		at cost	63,000
cluding the 1959 dividend		Loan to Lobster Ltd	1,500
received from Limpet Ltd		15,000 shares in Limpet Ltd	
but excluding the proposed		at cost	22,000
dividend for 1960)	21,500	Current assets	39,500
Creditors	32,500		
	£154,000		£154,000

Lobster Ltd

Issued share capital:		Fixed assets	£49,750
40,000 shares of £1 each	£40,000	Current assets	31,250
Profit and Loss Account:			
At 31st Dec. 1959 £16,600			
Add net profit 1960 5,700			
	22,300		
Loan from Shellfish Ltd	1,500		
Other creditors	17,200		
	£81,000		£81,000

Limpet Ltd

Issued share capital:		Fixed assets	£19,850
20,000 shares of £1 each	£20,000	Current assets	14,750
Profit and Loss Account:			
At 31st Dec. 1959 £3,600			
Add net profit, 1960 2,800			
	6,400		
Less proposed dividend 1,000			
	5,400		
Proposed dividend	1,000		
Creditors	8,200		
	£34,600		£34,600

Shellfish Ltd acquired the shares in both subsidiaries on 31st December 1959.

Lobster Ltd paid no dividend for 1959, and none is proposed for 1960.

The Profit and Loss Account of Limpet Ltd for 1959 was debited with a proposed dividend of £1600, which was paid in 1960.

You are required to prepare the Consolidated Balance Sheet of the group at 31st December 1960. Show your calculation of the items. Ignore taxation.

[I.B.

Profit and Loss Accounts

6. The following are the preliminary draft Profit and Loss Accounts of Magnum Ltd, and of its subsidiary Opus Ltd (both carrying on business as manufacturers) for the year 1961:

	Magnum Ltd	Opus Ltd		Magnum Ltd	Opus Ltd
General expenses	£4,800	£1,400	Unappropriated balance from 1960	£95,000	38,020
Audit fee, fixed by the members	1,730	920	Operating profit, 1961	52,000	28,548
Directors' emoluments:			Income from investments gross:		
Fees	1,400	600	Alpha Ltd (an associated company)	1,040	
Executive salaries	8,750	4,500	4% Consols (acquired in 1960)	480	720
Depreciation of plant	4,100	2,700	Opus Ltd dividends for 1961:		
Taxation:			Interim received in September 1961	4,000	
Income tax, 1962–3	11,000	5,000	Final, proposed	8,000	
Profits tax, 1961	4,200	1,650	Profits tax overprovision for past periods	800	
Income tax suffered by deduction	5,239	279	Transfer from general reserve		2,000
Income tax underprovided for past periods	2,200				
Appropriations made and proposed:					
Transfer to reserve	8,500				
Dividends (net) for 1961:					
Preference, paid	1,150				
Ordinary, interim paid		3,675			
final proposed	11,500	7,350			
Balances	96,751	41,214			
	£161,320	£69,288		£161,320	£69,288

You ascertain that:

(a) Magnum Ltd owns 40,000 Ordinary shares in Opus Ltd, which it acquired on 1st April 1961; the issued share capital of Opus Ltd is 60,000 Ordinary shares of £1 each fully paid.

(b) During 1961 Magnum Ltd redeemed at par, out of profits, 1500 redeemable Preference shares of £1 each fully paid, but that no entries had been made in the books in respect thereof other than those recording the cash payment.

(c) In the accounts of each company, depreciation of motor vehicles has been apportioned and charged to different departments and the operating profits shown are after charging such amounts, which totalled for Magnum Ltd £1800 and for Opus Ltd, £950.

(d) All the directors of Opus Ltd are directors of Magnum Ltd.

(e) Following a discussion with the Inland Revenue, it was agreed in October 1961 that a director of Magnum Ltd should be assessed to income tax, for the year 1959–60, on £500, representing the personal benefit to him of certain expenses paid on his behalf by the company during the year 1959.

(f) Magnum Ltd does not intend to publish its own Profit and Loss Account but, instead, to publish a Consolidated Profit and Loss Account as permitted by s. 149 of the Companies Act, 1948.

You are required to prepare in vertical form the Consolidated Profit and Loss Account, giving the minimum information required by the Companies Act, 1948. [C.A. (1963)]

7. The following are summaries of the Profit and Loss Accounts for the year ended 31st December 1960 of Purple Ltd and its three subsidiary companies, Red Ltd, Yellow Ltd and Green Ltd.

Purple Ltd

Proposed dividend	124,000	Net trading profit for the year	£42,370
Balance c/f	46,370	Dividends received	3,000
		Balance from 1959	25,000
	£70,370		£70,370

Red Ltd

Interim Preference dividend paid	£300	Net profit for the year	£830
Balance, c/f	780	Balance from 1959	250
	£1,080		£1,080

Yellow Ltd

Interim dividend paid	£4,500	Net profit for the year	£14,700
Proposed final dividend	4,500	Balance from 1959	18,000
Balance, c/f	23,700		
	£32,700		£32,700

Green Ltd

Net loss for the year	£4,160	Balance from 1959	£3,850
		Balance c/f	310
	£4,160		£4,160

The issued share capital of the subsidiaries is as follows:

	Red	Yellow	Green
Ordinary: Total	30,000	60,000	50,000
Held by Purple Ltd	24,000	40,000	50,000
6% cumulative Preference:			
Total	10,000	—	—
Held by Purple Ltd	Nil	—	—

All shares are of £1 each and all are fully paid.

Purple Ltd also held four-fifths of 150 5% Debentures of £1000 each issued by Yellow Ltd in 1956. Yellow Ltd paid no Debenture interest during 1960 and no provision for outstanding interest has been made in the accounts of either Yellow Ltd or Purple Ltd.

Purple Ltd acquired the shares in Red Ltd and Green Ltd on 31st December 1959. The shares and Debentures in Yellow Ltd were acquired on 31st December 1958, when the credit balance on the Profit and Loss Account of that company was £12,600. The net profit of Yellow Ltd for the year 1959 was £5400.

In January 1960 Green Ltd paid a final dividend of £2500 for the year 1959, which was correctly dealt with in the books of Purple Ltd.

In December 1960 Purple Ltd sold goods to Green Ltd for £360 and at 31st December 1960 these goods were included in the closing stock of Green Ltd at that amount. The cost of these goods to Purple Ltd was £270.

You are required to prepare a Consolidated Profit and Loss Account for the year 1960, showing your workings. Ignore taxation. [I.B.

8. Maryhill Ltd—ladies' garment manufacturer—in 1962 purchased 60,000 of the £1 Ordinary shares fully paid in Kirkintilloch Drycleaning Co. Ltd for £75,000, when the credit balance on Profit and Loss Account was £1400.

In 1965 Maryhill Ltd purchased the whole of the issued capital of Lochee Rainwear Ltd for £10,000, when the credit balance on Profit and Loss Account was £1700.

The draft Profit and Loss Accounts for the year to 31st December 1971 are given below and you are required to prepare a Consolidated Profit and Loss Account of Maryhill Ltd and its subsidiary companies, incorporating all transactions of the group as they affect the members of Maryhill Ltd. The holding company does not publish its legal Profit and Loss Account.

	Maryhill Ltd	Kirkintilloch Drycleaning Co. Ltd	Lochee Rainwear Ltd
Trading profit	£95,200	£60,700	£62,300
after charging:			
Depreciation	£20,000	£15,675	£10,720
Director's emoluments	17,500	10,200	14,500
	£37,500	£25,875	£25,220
Interests and dividends on trade investments		£2,100	£3,200
Dividend from subsidiary companies (gross)	£71,306		
	£166,506	£62,800	£65,500
Less Corporation tax	£79,806	£32,700	£29,500
Surplus after tax	£86,700	£30,100	£36,000
Brought forward	17,400	6,100	10,400
	£104,100	£36,200	£46,400
Transfer to general reserve		£24,000	
Dividends on Ordinary share capital	£50,000 (gross)	6,125 (gross)	£40,000 (gross)
	£50,000	£30,125	£40,000
Balance c/f	£54,100	£6,075	£6,400
Directors' emoluments:			
W	£10,000	£1,000	£3,000
X		7,200	1,000
Y	1,500	1,000	8,000
Z	6,000	1,000	2,500
	£17,500	£10,200	£14,500

[C.A. (S)

Balance Sheets and Revenue Accounts

9. Detail six adjustments which may be required during the consolidation of accounts and state the steps which an auditor would take to verify the accuracy of the adjustments.   [C.C.A.

10. From the following data prepare a Consolidated Balance Sheet of M Ltd and its subsidiaries at 31st December 19—.

Balances as at 31st December 19—:

	M Ltd	X Ltd	Y Ltd
Investments at cost:			
115,000 Ordinary stock of X Ltd	£100,000		
75,000 Ordinary stock of Y Ltd	100,000		
20,000 Ordinary stock of X Ltd			£20,000
Balances at banks	40,000	£20,000	10,000
Debtors	60,000	30,000	15,000
Stock in trade	80,000	30,000	40,000
Land and buildings at cost *less* Depreciation	200,000	100,000	50,000
Plant at cost *less* Depreciation	150,000	80,000	75,000
Payments in advance	10,000	5,000	2,000
	£740,000	£265,000	£212,000

	M Ltd	X Ltd	Y Ltd
Creditors	100,000	80,000	40,000
Mortgage on property	—	—	56,000
Ordinary stock (units of £1)	400,000	150,000	100,000
Profit and Loss Account	240,000	35,000	16,000
	£740,000	£265,000	£212,000

The Profit and Loss Account balances are made up as follows:

	M Ltd	X Ltd	Y Ltd
Balance at 1st January 19—	£200,000	£15,000	£20,000
Profit for year 19—	100,000	20,000	14,000
	300,000	35,000	34,000
Deduct dividends paid	60,000	—	18,000
	£240,000	£35,000	£16,000

M Ltd purchased its holding in X Ltd and Y Ltd on 1st January 19—. Y Ltd acquired its holding in X Ltd on the formation of X Ltd.
                [C.C.A.

11. Aurillac Ltd acquired the controlling interest in Bezier Ltd, cum dividend, on 30th June 1965, and Bezier Ltd acquired the share capital of Chatel Ltd on 30th June 1966. The following are summaries of the balances appearing in the books of the companies on 30th June 1967.

	Aurillac Ltd	Bezier Ltd	Chatel Ltd
Authorised and issued capital:			
Ordinary shares of £1 each, fully paid	£425,000	£120,000	£45,000
8% cumulative Preference shares of £1 each fully paid	—	37,500	—
Profit and Loss Account	106,800	68,550	11,475
7% Debentures		15,000	
Accumulated depreciation on fixed assets	98,000	56,000	17,000
Provision for accrued Debenture interest	—	1,050	—
Dividends proposed	45,000	16,800	—
Creditors	104,100	44,900	26,125
	£778,900	£359,800	£99,600
Fixed assets	£431,500	£215,100	£69,750
90,000 Ordinary shares in Bezier Ltd at cost	156,000	—	—
45,000 Ordinary shares in Chatel Ltd at cost	—	60,300	—
£9000 7% Debentures of Bezier Ltd	9,000	—	—
Debtors	151,500	62,400	24,600
Other current assets	30,900	22,000	5,250
	£778,900	£359,800	£99,600

The Profit and Loss Account balances of the subsidiaries are made up as follows:

	Bezier Ltd	Chatel Ltd
Balances as at 30th June 1965	£52,200	£8,325
Net profit for year ended 30th June 1966	6,150	1,800
Balances as at 30th June 1966	58,350	10,125
Net profit for year ended 30th June 1967	27,000	1,350
	85,350	11,475
Dividends proposed	16,800	—
	£68,550	£11,475

Provision had been made for the dividend of £3000 on the Preference shares and the proposed Ordinary dividend of £9600 in arriving at the balance of the Profit and Loss Account of Bezier Ltd on 30th June 1965. Both dividends were subsequently paid. The dividend received by Aurillac Ltd from Bezier Ltd had been credited to the Profit and Loss Account of Aurillac Ltd during the following year. No dividends were declared or paid by Bezier Ltd in respect of the year to 30th June 1966, and no accounting entries had been made by Aurillac Ltd in respect of Debenture interest due from, or dividends for, the year to 30th June 1967 proposed to be distributed by Bezier Ltd. The proposed dividends represent two year Preference dividends and a dividend on the Ordinary shares.

Goods purchased by Aurillac Ltd for £12,520 and invoiced to Bezier Ltd during 1966–67 for £18,480 remained unsold and were included at the latter figure in Bezier Ltd's stock in trade. The respective schedules of debtors and creditors of the two companies reflected a balance of £2500 owing by Bezier Ltd in respect of this stock.

You are required to prepare a consolidated Balance Sheet of the group as at 30th June, 1967, ignoring both taxation and the comparative figures for the previous financial year. [C.C.A.

12. Fore Ltd acquired the following shareholding in Aft Ltd:

9000 Ordinary shares on 31st December 1968 at a cost of £8750
3000 Ordinary shares on 31st March 1970 at a cost of £3860

and the skeleton Balance Sheets of the two companies at 31st December 1970 are as follows:

	Fore	Aft		Fore	Aft
Paid-up Ordinary shares			Plant etc. at cost	£75,639	£13,710
(£1 each)	£50,000	£12,000	Less Depreciation	16,943	3,422
Paid-up 8% Preference					
shares (£1 each)	20,000	nil		58,696	10,288
Profit and Loss Account	9,070	3,016	Investment in Aft Ltd	12,610	—
5% Debentures	7,500	5,000	Stock	16,849	9,420
Creditors	14,815	7,403	Debtors	15,121	7,610
Dividends received from			Cash	209	101
Aft Ltd	2,100	—			
	£103,485	£27,419		£103,485	£27,419

For many years the two companies have declared an Ordinary dividend of 10%, which is paid, with the Preference dividend, on 1st May in the following year. Provision is to be made for the same dividends this year.

The Profit and Loss Account balance of Aft Ltd is made up in the following fashion:

Balance at 31st December 1968	£744
Profit for the year 1969	1840
	2584
Less Dividend	1200
	1384
Profit for 1970	1632
	£3016

You are required to prepare a Consolidated Balance Sheet as at 31st December 1970 for the group in accordance with normally accepted principles. Taxation has been and is to be ignored and the full statutory form of Balance Sheet is not required. [C.C.A.

PART FOUR

INFORMATION FOR MANAGEMENT CONTROL

CHAPTER XIX

INTERPRETATION OF ACCOUNTS
(I) ACCOUNTING RATIOS

BEFORE proceeding with the more general aspects of the interpretation of accounts and Balance Sheet criticism, it may be helpful to consider first one of the useful aids available to the management accountant in assessing the position and formulating theories from the data given.

It must be emphasised at the outset that although accounting ratios are a useful guide in such work they are not normally exact enough to base definite statements on. They are *only* a guide and must always be used in conjunction with other information of a comparable nature.

In order to clarify their meaning, examples are given commencing with a simple illustration of their use, leading on to their practical application in the following order:

(*a*) Balance Sheet ratios.

(*b*) Profit and Loss Account ratios (or Operational ratios).

(*c*) Efficiency ratios.

(*d*) Practical application of ratios.

(*e*) Miscellaneous ratios.

Using the simple Balance Sheet and Revenue Accounts shown below the following ratios can be obtained. Some notes as to their application have been added.

BALANCE SHEET AT—

Ordinary share capital	£100,000	Fixed assets		£162,000
6% Preference shares	50,000			
Revenue reserve	30,000	Current assets:		
	———	Stock	£22,000	
	180,000	Debtors	51,000	
		Bills receivable	2,000	
7% Debentures	20,000	Bank	12,000	
Current Liabilities:			———	87,000
Corporation Tax	15,000			
Creditors	34,000			
	———			———
	£249,000			£249,000

459

TRADING AND PROFIT AND LOSS ACCOUNT FOR YEAR ENDED—

Opening stock	£16,000	Sales: Cash	£64,000	
Purchases	350,000	Credit	360,000	
	£366,000			£424,000
Less Closing stock	22,000			
Cost of sales	£344,000			
Gross profit c/d	80,000			
	£424,000			£424,000
Establishment expenses	£3,000	Gross profit b/d		£80,000
General and administration expenses	30,000			
Selling and distribution expenses	5,000			
Financial expenses (inc. debenture interest)	2,000			
Net profit c/d	40,000			
	£80,000			£80,000
Preference dividend (gross)	£3,000	Net profit b/d		£40,000
Taxation (say)	15,000			
Balance c/f	30,000	Balance b/f		8,000
	£48,000			£48,000

BALANCE SHEET RATIOS

1. TESTS OF LIQUIDITY (*i.e.* availability of funds).

(a) *Current ratio*

$$\frac{\text{Current assets}}{\text{Current liabilities and provisions}} \quad i.e. \quad \frac{£87,000}{£49,000} = \text{approx. } 1{\cdot}8{:}1$$

At one time 2:1 was considered ideal, but high ratios may be due to poor investment policies, excessive stocks, etc. A low ratio may signify a shortage of working capital.

In this case, as with accounting ratios in general, it is necessary to consider the type of business concerned. Only readily realisable investments and short term debts should be taken into the computation. If tax reserve certificates are held, they can be included too.

(b) *"Quick assets," "liquidity" or "acid test" ratio*

$$\frac{\text{Liquid assets}}{\text{Current liabilities}} \quad i.e. \quad \frac{£65,000}{£49,000} = 1{\cdot}3{:}1$$

1:1 is considered adequate.

Stocks may be a governing factor in the current ratio. The liquidity ratio is therefore more satisfactory from the point of view of the settlement of unsecured creditors.

A number of factors influence this ratio. Overstocking and falling profits, for example, or selling weakness without a corresponding decrease in output, may be the reasons for a fall. Thus it constitutes a critical test, for a business with bright prospects may run into danger if it is not in a position to meet its current commitments.

Since investors tend to be impressed by a seemingly "safe" liquid position, care has to be taken when this ratio is used, for the device of "window dressing" is sometimes resorted to: debtors pressed for payment before the Balance Sheet date, orders accelerated to bring them within the financial period. Another instance is the practice, after the declaration of interim dividends and dispatch of dividend warrants (some companies no longer declare final dividends), of not debiting cash with the amount of the dividend. Instead, an "Unclaimed Dividends Account" is shown on the Balance Sheet and the cash left intact. The practice is open to criticism since it is obviously done to show a larger bank balance by the amount of the unpresented dividend warrants.

This last case is quoted since it serves to reveal the need for careful use of the liquidity ratio as a guide to the financial soundness of a business.

Contrary to what might be expected, this ratio may fall in a time of prosperity, because increased activity may lead to larger stocks and more debtors but less cash. Conversely, when trade is slowing down stocks may be disposed of without renewal and debtors may decrease.

Increased liquid resources more usually indicate favourable trading, but on the other hand they may reveal an unwise use of funds which could be better employed.

2. CAPITAL GEARING RATIO

$$\frac{\text{Equity capital}}{\text{Fixed interest bearing securities}}$$

This is dealt with in Chapter III. In the present example the gearing ratio is

$$\frac{£100,000}{£70,000} = 1\cdot43$$

which is satisfactory, being neither too high nor too low.

3. CAPITAL EMPLOYED TO LIABILITIES (OR PROPRIETORS RATIO)

$$\frac{\text{Capital employed}}{\text{Liabilities (short and long term)}} \quad i.e. \quad \frac{£180,000}{£69,000} = 2\cdot6:1$$

"Capital employed" here means the amount of capital subscribed

and ploughed back into the company. A fall in this ratio may reveal
weakness due to reliance on "outside" capitalisation.

The proprietors should subscribe sufficient capital to cover the fixed
assets, intangible assets, investments in other companies and a reasonable figure for working capital. This ratio must therefore show an excess in respect of capital employed if the position is to be regarded as
satisfactory.

The so-called "proprietors ratio" can be inverted to give the creditors ratio (*see* 7 below).

NOTE

"Capital employed" should be distinguished from "capital subscribed."
Reserves ploughed back are funds put into the business just as much as those
paid in on capitalisation and are therefore employed through the use of the
assets they represent.

4. (a) CAPITAL EMPLOYED TO FIXED ASSETS RATIO

$$\frac{\text{Capital employed}}{\text{Fixed assets}} \quad i.e. \quad \frac{£180,000}{£162,000} = 1\cdot1:1$$

As mentioned in (3) above, it is normally expected that the proprietors—including any holders of Preference capital—shall provide
sufficient funds to cover the fixed assets of the business, since they
constitute the main structure of the company. If the margin is quite
small, it means the working capital is being supplied by outside sources
—a financial weakness unless, as in this case, the margin is increased by
a long-term debt. In such businesses as property owning companies,
however, it is quite usual for secured loan capital to cover a large
proportion of the fixed assets.

(b) FIXED ASSETS TO CAPITAL EMPLOYED RATIO (OR FIXED ASSETS TO NET WORTH RATIO—F/W RATIO)

If the figures shown in 4(a) are inverted they give the F/W ratio. It
is usually expressed as a percentage:

$$\frac{\text{Fixed assets}}{\text{Net worth}} \quad i.e. \quad \frac{£162,000}{£180,000} = 90\%.$$

The ratio serves to reveal the company's position with regard to
the points mentioned in 4(a) above, a high F/W ratio usually implying
a low current ratio with correspondingly inadequate liquid resources.
Conversely, a low F/W ratio may indicate a "top heavy" structure with
insufficient earning power.

This ratio must be used with discretion according to the type of
business concerned, as must the following ratio.

5. NET CURRENT ASSETS TO FIXED ASSETS RATIO

$$\frac{\text{Net current assets}}{\text{Fixed assets}} \quad i.e. \quad \frac{£38,000}{£162,000} = 1:4\cdot25$$

This ratio may vary according to the type of business concerned. It will be higher for a manufacturing company than for a trading company because plant and premises to house it are not called for in the latter case. The ratio may reveal an inadequate use of fixed assets as compared with similar concerns.

The net current assets constitute the working capital and if they are falling in comparison with the fixed assets, it may be a sign of weakness.

Care has to be exercised in the use of these last three ratios. They are very useful for comparative purposes, but comparison is often difficult because different policies are pursued by different companies. For example, the reserves to equity capital may be higher in one company than another owing to the creation of a capital reserve on the revaluation of properties. For the same reason the F/W ratio would vary as between two companies. Different depreciation policies would have this effect where historical cost bases are employed or where reserves are created for replacing as well as writing off existing assets.

Wherever possible, the revalued figures should be used, as in the valuation of securities (*see* Chapter XVI). If they are not available, the book figures must be used; an estimate of price increases would be too approximate.

CREDIT CONTROL

6 (a) DEBTORS RATIO

The average collection period can be calculated by this ratio. It will be observed that the credit sales (cash sales must obviously be excluded) are divided by 365. This enables the figure for "sales days" to be arrived at, so facilitating easy calculation of the period outstanding.

$$\frac{\text{Debtors}}{\text{Average daily credit sales}} \ i.e. \ \frac{£51,000}{360,000 \div 365} = 51 \text{ days or 7 weeks 2 days.}$$

If the division by 365 to arrive at the average daily sales were not used the fraction for the year shown above would be 10/72, which is an awkward figure for calculation and illustration purposes.

6 (b) CREDITORS RATIO

This is similar in application to the debtors ratio, the purchases figure being substituted.

$$\frac{\text{Creditors}}{\text{Purchases}} \ i.e. \ \frac{£34,000}{£350,000} \times \frac{365}{1} = 35 \text{ days or 5 weeks}$$

PERCENTAGE BALANCE SHEET

Now that we have dealt with the main Balance Sheet ratios, a percentage Balance Sheet is given below. Its usefulness should be apparent; for example, the position mentioned in (3) above with regard to capital employed and finance obtained from outside sources is made abundantly clear.

BALANCE SHEET AT —

Ordinary shares	£100,000	40%	Fixed assets		£162,000	65%
6% Preference shares	50,000	20	Current assets:			
Revenue reserves	30,000	12	Stock	22,000		
			Debtors	51,000		
	180,000	72	Bills re-			
7% Debentures	20,000	8	ceivable	2,000		
Corporation tax	15,000	6	Bank	12,000		
Creditors	34,000	14			87,000	35
	£249,000	100%			£249,000	100%

PROFIT AND LOSS ACCOUNT RATIOS
(OR OPERATIONAL RATIOS)

1. STOCK TURNOVER RATIO

This shows how often stocks "flow" through a firm in the course of a year. An increase usually indicates expanding business and a decrease the opposite. Again, it may be useful for purposes of comparison with concerns of a similar nature.

$$\frac{\text{Cost of sales}}{\text{Average stock}} \ i.e. \ \frac{£344,000}{£19,000} = 18 \text{ times}$$

The average stock held is taken to be:

$$\frac{\text{Opening} + \text{Closing stock}}{2}$$

The turnover rate in this case appears rather high. If it were decided to increase the stock held by £20,000 in the following year, with exactly the same sales and cost of sales, the average stock would be £32,000, i.e. (£22,000 + £42,000) ÷ 2. This would give a turnover rate of £344,000/32,000, i.e. 11 times, which is considerably less than the 18 shown above. This is an exaggerated case, but it shows how greatly turnover figures may be influenced by opening and closing stock figures.

Further ratios may be used for different types of product or for various departments. But any difference in the basis used for stock valuation would make the comparison useless.

The stock turnover may be expressed in various ways, e.g.:

(a) $\dfrac{\text{Cost of sales}}{\text{Average stock}} \ i.e. \ \dfrac{£344,000}{£19,000}$

= stock turned over 18 times per annum

(b) $\dfrac{\text{Average stock}}{\text{Cost of sales}} \ i.e. \ \dfrac{£19,000}{£344,000} = 0.055$ turnover ratio

(c) $\dfrac{\text{Average stock}}{\text{Cost of sales}} \times 100 = \dfrac{£19,000 \times 100}{£344,000}$

$= 5 \cdot 5\%$ stock turnover percentage

(d) $\dfrac{\text{Average stock} \times \text{Sales days}}{\text{Cost of sales}} = \dfrac{£19,000 \times 365}{£344,000}$

$=$ Period taken to turn over stock, 21 days

2. GROSS PROFIT RATIO

This ratio, which is invariably expressed as a percentage, reveals the average mark-up on goods sold above their cost. Expenses such as carriage inwards may be included in the cost of the goods, but otherwise expenses of any kind are excluded.

$$\frac{\text{Gross profit}}{\text{Net sales}} \ i.e. \ \frac{£80,000}{£424,000} = 19\%$$

Where a number of different products are sold, it is necessary to obtain the gross profit on each one, as the average by itself is of little use. It will be seen in the following example that the overall gross profit is shown as 18·8% yet none of the three products earns exactly that. It is possible for one or more of them to be showing a gross loss and for this to be covered by others which show a profit.

Example

If the sales of a company shown were made up of three different products, the position might be as follows:

Product	A		B		C		Total	
	£	%	£	%	£	%	£	%
Sales	180,000	100	100,000	100	144,000	100	424,000	100
Less Cost of sales	150,000	83·3	80,000	80	114,000	79·2	344,000	81·2
Cross profit	£30,000	16·6	£20,000	20	£30,000	20·8	£80,000	18·8

Gross Profit is also discussed in Chapter XXI.

3. NET INCOME AS A PERCENTAGE OF EQUITY CAPITAL

$$\frac{\text{Net profit (after taxation)} - \text{Preference dividend}}{\text{Equity capital}}$$

$$\frac{£25,000 - 3,000}{£100,000} = 22\%$$

Note however that the net income as a percentage of equity capital employed is 18%, *i.e.* £22,000/130,000.

4. TOTAL CONTRIBUTION TO SALES RATIO (OR PROFIT/VOLUME—P/V—RATIO)

"Contribution" may be explained as the difference between sales and the variable cost of the sales or as fixed costs plus net profit.

Marginal cost is in effect all the variable costs incurred in producing the sales, the remaining proportion of the sales figures being made up of fixed costs plus the net profit element.

This ratio shows the increase in profit which will be due to any given increase in sales and may be expressed in any of the following ways:

$$\text{P/V ratio} = \frac{\text{Fixed cost} + \text{Net profit}}{\text{Sales}} \times 100$$

$$\text{or}\quad \frac{\text{Contribution per unit}}{\text{Selling price per unit}} \times 100$$

$$\text{or}\quad \frac{\text{Sales} - \text{Variable cost}}{\text{Sales}} \times 100$$

Where sales are made up of various products, as in (2) above, it will be necessary to deal with each separately before aggregating them and deducting fixed costs to calculate a net profit figure. Net profit may be calculated by the formula:

$$\text{Net profit} = (\text{Sales} \times \text{P/V ratio}) - \text{Fixed costs.}$$

Thus if there are a number of products it will be necessary to calculate the net profit in the following manner:

Net profit = (Sales of Article A $\times$ P/V ratio of Article A) + (Sales of Article B $\times$ P/V ratio of Article B) etc. $-$ Fixed costs.

See Chapter XII.

5. NET INCOME TO NET SALES RATIO (OR PROFIT/SALES—P/S—RATIO)

$$\frac{\text{Net income}}{\text{Net sales}}\ i.e.\ \frac{\pounds 40,000}{\pounds 424,000} = 9 \cdot 4\%.$$

As the P/V ratio excludes the contribution, or fixed costs plus net profit prior to taxation, on every variation of the P/V ratio the P/S ratio will vary by an equivalent percentage.

Example

	(£000's)		(£000's)	
Sales		424		424
Less Cost of sales	344		320	
Other variable expenses, say	10	354	9	329
		70		95
P/V ratio		17%		23% (+6%)
Fixed expenses, say	30		30	
Net profit	40		65	
Contribution	—	70	—	95
P/S ratio		9%		15% (+6%)

If fixed expenses vary, this will also affect the P/S ratio. For example, had the fixed expenses risen in Year 2 to £40,000, then the P/V ratio would have remained as shown at 23% but the P/S ratio would have fallen by 2% to 13%.

The profit ratio is often associated with efficiency, a rise implying a reduction in costs or some other increase in efficiency. It is true that cost reduction may influence the ratio but the effect of sales volume should be recognised. The greater the volume of sales, the lower the fixed costs to sales (FC/S) ratio becomes. If sales are £100,000 with fixed costs at £20,000 (FC/S ratio 20%), then if sales rise to £150,000, the FC/S ratio falls to $13\frac{1}{3}$%. The P/S ratio may be expressed as:

$$P/S \text{ ratio} = P/V \text{ ratio} - FC/S \text{ ratio.}$$

The influence of sales may be traced from the following table:

Sales	P/V ratio	FC/S ratio	P/S ratio
£100,000	22%	20%	2%
150,000	22%	$13\frac{1}{3}$%	$8\frac{2}{3}$%
180,000	22%	11%	11%

6. NET INCOME AS A PERCENTAGE OF CAPITAL EMPLOYED (OR RETURN ON NET WORTH—P/W—RATIO)

$$\frac{\text{Net income} - \text{Preference dividend}}{\text{Equity capital employed}} \quad i.e. \quad \frac{£40,000 - 3,000}{£130,000} = 28\cdot4\%$$

See p. 516 where return on investment is dealt with.

7. RATIO OF RESERVES TO EQUITY CAPITAL

$$\frac{\text{Reserves}}{\text{Equity capital}} \quad i.e. \quad \frac{£30,000}{£100,000} = 30\%.$$

The previous two ratios are most useful for comparative purposes. The financial ratio, shown here for convenience although it is not an operational ratio, serves to clarify (6) since it reveals any policy pursued with regard to growth stocks, etc. If a conservative distribution policy has been maintained this ratio may seem unduly high.

EFFICIENCY RATIOS

Numerous ratios are employed to indicate the efficiency of a company's operations, although the first-named below is probably the most widely used. Many are used in respect of operations compared to sales.

1. *Profit to capital employed.* Despite the difficulties which sometimes arise in defining capital employed (should intangible assets be included? should gross or net assets employed be used? etc.) the return on capital employed, as invested both externally and internally, is of vital importance. It is also not always possible to compare percentage returns on various companies, as loan capital is sometimes excluded; it is recommended that the net or gross *tangible* assets figure should be

used, but in any case comparison should only be made between companies of a similar nature.

Some figures are very revealing under this ratio, for whereas in the electrical industry's profit to capital employed in the U.K. is, on average, about 13%, the General Electric Corporation of America has an average of approximately 23%, and although the method of computation may account for some slight variation, nevertheless the difference is significant. Profit here being calculated prior to taxation. This ratio is dealt with more fully in conjunction with return on investment (see p. 516).

2. *Profit to sales.* The P/S ratio has been mentioned above. It may vary quite widely from industry to industry. It should improve more rapidly, *i.e.* at a disproportionate rate on the sales above break-even point, owing to the lower incidence of fixed costs.

3. *Sales to capital employed.* As a comparative ratio this may not *appear* to vary widely, for example, a difference between such companies within the same trade as English Electric at 2·8 and I.C.I. at 1·3, but in fact this is quite a distinct variation considering the large amount of capital employed. But such ratios must be carefully examined. At the time of writing (1969), I.C.I. has been carrying out a modernisation programme and as yet may not be receiving the return it hopes to obtain at a later stage (*see also* 5 below).

4. *Sales to fixed assets.* This is a more specific measure than the previous ratio and is useful when similar companies are compared. A good example for comparative purposes is that of similar engineering companies—consider factory space and plant and equipment employed.

5. *Sales per employee.* This ratio is in turn dependent upon other factors, such as greater or less mechanisation. Returning to the I.C.I. comparison mentioned in 3 above, the modernisation would affect the sales per employee—this would be expected to rise per employee when the changes came fully into effect, but not before, owing to the necessity for redeployment of labour. Likewise, if the previous ratios are sound, then this ratio should consequently be satisfactory, as assets are being well utilised. Employees engaged on administration duties should be excluded from this ratio, as they should be dealt with on a comparative basis in administrative overheads.

6. *Sales to square foot of floor area.* This is of particular relevance with respect to such businesses as department stores—departmentally they would vary, but an overall comparison should be available with similar businesses and branches within a company.

7. *Sales to stocks held.* "Locking up" capital by holding excess stocks is an expensive process. Stocks should always be maintained at the lowest level consistent with efficient supplying of internal and external requirements. This implies efficient stock maintenance records and it would appear that at present British industry lags distinctly behind its American counterpart. Computerisation of stock records is already

widespread in the U.S.A., but it seems that investment would be justified in Britain in the establishment of sound record keeping, as this would more than repay the sums at present being lost by overstocking. In conjunction with such action, however, the ability to depend upon reliable delivery dates by suppliers is essential.

8. *Profits per employee*. This ultimate figure from the point of view of the deployment of labour is dependent again upon various of the foregoing ratios, but it does serve to reveal wide difference between similar companies, and in comparison with the U.S. is quite outstanding. There are various factors which affect it, such as mechanisation, wage rates, restrictive practices, etc.

The list of efficiency ratios might be extended, some being of more use within various trades and industries than others. We conclude with some further ratios which might be employed:

1. Production cost to sales.
2. Advertising and marketing expenses to sales.
3. Cost of materials to sales.
4. Cost of "bought out" parts to sales.
5. Direct labour cost to sales.
6. Material to average daily sales.
7. Work in progress to daily sales.
8. Finished goods to daily sales.
9. Sales per worker per year.
10. Sales per worker per hour.
11. Total operating cost as a percentage of wages.
12. Wages as a percentage of total operating cost.
13. Bad debts as a percentage of sales.

Commonsense is, of course, needed in applying these ratios. They must serve a useful purpose. There is no point whatever in calculating and explaining them to management unless they are going to be of some practical use.

The following illustration may be found useful in affording a practical exercise in the application of some of the ratios mentioned above.

Specimen question

BALANCE SHEET

1st January 19—

Authorised and Issued Share Capital	£100,000	Freehold Property		£80,000
		Plant and Machinery	50,000	
		Depreciation	15,000	
				35,000
				115,000
Profit and Loss Account	17,000	Stock	21,000	
		Debtors	20,000	
Current Liabilities	40,000	Bank	1,000	
				42,000
	£157,000			£157,000

The foregoing is the abridged Balance Sheet of a company. From the following information you are required to prepare in complete form, *i.e.* giving all details normally shown, the Trading and Profit and Loss Account and Balance Sheet at 31st December of the same year.

(*a*) The company was capitalised at the year end—the authorised and issued share capital being the same—as to:

Share capital	50%
Other proprietors' funds	15%
5% Debenture holders	10%
Trade creditors	25%

The Debentures were issued on 1st January, interest being paid on 30th June and 31st December.

(*b*) Freehold property remained unchanged. Additional plant and machinery had been bought and a further £5000 depreciation written off.

The total fixed assets then constituted 60% of total fixed and current (gross) assets.

(*c*) The working capital ratio was 8:5 or 1·6:1. The quick assets ratio was 1:1.

(*d*) The debtors (four-fifths of the quick assets) to sales ratio revealed a credit period of two months. There were no cash sales.

(*e*) The P/W ratio was 10%.

(*f*) Gross profit was at the rate of 15% of selling price.

(*g*) Stock turnover rate was eight times for the year.

Ignore taxation.

Answer

TRADING AND PROFIT AND LOSS ACCOUNT
for the year ended 31st December 19—

Opening stock	£21,000	Sales	£240,000
Purchases	213,000		
	£234,000		
Less Closing stock	30,000		
Cost of sales	204,000		
Gross profit c/d	36,000		
	£240,000		£240,000
Expenses	£17,000	Gross profit b/d	£36,000
Debenture interest	1,000		
Depreciation	5,000		
Net profit	13,000		
	£36,000		£36,000

BALANCE SHEET

31st December 19—

Authorised and issued share capital	£100,000	Freehold property		£80,000
Profit and Loss Account	30,000	Plant and machin-		
5% Debentures	20,000	ery	£60,000	
Current liabilities:		*Less* Depreciation	20,000	
Creditors	50,000			40,000
				120,000
		Current assets:		
		Stock	30,000	
		Debtors	40,000	
		Bank	10,000	80,000
	£200,000			£200,000

NOTE

The question is best dealt with by starting with the Balance Sheet and entering each item as calculated, so supplying additional information for each successive stage. For example, if the share capital of £100,000 remaining unchanged at the year end constituted 50% of the complete capitalisation, then the total must be £200,000. For the compilation of the trading account, the sales figure is obtainable from the debtors' period of credit allowed, the gross profit rate is given, and after calculating the cost of sales by using the formula

$$\frac{\text{Cost of sales}}{\text{Average stock}} = \text{Turnover, } i.e. \ \frac{£204,000}{(£21,000 + x) \div 2} = \frac{8}{1}$$

the closing stock and purchases may be inserted. The P/W ratio is given, facilitating the calculation of the net profit, and thereafter the remaining items in the Profit and Loss Account may be inserted, the expenses constituting the difference between the gross profit and the items calculated.

In conclusion a practical example is given, illustrating a number of useful ratios and their calculation, with brief comments thereon.

BH & CO. LTD

Abbreviated Trading and Profit and Loss Account

year ended 31st March 19—

Sales		£600,000
Opening stock	£65,000	
Purchases	335,000	
	400,000	
Less closing stock	40,000	
		360,000
Gross profit		240,000
General expenses		136,280

Trading profit before charging the following items:		103,720
Directors' emoluments	10,000	
Depreciation	6,200	
Audit fee	500	
Debenture interest	2,520	
		19,220
		84,500
Income from investments		8,700
Profit prior to taxation		93,200
Taxation:		
Corporation tax (42½%)		37,280
Profit after taxation		55,920
Balance b/f from previous year	10,580	
Overprovision for taxation written back	1,000	
		11,580
		67,500
Transfer to general reserve	10,000	
Transfer to dividend equalisation reserve	5,000	
	15,000	
Proposed dividends:		
5% Preference dividend (gross)	500	
30% Ordinary dividend (gross)	12,000	
		27,500
Balance of unappropriated profit c/f		£40,000

Balance Sheet at 31st March 19—

Fixed Assets	Cost	Aggregate depreciation	Net value
Freehold land and buildings	£50,000	—	£50,000
Plant and machinery	35,000	£21,000	14,000
Motor vehicles	15,000	7,500	7,500
Furniture and fittings	3,000	600	2,400
	103,000	29,100	73,900
Investments (market value £99,000)			87,000
Current assets:			
Work in progress	20,000		
Stock in Trade	40,000		
	60,000		
Trade debtors	50,000		
Bills receivable	1,100		
Tax reserve certificates	16,000		
Balance at bank	39,800		
		166,900	

Less current liabilities:

Trade creditors	45,000		
Accruals	5,500		
Taxation	39,800		
Proposed dividends	12,500		
		102,800	
Net current assets			64,100
			£225,000

Financed by:
Share capital—authorised and issued:

10,000 5% Preference shares, £1 each		10,000
40,000 Ordinary shares, £1 each		40,000
		50,000

Reserves:

Share Premium	4,000	
General reserve	90,000	
Dividend equalisation reserve	5,000	
Profit and Loss Account	40,000	
		139,000
		189,000
Loan capital: 7% mortgage Debentures secured on freeholds		36,000
		£225,000

ACCOUNTING RATIOS SUMMARISED

1. *Balance Sheet ratios*   *Comments*

(*a*) Current ratio
Current assets to Current liabilities
167:103   1·7:1 Satisfactory—used to be 2:1
                                (*see* p. 460).

254:103   2·4:1 Assuming investments read-
                                ily marketable.

(*b*) Liquidity ratio, or "acid test", ratio

          167
Less stocks 60
          ———
          107
Marketable
  securities 87 (at cost for conservative
                estimate)
          ———
          194
    to   103   1·9:1 Very good. 1:1, adequate.
          ———

(*c*) Trade debtors to trade creditors
          50:45   10:9 Well balanced. With an equal
                                period of credit debtors
                                should be greater by gross
                                profit.

(d) Capital gearing

(i) Based on nominal capital:

Debentures	£36,000	Highly geared.
Preference shares	10,000	40/46 = 0·87. Should be normally more than 1.
Prior charges	46,000	
Ordinary	40,000	
	£86,000	

(ii) Based in equity capital employed:

Prior charge capital			46	179/46 = 3·9 Very satisfactory. The contradiction with (i) above points to the need for capitalisation of reserves.
Equity			40	
Reserves				
Share premium	4			
Other	135	139	179	

(e) Utilisation of capital

Fixed assets	£73,900	33⅓% locked up;
Market investments	87,000	39% invested.
	£160,900	72%
Net current assets	64,100	28%
	£225,000	100%

(f) Structure of shareholders' funds

External—original capital	£54,000	28%
Internal—self-generating (reserves)	135,000	72% Shows heavy ploughing back.
	189,000	100%

(g) Shareholders' funds to liabilities £189,000 to

Debentures	£36,000	Liabilities completely covered. Indicates the extent to which liabilities are met by proprietors own funds.
+ Current liabilities	102,800	
	£138,800	

(h) Reserves ratio

Total reserves	139,000	=347%. Extent to which equity capital employed, £139,000 is in excess of equity capital subscribed.
Equity capital	40,000	
	£179,000	

(i) Debentures to total fixed assets — 36:74 48% (If near, difficult to raise loans, so capital issue necessary).

(j) Debentures to fixed assets on which secured — 36·50 (72%) Adequate.

(k) Provision for Depreciation to Depreciated fixed assets — 29:53 excluding freeholds (58%) This may reveal a need for further capitalisation for renewal.

2. *Revenue Account*

(a) Gross profit to sales   £240 to £600   40% Should be used comparatively with other companies.

(b) Expenses to sales
Trading Account   136
Profit and Loss Account   19

£155 to £600   26% Should be compared with previous periods.

(c) Trading profit before
tax to sales   £85 to £600   14% should be compared with previous periods.

(d) Net earnings to sales   £55·9 to £600   9·3%
Net trading income to sales
(deducting net investment
income £5111)   £50·8 to £600   8·5% approx. Trading profit margin on sales £0·08½ in £.

(e) Net cash flow
Net profit after tax   £56,920   Approximate amount available for future activities, to be compared with any capital commitments.
(having added back over
provision £1000)
Add depreciation   £6,200

£63,120
Less dividends (gross)   12,500

£50,620

(f) Rate of stock turnover
Cost of sales   £360   6·4 times—must be used comparatively.

Average stock   52

(g) Dividend policy and cover
Dividends   £12,500   22% Covered four times.
Retained profits   44,420   78%

£56,920   100% (*Note.* Inadequate dividends out of available earnings may cause danger of takeover bid.)

(h) Taxation impact on
current profits   £37,280   39% (not necessarily at current rate due to writing down allowances, etc.)
Less   1,000
————   36,280

93,200

3. *Balance Sheet in combination with Revenue Account*

(*a*) Earnings per equity share

Net income after tax	£56,920
Preference dividend	500
	56,420

	56,420	
	40,000	141% or £1·40 per share.

(*b*) Earnings yield
(Assuming share price £9)
141% × (£1/£9) = 15·6%

(*c*) Price-earnings ratio
Earnings per share £1·40
£9/£1·40 = 6·4

Here again the inadequate share capital aspect of the company is revealed. A more reasonable P/E ratio for such a company would be, say, 10, but inadequate dividend payments would keep the share price down.

(*d*) Credit control
  (i) Debtors (50/600) × 365   31 days. Quite tight.
  (ii) Creditors (45/335) × 365   47 days. Reasonable (per terms of trade).

(*e*) Net yield on capital employed   25%
(*f*) Sales to fixed assets at cost 600/103   6:1 (If buildings included). A comparison year by year indicates whether fixed assets are being used properly, subject to adjustment for purchases and sales and depreciation —which is a matter of policy.

(*g*) Working capital to turnover   64:600 or 11%

EXAMINATION QUESTIONS

1. *Trading and Profit and Loss Account for year ended 31st December 19—*

Opening stock	£130,000	Sales—cash	£80,000	
Purchases	420,000	credit	320,000	
				£400,000
	550,000			
Less closing stock	210,000			
	340,000			
Gross profit	60,000			
	£400,000			£400,000
Depreciation	13,100	Gross profit		60,000
General Expenses	20,900			
Directors' emoluments	10,000			
Net profit c/d	16,000			
	£60,000			£60,000

Balance Sheet, 31st December 19—

Issued share capital	360,000	Fixed assets	205,600
Profit and Loss Account	24,600	Stock	210,000
Creditors	140,000	Debtors	160,000
Bank overdraft	51,000		
	£575,600		£575,600

(*a*) The rate of stock turnover to be doubled.

(*b*) Stock is to be reduced by £60,000 by end of the financial year.

(*c*) The ratio of cash to credit sales is to be doubled.

(*d*) The rate of gross profit to sales is to be increased by $33\frac{1}{3}\%$.

(*e*) Directors' emoluments are to be increased to £15,000; general expenses and depreciation are to remain the same.

(*f*) The ratio of trade creditors to closing stock and the ratio of debtors to credit sales will remain the same as in the year just ended.

Draft the budgeted Trading and Profit and Loss Account and Balance Sheet as if all objectives had been achieved.   [B. & H.

2. The return on capital employed is often taken as a measure of the efficiency of an organisation. What are the aspects of control to which the board of a company should pay particular attention in attempting to increase this percentage return on capital employed?   [C.C.A.

3. You have been asked to make a financial analysis of a company to which a client of yours (a finance company) is considering making a substantial advance.

(*a*) Indicate the headings under which your examination would be conducted and in particular refer to the accounting ratios, valuation of which might reveal trends or weaknesses in the financial structure.

(*b*) Draft an evaluation of the main facts and ratios, using assumed appropriate figures.   [C.C.A.

4. Define the following ratios when used in reports on company accounts:

(*a*) Liquidity ratio.

(*b*) Current ratio.

(*c*) Turnover ratio.

(*d*) Gross profit ratio.

(*e*) Fixed expenses ratio.

(*f*) Earnings on shareholders' interests.   [C.C.A.

5. At the end of two consecutive trading periods of three months each, the Balance Sheet position of a company manufacturing light consumer goods is as follows:

	Period 1	Period 2
Issued capital:		
7% Cumulative Redeemable Preference shares	£100,000	£100,000
Ordinary shares	100,000	100,000
Reserves and Profit and Loss Account balance	50,000	44,000
	£250,000	£244,000

Land and buildings	30,000	30,000
Plant, machinery, vehicles, etc.	70,000	68,000
Raw material stocks	60,000	65,000
Work in progress at prime cost	70,000	72,000
Finished goods stocks	19,000	18,000
Debtors	100,000	95,000
Bank balance	1,000	1,000
	£350,000	£349,000
Creditors	100,000	105,000
	£250,000	£244,000

Annual rate of sales in period	£400,000	£350,000
Annual rate of materials purchased in period	250,000	240,000
Annual rate of materials usage in period	245,000	235,000

Prime cost may be taken at 60% of selling price, and total works cost, excluding selling and distribution expenses and profit, at 80% of selling price. The figures, generally, continue the trend experienced for some time.

(a) What ratios and other information would you give to reveal the salient features most effectively to the management of the company? Comment on each item you mention.

(b) Prepare a brief report to the management on these features.

(c) Note the lines of action you consider might be taken to improve the position.   [C.W.A.

6. Towards the end of 1964, the directors of Wholesale Merchants Ltd decided to expand their business. The annual accounts of the company for 1964 and 1965 may be summarised as follows:

	Year 1964		Year 1965	
Sales:				
Cash	£30,000		£32,000	
Credit	270,000		342,000	
		£300,000		£374,000
Cost of sales		236,000		298,000
Gross margin		64,000		76,000

	Year 1964	Year 1965
Expenses		
Warehousing	£13,000	£14,000
Transport	6,000	10,000
Administration	19,000	19,000
Selling	11,000	14,000
Debenture interest	—	2,000
	49,000	59,000
Net profit	£15,000	£17,000

	On 31st December 1964	On 31st December 1965
Fixed assets (*less* depreciation)	£30,000	£40,000

Current assets			
Stock	£60,000		£94,000
Debtors	50,000		82,000
Cash	10,000		7,000
		120,000		183,000

Less:

Current liabilities		
Trade creditors	50,000	76,000

Net current assets	70,000	107,000
	£100,000	£147,000

Share capital	75,000	75,000
Reserves and undistributed profit	25,000	42,000
Debenture loan	—	30,000
	£100,000	£147,000

You are informed that:

(*a*) All sales were from stocks in the company's warehouse.

(*b*) The range of merchandise was not changed and buying prices remained steady throughout the two years.

(*c*) Budgeted total sales for 1966 were £390,000.

(*d*) The Debenture loan was received on 1st January 1965, and additional fixed assets were purchased on that date.

You are required to state the internal accounting ratios that you would use in this type of business to assist the management of the company in measuring the efficiency of its operation, including its use of capital.

Your answer should name the ratios and give the figures (calculated to one decimal place) for 1964 and 1965, together with possible reasons for changes in the ratios for the two years. Ratios relating to capital employed should be based on the capital at the year end. Ignore taxation.   [C.A. (1966)

7. Timber Chests Ltd is a public company, and its shares are quoted on the London stock exchange. Its most recent accounts run as follows:

Balance Sheet as at 31st March, 1967

	(£'000)	(£'000)		(£'000)	(£'000)
Ordinary share capital: authorised,			Fixed assets:		
issued and fully paid		38,600	Land and buildings at cost		26,700
Capital reserves		11,900	Plant and machinery at		
Profit and Loss Account		13,600	cost	51,000	
		———	*Less* depreciation	26,600	
		64,100			24,400
					———
6% Debentures		15,000			51,100
Future taxation		1,500	Trade investments at cost		3,700
Current liabilities:			Current assets:		
Creditors	23,700		Stocks	34,300	
Current taxation	5,600		Debtors	17,800	
Proposed dividends	1,900		Quoted investments	2,400	
	———	31,200	Cash at Bank	2,500	
					57,000
		111,800			111,800

Profit and Loss Account for the year ended 31st March 1967

	(£'000)	(£'000)
Trading profit		15,850
Less Directors' emoluments	150	
Depreciation	4,600	
Debenture interest	900	
		5,650
Profit before taxation		10,200
Less taxation		4,900
Profit after taxation		5,300
Less Ordinary dividend, paid and proposed (gross)		4,600
		700
Add balance as at 1st April 1966		12,900
		13,600

You are required to define and calculate, from the figures in these accounts, the five accounting ratios which you think would be most helpful to a prospective investor in the company. Write a short note on the significance and limitations of each. [B. Sc. (Econ.)

8. The following information relates to an engineering company making consumer durables:

	Actual		Budget
	1963–64	*1964–65*	*1965–66*
Sales	£214,000	£235,000	£275,000
Production cost:			
Materials	79,180	82,250	96,250
Direct labour	34,240	32,900	37,125
Indirect labour	34,240	38,775	44,000
Other costs	26,322	28,670	35,750
	173,982	182,595	213,125
Administration	21,400	25,850	33,000
Selling	5,992	7,050	7,150
Distribution	2,568	2,820	3,850
	203,942	218,315	257,125
Net profit before tax	10,058	16,685	17,875
	214,000	235,000	275,000
Balance sheet at year end:			
Fixed assets at cost	120,000	155,000	175,000
Less depreciation	65,000	65,000	80,000
	55,000	90,000	95,000
Stock and work in progress	55,112	62,452	67,808
Debtors	35,178	32,192	33,904
Other current assets	4,210	3,500	2,750
	149,500	188,144	199,462
Less current liabilities	17,500	12,512	15,184
Total capital employed	132,000	175,632	184,278
Number of people employed (average during year):			
Direct	43	41	47
Works indirect	31	35	40
Administration	30	37	36
Sales	6	7	7
	110	120	130
Floor space occupied (square feet)	30,000	30,000	32,000

Give your interpretation of the production, commercial and financial management of the company over the period shown, illustrating your answer with a tabulation of selected key ratios. [C.W.A.

CHAPTER XX

INTERPRETATION OF ACCOUNTS
(II) DEPRECIATION AND APPRECIATION OF ASSETS

DEPRECIATION

THE nature of depreciation is not always easily grasped. It may be defined as that part of the cost of an asset not recoverable when disposed of by its owner; but it is often looked upon as an additional expenditure which reduces current profits. From the cash flow point of view, however, the liquid resources of the company are not depleted according to the amount of the charge: the capital funds have already been expended. The depreciation figure only reduces the profit which might otherwise be distributed, thus facilitating the putting aside of the amount concerned for replacement of the asset, and at the same time allowing the asset to be shown at its estimated current worth. This figure for depreciation may perhaps have already been absorbed into some form of asset other than cash and so is not available for investment. For this reason sinking funds with corresponding investments are often created to ensure that liquid resources are put aside.

THE EFFECT OF INFLATION

It is important that the student should have a clear idea of the subject, for depreciation and the replacement of assets are especially important nowadays, when rising price levels have led to additional complications. Even if the sum for depreciation is set aside in a specific investment—and this is not always done—it is unlikely to be enough to replace the original asset on final writing-off because prices will have risen so much in the meantime.

Example

Shown below are the abbreviated Balance Sheets of a company at the beginning and end of a ten year period. It has been assumed that:

(a) General prices have risen over the ten years from 100% to 150% and property prices from 100% to 250%.
(b) Stock turnover has been constant.
(c) Corporation tax at 40% in the £ has been charged.
(d) Lease to be written off over a life of 10 years.
(e) Plant and machinery to be depreciated at 10% on cost.

BALANCE SHEETS

	196–	197–		196–		197–	
Share capital	£200,000	£200,000	Leasehold premises	£80,000		£80,000	
Profit and Loss			Less Amortisation	—		80,000	
Account	50,000	113,000			80,000		—
Current liabilities	70,000	105,000	Plant and machinery	120,000		120,000	
			Less Depreciation	—		120,000	
					120,000		238,000
			Investments	—			
			Stock	50,000		75,000	
			Debtors	60,000		90,000	
			Bank	10,000		15,000	
					120,000		180,000
	£320,000	£418,000			£320,000		£418,000

TRADING AND PROFIT AND LOSS ACCOUNT FOR THE TEN YEARS ENDED 197—

Opening stock		£50,000	Sales	£3,550,000
Purchases		2,875,000	Closing stock	75,000
		£2,925,000		
Gross Profit c/d				
In respect of:				
Trading	£675,000			
Stock	25,000			
		700,000		
		£3,625,000		£3,625,000

Expenses	£270,000	Gross profit b/d	£700,000
Amortisation of lease	80,000	Investment income	
Depreciation:		(say)	25,000
Plant and machinery	120,000		
Net profit c/d	255,000		
	£725,000		£725,000

Dividends	£90,000	Net profit b/d	£255,000
Taxation	102,000	Balance b/f	50,000
Balance c/f	113,000		
	£305,000		£305,000

From the later Balance Sheet it will be observed that the fixed assets will have to be renewed. Ignoring the fact that the company might seek a freehold property or might prefer to rent premises, the assets would require renewal in the sum of:

Lease £200,000 (£80,000 × 250/100)
Plant and machinery 180,000 (£120,000 × 150/100)

380,000
Less Amount set aside in investments 238,000

Additional capital to be obtained £142,000

The example is simplified but it serves to reveal two very real problems which face business today, caused by (*a*) high levels of taxation and (*b*) the maintenance of depreciation and amortisation on a historical cost basis. The usefulness of the investment allowances against taxation which have been introduced in recent years is apparent, but the need to set aside additional sums above the normal depreciation rates is even more clearly revealed.

Actual methods of writing off depreciation are dealt with in financial accounting textbooks; suffice it to say here that at the moment the Institute of Chartered Accountants favour the straight line basis. But it is of vital concern to the management accountant to ensure that adequate funds are set aside for asset replacement and that production costing records take fully into consideration the additional burden imposed upon a business by rising price levels and obsolescence.

OBSOLESCENCE

Obsolescence is relevant because of the speed of technical progress nowadays. Even an apparently satisfactory combination of depreciation rates and replacement reserves may be upset through unforeseen obsolescence. Any particular machine may suddenly become outdated; when several machines are involved in a manufacturing process, a technical advance in one of them may make the others out of date too (though they may in fact be quite new) because the whole process has to be modernised to take advantage of the new development. Heavy expenses incurred in ways like this must be dealt with and reflected in process costs and selling prices, but it is not a simple matter to budget for them. It is here that the management accountant has to maintain a broad outlook and keep in touch with those on the production side of the business. With their co-operation he should both budget for losses and provide for asset replacement as accurately as possible.

DEPRECIATION CHARGE

(a) *Adjustment for inflation factor*

The necessity for the acquisition of additional finance where the replacement price of assets increases, owing to the influence of inflation, has been mentioned above. To meet this exigency companies have taken to setting aside further sums in addition to the normal depreciation charge. It has been recommended by the Institute of Chartered Accountants that any such additional amounts set aside shall not be regarded as charges against profit but appropriations thereof and should therefore be dealt with as transfers to reserve. These sums are often shown as Asset Replacement Reserves and it is advisable that they should be represented by investments of a realisable nature, in order to ensure that they, with any other sums set aside, are available when the replacement date falls due.

484   INFORMATION FOR MANAGEMENT CONTROL

The nature of the increases likely to arise and the calculations involved may be illustrated as follows:

Example

Machine Cost—£2000.
Life 5 years—no residual value.
Inflation factor—3%.

Year	Cost	Replacement Cost	Depreciation Straight Line	Depreciation Replacement Cost	Total Replacement Reserve	Annual Transfer to Reserve
1	£2000	£2060	£400	£412	£12	£12
2	2000	2122	800	849	49	37
3	2000	2186	1200	1312	112	63
4	2000	2252	1600	1802	202	90
5	2000	2320	2000	2320	320	118

NOTE

The depreciation rate for replacement purposes is calculated by taking the proportion of the expired life of the asset annually, *e.g.* 1st Year, one-fifth; 2nd Year, Two-fifths, etc.

(b) *Omission of depreciation charge.*

In Chapter XXIII will be found an example of a company which has been making losses and has various courses of action open to it (*see* p. 579). In the circumstances it is decided to ignore depreciation on the capital sunk in the assets.

Such a decision involves the use of marginal costing and consideration of how far depreciation can safely be ignored in such cases. Broadly speaking, depreciation cannot be ignored in dealing with a *continuing* business, but where, as with the WS Co. in Chapter XXIII, the object is to make the best of a situation where losses are inevitable anyway, the extreme circumstances warrant the elimination of depreciation. In order to clarify this point, a further, simpler illustration is given.

Example

Two partners purchase and equip between them for the sum of £6000 a motor vessel with an expected working life of six years. They budget for wages of £1500 a year and expenses of £500 a year. Their estimate of returns in the form of ferry charges is £4000 annually. After commencing business unexpected competition arises; receipts fall, and are budgeted for an income of £2800 a year. The original and revised budgets would appear as follows:

	Original budget	Revised budget
Receipt	£4000	£2800
Wages	1500	1500
Expenses	500	500
Depreciation	1000	1000
Net profit	£1000	Net loss £200

The boat would have to be sold at a heavy loss—since it is only suitable for a specific purpose—for £2200.

The question is, whether to sell out or continue in business? If the former, a loss of £3800 would be made on the capital expenditure. If the latter, and if depreciation were ignored, a profit of £800 a year could be made: £4800 over the six years. What is the present value of an annuity of £800 for six years at a rate per cent which takes into consideration the risk still involved? If 8% were considered a reasonable rate, the capital value would be £3696. Continuation in business is thus the best course to adopt despite the "loss" shown of £200 a year.

From this example it can be clearly seen that, given certain circumstances, it may be best to ignore depreciation in dealing with the overall affairs of a business.

The position where a company has recovered its fixed charges and may consider ignoring depreciation in fixing selling prices is of a more specialised nature and is dealt with in Chapter XI.

APPRECIATION

Besides the amount to be set aside for depreciation and the influence of rising price levels, the value to be set on an asset and its appearance on the Balance Sheet have to be considered. The valuation of assets is particularly important where take-over bids are concerned. If assets have increased in value, the position should be reflected on the Balance Sheet. In the past it has often been considered prudent to show assets at a low figure to obviate the risk of large sums having to be written off in the event of their being disposed of. But this kind of policy has led to much greater losses being suffered.

Assets which have not been properly re-valued will mean that the company's shares will be valued, on a Balance Sheet basis, at a price much lower than should really be the case. Hence shareholders can lose heavily if an offer is made and accepted accordingly, while the new controlling company will have acquired a subsidiary too cheaply. Freehold properties have tended to be the main items under-valued, but it could apply equally to any other type of asset.

For the purpose of sound management accounting it is recommended that the company shows a true and fair view of the worth of its assets. On appreciation to any material extent, the valuation as set by an expert should be shown, together with a corresponding reserve—preferably of a capital nature, indicating the desire not to distribute such profits as arise.

EXAMINATION QUESTIONS

1. Calculate (a) the replacement cost, (b) the written-down value, (c) the depreciation and (d) the amount set aside to capital reserve, for each year in respect of a fixed asset costing £1000 which is to be written off over five years and has no residual value. The annual inflation factor is to be taken as 4%.

[C.C.A.

2. Over the last few years there has been an increasing number of references in company reports and in the financial press (both American and British) to what is described as the "cash flow." This is usually taken to be the net profit after taxation, plus the provision for depreciation.

Such a reference might read:

"Because of the existence of excess plant capacity, originally constructed at the time of the Korean War, the company's current earnings are seriously restricted by heavy depreciation charges. Nevertheless, this depreciation money is still available to the company and the relatively high cash flow of $9·8 per $ of equity capital should be taken into account when considering the current earnings of $3·22 per $ and the dividend of $3·50 per $." (This is a composite example compiled from a number of actual reports, etc.)

Give your comments on the validity of this argument.   [C.C.A.

3. "The revaluation of assets is becoming too common a practice, especially in view of the fact that it is against prudent business policy. To assume the selling price of an asset—which is never certain—and then to create a capital reserve which still is available for distribution, is highly unsatisfactory and a method of encouraging the dissipation of resources which should be retained in the business." Comment on this statement.

4. The directors of your company consider that the Balance Sheet values of the fixed assets, having been substantially written down over the years, although maintained out of revenue in excellent and up-to-date working condition, give a misleading picture of their worth to the company. They have, therefore, decided to have them revalued.

(a) Describe the procedure you recommend for organising the revaluation by your own staff.
(b) Indicate how you would incorporate the results in the books.
(c) State the reasons frequently given for and against this practice.
          [C.W.A.

CHAPTER XXI

INTERPRETATION OF ACCOUNTS
(III) CRITICISM OF BALANCE SHEETS AND ACCOUNTS

SINCE management accounting involves the use of information disclosed in accounts to regulate future action, it is essential that the management accountant should be able not only to appreciate the immediate position but also to interpret the meaning, trends and policies such information reveals. This often demands commonsense and business acumen as well as knowledge of accounting procedures.

Although guidance can be given in the application of certain accounting rules and principles, they cannot in themselves provide a complete answer, since each problem requires analysis and investigation along the lines best suited to the undertaking concerned. Furthermore, the Balance Sheet and accounts of firms or companies are looked at from various viewpoints by those concerned with them, such as creditors, shareholders, bankers, etc. The management accountant must be able to interpret them from *all* these points of view because he may be required to advise from any one of them. For example, his company may contemplate taking up shares or Debentures in another company, or may hold some already and wish to know what action to take; or his company may be a creditor to the creditor of another. Why he should consider the accounts from the banker's position may be less obvious; but if he is to advise on the best way of raising new finance, the chances of success in raising a short term loan or overdraft, and to what extent it may be possible, he will need to work out some idea of the bank manager's likely reaction.

Besides examining the final accounts and Balance Sheets, any further information relevant to the business in hand should also be investigated. For example, the current trend of trading in the industry as a whole would be of great importance, as would any Government action that might increase or decrease trade.

When all such information has been considered, an opinion can be formed on:

(*a*) The recent trading and financial history of the concern and the policies it has pursued.

(*b*) Its present financial position.

(*c*) Its future trading and financial prospects.

It is emphasised that these will be opinions and assumptions: the warning about making definite statements in Chapter XXIII (*see* p. 460) should always be borne in mind.

The following heads may be taken as a guide to the most important points to be considered. In practice *every* item should be scrutinised. Those listed below are subsequently considered in detail.

(a) *Trading and Profit and Loss Account*

   (i) Stock turnover.
   (ii) Gross profit.
  (iii) Losses on sale of fixed assets.
  (iv) Directors' emoluments.
   (v) Net profit.
  (vi) Income tax and corporation tax.

(b) *Balance Sheet*

    (i) Share capital.
   (ii) Reserves.
   (iii) Debentures.
   (iv) Deferred Taxation Accounts.
    (v) Current liabilities.
   (vi) Investments
  (vii) Net current assets or working capital (including over-trading).
 (viii) Cash and bank balances (including funds flow statements).

Methods of analysing accounts differ and there is no single definite rule.

THE TRADING AND PROFIT AND LOSS ACCOUNT

1. STOCK TURNOVER

The frequency of stock turnover has been mentioned earlier (*see* p. 390). It will differ according to the nature of the trade or industry, and regular comparisons should be made to ensure that the rate of turnover is at least equal to that of the industry as a whole—although here again special circumstances (such as location) may affect the rate. Any increase or decrease should be investigated and the reasons for it discovered.

2. GROSS PROFIT

This should normally remain constant, subject to explainable variations caused by changes in the price of purchases or sales. Where there are a number of products they will have to be segregated (*see* Chapter XX).

Rates, however, change according to stock valuations and careful scrutiny is necessary. It is not difficult to over-value stock or under-value it, according to whether it is desired to increase or decrease the profit figures. It is sometimes argued that it is prudent business policy to under-value stocks, but such matters as the desire to lessen taxation assessments are also likely to be a reason. If, for caution's sake, it is wished to reduce the value, a stock reserve should be created and shown as such on the Balance Sheet. Where it is necessary to de-value stock materially, the figures should be shown on the final accounts, to avoid any large unexplainable variation in the gross profit rate due to the devaluation. The valuation of stock is dealt with in detail in Chapter xiv.

Falling gross profit rates have a direct effect on the P/S ratio and also increase the effect of fixed costs (see Chapter xx).

3. LOSSES ON SALE OF FIXED ASSETS

Any abnormal losses should be analysed, since they may result from inadequate depreciation rates which showed higher profits in previous periods than were justified, or poor management policies in the acquisition of assets.

4. DIRECTORS' EMOLUMENTS

It should be considered whether these are reasonable in view of the size of the company and its profits. It is a common practice in small private companies for directors to take out profits in the form of salaries so as to gain the benefits of earned income relief for taxation purposes, but it should not be overdone or it will prevent the adequate ploughing back of profits.

5. NET PROFIT

It is not enough merely to see that the company makes a net profit. If it is not earning an adequate return on the original capital invested and on any profits that have been ploughed back, the money would be more profitably invested elsewhere.

The P/S ratio and the P/W ratio are valuable guides to the adequacy or inadequacy of the returns. There is no point in specifying any parti-cular rate; it will vary according to the nature of the business—the greater the risk the larger the return expected. In any case, there should be sufficient net revenue to allow profits to be ploughed back and reason-able dividends to be paid.

6. INCOME TAX AND CORPORATION TAX

These should be fully provided for on the current profits as shown in the accounts. There is no legal requirement that taxation on cur-rent profits must be set aside out of those same profits, but it is advisable to do so. Any business that did not comply with the recommendation of the Institute of Chartered Accountants in this respect would immediately invite criticism.

Income tax arising owing to the receipt of investment income in excess of distribution of profit should be written off, although such tax is recoverable where subsequent distributions exceed franked investment income.

BALANCE SHEET

1. SHARE CAPITAL

The capital gearing should be examined, along with the points dealt with in Chapter III such as dividend cover.

The equity share capital should be sufficient in the first instance to provide for the fixed assets, any intangibles and for a further amount as working capital. Thereafter, sufficient profits should be ploughed back to provide for easy working without shortage of funds, for renewing assets and for expansion if necessary, though the latter may require additional capital issues. The capital may become "watered down" if there have been too many bonus issues, with the object of making tax-free profits by the sale of the shares. The P/S ratio is relevant here.

The existence of any Redeemable Preference share capital should be noted. If a redemption date is specified, it is important to see that there will be enough funds available and that a sinking fund or some similar provision carries enough distributable funds for transfer to a capital reserve fund. If this is not the case, a further issue of shares will be necessary (*Companies Act*, 1948, *s*. 58).

2. RESERVES

Reserves should be scrutinised, as they indicate the amount of profit ploughed back into the business. These should not be allowed to become out of balance with the equity share capital. The illustration given on p. 471 reveals heavy ploughing back without any capitalisation of the funds concerned. Such a policy may cause a company to become highly geared (*see* Chapter III). As there are only two *legal* types of capital reserve, recent policies have been to avoid the use of capital reserves, but they may still be created in order to show the desire to restrict the distribution of the profit element they represent, and nothing can be said against such a policy—which is sometimes desirable where liquid resources are short.

Capital reserves are often created when freehold properties are revalued. If they are not revalued the undervaluation of such assets may invite take-over bids. Thus when a Balance Sheet is being examined, it is desirable to obtain the dates when properties were purchased. If the purchase was recent it is unlikely that any material hidden capital reserve will exist. Some idea of the purchase date may be obtained when a number of Balance Sheets are being examined, because the "Freehold property" asset will obviously increase by the amount of the purchase during the period of the analysis.

3. DEBENTURES

This form of loan capital has been dealt with in Chapter I. The interest rate and redemption date should be noted and, particularly, whether a sinking fund has been created for their redemption. If the redemption date is not far distant and there is no sinking fund, the company may be tempted to over-capitalise (issue more shares than its profits justify), or it may have to borrow at an unfavourable rate in order to obtain the finance to cancel them.

If the Debentures are stated to be secured, the margin of the security should be noted. Such loan capital should be kept satisfactorily within the gear ratio, although in such cases as property companies the normal requirements do not apply.

Owing to the heavy incidence of taxation, the desire to lessen its effects by the charging of Debenture interest against profits has led to the danger of over-borrowing by means of Debentures when a more permanent form of capitalisation should take place. The capital gearing, as mentioned above, should be examined, together with the sufficiency of the cover given for the Debentures, as if this is not adequate it may be difficult to raise additional funds if these are required.

4. DEFERRED TAXATION ACCOUNTS

The Institute of Chartered Accountants, in their statement *Treatment of taxation in accounts of companies*, refer to this account as the "Deferred Taxation Account," stating that its use is usually restricted to those items which cause major differences between accounting profit and assessable profit. One of the main differences likely to arise is that caused between capital allowances and the charge made in accounts for depreciation.

From the interpretive point of view, which is of relevance here, it is worthy of note that the Institute consider that the balance on the account is in the nature of a deferred liability, not a reserve. But although the balance may not be considered as a sum for appropriation to anything other than future tax liabilities, nevertheless it reveals a conservative policy on the part of the company and points towards a healthy state of affairs, whereas another company less well managed might be inclined to ignore the difference between depreciation and capital allowances in particular (as other adjusting factors may be included, such as capital surpluses not immediately taxed) and hope that funds may become available when the actual liabilities arise.

When analysing accounts prior to 1966, it is necessary to observe that income tax was assessed on the financial year ending within the previous income tax year; profits tax was payable 28 days after the date of assessment. This meant that "current liabilities" in respect of income tax and profits tax appeared only if the financial year ended on any date between 1st January and 4th April. If an amount for future income tax ought to have been shown and was not, the position should be viewed with caution, for it might imply that current profits had been otherwise absorbed and were not available for setting aside to meet the income tax charge due to be made—revealing a state of financial weakness.

If the item for taxation normally shown under this heading or under "Current liabilities" is missing, it may imply that the company has been making losses and that they are being set off against the assessment which would be made on current profits.

5. CURRENT LIABILITIES

The liquid position and the extent of credit facilities being used may be ascertained as explained in Chapter XIX under "Current and quick assets ratios" and "Creditors ratio."

It is most important to observe any changes in the capital employed to current liabilities ratio, for a fall in it may imply that the business is relying on outside capitalisation. Conversely, a rise may imply a strengthening of the internal resources.

6. INVESTMENTS

If the investments are quoted on a stock exchange, the market value will be stated. But if a Balance Sheet is being examined any length of time after its date, the *present* market value should be ascertained, since it could be markedly different for a number of reasons (*see* Chapters XV and XVI).

If the securities are unquoted, then to obtain a reasonable valuation it will be necessary to investigate the final accounts and Balance Sheets of the companies concerned. Once again, it should be remembered that the equity share capital of the investing company ought to be sufficient to cover any investments besides the fixed assets and working capital. It would be highly irregular to invest moneys obtained from outside sources in such forms as extended credit facilities or loan capital.

7. NET CURRENT ASSETS, OR WORKING CAPITAL

The trend of a company's trading is often clearly revealed by a careful analysis of the constitution and balance of its working capital.

Certain transactions will not affect the balance of the net current assets. Thus if raw material stocks are increased, creditors will increase too; if creditors are paid, the bank balance will decrease correspondingly (*see* Chapter V). The balance will be varied, however, by the sale of stocks, so increasing the bank balance by an amount which includes the gross profit.

Rather less obvious are the variations in the working capital balance caused by such things as increases or decreases in:

(a) The price of sales (affecting the amount of debtors' balances).
(b) Efficiency, so varying costs (reduction of creditors for costs incurred).
(c) Credit control policies.
(d) Wages rates or expenses (quicker outflow of cash resources).
(e) The level of stocks of work in progress or finished goods.
(f) Production time, e.g. quicker conversion from raw materials to finished goods (as reflected in (e) above).

The net current balance cannot be considered in isolation, and of itself is insufficient to reveal the financial health of a business.

Example

	X Ltd	Y Ltd
Stocks	£20,000	£65,000
Debtors	42,000	30,000
Bank	8,000	1,000
	70,000	96,000
Less Current Liabilities	50,000	76,000
Net current assets (or working capital)	£20,000	£20,000

The working capital balance is the same in both companies, but the vulnerable position of Y Ltd is obvious, for with £31,000 in "Debtors" and "Bank," it could not settle its liabilities even if all the debtors were to pay at once. Stocks are no doubt due to be sold at a profit, but this pre-supposes that they *can* be sold—future sales and prices are never matters of certainty; furthermore, if raw materials and work in progress are involved, time is necessary for the conversion to finished goods.

Over-trading

The position of Y Ltd above is likely to arise where the company's policies have led to over-trading. In modern conditions, where delivery dates often cause more concern than the ability to find markets, there is every temptation to over-trade. "Over-trading" may be briefly described as an increase of activity without adequate financial backing. The following outlines briefly what takes place in such a case.

Where a company is trading satisfactorily on a good market, the management will wish to increase output so as to take full advantage of the prevailing conditions. More raw materials may be purchased (raising the figure for creditors), more production expenses are involved

—direct wages often forming a large part of them—and more fixed assets may be acquired for expansion. The time lag between the purchase of raw materials and the output of finished goods is extended. The immediate and increased expenses have to be settled, so creditors are forced to wait for settlement. The company now finds itself in a vulnerable position, and at this stage the bank manager may be called to the rescue. Banks, however, are not prepared to lend on a permanent basis, nor is it always easy for a small-to-medium sized firm to obtain additional capital. A further complication is that competitors too will take advantage of the favourable market conditions. Prices will fall and the company's income diminishes, reducing working capital resources even further.

But even without this further complication, difficulties are bound to arise where creditors are made to wait for settlement. Over-trading may overtake a quite promising concern; it does not signify inefficiency so much as misguided financial policy, and—often—over-zealous salesmanship in a new company. In the latter case, financial advisers may be regarded as over-cautious and their advice ignored. In practice, banks often come to the aid of such companies, but may insist on having a seat on the board so that they can prevent the resources they have made available from being used for further expansion by means of investment in further stocks or fixed assets, and can insist on the completion and delivery of current orders to strengthen the liquid position.

Example (1)

The following figures give an indication of the position of a company at the beginning and end of a year during which it has been over-trading:

	1st January 19—	31st December 19—
Stock	£28,000	£140,000
Bank and debtors	18,000	18,000
Trade creditors	28,000	140,000
Net realisable value of stock to settle creditors	10,000	122,000
Percentage of cost price	36%	87%

Provided outside help in the form of (say) a bank loan can be obtained, the company may be able to continue. If, however, it becomes necessary to cut selling prices or to sell the stock, it could be most difficult for the company to obtain 87% of the original cost price of the stock as a net realisable value; whereas at the beginning of the year, with the company in a sound position, it should always be possible to obtain at least 36% for the stocks.

Where a manufacturing company is carrying stocks of work in progress and finished goods, it is advisable to analyse the current assets on a percentage basis. This will reveal the trend of business more clearly than the actual figures themselves.

Example (2)

Note the distinctly less favourable position of a business carrying all three types of stock at the beginning and end of a trading period.

Current assets position at:

	1st January 19—		31st December 19—	
Stocks:				
Raw materials	£12,000	15%	£12,600	7%
Work in progress	20,000	25	79,200	44
Finished goods	9,600	12	48,600	27
	41,600	52	140,400	78
Trade debtors	29,600	37	37,800	21
Bank	8,800	11	1,800	1
	£80,000	100%	£180,000	100%

As mentioned in Example 1 above, the position with regard to creditors and the net realisable value of the stock at the year end will now be vital. The company's trading position should also be investigated, as it shows signs of having run into a period of over-trading.

8. CASH AND BANK BALANCES

The liquid position cannot be viewed in isolation: it is necessary to consider the current assets and liabilities at the same time.

Example

The following are extracts of the liquid position from the Balance Sheets of two companies:

	A Ltd	B Ltd		A Ltd	B Ltd
Current liabilities:			Current assets:		
Corporation			Investments (mar-		
tax	5,000	8,000	ket value		
Trade creditors	12,000	21,000	£12,400)	12,000	—
			Debtors	16,000	13,000
			Cash and bank	2,000	12,000

The fact that B Ltd has a reasonably large bank balance does not make its position better than A Ltd's. With the debtors and bank together there are not enough resources to meet the current liabilities; the remarks made earlier about debtors normally exceeding creditors by the amount of the gross profit rate, subject to equality of credit control, apply here. It appears to signify that B Ltd have pressed their debtors for payment.

In the case of A Ltd, the appearance of "Investments" under "Current assets" indicates that they can be realised easily, otherwise they should not be included there. The debtors-to-creditors position appears quite satisfactory.

Large bank balances do not represent financial strength; on the contrary, they may reflect unsatisfactory deployment of resources. The nature of the trade must be considered too, though, since it may be necessary to have immediate liquid reserves for particular purposes. The progress of a bank overdraft must be watched. If it tends to increase, it should be discovered why some other method of raising capital has not been used. Banks usually put some pressure on clients to reduce or to settle overdrafts that tend to be held over an extended period of time. If such pressure is resisted, the reason may be that the company cannot obtain capital apart from what it is borrowing. In itself this would be cause for further enquiry.

The funds flow statement

To obtain a clear picture of the deployment of funds over a period, a "funds flow statement" is most useful. It is possible to prepare one by accounting methods even when full information is not supplied.

Specimen question

The following balances constitute the Balance Sheets of X Ltd at the dates given. From the information supplied you are required to prepare a Funds Flow Statement for the year ended 31st December 19—.

	31st December 19—		31st December 19—	
Freehold property:				
At cost	£162,000			
As revalued			£256,000	
Plant and machinery:				
At cost	258,000		305,000	
Provision for depreciation		£88,500		£102,700
Investments in associated companies			55,920	
Stocks:				
Raw materials	34,000		45,200	
Work in progress	53,000		92,000	
Finished goods	12,600		24,800	
Debtors and creditors	78,000	61,500	86,000	67,400
Provision for bad debts		950		1,140
Taxation		12,000		17,200
Dividend (ignore tax)		10,000		
Cash	80		120	
Balance at bank	3,870			2,000
Issued share capital		200,000		250,000
Share premium		30,000		50,000
Capital reserve				109,000
Reserve for replacement of machinery		40,000		45,000
Profit and Loss Account		98,600		119,400
Profit for year		20,800		41,200
5% Debentures		40,000		60,000
Discount on Debentures	800		—	
	£602,350	£602,350	£865,040	£865,040

Other relevant information:

(*a*) The issue of Debentures was made on 1st January at 2% discount.

(*b*) Certain items of plant and machinery were sold for £6800. These items had been written down to £5000 at a rate of 10% on cost over the past eight years to 31st December 19—. The profit on the sale was transferred to the Profit and Loss Account and included in the profit for the year under review.

(*c*) The capital reserve includes the amount arising on revaluation of the freehold properties plus the profit made on the sale of a property which originally cost £8000.

(*d*) The liability to corporation tax was settled as finally agreed in the sum of £9000. Provision was made for corporation tax at £17,200 on the current year's profits. Income tax is £0·40 in the £.

Comments and answer

Before it is possible to draw up the required statement, it is necessary to prepare certain accounts in order to obtain additional details of the transactions which have taken place. Moreover, since a presentation of the movement of funds is required, items which are effected solely by book entries must be written back to reveal the increases or decreases caused by material transactions. Depreciation and Debenture discount are examples of such ledger adjustments.

In working out the details of the accounts, it is advisable to enter first the obvious movements shown by the opening and closing balances. After that, details can be added in conjunction with other accounts affected.

Plant and machinery

Balance b/d	£258,000	Transfer to plant dis-	
Machinery purchased	72,000	posal account	£25,000
		Balance c/d	305,000
	£330,000		£330,000

Depreciation: Plant and machinery

Transfer to plant dis-		Balance b/d	£88,500
posal account	£20,000	Profit and Loss Account	34,200
Balance c/d	102,700		
	£122,700		£122,700

Plant disposal account

Transfer from plant and		Cash on sale	£6,800
machinery account	£25,000	Transfer of depreciation	20,000
Transfer to Profit and			
Loss Account (profit			
on sale)	1,800		
	£26,800		£26,800

After the opening and closing balances have been entered, the cost price of the machinery sold is calculated and transferred to the Plant Disposal Account. The difference remaining must constitute machinery purchased.

The aggregate depreciation is transferred from the Depreciation Account to the Plant Disposal Account, the cash received on sale being entered there. As it is mentioned under (b) that the profit was transferred to the Profit and Loss Account, this can be shown. The depreciation charge for the year is then revealed in the Depreciation Account: it is the difference remaining after completion of the account into which the opening and closing balances and the transfer mentioned above have been entered.

The other accounts required are shown without further comment. A difficult point in the statement itself, however, may be mentioned: the Debenture discount written off.

As a further amount of discount was allowed during the year, it may seem strange that only £800 is written back as a book entry adjustment, and not £1200. But £400 Debenture discount was allowed during the year. If the increase in liabilities is shown for the gross amount of the Debenture issue of £20,000, it has the same effect during the current year as receiving £20,000 and paying back £400. If it were allowed to remain on the books until next year, its writing off would be a book-entry adjustment only and would have to be written back to the profit, as with the £800.

Capital reserve

Balance (constituting £8000 profit and £101,000 re-valuation)	£109,000

Freehold property

Balance b/d	£162,000	Cash on sale	15,000
Transfer to capital reserve	109,000	Balance c/d	256,000
	£171,000		£271,000

TAXATION ACCOUNT

Cash:		Balance b/d	£12,000
Corporation tax	£9,000	Debenture interest, tax deducted	1,200
Over-provision transferred back to Profit and Loss Account:		Profit and Loss Account: Corporation tax	16,000
Account	3,000		
Balance c/d:			
Corporation tax	17,200		
	£29,200		£29,200

FUNDS FLOW STATEMENT

for the year ended 31st December 19—

Opening bank balance			£3,870		
Increase in proprietors' funds:				Increase in assets:	
Share issue		£50,000		Plant and machinery £72,000	
Share premium		20,000		Stocks:	
		———		Raw materials 11,200	
		70,000		Work in progress 39,000	
Profit after taxation	£41,200			Finished goods 12,200	
Add Depreciation of				Debtors 8,000	
plant and machinery	34,200			Cash 40	
Provision for bad debts	190				£142,440
Reserve for replacement				Investments in associa-	
of machinery	5,000			ted companies	55,920
Debenture discount				Decrease in liabilities:	
written off	800			Dividend paid 10,000	
		81,390		Income tax and	
		———		profits tax paid 9,000	
		151,390		Income tax over-	
Less Profit on sale of				provided for writ-	
machinery		1,800		ten back 3,000	
		———	149,590		22,000
Decrease in assets:					
Sale of freehold		8,000			
Sale of plant and					
machinery (at writ-					
ten down value)		5,000			
		———			
		13,000			
Add Profit on sale of:					
Freehold	7,000				
Plant and machin-					
ery	1,800				
		8,800			
		———	21,800		
Increase in liabilities:					
Creditors		5,900			
Debentures		20,000			
Taxation		17,200			
		———	43,100		
Closing bank overdraft			2,000		
			£220,360		£220,360

We continue with an example of a type of examination question which is frequently set and is useful because it affords the opportunity to apply some basic principles of Balance Sheet criticism.

Specimen question

One of your clients has asked for your professional advice, as his accountant, on a further request for a loan of £6000 he has received from a relative. He points out that he would very much like to comply, but he has already made unsecured interest-free loans to the sum of £8000, and is worried about the financial soundness of the company his relative runs as sole working director. Enclosed is a recent Balance Sheet of the company, with other information, which may be summarised as follows:

XZ CO. LTD

Balance Sheet, 31st December 19—

19—				19—			
£25,000	Issued share capital		£25,000		Fixed assets:		
12,200	Profit and Loss Account		13,400	£8,000	Freehold factory premises at cost (purchased 1947)		£8,000
7,100	Amount set aside for income tax		3,900	26,500	Plant and Machinery at cost	£35,500	
2,000	Unsecured loan		8,000		Less Depreciation	15,500	
	Current liabilities:			13,000			20,000
25,600	Trade creditors	£44,950					
5,500	Taxation	7,100		13,500			
			52,050		Current assets:		
				32,200	Stock in trade	43,500	
				23,300	Trade debtors	30,050	
				400	Balance at bank	800	
							74,350
£77,400			£102,350	£77,400			£102,350

	19—	19—
Sales	£209,000	£223,000
Cost of sales	178,000	186,000
Directors' remuneration	3,000	6,000
Depreciation	6,200	

Answer

[Address)   [Address)

Dear Sir,   [Date)

XZ CO. LTD

Request for further unsecured loan

In accordance with your letter to me, dated ...., I have examined the enclosed Balance Sheet and relevant information, and report on the present position of the Company as follows.

1. Trading position

(a) *Gross profit.* The Company appears to have increased its trading activities over the year by £14,000, but this is not wholly due to increased turnover, as the gross profit rate was raised from 14·8% to 16·6% during the period. This may have been the result of an increase in selling prices with no corresponding rise in purchase prices. On the other hand, it could signify an over-valuation of stock-in-trade.

(b) *Stock-in-trade.* This has increased by over $33\frac{1}{3}$% on last year's figure which may indicate over-stocking, slowing down of turnover towards the end of the period, or over-valuation as mentioned above. It might conceivably be in anticipation of a coming peak sales season, however.

(c) *Depreciation.* The charge for depreciation appears inadequate. Although additions were made to plant and machinery during the year to the value of £9000, the charge for depreciation decreased by £3700 compared with the previous year.

(d) *Director's remuneration.* This figure is double the previous year's at £6000, which seems unwarranted in the circumstances.

(e) *Net profit.* The Profit and Loss Account from the information supplied might be summarised as follows:

Gross profit		£37,000
Director's remuneration	£6,000	
Depreciation	2,500	
Unspecified expenses	23,400	
		31,900
Net profit		£5,100

The figure so calculated for "Unspecified expenses" might be considered large for a company of this size but needs further elucidation.

The net profit figure of £5100, compared with sales of £223,000, reveals the unsatisfactory ratio of profit to sales of 2·3%. However, the figure of £5100 is itself open to doubt owing to the probably inadequate depreciation charge mentioned in (c) above.

The net revenue figure must also be considered in the light of the £6000 withdrawn as director's remuneration. If the director is almost the sole shareholder, the remuneration charged might in effect include part of the net profits, withdrawn in this way to gain the benefit of earned income relief against taxation. But in any case, it does not leave enough funds for ploughing back into the business, since taxation has to be provided out of the figure of £5100.

2. *Financial position*

(a) *Shortage of funds.*

(i) An obvious shortage of funds is revealed by the quick assets ratio of 1:1·7, *i.e.* the ratio of "Current liabilities" to "Trade debtors" and "Balance at bank." It shows that current funds are inadequate to meet current liabilities. This is confirmed by the sharp increase in the figures for "Creditors" of nearly £20,000 since 1st January 19—. On average, the creditors are having to wait three months for settlement. The period of credit allowed to debtors has increased from six to seven weeks, yet in view of the shortage of funds this period might be expected to decrease. It would be advisable, therefore, to look for overdue debts.

(ii) It is noted that your own unsecured loan was increased during the period from £2000 to £8000.

(iii) The actual movement of funds during the year may be clarified by the following statement.

FUNDS FLOW STATEMENT

for the year ended 31st December 19—

Balance at bank, 1st January			£400
Sources of funds:			
Increase in proprietors' funds (Profit and Loss			
Account)		£1,200	
Add Depreciation charge		2,500	
		3,700	
Increase in liabilities:			
Unsecured loan	£6,000		
Trade creditors	19,350		
		25,350	
			29,050
			29,450
Disposal of funds			
Increases in assets:			
Plant and machinery		9,000	
Stock in trade		11,300	
Debtors		6,750	
		27,050	
Net reduction in overall liability to income tax		1,600	
			28,650
Balance at bank, 31st December			£800

It will be seen that the main source of funds for expansion lay outside the business; the company provided only a total sum of £3700, and even this was subject to a charge for depreciation.

(b) *Fixed assets.* It appears from the reduced depreciation charge that the plant and machinery may be over-valued. On the other hand, the factory was purchased in 1947 and may be worth considerably more than the figure shown on the Balance Sheet.

3. Conclusions

(*a*) It is obvious that the company is running into difficulties through lack of finance and apparent over-trading. Its profit earning capacity is also inadequate. However, in view of the relatively high charges for "Unspecified expenses" and the director's remuneration—subject, of course, to an adequate charge for depreciation—it appears that with investigation and re-organisation the company might be made to operate more profitably.

(*b*) The company is in needs of capital funds, which should be supplied in a more suitable and permanent form than that of unsecured loans on an interest-free basis.

4. Recommendations

(*a*) In the company's present circumstances, a further unsecured loan of £6000 cannot be recommended.

(*b*) If, however, it is desired to make the loan for personal reasons, it is recommended that an expert valuation of the factory premises be requested. If, as is hoped, they are worth considerably more than the Balance Sheet value, security for the loan should be obtained on them. It would be advisable to seek security for the loans already made in like manner.

(c) A rate of interest should also be sought on these loans, since it should be pointed out that in any case the company cannot reflect a true revenue-earning position while it is operating on interest-free capital.

(d) Debentures might be issued in respect of the loans, but this would probably restrict further opportunities for borrowing later. If, after investigation, the company can offer evidence of more profitable trading, additional share capital should be raised.

Please let me know if I can be of further assistance.

Yours faithfully,

In conclusion, the method of enumerating the various points for inclusion in a report such as that shown above is illustrated.

Specimen question

BALANCE SHEET, *31st March 19—*

Authorised share capital:

50,000 £1 8% Cumulative Preference shares		£50,000
150,000 £1 Ordinary shares		150,000
		£200,000

Issued share capital:

50,000 8% £1 Cumulative Preference shares	£50,000		
75,000 £1 Ordinary shares	75,000		
		£125,000	
Revenue reserve:			
Profit and Loss Account		11,150	
Loan capital:			
5% Debentures (redeemable on or before 1st April 197–)		100,000	
			£236,150
			£236,150

	Cost	Depreciation	
Fixed assets:			
Freehold premises	92,000	—	92,000
Plant and machinery	204,800	49,850	154,950
	296,800	49,850	246,950
Investments (market value £54,600)			46,800
			£293,750

Current assets:
Stocks:

Raw materials	10,100		
Work in progress	5,600		
Finished goods	10,200		
		25,900	
Trade debtors		53,600	
Balance at bank	2,800		
Cash in hand	175		
		2,975	
			82,475
			£376,225

Current liabilities:

Sundry creditors	103,300	
Provision for current taxation	18,025	
Proposed Ordinary dividend (net)	18,750	
		140,075
Total net assets		£236,150

PROFIT AND LOSS ACCOUNT
for the year ended 31st March 19—

Trading profit		£86,400
Investment income		2,600
		89,000
Less Directors' remuneration	£25,000	
Depreciation	15,200	
Debenture interest	5,000	
		45,200
		43,800
Provision for taxation		18,025
		25,775
Preference dividend paid (gross)	4,000	
Proposed Ordinary dividend (25% gross)	18,750	
		22,750
		3,025
Balance brought forward from 31st March		8,125
Unappropriated profit c/f		£11,150

Above are the first draft Balance Sheet and Profit and Loss Account of an old-established company. The sales for the current year have reached £630,000 and the Profit and Loss Account is representative of those in previous recent years, save that sales have been steadily increasing on a widening market.

Orders are now being refused, although there is additional productive capacity available, as it is felt that the company is not financially strong enough to undertake further business.

Enumerate in list form, with brief comments, the items of particular relevance to the company's position, the conclusions to be drawn from them, and the recommendations which might be made as to future policy of the company.

Answer

1. Company's current position

(a) *Profit and Loss Account*

(i) The P/S ratio, at 6·5%, appears satisfactory, especially in view of (ii) below.

(ii) Directors' remuneration. This seems inordinately high at approximately 36% of the trading profits after deducting depreciation and Debenture interest but before deducting the remuneration figure.

(iii) Dividend on the Ordinary shares at 25% seems an unduly high proportion of profits after taxation, leaving insufficient funds to carry to reserve.

(b) *Balance Sheet*

(i) The company is highly geared at 2:1.

(ii) No Debenture redemption fund has been created in respect of Debentures redeemable in x years' time.

(iii) The current ratio is unsatisfactory at 1:1·7. It could be improved, however, to 1:1 by including "Investments" at market value.

(iv) The quick assets ratio is very poor at 1:2·5. It could be adjusted to 1:1·26 by including investments assumed to be readily realisable but would still be unsatisfactory even then.

(v) A revaluation may be possible of the freehold premises at cost.

(vi) Investments are included under "Fixed assets," but they bring in an income of just over 5%. In view of the company's position they have been considered with the current assets at market value, as it is necessary to obtain immediate funds in view of the amount of creditors outstanding (*see* (iii) and (iv) above).

(vii) Stocks appear low for a company with a turnover of £630,000. With sales at approximately £53,000 a month, by deducting a figure of (say) 25% for gross profit, the stocks of raw materials and finished goods can be reckoned in days rather than weeks.

(viii) Credit control on debtors is tight, at approximately one month.

(ix) The bank balance is low in view of current requirements.

2. Conclusions

(a) The company appears to be efficiently operated on the production side and has good prospects in this respect.

(b) The profit margin is adequate.

(c) But the financial management is inefficient, with:

(i) directors' remuneration and profit distributions too high,
(ii) inadequate ploughing back of funds,
(iii) a misguided investment policy,
(iv) inadequate working capital,
(v) irregular capitalisation and shortage of equity capital.

3. Recommendations

(a) Cut the proposed dividend to (say) 7% gross.

(b) Sell the investments.

(c) Use the major proportion of the proceeds from (b) above to reduce the creditors at once.

(d) If possible, revalue the freehold premises and create a capital reserve to improve the appearance of the Balance Sheet prior to action as in (e) below.

(e) Offer the remaining Ordinary shares for subscription. It would probably have to be at par, despite the previous high dividend distributions.

(f) Increase the working capital and accept additional orders, subject to a sufficient time lag for production to cope with the extra work load.

(g) Reconsider the amounts payable to directors in future and reduce them, if possible, until profits increase.

(h) Create a reserve for Debenture redemption as soon as funds are available, investing them outside the business and ensuring that they yield a reasonable rate of income.

EXAMINATION QUESTIONS

1. If you were acting on behalf of (a) a creditor, (b) a Debenture holder, (c) a prospective shareholder, to what points would you devote attention when examining the published accounts and directors' report of a limited company?   [C.C.A.

2. The summarised Balance Sheets of Flagstaff Ltd, a private company, at 31st March 1960 and 31st March 1961 and certain other particulars are given below.

Balance Sheets

	1960	1961		1960	1961
Issued share capital	£40,000	£45,000	Goodwill at cost	£15,000	£15,000
General reserve	12,000	18,000	Freehold property		
Profit and Loss Account	24,580	14,360	at cost	5,000	5,000
Income tax, 1960–61	3,470	—	Plant and machinery	21,000	34,000
Trade creditors	37,640	36,670	Investments, at cost (shares in X Ltd)	11,500	5,750
Accrued expenses	4,100	6,290	Stocks:		
Amount owing for new machinery	—	4,000	Materials	7,040	4,930
Bank overdraft (secured by mortgage on freehold property)	9,830	7,080	Work in progress	5,720	3,860
			Finished goods	26,080	28,150
			Trade debtors	40,280	34,710
	£131,620	£131,400		£131,620	£131,400

	at 31st March		
	1959	1960	1961
Plant and machinery:			
Cost	£85,000	£85,000	£100,000
Depreciation	56,000	64,000	66,000
	£29,000	£21,000	£34,000

No plant or machinery was scrapped or sold during the two years to 31st March 1961.

	Year to	
	31st Mar.	31st Mar.
	1960	1961
Sales	£402,600	£346,800
Overhead expenses, including depreciation of plant and machinery but excluding the items mentioned below	89,750	79,450
Interest on bank overdraft	250	520
Loss on sale of investments	Nil	3,200
Net profit	8,000	—
Net loss	—	4,200

At 31st March 1960 Flagstaff Ltd held 6000 shares in X Ltd. At the end of March 1961, 3000 of these shares were sold.

No dividends were paid during the two years to 31st March 1961.

The market value of the freehold property at 31st March 1961, was £8000.

The directors have asked the bank manager to increase the overdraft limit from £10,000 to £15,000.

You are required to write a report on the financial position and prospects of the company, drawing reasonable inferences from the figures and information given above.   [I.B.

3. The following are the summarised trial balances of Able Baker Ltd as at 31st March 1961 and 31st March 1962:

	31st March 1961		31st March 1962	
Issued share capital		£300,000		£300,000
Capital reserves		—		67,000
Revenue reserves		50,000		50,000
6% Debentures		—		100,000
Debenture discount			£2,000	
Freehold property at cost	£136,000			
Freehold property at revaluation			198,000	
Plant and equipment at cost	268,000		339,000	
Provision for depreciation of plant and equipment		123,600		144,800
Stocks and work in progress	117,000		229,000	
Debtors	84,000		144,400	
Creditors		61,000		82,900
Provision for bad debts		1,200		1,650
Profit and Loss Account balance		96,000		116,625
Net profit for year		20,625		59,000
Dividend (ignore tax)		18,375		
Trade investment at cost			63,025	
Cash in hand	120		150	
Bank balance	99,680			2,600
Taxation		34,000		51,000
	£704,800	£704,800	£975,575	£975,575

You are informed that:

(a) The capital reserve at 31st March 1962 represented:

(i) the profit on sale for cash of one property,

(ii) the surplus arising on the revaluation of the remaining properties.

(b) On 1st January 1962 £100,000 Debentures were issued at a discount of 3%.

(c) During the year, plant costing £22,000, with a written down value of £7,500, was sold for £12,000.

(d) The net profit for the year ended 31st March 1962 is arrived at after crediting the profit on the sale of plant and after charging accrued Debenture interest and writing off Debenture discount of £1000.

(e) The taxation account at 31st March 1962 is made up as follows:

1962 1st February:		1961 31st March:	
To cash	26,000	By balance	£34,000
31st March:		1962 31st March:	
Balance c/d	51,000	By Profit and Loss Account:	
		Corporation tax £51,000	
		Less over-provided 8,000	43,000
	£77,000		£77,000
		1962 31st March:	
		By balance	£51,000

You are required to prepare a statement for the directors showing how the reduction in the bank balance has occurred.   [C.W.A.

4. On 1st January 1961 the whole issued capital of LPG Ltd was acquired by HS and DY, who became the directors of the company immediately after the resignation of the former directors.

The summarised Balance Sheets of the company at 31st December 1960 and 31st December 1961 were as follows:

Balance Sheets

	1960	1961		1960	1961
Issued share capital	£80,000	£80,000	Goodwill	£32,000	£32,000
Profit and Loss			Freeholds, at cost	12,000	12,000
Account	38,400	41,000	Motor vehicles at		
Income tax 1961–2	27,600	27,600	cost, *less* depreciation	24,000	44,000
Income tax 1960–1	21,400	—	Stock in trade at		
Bank overdraft	4,600	31,200	cost	114,000	145,600
Trade creditors	94,000	174,400	Loans to directors	—	11,400
			Trade debtors	84,000	109,200
	£266,000	£354,200		£266,000	£354,200

The bank overdraft was secured by a mortgage on the freeholds, the market value of which, at 31st December 1961, was £40,000.

Income tax, 1960–1, is based on the profit of the year 1959 and was paid on 1st January 1961. Income tax, 1961–2, is based on the profit of the year

1960 and was paid on 1st January 1962. No income tax is payable by the company for 1962–3.

You are given the following particulars:

	1960	1961
Sales	£812,000	£832,000
Depreciation of motor vehicles charged in the Profit and Loss Account	16,000	4,000
Directors' remuneration charged in the Profit and Loss Account	5,000	13,000
Maximum bank overdraft	20,000	32,000
Minimum bank overdraft	Nil	18,400

The following is a summary of the stock in trade at the end of each of the years under review:

	31st Dec. 1960		31st Dec. 1961	
	Cost	Market value	Cost	Market value
Group A	£64,600	£82,600	£57,200	£73,800
B	49,400	65,000	51,600	67,400
C	—	—	36,800	8,000
	£114,000	£147,000	£145,600	£149,200

In 1961 the average selling price of the company's goods was 5% higher than in the previous year.

The company paid no dividends in 1961.

The directors have asked the bank manager to increase the overdraft limit from £32,000 to £60,000.

You are required to write, for the information of the bank manager, a report on the position of the company and the policy of the directors.

What, in your opinion, should the bank manager's answer be?

[C.I.S. (1962)

5. Transformations Ltd commenced business on 1st January 1960. On 1st January 1961 the company acquired additional premises and machinery and the business was extended by the manufacture of a new range of products.

The following are summaries of the company's Profit and Loss Accounts for 1960 and 1961 and of its Balance Sheets at the end of each year.

Balance Sheets

	31st Dec. 1960	31st Dec. 1961		31st Dec. 1960	31st Dec. 1961
Issued share capital	£120,000	£120,000	Freehold properties at cost	£31,500	£48,000
Debenture redemption reserve	—	1,200	Plant and machinery	58,050	70,500
Profit and Loss Account	15,000	15,600	Trade investment, at cost	—	11,000
5% Debentures	—	18,000	Discount on Debentures	—	360
Trade creditors	23,580	33,650	Stocks	34,200	47,710
Bank overdraft	—	27,180	Debtors	29,280	38,060
			Balance at bank	5,550	
	£158,580	£215,630		£158,580	£215,630

Profit and Loss Accounts

	1960	1961		1960	1961
Depreciation of plant and mach-inery	£6,450	£10,230	Balance, brought down	£21,470	£14,100
Debenture interest	—	900			
Bank interest	20	1,170			
Debenture redemp-tion reserve	—	1,200			
Net profit for year	15,000	600			
	£21,470	£14,100		£21,470	£14,100

The plant and machinery account was as follows:

1960			1960	
1st January	Cash	£64,500	31st December Depreciation	£6,450
1st January	Cash	7,560	31st December Depreciation	10,230
30th June	Cash	7,560		
31st December	Cash	7,560	Balance	70,500
		£87,180		£87,180

The three payments of £7560 each represent a deposit and instalments under a hire-purchase agreement. Two further instalments of £7560 each are due for payment in 1962 (ignore hire-purchase interest).

The bank overdraft is secured by a charge on the freehold property acquired in 1960 and the Debentures are secured on the property acquired in 1961.

Sales in 1960 amounted to £361,000 and in 1961 to £470,000, of which £109,000 represented the new products.

You are required:

(a) To compute the amount of the working capital at 31st December 1960 and at 31st December 1961.

(b) To prepare a statement showing the sources and application of working capital for the year 1961, in a form which reconciles the two amounts in (a) above.

(c) To discuss the changes in the company's position and to comment on the policy of the directors.

Ignore taxation. [I.B.

6. Bell Ltd acquired as on 31st March 1964 the current assets and goodwill of Drum Ltd.

(a) Detail the matters to which you would give attention when carrying out an investigation on behalf of the proposed purchaser of a limited company's shares.

(b) Illustrate your answer by reference to the abbreviated Profit and Loss Accounts and Balance Sheets of Drum Ltd—the company whose shares are to be acquired—for the period of three years to the 31st March 1964.

Profit and Loss Accounts, year to 31st March

	1962	1963	1964
Trading profit	£99,000	£75,000	£84,992
Surplus on insurance claim	3,500		
Income from investments:			
Trade	1,050	3,150	4,200
Government securities	240	240	
	£103,790	£78,390	£89,192
Depreciation of plant	£18,000	£10,000	£13,000
Plant replacement reserve	2,000	4,000	5,000
Bank interest	1,500	2,500	2,580
Written off preliminary expenses		500	500
Dividends paid	55,000	60,000	60,000
	£76,500	£77,000	£81,080
Balance for year	£27,290	£1,390	£8,112

Balance Sheet as at 31st March 1964

Authorised and issued share capital, £1 Ordinary shares		£100,000	Plant at cost (£300,000) *Less* Depreciation	£195,000	
Capital reserve		8,000	Goodwill	47,000	
Revenue reserves:			Trade investments	19,000	
Stock contingencies	£26,000		Stock at cost	75,720	
Plant replacement	25,000		Debtors	93,780	
Profit and Loss Account	87,000		Preliminary expenses	3,500	
		138,000			
Trade creditors		137,000			
Bank overdraft		51,000			
		£434,000		£434,000	

[C.C.A.

7. Mr Nova and his wife own all the shares in the Widget Manufacturing Corporation Ltd, a business which they started just over a year ago. You have prepared the accounts for the first year and they run as follows:

Profit and Loss Account

Direct manufacturing costs:	
Materials	£54,000
Labour	72,000
Cost of 2000 widgets	126,000
Less stock of 1000 finished widgets	63,000
	63,000
Depreciation of plant and machinery	55,000
Other factory overheads	34,000
General overheads	21,000
Research and development expenditure written off	17,000
	190,000
Sales: 1000 units at £130	130,000
Net loss for the year	£60,000

Balance Sheet

Ordinary Shares	£500,000	Plant and machinery—	
Less Profit and Loss		cost	£500,000
Account	60,000	*Less* depreciation	55,000
	440,000		445,000
Creditors, etc.	29,000	Stocks	63,000
Bank overdraft	65,000	Debtors	26,000
	£534,000		£534,000

Depreciation is provided at 11% p.a. by the reducing balance method. This rate will reduce the book value of the plant approximately to £50,000, its residual value, at the end of its life of twenty years.

Mr Nova writes the following letter to you:

Dear sir,

Thank you for sending me the accounts.

I was very surprised to see that these showed a loss of £60,000, for things seem to have been going rather well. I had planned to produce many more widgets than I could sell in the first year. At maximum capacity, I can produce only 3000 widgets per annum with this plant, and I expect to be able to sell a larger number once my product becomes known. In fact the sales of 1000 widgets during the first year were slightly better than I expected. In addition, the research department have been working on an improved model with excellent results. It should be possible to produce this soon and make a much higher profit per unit than with the current model.

At the end of the first year, someone offered to buy all the shares of my wife and myself in the company for £750,000. Since we invested only £500,000 in the business, this proves that we have made a profit.

How would you reply to Mr Nova?   [B. Sc. (Econ.)

8. The Major Company Ltd, a wholly owned subsidiary of Billings Ltd, a holding company, is unable to meet all of the demands for its products, in particular for the chemical compound SK 567, for which there were unfulfilled orders for the last twelve months of 245,000 cwts, and this is expected to increase to between 250,000–260,000 cwts. It is felt that the time taken to build new premises and install new plant is such that it would enable the

company's main competitors from overseas to satisfy this excess demand and to put them in a stronger position to compete for the company's other major customers. The Major Company have always managed to retain all of the big customers in this market and the overseas companies have been restricted to users whose combined demand is quite substantial but individual demand small. It has been decided, therefore, that existing facilities will have to be taken over. In particular, the management feel that the A.B. Company Ltd is ideal for this purpose. This is a privately owned company which only manufactures SK 567 for sale to many small users, and which has an annual capacity of 260,000 cwts. From the following information relating to the A. B. Company Ltd and the additional notes, prepare a report for management commenting: (a) on the current performance of the A.B. Company; (b) on the price to be offered for the Company; (c) the apparent profitability which would accrue to the Major Company, and (d) whether or not proposals to extend facilities by Major Ltd are reasonable.

Summary Profit/Loss Account of the A.B. Company
for year ended 31/5/69

Sales		£482,500
Trading Profit:		58,000
Less: Debenture interest	250	
Depreciation	12,500	
Directors' emoluments' fees	150	
Other	2,350	15,250
Profit before taxation		42,750
Corporation tax		21,140
Profit after taxation		21,610
Balance of profit brought forward		15,856
		37,466
Appropriations:		
Dividends 250% on Ordinary shares	10,000	
Transfer to reserve	7,674	17,674
		£19,792

Summary Balance Sheet of the A.B. Company
as at 31/5/69

Capital:			Fixed assets:	Cost	Depr. to date	
Authorised and Issued 4000 Ordinary Shares of £1		£4,000				
Reserves:			Land and building	15,000	—	£15,000
Capital reserve	20,500		Plant and machinery	102,500	48,950	53,550
Revenue reserve	153,543		Motor vehicles	3,490	2,490	1,000
Profit and Loss Account	19,792			£120,990	£51,440	£69,550
		193,835				
Deferred taxation account		15,000				
Debentures—5% 1974/75		5,000				
Current liabilities:			Goodwill			750
Creditors	19,860		Trade investments			2,500
Taxation	21,200		Current assets:			
Proposed dividends	10,000		Cash in Bank and on hand	3,495		
		51,070	Sundry Debtors	124,206		
			Stocks	68,404		
						196,105
		£268,905				£268,905

ADDITIONAL NOTES

1. The only other information, all of which has been estimated, about the A. B. Company is as follows:

(a) Sales were 240,500 cwts and this probably coincided with production.

(b) Fixed expenses are in the region of £124,000 per annum.

(c) Because of its smaller usage material prices will probably be 10% higher than those of the Major Company.

(d) There is no reason to believe that there will be a significant variation between the other variable expenses and those of the Major Company.

(e) It is thought that the owners of the A. B. Company regard $12\frac{1}{2}$% as a fair capitalisation rate for the pre-tax profits which the company earns.

2. For the Major Company the standard selling price and cost for SK 567, based on an annual output of 1,000,000 cwts is as follows:

Standard selling price	£2·00 per cwt
Standard cost:	
Material	£0·82$\frac{1}{2}$ per cwt
Labour	0·35
Variable expenses	·05
Fixed expenses	·47$\frac{1}{2}$
	£1·70

The Major Company have been set a profit target of 20% on capital employed by their holding company.   [C.C.A.

CHAPTER XXII

PROFITABILITY STATEMENTS AND
CAPITAL EXPENDITURE CONTROL

PROFITABILITY STATEMENTS

ONE of the most difficult problems which confront management is that of investment in fixed assets. Large amounts of money are often involved, and a decision to buy land, buildings or plant and machinery may influence the activity of the business for a considerable period of time. Capital is invested today in expectation of a return on it in the future, so it is important that in its decisions management should have available information that shows not only the amount to be invested, but also the expected earnings over a given period.

It is assumed here that in deciding whether or not to invest in fixed assets the sole criterion is the profit expected from the investment. The investment will arise from a projected expansion of business or replacement of existing assets. Of course, capital may be invested in projects on which it would be difficult to measure a return, such as:

1. *Safety precautions.* Provision of safety devices and equipment may be demanded by various legal requirements, including the Factories Acts.

2. *Service department projects.* The provision of buildings or equipment for non-manufacturing departments may be essential but the return cannot be evaluated.

3. *Welfare projects.* Provision of sports facilities for employees may contribute to employee morale, which cannot be evaluated financially.

4. *Research and development* may be initiated to improve company methods or products. It may prove unsuccessful or show no measurable return for a considerable time.

5. *Education projects.* Provision of a company training course may be instrumental in improving the efficiency of staff but here again results would be difficult to evaluate.

The advent of mechanisation and automation has resulted in management being confronted with ever more frequent and more difficult problems. Various techniques have been introduced to help management make its decisions, but the final choice still remains. It is the responsibility of the management accountant to see that management is presented with the most useful information about each project, so decisions are based not on guesswork but on reasoned calculations.

Of the techniques developed in recent years, some may be better than others according to the circumstances. In practice, it is usual to apply more than one technique in calculating the profitability of individual projects, so that management is presented with alternative choices which show what the result is likely to be according to the various factors considered. The techniques we shall consider are:

1. The return on investment.
2. The contribution related to a key factor:
    (a) where time is a key factor,
    (b) where shortage of resources is the key factor.
3. The pay-back period.
4. The discounted cash flow.

They can be applied to a variety of problems, such as, change in volume of output or selling price; the introduction of a new product; the optimum level of production; the purchase of a fixed asset to meet expansion requirements or to replace an existing asset; the purchase from suppliers of a component at present manufactured internally.

1. RETURN ON INVESTMENT

It is a reasonable assumption that shareholders invest money in a company to obtain a satisfactory return on their capital. What is regarded as a satisfactory return will be influenced by factors such as the nature of the industry, the risk involved, the risk of inflation, the comparative rate of return on gilt-edged securities, and fluctuations in external economic conditions. The shareholder can measure the success of a company in terms of profit related to capital employed. The return on capital employed can be used to show the efficiency of the business as a whole, or the profitability of an individual project.

What constitutes capital employed?

The capital employed in a business may be defined in a number of ways, but the two most widely accepted definitions are "gross capital employed" and "net capital employed." *Gross* capital employed usually comprises the total assets of the business, while *net* capital employed consists of total assets less current liabilities. However, in the commonly accepted sense the term covers capital, capital reserves, revenue reserves (including the Profit and Loss Account balance) and long term loans such as Debentures. But there is a good deal of controversy among accountants over which items should be included. A summary of the main assets found in a company Balance Sheet follows, with comments on whether each would normally be included in the computation of capital employed.

Fixed assets. All land and buildings, plant and machinery, fittings, motor vehicles, etc., should be included. The valuation of these assets gives rise to a difficulty. There are three recognised alternatives, (*a*) gross value, (*b*) net value, (*c*) replacement cost.

Gross value, (*a*), represents the original cost of the asset, and (*b*) net value the written-down value. Both methods have their supporters, but the latter appears to be more generally favoured. But recently, mainly because of the continuing problem of inflation, accountants have become increasingly conscious of the defects of historical cost and the advantages of (*c*) replacement cost. This technique recognises that the purchasing power of the £ is falling (or, to put it another way, that prices are rising). With replacement cost it is necessary to re-valuate fixed assets by assessing their current market values, either by reference to reliable published index numbers* or on valuations by experts. In calculating capital employed, therefore, the choice would seem to lie between the net value or the replacement cost of assets, with the latter steadily gaining favour.

It should be appreciated that if replacement costs are used in calculating capital employed, it will be necessary to re-calculate provisions for depreciation, because charges in the Revenue Account will have been based on the original cost of the assets.

If any assets are idle for a considerable period (*e.g.* owing to obsolescence or short working) it is considered advisable to exclude them from capital employed.

Goodwill is usually excluded from capital employed, because it is intangible and of uncertain value.

Patents and trade-marks. These are normally excluded; unless there is a potential sale for them, they too are of uncertain value. They should be written off to Revenue Account as soon as possible.

Investments made outside the business would be excluded but those made in associated companies to increase earnings may be included.

Stocks of raw materials, work in progress and finished goods should be valued at cost price and included in capital employed. Any obsolete stocks should be excluded from value of stock.

Debtors, reduced where necessary by a provision for bad or doubtful debts, should be included in the calculations.

Cash in hand and at bank. Cash is usually included. However, any excess or balance at bank which is beyond normal requirements should be excluded. Bank overdrafts should be included in the calculations, and either subtracted from current assets or treated in the same way as share capital.

Fictitious assets. Such items as formation expenses and deferred advertising costs should be excluded and written off to Revenue Account as soon as possible.

* See *Index Numbers* by W. R. Crowe (Macdonald & Evans, 1965) as a guide to those which are relevant and how they should be interpreted.

SUMMARY OF CAPITAL EMPLOYED

Capital and Liabilities	Assets
Issued share capital	(a) Fixed:
Capital reserves	Land and buildings*
Revenue reserves	Plant and machinery*
Debentures	Furniture and fittings*
	Motor vehicles*
	Investments made inside the business
	(b) Current assets
	Stocks
	Debtors *less* provision for bad debts
	Bank
	Cash
	Less Current liabilities:
	Creditors
	Bank overdraft

* at net value *or* replacement cost, less depreciation.

Example

The Balance Sheet of Jeraul & Co. Ltd is as follows:

BALANCE SHEET *as at 31st December 19—*

	Cost	Cumulative depreciation	Net
Fixed assets			
Freehold land and buildings	£200,000		£200,000
Plant and machinery	360,000	£120,000	240,000
Motor vehicles	50,000	30,000	20,000
	£610,000	£150,000	460,000
Investments			50,000
			£510,000
Current assets			
Stocks:			
Raw materials		£40,000	
Work in progress		10,000	
Finished goods		20,000	
			70,000
Debtors		80,000	
Less Provision for bad debts		2,000	
			78,000
Cash			2,000
			150,000
Less Current liabilities			
Creditors		50,000	
Taxation		30,000	
Bank overdraft		20,000	
			100,000
			50,000
Deferred advertising expenses			10,000
Total			£570,000

Capital employed

Authorised share capital:

200,000 £1 5% Preference shares	200,000	
300,000 £1 Ordinary shares	300,000	
	£500,000	

Issued share capital:

100,000 £1 5% Preference shares	100,000	
200,000 £1 Ordinary shares	200,000	
	300,000	

Capital reserves:

Share Premium Account		50,000	
Revenue reserves:			
General	100,000		
Profit and Loss balance	70,000		
		170,000	
			520,000
5% Debentures			25,000
Amount set aside for taxation equalisation			25,000
Total			£570,000

In order to ascertain the value of capital employed in the business, investigations have revealed the following:

(*a*) Freehold land and buildings are valued at £260,000.

(*b*) Plant and machinery has a replacement cost of £450,000. Depreciation on replacement cost would amount to £150,000.

(*c*) Motor vehicles would cost £60,000 to replace. Depreciation on replacement cost would amount to £36,000.

(*d*) Investments have been analysed to show the following:

Invested outside the business	£40,000
Invested inside the business	£10,000

(*e*) Included in the stock valuation are items now considered obsolete which amount to £2000.

CAPITAL EMPLOYED *as at 31st December 19—*

Fixed assets

Freehold land and buildings as revalued		£260,000
Plant and machinery at replacement cost	£450,000	
Less Depreciation provision based on replacement cost	150,000	
		300,000
Motor vehicles at replacement cost	60,000	
Less Depreciation provision based on replacement cost	36,000	
		24,000
Investments in associated companies		10,000
Total		594,000

Current assets
Stocks:

Raw materials	£38,000	
Work in progress	10,000	
Finished goods	20,000	
		68,000
Debtors		78,000
Cash		2,000
		148,000

Less Current liabilities:

Creditors	50,000		
Taxation	30,000		
Bank overdraft	20,000		
		100,000	
			48,000
			£642,000

Represented by:

Issued share capital	£300,000	
Capital reserve	50,000	
Revenue reserve	170,000	
5% Debentures	25,000	
Amount set aside for taxation equalisation	25,000	
		£570,000

Difference on revaluation:

Land and buildings	£60,000	
Plant and machinery	60,000	
Motor vehicles	4,000	
Stock	(2,000)	
		122,000

Assets not included in capital employed:

Investment outside the business	40,000	
Deferred advertising costs	10,000	
		50,000
		72,000
		£642,000

Profit

It should be realised that the figure for profit as used in return-on-investment calculations is the net profit with adjustments made (if necessary) for:

1. Any abnormal or non-recurring losses or gains.
2. Depreciation based on the replacement costs of assets.
3. Income from investments outside the business.

The profit figure is consequently brought into line with that used for capital employed; it will be recalled that assets were valued at replacement cost and only investments in associated companies were included in capital employed.

Example

The net profit shown in the Profit and Loss Account of Jeraul & Co. Ltd
was £83,000. Adjustments to be effected in calculating profit so as to find the
return on investment are:

1. Abnormal losses or gains:
   (a) Loss on sale of machinery, £2000
   (b) Bad debts recovered during the year, £1000
   (c) Interest on bank overdraft, £1200

2. Depreciation based on replacement cost:
   (a) Plant and machinery charged in Profit and Loss Account, £36,000.
This figure to be adjusted to £45,000
   (b) Motor vehicles charged in Profit and Loss Account, £10,000. This
figure to be adjusted to £12,000

3. Income from investments outside the business, £10,000.

Adjusted profit

Profit as per Profit and Loss Account			£83,000
Add Loss on sale of machinery	£2,000		
Interest on bank overdraft	1,200		
		£3,200	
Deduct Bad debts recovered	1,000		
Additional depreciation on plant and machinery	9,000		
Additional depreciation on motor vehicles	2,000		
Income from investments	10,000		
		22,000	
			18,800
			£64,200

Return on investment

(i) $\dfrac{\text{Profit}}{\text{Net capital employed}}$ *i.e.* $\dfrac{£64,200}{£642,000} = 10\%$

(ii) $\dfrac{\text{Profit}}{\text{Gross capital employed}}$ *i.e.* $\dfrac{£64,200}{£742,000} = 8\cdot6\%$

Specimen question

Jervid Ltd manufactures one standard product. The standard cost per unit
of output is as follows:

Element of cost	Per unit
Direct material	£6
Direct labour	3
Variable overhead	1
Marginal cost	£10

Budgeted output for the year, 10,000 units
Budgeted fixed overheads for the year, £50,000
It is company policy to assess profit as $33\frac{1}{3}\%$ of cost price.
Ignore taxation.
A budgeted Balance Sheet of the company is produced as follows:

Balance Sheet at 31st December 19—

Issued share capital:		Fixed assets:		
£1 Ordinary shares	£700,000	Freehold property at cost		£300,000
Profit and Loss Account	50,000	Plant and		
Creditors	20,000	machinery at		
		cost	£400,000	
		Less depreciation	60,000	
				340,000
		Motor vehicles		
		at cost	60,000	
		Less depreciation	20,000	
				40,000
		Current assets:		
		Stocks	30,000	
		Debtors	35,000	
		Bank	25,000	
				90,000
	£770,000			£770,000

You are required to calculate the return on investment.

Answer

PROFITABILITY STATEMENT

	Budgeted sales and costs	
Net capital invested	£750,000	
Output (units)	10,000	
Sales		£200,000
Element of cost:		
Direct materials	60,000	
Direct labour	30,000	
Variable overheads	10,000	
Marginal cost	100,000	
Fixed overheads	50,000	
Total cost		150,000
Profit		£50,000

Investment turnover	0·28
Percentage profit on turnover:	25%
Percentage return on investment:	6·6%

NOTES

This return on capital invested is quite inadequate. After deduction of tax it would result in a net return on capital of only approximately 3% if *all* profit were distributed to shareholders. This compares very unfavourably with the return from most gilt-edged securities and building societies, in which there is virtually no risk. In addition, the company may need to plough back some of the profits to meet future needs. It would appear that an immediate investigation into the company's methods is required, and the possibility of increasing the price of its product should be considered by the management.

In the profitability statement above, it will be observed that three measurements of profitability are shown. The first figure represents the relationship of sales to capital invested; the second represents the relationship of profit to sales, (*i.e.* the P/S ratio); the last represents the overall relationship of profit to capital invested. The return on investment consists of a combination of the two basic elements. This internal relationship of these elements can be expressed as follows:

$$\text{ROI} = \text{Profit/Sales} \% \times \text{Investment turnover}$$

or

$$\text{ROI} = \frac{\text{Profit}}{\text{Sales}} \times 100 \times \frac{\text{Sales}}{\text{Capital invested}}$$

Thus

$$\frac{\text{£50,000}}{\text{£200,000}} \times 100 \times \frac{\text{£200,000}}{\text{£750,000}} = 6 \cdot 6\%$$

This relationship is shown in more detail in Fig. 26.

Purchase of new assets

The return-on-investment technique is used frequently when considering the purchase of a new asset. A new machine may be required (*a*) to save costs by producing more cheaply than an old one, (*b*) to provide additional income by producing more output, or (*c*) to combine both advantages, saving costs and producing more output and doing it more cheaply.

Return-on-investment calculations can be used to show the relative profitability of investment in such projects. However, before giving an example of return on investment, it is necessary to consider a number of important points which will affect the calculations.

Rate of return

It is difficult to say what should be considered a satisfactory rate of return on capital employed. Perhaps the lowest rate should be that which would be paid on capital raised externally to finance the project, bearing in mind the points mentioned on p. 516. From research into the subject, it appears that an average figure would be around the order of 17% before deduction of tax.

Taxation

In the U.S.A. it is customary to show the return on capital employed *after* deduction of tax, and some accountants in the U.K. are inclined to follow this procedure. For convenience, taxation in the U.K. is considered to be about £0·50 in the £ or 50% of profits, so a return on capital after tax of about 8% would generally be considered satisfactory.

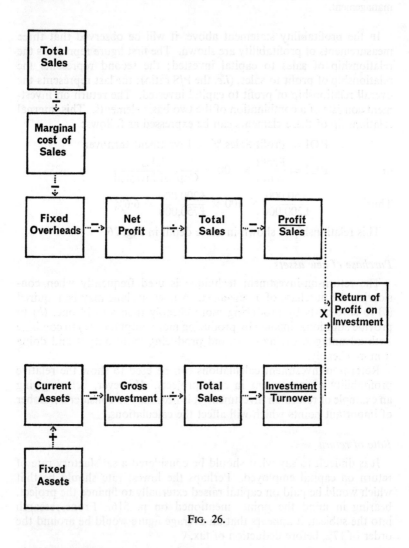

FIG. 26.

Average investment

There is some disagreement over how to arrive at the amount of investment in a project. Many accountants base their calculations on the average amount invested, the theory being that if £10,000 is invested in a machine today, at the end of its life of ten years it is worth nil, so the average amount is £10,000 ÷ 2 = £5000. Any residual value can be considered; if the residual value of the machine is expected to be £1000, the average investment is £10,000 + £1000 ÷ 2 = £5500. However, some accountants feel that £10,000 has actually been committed in the purchase of the machine, so this amount should be considered as the amount invested, irrespective of the fact that depreciation reduces the machine to a value of nil. In this book calculations will be based on average investment.

Residual value

There is controversy too as to the residual value of an old machine which is replaced by a new one. Many accountants consider that the residual value realised on the sale of an old machine should reduce the price of the replacement. Others feel that the cost of a new machine is unaffected by any cash from the sale of the one it replaces. There is no accepted rule. In this book, calculations will be based on the former theory.

Profitability formula

The return-on-investment formula which may be used for calculating profitability on investments in fixed assets is

$$\frac{\text{Average additional profit p.a.}}{\text{Average amount invested}} \times 100$$

Example

Chrisid Ltd is considering the purchase of a new machine to replace one which has been operating for six years. The following information is available:

	Present machine	Proposed machine
Cost of machine	£6000	£10,000
Estimated life of machine	10 years	10 years
Running hours per annum	2000	2000
Output per hour (units)	20	40
Costs:		
Power per annum	£300	£850
Consumable stores	£500	£700
Miscellaneous expenses	£600	£800
Wages cost per running hour	£0·40	£0·60
Material cost per unit	£0·10	£0·10
Sales price per unit	£0·22½	£0·20
Disposal value now	£2000	

Taxation is assumed to be 50% of profit.

PROFITABILITY STATEMENT

		Present machine		Proposed machine
Cost of machine		£6,000		£10,000
Life of machine		10 years		10 years
Output (units)		40,000		80,000
Sales value		£9,000		£16,000
Direct materials	£4,000		£8,000	
Direct labour	800		1,200	
Power	300		850	
Consumable stores	500		700	
Miscellaneous components	600		800	
Depreciation*	600		1,000	
		6,800		12,550
Profit before tax		2,200		3,450
Tax 50%		1,100		1,725
Profit after tax		£1,100		£1,725

Profitability

Return on investment:

Before tax $\dfrac{1250}{5000} \times 100$ 25%

After tax $\dfrac{625}{5000} \times 100$ 12·5%

NOTES
(i) Return before tax: £3450 − £2200
(ii) Return after tax: £1725 − £1100

The proposed project will yield a return on capital invested of 25% before tax, or 12½% after tax, which is probably considered to be quite satisfactory. If the company is willing to dispose of the old machine, it will reduce the amount invested in the new one:

(a) Average amount invested:
Amount invested   £10,000
Scrap value of present machine   2000
                        2) 8000   £4000

*Depreciation: some accountants consider that depreciation should represent the value of money forfeited by not selling the old machine. Thus, in this example, the machine can be sold now for £2000; its life with the company is estimated at another four years. By keeping the machine, £500 a year is sacrificed, and this figure is probably the correct amount for depreciation in a profitability statement which compares an existing machine with a proposed machine.

(b) Profit per annum:
Profit £3450
Reduced depreciation on £8000 invested £200 £3650

(c) Percentage profitability before tax $\frac{1450}{4000} \times 100 = 36\%$

(d) Percentage profitability after tax $= 18\%$

NOTE
Profit $= £3650 - £2200 = £1450$.

Advantages of return-on-investment technique
1. It is simple to operate and easy to understand.
2. It considers the profit of a project throughout its working life.
3. It acts as a yardstick when comparing the profitability of two projects.

Disadvantages
1. It ignores the fact that profits from different projects may accrue at an uneven rate.
2. It is difficult to assess a fair rate of return on capital employed.

COMPONENTS: PRODUCTION OR PURCHASE?

"Value analysis," developed in the United States, is a fairly recent innovation in Britain. Under this system, qualified staff review the design of components and other parts used in production to see if economies can be effected. They try to assess the value of the component, the necessity for it, the possibility of standardising it and of buying it from external sources. Management will be presented with information showing the price of the component as purchased from a supplier and the comparable cost of producing it internally. In the presentation of such information a useful calculation is that which compares the purchase price and the marginal cost of a component.

Specimen question

Chriseme Ltd manufactures three components, the cost of which is as follows:

Element of cost	Component		
	X	Y	Z
Direct material	£10	£8	£12
Direct labour	8	4	5
Variable overhead	2	4	3
Fixed overhead	5	2	10
Total	£25	£18	£30
Output per machine hour (units)	1	2	3

The key factor is a shortage of machine capacity.

You are to present a report to the management of the company, showing whether it should continue to manufacture these components (which are used in its main product) or whether it should buy them from a supplier, who has quoted the following prices: X, £30; Y, £15; Z, £25.

Answer

PROFITABILITY STATEMENT

	Component		
	X	Y	Z
Output per machine hour (units)	1	2	3
Purchase price	£30	£15	£25
Marginal cost	20	16	20
Fixed cost	5	2	10
Total cost	25	18	30
Difference between purchase price and total cost of production	5	(3)	(5)
Difference between purchase price and marginal cost of production	10	(1)	5
Per machine hour	10	(2)	15

NOTES

In an absorption costing system, it would be shown that the production cost of component Z is £5 more than the purchase price from the outside supplier. Similarly, component Y would be shown to cost £3 more to produce than to purchase. It would, then, seem advisable to stop producing Y and Z and to concentrate production on X.

However, with a marginal costing approach it can be seen that the most profitable component is Z because the saving in cost per machine hour is greatest. Y is unprofitable so, assuming output can be switched as desired, in all conditions component Y should be purchased, component X should be produced only when there are facilities available, and component Z should be manufactured at maximum level of activity.

2. OPTIMUM LEVEL OF PRODUCTION

When planning budgets or an expansion of output, management will no doubt wish to know what is the optimum level of output for the business; in other words, which is that highest level of output that can be achieved consistent with the lowest cost per unit? With most problems involving different levels of output it is beneficial to use marginal costing (*see* Chapter XI).

Key factors were discussed in Chapter IX, and a study of the items mentioned there suggests that the time factor itself may well be a key factor. However, key factors usually refer to some specific shortage such as shortage of direct materials or lack of capital. So, in this context, the time factor simply refers to a selected period of time, while the key factor may be any specified shortage of some important element in the production and sales of a product.

(a) *Contribution where time is the key factor*

This relates the contribution obtained from a product to the time taken to produce it.

Specimen question

Jeraul Ltd manufactures three products, the cost of which is as follows:

Element of cost	Product		
	A	B	C
Direct material	£15	£19	£25
Direct labour	7	5	11
Variable overhead	3	6	4
Marginal cost	£25	£30	£40

Other relevant information:

Selling price	£30	£38	£50
Output per day (units)	110 *or*	60 *or*	50

Management wishes to know the optimum level of production. On investigation you find the following:

If sales of Product A exceed 50 units a day, the selling price is expected to fall to £29 a unit for each additional unit; if sales of C exceed 20 units a day the selling price is expected to fall to £49 a unit; if sales of B exceed 15 units the price is expected to fall to £37.

The company works an eight-hour day and it is expected that 40 minutes will be lost daily in respect of machine setting-up time.

The key factor is a shortage of machine capacity.

Answer

PROFITABILITY STATEMENT (1)

	Product		
	A	B	C
Selling price	£30	£38	£50
Marginal cost	25	30	40
Contribution per product	£5	£8	£10
Profit–volume ratio	17%	21%	20%
Contribution per day	£550	£480	£500

Management would be recommended to produce Product A and sell it at £30 until the market has absorbed 50 units a day, when the selling price would have to be reduced. At this point it is necessary to find out which is better, to reduce the selling price of Product A or to produce B or C? The answer is shown by a new profitability statement.

PROFITABILITY STATEMENT (2)

	A	B	C
Selling price	£29	£38	£50
Marginal cost	25	30	40
Contribution	£4	£8	£10
Profit–volume ratio	14%	21%	20%
Contribution per day	£440	£480	£500

Management should be advised to produce 20 units a day of Product C, which will sell at the regular price of £50 each. A further statement will be prepared to determine additional output:

PROFITABILITY STATEMENT (3)

	A	B	C
Selling price	A	B	C
Selling price	£29	£38	£49
Marginal cost	25	30	40
Contribution	£4	£8	£9
Profit–volume ratio	14%	21%	18%
Contribution per day	£440	£480	£450

Management should be advised to produce B to sell at £38 a unit. The number to be produced cannot be determined until the capacity available is calculated. The capacity is as follows:

Product	Production time per day (minutes)	Output per day	Time taken per unit (minutes)
A	440	110	4
B	440	60	7⅓
C	440	50	8⅘

The optimum level of production will then be:

Product	Output per day (units)	Time taken per unit (minutes)	Time taken (minutes)
A	50	4	200
C	20	8⅘	176
B	9	7⅓	66
			442

The market can absorb 15 units of Product B a day, but the capacity available to manufacture it will only allow for an output of 9 units. In fact even then 9 units can be produced only if two minutes are available from the setting-up time of 40 minutes per day; this may result in only 8 units of

Product B being produced per day. It is assumed for simplicity that there is no possibility of introducing overtime or shift working.

In this example the time factor determines which products should be manufactured. Time is usually an important factor in determining production forecasts, except perhaps where sales are not keeping pace with output. Thus it is a key factor, and this technique relates contribution per product to this key factor.

(b) *Contribution where shortage of resources is the key factor*

The next example, in which contribution is related to key factors other than time, is very similar to the preceding one.

Specimen question

Dapher Ltd manufactures three products, which pass through three departments before completion. Department 1 is experiencing an acute shortage of skilled labour and there is no immediate prospect of the situation improving. In Department 1, total wages for the year are budgeted at £50,000 and will remain constant irrespective of which products are produced, assuming full production is maintained and that there is no need for overtime working. Standard costs for each product are as follows:

Element of cost	J	R	L
Direct material	£15	£10	£20
Direct labour: Dept. 1	5	4	8
2	3	3	4
3	2	1	2
Variable overheads	3	2	2

Fixed overhead for the year is budgeted at £40,000.
Selling prices per unit are: J, £35; R, £26; L, £45.

Answer

PROFITABILITY STATEMENT

	J	R	L
Direct material	£15	£10	£20
Direct labour: Dept. 1	5	4	8
2	3	3	4
3	2	1	2
Variable overheads	3	2	2
Marginal cost	28	20	36
Contribution	7	6	9
Selling price	£35	£26	£45
Percentage profitability	140	150	112·5
Contribution per annum	£70,000	75,000	56,250

Thus it is seen that:

(a) Maximum contribution per article is obtained by Product L.
(b) Maximum percentage profitability is obtained by Product R.

NOTES

(i) **Percentage profitability** is calculated by:

$$(\text{Contribution}/\text{Key factor}) \times 100$$

Product J	$(£7/£5) \times 100$	140%	
R	$(£6/£4) \times 100$	150%	
L	$(£9/£8) \times 100$	112·5%	

(ii) **Contribution per annum** is calculated by:

Direct wages cost of key factor department × Percentage profitability per product

Product J	£50,000 × 140%	£70,000	
R	£50,000 × 150%	£75,000	
L	£50,000 × 112·5%	£56,250	

(iii) Product R obtains the maximum use of the key factor, so production resources should be concentrated on that product. If the market can absorb as many units of it as can be produced under the present restricted conditions, then to achieve maximum profitability only R should be produced. This conclusion can be checked as follows:

Total wages of the department restricted by key factor are £50,000. Direct wages cost per unit of products, J. R and L is £5, £4 and £8 respectively. Output for the period would therefore be 10,000 units, 12,500 units or 6250 units respectively, or any combination of these units.

The level of production will be:

	J	R	L
Output (units)	10,000	12,500	6,250
Sales	£350,000	£325,000	£281,250
Marginal cost	280,000	250,000	225,000
Contribution	70,000	75,000	56,250
Fixed overhead	40,000	40,000	40,000
Profit	£30,000	£35,000	£16,250

It will be seen that:

(a) Maximum profit is obtained by producing Product R.

(b) Percentage profit to turnover: J, 8·6   R, 10·8   L, 5·8

3. PAY-BACK PERIOD

This method attempts to measure the period of time it takes for the original cost of a project to be recovered from the additional earnings of the project itself. "Earnings" in this context usually means profits from operation of the asset before charging any depreciation but after deduction of tax. It is a simple method of calculating the profitability of a machine and appears to be quite widely used both in the U.S.A. and in Great Britain.

Advantages

1. It is simple to operate and easy to understand.
2. It shows how soon the cost of purchasing an asset will be recovered.
3. Because the method considers only the years in which cost is recovered, estimates are not based on very long periods of time and so tend to be relatively more accurate than other methods in which the total life of the asset is considered.
4. This short term approach reduces the loss through obsolescence.
5. If a business is suffering from a shortage of cash, it is essential that capital invested should be converted into cash as soon as possible.
6. It acts as a yardstick in comparing the profitability of two projects.

Disadvantages

1. It considers only the recovery of purchase costs, not profits earned during the working life of the asset.
2. It ignores the fact that profits from different projects may accrue at an uneven rate. Thus a project which earns profit quickly, early in its life, may be considered a more profitable investment than another machine which earns profit slowly at first but at an accelerated rate later in its working life.
3. It stresses the importance of converting capital into cash. which may be unimportant in assets with a long working life.

Specimen question

Graemid Ltd is considering the purchase of a new machine which will carry out some operations at present performed by labour. E and F are alternative models. The following information, from which a profitability statement is to be prepared for submission to management, is available:

	Machine E	Machine F
Estimated life of machine (years)	5	6
Cost of machine	£15,000	£25,000
Estimated cost of indirect materials	600	800
Estimated savings in scrap	1,000	1,500
Estimated savings in direct wages:		
Employees not required	15	20
Wages per employee	600	600
Additional cost of maintenance	700	1,100
Additional cost of supervision	1,200	1,600

Taxation for convenience is to be regarded as 50% of profit.

Answer

PROFITABILITY STATEMENT

	Machine E	*Machine F*
Cost of machine	£15,000	£25,000
Estimated life of machines (years)	5	6
Savings per annum:		
Wages	£9,000	£12,000
Scrap	1,000	1,500
	£10,000	£13,500
Additional costs per annum:		
Indirect material	600	800
Maintenance	700	1,100
Supervision	1,200	1,600
	2,500	3,500
Profit (before tax)	7,500	10,000
Taxation	3,750	5,000
Profit (after tax)	£3,750	£5,000
Pay-back period (in years):		
(a) Before taxation	2	$2\frac{1}{2}$
(b) After taxation	4	5
Profitability:		
(a) Before taxation	£22,500	£35,000
(b) After taxation	3,750	5,000

NOTES

  (i) Pay-back period: Machine cost/Savings per annum.

Before tax	£15,000/£7,500	£25,000/£10,000.
After tax	£15,000/£3,750	£25,000/£5,000.

(ii) The pay-back period for machine E is less than that for F, and so E would be preferred. The simple pay-back period considers only the years during which the machine is paying for itself in savings, not the whole savings that accrue over its working life. It is frequently considered that this is too incomplete a picture, so a refinement can be introduced to show the additional amount of savings. In this example it would result in machine F having a profitability of £35,000 before tax, compared with £22,500 for machine E. The calculation is as follows:

Savings per annum	(Life of machine — Pay-back period)
E £7,500	(5 years — 2 years) = £22,500
F £10,000	(6 years — $2\frac{1}{2}$ years) = £35,000.

A similar calculation is made for both projects, showing profit after taxation.

In short: if the pay-back period is used, management would be advised to purchase machine E; but if profitability after the pay-back period is considered, management would be advised to purchase machine F.

(iii) *Taxation:* the question of including taxation in the computation of profitability was discussed earlier. In this example, taxation has been regarded as 50% of profit.

Pay-back reciprocal

The pay-back period expresses the profitability of a project in terms of years; it does not show any return as a measure of investment. The pay-back reciprocal has been utilised to rectify this situation, but it is only of value where the pattern of cash inflow is relatively consistent, and the life of the asset is at least double the pay-back period of the asset. The reciprocal is expressed as—

$$\frac{\text{Annual earnings}}{\text{Investment}} \times 100$$

Thus, using the figures in the foregoing illustration, based on annual earnings before taxation, we would have:

$$\text{Machine E } \frac{£7,500}{15,000} \times 100 = 50\%$$

$$\text{Machine F } \frac{£10,000}{25,000} \times 100 = 40\%$$

In this illustration, earnings before taxation have been used because the earnings after taxation do not cover a long enough period to warrant use of the reciprocal. Obviously, if the pay-back period were the same as the life of the asset, the reciprocal would be one. This pay-back reciprocal is often used as a guide to ascertain the discount factor in discounted cash flow calculations, which is discussed in the remainder of this chapter.

It should be noted that this method is not quite the same as the return-on-investment method. In any pay-back calculations, depreciation is ignored, while in return-on-investment calculations depreciation must be included. Thus, in the pay-back reciprocal method, annual earnings differ from the net profit used in the return-on-investment method by the amount of depreciation of the asset.

4. DISCOUNTED CASH FLOW

The discounted cash flow technique is a method of evaluating the profitability of investment in capital projects; it has been developed from the simple pay-back method. The D.C.F. calculations reveal not only the pay-back period, but also the profit accruing from the project. Many accountants claim that it is the most accurate method of evaluating the investment worth of capital projects because it reveals the estimated cash flow during the life of the asset and relates the discounted value of future proceeds in terms of current proceeds. In other words, it considers that £1 today (the original outlay) is worth more than £1 received at a future date (the cash flow) and it shows the estimated period during which the cash flow should continue. Management can be given guidance in its decision as to how much capital may be invested profitably in a project.

The D.C.F. technique considers the net cash flow as representing the recovery of the original investment plus a return on capital invested. The reader may be familiar with the mortgage principle, where the building society advances money which is repaid by equal instalments representing the recovery of money advanced plus an agreed charge for interest. The D.C.F. technique follows the same pattern, the main difference being that there is no certain rate of interest as with a mortgage, but, rather, an assumed interest rate. One of the difficult problems of using this technique is to determine a reasonable rate of interest.

Rate of interest

There is no rule to determine what rate of interest should be used in calculating the D.C.F. A possible rate to be required from a project could be similar to the satisfactory rate of return on capital employed discussed earlier in this chapter—17% before tax or 8% after deduction of tax. It is important that the required rate should be chosen with care, because it has a very important bearing on the result.

Life of the asset

The period during which the asset is expected to earn revenue is included in the D.C.F. calculation, but it is difficult to forecast the life of an asset with any degree of accuracy. Obviously a machine with an estimated life of ten years will show a different return from one with an estimated life of five years. Considerable care must be taken in assessing wear and tear of the asset and the possibility of obsolescence.

Cash flow

It is emphasised that it is the cash flow which must be considered, not revenue and costs expected during the period. A company may sell a product this year but not receive cash until the following year, and similarly may incur costs this year but not pay cash until next year. Only cash inflow and outflow must be considered. In most companies, receipts and payments of cash will take place throughout the year, but for D.C.F. purposes cash flow is assumed to take place at the end of each year. This assumption is purely for convenience of calculation, because it would be impracticable to calculate cash flow for every day of the year. In short, cash flow for the year represents total cash received from sales, less total cash paid in respect of costs incurred.

Present values

The D.C.F. technique is based on ascertaining the *present* value of earnings to be received in the *future*. It is, therefore, necessary to find a rate of interest which will discount future cash inflows so that the present value of these receipts will equal the capital cost of a project. This rate of interest may be obtained from special tables (*see* Appendix) or calculated as follows:

£1 is to be invested for a period of five years, from which is required a return before deducting tax of 20% per annum. The value of £1 at the end of each year can be calculated:

At the end of the

	1st	2nd	3rd	4th	5th

year, the value of £1 invested is

	$1 \cdot 2^1$	$1 \cdot 2^2$	$1 \cdot 2^3$	$1 \cdot 2^4$	$1 \cdot 2^5$
=	£1·2	£1·44	£1·7278	£2·0734	£2·4882

The present value of £1 earned at the end of each year is:

Year 1: £1/£1·2   = £0·83331
2: £1/£1·44   = £0·69440
3: £1/£1·7278 = £0·57877
4: £1/£2·0734 = £0·48240
5: £1/£2·4882 = £0·40188

Thus, for example, £1 earned in five years' time is worth £0·40 now, assuming a discount rate of 20% per annum. Reference to the Table in the Appendix will reveal the same results.

This present value factor may be derived from the formula:

$$P = \frac{S}{(1 + i)^n}$$

where P = Present value of a future sum of money,
S = Future value of a sum of money,
i = Interest rate,
n = Number of years.

Example

A sum of money is to be invested now to earn £50,000 in ten years. The rate of compound interest is to be taken at 8%. Find the present value.

The formula gives:

$$P = \frac{£50,000}{(1 + 8\%)^{10}} = \frac{£50,000}{(1 \cdot 08)^{10}}$$
$$= £23,150 \text{ approx.}$$

From the Appendix this can be checked:

£0·463 × 50,000 = £23,150 approx.

Specimen question (1)

Jeropher Ltd is considering the purchase of a machine which will have a working life of five years. The machine is expected to earn £10,000 per annum before deduction of tax. The company considers a yield of 20% necessary before investment is made in a project. How much could be spent in purchasing the machine?

Answer

Year	Cash flow	Present value of £1 at a discount factor of 20%	Present value of cash inflow
1	£10,000	£0·83331	£8,333
2	10,000	0·69440	6,944
3	10,000	0·57877	5,788
4	10,000	0·48240	4,824
5	10,000	0·40188	4,019
			£29,908

The company could afford to spend approximately £30,000 on this machine, so as to achieve earnings of £10,000 per annum for the next five years. This may be checked:

Year	Capital un-recovered at beginning of each year	Discount factor at 20%	Cash inflow	Capital re-covered during year
1	£29,908	£5,982	£10,000	£4,018
2	25,890	5,178	10,000	4,822
3	21,068	4,214	10,000	5,786
4	15,282	3,056	10,000	6,944
5	8,338	1,662	10,000	8,338
		£20,092	£50,000	£29,908

NOTE

Calculations for Year 5 have been approximated to allow for discrepancies incurred in "rounding off" figures to the nearest £1.

Specimen question (2)

Jeran Ltd is considering the purchase of a machine. Two machines are available, A and B, each costing £50,000. In comparing the profitability of the machines, a discount rate of 10% is to be used. Earnings after taxation are expected to be as follows:

Year	Cash flow Machine A	Machine B
1	£15,000	£5,000
2	20,000	15,000
3	25,000	20,000
4	15,000	30,000
5	10,000	20,000

PROFITABILITY STATEMENT

Year	Discount factor (10%)	Machine A		Machine B	
		Cash flow	Present value	Cash flow	Present value
1	0·90909	£15,000	£13,636	£5,000	£4,545
2	0·82645	20,000	16,529	15,000	12,397
3	0·75132	25,000	18,783	20,000	15,026
4	0·68302	15,000	10,245	30,000	20,491
5	0·62093	10,000	6,209	20,000	12,419
		£85,000	£65,402	£90,000	£64,878

This statement shows that machine A is the more profitable investment. Machine B will earn £5000 more than A, but the cash inflow is small to begin with and even though it rises steeply until the last year of its working life the present value of the cash flow is less than that of A. Machine A has a large cash inflow early in its working life, and so the present value of this flow is relatively high.

Comparison with pay-back period and return on investment

	Machine A	Machine B
Pay-back period	2⅘ years	3¼ years
Pay-back profitability	£35,000	£40,000
Return on investment	28%	32%
D.C.F. excess of present value of cash flow over capital cost	£15,402	£14,878

It will be observed from these figures that machine A would be preferred under (*a*) the pay-back period method and (*b*) the D.C.F. method while machine B would be preferred under (*a*) the pay-back profitability method and (*b*) the return-on-investment method. These results are as would be expected. Machine A gives a high return in the early part of its life and hence a favourable result with the pay-back period or D.C.F. methods. Machine B does not yield a good return until late in its working life, so the pay-back profitability and R.O.I. methods show more favourable results because they do not consider *when* the yield is obtained, merely the *extent* of the yield.

There are two basic methods of operating a system of discounted cash flow. Both methods involve discounting future inflows and, where necessary, cash outflows, and both are based on present value tables. Where they differ is in the calculation of the discount rate. The methods are: (1) the present value method, (2) the internal rate of return method.

1. *The present value method*

Management is required to select an acceptable minimum rate of return for any projects to be undertaken. This rate is regarded as the "cut-off rate," in other words, if a project cannot produce the required rate of return on capital invested, it will not be acceptable to the company. It is very difficult to ascertain which rate of return *would* be acceptable, but this rate may be arrived at by calculating the average cost of capital suitably adjusted to allow for the risk element involved in the project. Thus if management accepts that the cut-off rate is to be 20%, any project which returns discounted future earnings less than that figure would be unacceptable to the company: the net present value would be negative, and therefore the money to be invested today would be greater than the future earnings are worth today. Conversely, a project with a rate of return greater than 20% would have a positive value, showing that future earnings are worth more today than the cash invested today, and so would be acceptable to the company.

Example

Jereme Ltd wishes to expand output and is considering the purchase of a new machine. Two machines are available, machine X and machine Y, costing £25,000 and £35,000 respectively. The machines may be regarded as mutually exclusive, in other words, the company can buy only one or the other, not both. The cut-off rate required by the company is 20%. Earnings before taxation have been estimated as follows:

	Cash flow:	
Year	Machine X	Machine Y
1	£6,000	£5,000
2	7,000	10,000
3	10,000	10,000
4	10,000	10,000
5	8,000	10,000
6	5,000	10,000
7	2,000	6,000
8	—	4,000
9	—	2,000
10	—	—
	£48,000	£67,000

It is required to ascertain the more profitable machine.

PROFITABILITY STATEMENT

Year	Discount factor (20%)	Machine X Cash flow (£)	Machine X Present value (£)	Machine Y Cash flow (£)	Machine Y Present value (£)
0	1·000	(25,000)	(25,000)	(35,000)	(35,000)
1	0·833	6,000	4,998	5,000	4,165
2	0·694	7,000	4,858	10,000	6,940
3	0·579	10,000	5,790	10,000	5,790
4	0·482	10,000	4,820	10,000	4,820
5	0.402	8,000	3,216	10,000	4,020
6	0·335	5,000	1,675	10,000	3,350
7	0·279	2,000	558	6,000	1,674
8	0·233	—	—	4,000	932
9	0·194	—	—	2,000	388
		£23,000	£915	£32,000	£(2,921)

This statement shows that machine X yields a return of more than 20%, so is acceptable to the company, while machine Y does not give a return of 20% and so would be unacceptable. For machine Y, the present value of future earnings is £2921 less than the present value of the investment.

It must be appreciated, however, that no matter how refined the calculations may be, the validity of the conclusions depends on the accuracy of the data supplied. There are many variable factors included in the D.C.F. calculations, so unless the input figures are reasonably realistic, the output information will not be very useful. One must consider that in evaluating the cash inflow, a number of factors are involved, including: (a) future selling prices, (b) future sales volumes, (c) future costs of production, (d) estimated life of the asset, (e) estimated residual value of the asset.

These factors must therefore be borne in mind when deciding on a project. This is not to say that this technique is not a valuable tool of management, because it attempts to reduce decision making to a quantitative technique. All budgeting and forecasting techniques inevitably involve estimating, and it is important that a company must plan ahead as realistically as possible. Nevertheless, the technique is becoming increasingly regarded as an essential aid in decision making, especially when large projects are being considered.

2. The internal rate of return method

This method may be referred to as the "trial and error" method, because it involves making a number of trial calculations in an attempt to compute the correct interest rate which equates the present value of cash inflows with the present value of cash outflows; in other words, the rate of interest which discounts the cash flows to zero. Stated as a ratio,

Cash inflow/Cash outflow = 1.

When the present value method was discussed, it will be recalled that management determined the cut-off rate and this discount factor was used to calculate the present value of cash flows. In this method, the rate of return is not known, and this requires a series of trials at various discount rates.

Example

Graechris Ltd is planning to increase its present capacity, and is considering the purchase of a new machine. Machines C and D are available at a price of £40,000 and £45,000 respectively. The machines are mutually exclusive projects. Earnings before taxation have been estimated as follows:

Year	Cash Flow Machine C	Machine D
1	11,000	8,000
2	15,000	12,000
3	20,000	18,000
4	16,000	24,000
5	8,000	15,000
	£70,000	£77,000

It is required to ascertain the more profitable machine.

PROFITABILITY STATEMENT: PROJECT C

		Trial No. 1 (20%)		Trial No. 2 (24%)		Trial No. 3 (22%)	
Year	Cash flow	Discount factor	Present value	Discount factor	Present value	Discount factor	Present value
0	£(40,000)	1·000	£(40,000)	1·000	£(40,000)	1·000	£(40,000)
1	11,000	0·833	9,163	0·806	8,866	0·820	9,020
2	15,000	0·694	10,410	0·650	9,750	0·672	10,080
3	20,000	0·579	11,580	0·524	10,480	0·551	11,020
4	16,000	0·482	7,712	0·423	6,768	0·451	7,216
5	8,000	0·402	3,216	0·341	2,728	0·370	2,960
	£30,000		£2,081		(£1,408)		£296

This statement shows that in the first trial at 20%, the present value of cash inflows exceeds the present value of cash outflows by £2081. On the second trial at 24%, the present value of cash inflows is less than the cash outflow. On the third trial at 22%, cash inflows are marginally greater than cash outflows. Thus approximately 22% is the rate of return which equates the present value of inflows with outflows. Such approximation is usually adequate, but if, in the consideration of large projects, greater accuracy is required, interpolation may be used to find the required discount rate rather than the calculation of unlimited trials.

To apply interpolation techniques, a simple method is as follows (based on the above illustration):

$$22\% + (296/1704)\ 2\% = 22·34\%.$$

However, as stated previously, it is not possible to forecast accurately the data required for D.C.F. calculations, so it is normally unnecessary to work in decimals. Interpolation is discussed further on p. 548.

PROFITABILITY STATEMENT: PROJECT D

		Trial No. 1 (16%)		Trial No. 2 (20%)		Trial No. 3 (18%)	
Year	Cash flow	Discount factor	Present value	Discount factor	Present value	Discount factor	Present value
0	£(45,000)	1·000	£(45,000)	1·000	£(45,000)	1·000	£(45,000)
1	8,000	0·862	6,896	0·833	6,664	0·847	6,776
2	12,000	0·743	8,916	0·694	8,328	0·718	8,616
3	18,000	0·641	11,538	0·579	10,422	0·609	10,962
4	24,000	0·552	13,248	0·482	11,568	0·516	12,384
5	15,000	0·476	7,140	0·402	6,030	0·437	6,555
	£32,000		£2,738		(£1,988)		£293

Interpolation:

$$18\% + (293/2281)\ 2\% = 18·26\%.$$

These profitability statements show that, using the internal rate of return method, project C yields a rate of return of 22%, while project D yields approximately 19%. On this basis project C would be recommended.

Taxation

In this chapter the implications of taxation in investment decision making have not been considered seriously. In the discussion of pay-back and R.O.I. methods, an approximate figure of 50% was assumed as the reduction in profit due to taxation, while in the discussion of D.C.F. techniques, taxation was ignored. It is now desirable that the basic aspects of taxation should be considered. However, it must be appreciated that changes in the rate of taxation occur frequently, so it would be impracticable to revise the illustrations in this text on every occasion that the Government introduced new tax legislation. It is therefore proposed to use tax calculations which are relatively current at the time of printing, but are of a general nature rather than being exact at a particular time. For example, the authors will assume that corporation tax is 40%, which is a more manageable figure than (say) 42½%; in other words, we are illustrating general principles rather than the exact requirements peculiar to any fiscal year.

Example (1)

Chrisan Ltd is considering the purchase of an asset which is priced at £10,000. The estimated residual value at the end of its life of three years is £1000. The annual net cash savings are estimated at £3000. Capital grant is 20%, payable approximately eighteen months after purchase. The annual allowance is 20% and corporation tax is to be taken as 40%, payable approximately six months after the end of the year. Is the machine a profitable investment?

CASH FLOW STATEMENT

Details	0	1	2	3	4	5
Cash outflow	(10,000)					
Cash inflow						
Grant			2,000			
Trade in allowance					1,000	
Profit		3,000	3,000	3,000		
Taxation			(560)	(690)	(790)	1,240
Net	£(10,000)	3,000	4,440	2,310	210	1,240

Year column spans 1–5.

NOTES

(i) It has been assumed that the residual value for the machine was obtained.
(ii) Calculations of capital allowances:

Year 1	Investment	£10,000	
	Capital grant	2,000	
		8,000	
	Annual allowance	1,600	1,600
		6,400	
2	Annual allowance	1,280	1,280
		5,120	
3	Annual allowance	1,024	1,024
		4,096	
4	Residual value	1,000	
		£3,096	(3,096) balancing allowance

(iii) Corporation tax:

Details	Year			
	1	2	3	4
	£	£	£	£
Profit before taxation	3,000	3,000	3,000	—
Capital allowances	1,600	1,280	1,024	3,096
	1,400	1,720	1,976	(3,096)
Tax at 40%	560	690	790	(1,240)

PROFITABILITY STATEMENT

		Trial No. 1		Trial No. 2		Trial No. 3	
Year	Cash flow	Discount factor (30%)	Present value	Discount factor (20%)	Present value	Discount factor (5%)	Present value
0	£(10,000)	1·000	£(10,000)	1·000	£(10,000)	1·000	£(10,000)
1	3,000	0·769	2,307	0·833	2,499	0·952	2,856
2	4,440	0·592	2,628	0·694	3,081	0·907	4,027
3	2,310	0·455	1,051	0·579	1,337	0·864	1,996
4	210	0·350	74	0·482	101	0·823	173
5	1,240	0·269	334	0·402	498	0·784	962
	£1,200		£(3,606)		£(2,484)		£14

This statement shows the importance of tax computations in the consideration of purchasing new projects. When first reading the question, it would appear to be not worth consideration, when one observes that for an investment of £10,000, the savings will amount to only £9000 spread over the next three years, followed by a sale of the machine for £1000. However, after computing the tax payable and the tax allowances, the cash inflow is increased to £11,200. Discounting the cash flows shows that if this project were undertaken, there would be a rate of return of 5%. This rate, even though it is net, is probably much too low for the company; nevertheless, it is not disastrous. This example reveals clearly the implications of taxation in decision-making techniques.

Example (2)

Davan Ltd is considering the purchase of one of two machines which are mutually exclusive. Details of the machines are as follows:

(a) *Machine E*

Cost of machine: £1000.
Annual return before taxation: £250.
Estimated life of machine: ten years.
Residual value of machine at end of life: £50.

(b) *Machine F*

Cost of machine: £1000.
Annual return before taxation:

Year 1 £100   Year 2 £200   Year 3 £250   Year 4 £300   Year 5 £300
    6 £300   7 £300   8 £300   9 £300   10 £150

Estimated life of machine: ten years.
Residual value at end of life: £50.
Corporation tax is to be taken at 40%.
Investment grant for a non-development area to be taken as 25%, which is expected to be paid within twelve months of purchase. Annual allowance is to be taken as 20%.

CASH FLOW STATEMENT: MACHINE E

Taxation

Year	Outflow (£)	Inflow (£)	Allow- ances (£)	Profit less allow- ances (£)	Corpor- ation tax (£)	Profit less tax (£)	Net cash flow (£)
0	(1000)	—	—	—	—	—	(1000)
1	250	250	—	250	—	250	500
2		250	150	100	40	210	210
3		250	120	130	52	198	198
4		250	96	154	62	188	188
5		250	77	173	69	181	181
6		250	61	189	76	174	174
7		250	49	201	80	170	170
8		250	39	211	84	166	166
9		250	32	218	87	163	163
10		250	25	225	90	160	160
11	50	—	20	(20)	92	(92)	(42)
12		—	31	(31)	(12)	12	12
	£(700)	2,500	700	1,800	720	1,780	1,080

NOTE

Capital allowances:

Year 1 Cost	1000	Year 7	197
Grant	250		39
	750		158
Allowance	150	8	32
	600		126
2	120	9	25
	480		101
3	96	10	20
	384		81
4	77	11 Residual value	50
	307		£31 balancing allowance
5	61		
	246		
6	49		
	197		

PROFITABILITY STATEMENT: MACHINE E

		Trial No. 1		Trial No. 2	
Year	Cash flow (£)	Discount factor (20%)	Present value (£)	Discount factor (22%)	Present value (£)
0	(1000)	1·000	(1000)	1·000	(1000)
1	500	0·833	417	0·820	410
2	210	0·694	146	0·672	141
3	198	0·579	115	0·551	109
4	188	0·482	91	0·451	85
5	181	0·402	73	0·370	67
6	174	0·335	58	0·303	53
7	170	0·279	47	0·249	42
8	166	0·233	39	0·204	34
9	163	0·194	32	0·167	27
10	160	0·162	26	0·137	22
11	(42)	0·135	(6)	0·112	(5)
12	12	0·112	1	0·092	1
	£1080		£39		£(14)

This statement shows a return on investment of 22%; the difference of £14 is not considered to be enough to warrant the interpolation technique being used to obtain a more exact result.

CASH FLOW STATEMENT: MACHINE F

				Profit less allow- ances (£)	Taxation		
Year	Outflow (£)	Inflow (£)	Allow- ances (£)		Corpor- ation tax (40%)	Profit less tax (£)	Net cash flow (£)
0	(1000)	—	—	—	—	—	(1000)
1	250	100	—	100	—	100	350
2		200	150	50	(20)	220	220
3		250	120	130	32	218	218
4		300	96	204	62	238	238
5		300	77	223	89	211	211
6		300	61	239	96	204	204
7		300	49	251	100	200	200
8		300	39	261	104	196	196
9		300	32	268	107	193	193
10		150	25	125	110	40	40
11	50	—	20	(20)	52	(52)	(2)
12		—	31	(31)	(12)	12	12
	£(700)	2,500	700	1,800	720	1,780	1,080

PROFITABILITY STATEMENT: MACHINE F

		Trial No. 1		Trial No. 2	
Year	Cash flow (£)	Discount factor (20%)	Present value £	Discount factor (19%)	Present value (£)
0	(1000)	1·000	(1000)	1·000	(1000)
1	350	0·833	292	0·840	294
2	220	0·694	153	0·706	155
3	218	0·579	126	0·593	129
4	238	0·482	115	0·499	119
5	211	0·402	85	0·419	88
6	204	0·335	68	0·352	72
7	200	0·279	56	0·296	59
8	196	0·233	46	0·249	49
9	193	0·194	37	0·209	40
10	40	0·162	6	0·176	7
11	(2)	0·135	—	0·148	—
12	12	0·112	1	0·124	1
	£1080		(15)		13

This statement shows a return on investment of approximately 19%. Machine E is the more profitable project because it should yield a return of 22%. It will be observed that in both projects, the total cash inflow and the total taxation payable were the same, but the important difference was the cycle of cash flow. In the case of machine E, the early years in the life of the machine produced a greater return than those relating to machine F, while in the later years the reverse situation applied. It can be seen from the discount tables that the early years of a project are at higher rates than the later years; it will be appreciated that £1 to be received in one year's time is worth more now than £1 to be received in two years' time.

Establishing the trial rate

In the calculation of the discount rate, difficulty is often experienced in the selection of the first trial rate. Once the first trial rate has been computed, the second trial rate is determined by considering whether the cash inflow is greater or less than the cash outflow. If the inflow is less than the outflow, the second trial rate will be lower than the first trial rate; if the inflow exceeds the outflow, the trial rate will be higher than the first trial rate. However, the problem is to select the first trial rate. As an aid to this selection, a rough guide is as follows:

$$\frac{\text{Average savings p.a.}}{\text{Investment}} \times 100$$

Thus in the case of machine E above, a first trial rate of approximately 25% would be used:

$$\frac{250}{1000} \times 100$$

This guide, known as the pay-back reciprocal, was illustrated on p. 535.

Interpolation

On p. 542 the interpolation technique was mentioned briefly in connection with ascertaining the discount factor rate. A number of readers find difficulty in understanding how this technique works, so it is illustrated now in rather more detail. Interpolation is simply a means of ascertaining the desired discount factor rate with the minimum number of trial runs. It will be recalled that when using the internal rate of return method, it is necessary to process a number of trial runs in an attempt to discount the cash flows to zero. When after a number of trials the analyst has defined the area in which the required discount rate is situated—e.g. say that between 20% and 24% is the factor which will equate cash inflows with cash outflows—then by interpolation he can locate the actual rate, say 22·5%.

Example

The management of Pauleme Ltd is considering two mutually exclusive projects, P and L. Investment will amount to £10,000 in either case, and the life of the asset is expected to be ten years, with no residual value. Net profit is expected to be as follows:

Year	P	L
1	—	£2,000
2	£2,000	3,000
3	3,000	4,000
4	3,000	4,000
5	4,000	5,000
6	4,000	1,000
7	3,000	1,000
8	2,000	1,000
9	2,000	1,000
10	1,000	1,000
	£24,000	£23,000

To facilitate concentration on the interpolation technique, taxation is to be ignored in this example. Which project is the more profitable investment?

PROJECT P

		Trial No. 1		Trial No. 2		Trial No. 3	
Year	Cash flow (£)	Discount factor (10%)	Present value £	Discount factor (20%)A	Present value (£)	Discount factor (30%)B	Present value (£)
0	(10,000)	1·000	(10,000)	1·000	(10,000)	1·000	(10,000)
1	1,000	0·909	909	0·833	833	0·769	769
2	3,000	0·826	2,478	0·694	2,082	0·592	1,776
3	4,000	0·751	3,004	0·579	2,316	0·455	1,820
4	4,000	0·683	2,732	0·482	1,928	0·350	1,400
5	5,000	0·621	3,105	0·402	2,010	0·269	1,345
6	5,000	0·564	2,820	0·335	1,675	0·207	1,035
7	4,000	0·513	2,052	0·279	1,116	0·159	636
8	3,000	0·467	1,401	0·233	699	0·123	369
9	3,000	0·424	1,272	0·194	582	0·094	282
10	2,000	0·386	772	0·162	324	0·073	146
Total	£24,000		£10,545		£3,565C		£422)D

Interpolation:

From these three trial runs it can be observed that at 10% discount rate the inflow exceeds the outflow; similarly at 20%, but at 30% the outflow exceeds the inflow. Thus we have located the area as being between 20% and 30%. The formula for interpolation is:

$$A + \frac{C}{C - D} \times (B - A)$$

where A = discount factor of the low trial
B = discount factor of the high trial
C = present value of cash inflow of the low trial
D = present value of each inflow of the high trial

Thus:
$$20\% + \frac{3,565}{3565 - (422)} \times 10\%$$
$$= 20\% + \frac{3565}{3987} \times 10\%$$
$$= 20\% + 8\cdot94\%$$
$$= 29\% \text{ approximately}$$

NOTE

Cash flow is composed of net profit, to which must be added back depreciation of the asset. Thus year 2 profit £2000 + depreciation £1000 = £3000.

PROJECT L

Year	Cash flow (£)	Discount factor (10%)	Present value (£)	Discount factor (20%)	Present value (£)	Discount factor (30%)A	Present value (£)	Discount factor (40%)B	Present value (£)
		Trial No. 1		Trial No. 2		Trial No. 3		Trial No. 4	
0	(10,000)	1·000	(10,000)	1·000	(10,000)	1·000	(10,000)	1·000	(10,000)
1	3,000	0·909	2,727	0·833	2,499	0·769	2,307	0·714	2,142
2	4,000	0·826	3,304	0·694	2,776	0·592	2,368	0·510	2,040
3	5,000	0·751	3,755	0·579	2,895	0·455	2,275	0·364	1,820
4	5,000	0·683	3,415	0·482	2,410	0·350	1,750	0·260	1,300
5	6,000	0·621	3,726	0·402	2,412	0·269	1,614	0·186	1,116
6	2,000	0·564	1,128	0,335	670	0·207	414	0·133	266
7	2,000	0·513	1,026	0·279	558	0·159	318	0·095	190
8	2,000	0·467	934	0·233	466	0·123	246	0·068	136
9	2,000	0·424	848	0·194	388	0·094	188	0·048	96
10	2,000	0·386	772	0·162	324	0·073	146	0·035	70
Total	£23,000		£11,635		£5,398		£1,626C		£(824)D

Interpolation: as with project P, three trial runs were used at discount factors of 10%, 20% and 30%, but in this case even at 30% cash inflows exceeded cash outflows. A fourth trial run was made at 40%, when cash outflow exceeded cash inflow. Thus we have located the area as being between 30% and 40%. The formula is:

$$A + \frac{C}{C - D} \times (B - A)$$
$$30\% + \frac{1626}{1626 - (824)} \times 10\%$$
$$= 37\% \text{ approximately.}$$

NOTE

Cash flow is composed of net profit, to which must be added back the depreciation of the asset.
Thus year 1 profit £2000 + depreciation £1000 = £3000.

The interpolation graph

A graph can be constructed which shows clearly the required rate of discount factor at which cash outflow is equated with cash inflow. The cash inflow is divided by the cash outflow to produce the present value ratio which is used in the construction of the graph.

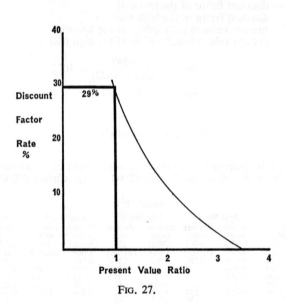

FIG. 27.

PROJECT P

	Discount factor			
	0%	10%	20%	30%
Cash outflow	£10,000	£10,000	£10,000	£10,000
Cash inflow	34,000	20,545	13,565	9,578
Present value ratio:				
$\dfrac{\text{Cash inflow}}{\text{Cash outflow}} =$	3·4	2·05	1·36	0·96

On the vertical scale of the graph is shown the discount factor. On the horizontal scale is shown the present value ratio. The present value ratios are plotted for each of the discount factors used in the trial runs, and a curve is drawn which joins together the points which have been plotted.

It will be recalled from earlier in this chapter that the internal rate of return method requires the discount factor where cash inflow divided by cash outflow is equal to 1. Thus on the graph the point where a perpendicular line drawn from the present value ratio of 1 meets the curve joining the points plotted, represents the required discount factor rate (*see* Fig. 27).

PROJECT L

			Discount factor		
	0%	10%	20%	30%	40%
Cash outflow	£10,000	£10,000	£10,000	£10,000	£10,000
Cash inflow	33,000	21,635	15,398	11,626	9,176
Present value ratio:					
$\dfrac{\text{Cash inflow}}{\text{Cash outflow}}$ =	3·3	2·16	1·54	1·16	0·92

For the graph of project L, *see* Fig. 28.

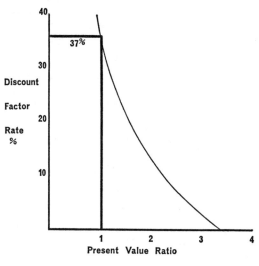

FIG. 28.

The M.A.P.I. system

This system was developed by George Terborgh, the research director of the Machinery and Allied Products Institute of the U.S.A. It provides a mathematical model which has been created to co-ordinate the important factors which should be considered in capital expenditure decision making. The M.A.P.I. system was introduced to cater particularly for relatively low value projects such as items of plant and machinery, rather than high-value projects such as new buildings complete with plant and machinery. The model is designed to eliminate long term forecasting, by considering the costs of operating this year with those of operating next year. In other words, it does not consider the life of the asset as do the other systems discussed in this chapter. Extracts are made of the net operating advantage which can be related to the project. These net operating advantages may be in terms of reduced costs or increased earnings.

The methods discussed so far in this chapter such as R.O.I., pay-back and D.C.F. are methods which are used in project evaluation as aids to management in a new project or to replace an asset. However, the M.A.P.I. system is designed primarily for use in evaluating the replacement of an old asset, the asset usually being a machine. To operate the system, estimates must be made of such factors as the following.

A, the net investment. This takes into consideration the total cost of the installation of the new machine, less the residual value of the old machine. From this figure should be deducted any costs which may be incurred in capital expenditure which would be necessary to maintain the old machine in service. Thus, for example, if an expensive part would be required for use on the replaced machine, the amount should be deducted from the investment in the new machine.

B, the consumption of capital which is allowed during the year in respect of the usage of the new machine. This amount represents the difference between the total cost of installing the machine and its disposal value expected one year later.

C, the consumption of capital which is avoided during the next year owing to the non-use of the replaced machine. This amount is not exactly the same as depreciation; it is the difference between the disposal value of the old machine now and the disposal value expected one year later.

D, the operating advantages expected during the next year. This amount represents the savings in cost and increases in revenue.

E, the effect of taxation, this being in respect of the operating advantages expected during the next year.

Example

Jeran Ltd is considering the replacement of machine X by a new machine, Y. The following data are available:

Residual value of machine X now: £4000.
Residual value of machine X one year later: £2000.
Investment in machine Y now: £20,000.
Disposal value of machine Y one year later: £16,000.
Operating advantages expected during the next year if machine Y is installed: £10,000.

Income tax next year based on the operating advantages expected, £5000. The M.A.P.I. formula is:

$$\frac{D + C - B - E}{A} \times 100$$

$$\frac{£10,000 + 2000 - 4000 - 5000}{20,000} \times 100$$

$$= 15\%$$

The figure shown above is known as the M.A.P.I. *urgency rating* and is used as a comparative figure in decision making. Thus, if no other project yields a return greater than machine Y (15% rating), investment will be made in machine Y to replace machine X.

The M.A.P.I. system may be used to determine whether to replace a machine now or to postpone its replacement to a future time, normally one year. In so far as factors are involved which are calculated only one year ahead, the M.A.P.I. system may be more easily operated than the other systems which involve forecasts of a number of factors spread over the economic life of a machine. However, this is also a great disadvantage of the system when different patterns of savings and investments are experienced. It would appear that this system is not widely used at present, but it may well be that, in the field of capital expenditure decision making when relatively small value projects are involved, there may be an increasing use of this technique in the United Kingdom. The M.A.P.I. system is certainly used by a number of companies in the United States.

PROFITABILITY PROJECT

A project is introduced now to give readers the chance to revise some of the techniques discussed so far in this chapter. The project involves a choice of five alternatives, each of which has a different pattern of net profit. Owing to the size of the projects, taxation has been ignored. With five alternative assets and with six alternative measurements of profitability to be calculated, it would be impracticable to bring in the complication of the taxation allowances and payments which were discussed earlier in this chapter. Readers who are particularly interested in the taxation implications of capital expenditure may care to re-work the project including taxation, using the allowances and rates given in the second illustration in the taxation section of this chapter.

Example

Graul Ltd is considering five alternative items of plant. The new asset is not a replacement of an old machine, residual value of each item of plant is to be taken as zero, and each item is a mutually exclusive project.

In respect of each asset you are required to show:

1. The pay-back period.
2. The pay-back profitability.
3. The pay-back reciprocal.
4. The return on investment.
5. The net present value (the company requires a return of 20% before taxation).
6. The internal rate of return.

Estimated cash inflows and outflows are as follows:

Year	G	R	Projects A	U	L
0	£(20,000)	£(20,000)	£(40,000)	£(20,000)	£(20,000)
1	12,000	6,000	—	6,000	12,000
2	14,000	6,000	15,000	6,000	10,000
3	14,000	6,000	15,000	6,000	10,000
4	—	6,000	15,000	6,000	8,000
5	—	6,000	15,000	6,000	6,000
6	—	6,000	10,000	6,000	4,000
7	—	6,000	10,000	6,000	—
8	—	6,000	10,000	—	—
9	—	6,000	10,000	—	—
10	—	6,000	—	—	—
	£20,000	£40,000	£60,000	£22,000	£30,000

Readers who are keenly interested in profitability techniques are advised to prepare their own statements to see how they compare with that shown by the authors. To complete the project will take a considerable time, but the effort should prove to be worthwhile if it provides a better understanding of the techniques discussed.

Pay-back period (Years)	1·6	3·3	3·7	3·3	1·8
Pay-back profitability (£)	£20,000	£40,000	£60,000	£22,000	£30,000
Pay-back reciprocal (%)	66·6	30·0	27·8	30·0	41·6
Return on investment (%)	66·6	40·0	33·4	31·4	50·0
Net present value (20%) (£)	£7,818	£5,158	£2,765	£1,624	£10,334
Internal rate of return (%)	43	27	22	23	44

From this statement, management can see that the projects rank in the following order:

PROJECTS RANKED IN ORDER OF PREFERENCE

	First	Second	Third	Fourth	Fifth
Pay-back period (years)	G	L	U	R	A
Pay-back profitability (£)	A	R	L	U	G
Pay-back reciprocal (%)	G	L	R	U	A
Return on investment (%)	G	L	R	A	U
Net present value (20%) (£)	L	G	R	A	U
Internal rate of return (%)	L	G	R	U	A

CALCULATIONS

1. *Pay-back period (years)*

Example: project R

Cash outflow		£20,000
Cash inflow: first year	£6,000	
second year	6,000	
third year	6,000	
fourth year		
($\frac{1}{3}$ × £6,000)	2,000	
		£20,000

2. *Pay-back profitability (£)*

Example: project A

Cash inflow	£100,000
Cash outflow	40,000
	£60,000

3. *Pay-back reciprocal (%)*

Example: project L

Cash inflow over six years	£50,000
Cash inflow per year	8,333·3
Investment	£20,000
Reciprocal $\frac{8,333 \cdot 3}{20,000} \times 100$	= 41·6%

4. *Return on investment (%)*

Example: project U

Cash inflow over seven years	£42,000
Depreciation over seven years	20,000
Net profit	£22,000
Average net profit p.a.	£3,143
Average investment	£10,000
Percentage	31·4

5. *Present value (20%)*

Example: project G

Year	Cash flow (£)	present value rate (20%)	present value of cash inflow (£)
1	12,000	0·833	9,996
2	14,000	0·694	9,716
3	14,000	0·579	8,106
			£27,818

6. *Internal rate of return*

Example: project U

		Trial No. 1		Trial No. 2	
Year	Cash flow (£)	Discount factor (20%)	Present value (£)	Discount factor (30%)	Present value (£)
0	(20,000)	1·000	(20,000)	1·000	(20,000)
1	6,000	0·833	4,988	0·769	4,614
2	6,000	0·694	4,164	0·592	3,552
3	6,000	0·579	3,474	0·455	2,730
4	6,000	0·482	2,892	0·350	2,100
5	6,000	0·402	2,412	0·269	1,614
6	6,000	0·335	2,010	0·207	1,242
7	6,000	0·279	1,674	0·159	954
			£1,624		£(3,194)

Interpolation:

$$20\% + £\frac{1624}{4818} \times 10\%$$

$$= 23\% \text{ approximately}$$

This can be checked as follows:

Year	Cash flow (£)	Discount factor (23%)	Present value (£)
0	(20,000)	1·000	(20,000)
1	6,000	0·813	4,878
2	6,000	0·661	3,966
3	6,000	0·537	3,222
4	6,000	0·437	2,622
5	6,000	0·355	2,130
6	6,000	0·289	1,734
7	6,000	0·235	1,410
			£(38)

WORKING CAPITAL INVESTMENT

Not all projects are completed as quickly as may have been suggested so far in this chapter. Of course, many projects, such as the purchase and installation of a machine, may be operational within a very short time, but a large number of projects may take years of planning, construction and/or installation, and then a period of "running-in" before regular production is achieved. In addition, a large amount of investment may be incurred in working capital, financing stocks and debtors. Working capital may be required at the beginning of the operation and additional amounts may be required at frequent periods during the life of the asset.

Investment in working capital must be considered in the total amount of capital invested in a project. Profitability statements must therefore allow for the outflow of such capital at required periods. This may involve the operation of separate cash outflow and cash inflow columns in the statement.

Example

Jervid Ltd is planning an extension to its factory, plant and equipment. Estimates of cash outflow and inflow have been prepared and are to be evaluated in terms of discounted cash flow. Completion of the extension will take two years. Estimates are as follows:

Year	Inflow (£)	Outflow (£)
1	—	100,000
2	—	50,000
3	40,000	10,000
4	60,000	—
5	100,000	5,000
6	100,000	—
7	80,000	—
8	60,000	—
9	60,000	5,000
10	50,000	—
11	30,000	—
12	20,000	—
	£600,000	£170,000

Taxation is to be ignored in order to keep this illustration relatively simple. In practice the use of computers or mechanised accounting machines would greatly facilitate the additional calculations involved.

PROFITABILITY STATEMENT

Year	Cash outflow (£)	Cash inflow (£)	Discount factor (30%)	Trial No. 1 Present value: Outflow (£)	Trial No. 1 Present value: Inflow (£)	Discount factor (35%)	Trial No. 2 Present value: Outflow (£)	Trial No. 2 Present value: Inflow (£)
−1	100,000	—	1·300	130,000	—	1·350	135,000	—
0	50,000	—	1·000	50,000	—	1·000	50,000	—
1	10,000	40,000	0·769	7,690	30,760	0·741	7,410	29,640
2	—	60,000	0·592	—	35,520	0·549	—	32,940
3	5,000	100,000	0·455	2,275	45,500	0·406	2,030	40,600
4	—	100,000	0·350	—	35,000	0·301	—	30,100
5	—	80,000	0·269	—	21,520	0·223	—	17,840
6	—	60,000	0·207	—	12,420	0·165	—	9,900
7	5,000	60,000	0·159	795	9,540	0·122	610	7,320
8	—	50,000	0·123	—	6,150	0·091	—	4,550
9	—	30,000	0·094	—	2,820	0·067	—	2,010
10	—	20,000	0·073	—	1,460	0 050	—	1,000
				£190,760	£200,690		£195,050	£175,900

By interpolation, this results in a yield of approximately 32%.

NOTES

(i) The first trial of 30% was obtained by using the pay-back reciprocal method which was discussed on p. 547. Thus:

$$\frac{\text{Annual earnings}}{\text{Investment}} \times 100$$

$$\frac{£60,000}{170,000} \times 100 = 35\% \text{ approximately.}$$

In this example, the pay-back reciprocal method has proved to be reasonably accurate, but, as mentioned earlier, it is simply a guide to choosing the approximate area in which to base calculations.

(ii) The annual earnings figure is calculated as follows:

$$\frac{\text{Total earnings}}{\text{Life of asset in years}} = \frac{£600,000}{10 \text{ years}}$$

RANKING ALTERNATIVE PROJECTS

It is usually found in practice that there are more requests for capital expenditure projects than capital available to finance them. The management accountant should be able to assist management in selecting the projects which appear to offer an adequate return. Many companies establish a minimum required return on investment, and any project which does not measure up to it is not considered. Earlier in this chapter it was suggested that many accountants regard 17% before tax as a reasonable return, in which case only projects offering at least 17% would be considered.

It may be found that in some cases there is an alternative, for example to repair rather than to replace or to lease instead of purchase (the latter is becoming increasingly popular). Such projects will therefore be excluded from the capital expenditure procedures described above, but will be closely investigated by the management accountant, who will then submit details of cost and performance to the management.*

When a number of projects appear to offer an acceptable return on investment, it may be necessary to rank them in order of profitability so that the available capital is put to the best use. The usual procedure is to list them in order of increasing capital expenditure, so that comparisons can be made between them.

Example

The Paulon Co. Ltd is considering six capital projects. The minimum return on investment accepted as company policy is 17% before taxation. The projects are as follows:

Project	Capital expenditure	Estimated savings	Return on investment
P	£10,000	£1,000	20%
A	12,000	1,500	25
U	15,000	1,500	20
L	20,000	1,800	18
O	25,000	5,000	40
N	30,000	5,550	37

From the ranking of alternatives, it would appear that Project O is the most profitable investment. However, this is not necessarily so: much depends on whether any surplus capital can be invested more profitably elsewhere. Thus, taking the above figures, Project N shows a saving of £550 more than Project O because an extra £5000 was available and invested elsewhere at 22% (£550/£2500). In other words, if the company had £30,000

---

* Those who wish to pursue the subject are referred to "Rent or buy?" by J. N. H. Cameron and "Plant leasing" by R. Ogden in *The Cost Accountant* for February and December 1963 respectively, also "Economic Analysis of Lease *v.* Buy and Borrow Decisions" by C. A. Burrows, in *Accountancy*, May 1969.

capital available for investment, it would be more profitable to invest in Project N than any of the alternatives shown, unless it was possible to invest in Project O and then invest the remaining balance of £5000 elsewhere at an even better rate than 22%. This can be checked:

Invest 25,000 to earn 5,000: return on investment, 40%
Invest 5,000 to earn 550: return on investment, 22%

£30,000   £5,550

NOTE

Earnings on £5000 at 22% would be £550. Thus £25,000 invested in Project O to return 40% and £5000 invested elsewhere to return 22% would yield £5550, which is the same return as on Project N.

Present value index

When the present value method of discounted cash flow is used, difficulty may be experienced in ranking alternative projects which have a different pattern of investments. Each project may have a yield which is greater than the "cut-off point." But if the amounts to be invested vary considerably, it is not easy to ascertain quickly and clearly which is the most profitable investment. A simple aid to management is the use of the present value index, which relates the present value of the cash flows of each payment to the amount invested.

Example

The Jervid Co. Ltd is considering a capital project. The minimum return on investment required is 20% before taxation. The alternatives are as follows:

Project	Capital investment (£)	Present value of cash flow (£)	Present value index	Ranking
J	50,000	49,000	0·980	6
E	40,000	43,000	1·075	3
R	60,000	62,000	1·033	5
V	30,000	31,500	1·050	4
I	35,000	38,000	1·085	2
D	45,000	49,500	1·100	1

This statement shows that using the method of calculating capital expenditure, project D is ranked most favourably, followed by project I, project E, project V and project R. Project J does not meet the required minimum acceptable yield and would be rejected—provided, of course, that it was not a project necessitated by law (a possibility discussed in (2) on p. 561).

Specimen question

The following is a typical examination question set by a professional body.
The Alpha Company Ltd is considering the purchase of a new machine which will cost £40,000. It is estimated that the machine will have a life of seven years, at the end of which it will have a scrap value of £1000. This will

also involve an investment in working capital of £10,000. The net pre-tax cash flows which this will produce are as follows:

Year 1	£10,000
2	10,000
3	14,000
4	13,000
5	11,000
6	12,000
7	10,000

The Company has a target return on capital of 15% and on this basis you are required to prepare a statement evaluing the above project.

Taxation. Assume the following:

(a) Corporation Tax 40% in the £.
(b) Investment allowance, 30%. Initial allowance, 10%.
(c) Annual allowances, 25%.

The company carries on other trading activities from which it derives taxable profits.

Note: the present value of £1 due in one year's time at 15% = £0·870

two	0·756
three	0·658
four	0·572
five	0·497
six	0·432
seven	0·376
eight	0·327

[C.C.A.

Answer

Year	Cost	Cost of machine (£)	Capital allow-ances (£)	Cash flow (£)	Taxable income (£)	Tax burden (£)	Year of payment
1	Cost	40,000					
	Investment allowance		12,000				
	Initial allowance £4,000						
	Annual allowance 10,000						
		14,000	14,000				
		26,000		10,000	(16,000)	(6,400)	2
	Written down value	26,000					
2	Annual allowance	6,500	6,500	10,000	3,500	1,400	3
	Written down value	19,500					
3	Annual allowance	4,875	4,875	14,000	9,125	3,650	4
	Written down value	14,625					
4	Annual allowance	3,656	3,656	13,000	9,344	3,738	5
	Written down value	10,969					
5	Annual allowance	2,742	2,742	11,000	8,258	3,303	6
	Written down value	8,227					
6	Annual allowance	2,057	2,057	12,000	9,943	3,977	7
	Written down value	6,170					
7	Scrap value	1,000					
	Balancing allowance	5,170	5,170	10,000	4,830	1,932	8

NOTE

As the discount table only extends to year 8, it has been assumed that the machine is to be sold in year 7.

ALPHA COMPANY LTD

*Evaluation statement for
proposed acquisition of new machine*

Project ref: ....   Date ....

CASH OUTFLOW

Year	Capital expenditure (£)	Working capital (£)		Discount factor (15%)	Present value (£)	£
0	40,000	10,000		1·000	50,000	
7	(1,000)	(10,000)	(11,000)	0·376	(4,136)	
					45,864	45,864

CASH INFLOW

Year	Pre-tax cash flow (£)	Taxation (£)	Net cash flow (£)	Discount factor	Present value (£)
1	10,000	—	10,000	0·870	8,700
2	10,000	(6,400)*	16,400	0·756	12,398
3	14,000	1,400	12,600	0·658	8,291
4	13,000	3,650	9,350	0·572	5,348
5	11,000	3,738	7,262	0·497	3,609
6	12,000	3,303	8,697	0·432	3,757
7	10,000	3,977	6,023	0·376	2,265
8	—	1,932	(1,932)	0·327	(632)
					43,736	43,736

(£2,128)

At the target return of 15% net for this project, it cannot be recommended as expenditure would be in excess of income at that rate.

ESTABLISHING CAPITAL PRIORITIES

When the capital available is limited, it is essential to establish a system of priorities so that best use is made of it. The accountant will establish what he considers to be the most important items to be developed, and will make recommendations to management accordingly. Such a list of priorities may be as follows:

1. *Projects already in hand:* projects which are incomplete but require additional expenditure for completion will normally receive top priority. Investigations should be made to find out why the situation has arisen, but it will be realised the project must be completed.

2. *Projects necessitated by law:* where expenditure is essential to comply with safety regulations (*e.g.* the provision of dust extraction plant) it must receive priority.

* Taxation refund to be set off against other income.

3. *Projects to maintain capacity:* plant required to maintain present capacity, *e.g.* the replacement of a machine.

4. *Projects to increase earnings:* plant which will reduce costs or increase sales of existing products.

5. *Projects to develop new products.*

IMPROVING PROFITABILITY

The management accountant must be concerned to improve the profitability of capital employed in the company. He must investigate the possibilities of increasing the rate of profit obtained and/or reducing the investment in working capital and capital projects. Possible ways of increasing profitability include:

1. *Increasing turnover:* an attempt should be made to increase the sales of products which are yielding a favourable return.

2. *Increasing selling prices:* can the market absorb the company's products at a higher price?

3. *Reducing costs:* can savings be effected in fixed and variable costs?

4. *Improving methods of production and distribution:* an organisation and methods study may suggest better methods with corresponding savings.

5. *More efficient use of equipment:* time study engineers may be able to suggest improvements.

6. *Reducing the investment in stocks:* the adoption of maximum and minimum stock levels should enable reductions to be made here and hence in the working capital invested.

CAPITAL EXPENDITURE CONTROL

The control of capital expenditure is growing in importance as mechanisation and automation are introduced and extended; larger sums are being locked up in fixed assets then have been in the past. In most companies there is usually no lack of ideas for capital development, but there *is* usually a lack of available funds to carry it out, worthy though the ideas may be. One of the duties of top management is to make decisions on capital expenditure projects, decisions which will possibly affect company policy for some time in the future. The management accountant may operate a system of capital expenditure control which will incorporate the following features:

1. *Planned development.* Investment in capital expenditure should be carefully planned to include developments in each site or department to ensure that each unit in the group or company is developing in step with the overall plan.

2. A *capital budget* will be essential, even in companies which do not operate a complete system of budgetary control. Capital appropriations

and payments must be planned well in advance to ensure cash availability and asset procurement. Budgets were discussed in Chapter IX.

3. A *progress record* should be kept, to show the progress of each capital project. The budget and actual expenditure will be compared so that management is regularly informed of any variations.

4. *Profitability audit:* when a capital project is completed and in operation, the management accountant should compare actual profitability with that estimated. Return-on-investment calculations will obviously be affected if either the actual cost or the actual earnings of the project differ from what was forecast. This review can be very important because it may reveal inefficiencies in the system, and it provides experience which should enable repetition of mistakes to be avoided.

5. *Forms and procedures:* there should be a routine for controlling capital expenditure. A procedure should be adopted for the various stages: requesting, authorisation, progress and audit. Forms should be available which can be completed and presented to management as and when required: examples are given below and overleaf.

Capital expenditure project

REQUEST TO CAPITAL EXPENDITURE COMMITTEE

Department: Project No.:

Factory: Date:

1. Classification: Replacement
                   Development
                   Amenity
2. Description of project:
3. Reason for proposed expenditure:
4. Supplier:
5. Commencement of project:
6. Completion of project:
7. Budget periods affected:
8. Estimated expenditure: (*give details of all expenditure to be incurred, including any incurred by own labour*)
9. Estimated increase in earnings: (*if applicable*)
10. Profitability: (*if applicable, show here relevant calculations of return on investment, pay-back period, present value index, etc.*)
11. Any further capital expenditure to be incurred: (*give details of any further projects which may be required as a consequence of authorising this project*)
12. Estimated life of project:

Submitted by: Approved by:

Date: Date:

Budget Committee approval/rejection

Date:

Remarks (if any):

(Signed)....................Chairman

Capital expenditure project

PROGRESS RECORD

Department: Project no.: *X57*

Factory: Date:

Description: *Additional store room*
Budgeted expenditure: £50,000

Reference number	Description	Degree of com-pletion %	Budgeted amount £	Actual amount £	Actual variation £
X57/1	*Building*	80	25,000	22,000	+2,500
2	*Shelving*	50	2,000	900	−150
3	*Furniture, cabinets*	100	1,000	1,020	+20
4	*Company labour, etc., etc.*	40	12,000	5,000	+500

Original estimated completion date: *31st August*
Now expected to be completed: *15th September*

Remarks:

Signed:

Date:

Requests for capital projects are usually made out by the head of a department and forwarded to the management for approval. In most companies, only projects which have been allowed for in the capital budget will be approved, with a possible exception for real emergencies. Many large companies classify projects according to the amount of capital involved, *e.g.* minor, medium and major projects. Approval for minor ones may be given by area executives, for medium projects by group executives, and for major projects by the board of directors. In some companies, approval for any project can be given only by the board of directors, but this not only wastes time which the board could spend on more important matters, it deprives junior executives of valuable experience.

Accounting entries

All charges invoiced by suppliers, and any internal costs in respect of materials and wages incurred on capital projects, will be recorded, and, where appropriate, overhead costs will be charged. Accounts will be maintained for each capital project so that costs of each can be ascertained and expense accounts cleared.

Example

Jerdav Ltd operates an integral accounting system. During the year the following costs were incurred in respect of capital project No. 57:

Invoiced from suppliers	£50,000
Direct materials charged	30,000
Direct labour costs	25,000
Overheads absorbed	15,000

The appropriate entries will be as follow:

Capital project No. 57

Creditors	£50,000	Fixed assets	£120,000
Stores	30,000		
Labour	25,000		
Overheads	15,000		
	£120,000		£120,000

Fixed assets

Capital project No. 57	£120,000

Creditors

Capital project No. 57	£50,000

Stores control

Capital project No. 57	30,000

Wages control

Capital project No. 57	25,000

Fixed overheads

Capital project No. 57	15,000

EXAMINATION QUESTIONS

1. Profit is very often expressed for comparative purposes as a percentage of sales or of the cost of goods sold.

As management accountant of a long-established manufacturing company, enumerate the advantages and disadvantages of using capital employed for this purpose instead of sales or cost. [C.W.A.

2. It has been argued that the important relationship in the measurement of efficiency is not that of the margin of profit to sales turnover, but rather that of the profit margin to the physical volume of resources utilised.

Comment on this statement, and suggest possible measurement for the second relationship mentioned, bearing in mind the different ways of expressing profit margin and resources. [C.W.A.

3. Most businesses are today faced with alternative uses for available funds. What criteria would you, as an accountant, recommend should be used to decide which use should be satisfied? What problems would the application of your criteria bring?

Give a formula for the evaluation of a capital expenditure project by the

discounted cash flow method, explaining how each term in the formula
is obtained. [C.C.A.

4. The works manager of Jigs Ltd has proposed the introduction of an
automatic machine to replace existing manually controlled machines used in
the production of a particular component.

At present, one component is produced every half-hour, by an operator
using a set of tools costing £100 on a manually controlled machine. The
operator earns £0·40 an hour.

The design of the component is changed at intervals, necessitating complete
sets of new tools, the average run between changes being 40,000 components
and the tools outlasting the run of components.

The programme is 800 components a week; 10 operators and machines are
engaged in producing them, each working a 40-hour week for 50 weeks a
year.

Overheads amount to $87\frac{1}{2}\%$ of productive labour cost, made up as
follows:

Depreciation of machines	$12\frac{1}{2}\%$
Tools	$12\frac{1}{2}\%$
Other expenses varying with productive labour	25%
Other expenses of a fixed nature	$37\frac{1}{2}\%$
	$87\frac{1}{2}\%$

The proposed automatic machine would produce one component every
three minutes, the necessary setting up and maintenance being carried out,
as at present, outside normal working hours, and the machine would be
worked the same hours as the existing machines.

The cost of the new machine, including installation, would be £25,000
and it may be assumed to have a life of ten years and no residual
value.

It would require supervision by an engineer earning £0·50 an hour and the
tools for each design of the component would cost £2000 and would outlast
the maximum run of such design.

The aggregate of "Other expenses varying with productive labour" would
be reduced by a quarter while the "Other expenses of a fixed nature" would
be unchanged in total.

The cost of materials used in producing the component would remain
unchanged at £0·25 per component. You are required:

(a) to prepare a statement showing the cost of the component when
produced by the present methods, and the comparative cost if produced
on the proposed machine (interest on capital to be ignored);
(b) to show the comparative costs if the average run between changes of
design were 10,000, and
(c) to add a note of any other points which should be taken into account
by the directors when considering the proposed change. [C.A.

5. A cigarette manufacturer proposes to replace his existing cigarette
making machines, which produce at the rate of 1200 cigarettes a minute, by
the latest type of high-speed machine, to operate at the rate of 2000 cigarettes
a minute.

The existing machines cost £6000 each, ten years ago. New and old
machines have an estimated total useful life of 20 years. The depreciation

provision is by the "straight line" method, the residual value for each being £1000. The price of the new machine is £10,000. The present part-exchange value of the existing machines is £1500 each.

The new machine will occupy only 80% of the effective floor space of an old machine, the cost being £50 a year.

The following details also apply:

	Old machine	New machine
Annual operating hours	1500	1500
Operator's annual wages	£550	£550
Annual repair and maintenance cost	150	190
Annual power cost	50	110

Any probable capital loss on the old machines is to be included in the stimated costs of the new machines.

(a) Tabulate a comparative cost estimate for one year for an old and a new machine.

(b) Calculate how many cigarettes must be produced by the new machine to yield savings equal to the extra capital outlay it involves. Ignore tax.
[C.W.A.

6. A company has invested £300,000 in a small manufacturing plant which includes buildings beyond present manufacturing requirements. A proposal is made to increase output in order fully to utilise the premises and services available. Additional capital expenditure of £20,000 is necessary.

The following are the budgeted figures for a year ahead:

	Existing programme	Proposed additional programme	Total
Direct materials	£12,600	£6,400	£19,000
Direct wages	19,500	14,500	34,000
Factory overheads, variable	11,500	5,500	17,000
Selling, administration and distribution overheads, variable	19,000	20,000	39,000
Sales	112,000	56,000	168,000

Fixed costs—factory and other—are £26,500 for the present programme and would increase by a further £1500 if the proposed expansion takes place. Of the existing fixed costs, £12,000 may fairly be allocated to the proposed additional output.

(a) Tabulate figures, on a marginal costing basis, to show budgeted contribution for present and for additional working, with net profit or loss overall.

(b) Tabulate figures to show net profit or loss for the proposed additional programme but without using the marginal costing basis.

(c) Calculate returns on capital before and after the additional programme.

(d) Comment, for the guidance of management, on the figures prepared.
[C.W.A.

7. Your directors are contemplating the purchase of a new machine to replace one which has been in operation in the factory for five years. From the following information prepare a statement for submission to the board showing the effect of the installation on costs and profits, and comment on the results shown. Ignore interest.

	Old machine	New machine
Purchase price	£4000	£6000
Estimated life of machine	10 years	10 years
Machine running hours per annum	2000	2000
Units produced per hour	24	36
Wages per running hour	£0·30	£0·52½
Power per annum	£200	£450
Consumable stores per annum	£600	£750
All other charges per annum	£800	£900
Material cost per unit	£0·05	£0·05
Selling price per unit	£0·12½	£0·12½

[C.W.A.

8. A group holding company has several subsidiary companies manufacturing and selling electrical appliances. Describe briefly the main ways of defining profit and capital employed for the purpose of comparing return on capital employed in each subsidiary, and the factors involved in deciding which to use in practice.   [C.A. (1965)

9. A client is considering buying a factory to make a new product which he has developed. He asks you which is the best method to use to assess the profitability and risk of the venture and says that he has heard of three methods, namely: (a) discounted cash flow, (b) return on investment, (c) the pay-back method. You are required to explain briefly two of these methods of appraising capital expenditure and state the advantages and disadvantages of each.   [C.A. (1968)

10. Planrite Ltd is considering what products to manufacture during the coming year. The available products are A, B, C, D and E, there is complete flexibility as regards mix. The following table (showing costs, etc., per unit of each product) has been drawn up by the firm's accountant to assist management in their decision:

Available products:	A	B	C	D	E
Skilled labour hours required	10	8	8	6	4
Unskilled labour hours required	4	20	8	16	12
Selling price	£28	£38	£37	£42	£29
Direct costs:					
Materials	£8	£11	£12	£15	£7
Skilled labour	5	4	4	3	2
Unskilled labour	1	5	2	4	3
	14	20	18	22	12
Overhead expenditure—50% of direct cost	7	10	9	11	6
	£21	£30	£27	£33	£18
Profit per unit	£7	£8	£10	£9	£11
Net profit per £1 spent on labour	£1·17	£0·89	£1·67	£1·29	£2·20
Estimated demand for the year (units)	500	600	300	200	400

Overhead expenses will be the same regardless of what combination of products is manufactured. The firm can employ up to five skilled men and eight unskilled men; each man works for 2000 hours per annum.

You are required to criticise the accountant's statement as a basis for management's deciding what to produce in the coming year. If you think some other calculation would be more appropriate, describe the method and include a formulation of the problem; a numerical solution is *not* required.

Add a short note on factors which might influence the decision but would not be reflected in your calculations. [B.Sc. (Econ.)

11. I am planning to build a motel with one hundred double bedrooms. The initial costs are:

Land	£20,000
Architect's and other fees	15,000
Construction	220,000
Furnishing	70,000

I can borrow the needed funds at 7% per annum by mortgaging this and other property.

Running costs (less the net contribution from bars and dining rooms, etc.) will come to some £65,000 per annum. This includes maintenance of buildings, but excludes their depreciation; it also includes renewals of furniture.

I expect a room to be let for about 220 nights a year, on average, with one and a half persons per room.

Required:

(a) Calculate the minimum room charge per person per night to break even on the alternative assumptions that:

(i) The building will have a life of 30 years with residual site value £40,000.

(ii) The building will have an indefinitely long life.

(b) If inflation raises the net running costs, and enables me to put up charges (above the amount calculated in (a) (ii)) by $2\frac{1}{2}\%$ per annum, what will be my profit per annum at the end of 20 years on the assumption that the building will have an indefinitely long life? [B. Sc. (Econ)

12. X Ltd has established a new department which commenced production at the beginning of 1966. The department was housed in available unutilised space at the company's own factory, no additional rent being payable (and none being charged in the undernoted profit forecast) and the space not being a practicable letting subject. You obtain the following particulars in respect of the new department:

Cost of fixed plant required (paid 1st January 1966) £100,000
Average working capital required:

1966	£50,000
1967	80,000
Thereafter	100,000

Profit forecast:

	Profit before depreciation and taxation	Depreciation
1966	£21,000	£20,000
1967	35,000	20,000
1968	60,000	20,000
1969	65,000	20,000
1970	58,000	20,000

The company estimates that the department's life will end at 31st December 1970, and it is thought that the plant may have become worthless by that time, although annual allowances for taxation purposes are at the rate of 15%.

The company has been in business for many years and, apart from this project, its taxable profits are forecast at rates between £200,000 and £300,000 per annum.

It has been suggested to the company that it might have carried out this expansion in a "development district" and for this purpose it had in fact been offered a lease of a suitable factory at £3000 per annum. It is estimated that other extra costs arising from operating in the new location would have been £1000 per annum.

In addition to the taxation advantages conferred in development areas, the company would have received a direct grant from the Board of Trade of 10% of the cost of plant installed. It may be assumed that this grant would have been received on 1st January 1966.

On the basis of interest at 10% you are required to compute the "present worths" of the new venture (*a*) as it has been established and (*b*) on the basis of the alternative suggestion, and to comment on the significance of the results disclosed.

You may assume that the rate of corporation tax throughout the period will be 40%.

To simplify calculation you may regard all profits as accruing on the last day of the financial year. [C.A. (S)

13. A company, which you are advising, is earning profits in excess of £100,000. It is operating in a development area and has purchased an item of plant on the last day of its financial year—*i.e.* 31st March 1964, for a sum which, after setting off the Government grant relative thereto, amounted to £20,000. You are required:

(*a*) To explain:

(i) What is meant by the "discounted cash flow" technique and the reasons for its increased use in assessing financial proposals.

(ii) The reasons why the charge for depreciation should not be deducted in computing the cash inflow.

(*b*) To prepare a statement showing the cash inflow, appropriately discounted, of the taxation reliefs arising from the purchase of the plant, assuming that all possible allowances are claimed.

(*c*) To state the percentage recovery of the initial capital expenditure resulting from the taxation reliefs.

In this connection you are provided with the undernoted discount factors based on an interest rate of 7%:

Year	Discount factor
0	1·00
1	0·94

NOTE. In preparing your answer you should ignore the provisions of the Finance (No. 2) Act, 1965. [C.A. (S)

14. Discuss the significance of cash flow in management accounting.

(*a*) The AB Co. Ltd is proposing to make a capital investment of £200,000 which it is estimated will produce the following profit figures after allowing for depreciation over five years on a straight line basis:

Year 1	£30,000	Profit
2	£30,000	Profit
3	£20,000	Profit
4	£10,000	Profit
5	£15,000	Loss

To undertake this, the company will require to issue loan stock at 6% per annum. Over the past few years the company's profits have been of the order of 20% on the equity interest. You are required to prepare a statement for management indicating the apparent profitability, or otherwise, of this proposal and to state, giving reasons, whether you think that management are acting in the best interests of the shareholders in undertaking this.

NOTE. The present value of £1:

one year hence at 6% is £0·943	at 20% £0·833
two years ,, ,, ,, 0·890	,, 0·694
three ,, ,, ,, ,, 0·840	,, 0·579
four ,, ,, ,, ,, 0·792	,, 0·482
five ,, ,, ,, ,, 0·747	,, 0·402

Taxation can be ignored.

(b) In present-day circumstances do you think that taxation can be ignored when investment opportunities are being considered? Give reasons for your answer. [C.C.A.

15. The Alpha Co. Ltd is considering the purchase of a new machine which will cost £40,000. It is estimated that the machine will have a life of seven years, at the end of which it will have a scrap value of £1000. This will also involve an investment in working capital of £10,000. The net pre-tax cash flows which this will produce are as follows:

Year 1	£10,000
2	10,000
3	14,000
4	13,000
5	11,000
6	12,000
7	10,000

The company has a target return on capital of 15% and on this basis you are required to prepare a statement evaluing the above project.

Taxation: assume the following:

(1) Corporation tax 40%.
(2) Investment allowance, 30%. Initial allowance, 10%.
(3) Annual allowances, 25%.

The company carries on other trading activities from which it derives taxable profits. [C.C.A.

16. An automatic machine tool, which is used for one product only, is still producing the required volume of output but is costly to operate. Two alternative machines (A and B) have been suggested to replace it.

Given the following information, state:

(a) Which alternative you consider financially preferable.
(b) What discounted rate of return that alternative will yield.

	Existing machine	Alternative A	Alternative B
Cost now		£9,500	£20,000
Realisable value now	£10		
after five years		£3,800	£8,000
Production capacity (units per annum)	510,000	680,000	1,020,000
Routine maintenance cost per annum	£600	£100	£250
Direct material cost, per unit produced	£0·04	£0·03	£0·02½
Machine running costs, and other variable costs of production, per working hour	£0·15	£0·80	£1·10
Variable labour cost of operating machine (1700 hours)	£1,224 per annum		

Assume throughout that output will remain at the existing level of 510,000 units per annum.

The current rate of other factory and administration overheads (excluding depreciation) is $66\frac{2}{3}\%$ on direct labour cost.

The sales value of the product is £12·50 per 1000.

A cash subsidy of 20% of capital cost is receivable from a government department one year after expenditure.

Annual allowances of 20% per annum (straight line) on the balance, and the appropriate balancing allowance or charge on sale.

The written down value for tax purposes of the existing machine is £30.

The applicable rate of tax is 40%.

All taxation adjustments are made one year after the events to which they relate.

Cash flows may be assumed to take place at year end, except for cost of new machine and sale of old machine which take place at the beginning of first year. [C.W.A.

17. It is recommended that profits should be sufficient to finance the replacement of assets as this becomes necessary, to make a contribution towards growth, to provide adequate dividends on share capital and to cover taxation on these items so far as they are not allowable for tax purposes.

You are given the following information relating to the present position of the company:

Fixed assets at cost (replacement value £17,500)	£10,000
Current assets (net)	10,000
Total capital employed	£20,000
Represented by:	
Ordinary share capital	8,000
Retained earnings	12,000
	£20,000

Capital allowances for the year on existing fixed assets: £1000 at 40% = £400.

Average overall life of fixed assets: 25 years.

Target dividend on ordinary share capital: 15% (gross).

Target growth rate per annum in new capital investment in fixed assets (at replacement values): 3%.

Proportion of new capital investment to be financed out of retained earnings from current year's profits: 70%.

Rate of taxation: 40%.

Capital grants (not taxable) on capital cost of new assets: 20%.

Annual allowances for tax purposes on capital cost of new assets after deducting investment grant: 20%.

On the basis recommended in the first sentence of this question state:

(a) The target profit you would aim for in the year ahead.

(b) The rate of return it would represent on the total capital employed at the commencement of the year. [C.W.A.

18. The AB Company Limited uses the payoff criterion for selecting investments in that a project which does not recoup all the capital outlays within four years is automatically rejected. The cash budget for the ensuing year indicates that there will be £100,000 available for investment. Three projects have been submitted to the directors, all of which pay back within four years and all of which, over this period, show an identical surplus cash inflow.

Prepare a report advising the directors as to which should be accepted, commenting on the present method for selecting investments and any other matters you think relevant.

Project A—Lend the £100,000 to a subsidiary company at 8% interest for four years; the interest to be withdrawn each year.

Project B—A property developer with whom the AB Company is associated wishes the company to construct a supermarket, which will cost in total £100,000. It is anticipated that the net cash inflow for the first two years will be £3,000 and £5,000 respectively, all of which will go to the company and at the end of the second year the property developer will purchase a half share in the supermarket for £52,500. During the next two years the net cash inflow will be £12,000 and £16,000 respectively, to be shared equally between the company and the developer, and at the end of the period the property developer will purchase the remaining share in the supermarket for £57,500.

Project C—Invest the £100,000 in new machinery which will provide net cash inflows for four years of £30,000, £35,000, £35,000 and £32,000 respectively.

NOTE.

(1) Taxation and investment grants can be ignored.

(2) The AB Company's capital structure is as follows:

	£
8% debentures	600,000
5% redeemable preference shares	200,000
Ordinary £1 shares	200,000
	£1,000,000

(3) Ordinary dividends of the AB Company have been: 1963—9%; 1964—9%; 1965—9½%; 1966—10%; 1967—10%.

(4) For present value of £1 from 1 to 5 years at 2% to 12%, see Appendix. [C.C.A.

19. Vesta Ltd makes scientific instruments. It relies on its own research department to suggest possible new products. The company budgets to spend about 5% of its turnover on research department salaries; the department is required to undertake general research if it is not fully occupied in the development of specific projects. The average salary rate in the research department is £1·25 per man-hour.

Early in 1966, a proposal was received for the development of a new product, the "Elektrap". The board instructed the research department to carry out a preliminary feasibility study, which cost £5000, and this produced the following information:

(a) The development could be started immediately and the company could then start production on 1st January 1967.

(b) 20,000 man-hours of the research department time would be needed.

(c) The development would require additional cash expenditure in the works of £8500 on special equipment.

(d) Sales potential for the first three years is estimated at:

1967	2000 units
1968	2500 „
1969	2000 „

It is the company's policy to assume (for the purposes of project appraisal) that no sales will be made after three years because rapid technological progress in the industry commonly causes early obsolescence.

(e) Competitive considerations would cause the company to set its selling price at £20 per unit. Variable costs per unit would be: materials £9, and direct labour 12 hours at £0·50 per hour. Overhead expenses of the company would not be altered by the manufacture of this product.

(f) One machine of Type XL 120 would be required for the manufacture of "Elektraps." One is already owned by Vesta and used in the manufacture of a product which is to be discontinued on 31st December 1966; there would be no other use for this machine within the company. Its book value at 31st December 1966 (cost less depreciation) will be £4800, though if it were then sold it would fetch £5500; a precisely similar machine could be purchased for £6000. The machine at present owned would, if used, be expected to have a scrap value of £500 on 31st December 1969.

The manufacture of "Elektraps" would also require some time on a machine Type WL 200, one of which is also owned by Vesta. Other products will in any event use 70% of the capacity of this machine and the remaining 30%, which would otherwise remain unused, is just sufficient for the requirements of "Elektrap" production. Machine WL 200 will have a book value of £2500 at 31st December 1966; it could then be sold for £1500. Another exactly like it could be purchased for £2000. The machine already owned would in any event have no residual value at 31st December 1969, as it will by then be obsolete.

You are required to make a calculation showing whether manufacture of "Elektraps" is worth while. Add a brief note describing any considerations not reflected in your calculation which management should weigh in taking a decision. Assume that the cost of capital of Vesta Ltd is 10%; also that, as a reasonable approximation, the development cost under (c) is all incurred on 1st January 1967 and cash receipts from sales and payments for variable costs arise on 31st December in each year. Ignore taxation.

Compound interest table
10 per cent

n	a_n	v^n	s_n
1	0·9091	0·9091	1·000
2	1·7355	0·8264	2·100
3	2·4869	0·7513	3·310
4	3·1699	0·6830	4·641
5	3·7908	0·6209	6·105
10	6·1446	0·3855	15·937
20	8·5136	0·1486	57·275

Note: The symbols have the following meanings:

　n　number of years
　a_n　present value of £1 receivable at the end of each of n years
　v^n　present value of £1 receivable at the end of n years
　s_n　amount of £1 receivable at the end of each of n years.

[J. Dip. M.A.

20. The MN Co. Ltd. has decided to increase its productive capacity to meet an anticipated increase in demand for its products. The extent of this increase in capacity has still to be determined and a management meeting has been called to decide which of the following two mutually exclusive proposals

—I and II—should be undertaken. On the basis of the information given below you are required to:

(1) evaluate the profitability (ignoring taxation and investment grants) of each of the proposals and

(2) on the assumption of a cost of capital of 8% advise management of the matters to be taken into consideration when deciding between Proposal I and Proposal II.

Capital Expenditure	I	II
Buildings	£50,000	£100,000
Plant	200,000	300,000
Installation	10,000	15,000
Working capital	50,000	65,000
Net income		
Annual pre-depreciation profits (Note (i))	70,000	95,000
Other relevant Income/expenditure		
Sales promotion (Note (ii))	—	15,000
Plant scrap value	10,000	15,000
Buildings disposable value (Note (iii))	30,000	60,000

NOTES

(i) The investment life is ten years.

(ii) An exceptional amount of expenditure on sales promotion of £15,000 will require to be spent in year 2 on Proposal II. This has not been taken into account in calculating pre-depreciation profits.

(iii) It is not the intention to dispose of the buildings in ten years time, however, it is company policy to take a notional figure into account for project evaluation purposes.

The present value of £1 due annually to 11 years hence at 8% see Appendix.

[C.C.A.

21. The Board of the Gamma Power Corporation has decided that, for the purpose of testing whether its capital investment projects are acceptable, a compound interest (DCF) rate of 7% per annum will be used in the usual discounting formula.

An investment project is now under consideration. Estimates of the expected cash flows, over forty years, are as follows:

	Expected cash flow during each year	
	Net receipts	Net payments
Years	£million	£million
1–5	—	2·0
6–10	1·5	—
11–20	0·8	—
21–40	0·4	—

The expected residual value of the assets is zero.
You are required to:

(a) Show whether the project satisfies the normal capital budgeting criterion for acceptance.

(b) Show how sensitive the calculation in (a) is:

    (1) to an increase in the residual asset value from zero to £1 million;
    (2) to a 1% increase in the initial capital outlay (during each year of the outlay);
    (3) to a 1% decrease in the estimate of expected cash flow during each of the years from 6 to 10.

(c) Show the effect of adopting the project on the ratio of reported profits in years 5 and 6 to net Balance Sheet value of assets at the beginning of those years. Comment briefly on the usefulness of the latter type of ratio in the interpretation of accounts in the light of your calculation. (Assume that the expenditure in years 1 to 5 is capitalised, that straight line depreciation is charged after year 5 at 5% per annum and the actual cash flows are according to plan.)

You can assume (for simplicity of calculation) that all cash flows arise on the last day of each year, that all figures are net of tax and expressed in terms of constant price levels, and that working capital for the investment project can be ignored. [J. Dip. M.A.

22. Your company is considering investing in a project for which the investment data are as follows:

Capital outlay £200,000.
Depreciation charge 20% per annum.
Forecasted annual income, before charging depreciation, but after all other charges.

$$
\begin{array}{rr}
\text{Year 1} & £100,000 \\
2 & 100,000 \\
3 & 80,000 \\
4 & 80,000 \\
5 & 40,000 \\
\hline
& £400,000 \\
\end{array}
$$

In connection with the foregoing you are asked to employ methods of measuring the return on the capital employed with a view to ascertaining the value to the company of the proposed investment.

On the basis of the figures given above, set out calculations illustrating and comparing the following methods of evaluating the return on capital employed:

(a) Pay-back period.
(b) Rate of return on original investment.
(c) Rate of return on average investment.
(d) Discounted cash flow.

State clearly any assumptions you make. Taxation to be ignored. Calculations may be approximate. [C.C.A.

23. The authority of the board of directors is being sought for the expenditure of a considerable sum of money on new plant to perform automatically work at present done by hand. The engineering department has completed the technical details and now ask for the assistance of the cost department in putting their case forward for the board's approval.

Draft the headings of such a capital proposal form, showing the major considerations involved. [C.W.A.

24. The board of your company has decided upon a major scheme of

capital expenditure on additional buildings and plant for the purpose of extending its activities. Explain how this expenditure could be controlled.

[C.W.A.

25. Set out, point by point, the purpose of and procedure for preparing an annual capital expenditure budget in a medium-sized manufacturing company.

[C.W.A.

26. Your board complains that it is presented with requests for the sanction of capital expenditure which may be sponsored by any one of a number of company officials and supported by information varying widely in content, presentation and degree of details. You are asked to advise on a uniform procedure for the sponsoring and mode of presentation of such requests.

[C.W.A.

Chapter XXIII

REPORTS TO MANAGEMENT
(I) THE WRITTEN REPORT

STYLE OF THE REPORT

It is essential that after expending much effort and the variety of skills involved in management accountancy, there should be no doubt about the meaning and implications of the facts and figures.

Adequate time should always be allowed for the final collation of information and the preparation of the report prior to the meeting, etc., for which it is required. A hastily compiled report may lead to misunderstanding and the wrong action being taken.

Below are listed some guiding principles for preparing reports, but particular circumstances or the purpose of the report will obviously mean modifications in detail:

1. The report should be addressed to those for whom it has been prepared; it should state by whom it is submitted, be dated and duly signed.

2. Sections should be headed and paragraphs numbered for easy reference.

3. The language should be clear and unambiguous. Greater brevity of expression is permissible than would be justified in other forms of writing. The report should be impersonal. Professional jargon should be avoided, since those who receive the report may be quite unfamiliar with expressions the accountant takes for granted.

4. The contents should follow a logical sequence:

   (a) Summary of present position.

   (b) Courses of action which might be taken and the expected results.

   (c) Recommendations and reasons for their submission.

5. Professional opinions should not be expressed assertively, since they are opinions and *not* facts. If a conclusion is based on a reasoned argument and events do not subsequently turn out as anticipated, there is no reflection on the professional capacity of the person concerned. But a definite statement, *e.g.* that profit will or will not increase, which turns out to be wrong will be viewed as a serious failure, especially if others have relied on the statement to their detriment. Expressions of caution such as "it would appear that," "from the

evidence supplied it would seem that," etc., should always be used to show that assumptions or opinions are expressed.

6. Discrimination must be used in selecting the facts to be submitted. There is no need, usually, to mention every contingency that may arise, and the difference between significant and insignificant facts must be appreciated. Since "management by exception" is now the rule rather than the exception, a board will not want to waste time grasping the implications of an unduly long report before it can decide the appropriate measures.

7. Where it is necessary to provide additional documents, such as plans or graphs, they should be appended rather than included in the body of the report and clearly referenced by number.

8. With examination questions, care should be taken to observe by whom the opinion is to be given. For example, if by an accountant, then financial matters will take precedence; if by a cost accountant, then costs, overheads, budgets and variances will predominate.

9. In all cases, reports should be impartial.

Two examples follow, one an external appraisal, the other an internal report on the affairs of an organisation. It will be noted that in the second case quite lengthy information of a "domestic" nature is supplied, as it may be assumed that the people dealing with such a matter would have more detailed knowledge than those discussing an external affair affecting the company more generally. In the latter case the board of directors would be concerned with establishing the broad principles of future action.

The opportunity has been taken to incorporate into the following question the subject of establishing present values on future courses of action (see Chapter XXII). This means applying the principles governing annuities, with which the management accountant should be familiar. They are briefly exemplified in the following report.

Specimen question

The managing director and majority shareholder of a private company, H Co. Ltd., has asked your opinion as an accountant on the best course of action to be taken in the following circumstances.

The company has a wholly owned subsidiary, WS Ltd, which is run efficiently but was taken over in a boom period. The subsidiary supplies specialised components to the holding company at current market rates. Owing to the fall in prices and the writing down of the company's assets at the rate of £70,000 a year, the company has been showing losses recently at an average of £42,000 a year. As no foreseeable change in market conditions is likely, the position is expected to continue, and cessation of business has been contemplated.

WS Ltd has now received the offer of a long term contract for the supply of certain components to the value of £75,000 annually, the additional cost of production being estimated at £45,000. At the same time an outlay of £100,000 would be required for additional working capital and machinery. The offer of the contract is not considered by the board of the holding company to be very acceptable, since estimated losses of £12,000 a year would still be incurred besides the capital outlay required; nevertheless, some hesitation is felt, as in effect, for £12,000 a year, the delivery of the specialised components required by the holding company could be assured.

In view of the hesitation of WS Ltd, the company offering the contract has made a further offer, to take over the subsidiary on a share-exchange basis of 120,000 of their £1 shares quoted at £1·66½, which is considerably more than would be obtained in the event of a shut-down.

The managing director has intimated that for personal reasons he would not consider any proposal likely to exceed a period of eight years; he suggests that cessation of business at the end of that time be assumed, when the assets at present held by WS Ltd might be sold for £50,000. If the company accepted the offer of the contract and acquired the additional assets, the total saleable value of its assets in eight years' time would be about £110,000.

Investments in other companies like WS Ltd are expected to yield 10% per annum. Relevant figures obtainable from interest tables are:

Present value of £1 in eight years,   £0·474
Present value of £1 p.a. for eight years, £5·335

Further and more detailed information is to follow, but you are asked to give a preliminary report according to the details supplied.

Answer

The Managing Director,   Address
H Company Ltd,   Date
[Address].

Dear Sir,

Preliminary report on the proposed future policy of WS Ltd

In accordance with the information supplied in your letter dated ....,
I have pleasure in submitting my preliminary report as follows.

1. *Present financial position of the Company*

(a) *Losses.* The Company is at present sustaining average losses of £42,000 per annum with no foreseeable likelihood of improvement. This figure is arrived at after writing down losses on assets of £70,000 per annum.

(b) *Depreciation of assets.* While it is necessary to write down the value of the Company's assets by depreciation charges, as losses have been sustained on assets and the business will not continue for more than eight years, it is expedient in this instance to ignore the losses already sustained and to concentrate on the profits which may be obtained by current trading.

If this course is taken and depreciation omitted, the Company's Revenue Account will reveal a profit on current trading of £28,000 per annum. In view of this, any of the courses mentioned below are likely to prove more profitable than an immediate cessation of the Company's activities.

2. *Courses of action available*

(a) *Sale on a share-exchange basis.* As sale on cessation of business would bring in considerably less than the offer for purchase as a going concern, the latter would be preferable. Sale would yield a present value of:

120,000 shares, value £1·66½ each, say   £200,000

(b) *Continuing present operations.* This is obviously a less profitable course than accepting the long term contract, but is worth considering because the further outlay of £100,000 if the contract were accepted would not be required. The present loss figure of £42,000, after omitting the depreciation charge according to 1 (b) above, would be adjusted to £28,000 profit. The present value which might be set upon this course of action is:

Present value of an income of £28,000 per annum for eight years at 10%, (£28,000 × 5·335)		£149,380
Present worth of saleable value of assets at end of eight years, (£50,000 × 0·474)		23,700
(say)		£173,000

(c) *Acceptance of the long term contract.* If the long term contract is accepted, the present loss figure might be adjusted as to:

Average annual net loss		£42,000
Less Depreciation charge written back	£70,000	
Additional net income on contract	30,000	
		100,000
Annual income		£58,000

The present value if this course were adopted would then be:

Present value of an income of £58,000 per annum for eight years at 10%, (£58,000 × 5·335)		£309,430
Present worth of saleable value of assets at end of eight years, (£110,000 × 0·474)		52,140
say		362,000
Less Additional outlay required		100,000
		£262,000

3. *Financial summary of alternative policies*

(a) Sale on share-exchange basis	£200,000
(b) Continuance of present operations	£173,000
(c) Continuance of operation on acceptance of long term contract	£262,000

4. *Recommendations*

The most profitable course of action would be acceptance of the long term contract and, provided the necessary finance can be raised, this course is recommended.

The next most profitable alternative would be the sale on a share-exchange basis, but it would then be necessary to get a firm assurance that supplies for H Co. Ltd would still be forthcoming. Despite the financial attraction of selling out, the company might deem it wiser to continue trading so as to ensure regular supplies. In any case, the difference financially between the second and third alternatives is not so great as between either of them and the first.

I shall be pleased to supply a more detailed report on receipt of further information.

Yours faithfully,

Chartered accountant

NOTES

(i) The first reaction on reading this report may be that a difference of £62,000 between the most profitable policy (*c*) and sale of the business (*a*) does not justify expending an additional £100,000 and trading for eight more years. This is to misunderstand the method of applying present values to future income. Under the recommended scheme, income is increased from £28,000 to £58,000 per annum, and this alone would give an additional actual income over the eight years of £240,000. (The figure of £30,000 is chosen arbitrarily for convenience but it is quite valid.)

(ii) Objection may be raised to the ignoring of depreciation. It is true that in a company which expects to continue trading the replacement of assets cannot be overlooked; but if a company is making heavy annual losses, urgent steps must be taken to retrieve the situation before it is too late. The subject is dealt with more fully in Chapter xx.

As remarked earlier, the following example goes into more detail because it is an internal report and those responsible for it will be more familiar with the business. The appendixes marked with an asterisk (*) are not reproduced here.

Example

17th May 19—

From: *Internal Audit Department*

To: *Financial Director*

Subject: *Stores depot at Doncaster Road, Battersby, Yorkshire*

Findings

1. We were instructed by your internal memorandum No. 714/C to visit the above-mentioned depot and conduct an investigation into the general organisation and control existing there.

2. We attended the stores for three consecutive days, 10th to 12th May.

3. The standards against which the stores were compared were those as generally practised in the Company and as covered by sections 31/116 to 34/134 of the operations manual.

4. The only records kept there are of a stores recording nature, with the exception of a £10 petty cash float under the control of the cashier's office and which was not inspected by us.

5. *Location and security arrangements:* we noted that considerable quantities of stores were kept outside the main storage building. While most of them were not easily portable, there was a considerable quantity of material of some value, *e.g.* strips of duralumin, crates of tinfoil and boxes of chromium-plated door handles, which we feel would be better placed inside. The premises are adequately protected by the boundary wall, but it is doubtful whether they are proof against a determined thief. Only one night-watchman was employed to safeguard more than an acre of grounds and buildings.

6. *Maximum and minimum stores control:* we made a test check of 45 different types of stores (out of a total of 200) for the efficiency of the general input/output control. We discovered that:

(*a*) On eight different types of stores (all of the nuts, bolts, screws and washers type—for details see the attached Appendix I*) there was under-stocking greater than 10% of the regulation minimum. No explanation was available about the cause of this state of affairs and we feel that the enforcement of this most important control could be profitably tightened up.

(b) On seven types of stock (bulk stores of bulbs, electric wiring and electrical accessories—for details see Appendix II*) there were quantities in excess of 10% of the regulation maximum. We were informed by the Depot Manager that this was due to the eccentricity of demand from the 22 depots which his stores supply. Investigation supported this explanation.

7. *Stores records and system:* on the whole, the standard of recording was on a par with the rest of the organisation. We feel, however, that the present staff are under too much pressure to avoid making minor mistakes, of which we found an above average number. At present four clerks have an approximate constant average of 400 postings each to make daily, as compared with 300 in other locations.

We were informed that the quantity of work will soon increase by approximately 10% owing to the new Government production contracts.

The system in use was installed by the existing staff to comply with the stores manual (amended) last September, and is functioning satisfactorily with two exceptions (*see* (8) below).

8. The "Goods inwards" book has not been initialled every day by the Depot Manager. It is a most important link in the chain of internal control and it is essential that this omission should not be repeated. We feel that there is some excuse for the omission as a great deal of extra work, resulting from the change of ownership, has devolved on the Depot Manager. He informed us that in future it would be done without fail.

By an oversight the "Goods inwards" notes prepared by the gatekeeper were not printed with consecutive numbers. This omission was supposedly overcome by the gatekeeper himself writing in the number. However, such a proceeding was inadequate: it was important that it should be rectified immediately and in the course of our visit a set of appropriately numbered duplicate notes was obtained.

9. *Perpetual inventory:* this necessitates three full-time employees at present —largely, in our opinion, because of the considerable amount of time required by the present manual counting methods. If they were brought into line with the normal practice of using weighing machines for the large number of small but numerous stock types, we feel a considerable increase could be made in the frequency of counts. We think the latter are not frequent enough at present—only five times a year—and that the target should be at least twice as often.

Recommendations

10. Re (5) above, we feel that it is urgently necessary to employ another watchman for night duties. The Depot Manager strongly supports this recommendation, and we are informed by him that he had made repeated representations to the previous proprietors about it.

11. Re (6(a)) above, the controls described in this paragraph are most important, and we indicated to the chief clerk and to the Manager the desirability of adhering strictly to the standards laid down. We were informed that great efforts would be made to do so in future. In this connection we would recommend the installation of Form B652A for monthly returns of stocks, with memoranda columns for maximum/minimum limits.

12. Re (7) above, to equate the clerical work with a reasonable output we would further recommend the employment of another stores clerk. This suggestion meets with the approval of the Manager.

13. Re (6(b)) above, in our opinion this depot should adopt the practice that applies at the Southern and North-western area stores, *i.e.* ordering

items of this nature direct from the manufacturers, since delivery dates are now very prompt and the need for these and similar items (see Appendix III*) is never urgent.

14. Re (9) above, we would recommend the purchase of three Jones & Jones scales of the type in use at the Screws, Nuts and Bolts Main Depot at Wexborough. We would also recommend that the items counted should be so marked on the monthly stock return B652A already mentioned. Both of these suggestions meet with the approval of the Manager.

General conclusions

15. Our impression of the calibre of works and clerical staff and of the executives was favourable.

16. It would have been reasonable to expect considerably more variances from our standard practice such a short time after their installation and the accompanying upheaval.

17. We received the highest measure of co-operation from all with whom we had to deal, especially the Manager, Mr Johnson.

18. We propose to re-visit this depot in approximately three months' time.

(Signed) *G. W. Green,*
Senior Internal Auditor

EXAMINATION QUESTIONS

1. Your organisation has a plant at Barchester which, owing to technological developments, will shortly have to cease production of the existing lines as the demand for them is coming to an end. Hence your board has to consider what to do with the Barchester factory. The buildings are comparatively new and good for another 50 years—although it would be wise to reckon on maintenance of the fabric of the premises at around £500 per annum. An offer has been received for a seven-year lease at £10,000 per annum; alternatively, they would fetch £100,000 if sold. The existing equipment is obsolete and will fetch no more than the cost of dismantling and carting away.

At this time your company is considering launching on the U.K. market one or both of two new products, "Ace" and "Trumps," for which an excellent demand is expected until superseded by further technical advances expected 7–8 years hence. The factory at Barchester, suitably re-equipped, would allow for the production of either of these products at a normal budgeted production of 100,000 units per annum. The new plant required (estimated life seven years) would cost £40,000 for the manufacture of "Ace" and £50,000 for "Trumps." In addition, £10,000 manufacturing working capital would then be required for each product.

The normal production capacity could be extended to 150,000 units per annum by overtime working. The additional costs for stepping up production (by overtime working or extra shifts), etc., and conversely the under-recovery of overheads and other losses due to under-production, are estimated as: "Ace," £0·10 per unit and "Trumps," £0·30 per unit. The products are perishable and cannot be stored for longer than to allow for the carrying of the usual small buffer stocks.

(*On normal production basis*)	*Ace*	*Trumps*
Production costs per annum	£52,000	£47,000
Distribution costs per annum	19,200	18,300
Selling costs per annum	5,000	4,000
Administration costs per annum	10,000	10,000

The products could be brought in completed from Germany which, with selling, distribution and administrative costs, would amount to a price per unit of: "Ace," £1 and "Trumps," £0·87½. Both products are expected to sell at £1·10 per unit delivered to wholesalers and bulk buyers.

A market research survey has been conducted, and from this the following annual demand pattern has been forecast for the seven years' period:

Year	Ace	Trumps
1	50,000 units	20,000 units
2	90,000	80,000
3	120,000	120,000
4	120,000	150,000
5	110,000	120,000
6	100,000	100,000
7	50,000	70,000

You will appreciate from the foregoing that your board is faced with a policy decision as to whether to sell or let out the Barchester premises or to continue manufacture there with a new product—and there may be other factors which should be taken into account. You are to appraise the position fully and write a report, including in it any statements you consider relevant, to assist the board to make a decision.

The board considers 7% per annum as a reasonable return for capital tied up. The annuity which may be obtained for a current outlay of £1 (that is, to return capital and provide an interest rate of 7% on the remaining balance), is, for a seven-year period, £0·185553.

To provide for return of capital only and taking into account 7% compound interest on the annual amounts set aside requires an annuity of £0·00246 for a fifty-year period. [C.C.A.

2. The managing director of a manufacturing company and his chief departmental executives hold regular monthly meetings at which the trading and financial position of the company is reviewed. As the Chief Accountant, draft in outline a one-page monthly report suitable to be laid before the meeting. [C.W.A.

3. XY Ltd, an engineering company, has had one-third of its capacity idle for some time owing to lack of orders, and the number of employees has dropped to 240 from the normal level of about 300.

It is approached by a large manufacturing group, AB Ltd, which wishes to find a regular source of supply of specialised pieces of equipment required in connection with its experimental and development work. AB's orders would be of a miscellaneous character with little likelihood of repeat orders, and the volume of work might vary widely from one period to another. A quick delivery service is essential for AB's purpose.

In general, the work would call for a higher standard of precision than XY is accustomed to, and would necessitate the engagement of additional design, drawing office and tool room staff at an estimated cost of £15,000 per annum.

AB makes a proposition to XY on the following lines:

(a) XY to reserve one-third of its capacity for AB's orders in return for a fixed annual retaining fee.

(b) In addition to the retaining fee, XY to be paid for the cost of work carried out for AB with an allowance for profit of 10% of the capital actually employed on the orders.

(c) AB to have absolute priority for its orders over all other customers of XY in respect of the one-third capacity reserved to it, but XY to be permitted to use that capacity on work for other customers when not required for AB's work.

(d) The amount of the retaining fee and the precise definition of "cost" and "capital employed" to be matters for negotiation.

You are asked to prepare a report for the board of XY, setting out the economic factors to be considered in negotiating with AB and suggesting an equitable basis for arriving at the amount of the retaining fee and for calculating the cost of AB's orders and the capital employed on them.

[C.W.A.

4. The data below have been made available to you in connection with an exempt private company in which your organisation, XY Ltd, a public company, has been offered a 50% interest for £500,000.

Your managing director has asked you to study the information in readiness for an exploratory meeting with the board of the AB Co Ltd.

Write a report setting out your impressions from the limited data so far available, indicating what other information, if any, you require; and generally supporting your report with any arguments you consider relevant.

AB CO. LTD

	1968	1969	1970
Sales	£1,000,000	£1,200,000	£1,500,000
Net profit (before tax)	90,000	100,000	120,000
Ordinary share capital	500,000	500,000	500,000
General reserve	40,000	90,000	160,000
Trade creditors	60,000	110,000	140,000
Plant and equipment (written down value)	400,000	450,000	500,000
Stocks and work in progress	90,000	160,000	230,000
Debtors	70,000	60,000	50,000
Cash	40,000	30,000	20,000
Gross profit to sales	30%	$33\frac{1}{3}$%	34%
Net profit to share capital	18%	20%	24%

The company manufactures three products, "Bugs," "Cugs" and "Dugs." The industry generally has good prospects—having doubled the level of activity in this field over the past three years. AB's policy is to be able to meet customers' requirements at very short notice. Sales are direct to customers—*via* representatives on the road or orders received through the post.

SALES PATTERN

Products (percentages)

To:	Bugs	Cugs	Dugs	Total
Two large customers	25	18	2	45
4000 retailers	30	1	9	40
Government institutions	—	—	15	15
	55	19	26	100

Gross profit 1968	£135,000	£95,000	£70,000	£300,000
1969	262,000	70,000	68,000	400,000
1970	399,000	40,000	71,000	510,000

[C.C.A.

CHAPTER XXIV

REPORTS TO MANAGEMENT
(II) GRAPHS AND CHARTS

FACTUAL information is often clearer and easier to understand if presented in graphical form. This in itself justifies the use of graphs in reports to management, but care is necessary because the presentation of facts other than in figures can lead to distortion.

1. GRAPHS

Graphs, and similar methods of displaying facts or estimates, suffer from the disadvantage that (a) they are not precise in their definition, or, if they are, that (b) they cannot be read to the degree of exactness to which they were drawn. Nevertheless, they can save much time and effort and, provided the following points are borne in mind when compiling them, graphs can be most useful.

(a) A graph is used to show the relationship between two variables by means of either a curve or a line. It is based on the use of two lines drawn at right angles, known as *co-ordinate axes*, which meet at a point of intersection called the *origin*. In normal business statistics, only the YOX quadrant is used.

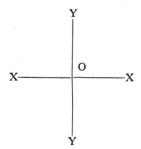

FIG. 29.—*Co-ordinate axes.*

(b) When plotting information, it is necessary to decide which is the independent variable, *i.e.* the one against which the other is measured; thus of the two variables, sales and time, the independent variable is time. The independent variable should be plotted along the X axis.

(c) Where the graph depicts absolute changes, the zero line should normally be shown, otherwise a wrong impression may be given.

(d) Too many lines should be avoided on one graph or they will lead to confusion.

587

(e) A proper heading should be provided, with further elucidation by means of sub-titles or footnotes.

(f) Wording should not be shown vertically; any explanation should be shown on the left-hand side of the graph, to ensure that the graph can be read naturally and without inconvenience.

(g) The scale should be given on the left-hand side; it may be repeated, if this would be helpful, on the right-hand side.

(h) Where a number of curves are necessary, colouring or differentiated lines (e.g. dotted, pecked, etc.) should be used.

Specimen question

From the graph in Fig. 30, which shows information taken from the final accounts of the company for five years, you are required to state such facts about the history and policy of the undertaking as you are able to deduce.

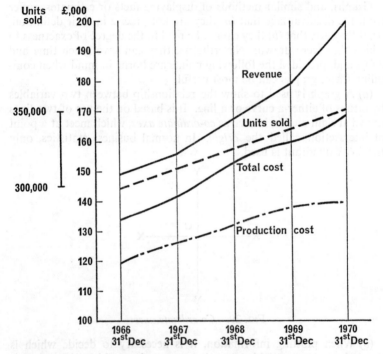

FIG. 30.—X Company Ltd: revenue, production, total costs and units sold for the years 1966–70 inclusive.

Answer

It is assumed that the production cost line refers to the cost of producing the units sold, since the production cost as revealed in the annual accounts woud not usually refer to sales but rather to units produced, including stocks carried forward.

The following facts may be observed from the graph shown above:

(a) Unit sales during the period have increased at an even rate, whereas revenue and expenses have varied.

(b) Production expenses have increased, but to a lesser extent than output. This is particularly noticeable near the end of 1969 and during 1970, and would indicate some change in production methods, probably modernisation of some kind.

(c) The general expenses have increased out of all proportion to output and sales, reducing the P/S (profit to sales) ratio, which would otherwise have increased.

(d) Revenue has increased, but not in proportion to units sold. From the revenue curve it would appear that the company's pricing policy has been to make sharp increases at too infrequent intervals; smaller ones more often would seem more suitable.

NOTE

It is observed that no zero line is given, contrary to (c) above. The reason, doubtless, is that comparative movements are more important here than absolute changes.

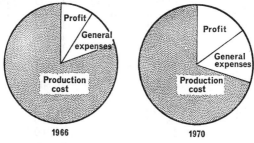

FIG. 31.—*Pie charts: comparison of costs and profits of X Company Ltd for 1966–70*

2. PIE CHARTS AND AREA DIAGRAMS

"Pie charts" are used to show the relationship of parts to the whole. They are formed on the basis of a circle divided into sectors, after the fashion of slices from a cake or pie, hence the name. Using the data in the example above, the revenue constitutes the whole circle and the relative proportions of the production and general expenses and the profit are shown by the size of the sectors (*see* Fig. 31).

The drawback with pie charts, as can be seen in this case, is that it is difficult to judge from them the difference between the size of the "slices." They are therefore of little use for management control purposes. This applies equally to *area diagrams*, which show relative differences by squared blocks of various sizes.

3. Z CHARTS

Comprising three curves on a single graph, the Z chart is so called because on completion it is similar in shape to the letter Z.

The three curves display:

(a) The current figure for the period concerned.
(b) The cumulative amount to the latest date.
(c) The moving annual total, or "trend."

This useful chart suffers from one disadvantage: because the trend curve begins at the cumulative figure for the previous period, it is separated rather widely from the current monthly or other period figure. Nevertheless, this type of chart can be used to advantage for graphical portrayal of such things as the progress of sales figures over a period.

Example

SALES FIGURES OF TWO NEWLY OPENED BRANCHES

| | Branch A | | Branch B | |
	1st year	2nd year	1st year	2nd year
January	£4,000	£10,100	£12,000	£16,500
February	5,200	10,400	12,600	16,800
March	6,800		14,000	
April	6,300		13,200	
May	5,900		13,600	
June	7,000		14,320	
July	7,390		15,400	
August	9,200		16,800	
September	8,600		18,580	
October	7,910		17,100	
November	8,900		19,300	
December	12,100		22,100	
Total	£89,300		£189,000	

INDUSTRIAL SALES OVER SAME PERIOD

	1st year	2nd year
Quarter 1	£3·2 million	£5·8 million
2	4·2	
3	4·4	
4	4·8	

The trend figure is calculated by taking the total sales figure of the previous twelve months, adding the figure for the current month and deducting the corresponding month in the previous year:

Total sales for year	£89,300
Add January, second year	10,100
	99,400
Less January, first year	4,000
Trend figure at 31st January in second year	£95,400

Using the information given for Branch A above, the chart would appear as in Fig. 32.

NOTES

(i) In order to reveal the current year movements more clearly, it is advisable to show the current figures on a larger scale than the trend and accumulated sales. To show the effect of this, the current year's figures have been superimposed on the complete Z chart. It would not be necessary normally to give both lines for current sales.

(ii) As figures for the previous year are not available, a budgeted trend curve has been entered on the chart in Fig. 32 for illustrative purposes.

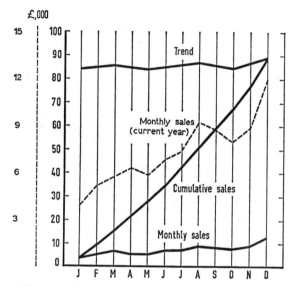

FIG. 32.—*Z chart: graph of sales of Branch A for the year 19— (monthly, cumulative and trend).*

4. SEMI-LOGARITHMIC SCALE GRAPHS

An example will best show the purpose of this type of graph.

Example

Using the information given in the preceding example:

(a) Branch A has increased its sales by £8100 in December as compared with January.

(b) Branch B has increased its sales by £10,000 over the same period.

Superficially, it would appear that Branch B is trading more successfully. Figure 33 shows the two trading positions on an ordinary line chart. Branch B's total sales figure is greater, but *relatively* Branch A is doing much better;

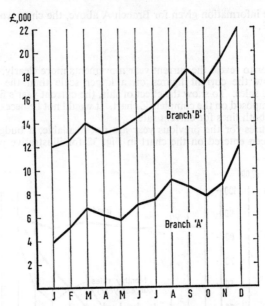

FIG. 33.—*Sales of branches A and B for the year ended 31st December 19—, shown as an ordinary line chart.*

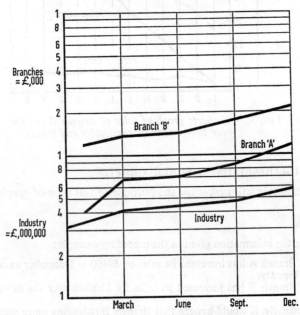

FIG. 34.—*Sales of branches A and B for the year ended 31st December 19—, shown as a semi-log graph.*

a comparison of the two on a percentage basis reveals the following increase in sales at December since they began trading in January:

$$A: (12{,}000/4000) \times 100 = 300\%$$
$$B: (22{,}100/12{,}000) \times 100 = 184\%$$

The actual position is more truthfully shown in graph form by a semi-logarithmic scale graph as in Fig. 34. Here the relative increase is revealed, as well as the varying rates of increase. Thus the purpose of such charts is to show the *relative* rate of change of data, not absolute changes as with the more common graph or line chart.

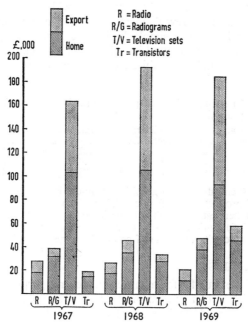

FIG. 35.—*Bar chart: home and export sales of Electrical Ltd for the three years 1967–69.*

Figure 34 shows an additional use: the performance of the industry as a whole has been added. Where figures are available, it is obviously useful for management to be able to compare the national trend with its own performance at a glance. Such additional comparisons are easily made in a semi-logarithmic scale graph.

Continuing with our example, the semi-logarithmic scale chart reveals the following points:

(*a*) The initial rise in sales in both branches, the more spectacular being that in Branch A.

(b) While Branch B's sales progressed more slowly at the end of the period, its relative increase was nearly as great as that in Branch A.

(c) In both branches, sales were satisfactory in comparison with national figures.

(d) With respect to (c) above, however, except for the initial increase of sales in Branch A, the improvement over the national figures was not outstanding: further efforts in the field of advertising, etc., might be advisable, for if national demand is increasing, the more efficient firm will have opportunities to expand.

5. BAR CHARTS

This type of chart facilitates quick visual comparison. It must always commence at zero, otherwise the comparison will be distorted.

The simple bar chart reveals increases or decreases in magnitude of any particular item. The simple basic type is not illustrated here, but Fig. 35 shows a compound bar chart, *i.e.* one that allows for the comparison of a number of subjects on the same chart.

Example

An electrical manufacturing company has made the following sales over the past three years (in £000's):

	Radios		Radiograms		Television sets		Transistor radios	
	Home	*Export*	*Home*	*Export*	*Home*	*Export*	*Home*	*Export*
1967	19	9	31	7	102	60	15	4
1968	17	8	35	9	114	76	29	6
1969	12	9	37	9	92	91	45	13

To set out such information graphically should not be difficult but, with four types of product and a further division into home and export sales, care must be taken lest too much information on one chart causes confusion.

The above information could be arranged in the form of a bar chart as in Fig. 35. The clarity and ease of comparison are an obvious advantage.

6. FLOW CHARTS

This type is very useful for management control purposes. It enables an overall picture of a system or systems to be obtained, and when adjustments are made to increase efficiency or eliminate unnecessary procedures, the prevailing flow of work and the probable effects may be seen clearly.

It is useful for internal audit purposes; it can facilitate planning and lead to the organisation working more efficiently, as well as elucidating procedures for instituting or improving an internal check system. Fig. 36 shows an example used in production control.

7. GANTT CHARTS

These charts are widely used in industry for planning purposes. Production must be budgeted in order to ensure sufficient use of assets as well as ascertaining that no orders are taken that cannot be fulfilled. The Gantt chart serves both these purposes as well as facilitating comparison of actual production with that budgeted. It takes the form of

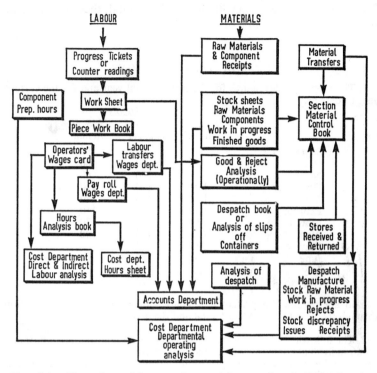

FIG. 36.—*Flow chart: labour and material control and production in X Company Ltd.*

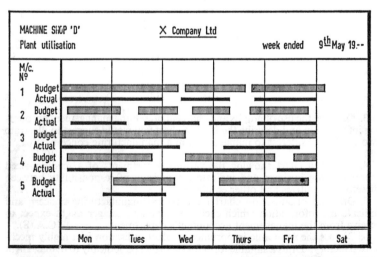

FIG. 37.—*Gantt chart: X Company Ltd.*

596 INFORMATION FOR MANAGEMENT CONTROL

a compound bar chart, but with the bars horizontal; they can represent
any unit of quantity, time or value (*see* Fig. 37).

1. The monthly sales figures for the last financial year and for the current
year to date are:

Sales in £000's

	1966–67 Actual	1967–68 Budget	1968–69 Actual
September	60	70	80
October	70	70	60
November	90	100	60
December	100	110	110
January	120	130	120
February	120	130	110
March	120	120	130
April	150	150	140
May	100	110	
June	100	110	
July	80	90	
August	70	70	

You are required to present a Z chart showing the budgeted position
through the year to 31st August 1968 and the actual position to date.
[C.A. (S)

2. The following table shows the sales made by an industry as a whole and
by an individual company within that industry over the same period. Draw
up a semi-logarithmic scale graph from the data and state what conclusions
you would draw.

	Company (£000's)	Industry (£ millions)
1956	12	6·2
1957	18	8·3
1958	32	9·1
1959	41	9·4
1960	60	11
1961	72	12·4
1962	88	13·6
1963	104	14·2

3. Describe the use of graphs and charts in presenting management accounting information and describe the kind of chart you would suggest to illustrate
two matters of interest to management in a manufacturing concern.
[C.C.A.

4. Prepare a chart showing the various departments of a medium-sized
manufacturing business and indicate the division of responsibility between
directors, executives and other employees. [S.C.A.

5. Draw an organisation chart for a typical manufacturing concern and
indicate the information which each executive or manager might expect to
receive from the management accountant's department. [C.A.(S).

6. Discuss the economic importance of plant utilisation in a highly mechanised factory. Draft a suitable form for reporting periodically to management
upon plant utilisation. [C.W.A.

7. Discuss the application of (*a*) flow charts and (*b*) work studies to office routines. Illustrate your answer by reference to an office organisation with which you are familiar.   [S.C.A.

8. Describe the advantages and disadvantages of using logarithmic ruled graph paper instead of graph paper ruled using an arithmetic scale.
                                                                                     [C.A.(S).

APPENDIX

Present value of £1 to be received in one payment at the end of a given number of years $(1 + r)^{-n}$

Discount rates of 1% to 9%

Future years	Percentage rate of Discount								
	1	2	3	4	5	6	7	8	9
1	0·990	0·980	0·971	0·962	0·952	0·943	0·935	0·926	0·917
2	0·980	0·961	0·943	0·925	0·907	0·890	0·873	0·857	0·842
3	0·971	0·942	0·915	0·889	0·864	0·840	0·816	0·794	0·772
4	0·961	0·924	0·888	0·855	0·823	0·792	0·763	0·735	0·708
5	0·951	0·906	0·863	0·822	0·784	0·747	0·713	0·681	0·650
6	0·942	0·888	0·837	0·790	0·746	0·705	0·666	0·630	0·596
7	0·933	0·871	0·813	0·760	0·711	0·665	0·623	0·583	0·547
8	0·923	0·853	0·789	0·731	0·677	0·627	0·582	0·540	0·502
9	0·914	0·837	0·766	0·703	0·645	0·592	0·544	0·500	0·460
10	0·905	0·820	0·744	0·676	0·614	0·558	0·508	0·463	0·422
11	0·896	0·804	0·722	0·650	0·585	0·527	0·475	0·429	0·388
12	0·887	0·788	0·701	0·625	0·557	0·497	0·444	0·397	0·356
13	0·879	0·773	0·681	0·601	0·530	0·469	0·415	0·368	0·326
14	0·870	0·758	0·661	0·577	0·505	0·442	0·388	0·340	0·299
15	0·861	0·743	0·642	0·555	0·481	0·417	0·362	0·315	0·275
16	0·953	0·728	0·623	0·534	0·458	0·394	0·339	0·292	0·252
17	0·844	0·714	0·605	0·513	0·436	0·371	0·317	0·270	0·231
18	0·836	0·700	0·587	0·494	0·416	0·350	0·296	0·250	0·212
19	0·828	0·686	0·570	0·475	0·396	0·331	0·277	0·232	0·194
20	0·820	0·673	0·554	0·456	0·377	0·312	0·258	0·215	0·178
21	0·811	0·660	0·538	0·439	0·359	0·294	0·242	0·199	0·164
22	0·803	0·647	0·522	0·422	0·342	0·278	0·226	0·184	0·150
23	0·795	0·634	0·507	0·406	0·326	0·262	0·211	0·170	0·138
24	0·788	0·622	0·492	0·390	0·310	0·247	0·197	0·158	0·126
25	0·780	0·610	0·478	0·375	0·295	0·233	0·184	0·146	0·116
30	0·742	0·552	0·412	0·308	0·231	0·174	0·131	0·098	0·075
35	0·706	0·500	0·355	0·253	0·181	0·130	0·094	0·068	0·049
40	0·672	0·453	0·307	0·208	0·142	0·097	0·067	0·046	0·032
50	0·608	0·372	0·228	0·141	0·087	0·054	0·034	0·021	0·013

PRESENT VALUE FACTORS

Present value of £1 to be received in one payment at the end of a
given number of years $(1 + r)^{-n}$

Discount rates of 10% to 18%

Future years	Percentage rate of Discount								
	10	11	12	13	14	15	16	17	18
1	0·909	0·901	0·893	0·885	0·877	0·870	0·862	0·855	0·847
2	0·826	0·812	0·797	0·783	0·769	0·756	0·743	0·731	0·718
3	0·751	0·731	0·712	0·693	0·675	0·658	0·641	0·624	0·609
4	0·683	0·659	0·636	0·613	0·592	0·572	0·552	0·534	0·516
5	0·621	0·593	0·567	0·543	0·519	0·497	0·476	0·456	0·437
6	0·564	0·535	0·507	0·480	0·456	0·432	0·410	0·390	0·370
7	0·513	0·482	0·452	0·425	0·400	0·376	0·354	0·333	0·314
8	0·467	0·434	0·404	0·376	0·351	0·327	0·305	0·285	0·266
9	0·424	0·391	0·361	0·333	0·308	0·284	0·263	0·243	0·225
10	0·386	0·352	0·322	0·295	0·270	0·247	0·227	0·208	0·191
11	0·350	0·317	0·287	0·261	0·237	0·215	0·195	0·178	0·162
12	0·319	0·286	0·257	0·231	0·208	0·187	0·168	0·152	0·137
13	0·290	0·258	0·229	0·204	0·182	0·163	0·145	0·130	0·116
14	0·263	0·232	0·205	0·181	0·160	0·141	0·125	0·111	0·099
15	0·239	0·209	0·183	0·160	0·140	0·123	0·108	0·095	0·084
16	0·218	0·188	0·163	0·141	0·123	0·107	0·093	0·081	0·071
17	0·198	0·170	0·146	0·125	0·108	0·093	0·080	0·069	0·060
18	0·180	0·153	0·130	0·111	0·095	0·081	0·069	0·059	0·051
19	0·164	0·138	0·116	0·098	0·083	0·070	0·060	0·051	0·043
20	0·149	0·124	0·104	0·087	0·073	0·061	0·051	0·043	0·037
21	0·135	0·112	0·093	0·077	0·064	0·053	0·044	0·037	0·031
22	0·123	0·101	0·083	0·068	0·056	0·046	0·038	0·032	0·026
23	0·112	0·091	0·074	0·060	0·049	0·040	0·033	0·027	0·022
24	0·102	0·082	0·066	0·053	0·043	0·035	0·028	0·023	0·019
25	0·092	0·074	0·059	0·047	0·038	0·030	0·024	0·020	0·016
30	0·057	0·044	0·033	0·026	0·020	0·015	0·012	0·009	0·007
35	0·036	0·026	0·019	0·014	0·010	0·008	0·006	0·004	0·003
40	0·022	0·015	0·011	0·008	0·005	0·004	0·003	0·002	0·001
50	0·009	0·005	0·003	0·002	0·001	0·001	0·001	0·001	

PRESENT VALUE FACTORS

Present value of £1 to be received in one payment at the end of a
given number of years $(1 + r)^{-n}$

Discount rates of 19% to 26%

Future years	Percentage rate of Discount							
	19	20	21	22	23	24	25	26
1	0·840	0·833	0·826	0·820	0·813	0·806	0·800	0·794
2	0·706	0·694	0·683	0·672	0·661	0·650	0·640	0·630
3	0·593	0·579	0·564	0·551	0·537	0·524	0·512	0·500
4	0·499	0·482	0·467	0·451	0·437	0·423	0·410	0·397
5	0·419	0·402	0·386	0·370	0·355	0·341	0·328	0·315
6	0·352	0·335	0·319	0·303	0·289	0·275	0·262	0·250
7	0·296	0·279	0·263	0·249	0·235	0·222	0·210	0·198
8	0·249	0·233	0·218	0·204	0·191	0·179	0·168	0·157
9	0·209	0·194	0·180	0·167	0·155	0·144	0·134	0·125
10	0·176	0·162	0·149	0·137	0·126	0·116	0·107	0·099
11	0·148	0·135	0·123	0·112	0·103	0·094	0·086	0·079
12	0·124	0·112	0·102	0·092	0·083	0·076	0·069	0·062
13	0·104	0·093	0·084	0·075	0·068	0·061	0·055	0·050
14	0·088	0·078	0·069	0·062	0·055	0·049	0·044	0·039
15	0·074	0·065	0·057	0·051	0·045	0·040	0·035	0·031
16	0·062	0·054	0·047	0·042	0·036	0·032	0·028	0·025
17	0·052	0·045	0·039	0·034	0·030	0·026	0·023	0·020
18	0·044	0·038	0·032	0·028	0·024	0·021	0·018	0·016
19	0·037	0·031	0·027	0·023	0·020	0·017	0·014	0·012
20	0·031	0·026	0·022	0·019	0·016	0·014	0·012	0·010
21	0·026	0·022	0·018	0·015	0·013	0·011	0·009	0·008
22	0·022	0·018	0·015	0·013	0·011	0·009	0·007	0·006
23	0·018	0·015	0·012	0·010	0·009	0·007	0·006	0·005
24	0·015	0·013	0·010	0·008	0·007	0·006	0·005	0·004
25	0·013	0·010	0·009	0·007	0·006	0·005	0·004	0·003
30	0·005	0·004	0·003	0·003	0·002	0·002	0·002	0·001
35	0·002	0·002	0·001					
40	0·001	0·001						

APPENDICES

PRESENT VALUE FACTORS

Present value of £1 to be received in one payment at the end of a given number of years $(1 + r)^{-n}$

Selected discount rates from 28% to 60%

Future years	Percentage rate of Discount							
	28	30	35	40	45	50	55	60
1	0·781	0·769	0·741	0·714	0·690	0·667	0·645	0·625
2	0·610	0·592	0·549	0·510	0·476	0·444	0·416	0·391
3	0·477	0·455	0·406	0·364	0·328	0·296	0·269	0·244
4	0·373	0·350	0·301	0·260	0·226	0·198	0·173	0·153
5	0·291	0·269	0·223	0·186	0·156	0·132	0·112	0·095
6	0·227	0·207	0·165	0·133	0·108	0·088	0·072	0·060
7	0·170	0·159	0·122	0·095	0·074	0·059	0·047	0·037
8	0·139	0·123	0·091	0·068	0·051	0·039	0·030	0·023
9	0·108	0·094	0·067	0·048	0·035	0·026	0·019	0·015
10	0·085	0·073	0·050	0·035	0·024	0·017	0·012	0·009
11	0·066	0·056	0·037	0·025	0·017	0·012	0·008	0·006
12	0·052	0·043	0·027	0·018	0·012	0·008	0·005	0·004
13	0·040	0·033	0·020	0·013	0·008	0·005	0·003	0·002
14	0·032	0·025	0·015	0·009	0·006	0·003	0·002	0·001
15	0·025	0·020	0·011	0·006	0·004	0·002	0·001	0·001
16	0·019	0·015	0·008	0·005	0·003	0·002	0·001	0·001
17	0·015	0·012	0·006	0·003	0·002	0·001	0·001	
18	0·012	0·009	0·005	0·002	0·001	0·001		
19	0·009	0·007	0·003	0·002	0·001			
20	0·007	0·005	0·002	0·001	0·001			
21	0·006	0·004	0·002	0·001				
22	0·004	0·003	0·001	0·001				
23	0·003	0·002	0·001					
24	0·003	0·002	0·001					
25	0·002	0·001	0·001					
30	0·001	0·001						

INDEX